DATE DUE

OCT 30			
DEC 15			
MAY 15			
DEC 15			
MAY 3			
FEB 23			
NOV 30			
JAN 31			
MAY 21			
DEC 9 '75			
GAYLORD			PRINTED IN U.S.A.

THE OUTLINE OF MUSIC

ARCO MUSIC LIBRARY

THE OUTLINE OF MUSIC

EDITED BY

SIR MALCOLM SARGENT

ASSOCIATE EDITOR

MARTIN COOPER

ARCO PUBLISHING COMPANY, INC.

NEW YORK 17, N.Y.

FOREWORD

THERE are so many excellent books available to the music-lover that I would hesitate to add to their number if it were not for the fact that I believe this "Outline" to be more thorough than many popular books on musical appreciation, but less bulky and perhaps less exacting in reading than the mighty tomes of the all-embracing Dictionaries and Histories.

This book is intended for the use of the "adult" concert-goer of any age who is sufficiently interested in the art of music to wish to know more about it than can be learnt from only hearing performances and recordings. The better the work of art, the greater will be its emotional impact through the senses—provided the hearer is sufficiently sensitive. But this sensitivity can be accentuated by a preliminary mental interest or foreknowledge of the circumstances of the composition, the conditions, customs of the period when it was written or first performed, and the character and intentions of the composer.

All "knowledge" is but a preliminary to the actual appreciation, which must be one of "feeling". Music exists that the spirit of one man may speak to the spirit of mankind, and I warn the reader that he will not find in this book, or in any book, the secret of this revelation, which is a spiritual mystery, and is Music.

As editor, I have made myself responsible for a compilation—or symposium—of knowledge which is wide in interest but does not profess to be all-comprehensive.

I realise that not every chapter will be of equal interest to every reader. For instance, Chapters II to V are designed primarily to give information to the student and may be heavy going to those who have little interest in musical history *per se*. I recommend the latter readers to begin at Chapter VI, where they will find information on music they probably have heard. The earlier chapters should be of interest eventually.

Chapter XXVI gives elaborate and rather formidable information on the modern revolutions in music-making—serialism, electronic music, and *musique concrète* are described and methods explained in some detail. It is hoped that the relative value of these new types of sound production will not be judged by the amount of space given to them as compared with that allotted to more conventional music. There is at the present time a great youthful interest in these new inventions, and an exposé of their intricacies may perhaps help the discerning listener to separate the dross of

v

calculation from the gold of inspiration. The book has been planned at all times to give information rather than to express critical evaluations.

It has been difficult, and at times proved impossible, to avoid " over-lappings ", as subject headings seemed to be of probable convenience to the reader. One can only hope that information twice given may be the more easily remembered.

The demands of actual music-making have made it impossible for me to undertake a book of this size without the help of others, and I am particularly grateful to Mr. Martin Cooper, who has been invaluable in correlating material provided by a team of experts to whom I am also greatly indebted. Messrs. Ernest Bradbury, A. V. Coton, Scott Goddard, Dyneley Hussey, Arthur Jacobs, Robert Jacobs, Edward Lockspeiser, Malcolm Macdonald, Henry Rayner, Gilbert Reaney, Charles Reid, and Reginald Smith-Brindle have all contributed of their knowledge in special branches of musicology.

Mr. Lionel Salter has also been of indefatigable help in checking detail and correcting proofs.

This book is humbly presented as an " Outline " which may easily be criticised for its irregularities of contour. There may be bulges and con-cavities in unexpected places, but no two people would agree as to the shape of an Outline of Music. I can only hope that the reader may be excited to supplement his knowledge from more informed sources, and especially that his pleasure in listening to music may be enhanced.

London, 1962

vi

CONTENTS

vii

CONTENTS

COLOUR PLATES

MONOCHROME PLATES

MONOCHROME PLATES

THE OUTLINE OF MUSIC

I

MUSIC AS A EUROPEAN ART

TO survey the whole art of music in a single volume is manifestly impossible, and the present work has been designed for the practical use of a concert-going public which is most interested in music it is likely to hear. This fact explains the proportions of the book, in which works written for the concert-hall or the opera-house receive much fuller treatment than those written for the church or the " chamber ", and only the last four centuries are covered in any detail. Although only one age and one province in the history of the art of music, it is well to remember that these centuries in Western Europe have seen a development of the art unique both in quantity and quality, and that no other four centuries in any other part of the globe could possibly provide material for a study of comparable size.

These centuries have seen, in particular, the emergence of great individuals, whose names have become household words throughout the whole civilised world, their greatest works studied and loved with an intensity which earlier generations brought to the study of the Bible. Bach, Handel, Haydn, Mozart, Beethoven, Schubert, Chopin, Schumann, Brahms, Verdi, Wagner, are to countless music-lovers not simply the creators of music which never seems to lose its freshness, but personal friends. We turn to them rather as the devout of the Middle Ages turned to the saints—in joy and in sorrow, for exhilaration and consolation. Each music-lover will have his own favourites, as the medieval man chose his patrons among the saints ; and no detail of a favourite's life, no trait of character, is too small to arouse our interest. It is for this reason that, whenever possible, biography as well as musical history figures largely in this book, and an attempt has been made to connect an artist's works with his life. Composers of an earlier age—before Bach, roughly—and those of the present day have not the same personal appeal. It is difficult for us to enter the musical world of, say, Palestrina or Schütz, to feel either as personal friends ; and composers of the present day have hardly yet been canonised by popular acclaim. They are, as it were, our brothers, rather than father-figures in our emotional lives. Slowly, almost imperceptibly, this situation is altering, and Strauss, Debussy, Bartók, and Stravinsky are shifting towards canonisation.

I

Our whole conception of music has been enormously enlarged during the last fifty years. To the ordinary music-lover in this or any other Western European country during the nineteenth century, " music " meant the music written by Italians, Germans, and Austrians since about 1700. All but a few specialists regarded medieval and renaissance music as dull and primitive, and non-European music as a curiosity. Even Gregorian plainchant was referred to as " droning " and accorded a purely functional place in religious rites. This narrowness of interest was due simply to ignorance—not only of the music itself, but of the multifarious cultures from which it sprang. While faith in the " inevitable progress of mankind " was unquestioned, so the superiority of the new over the old seemed indisputable. It was understood, if not always openly stated, that the emergence of the major-minor scale system at the beginning of the seventeenth century marked the first rays of light in a day whose noon was Beethoven, while all subsequent music was depicted as a solemn and often gorgeous afternoon and evening, finally declining into darkness with Richard Strauss. This is in fact a conception based on the rise and fall of Germany as a first-class musical power, whose primacy was disputed only by Italy, and even then only in the field of opera.

This conception was challenged by the revival of interest in " national " or folk music, first in the Slavonic countries and later all over Europe. The Romantics had indeed turned their eyes to the past, but in search of inspiration for their own music rather than in the hope of discovering any fresh musical world whose laws and ideals could be expected to have a validity equal to their own. Wagner, for instance, based *The Mastersingers* on medieval German musical history, but he never intended to revive practical interest in the music of Walther von der Vogelweide and Wolfram von Eschenbach. Even Debussy, the first major European composer to take an interest in Oriental music, looked for " exotic " timbres in the Javanese *gamelans* of the Paris Universal Exhibition of 1889, and had no real interest in autonomous musical cultures outside Western Europe. Only the devastation of two world wars and the subsequent questioning of all æsthetic values have humbled us sufficiently and opened our eyes to the fact that music is a universal phenomenon, an integral part of every culture in every age and to be judged by the standards of that culture, rather than by a single universally applicable yardstick of modern Western European fashioning. The fact is that our yardstick has broken in our own hands. Our horizons have suddenly spread, our own music reflects the confusion of values inseparable from an age of transition, and our former confidence in our own superiority begins to look like that of ignorant provincials. Conceptions of music that were until recently dismissed as primitive—music as number, magic, esoteric meaning or a means of inducing physical ecstasy

2

—crowd upon the composer of to-day for serious consideration. No sensible music-lover in these days can dismiss the art of any civilisation, however remote in time or place, as meaningless or uninteresting. His mind and senses may not be trained to distinguish its characteristic beauties, and he will certainly have to make many mental adjustments before he can hope to understand its nature ; but we are gradually establishing the conception of music as a single world-wide art of enormous antiquity and subject to an infinity of various laws in different ages. Scholars have as yet touched only the fringes of many musical cultures, but already they are beginning to establish universal types and parallel lines of development. The music that we know—that of Western Europe during the past four centuries—appears now as that of an age and a province rather than the whole art. It may be that ours is incomparably the richest and most varied musical tradition known to history, but it no longer appears as absolutely unique.

THE ORIGIN OF MUSIC

We cannot hope to discover any single origin for an art whose most primitive forms to this day include whispering, speaking, humming, singing, shouting, stamping, and the production of pitched and unpitched sounds from almost every conceivable form of "instrument", from a hollowed tree-trunk or a pair of one's enemy's knuckle-bones to a well-tempered pianoforte. To make rhythmic sounds is an instinct observable in every human baby, and it seems certain that, like babies, primitive man's musical instinct was invariably connected with the desire to express some emotion or idea. Pattern-making for its own sake is a much later and more sophisticated activity. We can see this from the fact that even to-day a primitive man introduced to a new melody will at once ask what it is "about" and will spontaneously add words of his own. Even songs whose texts have no intelligible meaning will be found to consist of syllables credited with a magic power of some kind. In primitive societies music is much more closely integrated with everyday life than in our own. Melodies acquire different meanings from different styles of performance ; some may be sung only by men, others only by women. Some belong to a single office and are inheritable, others are tabu except on certain occasions. Although what the psychologists speak of as pure "play-instinct" has a great part in the shaping of a melody, even the most ecstatic songs and dances often exhibit conscious and well-regulated structure.

In primitive societies the same power that is attributed to a name is often attributed to a sound. If a man's name or his likeness are in some

3

way identical with him, so the man who can perfectly imitate the roar of the lion or the hiss of the snake becomes partaker in some of the animal's powers. " One must have heard them to realise how extremely realistically aboriginals can imitate animal noises and the sounds of nature", writes Professor Marius Schneider. "They even hold ' nature concerts' in which each singer imitates a particular sound—waves, wind, groaning trees, cries of frightened animals—' concerts' of surprising magnificence and beauty." In totemistic societies " similarity of voice " betokens a fundamental relationship. From this it follows that it is only at puberty, *i.e.* when his voice breaks, that a young man is finally named, assigned to the totem and introduced to his ritual duties. Even musical instruments are endowed with sexuality, *e.g.*, the male flute and the female drum, and " the player, the instrument, and the sound are related as father, mother, and child " in cases where a predominantly female instrument is played by a man or vice versa. Such characteristic conceptions reveal the width of the gulf dividing the place of music in primitive cultures from that which it occupies in our own, and also explain the significance of what may seem to our ears monotonous repetitions or nursery imitations of natural sounds such as birdcalls.

Since Western European music is rooted in the great civilisations which have contributed to the formation of European culture—Greece, Rome, Islam, and Israel—it will be as well to say something briefly of each.

THE MUSIC OF ANCIENT GREECE

The absence of a written musical notation is the first and greatest of the many difficulties that beset our understanding of ancient music. It has been well said that " the scholar who seeks to understand ancient Greek music is in much the same position as a musicologist two thousand years hence who might try to reconstruct our music with only the following documents—three bars from the St. Matthew Passion, a drinking song from the eighteenth century, a Mass by Bruckner, half a dozen modern pieces for the piano and a large number of theoretical works, from Fux's *Gradus ad Parnassum* to a modern textbook on harmony ". On the one hand, we know that musical theory was highly regarded by the Greeks as a branch of both mathematics and philosophy ; on the other, we have only the scantiest evidence of Greek musical practice. We know that it was predominantly homophonic, *i.e.* single lines of melody without harmonic support, and that both rhythm and melodic shape depended largely on the rhythm and natural pitching of the spoken language. The amateur's instrument was the lyre. The *kithara* (also plucked strings) and the *aulos* (a blown reed-pipe) were regarded as the preserve of professional

4

performers, who competed at many of the festivals. The Greeks employed a greater variety of intervals than modern European music and were plainly very sensitive to variations in styles of performance and particularly in tonality or *mode*, which determined the character of the music. It is a bitter fact that although we know that the performance of a Greek tragedy would strike us to-day as more than half-way towards what we mean by opera, the music to which the immortal choruses of Æschylus, Sophocles, and Euripides were chanted is irretrievably lost.

From the fourth century B.C. onwards, music in Greece fell into the hands of professional performers who regarded themselves, and were popularly regarded, with an esteem as great as that of the *castrati* in eighteenth-century Italy. Fees were enormous, but instrumental virtuosity was regarded as incompatible with good breeding in a man, or good morals in a woman.

THE ROMAN EMPIRE

Music in Rome seems not to have been a native art but to have been borrowed from the Etruscans, the Greeks, or the East. Native " Italian " music was possibly to be found in the popular music of the Empire, rhythmic and percussive ; but the Greek musicians who came to Rome in 167 B.C. met with total incomprehension and were laughed off the stage. Brass instruments (*tuba*, *buccina*, and the Etruscan *cornu* and *lituus*) were used in military and state ceremonial, and lyres, harps, and various forms of pipe were frequent in social—and particularly in what we should call " night-club "—life. Under the Empire the Roman public developed that taste for the brilliant virtuoso soloist that still persists. " Successful players were mobbed by the crowd," says J. E. Scott, " paid fantastic engagement fees, and allowed to indulge in any amount of artistic temperament on and off the stage. These artists, too, banded themselves into professional groups not unlike trade unions, and by the second century A.D. had a practical monopoly." We know virtually nothing of the music performed, but purely physical qualities—volume and duration of a single note—probably played a large part in determining popular enthusiasm.

ISLAM

Despite the early Puritanism of Islam, which regarded music as one of the forbidden pleasures, music was widely cultivated in the civilisation which spread from Samarkand in the East to Cordova in the West. The chief centres of musical influence were Persia and Syria on the one hand, Spain on the other. Since there is no proper Islamic liturgy, religious music consisted of hardly more than chantings of the Koran and the formal call to prayer. Secular music was developed in working songs and domestic lullabies, marriage and funeral chants ; but it was at the court of the great Mohammedan princes, with their retinues of foreign slaves and professional singing-girls, that art-music was chiefly cultivated. Vocal music was more highly valued than instrumental, as was common in the ancient world, and the melodic ornamentation and rhythmic varying of a single line remains even to-day the characteristic form of musical expression in Islamic countries. A wide variety of drums, tambourines, pipes, and stringed instruments was employed, but by far the most important from the historical point of view was the lute (Arabic *al-ud*), an instrument with strings plucked by the right hand, and the length of the strings being shortened at will by the left hand, thus raising the pitch. (This also accounts for the strange fact that it is the violinist's *left* hand which has the most intricate work to do.) Introduced into Spain by the Moslem invaders, the lute was not in common use in the rest of Europe until after the period of the Crusades, and its form was not stabilised until the fourteenth century, the golden age of lute music (1500–1630) following two centuries later.

ISRAEL

Whereas Islamic music is predominantly secular in character, the great contribution of the Jews to the art of music has been in the religious sphere. The Bible mentions an impressive array of instruments—trumpets, timbrels, harps, and *shofar* (ram's-horns)—in the ritual of the Temple, and in Biblical times Hebrew song seems to have been normally accompanied by instrumental music. Yet even before the destruction of the Temple by the Emperor Titus in A.D. 70 there appears to have been a growing opposition to the use of anything but the human voice in the worship of Jehovah. Instrumental music for the Jews, as for the first Christians and Moslems, was suspect because of its associations with the orgiastic and licentious rites of their neighbours' pagan religions. Worship in the synagogue, which was all that remained after the destruction of the Temple, found a place only for the chanting of Scripture, a practice deeply rooted in the metrical symmetry (or " parallelism ") that we can see most clearly in the Psalms, even when translated from the Hebrew. " Whoever reads Scripture without chant," says the Talmud, " to him the Scriptural word is applicable, ' I gave them laws and they heeded them not.' " There is great variation, regional as well as liturgical, in the character of the Jewish chant—from the most ancient forms employed by the Yemenite Jews to the Ashkenazim of central and western Europe and the Sephardim of Spain and Portugal. It has been established beyond question that the early Christian liturgies of Jerusalem and Antioch took over this chanting of Scripture from the Jewish synagogue, and Christian chant (both Byzantine and Roman) developed from this with strong cross-fertilising from other, especially Syrian, sources. After the geographical dispersion of the Jews, synagogue music in every country underwent local changes and modifications, but in the Near East we can observe a decline to a kind of standardised folk-music, a change from genuine flexibility to an almost petrified musical system.

MUSIC AND EMOTION

To the ordinary man in Europe and America, who is indifferent to æsthetic philosophising, music remains an art of emotional expression and communication, just as it is to the primitive man. Exactly what is expressed may be difficult to determine, still more difficult to state in philosophical language. Although there can be no question of disregarding or disparaging music's intellectual character, either in matters of construction or logical development, yet any music (if such exists) which is conceived purely intellectually and corresponds to no recognisable emotional experience in the composer's life is doomed to sterility. The Greek philosophers made the sensible distinction between the mathematical and philosophical theory of music and the practical art of live, sounding music. Treatises remained treatises, and mathematical demonstrations did not masquerade as songs or dances, which kept their direct appeal to the ear. The invention and complication of musical notation, which permitted a composer to develop a musical idea at much greater length than formerly, brought with it the danger of " eye-music "—in which the beauties appeal to the brain through the eye, leaving the ear starved or untouched. Our age of scientific exploration has seen a recrudescence of this music which, in the late fifteenth-century Netherlands School, had already provoked a strong reaction. History is repeating itself to-day, and in the middle of the twentieth century we are witnessing an enormous increase in popular interest in music which may well lead to a new and as yet unimagined flowering of the art.

II

THE EARLIEST DAYS—CHURCH, COURT, AND PEOPLE

FOLK-SONG and folk-dance in everyday life and the ritual chant of the Church between them form the foundation of our whole Western European art of music. Music was made, instinctively, long before men began to theorise about its nature, and even longer before any attempt was made to find a system of notation—to perpetuate, that is to say, individual melodies and rhythms by writing them down. The history of music, owing to this absence of notation, starts with theory (scientific acoustics and philosophical mysticism), and we are in the tantalising situation of knowing more of what learned men thought about music than of the actual sounds produced by singers and instrumentalists. Apart from a small number of specifically Christian features, the Roman musical writers of late antiquity simply passed on Greek theory to the West. Typical instances from the sixth century A.D. are Boethius and Cassiodorus, both counsellors of the Gothic King Theodoric. The characteristically philosophical or scientific approach of these early writers is only superseded by something more practical after *plainsong* became solidly established throughout Europe.

PLAINSONG

Christian liturgical chant—St. Paul's " psalms, hymns, and spiritual songs "—was directly inherited from the chanting of the Jewish synagogue. Like all ritual music, this had a double origin, practical and spiritual. In a large building chanting is clearer and more intelligible, as well as more solemn, than speech, and the inflections and ornamentations at points of special importance, at the beginning or the end of a text, serve as guides to the congregation as well as expressing man's instinctive beautifying of all that he offers to God. Before the advent of plainsong we have many references to music—Sumerian harps, quantities of sculptures and bas-reliefs showing musical scenes in ancient Egypt, accounts of performances and instrumental tunings and scales of the Greeks. But the only actual music that survives from those days is a handful of Greek fragments whose interpretation is disputed by scholars. It was probably the desire for ecclesiastical uniformity that led to the eventual notation of ecclesiastical chant.

Until the time of Charlemagne, who died in 814, the liturgical chant of Western Europe was divided into four principal dialects, but both Pope and Emperor were determined to establish uniformity. And so it happened that the Gallican rite was virtually eradicated from France, and the Visigothic (or Mozarabic) rite from Spain, while the Ambrosian rite was allowed to subsist—as it still subsists to-day—only in the diocese of Milan. This left the *Roman* rite supreme. In England the Roman liturgy and chant were introduced in 597 by St. Augustine, the personal emissary of Pope Gregory I, who had reorganised the school of chant in Rome and who gives his name to what is now called *Gregorian* chant. The council of Cloveshoe (the modern Glasgow) in 747 made it plain that all British churches were expected to adopt the plainsong according to the antiphoner, or service book, brought from Rome. Two centuries later we find two monks from Corbie, in France, being sent to teach the monks of Worcester to chant after the manner of an antiphoner sent by the Pope from Rome.

The earliest plainsong manuscripts date from the ninth century, but they can be deciphered only with the help of later sources, since they contain no indication of pitch. A few early pieces can be transcribed, because they are written in letter notation (A,B,C,D, etc.) but this method was generally reserved for teaching purposes. The use of the *stave*—or the scheme of lines and spaces on which our music is written to-day—was made general by Guido d'Arezzo, who lived in the eleventh century, and the four-line stave is still normally used for plainsong to-day. Our usual five-line stave was invented with the advent of wider-ranging melodies in the late twelfth century. It is a strange fact that the main body of plainsong, which was composed between the fifth and eighth centuries, is known to us from manuscripts dating from four, five, or even six hundred years later.

The chants of the Mass are divided into two kinds—those of the *Ordinary*, whose texts never change, and those of the *Proper*, whose texts change according to the feasts and fasts of the church's year. The Ordinary of the Mass consists of the Kyrie, Gloria, Credo, Sanctus, and Agnus Dei. Most of the plainsong for these texts dates from between the ninth and twelfth centuries. The Proper consists of Introit, Gradual, Tract, Offertory, and Communion, and the chants for these—mostly fragments of psalm or scripture—are considerably older. These earlier chants developed from psalmody, a simple and recitative-like form of intonation which came to be varied by antiphons, short refrains or links between the verses of a psalm. In *antiphonal psalmody* the two halves of a chorus sang the two halves of a psalm-verse ; in so-called *responsorial psalmody* the division was between soloist and chorus, the soloist singing each psalm-verse and the chorus answering with Amen or a short refrain. There are few chants left in the repertory that show this alternation between verse and antiphon or verse and respond.

Plainsong is difficult for the modern listener to appreciate because it is unharmonised, has no regular rhythm in the modern sense, and its tonality is that of the now superseded *modes*. These were inherited from the Greeks, and correspond roughly to the scales formed by consecutive ascending white notes of the piano keyboard. The mode corresponding to the scale D–D was called Dorian; that between E and E, Phrygian; F–F, Lydian; G–G, Mixolydian; A–A, Æolian; B–B, Hypophrygian; and C–C, Ionian. The mode of any melody is determined by its final note; but its beginning, the cadences of intermediate phrases and the compass of the whole melody also help to establish its underlying mode.

SECULAR MUSIC

Unlike plainsong, medieval secular music employed what is now called the "major" scale. The secular music of the early period is generally in staffless notation and therefore indecipherable. There survive songs with Latin texts (Horace and Vergil) and laments for a Visigothic king and queen as well as for the great Charlemagne. One of Horace's odes appears with the same melody as the hymn *Ut queant laxis* (which Guido d'Arezzo used to teach his pupils the sol-fa system) and this has the same square rhythms as the Latin song *Aurea personet lyra*, popular in the eleventh century. Such occasional pieces as these are all that we possess from the time before the troubadours, though semi-religious, moralising songs form a kind of half-way house between sacred and secular music. Outstanding among these are the so-called *Carmina Burana*, a collection of Latin songs from the Bavarian monastery of Benediktbeuern, which also includes drinking and love songs. This collection, although as late as the beginning of the fourteenth century, is in staffless notation and therefore indecipherable. The manuscript has been generally ascribed to the "Goliards", or wandering scholars; but in fact only a small portion of it is devoted to their songs, and these have no notation at all.

TROUBADOURS AND TROUVÈRES

The gradual development of the French and Provençal languages brought with it a body of lyric song of remarkable individuality. Both troubadours in the South and, later, trouvères in the North—minstrels wandering from one small court to another—were often of noble birth, and song-composition was considered an aristocratic distinction. Among the earliest troubadours were William IX, Count of Poitiers and Duke of Aquitaine, who died in 1127, and Thibaut IV, a prolific trouvère who was Count of Champagne and King of Navarre and died in 1253. On the other hand, perhaps the most famous of all troubadours (partly owing to his mention by Dante) was Bernard de Ventadorn, who was a kitchen servant in the castle of Count Eble de Ventadorn and died in 1195. The art of the troubadours, which flourished roughly between 1100 and 1300, spread not only northwards but also to the south—Germany, Italy, and Spain, where Catalonia was an early home of the movement. The poetry of the troubadours was devoted to the glorification of ideal womanhood, and underwent a gradual refining process almost certainly influenced by the cult of the Blessed Virgin. Bernard de Ventadorn's beautifully balanced combination of poetry and music still contains unmistakably sensual elements, but his best songs have a Spring-like freshness, sincerity, and simplicity which still appeal to the modern listener. His whole output amounts to hardly a score of songs, and the whole troubadour repertory that survives consists of hardly three hundred pieces. Almost fifty of these are by Guiraut Riquier. Other famous troubadours are Guiraut de Bornelh (known as " Master of the Troubadours "), Folquet de Marseille, Peire Vidal, and Raimbaud de Vaqueiras.

After the forcible suppression of the Albigensian heresy—a form of Puritanism of Oriental origin—in the first quarter of the thirteenth century, the Provençal troubadours found it difficult to obtain employment. The nobles had lost their power and wealth, love poetry was suspect, and the school gradually dispersed. Several troubadours took refuge in Italy and founded the new school of Italian lyric poetry. Guiraut, generally known as the last of the troubadours, stayed on at the court of the Count of Rodez, whose wife appears in his songs under the name of Belh Deport (Lovely in Movement).

The work of the trouvères in the north of France was far more extensive, or at least far more of it—some 1500 melodies—has survived. Many of the composers are anonymous, but the names of Blondel de Nesles (celebrated in legend for his association with our own king Richard Cœur-de-Lion) Conon de Béthune, and Adam de la Halle have remained famous. The trouvères were first active in the second half of the twelfth century and their work was continued into the fourteenth by Guillaume de Machaut. Their forms were the same as those used by the troubadours ; they themselves were drawn from all classes of society, with a noticeably smaller aristocratic element. The performers of this music—the minstrels with their viols, that is to say—played an even larger part in the art of the trouvères than in that of the troubadours. Competitions in the composition of songs by minstrels were arranged, and musical debates, or *jeux partis*, were used to discover the best artists to entertain the nobility in all parts of the country.

The *jeu parti* was the chief feature of the " Courts of Love " which were popular from early troubadour times until well into the fifteenth century. At these courts the artists discussed in music the various difficulties that might arise in love. A standard melody would be chosen and developed by several contestants, and a judge would sum up. Music played a particularly important part in dance-songs such as the *rondeau*, of which many anonymous examples survive. These have only two musical phrases, but they are often gracefully strung together and varied. The triple-time melodies so common in thirteenth-century music are certainly naïve-sounding to our ears, but therein lies a great part of their charm. Thibaut de Navarre's song *Por conforte ma pesance* is a good example of the song which later developed into the *ballade*, the first part of the melody being repeated to new words in each of a varying number of stanzas.

LAYS

" Lays " probably suggest to most people the picture of an ancient bard with a harp, and the image is not much mistaken. The medieval lay was a long lyrical poem with stanzas of varying designs and frequently short lines of verse fitted to equally simple musical motifs. The relation between poetry and music is unusually close : a rest often corresponds to the end of a line or verse, and two or three short lines will be paralleled by the same number of melodic sequences in the music. The original Breton lays, often recalled by the lyric poets of the twelfth or thirteenth centuries, must have been narrative poems sung to a scrap of music probably identical for each verse, as in the few *chansons de geste* (or heroic narrative poems) that we know. They were probably accompanied by harp, viol, or lyre. The instrumental part was never notated but probably consisted of a short prelude, interlude, and postlude, and probably a simple strummed harmony supporting the voice. The lays that we possess, however, are considerably more complex, and almost every stanza is different from the last in verse-form and music. The anonymous lays are the simplest and often employ stock melodic phrases, but Thibaut de Navarre and Guillaume de Machaut evolved satisfactory artistic wholes despite the restrictions of the conventional " courtly love " themes.

Closely connected with the lay is the *estampie*, one of the earliest of instrumental forms, based on the principle of progressive variation. Very few of these pieces exist, as they were generally improvised, with viol, rebec, bagpipe, shawm, or portable organ, and plenty of percussion to accompany them.

GERMANY

Lyric song certainly flourished in medieval Germany, but even less of this has been preserved than in the case of France, since German notation was less developed than French. There can be little doubt that French and Provençal songs were the models for these German poet-composers, and in the case of one, Friedrich von Husen, there exist melodies by Guiot de Provins, Bernard de Ventadorn, Folquet de Marseille and Conon de Béthune, to fit his poem in four instances. The characteristic French triple rhythms are not so easy to apply to German words, but there is evidence of their use in the simple " summer and winter songs " of Neidhart von Reuental, who lived in the first half of the thirteenth century. Contemporary with Neidhart were the famous *Minnesinger* (*i.e.* singers of courtly love) Walther von der Vogelweide—remembered by a single song, written on first seeing the Holy Land—Tannhäuser, and Wolfram von Eschenbach, who in fact competed like French minstrels, very much as depicted in Wagner's *Tannhäuser*.

Among the forms used by the German poet-composers one of the most popular was the *Bar*, which resembles the *ballade*. The equivalent of the *lay* was the *Leich*, and the Provençal *alba* (dawn-song or *aubade*) had its parallel in the *Tagelied*. Many of the Minnesinger songs are religious, even mystical, in tone ; and devotion to the Blessed Virgin becomes particularly noticeable in the fourteenth century with the songs of Frauenlob and Hermann of Salzburg, in whose songs (sacred and secular) there is clear indication of folk-song influence.

If we wish to find a typical Minnesinger poet, we can hardly do better than take Oswald von Wolkenstein, who died in 1445. He was a member of the lesser nobility, a man whose travels had brought him into contact with French and Italian models, which he used for his songs of love, drinking, and politics. The Mastersingers, who owe their modern reputation entirely to the fact that Wagner made them the subject of his one comedy, flourished in the fifteenth and sixteenth centuries and reflected the glories of a past age of musical creation. Textbook regulations governed their songs, and competitions were in fact marred by the presence of a " marker " who chalked up each performer's offences against the rules—a feature which suggested to Wagner a parallel between himself (represented by the " free " artist Walter von Stolzing) and his chief critic Eduard Hanslick, whom he parodied as Beckmesser.

ENGLAND

English music seems to have been little affected by the troubadours. The English language was rarely used for songs, since French had been the language of the nobility since the Norman Conquest and the art-song was still an aristocratic or courtly form. The rare English texts of the Middle Ages (*Mirie it is while sumer ilast* or *Worldes blis*) are mostly sad reflections on the brevity of life. There was, however, one peculiarly English form of song which developed during the fifteenth century into a popular polyphonic piece, and this was the *carol*. The few monodic, or single-voice, carols that survive probably belong to the fourteenth century. With text in Latin or English and marked by a characteristic refrain, the carol may be religious, amorous, or even political, and the modern exclusive association with Christmas represents the persistence of a single type of what was originally a much wider form.

SPAIN AND ITALY

Many collections of Spanish and Italian medieval songs survive, and in both cases the texts are religious although in the vernacular. The *Cantigas de Santa Maria*, compiled by King Alfonso of Leon and Castile in the second half of the thirteenth century, bear witness to the strong Spanish cult of the Blessed Virgin. They are written in rhythmic notation, with triple rhythms slightly preponderating over duple. A similar Italian form of song—the *laude* (or " praise ")—grew up in association with the secular companies formed in many Italian towns during the thirteenth century to perform religious plays. In both Spain and Italy these songs had a popular style and vigour in marked contrast with the character of liturgical plainsong. The troubadours who fled to Italy after the Albigensian Crusade seem to have left no music and to have concentrated all their interest on poetry. The *laudi* are probably the source of the few single-voice ballades (*ballate*) which date from the early fourteenth century.

TROPE AND CONDUCTUS

It was not only secular music that proliferated in new forms during the Middle Ages. Textual and musical interpolations were gradually introduced into the more ornamental passages of the plainsong of the Mass—such as the *Kyrie eleison*, the word " Alleluia " or the final *Benedicamus Domino*. These interpolations were called *tropes*, and a " troped *Kyrie* ", for instance, would have new words added to the long ornamental musical phrases between the two words " Kyrie " and " eleison ". The word " Alleluia " had been from earliest times ornamented with rich musical " coloratura " to emphasise its ecstatic, jubilant character. When words were added to this coloratura it often happened that two stanzas covered a single musical passage, and this was the origin of the *sequence*, with its paired stanzas and simple syllabic melody. Some of the most famous Latin hymns are in fact sequences—*Dies Irae* and *Veni Sancte Spiritus* are good examples.

Conductus is the name loosely applied to almost any Latin song with religious or moralistic text written between the twelfth and the fourteenth centuries. It may be in the form of a sequence or a " troped " *Benedicamus Domino*. The school associated with St. Martial in the early twelfth century, and later with Notre Dame in Paris, produced conductus-compositions that are still fascinating in their melodic skill and beauty, and lively with their characteristic triple rhythm. As the name suggests, the conductus was associated with processions, and some of the finest examples were written for the coronations or funerals of French kings. There is an interesting two-part example, *Redit aetas aurea*, written for the coronation of Richard Cœur-de-Lion in 1189.

III

THE RISE OF PART-MUSIC

HARMONY is so important in all the music that we really know and love that it is hard for us to appreciate the fact that music in several parts was quite subsidiary in the early Middle Ages—at least from the ninth to the twelfth century, when we first hear of the use of consonance.

It is possible that the doubling of a melody at the fourth, fifth or octave was an instinctive practice in the Middle Ages, as it is among some primitive peoples to-day. Although ancient Greek music was essentially melodic (*i.e.* single-voiced), composers certainly doubled at the octave (natural when boys' or women's voices sing the same tune as men) and seem to have used other intervals when accompanying a voice on the lyre, but probably only occasional notes of the accompaniment diverged from the unison. A musical treatise of the ninth century gives details of parallel doubling of a melody at the fourth, fifth, octave, and twelfth against a plainsong chant.

Two parts were enough for the first experimenters, and we find a second voice singing a fifth, fourth, or third above a plainsong melody. Parallel movement was soon found to be unsatisfactory, and it was generally recommended that when one voice moved upwards the other should descend, a precept still followed by every student of elementary two-part harmony.

The next problem was that of the rhythmic adjustment of the different parts. This was easy while one note of the second part corresponded to one note of the original line of melody ; but difficulties arose as soon as there were two, three or more notes in the new "voice", and it was necessary to sing them at the right speed and in the right rhythm against the original. Such pieces were generally written in score, with occasional bar-lines to align the parts. As with plainsong, the melodies in manuscripts earlier than the twelfth century have first to be deciphered, and from our point of view it is a tragedy that the Winchester Troper (containing 164 two-part *organa* and by far our largest collection of early part-music) is written without staves.

FRANCE—ORGANUM AND MOTET

The word " organum " was used to mean first of all harmonised music in general and then a particular form of part-music. One of the early methods of avoiding the difficulties inherent in adding a new part to a plainsong melody was the so-called " free organum "—a method still used to-day among primitive peoples, *e.g.*, on the island of Madagascar. The lower voice sings the original melody in very long drawn out note-values, while the upper voice has soaring coloraturas with perhaps dozens of notes to one note in the lower part, which is called the *tenor* from its " holding " the melody.

This method of composition is already found in the St. Martial manuscripts, but it was particularly developed at Notre Dame in Paris under Leoninus in the twelfth century. (An anonymous Englishman writing a hundred years later speaks of Leoninus as " optimus organista "—not the best of organists but the best composer of *organa*.) This was clearly a solo art-form, and so it was that the solo passages of the liturgical plainsong of the Mass—the Gradual and the Alleluia—were the first to be set polyphonically. Leoninus was active between 1160 and 1180, when the present Notre Dame was being built, and he was succeeded at the end of the century by Perotinus, who developed a new form called " discant organum ", in which the voices move more uniformly and the rhythm is much more tightly organised. His masterpieces are the three- and four-part organa, *Viderunt* and *Sederunt*. Perotinus uses strict rhythmic patterns or modes, and the most frequent of these—consisting of longs and shorts which fall naturally into bars of 6/8— makes the combination of several voices comparatively easy. The lowest voice, or *tenor*, still has very long notes, but the upper voices are given plenty of rhythmic variation. (We may compare this with the use of " discant " in church choirs to-day.) It was probably Perotinus who laid the foundations of a new musical form by adding words to the upper parts. Hence arose the *motet*, so called because almost every note has a syllable of text (French *mot*—word). The individual discant sections were short and the largest manuscript of the Notre Dame school contains hundreds of these " little sentences " or *clausulas*. A slightly later source shows the next stage of the process, in which the first few words of the *motet* have been added in the margin, though the music is simply that of the textless *clausulas*.

Organum and *motet* were by definition polyphonic (*i.e.* many-voiced) forms. On the other hand, *conductus* was often written for a single voice, and the two or even three parts that appear in some manuscripts may be later accretions. The medieval system had no harmonic system or chords like our own. Composers built upwards, voice by voice, from the *tenor*, and each part was given an independent melody. The longer pieces—such as Perotinus's three-part *Salvatoris hodie*—often have textless passages at the beginning or the end, or even both. These passages have the same dance-like character as the two-part English dance-songs in the *Sumer is icumen in* manuscript. The gradual development of the note-against-note style plainly carried with it the implications of what we understand as "harmony".

In the motet, based on a plainsong *tenor*, the upper voices soon attained greater individuality and were given texts quite independent of one another, sometimes in French and sometimes in Latin. Thus a three-part motet might have a French love-song at the top, a Latin prayer to Our Lady in the middle voice, with a plainsong melody, of course, in the *tenor*. The English motet developed more slowly and showed a marked economy of material : in a three-part work the two upper voices would sing a phrase and then exchange parts while the *tenor* repeated the phrase. During the thirteenth century French musicians fitted an increasing number of notes into a single bar of the highest voice in a three-part motet, and the *tenor* notes grew longer. French texts were more commonly used, and by the end of the century even the *tenor* might be based on a popular rondeau. Two-part motets became, to all intents and purposes, solo songs, and the plainsong *tenors* were probably played on instruments. In the rondeau motet the upper voice is, in fact, a completely independent rondeau.

ARS NOVA—GUILLAUME DE MACHAUT

Philippe de Vitry, whose life covered the first half of the fourteenth century, was the author of a treatise entitled *Ars Nova* (The New Art), which gave its name to the new movement in France. Only fourteen of his motets survive, but in them we find examples of 2/4, 3/4, 6/8, and 9/8 ; and the expansion of the hitherto small rhythmic groups is one of the most important features of the fourteenth century. A single repeating rhythmic pattern might cover twenty bars or so in the upper voice of a motet, and this practice, known as *isorhythm*, was eventually extended first to the two lower voices of a four-part piece and finally to all four voices.

Guillaume de Machaut (*c.* 1300-77) was one of the main architects of the motet in this early period. He was a minor canon of Rheims and used mostly French texts, except in his later works, where Latin is more common. Only a few of Machaut's motets show isorhythm in the upper voices, and it was only in the following century, with Guillaume Dufay, that the isorhythmic motet achieved its greatest expansion.

ACCOMPANIED SOLO SONG

Although the motet was a popular form in the early fourteenth century, Machaut's accompanied solo songs soon caught the fancy of music lovers. His early works in ballade form are for solo singer and instrument, and there is no longer any question of a *tenor* derived from plainsong. In Machaut's earliest three-part songs the third part lies above that of the voice and it is given the same name as the highest voice in a three-part motet ; but with the gradual standardisation of both poetry and music, the *tenor* and *contratenor* were set beneath the voice. In the rare four-part works there is another instrumental part above the voice, but the three-part song was to remain the norm until the end of the fifteenth century. There is no indication in the manuscripts of the precise nature of the accompanying instrument, but the Middle Ages had a wide choice—viol, portable organ, small harp, shawm (oboe), trumpet, recorder, flute, lute, or bagpipe. Most of these were treble instruments, but lower parts could of course be provided by viols. As the century progressed, the slide trumpet also became popular and the larger oboe-type *bombards* were often used.

Similar in form to the Spanish *cantigas* and Italian *laudi* were the *virelais*, a solo-song form used by Machaut, whose most attractive compositions in this form have also an accompanying *tenor*. Machaut also has the distinction of having composed the first complete four-part setting of the Mass—including the *Ite missa est* as well as the usual movements of the Ordinary. His Gloria and Credo are in *conductus* style, and the other movements follow the pattern of the isorhythmic motet. The increasing complexity of fourteenth-century church music earned the rebuke of Pope John XXII, whose complaints led to the adoption of a simpler three-part song style which remained popular until the time of Dufay.

ITALY—MADRIGALS

It was hardly to be expected that fourteenth-century Italy, the cradle of the Renaissance, would lack a developed musical culture of its own, and in fact the second quarter of the century saw a flourishing school whose leaders were Giovanni da Cascia, Jacopo da Bologna, Donato da Cascia, and Gherardello da Firenze. They wrote *madrigals*—two-part vocal duets in which instruments were probably used to support the voices, although there are no separate instrumental parts. The subject-matter of these madrigals is the " courtly love " of the troubadours, and the musical origin of the madrigal seems to be the two-part *conductus*. They differ from contemporary French works chiefly in rhythm and in the greater emphasis on melody. The Italian composers make frequent changes of rhythm, whereas in France the bar-length generally remains the same throughout.

A form that was common in both countries was the *chace* (It. *caccia*), so called because in it two upper voices form a canon—in fact " chase " or pursue each other—and the *tenor* serves the purposes of a harmonic bass.

The most prolific Italian composer of this period was the blind organist Francesco Landini, who died just before the end of the fourteenth century. His two-part ballades (*ballate*) are in the style of the madrigal, but his three-part works are closer to the solo ballade of the French composers. His *Gran' pianto agli occhi* is a two-part duet with an instrumental *contratenor*. In Italy both vocal and accompaniment parts are generally smoother and more continuous than in French *ars nova* music, which is often broken up by a large number of rests. Even so, by the beginning of the fifteenth century French influence was very strong in Italy, and foreigners in general seem to have been valued more highly than native musicians.

GERMANY AND SPAIN

In Germany and Austria polyphony developed at a much later date than in France, and even in the fifteenth century German liturgical music reveals the most primitive *organum* technique. The few polyphonic songs by Hermann of Salzburg are very elementary, though certain *tenors* suggest the use of trumpet or bombard. They are mostly two-part works, like those by Oswald von Wolkenstein, who borrowed heavily from French models.

In Spain *ars nova* solo songs with French texts were very popular at the court of Aragon. Elsewhere we find traces of simple rounds or motet-like songs, with religious texts.

THE END OF THE MIDDLE AGES

Towards the end of the fourteenth century the rhythmic complications in French song had become excessive. Yet by means of syncopation and the simultaneous combination of different rhythms composers like Philip of Caserta and Jacob de Senlèches created music of great sophisticated beauty. Within the framework of the ballade there was little change, but it may have been Italian influence in general and that of Landini in particular that led to a gradual change which can be traced in the rondeau with simple 6/8 rhythms. The key-figure in the period of transition was Johannes

Ciconia de Liège, who was active in Italy about 1370, composing Italian madrigals and *ballate*, Mass movements and motets, but few French songs. He was perhaps the first composer to realise the potential importance of the harmonic bass provided by the *tenor* of the *chace* or *caccia*, while the Italian interest in melody prompted him to develop melodic imitation and sequence between the various parts. His motets show a new rhythmic freedom, and the *tenor* and *contratenor* parts are linked to form a harmonic support which may well have been strengthened by the use of slide trumpets.

JOHN DUNSTABLE (*d.* 1453)

Complete settings of the Mass are rare at this period, but we find many instances of single movements or such pairs as Gloria and Credo, or Sanctus and Agnus Dei. England led the way in the development of liturgical music during the fifteenth century, and the technique of improvising a harmonisation of plainsong in thirds and sixths played an important part in establishing these intervals as consonant. During the fourteenth century Mass movements composed in this " English discant " are common, and the composers of the English Chapel Royal gradually moved away from strict isorhythmic patterns to the freer style of the continent.

Henry V's victories in France helped to spread the fame of English musicians, and among them none was more highly esteemed than John Dunstable. He may have gone to live in France in the suite of the Duke of Bedford, brother of Henry V, but in any case he seems to have gone less to learn from French musicians than to instruct them. Although the author of a number of isorhythmic motets, he is most successful in his freer motets and Mass movements, where he introduces a smoothly flowing type of melodic sentence based on the interval of the third. English composers in general seem to have been the first to give unity to complete settings of the Mass by using the same plainsong phrase as the *tenor* throughout.

GUILLAUME DUFAY (*d.* 1474)

The most celebrated French composer in the first half of the fifteenth century was Guillaume Dufay, whose works show great variety and a clearly traceable development under foreign influence. His early songs, Masses, and isorhythmic motets do not differ greatly from those of his contemporaries at the beginning of the century, but between 1420 and 1430 we find Dufay experimenting with *faburden* (the " English discant " technique with the plainsong in the treble) and contrasting solo-voice duets with three-part choruses. In his later Masses he uses the English consonant style and also the "cyclic" *tenor* technique mentioned above. It is significant that the *cantus firmus* (or basic melody) of his *Caput* Mass is an antiphon from the Sarum, or Salisbury, Use. Dufay was also responsible for another practice which became common in the fifteenth and sixteenth centuries— the use of a secular theme, such as his own ballade *Se la face ay pale*, as *tenor* of a Mass. From Dufay's time, too, four-part writing becomes the rule in liturgical music, and occasionally five parts are found, though not often before the sixteenth century. In this matter, too, the English led the way. The six-part *Sumer is icumen in*, dating from the thirteenth century, is admittedly an exception, but several five-part English compositions have survived from about 1400, when none are known to have existed on the continent.

Finally, the gradual extension of the text to the lower as well as the upper voices in a liturgical composition gradually led to the completely vocal performance of such works. Instruments were retained, to give colour and support to the voices, but they were no longer essential. Most polyphony during the fourteenth and early fifteenth centuries was in fact difficult solo music, and even a good cathedral choir might contain only one or two singers able to perform it without instrumental support. Full choral polyphony is a product of the fifteenth century. In Dufay's most mature Mass, *Ave Regina Coelorum*, there is still some alternation between duets, trios and full four-part writing ; but the use of the text in all four parts is an indication that these sections were unquestionably choral. The development of college chapel choirs, such as those at King's College, Cambridge, and Eton, made polyphony a practical possibility, and the "Eton Manuscript" represents an important school of church music. Half of the 93 original manuscripts are lost, but there are still 39 motets and 4 Magnificats by Browne, Davy, Lambe, Wilkinson, and other composers. Five-part writing is the norm here, though six parts are not uncommon, and two of Wilkinson's pieces are for nine and thirteen voices respectively. Imitation between the voices is not very common, though John Plummer had made considerable use of it in the middle of the century.

THE BURGUNDIAN SCHOOL—
OCKEGHEM, OBRECHT, AND JOSQUIN DES PRÉS

The dukedom of Burgundy was founded in 1363, when John II of France gave it, with hereditary rights, to his son Philip. Marriage, inheritance, conquest, and purchase very quickly enlarged the Burgundian domain to include almost the whole of the modern Holland and Belgium as well as Lorraine, and during the Hundred Years War Burgundy joined the invading English forces against the French monarchy. Under Philip the Good and Charles the Bold—roughly, that is to say, from 1420 to 1480—the Burgundian court was a great centre of the arts, employing Guillaume Dufay among its musicians and Jan van Eyck among its painters. Dufay's work was continued in the second half of the fifteenth century by the Flemish–Burgundian composers Obrecht, Ockeghem, and Josquin des Prés. Ockeghem's Masses continue the long, flowing melodic phrases of Dunstable, but Obrecht and Josquin began to emphasise and to develop the vertical, *i.e.* harmonic, aspect of choral music. In his Masses Josquin makes plentiful use of imitation, and instead of prolonging the plainsong notes of the *tenor* introduces it with great skill into all the voices, so that horizontal and vertical forces are perfectly combined.

Another method used by Josquin, and one to become very popular in the sixteenth century, was the " parody " Mass. In his *Mater patris* Mass, for instance, Josquin took a three-part motet by his contemporary Brumel and used quotations from it to open and to close the movements of the Mass. One, two, or all three voices of the model could be used, either as a basis for the development of the composer's own ideas or as a ground for the stricter form of variation. With the standardisation of four-part writing, harmony began to take on something of its modern complexion. If this later medieval music still sounds strange to our ears, this is due to the use of a single mode throughout each piece instead of the key system with its modulations. This was not to be developed until the seventeenth century.

EARLY KEYBOARD MUSIC

The recent discovery of an early fifteenth-century Italian keyboard score has given us new information about the few extant pieces of keyboard music that survive from the fourteenth century. The manuscript consists chiefly of keyboard arrangements of well-known songs by Guillaume de Machaut, Jacopo da Bologna, and Francesco Landini, and some settings of plainsong from the Ordinary of the Mass. These pieces are in two parts only, the original song appearing in the *tenor* while the upper part provides a highly ornamented paraphrase of the melody. The organ settings of the Mass movements, on the other hand, are entirely new compositions intended to alternate with choral plainsong, whose melody appears in long notes in the lower part.

Two important collections of organ music survive from mid-fifteenth century Germany—the Buxheim Organ Book and Conrad Paumann's *Fundamentum Organisandi*, a handbook for organ composers. Like Landini,

Paumann was a blind organist who was also master of many other instruments. The *Fundamentum* is an elementary guide to counterpoint at the organ, and the other compositions in this, as well as in the Buxheim collection, consist of well-known songs set in long notes in the *tenor* with florid new melodies in the treble. The Buxheim book, which clearly indicates the use of the pedals, contains German as well as French polyphonic songs and Mass movements.

IV

THE GOLDEN AGE OF CHORAL MUSIC

FRANCE

THE sixteenth century was an age of development and fruition in many forms of music, but it is in vocal polyphony that the age was outstanding. The musical setting of the Mass had reached a classic form with Josquin des Prés, and the motet might either follow a similar pattern or else take the simpler form of a polyphonic hymn. With secular music it was different. About the same time that Louis XI of France reincorporated Burgundy in the French state (1477) the obsolete three-part song was replaced by a new form developed by Josquin from the motet. It is true that Josquin uses a Latin *tenor* in long notes (the introit *Requiem æternam*) in his five-part lament for Ockeghem, who died about 1495 ; but other works of his of the same date are not based on any pre-existent material, and the imitative counterpoint of his six-part *Petite camusette*, for instance, clearly foreshadows the typical French song of the sixteenth century, as we see it in the works of Claudin de Sermisy and Clément Jannequin.

Jannequin is best known for his picturesque (or as we should now say " programmatic ") battle and birdsong pieces and " cries of Paris "—four-part, chordal music for the most part. Such printers as Attaignant and later Le Roy and Ballard helped to popularise this music, which also received a strong additional impetus from the French classical revival that we connect with the name of Ronsard and the Pléïade poets. In the second half of the century, on the other hand, we find a more dignified contrapuntal style, in five or more parts, and the solo voice with instrumental accompaniment in the lute songs. Claude Lejeune practised both forms and also attempted the so-called " measured verses ", in which the long and short syllables of Greek and Latin poetry were substituted for the regularly recurring bar-lines of the predominant " common time ".

The lightheartedness of the typical French *chanson* attracted foreign composers also, and we find Roland de Lassus (1532–94) writing German *Lieder*, Italian *frottole* and madrigals, and French *chansons*, including settings of Ronsard and du Bellay.

PALESTRINA AND LASSUS

During the second half of the fifteenth century the fame of Netherlands or Flemish composers had grown to such an extent that it was a recognised thing for these Northern masters to travel to Italy, not as pupils but as instructors. Adrien Willaert's position as *maestro di cappella* at St. Mark's, Venice, and Cyprien de Rore's at Ferrara, were characteristic of the age, and Lassus held high posts of honour in Italy as well as at Munich. Italian composers were not, however, long in learning. Luca de Marenzio and Gesualdo were soon supreme in the field of the madrigal, Palestrina in the ecclesiastical domain. Andrea and Giovanni Gabrieli developed a branch of choral music for several choirs and instruments that held the seed of much that was to come. The Cavazzonis and Francesco da Milano made great names in the field of organ and lute music.

Giovanni Pierluigi da Palestrina (1525–94) is chiefly remembered as the composer of some hundred Masses and six hundred motets and other liturgical music. Within its consciously accepted limits—the limits of any strictly liturgical art—his music is flawless. He did not aim at innovation, but at the perfect balance between horizontal and vertical voices (*i.e.* counterpoint and harmony) that Josquin des Prés had foreshadowed. Palestrina, however, weeded out many of the dissonances that still persisted in Josquin's harmony, and this discipline produced the most perfectly consonant style, with the smoothest possible movement in all the parts. The lines of his melodies are small in compass, and rests at the end of phrases are made as small and as rare as possible. Despite the extremely severe discipline of this style, Palestrina's music—like all great art—gives the impression of freedom and naturalness.

If Palestrina is chiefly remembered for his Masses, the best and most characteristic of Lassus's work is to be found in his motets. This exuberant and powerful music, with its great variety of tenderness and vivid pictorialism, is a pure expression of human nature, as Palestrina represents the best religious feeling of the age. Lassus allows his texts to dictate the form of his motets, and his writing is on the whole more chordal, less polyphonic than Palestrina's. In works for eight or more parts he seems to be anticipating the choral style of the Gabrielis, but he rarely divides his forces into contrasting groups. An excellent example of his illustrative style is the six-part *In hora ultima*, where he imitates the sounds of trumpet and harp, and even of laughter.

VENICE—ANDREA AND GIOVANNI GABRIELI

Andrea Gabrieli was a contemporary of Lassus, and both he and his nephew Giovanni developed the antiphonal style of chordal writing in many parts, prompted by the disposition of several separate choirs in the Venetian basilica of St. Mark. Giovanni Gabrieli, in particular, worked on a magnificent scale. His *Salvator noster* is written for three five-part choirs, and his *Ascendit Deus* for four four-part choirs. *In ecclesiis*, on the other hand, has solo passages for both soprano and tenor voices, which are also combined in a number of different ways with a four-part chorus, a six-part instrumental ensemble (three cornetts, violin, and trombone), and two four-part choruses.

SPAIN AND GERMANY

Polyphony also flourished in Spain and Germany at this time. During the first half of the sixteenth century the name of Cristóbal de Morales overshadowed all others, but was in turn overshadowed by that of Tomás Luis de Victoria, who died in 1611. Victoria used a technique very similar to that of Palestrina, but his motets have a passionate intensity that we can recognise as typically Spanish. Most remarkable among his Masses is the Requiem written on the death of the Empress Maria in 1603.

German composers in the second half of the fifteenth century were strongly influenced by Netherlands models, and the Masses of Heinrich Finck and Heinrich Isaac clearly show the break with the archaic polyphony found in German manuscripts dating from the earlier part of the century. The Reformation made German hymn-settings popular (generally in four parts, with the melody in treble or tenor), but religious differences did not prevent composers from working on both sides of the line which divided Europe so sharply. Ludwig Senfl, a Swiss, was a composer in the Netherlandish tradition who completed Isaac's gigantic collection of polyphonic Mass settings, the so-called *Choralis Constantinus*. Lassus and Philippe de Monte continued the Catholic tradition, and even Hans Leo Hassler, though a Protestant, continued to write settings of the Mass. His motets show the influence of Lassus, but the Venetian School of the Gabrielis clearly suggested the division of his eight-part works into two four-part choruses.

ENGLAND

The religious situation was nowhere more confused than in England. Taverner, a fanatical Protestant, wrote eight Masses and many motets before renouncing the composition of elaborate church music. William Byrd

(1543-1623), whose life covers the reigns of Elizabeth and James I, remained a staunch Catholic, and his three Masses (in three, four, and five parts), the motets of the *Cantiones Sacrae*, and liturgical composition of the " Gradualia," show him at his best, comparable in stature to Palestrina, but with a warmer, more human temperament. Yet Byrd worked for the Anglican Church and his " Great Service " is one of his finest works.

The composer whose work has left most mark on the music of the Anglican rite is Thomas Tallis (*d.* 1585), who belonged to an earlier generation than Byrd. He, too, wrote settings of the Mass and many Latin motets, but his Anglican " Short Service " is written according to the Lutheran principle of securing the maximum of verbal clarity by means of simple chordal writing, as opposed to the elaborate interweaving of melodic strands which often make the texts of polyphonic pieces unintelligible. Anglican polyphony was at first a rather dull imitation of the Catholic motet, but Tye's *Acts of the Apostles* already shows a more interesting musical style, with frequent imitation between the parts ; and Weelkes, Gibbons, and Tomkins wrote splendid works in four, five, six, or more parts. These men lived on well into the seventeenth century. It was the influence of solo song that led them to elaborate the so-called " verse anthem ", which alternates solo voices and instruments with full chorus sections. Both Morley and Tomkins wrote an *Out of the deepe* in this style, and Gibbons's *This is the record of John* is one of his masterpieces.

MADRIGALS

During the sixteenth century the French, as we have seen, delighted in the polyphonic *chanson* and the Italians excelled in the madrigal. This form seems to have developed from the *frottola*, a simple, generally four-part song of a popular character. Such songs would be sung during the celebration of Carnival, and their religious equivalent was the *laude*. The sixteenth-century madrigal was free in poetic structure, and the music was in imitative counterpoint, generally in four or five parts. Such early madrigalists as Verdelot, Arcadelt, and Festa, who wrote in the 1530s and 40s, are nearer in style to the simpler *frottola* writers, though they chose texts of superior literary quality. The *villanesca*, which was popular at this time, is of Neapolitan origin and shows its humble, popular origin clearly in the " parallel fifths " (possibly imitating the drone of the bagpipe).

Later in the century the madrigal-writers show increasing preoccupation with the expression of mood and pictorial illustration of the text. An extreme instance of chromaticism used to express emotional tension is to be found in the works of Prince Gesualdo of Venosa. In a work such as his *Io pur respiro* the constant progression from one out-of-the-way chord to another eventually weakens the sense of tonality, despite the fact that he begins and ends the piece conventionally. The true greatness of Luca Marenzio (1553–99), on the other hand, lies in his many-sidedness and his classical balancing of the elements of each composition. His pastoral pieces are elegant in the extreme, but he can be powerful, tender, or lively as occasion demands, and word-painting is an important feature of his music. (In *Gia torna*, for instance, he depicts the movement of waves by a gently undulating phrase.)

In the works of Claudio Monteverdi (1567–1643) we can see the transition from the purely vocal madrigal to accompanied solo song. The first three books of his five-part madrigals are comparatively conventional, but Book IV contains many examples of choral recitative and counterpoint simplified in order to make the text more easily intelligible. In Books V and VI, five-part sections alternate with solo passages, and Monteverdi even employs an instrument (harpsichord or lute) as " continuo ", *i.e.* to strengthen the bass and emphasise the harmony.

In Germany Heinrich Isaac, whom we have already met as a composer of church music, provided the impetus needed to convert late medieval secular polyphony into newer forms in keeping with the spirit of the sixteenth century. These German songs were often based on an original melody used as a *tenor*, and Isaac's squarely German *Zwischen perg und tieffem tal* is a fine example. At the end of the century Hassler published, beside German songs in madrigal style, a number of Italian madrigals, and he even imitated the *balletti*, or dance-like songs, which were also to attract Thomas Morley in England. In Spain the *villancico* corresponded to the Italian *frottola*, and the master of this form was Juan del Encina, who wrote in a predominantly chordal style, in two to five parts.

INSTRUMENTAL MUSIC

A purely practical consideration provided the most powerful stimulus to the composition of instrumental music in the sixteenth century. This was the invention of a notation for lute music, which made it possible to copy out collections of dances, arrangements of vocal music, and new instrumental works that appeared after 1507. Among the dances the slow *pavanes* and quick *saltarellos* predominate, and the independent *ricercare* started as a showpiece like the later *toccata*. The *ricercare* soon became the instrumental equivalent of the motet, with rich imitative counterpoint, and we find examples for organ and various instrumental groups. Although superseded in Italy by the *passamezzo* about the middle of the century, the *pavane* maintained its popularity in England and is to be found in all the virginal books of the later half of the century. It is often paired with the sprightlier *galliard*, and sometimes both pieces are based on the same musical material. Organ and harpsichord music is generally found without differentation in the same volume, but plainsong settings (such as Tallis's virtuoso *Felix namque*) obviously belong to the organ, while Bull's *Walsingham* variations are equally clearly meant for the harpsichord.

A peculiarly English form of instrumental composition was the *In nomine*, which originally drew its material from the *Benedictus* section (which of course includes the words " qui venit *in nomine* Domini ") in Taverner's Mass *Gloria tibi trinitas*. No clear distinction in the matter of form exists between compositions for lute, keyboard, or strings (" consort " of viols). In Italy the organ Mass, with alternating organ and plainsong, was developed by Girolamo Cavazzoni, who also wrote *ricercari* and *canzoni*, the latter in the style of the French chanson. The Venetians were especially famous as organists, and the toccatas of Claudio Merulo are not simply virtuoso showpieces but also contain sections in imitative polyphony.

Lute music was popular all over the Continent at this time, and the prevalent polyphonic style was used even for lute music, so that an instrument whose natural genius was for chordal music was asked to perform contrapuntal *ricercari* and fantasias. It was in these that Francesco da Milano particularly excelled. The Spanish *vihuela* (an early form of guitar) had a repertory very like that of the lute, and included *pavanes* and fantasias as well as variations on well-known themes. The blind Antonio de Cabezón was the chief Spanish keyboard composer of the mid-sixteenth century.

The Germans had been well known as lute-makers and organists for more than a century, and the *cantus firmus* (or variation) technique of hymnsettings by Arnolt Schlick and Paul Hofhaimer in the early sixteenth century provides the first examples of an art which was to be brought to perfection by J. S. Bach in his chorale preludes. Renaissance Germany particularly favoured the improvisatory form of prelude or preamble, consisting of chordal passages interspersed with ornamental scales, both in lute and organ pieces. The lute manuscripts of the period contain many dances, some based on Italian models but many on the German *Tanz*. This was divided into two parts—the first generally in duple time and the second (or *Nachtanz*) usually in more lively triple time.

Instrumental consorts of wind instruments, with a few strings added, were widely used in court and municipal music. Unfortunately the exact instrumentation of these pieces is not often indicated, but a notable exception is Giovanni Gabrieli's *Sonata pian e forte*. Here there are two instrumental choruses, one of which plays loudly and the other softly. Both groups contain three trombones, but one has an additional cornett (a woodwind instrument with finger-holes but a cup-mouthpiece) and the other a violin. With this baroque-sounding piece we are on the threshold of a new era.

ENGLISH MUSIC 1500–1700

The population of England and Wales at the end of the sixteenth century —the century in which we may properly speak of the Renaissance as a formative influence in British music—is reckoned by modern historians to have been slightly over four million. We may wonder what music most of those four million heard. What did the farm labourers sing at a harvest feast ? What music on what instruments accompanied a guild celebration in York or Bristol ? What ditties had the sailors who brought the sea-coal (so named from its mode of transport) from Tyneside to warm the hearths of London ? Many indeed are the contemporary references to music-making of a social kind. The wealthy clothier John Winchcomb (d. 1520) became, as " Jack of Newbury ", the hero of an Elizabethan folk-ballad which gives us one such reference. Though G. M. Trevelyan in his *English Social History* warns us that the numbers of people mentioned must be exaggerated, the ballad is still worth quoting :

> Within one room, being large and long
> There stood two hundred looms full strong.
> Two hundred men, the truth is so,
> Wrought in these rooms all in a row.
> By every one a pretty boy
> Sate making quilts with mickle joy.
> And in another place hard by
> A hundred women merrily
> Were carding hard with joyful cheer,
> Who singing sat with voices clear.

Of the substance of this popular kind of music-making we can know very little. True, we have the variations written by scholarly masters on popular tunes (such as William Byrd's on *The Carman's Whistle*), for in those days there was no gap such as yawns to-day between " serious " and " popular " music. True, we know the names of certain popular tunes from literary references (not only Shakespeare), and some of these tunes retained their popularity sufficiently long to appear in printed collections of song-tunes and dance-tunes in the second half of the seventeenth century. But for most of the sixteenth century printed music was at an early stage and furnished the material for only a small corner of English music-making. Even when we turn to manuscripts, those which survive—such as the famous *Mulliner Book*, a collection of pieces mainly for the virginals or organ, probably compiled by one Thomas Mulliner some time between 1550 and 1575—bring us into contact only with the world of the cathedral organist, or of the professional musician in service to a noble family.

In considering, therefore, the high achievement of the music of the sixteenth century in England—an achievement which has led some historians to call this the Golden Age of English music—we are basing our judgments on the art of professional musicians serving a restricted and cultivated section of society. What is sometimes called " Tudor Church Music " was not the repertory of every village church ; it was music written for the special resources of cathedrals and such establishments as the Chapel Royal. Nor can we think of a favourite madrigal, or a fantasia for viols, or a dance-movement for virginals, as having a circulation comparable with that of a Beethoven symphony in modern times.

" TUDOR CHURCH MUSIC "

Exceptionally, however, we have evidence of one kind of " vernacular " music of lasting importance. It was at this period that English Psalters—translations of the Psalms into English metrical verse—began to be printed with tunes. One such collection was brought out by the religious reformer Miles Coverdale, but suppressed for its Protestant tendencies by Henry VIII in 1539. Six years previously, a Psalter had appeared of which the music has been ascribed by later scholarship to Christopher Tye (*c.* 1500–*c.* 1573). The Psalter which achieved the greatest acceptance was that which came to be known as " Sternhold and Hopkins " and went through several editions to achieve a definitive form in 1562. In 1567 or 1568 a Psalter was prepared by Archbishop Parker but was never, apparently, published. It was for this that Thomas Tallis wrote nine tunes—one of which is the source of the famous *Tallis's Canon* (incorporated by Benjamin Britten into *Noye's Fludde*) and another one of which is the basis of Vaughan Williams's *Fantasia on a Theme of Tallis*.

The considerable activity in publishing Psalters is to be seen as a sign of Protestantism, and indeed musical activity was deeply involved in the religious controversy of the period. Nowhere is that better seen than in the career of John Taverner (*c.* 1495–1545), who wrote a number of Masses and other church works in Latin for the Catholic rite, but afterwards changed his views and underwent imprisonment for Protestant heresy. From a contemporary source we learn that his profession earned him a special pleading : " The Cardinal for his musick excused him saying that he was but a musitian, and so he escaped." Later Taverner quitted music and became an agent in the enforcement of the dissolution of the monasteries.

Taverner's Masses are regarded as bringing to a climax the strength of English choral music in the generation before Tye and Tallis. With Taverner's name may be coupled that of Robert Fayrfax, who lived from 1464 to 1521 and accompanied Henry VIII to the Field of the Cloth of Gold in 1520.

As already stated, Taverner has peculiar interest as the originator of a characteristic form of English instrumental music, the *In Nomine*. Taverner, having written a Mass based on the plainsong melody *Gloria tibi trinitas*, transcribed for the virginals the part of his Mass beginning with the words " In Nomine Domini " and used the words " In Nomine " as a title for his transcription. Other composers developed the custom of writing fantasias for viols or virginals on this particular plainsong and of entitling such works *In Nomine*, apparently in tribute to Taverner's example.

VOICES AND INSTRUMENTS

Voices, virginals, viols—here were the three most important media for English composers of that period. As far as professional music-making was concerned, the voices were chiefly those of boys and men, including the adult male alto (often styled " counter-tenor " in the mid-twentieth century secular revival of this type of voice—although, strictly speaking, a male alto is a baritone singing falsetto, and a counter-tenor is a light high tenor). The virginals was a keyboard instrument—in effect, a small harpsichord with one manual. Despite legend, it was not named after the Virgin Queen and it was known before her time. Just possibly it was named through being played by young girls, but more probably from the Latin *virga*, a rod or jack (part of the mechanism).

The viols, bowed stringed instruments with frets (like those of a guitar) along the fingerboard, formed a " family " of instruments from high to low pitch. They were frequently used on their own as a " consort ", to use the sensible English word which was then current for " ensemble ". A " broken consort " was a mixture of stringed and wind instruments. The most popular wind instrument of the time was the recorder, made, like the viol, in several sizes, and familiar in many literary references (including *Hamlet*). We must also mention the lute, whose plucked strings were a familiar sound in Elizabethan England. The theorbo was a large lute ; the cittern and gittern were two other (not identical) plucked instruments of lute or guitar type.

Henry VIII (1491-1547) was himself a composer, though an unimportant one. The motet *O Lord the Maker of All Thing*, formerly attributed to him, was really by William Mundy. Elizabeth I (1533–1603), though she played the virginals, did not compete in composition with the great musicians who came under her sway. But this sway was direct ; Tallis and William Byrd jointly held the position of organist at the Chapel Royal from 1572, and three years later received from the Queen the lucrative monopoly of music-printing in England. Until very recently, Elizabeth has always been mentioned in musical history as the person in whose honour there appeared the compilation of madrigals called *The Triumphs of Oriana* (published in 1603). But recent scholarship has now shown that " Oriana " was not Elizabeth I but Anne of Denmark, the wife of Elizabeth's successor, James I.

Tallis and Byrd published in 1575 a joint set of Latin motets (short choral compositions to religious words) with the title *Cantiones Sacræ* or sacred songs. Church music, first in Latin and then in English, seems indeed to have occupied Tallis almost entirely. His is the astonishing feat of having written a motet in forty parts (that is, for eight choirs each of five voices, all independent) *Spem in alium nunquam habui*, a work of great musical effectiveness, apart from all technical considerations. Tallis culti-vated a predominantly solemn style, and his Latin and English church music remains in modern use.

William Byrd's output was broader. As we have seen, he composed notable music both for the Catholic rite in Latin and for the Anglican rite in English, and also madrigals and other secular vocal music. His many pieces for the virginals include a descriptive suite of fourteen movements entitled *The Battell*, of which one movement is headed " The marche to the fighte—Tantara, tantara—The Battels be joyned ". In the fashion of his time, Byrd wrote a number of sets of variations for keyboard, either on popular songs or on a " ground ", that is, a phrase repeated again and again, usually in the bass. It was also typical of this period, when the boundary between vocal and instrumental music was not as clearly defined as it later became, that Byrd should include two fantasias for viols in the collection entitled *Psalms, Songs, and Sonnets* (1611).

A pupil of Byrd, and a composer who generally shows a lighter touch than either Byrd or Tallis, is Thomas Morley (1557–1603). He composed a setting of " It was a lover and his lass " for Shakespeare's *As You Like It* in 1599. Morley is the author of the most famous English musical textbook of the period, *A plain and easy introduction to practical music*, in which he describes an imagined occasion when a guest finds himself put to shame because he could not sing at sight. (This passage, formerly thought to be evidence of an astonishingly high standard of general musical education in Elizabethan England, is now considered to correspond rather to well-written advertising " copy ".) Though he also wrote instrumental pieces and church music in Latin and English, Morley is chiefly famous for his madrigals and *balletts*. He was the editor of *The Triumphs of Oriana*, as well as a contributor to it.

MADRIGALS

The English madrigal, of which the *ballett* is a variant, is generally held to be the form which (apart from church music) crowns the musical achievement of the age. The Golden Age of the madrigal lasted some forty years, from 1588, the year of the Armada, to 1627. The madrigal was in two significant ways typical of its time—in its debt to Italy (a debt to be seen also in contemporary English literature) and in its reluctance to make a firm demarcation between vocal and instrumental music. Although the English madrigal is in essence a contrapuntal composition for four or more voices, to think of it as remote from instrumental music is a mistake. It seems clear that viols could and occasionally did replace the singers. We may get some idea of the interchangeability of voices and instruments from Byrd's *Psalms, Sonnets and Songs of Sadness and Piety* which show an approximation to madrigal style and which appeared in 1588 ; in these the five-part vocal setting is an adaptation from what had originally been scored for one voice with accompaniment for viols.

Later in the same year appeared a volume called *Musica Transalpina*, a collection of Italian madrigals with words translated into English. The chief composer represented there was Luca Marenzio, and it was this Italian example which led to the flowering of the madrigal in the hands of English composers. The poetry they set was, like the Italian, chiefly the poetry of sensual love. An erotic significance is conveyed by expressive musical settings of such words as "sigh" and "die", precisely as in the Italian. Lighter in touch are the *balletts*, chiefly distinguished by their "fa-la" refrain ; these too, follow an Italian exemplar, Giovanni Giacomo Gastoldi (*d.* 1622).

But it would be wrong to think of the English madrigal as simply the Italian madrigal transplanted. In such composers as Morley, Thomas Weelkes (*d.* 1623), and John Wilbye (1574–1638) we can speak of a great and specifically English school of madrigalists. Another such composer is Orlando Gibbons (1583–1625), whose madrigals include *The Silver Swan*. Though it is sometimes supposed that the contrapuntal nature of the madrigal implies that all voices are equally important in providing the "tune", this is by no means always so. Gibbons's *The Silver Swan* and Morley's *ballett Now is the month of Maying* provide familiar examples of how the topmost voice tends to grasp the chief melodic interest. This tendency eventually asserted itself fully in the " ayres " of John Dowland (1563-1626). The madrigal had a late exponent in Thomas Tomkins (1572-1656) who, like Morley, was a pupil of Byrd ; but the special interest of Tomkins's work lies in his church music.

JOHN DOWLAND

Composer and poet are linked in a famous sonnet which, though it has in the past been attributed to Shakespeare, is now thought by some to have been written by Richard Barnfield :

> If music and sweet poetry agree
> (As they must needs, the sister and the brother)
> Then must the love be great 'twixt thee and me,
> Because thou lov'st the one and I the other.
> Dowland to thee is dear, whose heavenly touch
> Upon the lute doth ravish human sense ;
> Spenser to me, whose deep conceit is such
> As, passing all conceit, needs no defence. . . .

John Dowland was a virtuoso of the lute whose renown went well beyond England. In 1598 he was appointed court lutenist to Christian IV of Denmark at a handsome salary. Not only did he compose remarkably expressive solo pieces for his instrument ; he was also the apparent inventor of the vocal form now usually called the English " ayre " (the old spelling of the word " air " being retained for this special meaning). The madrigal in principle allotted equal musical interest to each of its combining vocal strands (though we have seen that the principle was not always adhered to) ; the ayre firmly placed the melodic line on top, and supporting harmony was supplied either by other voices or by a lute. The ayres or lute-songs of Dowland are chiefly notable for their expressive treatment of words, both in the melody and the harmony.

Thomas Campian or Campion (1567-1620) and Philip Rosseter (1568-1623) brought out a joint publication of songs to the lute in 1601 ; each was a distinguished poet as well. Another composer of lute songs was John Cooper (c. 1575-1626), who journeyed to Italy about 1604 and, on returning, used an italianised form of his name, Coperario. (He was not the last Englishman to find that a foreign name improved his professional chances at home.) English musicians of the period indeed kept in touch with Continental developments and were themselves highly esteemed abroad. John Bull (1563-1628) died in Antwerp, where he was the cathedral organist. He is chiefly remembered as a composer of music for the virginals. Among

DETAIL SHOWING ANGELIC CHOIR FROM " CHRIST GLORIFIED IN
THE COURT OF HEAVEN " (*circa* 1430) BY FRA ANGELICO

The instruments shown are tabor, portative organ, harp, trumpet, lute, psaltery
(a stringed instrument of the zither type) and rebec (a precursor of the violin).
These were all in use at the time the picture was painted.

his keyboard pieces is one in the minor mode which may have been an ancestor of *God Save The Queen*. (The present version dates from the eighteenth century and its composer is unknown.)

WILLIAM LAWES

A pupil of Cooper (Coperario) was William Lawes, who was born in 1602 and was killed in 1645 when fighting on the Royalist side in the Civil War. The writing of chamber music in the form of fantasias for viols, and also for " broken consorts " of various instruments, is his particular achievement. His brother Henry Lawes (1596–1662) is more celebrated, not perhaps because of any decided musical superiority but because of his association with the poet Milton. It was Henry Lawes who provided the music to Milton's masque, *Comus*, in 1634, and Milton later wrote a sonnet beginning :

> Harry, whose tuneful and well-measured song
> First taught our English music how to span
> Words with just note and accent. . . .

This may seem to us exaggerated praise, especially when we remember Dowland's achievement in just this respect ; but it was praise echoed by other musicians and poets of Lawes's day. *Comus* was a mixture of song, dancing, speech, and pageantry. It was in fact a herald of English opera, and, as we shall see, Henry Lawes was a composer involved in the production of the first English opera to be so called (*The Siege of Rhodes*).

A four-part round by William Lawes, *She weepeth sore in the night* (beginning with a striking chromatic descent), is an exceptionally serious example of a form which was more often adapted to frivolous and convivial moods. Thomas Ravenscroft (*c.* 1590–*c.* 1633) had published in 1609, under the title of *Pammelia* (from the Greek for " all-honeyed "), the first English printed collection of canons, rounds, and catches of this sort, among them *Three Blind Mice*. (A round is, technically, a variety of canon ; a " catch ", possibly derived in this sense from the Italian song of the type called *caccia*, involving a play on words or a similar trickery evident in performance.) Those eminent exponents Sir Toby Belch and Sir Andrew Aguecheek show us that this type of thing was not new, but the seventeenth century was its heyday. Another famous collection was published by John Hilton (1599–1657) under the title of *Catch That Catch Can* in 1652. Later examples of catches include some by Purcell to bawdy words suppressed in modern publications. The form continued in favour well into the nineteenth century.

DANCE TUNES

The English Dancing Master (1650) represented another type of popular music of the period. A collection of dance tunes, with instructions for dancing, it was the first musical work to be issued by the publisher John Playford (1623–86) and retained great popularity through many editions. The publishing of music in general was more intense during the period of the Commonwealth and Protectorate (1649–60) than in the periods immediately before and immediately afterwards. Though the Puritans suppressed the use of professional choirs and of organs in church—a suppression which affected some of the finest English music—the idea that the Puritans had any objection to music in general is a legend which has now been thoroughly exploded. Cromwell himself engaged a musician as his private organist (for secular occasions) and as music-teacher to his daughter. Since Cromwell's régime closed the public theatres, it was thus on non-theatrical premises that the first English opera was produced—*The Siege of Rhodes* (1656) with libretto by Sir William Davenant (who had formerly been imprisoned for royalist activities) and with music (now lost) by two major composers, Henry Lawes and Matthew Locke (*c.* 1630–77) and three lesser ones, Henry Cooke, Edward Coleman, and George Hudson.

The idea of opera, like the idea of the madrigal in the previous century, came to England from Italy; and so did the declamatory style of setting words to music which was incorporated in *The Siege of Rhodes* and which contemporaries called " the recitative music ". But English opera in the seventeenth century is not opera as we know it so much as a kind of spectacular play with fairly elaborate music; and Purcell's *Dido and Aeneas*, as we shall see, is an exception. The Restoration theatre made a prominent use of music. It was for Davenant's adaptation (barbarous according to modern standards) of *Macbeth*, in 1674, that there was composed some incidental music which long remained in favour and which was formerly ascribed to Locke. He is now known not to have written it, but it is not known who did.

The lute went out of fashion towards the end of the seventeenth century; Arabella Hunt (*d.* 1705), a singer for whom Purcell and Blow wrote many songs, and a court favourite of Queen Mary, was one of its last celebrated exponents. The large harpsichord, more powerful than the small virginals, became the favoured instrument for accompanying songs and for keyboard solos. The viol family lost ground to the new violin family; Charles II, in emulation of Louis XIV, had a court orchestra of twenty-four strings of this type and even used it in the Chapel Royal. (The sound, said the diarist John Evelyn, was " better suiting a tavern or playhouse than a church ".)

But one of the old family, a small bass viol (rather smaller than the cello, its approximate counterpart among the newcomers) long retained favour as a solo instrument. It was used particularly for the playing of variations (mostly exploiting runs) called "divisions", and the instrument itself, therefore, was sometimes called a "division viol". Christopher Simpson (d. 1669) was a notable exponent of the instrument, and it is significant that his treatise on playing it was reprinted as late as 1712.

TAVERN MUSIC

Evelyn's remark, just quoted, may make us wonder just what music was in fact played in taverns in those days. Of the compositions generally chosen for performance we are indeed ignorant, but a host of references in the literature of the seventeenth century make it clear that fiddlers and sometimes other musicians visited inns to make money by playing to the customers. Organs were also sometimes found in inns. Apparently a few tavern keepers specialised in providing regular musical entertainment, and from there it was but one step to the institution of public concerts. It seems that the world's first such concerts (by which is meant the first to which the general public was admitted on payment of a fee at the door) were those held in London by John Banister from 1672 to 1678. A longer-lived London series, lasting thirty-six years, was begun in 1678 by Thomas Britton, whose regular business as a charcoal seller earned him the name of "the musical small-coal man".

HENRY PURCELL

From our perspective the dominant composer in England towards the end of the seventeenth century was Henry Purcell (1659–95). Because he is so much better known to-day than his contemporaries, we tend to ascribe to him personally certain musical characteristics which were really those of his period in general—melting chromatic harmonies, songs built on a repeated ground bass, a light 3/4 rhythm with frequent minims on the second beat, and so on. The same is true of Purcell's very flexible treatment of the English language—an almost pictorial treatment of emotional words like "die" and "rise", but at other times a light, tripping, conversational kind of music reproducing the inflections of the spoken language. This "conversational" music was much in fashion; but though Purcell composed in the manner of his time, he did it better than other composers. We shall look in vain elsewhere for anything so consistently good as the music of the opera *Dido and Aeneas*.

This is a work set to music throughout, without spoken dialogue ; and that makes it an exception in Purcell's work for the stage (just as *Trial by Jury* is an exception among Gilbert and Sullivan operettas). *Dido and Aeneas* (with a libretto by Nahum Tate) was written not for a public theatre but for a girls' school in Chelsea run by a dancing-master called Josias Priest. It was produced there, probably in 1689. Its climax is the famous air sung by Dido before her suicide, " When I am laid in earth ". The melody of this song is written over a " ground bass ", a bass melody which repeats itself over and over again—that is, the piece is a *chaconne*, a form in which Purcell wrote many masterly movements both as songs and as instrumental pieces. The jollity of the sailors' music and the exact fitting of music to the words of the recitatives are also notable.

Purcell's other so-called operas are also called, perhaps more helpfully, semi-operas ; that is, they have much spoken dialogue, and a good deal of the drama is carried on without music. *King Arthur* (1691) is an example. Its text by Dryden to-day appears somewhat ridiculous on the stage, since for us the heroic manner has become the mock-heroic. The music is splendid not only in its quality but in its range—from the broad " common touch " of the *Harvest Home* song to the vocal chaconne of *How happy the lover*. From *King Arthur* also comes the famous song *Fairest Isle*, in which Purcell's characteristically bold harmony is wickedly bowdlerised in some modern editions. Purcell's other semi-operas are *The Prophetess*, or *The History of Dioclesian* (1690 : also known just as *Dioclesian*) ; *The Indian Queen* (1695), and two examples of how the taste of that time barbarously adapted Shakespeare—*The Fairy Queen* (1692, after *A Midsummer Night's Dream*) and *The Tempest*, probably composed in 1695. In addition, Purcell composed songs and incidental instrumental music for dozens of plays, and it is in one of these, Aphra Behn's *Abdelazar* (1695), that there occurs the tune used by Benjamin Britten in his *Young Person's Guide to the Orchestra* (*Variations and Fugue on a Theme of Purcell.*)[1]

Purcell wrote much church music, some of it seeming too worldly and even frivolous in style for church use to-day. A number of his anthems (including the so-called " Bell " anthem, which imitates the sound of bells) have accompaniment for the string orchestra which was brought into the Chapel Royal under Charles II.

His vocal music also includes odes for various public occasions, four of them for St. Cecilia's Day, which was at this time beginning to be publicly observed in England as a celebration of the patron saint of music.

[1] See page 444.

Of Purcell's numerous solo songs, a number have been brought out in modern editions, though some fine examples, such as *Anacreon's Defeat*, are still virtually unknown.

Less important is Purcell's harpsichord music, which includes an arrangement of *Lilliburlero* (topical at that time) under the title "A New Irish Tune". But his music for strings constitutes a distinctive side of his art and shows how he bridges an historical gap. He followed older models in composing fantasias and *In Nomines* for strings without a keyboard instrument ; but he also wrote " sonatas " for two violins, bass viol and a keyboard " continuo " (the harpsichord-player filling in the harmonies as directed by the figured bass, but using inventive touches of his own) in the newly fashioned Italian style. The nickname of " The Golden Sonata " has given an undeserved special celebrity to one of them.

Purcell's contemporaries include several composers worth mention. Among them are John Eccles (1668–1735), who wrote many attractive songs ; Pelham Humfrey (1647–74), even more short-lived than Purcell, and whose *Hymn to God the Father* on Donne's verse is one of the masterpieces of English song ; Daniel Purcell (*c.* 1660–1717), whose melodic gifts are somewhat unfairly overshadowed by those of his famous brother ; Jeremiah Clarke (*c.* 1673–1707), the composer of *The Prince of Denmark's March* (often erroneously called " Purcell's *Trumpet Voluntary* ") ; and John Blow (1649–1708). Blow was Purcell's teacher and his predecessor as organist of Westminster Abbey ; and Blow returned to that post after Purcell's death. His church music is notable ; and his masque *Venus and Adonis*, presented at court about 1682, interests historians as a genuinely operatic work, without spoken dialogue and with some ingeniously expressive music.

V

THE BEGINNINGS OF OPERA

THE terms "renaissance" and "baroque", as applied to music, are useful borrowings from the history of the visual arts, but they are not in themselves exact, and their application varies greatly in different countries. In Italy the baroque period started in the last quarter of the sixteenth century, whereas in the Northern countries it can only be dated from nearly half a century later. Without going into too much detail and distinguishing between early, middle, and late baroque, it is still possible to discover salient characteristics and movements in all the music of the period between roughly 1600 and 1750. In the first place, this period witnessed the progressive secularisation of the art in Western Europe. Church music, instead of dominating the scene, became one of many forms, still of great but no longer of exclusive importance. Even more important was the gradual emergence of instrumental music with a style of its own, in place of one equally "apt for viols or voices", and with it the gradual development of the instruments familiar to-day in the modern symphony orchestra. Most important of these were the members of the violin family, whose more brilliant and incisive tone and greater potentialities for virtuosity slowly brought about the disappearance of the softer-voiced viols. The same period saw the rise and fall of the clavichord and harpsichord and, at its end, the appearance of the ancestor of the modern pianoforte. Music was in fact moving from the church and the "chamber" into the theatre and the "hall", not yet approaching the modern concert-hall in size, but a public and no longer a private place, where volume and incisiveness became increasingly important.

One of the most characteristic developments of the baroque age is to be found in the *basso continuo* or "thorough-bass", an efficient system of musical shorthand which outlined, below the bass line, the chordal structure of a work by means of figures ; these were interpreted, or "realised", by a keyboard (or sometimes a lute) player, who added decoration to the bare harmonic bones, using his own skill, taste, and judgment. The origin of this practice of "figured bass" is to be seen in the late sixteenth-century habit of doubling the bass line of a polyphonic vocal work by the organ ; but during the baroque period the increasing tendency to elaboration of a single, simple line—most obvious in opera—determined the character of much instrumental music also. The Venetian organists Andrea Gabrieli and his nephew Giovanni hardly show signs of this rhapsodic, improvisatory style in their music, but Girolamo Frescobaldi (1583–1643) developed the old form of organ improvisation on a Gregorian melody in brilliant toccatas, preludes, and capriccios, often with strong chromatic colouring. In the predominantly Protestant North Germany and the Netherlands Jan Pieterszoon Sweelinck (1562–1621), Hans Leo Hassler (1564–1612), Michael Prætorius (1571–1621), Heinrich Schütz (1585–1672), Johann Hermann Schein (1586–1630), and Samuel Scheidt (1587–1654) grafted the new virtuoso Italian style on to the traditional chorale motet, using the thorough-bass continuo in polyphonic compositions with brilliant instrumental and vocal choruses and lively solo ornamentation. The most characteristic form invented in the baroque era, however, was the opera.

THE BEGINNINGS OF OPERA

Although there had been dramatic performances before the end of the sixteenth century in which music played some part, the function of music in these religious mysteries or secular masques and pastorals was incidental. It was, indeed, only in the seventeenth century that music was in a position to assume paramount place in a combination of the arts of dramatic poetry, spectacle, and music. The sixteenth century saw, as we know, the final flowering of the great polyphonic school of music, of which the chief ornaments were Lassus and Palestrina, Victoria, Byrd, and the galaxy of English madrigalists. By the turn of the century the decrees of the Council of Trent had effected a simplification in the setting of liturgical texts, while in the Reformed Churches of Geneva and Germany there was a strong reaction against any kind of polyphony, that is, the simultaneous singing of different melodic lines and often of different words. In England, for all that Archbishop Cranmer advocated the principle of " one word, one note ", there was a characteristic compromise between tradition and reform. So there was precedent in other departments of music for the enquiring minds who, stimulated by the re-discovery of the masterpieces of ancient Greek and Roman literature, began to react against the established musical style. Desiring to create new dramas on the principles of Greek tragedy as they understood, or perhaps one should say misunderstood, them, these pioneers set themselves to create a new musical style (which they termed *stile rappresentativo*, or imitative style), which would enable them to compose musical dramas. Polyphony was useless for their purpose, since they needed a style in which dialogue could be set to music and individual characters could express their thoughts. They had no precedents to guide them, nor any classical model of ancient music, except one spurious example which they interpreted incorrectly. The only existing music for the solo voice consisted of songs, and the song-form did not suit their purpose of presenting a dramatic action in music—though it might be used for the expression of emotion and the summing-up of a dramatic situation.

THE "NEW" MUSIC

What was needed was a new kind of music for solo voices, in which dramatic dialogue could be carried on swiftly and, as it were, naturally—a kind of music which came to be known as *recitative*. Recitative, if it is not to wander aimlessly, requires a stable harmonic support. It happened that in the last years of the sixteenth century the modal scales were tending to give way to the dominance of the two modes which we know as the major and minor diatonic scales, and these were to form the basis of harmonic practice during the succeeding three centuries.

This precipitation of the major and minor scales from the body of the modes was largely affected by the chromaticism employed by both church and secular composers in the later sixteenth century, and it coincided with the invention of the thorough-bass as an accompaniment to voices or to other instruments. It is significant that this new technical device appears first in music by Cavalieri, Peri, and Caccini, all of whom were closely concerned with the Florentine experiments in opera. Cavalieri, a Roman, had written music for pastorals produced at the Florentine court. In 1600 his *Rappresentazione di anima e di corpo* (" Representation of Soul and Body"), a sacred drama or " morality ", was produced in Rome and published with a figured bass (*i.e.* the harmony was indicated by figures placed under the fundamental notes in the bass). Peri's *Euridice*, the first true opera that has survived, was performed in the same year ; Caccini, who contributed some of the music to the opera, published a complete version of his own in 1601, and in 1602 issued a collection of madrigals and canzonets called *Le nuove musiche*. In his preface Caccini explains that he sought to compose " a kind of music whereby people could speak in tones . . . imposing therein a noble restraint upon melody ". The ultimate aim of Caccini and his fellow-theorists was the setting of words to music that did not merely underline graphic details in the text, but interpreted the whole feeling of the scene or poem. This was to enunciate one of the fundamental æsthetic principles of opera, even though they had not the musical genius to give it full effect. Caccini's " New Music " included airs composed in the novel monodic style and embellished with vocal ornaments (called *gorge*) which were soon to become an important element in operatic music.

THE FIRST OPERA AND THE FIRST ORATORIO

Cavalieri's *Rappresentazione* initiated the "opera on a sacred subject" which we know as oratorio. This name comes from the Oratory of St. Philip Neri in the newly built Roman church of Sta. Maria in Vallicella. The Congregation of the Oratory founded by St. Philip (which gives its name to the Oratories in London and Birmingham to-day) had as its main purpose the moral and religious instruction of the young and uneducated. Philip Neri—the "humorous saint", whose life is described by Goethe in his *Italian Journey*—had the idea of making Biblical stories and saints' lives more interesting by having them set to music, and these dramatised sermons soon assumed the name of the chapel in which they were given. Palestrina himself was among the company of distinguished musicians who worked with Philip Neri. The idea was not, of course, new. It had long been the custom of the Church during Holy Week to recite the story of the Passion in dramatic form, with a tenor voice singing the words of the Evangelist, two solo voices taking the principal characters of the story, and a chorus representing the disciples and the Jewish people. Moreover, the mysteries and miracle-plays of the Middle Ages—dramatised and much expanded versions of biblical stories, often with musical interludes—had retained their popularity with the common people, even if they were not wholly approved by the Church, which understandably frowned upon certain abuses that crept into their performance.

THE RISE OF THE MODERN ORATORIO

On this groundwork, then, oratorio as an art-form began to flourish, in common with other revolutionary musical forms that spread across Italy at the beginning of the seventeenth century. The old church style of polyphony and counterpoint was giving way to the "new music", with its emphasis on harmonic accompaniment and the qualities arising from the intentional combination of vocal and instrumental ensembles. Cavalieri's *Rappresentazione* was styled by the composer, however, a "spiritual opera", and was actually performed with costumes and scenery. Equally it can be regarded as a morality set to music. The score demands the use of soloists, chorus, and orchestra, and was also important for its use of dramatic recitative which, but recently invented, was to exercise a marked influence on oratorio.

Though opera was becoming increasingly the representative type of music in Italy, its chief characteristics—melodious treatment of the voice, contrasts between voices and instruments, the new " expression " that music was giving to words—also dominated other musical forms, especially oratorio, to which it was inevitably bound. The story of the rise of oratorio from this point is the story of the greater experience and competence of composers themselves. Giacomo Carissimi (1605–74), Alessandro Stradella (1642–82), and Alessandro Scarlatti (1660–1725) developed the new form by, respectively, greatly improving the character and musical expressiveness of the recitative, by venturing more boldly into the field of choral writing, and by the cultivation of what became known as the *da capo* aria. Carissimi's *Jephtha* is a particularly beautiful example of lyrical writing, depth of pathos and strength of harmony, that still sounds surprisingly " modern " in the concert hall to-day.

PERI'S " EURIDICE "

Peri's *Euridice*, which was performed before a distinguished company during the festivities accompanying the marriage of Maria de' Medici to King Henry IV of France in 1600, conforms to the pastoral style of earlier court entertainments. It opens with a formal prologue uttered by the Muse of Tragedy, who, after compliments to the royal bride, begs the company to attend to the tale of Orpheus. The opera then begins with a chorus celebrating the wedding of Eurydice. Orpheus enters, and in a song expresses his longing for the oncoming of night. His joy is turned to grief by the entry of a shepherdess bringing news that Eurydice has been bitten by a snake and is dead. This narration, obviously modelled on the messenger's speeches in Greek tragedy, is a remarkably expressive and dramatic account of the incident. There is a chorus of lamentation, after which another messenger tells how Orpheus has fainted at the sight of the dead Eurydice and has had a vision of Venus.

Directed by Venus, Orpheus goes to the gates of Hades and so moves Proserpina by his singing that she intercedes with Pluto on his behalf. Pluto yields to Orpheus's entreaties and allows Eurydice to accompany him back to earth, where the opera ends with a chorus of rejoicing in praise of Orpheus's daring and with a hymn to Apollo.

It is all very simple in construction ; and the poet, Rinuccini, besides providing the happy ending that was obviously required at a court function of this nature, has even sacrificed the most dramatic feature of the legend— Eurydice's release on condition that Orpheus does not look upon her face until they have returned to earth, and his failure under this test.

FRANCE

It is easy to smile at the crude result of this experiment. But if we consider the lack of any musical precedent for what the Florentines were attempting, their achievements seem worthy of respect. At least they made a serious effort to bring back to life the spirit and æsthetic power of Greek tragedy. In this their work differed from contemporary experiments in Paris, where, in the 1570s, a group of poets and musicians, headed by Antoine de Baïf, and including the famous Ronsard, were speculating on the nature of ancient Greek music. They evolved a new kind of versification, in which they sought to apply to the French language the metres characteristic of the Greek. Although such an attempt to revive the dead letter of classical poetry was bound to be sterile, these experiments did produce a declamatory musical style which outlived the original purpose of its creators. The music had, naturally, to consist of a single melodic line in order to preserve the uniform accents and quantities, and to avoid the repetition of words, on which the poets frowned. Here was the seed from which, a hundred years later, a French operatic style grew. If the period of germination was long, that was due to the failure of France to produce a musician of genius who could transform a rudimentary experiment into a positive musical language. Meanwhile French composers turned their attention to the *ballet de cour*, the equivalent of the English masque, in which spectacle and dancing were the chief ingredients.

MONTEVERDI'S " ORFEO "

The court *opera in musica* might have gone out of fashion in Italy too but for the work of Claudio Monteverdi, a musician of genius who was in the service of Vincenzo Gonzaga, Duke of Mantua. The duke was present at the performance of Peri's *Euridice* in Florence, and it is probable that Monteverdi was in attendance on his master. A Gonzaga was not to be outdone by a Medici, and, at the instigation of the duke's two sons, Francesco and Ferdinando, Monteverdi composed his first opera, *La favola d' Orfeo*, in 1607. In the following year the marriage of Francesco Gonzaga was the occasion of the composition of *Arianna* (of which all but the well-known " Lament " has been lost) and the satirical *Ballo delle Ingrate*.

Monteverdi was forty years old when he composed *Orfeo*, a mature and " advanced " musician who may be styled the last of the great madrigalists and the first great composer of opera. For in *Orfeo* all the elements that we recognise as essential to opera are present ; spirited recitative in which the action is carried forward, heightened by melodic arioso at moments of tension and sometimes blossoming out into elaborate embellishments (as in Orpheus's long plea to the infernal deities, with its accompaniment for various solo instruments) ; choral movements and dances ; and all enriched by the appropriate use of different kinds of orchestral colour. Though the orchestra employed in *Orfeo* was a fortuitous collection of the instruments that were available at the Mantuan court, Monteverdi used them individually and in combination to create dramatic contrasts of texture and to underline the emotional character of the scenic action. Beside Peri's monotonous treatment of the Orpheus legend, Monteverdi's is full-blooded and passionate and it can still move us in the theatre.

ROMAN OPERA AND THE BAROQUE STYLE

Rome, too, followed the example of Florence, at first with operas in the pastoral style of Peri's *Euridice*. A more important development occurred under the patronage of the Barberini family, headed by Pope Urban VIII, of whose nephews two were cardinals and the third was prefect of Rome. This powerful and wealthy family was responsible for some of the most important baroque monuments in Rome, including the Barberini Palace itself with the Triton Fountain by Bernini, who was under their patronage. It was quite natural that opera, the typical product of the baroque age, should also have found patrons in the Barberinis. They added to their palace a theatre of great size and splendour capable, it is said, of holding three thousand spectators. Here, before a distinguished assembly of princes of the Church and State, was presented during the Carnival of 1632 *Sant'Alessio*, by Stefano Landi, a singer in the Cappella Giulia.

Sant'Alessio, based on the life of the fifth-century Saint Alexis, represents a break with the classical mythology that had hitherto supplied operatic themes. Suitable though this subject might appear as a Lenten entertainment for the reverend patrons of opera, the libretto by Giulio Rospigliosi (later Pope Clement IX) was by no means wholly edifying. The tale of the saint's abnegation was enlivened with comic scenes, evidently based on contemporary life, and ample opportunity was given to Bernini, who was responsible for the scenic designs, to exercise his ingenuity in the manipulation of striking changes of scene, spectacular tableaux and " machines ", in which angels could fly singing through the air.

Here was already a swift decline from the lofty ideals of the Florentine theorists and the practice of Monteverdi in his Mantuan operas. The patrons of Bernini, who had not scrupled to rob the Pantheon of its bronze columns so that the sculptor might use the metal for a new canopy in St. Peter's, were not likely to be content with austere imitations of ancient tragedy. Indeed, they soon tired even of the pretence of sacred subjects for these Carnival entertainments, and resorted to Tasso, Ariosto, and Marini, whose works supplied material more congenial to their taste.

Although the music of *Sant' Alessio* is by no means undistinguished and has been summed up as having " energy, simplicity, and depth of feeling ", and although it also contains the earliest examples of concerted music for two or three voices in opera, the importance of the work from the historical point of view lies in the fact that it is the first example of opera to which the term *baroque* can be accurately applied.

THE BAROQUE STYLE

Since this term *baroque* has been the subject of much confusion and misunderstanding, it will be well to define what is meant by it in the present context. Baroque art originated in the architecture of the Catholic Church, which had always sought to provide for the Divine Presence the most beautiful imaginable shrine. Under the stimulus of reaction against the Protestant Reformation, a special impetus was given to the building of new churches and the fresh adornment of old ones in a new style which, originating in Spain, quickly spread to all the Catholic countries of Europe. The new style took advantage of advances in the techniques of architectural construction and decoration to achieve the maximum of magnificence. The architects sought to excite and dazzle with resplendent and elaborate effects of combined richness and mystery. To this end they employed every means to produce in the interiors of their churches an appearance of grandiose proportions and a luxuriousness of ornament. They applied to the stone-work stucco which could be fashioned into florid designs and then coloured or gilded ; they employed statues larger than life-size in attitudes of rapt ecstasy ; they had the ceilings painted with subjects such as the Assumption of the Virgin, which could be represented in such a way that the spectator seemed to be looking up, not at a roof, but at a miracle taking place in the open sky above his head. " The ideal of the baroque ", it has been said, " is a composition of bold and flowing curves, in which all possible elements of the grandiose, the florid and the delicate are fused so as to create the greatest impression on the beholder." The aim of the artist was to weld all the diverse elements of his intricate design into a satisfactory whole, without so much regard to that perfection of detail which had been one of the hall-marks of Renaissance art.

There have been objections to the application of the term *baroque* to the art of music. But, in so far as opera is concerned, no description could be more appropriate. For although the baroque style was evolved in the first instance by architects for the embellishment of churches and palaces, one of its main characteristics was, as we have remarked, the simultaneous use of all the visual arts in combination to produce a grand and unified effect. It was essentially a dramatic, not to say theatrical style. And it is at least arguable that in opera this style found its most complete expression. For here the visual arts of painting, sculpture, and architecture combined with those of music, dramatic poetry, and dancing to produce the most elaborate synthesis of the arts. The theatrical designer had the further advantage over the architect that he was not bound by the laws of physical science applicable to structures of brick and stone. With plaster and paint on canvas he could allow his fantasy to soar high above the dreams of the practical architect.

It was in the nature of baroque art to be extravagant in emphasis and to exaggerate every gesture. This quality persisted in opera long after the baroque style itself had gone out of fashion. A good deal of the misunderstanding from which opera has suffered is due to the survival of these " irrational " elements.

SPECTACLE IN OPERA

Spectacle was one of the main features, sometimes even the most important feature, in baroque opera. There are good reasons for the prominence accorded to this spectacular element. In a spoken drama our minds are fully occupied with the words and gestures of the actors, and spectacle may be a positive distraction ; in an opera it is the music that chiefly engages our attention, so that the eye needs something more interesting to rest on than a bare stage with a minimum of " properties " on it. It is a little difficult in an age of utility and economy to visualise the effect of the extravagant splendours of the seventeenth-century court entertainments. In them some tenuous and conventional story was the occasion for a series of magnificent processions and dances, with frequent transformations of elaborately painted scenery ; and at the end the divinities of ancient mythology descended from heaven in complicated machines to solve the problems of perplexed mortals. There is no exact parallel for such mechanical ingenuities and profuse spectacles in the modern theatre. Elements of the style survived in Parisian grand opera (of which Verdi's *Aida* is the most familiar example), in the transformation scenes of the Drury Lane pantomimes of a generation ago, and, more recently, in productions of such ballets as Tchaikovsky's *The Sleeping Beauty*.

THE VENETIAN OPERAS

It was in Venice that this baroque style of opera was first fully exploited. Still enormously rich as a centre of trade between East and West, Venice had already become the great pleasure-city of Europe. Instead of the closed circle of the aristocratic court which ruled in Mantua and Florence, there was an oligarchy of patricians and merchant princes who, however much they curbed political opposition, encouraged the free development of the intellect and the arts.

So it is not unnatural to find in Venice the first public opera-house. This was the Teatro San Cassiano, opened in 1637. The venture was so successful that very soon several theatres were presenting opera simultaneously. They were mostly built by patrician families and supported by wealthy subscribers to the boxes, the general public being admitted to the inferior parts of the theatre for a small sum. Though built at a later date and larger in size, the Fenice Theatre in Venice still preserves the general plan of these early opera-houses—a horse-shoe of boxes rising tier upon tier to the roof, with a parterre for the poorer opera-goers.

MONTEVERDI'S " THE CORONATION OF POPPÆA "

At first the Venetian operas were provided by two musicians from Rome, Francesco Manelli and Benedetto Ferrari. But soon Monteverdi began to compose for the Venetian theatres. He had left the service of the Gonzagas in 1612, and in the following year was appointed *maestro di cappella* of the Basilica of St. Mark's. For several years he continued to supply dramatic pieces for the Mantuan court. Now he entered the public theatre. *L'Adone*, of which only the libretto by Paolo Vendramin survives, was produced in 1639, and in the same year the Mantuan opera, *Arianna*, was revived. Of Monteverdi's four Venetian operas two—*Il Ritorno di Ulisse* (" The Return of Ulysses ") produced in 1641, and *L'Incoronazione di Poppea* (" The Coronation of Poppæa ")—have survived. *L'Incoronazione di Poppea*, composed in 1642 when Monteverdi was seventy-five, is his masterpiece. In it he shows a complete understanding of all the resources of opera. The recitative is free and flexible, responding to the inflexion of the words without lapsing into the monotony of the Florentine *stile rappresentativo*. Moreover, in his last two operas Monteverdi eliminated, as far as possible, set pieces and composed his scenes as continuous musical entities. Here the old composer seems to stretch his hand across the centuries to grasp that of another septuagenarian, the Verdi of *Otello*. The characters in *Poppea* range from the coquettish heroine and the passionate Nero to the noble Seneca and the tragic Octavia, and include also comic subsidiary characters. All are clearly defined in their music. The whole action is presented with great vividness, whether in the grandly tragic scene of Seneca's leave-taking of his friends, in the sensual comedy of the pageboy's flirtation with a maid-servant, or in the passionate love-duet with which the opera ends.

Monteverdi had the adaptability of the great artist and turned to account the limitations of a public theatre that must balance expenditure against receipts. The chorus (an expensive item and one which does not seem to have interested the Venetian audiences) is reduced to the status of " supers ", lending importance to the entry of some personage. The orchestra, shedding the odd assortment of instruments used in *Orfeo*, has become stabilised on the basis of string-tone in three or four parts, with a harpsichord *continuo* to fill in the harmony. The brass appears occasionally to give special solemnity to scenes dealing with the supernatural—a convention that persisted until the time of Gluck—to add excitement to some war-like scene, or splendour to a processional entry.

The very subject of *Poppea* is indicative of a change in public taste, corresponding with that which was taking place in Rome. The gods and legendary heroes of Greece, who had fascinated the men of the Renaissance, no longer seemed so interesting in the Baroque Age. They were replaced, as subjects for opera, by historical personages who could be made to appear more human. Even the legendary Penelope and Ulysses became, in Monteverdi's hands, characters of flesh and blood, with comic foils in their servants, Melanto and Eurimaco, who burlesque the love-making of their master and mistress. The comic relief, introduced by the Roman composers, was becoming an integral part of opera, even as it had been in the tragedies of Shakespeare, where, however, the Osrics and Roderigos are much more skilfully worked into the tragic context by the hand of a great master of the theatre.

THE OPERAS OF CAVALLI

Monteverdi was an exceptional genius, and the general standard and character of Venetian opera is not to be judged by his works. The type is to be found, rather, in the operas of Pietro Francesco Cavalli (1602–76), Monteverdi's pupil and eventually his successor at St. Mark's, or Marc' Antonio Cesti (1623–69). The subjects of Cavalli's forty-two operas, pro-duced over a period of thirty years from 1639, range from the traditional classical legends (Peleus and Thetis, Dido, Jason) through romantically named personages from Tasso and other poets (Bradamante, Orimonte, and

GIOVANNI PIERLUIGI DA PALESTRINA (1525–1594)

Copy of an original in the musical archives of the Vatican

JOHANN SEBASTIAN BACH (1685–1750)

Oil painting by Hausmann

Statira, Princess of Persia) to the historical figures of Julius Cæsar, Scipio, and Pompey. It cannot be said that Cavalli's librettists, among whom Busenello (the author also of *L'Incoronazione di Poppea*) and Cicognini were the most distinguished, had much respect for the original " facts ", whether of legend or history. How far Venetian opera in the mid-seventeenth century had fallen below the dignity and dramatic propriety of Monteverdi may be judged from the synopsis of the first act of Busenello's libretto for *Statira* (1655), which has been cited as one of the better examples of its kind.

Statira, the Persian Princess, is walking in the garden with the Arab Prince Cloridaspe, whom she has cured of his wounds and with whom she has fallen in love. She has as a confidante Ermosilla, who is in reality a prince in disguise and in love with her. The comic character of the piece is a negro servant, who is smitten by the beauty of " Ermosilla ", who also attracts the attentions of Prince Nicarco. " Ermosilla " plays these two off against one another and tries to induce Nicarco to murder Cloridaspe.

This is nothing to the absurdity of a fantasy about Helen, *Elena rapita da Teseo* (1653), in which Menelaus disguised as a girl wrestles in Spartan fashion with Helen. They are surprised by Theseus and Pirithous, who carry them off, while Helen's nurse laments that she has been overlooked by the ravishers. Even this is surpassed in absurdity by an opera called *La Costanza di Rosmonda* (1659) composed by a follower of Cavalli, of which a synopsis is given in E. J. Dent's *Opera*.

It will be evident that, like other manifestations of the baroque style, seventeenth-century opera at its worst could be pompous, mannered, and absurd. It should not be overlooked, however, that the Venetian operas were not designed for a " highbrow " audience, but, like their successors in Italy two centuries later, as a form of popular entertainment. The Venetian audience evidently demanded complex intrigues, in which female characters dressed up as young men in order to pursue unfaithful lovers, and themselves attracted other women in the cast. There needed also to be a spice of low comedy and *double-entendre*, to which the appearance of girls in men's clothes naturally lent itself, even as did the boy-players of Shakespeare's heroines.

THE VOGUE OF THE CASTRATI

There was the additional complication (and attraction) that some of the singers were male sopranos and contraltos—a phenomenon which demands some explanation, since it largely conditioned the character of opera in the eighteenth century.

The *castrati*, or eunuch singers, first appeared in the Roman church choirs at the end of the sixteenth century, when they began to replace the Spanish-trained "falsettists". Women were not allowed to sing in church choirs any more than they were permitted to appear on the Roman stage. Hence the demands made by baroque taste for greater emotional expressiveness, consonant with the ecstatic spirit of the new style, favoured the employment of singers who, by a simple operation before puberty, had preserved the high pitch of a boy's voice while developing it to the full strength of a man's. Although ecclesiastical officials frowned in principle upon the mutilation whereby such singers were produced, they none the less readily employed them, with the result that the demand created a supply. The *castrati* appeared in opera from the first, for Monteverdi's *Orfeo* was sung by Giovanni Gualberto Magli (a male soprano trained by Caccini), who was borrowed by the Mantuan court from the Grand Duke of Tuscany. In Venice the *castrati* soon established themselves, and we find them in Monteverdi's *Poppea* singing the parts of Nero and Ottone, both written for sopranos, while Ottavia and Poppæa were sung by female contraltos. Odder still, *castrati* appeared in Cavalli's *Eliogabalo* in the parts of Heliogabalus, Cæsar, and Alexander, while the female part of Zenia was allotted to a tenor. The tenor, indeed, soon became the exponent of low-comedy parts, old women, nurses, and so on, who indulged in the kind of bawdiness relished by the Nurse in Shakespeare's *Romeo and Juliet*.

THE SPANISH INFLUENCE—CESTI'S " ORONTEA "

The middle of the seventeenth century saw a tendency for Venetian opera to adopt a fantastic, picaresque manner derived from Spanish drama. A great part of Italy was at this time under the rule of Spain, and Spanish influence penetrated to the rest of the country. This was the " golden age " of Spanish drama, of which the chief ornament was Lope de Vega, while among the notable products of the school were Guevara's *El Diablo Cojuelo* (the source of Le Sage's *Le Diable Boiteux*) and the original Don Juan play of Tirso de Molina.

The Spanish influence is most obvious in Cesti's first opera, *Orontea*, produced at the inauguration of the S.S. Apostoli Theatre in Venice in 1649. The libretto by Cicognini is the usual farrago of intrigue, involving a prince in disguise (as a portrait-painter), and a girl in boy's clothing. But Cicognini was a genuine poet, and his verse is quite free from the inflated rhetoric that later became fashionable. The interesting fact about it is that it is not heroic drama, like those we have been considering, but a comedy of sentiment, like *Twelfth Night*, with which it has several situations in common, so that one may suspect a common ancestry in some forgotten Spanish drama.

Orontea is Queen of Egypt, a great lady who (like Olivia in *Twelfth Night*) is at first scornful of love, but who falls in love with the painter, who turns out to be a prince and therefore a suitable husband. There are rivals for his affection, to provide a wrathful outburst for the jealous queen. Comic relief is provided by a drunken buffoon, Gelone, and a boastful valet, Tiberino, whose scenes are mostly irrelevant to the main story. It is the buffoon, however, who effects the dénouement when he cries, " Stop thief ! " on seeing the painter with the jewelled locket that proves his identity as a prince.

The most remarkable of these comic interventions is the scene where Gelone, during a love-scene, parodies the words of the two lovers, extolling the pleasures of drinking where they discourse of love's delights. Presently Tiberino joins in and the trio becomes a quartet, which anticipates the late eighteenth-century type of ensemble in which several characters give expression to different points of view.

Orontea is notable for the fluidity of the music. Only six years after Monteverdi's death, here was a young composer writing his first opera with assurance and individuality in the handling of the musical drama. The music is no longer grand and statuesque, as it had been in Monteverdi's operas. Cesti's style is more lyrical and tender, and by so much the less " great " ; but it has more flexibility and continuity, because the melody does not make frequent halts on well defined cadences. There is, too, a clearer division of the music into recitative and aria, bringing with it a more evident sense of tonality, which became well developed by the time Cesti came to compose his most famous opera, *Il Pomo d'Oro* (" The Golden Apple "), where the arias nearly always modulate to the dominant (or relative major) key and back to the tonic.

THE DEVELOPMENT OF THE ARIA

In the later Venetian operas this distinction between the recitative, in which the dramatic action is carried on in speech-like declamation with a simple harmonic accompaniment, and the aria, in which the emotional situation is summed up, became definitely crystallised. The aria developed naturally out of the arioso passages in the recitative, where, to give special emphasis to some important or emotional utterance, the composer set the words to music of a more definitely melodic kind. The aria acquired more importance, both from its embellishment with vocal ornament by the singers and by its more elaborate orchestral accompaniment. Monteverdi generally adhered to the free arioso type of expression without formal repetitions of phrases or melodies. Even Orpheus's strophic song with which he seeks to charm Charon is set as arioso, each verse having quite different music ; and in *Poppea* Octavia's lament is a development of the same free musical form. Monteverdi's successors, however, soon developed the song in ternary form, in which the opening strain is repeated after a contrasted central section. This form, much elaborated as the *da capo* aria, became the stock pattern in opera during the succeeding century.

DRAMA AND SPECTACLE

The librettos of Venetian opera in the last half of the seventeenth century became as stereotyped as the musical forms. The names of the characters in each opera might be different, but their actions differed little from one piece to another, and the old legends became so encrusted with intrigues designed to interest and amuse a popular audience that they were hardly recognisable. The prime motives of the action were invariably ambition and desire.

If, however, the characters and their actions differed little from one opera to the next, there was plenty of variety in the scenery ; this was changed with great frequency, and by a series of transformations moved to a grand spectacular climax. Though the resources of the Venetian theatres could not vie with the extravagances of the Barberinis or the courts of Versailles or Vienna, the fame of Giacomo Torelli's designs for *Andromeda* and *Bellerofonte* at the Teatro Novissimo soon spread throughout the civilised world, and attracted tourists to Venice as they are attracted nowadays by a new opera of Stravinsky or Benjamin Britten. Those interested in the detail of stage design may be referred to Dr. Towneley Worsthorne's *Venetian Opera in the Seventeenth Century*, which contains a translation of the scenario of Francesco Sacrati's *Bellerofonte* as well as numerous reproductions of the scenery and technical apparatus used in its production in 1642. A perusal of these details makes it clear that to the seventeenth-century audience the spectacle was paramount ; the drama and the music were secondary considerations.

Although this attitude represents a lapse from the ideal of dramatic propriety sought by the Florentine theorists and at least partly achieved by the genius of Monteverdi, the Venetian opera marked an important stage in the development of the form : it brought opera definitely into the theatre as we understand it. The court operas of Florence and Mantua never presented a purely optical picture, because in them the stage was not independent of the auditorium, and the scene was not framed by a proscenium. As may be seen in the old prints of these productions, the singers performed in the midst of the spectators, who were thus to some extent partners in the performance. In the Venetian theatres, though privileged persons might be in stage-boxes and so practically on the stage, the main audience was separated by an orchestra-pit, as nowadays, from that magical world where so many strange happenings take place when the curtains part.

ITALIAN OPERA ABROAD

By the middle of the seventeenth century opera began to make its way northwards from Italy to other countries. Owing to its comparative nearness to Venice and to the musical enthusiasm of the reigning Hapsburgs, Vienna was a natural centre for its development. The Emperor Ferdinand III, himself a prolific composer, had several Italian operas performed at his court. But it was not until after the end of the Thirty Years War in 1648 that Vienna could afford the time or the money for such entertainments, and it was in the reign of Ferdinand's successor, Leopold I, that the Austrian capital became an important centre of operatic activity.

Unlike the commercial theatres in Venice, the operas produced for the Viennese court did not have to " pay ", and so it was here that the vogue of spectacular scenery and elaborate " machines " reached its highest splendour. Ludovici Burnacini was the chief architect of these lavish devices. Moreover, under the exigencies of court etiquette which insisted that the Emperor and his family should receive flattering compliments during the course of the entertainment, Italian opera in Vienna developed a form more pompous and ceremonious than befitted the public theatres of Venice. The most famous example of this style, which was later to be adapted by Lully at Versailles, was the sumptuous *Il Pomo d'Oro* (" The Golden Apple ") of Cesti, produced during the Emperor's wedding festivities in 1667. The opera, whose libretto purports to tell the story of Paris and the golden apple, began with a prologue in which personifications of all the provinces of the Empire appear, while the climax of the five acts that follow is the award by Jupiter of the golden prize of beauty to " the most excellent Princess the world has ever known ", namely, the Emperor's rather plain little Spanish bride.

Whatever the dramatic faults of the Viennese operas, they nevertheless became the focal point of enterprise in all the arts—poetry, music, dancing, architecture, and painting. These supreme manifestations of the baroque style fulfilled in their own way, if only for their own age, the ideal of opera as a synthesis of all the arts of the theatre.

OPERA IN GERMANY

In Northern Germany the various princely courts followed the example of Vienna, though less lavishly, in keeping with their more limited resources. At Dresden and Munich were established court opera-houses that were to flourish under different auspices in a later age. In the Bavarian capital a hint of future developments is given by the early adoption of subjects from German history, in preference to those drawn from classical mythology. Here, too, the orchestra began to assume a greater prominence than it was allowed by the average Italian composer of the time, a presage of the distinguishing characteristic of German opera.

In Germany there existed no indigenous form of dramatic entertainment which could compete with the imported Italian opera. In France and in England no such vacuum existed. In France the drama was already flourishing by the beginning of the seventeenth century, and Corneille (born in 1606), and Racine in the next generation, were to raise French tragedy to the greatest height it has attained. For musical entertainment France also had the court ballet, which corresponded somewhat to the English masque, being a spectacular entertainment with songs and dancing accompanied by music. As has already been mentioned, a group of poets, led by Antoine de Baïf, had experimented in the musical setting of verse in what they supposed to be the classical Greek style.

THE CASE OF ENGLAND

As for England, it is perhaps necessary only to mention the name of Shakespeare, beside whose fully developed drama even the masterpieces of Monteverdi seem of puny stature. It is not surprising that the drama should have satisfied English appetites for theatrical entertainment, while at court the masque supplied the musical festivities in celebration of marriages, birthdays, or accessions which in Italy were furnished by opera. The splendid flowering of the English poetic genius in the theatre may well explain the failure, through three centuries, of England to produce an indigenous operatic tradition.

There was certainly no lack of musical genius in the England of Elizabeth I and James I, and there seems no reason why an English opera should not have been created had the impulse in that direction existed. But composers received no such stimulus and were content to make use of the opportunities afforded by the masques of Ben Jonson and the masque-like plays of which *The Tempest* is the type. Shakespeare's last play has many musical scenes,

and ends with a masque. The musical scenes are associated with the supernatural interventions of Prospero, where music would seem quite in place.
Here was established a theatrical tradition and a dramatic form, providing
long supernatural or allegorical scenes designed for musical setting and
including dances, which attained its highest point in the so-called "operas"
of Purcell, *The Fairy Queen* and Dryden's *King Arthur*.

THE BEGINNINGS OF FRENCH OPERA

Meanwhile, in France during the minority of Louis XIV, Cardinal
Mazarin made a determined attempt to acclimatise Italian opera in Paris.
Mazarin had been brought up in Rome and, as a young man in the service
of Cardinal Barberini, developed a taste for the spectacular Roman operas.
He also hoped by this means to distract the French nobles from their political
hostility to the foreign Regent, Anne of Austria, whose chief minister he was.
Despite the lavish productions supervised by the famous Venetian scene-
designer, Giacomo Torelli, the French obstinately refused to take an interest
in Italian opera, especially as most of the libretti were ludicrous perversions
of the kind of classical fables which French dramatists were treating with
an austere nobility. They also disliked the eunuch singers, whose condition
provoked ridicule. Mazarin died shortly before the completion of his most
ambitious operatic project, Cavalli's *Ercole amante* ("Hercules in Love")
which was commissioned to celebrate the Cardinal's most ambitious stroke of
policy, the marriage of the youthful Louis XIV to the eldest daughter of the
King of Spain. The only really successful part of this huge entertainment
was the ballet, including a majestic entry for the king and his bride attended
by their court. The music for these ballets was composed by a young
Florentine musician recently arrived in Paris, Jean Baptiste Lully (1632–87).

THE RISE OF LULLY

Lully had managed to attract the attention of the king, and when, on
Mazarin's death, Louis assumed the royal powers, he was quickly advanced
in favour. Lully had been astute enough to hold aloof from his compatriots
who came to perform the Italian operas. He confined himself to composing
ballets for them, including the royal entries, thereby delighting the king,
who fancied himself as a dancer. He was given a band of violins of his own
which he quickly trained to a pitch of excellence surpassing that of the court
orchestra, the famous "Vingt-quatre Violons du Roi". Lully seems to
have perceived instinctively that Italian opera would never please French

taste, and set himself to master the musical setting of the French language. This he achieved by an intensive study of the declamation of the great French tragedians. His first dramatic compositions, apart from the ballets supplied for operas by other composers, were written in collaboration with Molière. They were either plays with musical interludes, of which *Le Bourgeois Gentilhomme* is the most famous, or fantastic entertainments of a masque-like character like *Les Plaisirs de l'isle enchantée*, which was performed at Versailles in 1664.

LULLY AND QUINAULT

In 1673 Lully began a collaboration with Philippe Quinault in the composition of a series of *tragédies-lyriques*, in which the emphasis was laid upon the ordered design of the drama and the intelligibility of the text ; and these established the character of French opera. In accordance with his practice of regulating the arts and sciences through official academies, Louis had in 1669 established the *Académie royale de musique* (still to-day, with the omission of *royale*, the official title of the Paris Opéra). As soon as Lully felt sure of himself, he used his influence with the king to have himself appointed to the management of this institution with an exclusive control over the production of opera. His action, unscrupulous though it was, had some justification in the poor quality of the works produced by the Academy and the disorder created there by the quarrels of jealous musicians. Lully brought order to the Academy of Music and, though he allowed no potential rival any opportunity to compete with himself, he created a series of masterpieces whose quality made his selfish precautions unnecessary.

It is difficult for the twentieth century to appreciate the worth of Lully's operas, because the conditions of their performance no longer exist. It is especially difficult for Englishmen who, bred in the tradition of Shakespeare, find the tragedies of Racine stiff and cold. Quinault was certainly no match for Racine as a poet. As a librettist he had no need to be. He provided Lully with exactly the kind of material the composer could turn to advantage, and he was, moreover, an adaptable colleague. Lully for his part had for ten years studied French declamation until his ear had completely mastered the inflections of the language as spoken in the theatre. It was his grand achievement to create in his recitatives a musical idiom for the French language which set a standard for the musical declamation of French. Nor had he failed to learn from the Italian operas imported by Mazarin all that would serve his own original purposes. In particular, he appreciated the virtue of Cavalli's spacious simplicity of style and his refusal to become involved in the elaboration of musical detail which too often cluttered the scores of his Roman contemporaries. In his understanding of the importance of the architectural principles of musical form Lully was in step with the great men of his time in other spheres. " He wanted ", says W. S. Mellers, " to establish a criterion of order in music, just as Mansart established it in architecture, Boileau in poetic technique and Colbert in state administration " . . . and, he might have added, Poussin in painting.

CHARACTERISTICS OF LULLIAN OPERA

Lully perceived that French taste with its strong literary bias would never tolerate the absurdities of the Italian librettists. He devised exactly the right alternative—the *tragédie-lyrique*. " My recitative ", he claimed, " is simply made to be spoken "—even though it was the special kind of speaking used by the actors in Racine's tragedies, strictly syllabic and therefore falling into set rhythmical patterns, yet capable of expressing intensity of feeling with perfect naturalness. Lully's recitative was, in fact, conceived as rhetoric rather than as music, and its frequent changes of metre follow the flow of the verses, enabling the singer to make them flow easily. In this respect for the dramatic and literary quality of the text lay the difference between French and Italian opera, which has persisted from Lully's day to our own.

With their first opera, *Cadmus et Hermione* (1673), Lully and Quinault established the form which all their succeeding operas were to take. They might move out of classical legend into the more romantic world of Tasso, but their architectural scheme remained constant. The operas were always in five acts (a convention that survived into the nineteenth century and caused Verdi to groan at the excessive length of his Parisian commissions) preceded by a Prologue devoted to the glorification of *Le Roi Soleil*, then at his zenith, with allusions to important topical events such as a diplomatic or military victory, a royal marriage or birthday. In the opera itself the action proceeded with majestic deliberation, the stately personages of the story discoursing upon love and fame in the intervals of their often surprising adventures. Comic relief was rarely allowed and, indeed, after *Alceste*, the second of Lully's operas, dropped out altogether. The drama was presented in a wholly formal manner, like a court ceremony in honour of the very embodiment of the national genius. These operas were not designed, like those of the Italian courts, to entertain the aristocracy, nor, as in Venice, to please a wider public ; they were addressed entirely to one individual, the king, whose word was law and whose approval meant success. Lully maintained this success until his death in 1687.

If court etiquette stands between us and a full understanding of Lully's operas, we can at least perceive the greater warmth and humanity which give life and even individuality of character to the personages of his later operas. Possibly the more romantic world inhabited by Roland and Armide assisted in the change, which included also a heightened expressiveness in the recitative and the fusion of the dramatic and picturesque elements into a more coherent whole. The orchestral descriptions of natural phenomena, of battles, storms, and the like, became more closely linked with the action and so acquired a psychological justification for their existence, whereas they were in the early operas merely ornamental. In his last works Lully achieved a singularly successful equilibrium in a musical style which ignored the contemporary Italian practice of crystallising emotional passages in formal *da capo* arias and reverted towards the ideal of that more or less continuous *arioso* of which Monteverdi had been the great exponent fifty years before.

ORATORIO IN FRANCE

Of Lully's contemporaries the most important was Marc-Antoine Charpentier (1634–1704), who was a pupil of the Italian Carissimi. More important than his secular operas were his " Sacred Histories " composed for the Maison Professe of the Jesuits in Paris, where he was *maître de musique* during the 1680s. These were in fact oratorios with Latin texts recounting in dramatic form such Biblical stories as those of Abraham, Esther, and Saul and Jonathan from the Old Testament, and the Prodigal Son, the Massacre of the Innocents, and St. Peter's Denial of Christ from the New. The introduction of the Narrator, or *Historicus*, made necessary by the gradual abandonment of scenic representation in Carissimi's oratorios is no evidence that Charpentier's oratorios were given " in concert form ", and the dramatic character of the music as well as the Jesuit tradition of educational theatrical performances make this most improbable.

VI

THE AGE OF BACH AND HANDEL

ALTHOUGH the late seventeenth and early eighteenth centuries were starred with many composers of merit, to our eyes to-day two of these stand head and shoulders above the rest. They are Johann Sebastian Bach (1685-1750) and George Frideric Handel (1685-1759). As we have seen, England had Purcell and France Lully ; but neither of these achieved anything comparable in scope, variety, or historical importance to the great output of these two German musicians. Before we deal in detail with their music, it may be as well to consider the characteristics of their age, and some of their immediate predecessors.

The seventeenth century was a period of change from one richness to another, from textures conditioned by power and range of the voice to those which were to command greater power and extend over the wider ranges of instruments. Not only have many instruments a wider compass of available notes than have voices, but it must be realised that not many singers have absolute pitch (*i.e.* the power to hit any written note at will) : they must derive each note as an interval easily singable from the previous note. This was the essence of good vocal writing. But with most instruments any note within their compass can be played without relation to its predecessor. This allows the composer a greater freedom—a freedom which has become in modern music virtually unbounded. As we shall see, the trumpets and horns were still limited to certain notes of their harmonic series—a limitation which definitely restricted composers up to well into the nineteenth century ; but most instruments of the woodwind, strings, and keyboard suggest and allow a freedom in ornamentation, in speed, and in variety and range of interval quite unsuited to the human voice. It must be noted also that when instruments of different types are combined, a contrast in tone-colour is made available—a contrast to the ear far greater than that of soprano, alto, tenor, and bass.

But although the change was significant, it was never absolute. The two textures, vocal and instrumental, were to mingle, to the great enrichment of musical thought and practice. There is no single moment in the history of music on which we can lay a finger and say that that is the point at which the old régime gave way finally to the new. Certain moments, however, now appear to us as outstanding. One is the appearance of Bach's Brandenburg Concertos, another the production of Handel's masque *Esther* as an oratorio.

Both Bach and Handel reacted to the challenge of a new age in their different ways and according to their different situations in the social framework of their time. Handel went out into the world, and coming into contact with the new tendencies in art, became aware—slowly and with great difficulty in his one particular, cripplingly conventional sphere of opera—of the new spirit in music. Bach's awareness of that spirit was less acute and his contribution to it less apparent, for his whole career was confined within a narrow geographical boundary and his chief sphere of activity was the church. It was not by way of the church, in any case, that that change was to come. Bach's son Carl Philipp Emanuel was one of the most vital forerunners of the new age of change, and he wrote sonatas and concertos where his father had written cantatas and motets.

Handel seems to have become aware of the change by the time he reached mid-career, at least as far as it was beginning already to shift the interest of composers from church to secular surroundings. If it seems paradoxical at first glance that Handel should have taken his music away from the stage and moved it bodily into the realm of religious art, it must be remembered that his oratorios were, for all their religious character and quasi-devotional quality, essentially dramatic works. They were not very far removed from the stage upon which Handel's operas appeared in London. Handelian oratorio was within comfortable hailing distance of Handelian opera.

The age of Bach and Handel starts with the birth of the two men in 1685, and ends with Handel's death in 1759, Bach having died in 1750. The period comprises a good deal of the effective working life of Alessandro Scarlatti and that of Henry Purcell. When this period ends, Josef Haydn (1732–1809) was twenty-seven. Let us look back a moment.

PURCELL'S PLACE

As we have seen, Henry Purcell lived during an inauspicious time which gave him little opportunity to exercise his great gift for dramatic expression. Had he been able to command enlightened patronage and had the spoken drama in England been less well developed, he would have written more than incidental music to stage plays, such as forms the larger part of his output in that sphere. He would surely have produced true opera, and had that been the case, Handel's position when he reached London fifteen years after Purcell's death would have been different. In fact, he might never have come to England if native opera, well grounded by Purcell and continued from such a secure basis, had flourished ; for the outlook for Handel's type of exotic, sophisticated Italian opera for the aristocracy would have been by so much the less attractive. As it was, the climate of opinion was unfavourable to Purcell's operatic ambitions and his genius was expended on other types of composition. In that he was less fortunate than Handel and Bach, both of whom found, if not a wholly congenial social surrounding, at least a sufficiently receptive audience for their music at some period in their careers. Purcell, on the other hand, appears as a composer who poured out a strong stream of exquisite and splendid music before a heedless audience. For him there was no Burlington to give princely hospitality, not even a Margrave of Brandenburg to accept a new composition.

Handel knew Purcell's music well enough to model his Chandos Anthems and Te Deum and the Utrecht Te Deum largely upon Purcell's church music. He presumably studied Purcell's manner of setting English, a tongue foreign to Handel and one in which he was never completely at home. If in fact he was closely conversant with Purcell's songs, he took a dangerous course for a foreigner anxious to become fluent in the musical setting of English, for Purcell's scansion is by no means always kind to English prosody, and he is capable of forcing his texts into a strait-jacket to suit the rhythm of a given melody. This Handel did too, but he could claim the distinguished precedent of Purcell.

Purcell's church music is elaborate and dramatic, and capable of exquisite simplicity and great dignity ; and like his incidental stage music, it forms a link between the Italian-French Lully's court ballets and operas and the operas which Purcell himself was never given the opportunity to write, those which eventually Handel was to write for the London stage. He was peculiarly English in the style and type of his melodic inspiration, and it was this quality that he passed on to Handel, always an intrepid assimilator of other men's ideas. In more than one way Purcell's mentality joined Handel's, and there is a kinship between the worldly Restoration musician, with his intense spirituality and sensuality, and the worldly Hanoverian musician, equally if not more spiritual and equally sensitive to outward manifestations of beauty.

When Purcell died there was no one to carry on the succession in native music. Those who cherished national ideals, who may have wished to foster native music at the expense of importations from the continent, had to accept something that was hardly less of an enrichment to music in England, the importation from abroad. They may well have felt that the defences had been breached and were now left open to any foreign marauder. For good or ill, such was the situation, and through that gap Handel was to step.

GERMANY—SCHÜTZ

In Germany the situation as it affected the young Sebastian Bach was different. Heinrich Schütz (1585–1672) was long dead. The greatest figure in German music in the first half of the seventeenth century, Schütz was a musician of wide education and sympathies far removed from the somewhat narrow and bourgeois musical life of most of his colleagues. He had received training in Italy and was thus acquainted with the new ideals prevailing there. Moreover it was his task, on becoming *Kapellmeister* to the Elector of Saxony in 1614, to organise both sacred and secular music on Italian models. Soon after this appointment at Dresden, Schütz wrote his oratorio *The Resurrection*, which, while bearing the imprint of his own strong musical personality, yet shows some resemblance in its free recitative to the works of Carissimi. But at the end there is a short chorus on a chorale, which foreshadows the later Passion oratorios. Schütz wrote these German Passions late in life, and so skilfully combined recitatives and choruses as to create a complete work of art, an entirely new kind of church music which was to reach its highest point in the works of J. S. Bach. Before Bach, however, Passion-oratorios were represented by several other remarkable works, notably by Reinhard Keiser (1674–1739), who was born only just more than a year after Schütz's death. His music exerted a strong influence on Bach himself.

One of the most important figures of the North German school of organists which also had so great an influence on Bach was the Danish composer Diderik (or Dietrich) Buxtehude (1637–1707). He made Lübeck, where he was organist of the Marienkirche, a place of pilgrimage for German musicians, both by his performance and by the concerted pieces for chorus and orchestra which he wrote and directed for the " evening concerts " called *Abendkonzerte* or *Abendmusik*. In his handling of the organ " chorale-prelude " Bach was also influenced by the South German, Johann Pachelbel (1653–1706). Bach was in his early twenties when Buxtehude died, and in some ways he may be considered to be a successor, though by then Bach was in his first maturity and already evincing qualities of mind and technique as subtle and profound as any that even Buxtehude, great and original craftsman as he was, had displayed.

NEAPOLITAN OPERA

Towards the end of the seventeenth century the centre of interest for Italian opera shifted southwards from Venice to Naples. There, after an apprenticeship in Rome, Alessandro Scarlatti poured out a copious stream of operas, and by his success established the form that prevailed in the opera-houses of Europe for nearly a century. Scarlatti's early operas follow Venetian models, and it was only after his arrival in Naples in 1683 that his style assumed its characteristic form, and in the process lost something of its native charm, compounded of tender pathos and elegant playfulness.

The chief architect of the change that took place at the turn of the century was the poet, Apostolo Zeno. A Venetian born in 1668, he reacted against the ludicrous fantasies and incoherent form of the Venetian operas. Under the influence of Racine, he sought to restore opera to the world of ideal tragedy from which it had strayed. He purged it of its comic characters who, as we have seen, brought light relief to the more solemn scenes. Moreover, he altered the musical style of opera by making a hard-and-fast distinction between the recitative and the aria, allowing no opportunity for the arioso-type of music which is something between the two.

As a poet, Zeno was sententious in the fashion of his day. His verses are full of conceits and affected jingles, of strained similes or antitheses. But he provided the early eighteenth-century composers—and his libretti were set by most of them, great and small, including Handel and Scarlatti, Hasse and Vivaldi—with exactly the kind of text they needed. His favourite device was the "simile" aria, in which the character likens his or her emotions to some natural phenomenon. A familiar example of the type in English is *As when the dove* or *O ruddier than the cherry* in Handel's *Acis and Galatea*, while Fiordiligi's *Come scoglio* ("Firm as a rock") in Mozart's *Cosi fan tutte* is a parody of the convention. Zeno's texts, written in polished verse, required of the composer only a smooth and generalised response to the emotion expressed, without picturesque reference to individual words.

While Zeno, with the help of an assistant, turned out two librettos each year, Scarlatti often composed three operas in the same period. The rapidity with which he and other composers of the time worked inevitably tended to stereotype their music. In his early operas Scarlatti showed himself skilled in contrapuntal writing, and made a daring use of dissonance comparable with that of his English contemporary, Purcell. As he became successful and more busy, he adopted a simpler style and became less adventurous in his harmony. His operas deal ostensibly with the heroes of ancient history—Pompey, Scipio, Lucullus, Gracchus, and so on—with occasional excursions into Greek mythology or the Orient—Hercules, Tamberlane, and Tigranes. But they are, in reality, all variations upon the themes of amorous intrigue and political conspiracy played out by a group of pasteboard figures, who became more and more conventional and dehumanised in the works of Scarlatti's successors. Lofty sentiments, lengthy metaphors, and heroic acts of magnanimity designed to resolve the dramatic situation happily were the chief ingredients of the librettos.

THE DA CAPO ARIA

Although its rigid formulas and conventions make its revival on the modern stage (save for special occasions) an impossibility, Neapolitan *opera seria* is historically of great importance. In contrast with the aristocratic opera of Northern Europe centred in Vienna, Neapolitan opera was more popular in its appeal and consequently simpler in style. National taste may also have influenced composers writing for Vienna, Dresden, and Leipzig to give their music a greater contrapuntal interest than was required by the melody-loving Southern Italians, who wanted nothing better than a good tune well sung. So the whole interest in the operas of Scarlatti and his followers is concentrated in the arias, in which he stabilised the *da capo* form, and the singer's performance became more important than the dramatic effect.

The *da capo* aria, which first appears as a musical form in the middle of the seventeenth century, is a simple example of ternary form; that is, a piece of music in three parts, the third being an exact repetition of the first. The second part has new words and music, usually in the key of the dominant or relative major or minor, after which the first part returns. Scarlatti found in this form the means for a wide range of emotional expression, and sometimes achieved strokes of real dramatic power. In general, however, the arias of early eighteenth-century opera are completely static ; they express a single mood or *affetto* and there is no movement, either physical or psychological, during their progress.

THE OVERTURE

Another feature of Scarlatti's procedure is important on account of its influence on musical history outside opera. In place of the " French " overture copied by the Northern composers from the example of Lully (who himself developed it from Venetian models), Scarlatti adopted the " Italian " overture or *sinfonia* which derived from the instrumental concerto. The distinction between these forms lies not so much in the difference in the order of the movements—the French having *Largo–Allegro–Largo*, the Italian having a slow movement between two quick ones—but in musical style and texture. The French overture was polyphonic and derived from the past ; the *sinfonia* was homophonic, *i.e.* its melodic themes were supported by simple harmonies derived from the melody and not accompanied by more or less elaborate counter-themes. From its manner of developing clearly defined themes, as well as from the very order of its movements, the classical symphony acquired not merely its name but its general form and characteristics.

Scarlatti's overtures were small in scale, the individual movements often not exceeding twenty bars, so that no elaborate development was possible. They were, in fact, theatre music simply designed to catch the attention of the audience before the opera began. Apart from the overture and the arias there was little formal music in Scarlatti's operas. The descriptive orchestral passages, which are so important in the operas of Lully and Rameau, had no place in them. All that Scarlatti offered was an occasional march or processional music to accompany a ceremonial entrance on the stage. The music of the dances seems generally to have been composed by someone else.

Scarlatti lived at a time when the harmonic system based upon the major and minor scales was becoming consolidated. Perhaps his most important contribution to the development of his art was the impetus he gave to the system by his own practice. He has been admirably summed up as " the founder of that musical language which served the classical composers for the expression of their thoughts down to the close of the Viennese period ".

THE CONCERTO

One of the most characteristic forms of baroque instrumental music, the *concerto*, had clear origins in the immediate Italian past—the contrast between solo and " chorus " of large and small instrumental groups in the Venetian composers of the late sixteenth century, in the *sinfonia* of Alessandro Stradella and even in the orchestral *chaconnes* of Lully's operas. Two slightly later Italian contemporaries were to crystallise the form more clearly, Giuseppe Torelli (1658–1709) and, more particularly, Arcangelo Corelli (1653–1713), perhaps the most important figure in the development of the *concerto grosso*.

Corelli was a superb virtuoso violinist, and that alone sufficed to give him contemporary fame. Posterity is fortunate in that he possessed more than this ephemeral gift. He was also a creative musician of the finest subtlety, a profoundly versed artist with a mind as active as were his fingers. It is remarkable that a man who could command such astonishing virtuosity as a performer should have been impelled to create a type of *concerto grosso* in which virtuosity is tamed and its exuberance brought within the limits of a corporate work of art. Instrumental music owes much to Corelli in that he nurtured it carefully in its youth and thereby saved it to a great extent from the tyranny of the virtuoso, which already threatened opera in the castrato and the prima donna. The noble outlines and textures of Corelli's *concerti grossi* were continued by both Handel and Bach. Each gave his own particular turn of individuality to the type—Handel an especially grand style of melody, Bach the extra brilliance of the instrumental forces which he brought into play in the Brandenburg Concertos and the Overtures.

ANTONIO VIVALDI

Antonio Vivaldi (*c.* 1675–1741) was considerably younger than Corelli and altogether a composer of a quicker habit of mind ; perhaps more brilliant but certainly less solid, he wrote a seemingly infinite succession of concertos and other instrumental works. It was his solo concertos that came to Bach's notice and influenced his technique, though influencing hardly at all his individual style of melodic and harmonic utterance. Bach's solo concertos, notably the works for violin and orchestra, benefited from Vivaldi's example in a certain lightening of the texture, an Italianate injection that had the same vivifying effect as had the example of Gabrieli's bright instrumental antiphony upon Schütz.

More influence than this preponderantly technical one Vivaldi could not have over Bach. The profoundly thoughtful exponent of the ideas and ideals of German Protestant church music could hardly have been expected to come into any closer contact with the delightfully worldly Italian. But it is probably just to credit Vivaldi with the example of that muscular energy which characterises Bach's quicker concerto movements and is to many listeners more invigorating than any other music of its time. Between them, Corelli and Vivaldi put the finest Italian musical culture within reach of Bach and Handel.

DOMENICO SCARLATTI

The exact contemporary of both Bach and Handel was Domenico Scarlatti (1685–1757), the brilliant son of a no less gifted father. Between them Alessandro and Domenico Scarlatti spanned but two years short of a century, and eighteenth-century music, its development and enrichment, goes under their name as much as under those of the two great figures then active in Germany and England.

Domenico Scarlatti was born in Naples and died in Madrid, having lived for more than a quarter of a century during the most mature period of his career in Spain, where he held court posts. He was a virtuoso harpsi-chordist of the highest order, though he was wont to protest that Handel, with whom he had been friendly in his youth, was the better organist. At the age of 23 he was in Venice, where it appears he first met Handel, and in the following year he was in Rome as a musician in the service of the exiled Queen of Poland, composing operas for her private theatre. Handel's admiration for Scarlatti was warm, and Mainwaring said that he "often used to speak of this person with great satisfaction ; and indeed there was reason for it ; for besides his great talents as an artist, he had the sweetest temper and the genteelest behaviour."

Besides his operas Domenico wrote music for the church, and for five years was in the service of the Vatican ; but it is by his (mostly one-movement) keyboard sonatas that he is known, such witty, elegant and vivacious writing as hitherto had not been expended on any secular keyboard instrument. Nor is it variety of lively adornment alone that gives these sonatas such individuality. There is, too, the astonishing depth of feeling that Scarlatti lays bare in the slower movements, particularly those cast in a minor key. This sensuous quality and the markedly Spanish influence in rhythm and harmony struck a new note in keyboard music, while to the technique of actual finger dexterity he contributed more than any composer before him. Such a conjunction of brain and heart Scarlatti at his best could command with what seems effortless inevitability.

GERMAN KEYBOARD WRITERS

In Germany Johann Kuhnau (1660–1722) developed a form of the sonata that was in fact unique, though very much in accordance with the taste of the day. In his *Biblische Historien* (Bible Stories) of 1700 he used a large variety of instrumental forms, ranging from the dance to the chorale-prelude, for descriptive scenes—what a later age was to call " programme music "—drawn from the Bible. Characteristic is *The Illness and Recovery of Hezekiah*, in which rhythmic transformation is used to give a chorale-prelude a new, " literary " significance.

Kuhnau wrote under French influence, for French composers had shown a preference for visual or literary programmes ever since late medieval times. Similarly Johann Jacob Froberger (1616–67), a pupil of Frescobaldi, spent some time in France and came under the influence of Jacques de Chambonnières (1602–72), who characteristically sought for variety in his harpsichord suites, where the Germans were already concerned with thematic unity and integration.

FRANCE

François Couperin (1668–1733), the slightly older contemporary of Domenico Scarlatti in France, and, like him, a refined composer for the keyboard, brought out his famous treatise *L'Art de toucher le clavecin* the year before Bach began his duties at Cöthen. Like the Bachs, the Couperins were a family of musicians, though unlike them they lived and worked in the fashionable world of a great court. François Couperin, called " Le Grand ", became organist of the private chapel of Louis XIV, "Le Grand Monarque ", at Versailles.

His reputation rests upon his keyboard suites, the *Ordres*, as he termed them. Both Bach and Handel composed keyboard suites, and both show that they were at least aware of Couperin's treatment of dance tunes as he formed them into suites of courantes, sarabandes, gavottes and so forth. Couperin did not venture far afield ; and in that he differed from Domenico Scarlatti, who was never averse to experiment and the exploration of new ideas. Couperin, on the other hand, was more intent on consolidating what had already been gained. His exquisite art was designed primarily for the entertainment of sophisticated, easily bored, listeners, and in that it succeeded wonderfully.

TELEMANN

Among the outstanding contemporaries of Bach, Handel, and the Scarlattis, is the German composer Georg Philipp Telemann (1681–1767), a colleague of Keiser at the opera in Hamburg, a friend of Handel and an applicant for the cantorship in Leipzig which he rejected before Bach was considered. His output was immense ; but his fluency, though it may have increased esteem during his lifetime, has worked against him with posterity, which has continued to refuse him a place with the really great, as that term is understood. Yet on the rare occasions when his work, such as some of the *Tafelmusik*, is heard, one wonders whether the judgment of posterity is, in this case as in others, founded on hearsay. Admittedly Telemann was, like Couperin and unlike Bach, Handel, and the Scarlattis, a confirmed consolidator. But his music has a remarkable quality of fine workmanship, and it cannot wholly be ignored.

And now, having glanced at their immediate predecessors and most distinguished contemporaries, we must go on to the study of the giants who, at least in retrospect, dominate between them the age that they so signally adorned.

VII

J. S. BACH

NOT far in the background of the age of Bach and Handel in Germany lay the spectre of the Thirty Years War, in which France and the Catholic Empire were locked in a struggle involving Germany and the Protestant powers. The parents of Bach and of Handel had been close to that terrible period ; their grandparents would have known it from bitter experience. At the time of the Peace of Westphalia, which put an end to the fighting in 1648 (though feuds continued to menace the tranquillity of Europe for many years after), Handel's father was 26, while Bach's was three years old. Conditions after the war are thus described in the Cambridge Modern History :

These effects . . . furnish perhaps the most appalling demonstration of the consequences of war to be found in history ; . . . whole districts converted into deserts . . . a full third of the land in northern Germany left uncultivated (during more than a generation after the conclusion of the war) . . . the deadliest promptings of religious hatred were designedly fostered and the whole savagery of religious fanaticism was deliberately let loose upon its prey . . . the order, the comfort, the decency which had so long distinguished German town life had come to an end.

In such social and spiritual conditions Handel's and Bach's parents grew up, married and produced their families.

Looking back to this fateful period in German history, we begin to understand the point of view of Handel's elderly father and his insistence that his son should be given some settled training such as a University education and the law, rather than undertake the unsettled existence of a musician. This offered no likelihood of economic stability, and indeed seemed to lead to that lack of family order, domestic comfort, and social decency which a man of the elder Handel's mentality would rate high, since he had known something of the lawless conditions during the war and was now in a good position at the court of Weissenfels.

Bach's father had less direct experience of the horrors of the Thirty Years War and belonged to a different social order ; he had no such qualms when it came to deciding the way Johann Sebastian should go. Being younger than Handel's father, he could expect to supervise his son's education. The wide ramifications, too, of the Bach family around Eisenach manifestly made for stability even in times such as those. But the real reason for Ambrosius Bach's confidence lay in the fact that music had for long been accepted by generations of past Bachs as a thoroughly reputable career. Where Handel's father may have feared the life of an unattached musician, Bach's father knew that playing in a town band and being a church organist were jobs that could well keep a young man in one place for a dependable length of time.

The Bachs were inhabitants of small towns, unlike Handel's family who lived in Halle (a university town) and had direct contact with a ducal court, from which it was no great step to Berlin and Hamburg, so that the young Handel was from the start in the way of a European career. The young Bach had no opportunities of that kind. His experiences as a court musician did little to widen his horizon. In 1618, the start of the Thirty Years War, Anhalt was scarcely larger than Essex, and in that minute area were no less than four separate principalities—Zerbst (which was to send a princess to Russia who became Catherine the Great), Dessau, Cöthen (where Prince Leopold was to secure Bach as his *Kapellmeister*), and Berenburg, whence came Leopold's wife. Leipzig was Bach's most imposing post, the climax of his career. On the other hand, so far as Handel was concerned, Hamburg was but a stepping-stone for Italy ; and even Italy, and later Hanover, appear as milestones on his journey to London, which became his home. He was destined to become a man of considerable breadth of culture and in time a composer of European fame. Bach remained confined within his small Thuringian sphere, with none of Handel's worldly brilliance but with a profound sense of spiritual values such as had not been expressed in church music so intensely since the time of Palestrina.

We have comparatively little information about the state of music during the war, but those thirty years of turmoil which vitally harmed the whole intellectual life of Germany threatened music no less severely. Schütz worked at the court of Dresden during the war, the miseries of which were such that three times he tried to escape to Denmark. He had been twice to Venice in happier days, had been in the first instance a pupil of Giovanni Gabrieli, and later came under the influence of Monteverdi. With his powerful intellect he was able to fuse the musical ideals of northern Italy with those of his own northern Germany, a valuable activity that demanded a very great musical mind.

Organists and organ-music composers persisted in some regions during the war, and as soon as peace gave men some leisure in which to think, musicians such as Pachelbel and Buxtehude came into prominence. In the courts and the large commercial centres dramatic music began to revive, and Italian influence in opera to be significant—in, for instance, Hamburg, where Reinhold Keiser had established a German operatic form which Handel discovered when he arrived there in 1703 as a youth of eighteen.

BACH'S EARLY YEARS

The first formative years in the life of a genius, the earliest years of childhood, are the years of which we often wish to know more. The fluent writing of notes on a stave is an activity of its own and need not presuppose a like fluency in the writing of words. It is relatively seldom that a Richard Wagner appears, or a Berlioz with a literary gift equal to his musical powers. Beethoven seldom wrote revealingly about himself, and we owe something to his deafness, which has given us the notebooks where he would sometimes jot down a mite of his conversation. Haydn was an acute observer with a sense of the humorous, and there again we should be glad to have more from his own pen in reminiscence and comment. Of Bach, as of Handel, we have almost nothing to go on, and we must be content with tales, not always reliable.

Johann Sebastian Bach was born in 1685 at Eisenach in Germany, a town lying midway between Hanover and Frankfurt. The family of Bach had been musically inclined for many generations before Johann Sebastian was born, and to this day men of that name are practitioners in music—there is, for instance, a Bach famed in Poland as an organ builder.

With the appearance of J. S. Bach, the family won a great creative artist in whose achievement the work of his ancestors, either as performers or as composers, is forgotten. His father, Johann Ambrosius of Eisenach, was of the fourth generation of Bach musicians, in direct descent from the first recorded bearer of the name, Hans Bach, who is known to have lived at Wechmar in 1561. When J. S. Bach was ten, his parents died and he went to live with his brother, who was then organist in Ohrdruf. There he began his general and musical education.

In 1700, when he was fifteen, Bach went to school in Lüneburg, which offered more, especially in music. Bach became a choirboy with "a beautiful soprano voice" and, more important for his future, began the serious study of the theory and technique of composition. His talent unfolded rapidly, and he studied the finest examples that were available to him, notably the playing of the organist of St. John's Church in Lüneburg, Georg Böhm (1661–1733), who was a pupil of the great Jan Reinken, at that time organist of the Church of St. Catherine in Hamburg. From Lüneburg to Hamburg was a journey of nearly thirty miles, and more than once Bach went there on foot to listen to Reinken's playing. By the time he had reached the age of nineteen and taken his first post as professional musician, he had become a reputable string player and an even better organist and clavier player. He was, in fact, ready to fend for himself.

THE ACCOMPLISHED MUSICIAN

Early in 1703 Bach had become a violinist in the court band at Weimar, but left later that year to take up his first considerable post, that of organist at Arnstadt. This was what may be called a family job ; the name of the town continually occurs in the history of the Bachs, either as birthplace or place of work. It lies in the midst of what we may call the Bach country, an area some hundred kilometres square between Erfurt, Eisenach, and Mühlhausen, all places that come into the biography of Johann Sebastian.

It is as an organist that Bach became a musician of noteworthy stature. At Arnstadt he found an excellent instrument for his use. It was moderate in size but good in quality ; a Great organ of ten stops, a Choir organ of seven stops, among them those mixture combinations that gave organ tone at that time its characteristic baroque brightness, and finally a pedal range of five stops. In addition Bach trained the church choir, besides being able to call on the local choral society and some sort of an orchestra. The means at his disposal, therefore, were large, and making the most of his local musical material, he became active in creating new works, such as the early cantata *Denn wirst Du meine Seele nicht in der Hölle lassen*, which almost certainly belongs to this period.

CAPRICCIO

Less significant, though momentarily more interesting, is another work written at this time. Bach's brother Johann Jakob left home during 1704 for Sweden to take the post of oboist in the Royal Guard. The Bachs may be presumed to have been clannish, and the departure of a brother was an event of some importance ; and thus we find Johann Sebastian writing a keyboard *Capriccio on the departure of a beloved brother*. The interest of the work lies in the fact that this is " programme music ", almost the only example of that style of composition in all Bach's output.

Bach's personality was ripening and his individuality becoming strong and determined. He was already a man to be reckoned with, as his employers were to discover. In October 1705 he applied for leave of absence to visit Lübeck, some fifty miles to the north, to hear the great

Buxtehude play the organ in the Marienkirche and to listen to the *Abend-musik* there, the famous church concerts. The Arnstadt authorities gave the necessary permission but were understandably displeased when Bach overstayed his leave and did not appear again in Arnstadt until the following February. He was accepted back, but it is not surprising that in 1707 he left to take up a new post as organist at the church of St. Blasius in Mühl-hausen. A few months later he married his cousin Maria Barbara Bach, and took in hand the reconstruction of the St. Blasius organ. But his stay at Mühlhausen was short, and the next year found him in Weimar again, now in an altogether more secure position, that of court organist, to which was added in time the position (with some slight increase in salary) of *Konzertmeister* and then *Kapellmeister* or Director of Music. Bach stayed contentedly enough in Weimar for nine years, his longest term of service up to then. His master, the Duke of Saxe-Weimar, was a fair employer, a man of earnest disposition and considerable integrity, a matter of the first importance to Bach, who would inevitably be influenced by the personal tastes and dispositions of the autocrats with whom he stood in the relation of servant to master.

ORGAN WORKS AND CANTATAS

In Weimar Bach had at his disposal an organ of the size of that which he had found at Arnstadt. His Weimar years were to be the great period of organ composition. His master was no Pietist but an orthodox Lutheran, who allowed music a fair place in the church services and gave Bach that freedom to compose for his chapel which resulted in a large number of remarkable cantatas. There was opportunity for instrumental work as a performer on violin and keyboard, and this meant that composition in the domain of chamber music came within Bach's sphere of activity. Weimar was, in fact, a rich field of creative activity which Bach, still young, energetic, and hopeful for his future, cultivated assiduously.

Bach's development in the technique of writing for the organ, based on the music of Buxtehude, Pachelbel, and Froberger, began at Weimar. It was during this period that he began to explore territory that had come within his vision alone—such immense works as the D minor Toccata and Fugue among the earlier Weimar compositions and the Fugue "in modo Dorico" among the later organ works. These show the first signs of Bach's profoundly romantic outlook, his towering poetic genius.

In the same way, though in the nature of the case more strikingly exemplified, the cantatas of this date show remarkably profound expression of human feeling, such as the Actus Tragicus *Gottes Zeit ist die allerbeste*

Zeit (" God's time is the best "). This intensely affecting work opens with a short slow introduction for instruments accompanying a flute melody, one of Bach's first great instrumental textures, music that looks ahead to the next period in his career, when at Cöthen he was to write the Brandenburg Concertos and to establish his right to be considered as a subtle manipulator of the orchestra.

By now his fame had begun to spread. He was asked to advise on organs in his neighbourhood. He himself, hearing that Handel's master Zachow had died, put in for the post of organist in Halle ; but he (or the authorities there) failed, and he stayed on at Weimar. The famous French organist Marchand (1669–1732) was in Dresden during 1717, and one of those contests between executants which were then so much in vogue was staged there. " A large company of both sexes and of high rank assembled . . . Bach did not make them wait long, but Marchand did not appear . . . and the company learned to their great astonishment that he had left Dresden in the morning. . . ." (Forkel). It appears that Marchand, suddenly aware of Bach's brilliance as a player, had turned tail. Bach returned to Weimar, his reputation enhanced. In that December we hear that he was released from gaol, wherein he had been confined " for too stubbornly forcing the issue of his dismissal ". He had asked to go but had offended the authorities by the manner of his request. At length he was free to leave and to take up his next post at Cöthen.

For one fleeting moment we seem to catch sight of the man behind the musician Bach ; a man, it appears, who was probably over-hasty when it came to a crisis that called for a decision, but who would not be put upon by authority when it got in the way of his advancement. At this moment Bach had more than his own future to consider ; he was a husband and a father, and the competition for good musical posts was probably no less keen then than it is to-day. The note contained in the reports of the Court Secretary in Weimar says that he was freed from an arrest of over three weeks' duration with notice of his " unfavourable discharge ". He knew he was wanted in Cöthen and could be sure of a welcome there. His new master had, in fact, started to pay him his salary in the previous August, and it was perhaps that which annoyed the Weimar authorities.

CÖTHEN

It would be interesting to know precisely what were the reasons which caused Bach to give up his Weimar post, where he had a good organ at his disposal and ample resources for choral and instrumental works on a large scale, for one in a small court with no adequate organ or choir and no theatre from which to obtain singers and players. This was the situation he knew he would find at Cöthen, yet he eagerly accepted the new post. The young Prince of Anhalt-Cöthen, however, was an agreeable young bachelor of twenty-three, intelligent, and much given to the enjoyment and study of music. He must have given Bach plentiful assurances of his esteem (which seems in time to have developed into mutual affection) before finally persuading him to leave Weimar.

Bach now entered upon the happiest, most contented period of his life. He was treated with friendly sympathy by his Prince, and he had material enough for the exercise of his art, restricted in comparison with Weimar yet sufficient to produce some of his most splendid works. Leopold of Anhalt-Cöthen, proud of his *Kapellmeister*, let him go free when Hamburg called, or took him in his suite to Carlsbad. There was one black cloud in Bach's Cöthen years, the death of his wife, news of which awaited him when he returned from Carlsbad in July 1720. But it was not long before, of necessity, he married again, this time the intelligent, musically cultured Anna Magdalena Wilcken, and he was fortunate in her to the end of his life. Another cloud came over his professional horizon—the marriage, a few weeks after his own, of Prince Leopold. Bach wrote during 1730, when he had already left Cöthen, to a friend : " There I had a gracious Prince, who both loved and knew music, and in his service I intended to spend the rest of my life. It must happen, however, that the said Serenissimus should marry a Princess of Berenburg, and that then the impression should arise that the musical interest of the said Prince had become somewhat lukewarm. . . ." He called her *eine amusa*, a girl (she was only nineteen) who had no real feeling for the Muses, that is for music. Leopold was too much taken with his young wife's entrancing company to do anything that would assuage Bach's jealousy. The *amusa* easily won the contest with the musician.

After her death a couple of years later it was too late for the two men to come close again. Bach had by then applied for the post of organist and cantor in Leipzig ; and by the end of May 1723 he was duly installed there. Nevertheless he and the Prince of Anhalt-Cöthen were not wholly estranged. Leopold gave Bach the title of honorary *Kapellmeister*, and when he died at the age of thirty-two Bach wrote his funeral music and went to Cöthen to direct the performance.

SECULAR INSTRUMENTAL WORKS

Deprived as Bach was during his six years in Cöthen of an expert choir and a really good organ, he turned his attention to secular instrumental music. To circumstances at Cöthen we owe the solo partitas for violin and for violoncello ; the sonatas for violin, gamba, and flute ; the first book of the *Well-tempered Clavier* ; and the orchestral suites and the six Brandenburg Concertos. It seems now unthinkable that these works might not have appeared. Yet if Bach had found at Cöthen the same kind of musical material as he had employed at Weimar, instead of secular instrumental works he might have continued to compose church cantatas and organ music.

THE BRANDENBURG CONCERTOS

One of the most striking signs of Bach's interest in the composition of instrumental music was the set of Brandenburg Concertos for orchestra, the outcome of a meeting between Bach and the Margrave of Brandenburg in, presumably, 1718 or 1719. In the dedication dated March 24, 1721, Bach speaks of having had "the pleasure of appearing before Your Royal Highness, by virtue of Your Highness' commands" which must mean a command concert, probably when the Margrave was visiting Cöthen. The "command to send Your Highness some pieces of my composition" suggests no precise commission, but an invitation for Bach to send works of his own choice. Ludwig of Brandenburg was a man of considerable musical enthusiasm, but there is no evidence that he ever heard these six works, and he appears not to have acknowledged their arrival in Berlin.

SOLO CONCERTOS AND CHAMBER MUSIC

The orchestra at Cöthen may have been small but, on the evidence of Bach's compositions while he was *Kapellmeister* there, it seems to have comprised some able players. If we take into account the solo partitas (sometimes called suites) for violin and for violoncello, then we may conclude that there were players available who were quite out of the ordinary run in technical accomplishment.

Whereas the six Brandenburg Concertos explore new territory, the violin concertos, the sonatas for violin, gamba, and flute with clavier, and (but for the extreme technical mastery demanded) the solo partitas, come within the province of contemporary Italian instrumental music, as exemplified in the work of Antonio Vivaldi and Arcangelo Corelli. It was during his Weimar period that Bach had turned to the work of Vivaldi, not only for study but in definite note-for-note emulation, taking Vivaldi's violin concertos and transcribing them for keyboard and string orchestra. To copy out the works of great masters, as Zachow set Handel to do, was a traditional method of discovering technical solutions ; to transcribe them as Bach did was the same method carried into the regions of creative art. How far Vivaldi's Italian mentality is reflected in Bach's transcriptions is a matter still in dispute. His original works in concerto form are purely his own mind and spirit. One example will suffice, namely the concerto in D minor for two violins and string orchestra. It is conceivable that Corelli, but not Vivaldi, could have fashioned the two outer movements. No other composer than Bach could have created the slow movement, which contains the essence of his style at that time.

THE ORCHESTRAL SUITES

Bright as the Brandenburg Concertos are in their orchestration, the four Overtures which are generally held to belong to this period are hardly less brilliant. What Bach's intention was in writing these works and specifically naming them not Suites (as future generations have been led to call them because of the number and scheme of their movements), but Overtures, is not certain. The conjecture still holds good that Bach's mind was occupied with the form and content of the French style of overture with the slow introduction, such as had been employed by Lully and many others, including Handel, not only in his operas but in an oratorio such as *Messiah*. Bach's slow introductions to these overtures are a development, extension, and deepening of the original Lullian pattern ; not so much a separate short movement as an introduction strongly contrasting with the musical (one might even say psychological) atmosphere of the music that follows. As regards the craftsmanship of orchestral manipulation, the four Overtures consolidate the achievement attained in the Brandenburg Concertos.

THE SOLO PARTITAS

The two sets of six partitas or suites, one for a solo violin and one for a solo violoncello, are unique works. To this day they are among the most exacting of Bach's works to listen to with full concentration. They are player's music, a delight for the executant faced with such wonderful problems not only of performance but of the finest, most profound interpretation. These remarkable exercises in abstract thought demand the greatest players to do them justice, and the music is of that rare kind that can only be continuously shared when the player has with him an equally devoted listener.

KEYBOARD MUSIC

One work from the Cöthen period poses a special problem of scientific character apart from its æsthetic value. It is the set of keyboard preludes and fugues in all twenty-four keys called *Das Wohltemperierte Clavier*. Bach's title-page reads : " The Well-Tempered Clavier, or Preludes and Fugues through all the tones and semitones both as regards the *tertia major* or Ut Re Mi and as concerns the tertia minor or Re Mi Fa." This is the first half of the celebrated " 48 ", the second half being added some years later during the Leipzig period.

The recent new " tempering " (tuning) of the scale, to which Bach now gave his definite and, as it were, public allegiance, came about through sheer physical necessity. As instrumental music arose and developed, some comprehensive system of tuning orchestral and keyboard instruments became imperative, a system that would make it possible for music to move from key to key with an overall relative similarity of measurement. The human voice, which hitherto had ruled music, never submitted to scientific- ally exact tuning, for obvious physical reasons ; the ear sufficed, at least so long as the music did not modulate widely. Instruments could pitch intervals beyond the limits of the human voice ; but if instrumental music, tuned to a relative set of values proper to one key or mode alone, strayed far beyond those limits, it found itself in a region where chaos reigned and the ear was perpetually assaulted by jarring mistunings. Gradually the more scientifically minded among musicians evolved a system by which free modulation could be made ; tuning had to be adjusted to comply with this new desire for harmonious texture and so the scale was " tempered ".

Having set the seal of his approbation on this system, Bach proceeded to create what are, in effect, not works of scientific character but of high art. The variety of craftsmanship and mood in these preludes and fugues (and here we must also take into consideration the second volume, making the grand total of forty-eight) is remarkable. As for the fugues, once and for all Bach made it evident that, far from being a dry, pedantic exercise, fugue in the hands of a poet among musicians can be intensely dramatic and moving.

THREE " LITTLE BOOKS "

Certain collections of pieces designed for domestic use belong to this period. The *Little Organ Book* in which " a Beginner at the Organ is given Instruction in Developing a Chorale . . . and at the same time in Acquiring Facility in the Study of the Pedal " (from the title page, the first to bear

Bach's name as *Kapellmeister* at Cöthen) was meant to help a young organist, such as, for instance, Bach's son Wilhelm Friedmann. These exquisite short movements have a value beyond that of instruction, and as examples of the art of treating the chorale or hymn-tune they are of inexhaustible interest.

We know that the next domestic collection made by Bach, the 1720 *Clavier-Büchlein*, was directly designed for the use of the nine-year-old W. F. Bach. The title page is explicit and gives the actual date when the little book was begun—January 22, in Cöthen. Here Bach includes figures for fingering, a matter to which he attached considerable attention, and which he reorganised.

The third collection made by Bach for family use bears the title " Little Clavier Book for Anna Magdalena Bach. Anno 1722 ", and to that Bach added his personal description of the book as " antiCalvinismus und Christen Schule, item anti Melancholismus ", a broad hint of his attitude towards a narrow contemporary piety when it came to his intimate dealings with wife and children.

LEIPZIG

When Bach left Cöthen at the end of May 1723 to take up the post of Cantor at the Church of St. Thomas at Leipzig he entered upon his longest, most creatively fruitful, and most taxing period of service. His duties were manifold. Besides the Cantorship he undertook responsibility for the music of the Church of St. Nicholas and the very important post of Cantor of the Thomas-Schule, that is to say, music teacher of the scholars from among whom the choristers for the two main churches were chosen. This " charity school for poor children as well as nursery for choirboys " drew on a low class of boy, and Bach was to have difficulty in controlling the rough humour and natural boisterous spirits of his pupils. His mind was occupied with creative work and he had little time for considerations of boyish behaviour. His written undertaking to " set the boys a shining example of an honest, retiring manner of life, serve the School industriously and instruct the boys conscientiously " puts on record the ideal he strove to follow. To this source of supply there should have been added, if Bach's scheme for unifying the musical resources of Leipzig had succeeded, the students of the University where Bach retained the title of Director of Music. But local jealousy and the vanity of the Council came between Bach and his scheme. Leipzig was to become a stormy place for him. With his private pupils it was quite otherwise, and with them he was able to do great things without interference from the authorities. But his official salary was small, his family large, and his life one of incessant hard work.

CANTATAS

In Leipzig Bach found himself working in surroundings new to him. In the past he had been employed in small towns and at small princely courts. Here he worked in a large and flourishing city. His employers were neither townsmen nor courtiers such as he had known, but a council of city fathers.

Bach's duties to the two churches entailed much creative work, for besides organising the services he was required to provide music of his own. Hence came the church cantatas which, together with the few written in previous years, number nearly three hundred. When we realise that this was only a part of his creative work—there was also the St. Matthew Passion, the Mass, and more—and that meanwhile he had a heavy burden of teaching, we cannot help marvelling at Bach's assiduity. That his employers were dissatisfied and found his church music distasteful can be understood, in the special circumstances of the time and place. The cantatas, as Bach's adverse critics in Leipzig held, are often elaborate to the point of taking a worshipper's attention from his devotions. But musically they provide a wonderfully rich area of study and, for those so inclined, an ineffable enjoyment. Their range of mood is wide. This music can be withdrawn and contemplative as well as instantly dramatic. The means employed are very varied, both in vocal or instrumental texture. The cantatas lie at the very centre of Bach's achievement and are among his most personal utterances. The so-called *Christmas Oratorio* consists of a succession of six cantatas.

THE PASSIONS

Bach came to Leipzig with a new work, a setting of the Passion according to St. John, which was evidently meant to display his creative gifts before his new audience. The Passion according to St. Matthew was written some years later (1727–8). These works and the Mass in B minor are, of all Bach's choral compositions, the ones most frequently performed to-day. They are notable examples of German polyphonic music at its most elaborate, and as far as Bach's art is concerned they are among the greatest of his compositions.

Lutheran Passion Music, with its origins in the earliest medieval era, had reached remarkable heights of expressive interpretation of the Scriptures in the settings from all four gospels by Heinrich Schütz. By Bach's time the general scheme of that style of work had become crystallised—a solo

GEORGE FRIDERIC HANDEL (1685–1759)

Marble statue by Louis Roubiliac, 1738

FRANZ JOSEPH HAYDN (1732–1809)

Pencil sketch by George Dance, London, 1794

Evangelist (for which Bach, as was traditional, used a high tenor voice), a number of solo parts for the main characters in the story, and a chorus employed both as a clamorous crowd (called the *turba*) and for more contemplative comment in chorales.

Only a careful and detailed examination of the score of the St. Matthew Passion will reveal the subtle mastery that lies behind the imposing grandeur of this remarkable work. In particular one might mention the imagery employed by Bach. Any line, or even a word, in the text would suggest to Bach a particular musical idea, and most of the formal arias, besides many smaller details, will be found to reflect Bach's striving for this kind of expressiveness. Peter's sobbing, after his denial of Christ, is reflected in the long and tender violin solo of the following aria. The final chorus is a solemn sarabande, a reverent lullaby or lament for the Saviour laid to rest, and so on. The Passion is therefore a lyrical and personal, as well as dramatic, utterance, and it remains something unique in the whole realm of music.

In the past there have been ridiculous examples of " word-painting " cited and repeated *ad nauseam* by writers who read books rather than music. One is that a cross is depicted in music when the word " crucify " occurs. A horizontal line across a vertical can only be expressed in music by a melodic line across a sustained harmony. Music abounds in such examples. Another amazing instance is continually being quoted, *i.e.* that Bach set the words " Is it I ? " eleven times to portray accurately the disciples' question to Christ at the Last Supper, Judas having left. Looking at the music one sees that the sopranos sing " Bin ich's ? " five times, the altos seven, the tenors seven, and the basses five times. How is the figure of eleven reached in this disposition ?

Rival to the St. Matthew Passion, though less personal and more universal in outlook, is the great Mass in B minor, put together by Bach at various dates but remaining, for many listeners, one of the most impressive statements of religious faith in existence. The setting of the Latin text here reminds us again how the Lutherans, unlike other branches of the Reformed church which provided a separate liturgy to supersede the Roman Mass, continued to treat the Communion Office as the principal form of worship. To this piece of good fortune, more perhaps than to any other, we owe the origin of Bach's masterpiece, although, of course, its monumental proportions would preclude its ever being used as part of the liturgy. With its unparalleled resources of polyphony, the expressiveness of its solos, its mighty choruses and above all its noble *Sanctus*, the Mass has for long been regarded by all musicians as one of the great musical works of the world.

The Mass in B minor appeared in sections. The *Kyrie* and *Gloria* were sent to the Elector of Saxony in 1736 with a petition that Bach be given the title of Court Composer—which was granted. The *Credo* may have been written before that, the *Crucifixus* still earlier, and the monumental *Sanctus* came into being some time after 1735. For all this piecemeal production, the work has a complete unity, like that of a building well founded and perfectly proportioned.

"THE MUSICAL OFFERING"

The material facts of Bach's life, the activities of the man other than the work of the musician, are disappointingly sparse. A few anecdotes have been preserved, and we eagerly scan these scraps of history or gossip searching for an indication of Bach's character in, for example, the tale of his meeting with Frederick the Great of Prussia in 1747. Frederick was musically inclined and a very fair flautist. Bach's second son, Carl Philipp Emanuel, had been *Kapellmeister* to Frederick in Potsdam since 1740, and it is reasonable to suppose that the name at least, if not the fame, of Bach himself had penetrated thither. (We have to remember in Bach's case that, unlike Handel's, his contemporary fame spread over a very restricted area.)

The tale of Bach's journey to Potsdam, accompanied by Wilhelm Friedmann, is charming. " At this time the King used to have every evening a private concert, in which he himself generally performed some concertos on the flute. One evening, just as he was getting his flute ready, an officer brought him the written list of the strangers who had just arrived. . . . With his flute in his hand, he . . . turned to the assembled musicians and said, with much excitement : ' Gentlemen, old Bach is here.' " (" Old Bach " sounds condescending from a man who had cherished Voltaire ; but Frederick, having a younger Bach in his service, probably meant by that phrase simply to distinguish between the generations.)

Bach played for Frederick, who then gave him a subject for an extempore fugue, and desired " to hear also a fugue with six obbligato parts ". When Bach got back to Leipzig, his last journey, he composed " the subject he had received from the King in three and six parts, and added several intricate pieces in strict canon ". This was *The Musical Offering*, dedicated by Bach to Frederick the Great.

"THE ART OF FUGUE"

Bach's last extensive work was the collection of movements that he called *The Art of Fugue*. He had spent his life pouring poetry into what is sometimes still considered the most arid of forms. It was perhaps inevitable, certainly natural, that at the end of his life he should sum up what he had done, not by writing even more dramatic, emotionally rich fugues, but by demonstrating the vast possibilities of the scientific manipulation of that style of musical texture.

The Art of Fugue consists of movements of high ingenuity that display all the known possibilities of fugal construction, interspersed with canons. Three subjects (themes) are worked upon, and the end was to have been the most complete movement of all, a complex fugue on the three subjects with a fourth that spelt out the letters of his own name in addition, as though he were signing the work with his own hand. He did not live to complete that movement.

This work is a practical manual of the science of fugal construction; it is also a token that Bach had reached the stage where he could successfully merge the two sides of his nature, the emotional and the practical. For besides all the ingenuity displayed to such a bewildering extent, there is poetry here too, sometimes hidden but still present, and at moments, as in the eighth and eleventh fugues, overwhelming.

THE FINAL YEARS

Bach's visit to Potsdam is the last clear sight we have of him. Three more years were left, and during that time he disappears, departing as quietly as he came, unnoticed by all except his narrow family circle. Handel was to die nine years later, having reached great eminence in his own country and considerable fame throughout Europe. Bach never attained either of those heights. His country, at that time a collection of small princely states, hardly knew of his existence as a musician of towering mental stature, and knew even less of him as a man. Only in exceedingly rare instances, such as Frederick's acknowledgment of his gifts as a musician cleverer than most at constructing fugal puzzles, did Bach ever penetrate further than the small circumference of the places wherein he worked. Of wide European fame he knew nothing.

Returning from Potsdam that summer, he resumed his life as servant of the municipality, provider of music for the services of the two churches, and choir-trainer. His private pupils had his usual close attention, his family was there to help and be helped. Of his works there remained still the *Musical Offering* and the *Art of Fugue* to be created. In these last years he wrote the set of variations on the Christmas chorale *Vom Himmel hoch* which, like the Goldberg Variations, written for his pupil of that name to play Count Kaiserling to sleep, are based on canonic invention. That was in 1747, and the manuscript already shows signs of Bach's failing sight.

THE END

It was in 1749 that Bach, then sixty-five, fell seriously ill. He suffered a paralytic stroke, and though he recovered and could still work, his employers thought otherwise. The Town Council at once set about electing a successor—with indecent haste, as it seems to us now, as though they were eager to shuffle off this old, stubborn man whose music they had never understood or liked. After the stroke his sight dimmed perilously. His mind was as clear as ever and he could dictate his last works to his son-in-law Altnikol. By then he was quite blind and had to face an operation, which was duly performed by an English oculist called Taylor. (This was the same John Taylor the Elder who operated on Handel.) The operation was not successful, and although for a moment afterwards Bach's spirits rose—" I can see ! ", he exclaimed—he was a doomed man. In mid-July 1750 he had a second stroke, and ten days later he died.

In those final months Bach turned to the writing of chorale preludes. Chorales had always been his great love and enjoyment. In the elaboration of such beloved tunes he found instant inspiration—as in the prelude on *Schmücke dich, O liebe Seele* (" Deck thyself, dear soul "), or that based upon *Wachet auf* (" Sleepers, wake ! ")—and in such work he most easily combined ingenuity with poetry. His last essay in this type of composition was the final prelude upon *Wenn wir in höchsten Nöten sein* which he had already worked upon in the *Orgelbüchlein* of the Weimar and Cöthen years. This hymn tune is associated with another to the words *Vor deinen Thron tret' ich* (" I come before Thy throne ")—and those words he asked Altnikol to place at the head of this, his last composition.

THE MAN AS HE WAS SEEN

It is unfortunate that Bach never came in touch with a good portrait painter, let alone a profound artist. Handel at least had Roubiliac to make a statue of him, and there exists an early miniature that can be accepted as a fair likeness. Of Bach there is only a poor, stiff portrait by Elias Gottlieb Haussmann for us to study, with, it must be owned, growing disappointment and distaste. It shows Bach, his face devoid of individuality, holding the manuscript of the canon he presented to the Musical Society in Leipzig on his election as a member. The heavy face seems little more than a façade, and we are left guessing what Bach really looked like. His son Carl Philipp Emanuel left the most authentic account of him :

With his many activities he hardly had time for the most necessary correspondence. . . . But he had more opportunity to talk personally to good people, as his house was like a beehive and just as full of life. Association with him was pleasant for everyone and often very edifying. Since he never wrote down anything about his life, the gaps are unavoidable.

Bach left a lasting imprint upon music, and influenced succeeding generations of composers, and indeed of listeners, as profoundly as any composer before or since. The final stage in his career was hard. Leipzig did not give him the spiritual contentment he found in the service of young Leopold in Cöthen. We see him struggling against conditions that irked him and that he combatted, often with stubborn insistence on rights which his employers could not understand and refused to grant. Yet out of this he forged much of the finest of his music.

THE EIGHTEENTH-CENTURY ORCHESTRA

Bach's career coincided with a period of signal importance in the development of the orchestra. To that development he contributed works, such as the Brandenburg Concertos and Overtures, that widened the scope of orchestral composition to a degree unthought of until then. This was partly through his command of the actual musical material, in counterpoint of extremely individual quality, and in harmonic procedures of extraordinarily rich textures, and partly through his feeling for the individual characteristics of the instruments he employed.

In sheer bulk Bach's purely orchestral music is sparse in comparison with his vast output of vocal music, music for organ, and for chamber ensembles. It is in the quality of his orchestral textures, the strange balance of instrumental tone qualities—strange because seemingly fortuitous—that Bach's widening of the range of orchestral music can be felt. Though it seems to have made little immediate impression, and certainly fell into disrepute, his orchestral writing has imposed itself on the thought and imagination of later generations of composers. For all his intensity of vision, his instrumental treatment was of his time. It was Handel and Alessandro Scarlatti who adopted the newer ideas of instrumental usage, taking into closer account than did Bach the individual proclivities of the different instruments. Bach's flashes of insight into these fresh potentialities for individual expression among the various orchestral instruments are intermittent and not part of the normal workings of his mind.

Bach was an opportunist in his choice of the type and character of work, whether choral, solo vocal, instrumental, or in smaller chamber ensembles, to which he set his hand. The commission that came to him, or rather the opportunity he took from the Margrave of Brandenburg, to write the famous concertos, is one example. Few others presented themselves, and thus it is that he wrote lamentably few other works of that nature. Had he been able to give his attention to the individual characteristics of instruments over a longer space of time, his sensibility aided by his keen faculty for research might well have resulted in wonderful works. As it is, his sudden inspirations remain startling to this day.

There is, for instance, his use of the radiant top register of the trumpet, which he employs as though the limitations of that early form of the instrument did not exist, framing his trumpet parts daringly but in such outlines as preserved and enhanced the purely musical quality of whatever movement he was then forming. Many trumpet passages come to mind, but two may be mentioned here. There is the brilliant trumpet part in the introduction of the second D major Overture, notably the re-entry of the instrument at the close of that section after bars of silence. Again, in a different texture, there is the high trumpet part in the *Gratias agimus* and in the *Dona nobis* of the Mass in B minor. There is a miraculous moment at the end of the Mass when Bach makes his trumpet plane high above the sound of voices and instruments as a final enhancement of the intense emotion in that music.

In the *Crucifixus* of that work too there is the use of the tone, at once warm and impersonal, of flutes. We meet the same mingling of the intimate and the abstract in the twin oboes accompanying the lullaby in the first part of the Christmas Oratorio, and in the violin, less abstracted from human problems, which accompanies the aria *Have mercy, Lord* in the St. Matthew Passion. All these instances seem now the inevitable choice in the particular context.

The Brandenburg Concertos occupy a significant position mid-way between Monteverdi and Haydn in the development of the orchestra. The time was not ripe for the stabilising of the orchestra into the main groups of strings, brass, woodwind, and percussion such as were ready for the organising genius of Haydn to use in his symphonies. Bach, working within the limits of contemporary instrumental technique, as he worked within the contemporary climate of musical thought, still relied upon the harpsichord continuo to fill in the spaces in the contrapuntal texture. Gabrieli in Venice and his pupil Schütz in Dresden had already explored the possibility of using wind tone as a sustaining element, and with that had begun to display the dramatic contrast between linear string counterpoint and interspersed wind chords which was to lead to the modern conception of orchestral texture when the harpsichord continuo had been superseded.

The mere recounting of the instruments used in the six Brandenburg Concertos shows how fecund was his imagination when occupied with the problems of instrumental tone. The first concerto shows at once that the Corelli type of *concerto grosso* (in which two contrasted bands of strings are deployed, each with its own continuo) was not to hold Bach's attention exclusively. This work is scored for strings (among them a *violino piccolo*, a violin of small size, tuned higher and having thinner strings which gave it a special tone quality), three oboes, two horns, a bassoon. The second Brandenburg work is for a main body of strings with solo violin, flute, oboe, and trumpet. In the third Bach returns to the Corelli type of *concerto grosso* for strings, but he divides them for purposes of antiphonal question and answer into groups of violins, violas, and cellos, three parts for each, plus a string bass. The fourth concerto is for strings with a solo violin and two solo flutes. In the fifth there is an elaborate solo part for the harpsichord, with violin and flute solos in addition. The sixth is scored for strings alone, and Bach shows daring as well as unusual sensibility to instrumental tone in dispensing altogether with violins, giving the violas the highest part.

CONCERTOS FOR VIOLIN AND FOR KEYBOARD

The solo concerto in Bach's day begins to show an approach different from that needed by the more homogeneous *concerto grosso* and the overture or suite. It also provided a means of exploring other structural forms, since the confrontation of solo and chorus (the instrumental *tutti*) brought with it a fruitful opportunity for the dramatic, an element that Bach exploits splendidly in the keyboard concertos. We need only listen to the great concertos in C major and C minor for two harpsichords to hear how strongly his mind reacted to that challenge, and how richly he developed his themes as he displayed them on those instruments.

The violin concertos have another quality. Here it is the warm lyrical tone and phrasing of a stringed instrument that he explores, and the result is less of a vivacious mental conflict expressed in terms of music than a lyrical style of utterance with relatively restrained contrasts. The slow movements are particularly significant here. Bach created a type of intimate dialogue between solo and *tutti* (or in the superb D minor concerto for two violins, a dialogue between the two solo parts and the *tutti*) distinguished by a notable formal elegance as well as profound emotional penetration. His models were the concertos by Vivaldi, but for the essence of the music he relied on his own vision and produced works that are still intrinsically personal.

THE GERMAN CANTATA

The place of Bach's cantatas in his achievement is undoubtedly high, and their position in the general development of choral music is so important as to make one wonder whether after all they do not provide the most complete evidence of Bach's supremacy. Certainly the cantatas have a unique quality of devotional expressiveness, a quality that comes neither from the words nor from the music alone, but from the interaction of the one upon the other.

The texts are strangely moving even when they appear, to our vision, sentimental yet curiously arid. That naïve simplicity in expressing ineffable spiritual experiences, and in teaching such truths as appear to arise from them, belongs to the religious utterances of all ages and creeds. It is present in the writing of the true Pietists and Lutheran religious writers of Bach's time in Germany, was accepted by him as a normal manner of religious exposition, and was mirrored and echoed in the music he created as an accompanying medium designed to enhance the expressive content of the texts. Not all those cantata texts were of a high artistic level comparable with that of the music. We cannot but regret that their poetic insight was often weak and their literary merit often non-existent ; so that Bach, hard pressed to find texts for the continual succession of cantatas which he had to supply for his Leipzig employers, was too often forced to set deliberately contrived compilations, and often so desiccated and lacking in any warm human emotion, or else so sentimental, that we are amazed by the devotion that Bach brought to his manipulation of such poor stuff and the splendour, as much as the ingenuity, of his music.

Even the poorer texts, however, provided him with subjects on which he could exercise his thought and find scope for his visionary flights into the regions of spiritual experience, as well as furnishing innumerable opportunities for his gift of pictorial musical allusion—a matter that he did not press beyond the bounds of artistic propriety but of which he was perpetually aware, a device that he was instinctively ready and able to employ.

The cantatas cover the whole span of Bach's mature creative existence, from the first belonging to his Arnstadt days when he took over the post of organist there as his first settled appointment, to the last, the date of which can exactly be determined, and which appeared within a few years of his death in Leipzig. At every stage of his career he wrote church cantatas and secular cantatas, their number in relation to his other forms of composition depending on the musical material available. Thus at Weimar there were more than at Cöthen, and by far the largest number were written during the final Leipzig period.

The cantatas are wonderfully varied in form and style. Fundamental to them all is Bach's intense spirituality, while from the purely musical point of view they show an astonishing technical mastery and an unfailing resourcefulness in creating illuminating settings of the texts. The words seem to have acted immediately upon his imagination, whether in an aria expressing the lyrical emotion of the church adoring the Saviour, in elaborate choruses celebrating the ecstasies of the soul of man in its journey through life to eventual heavenly bliss, or in movements for a single voice or for chorus in which one of the church chorale melodies was woven into the fabric of that Sunday's cantata. Such a work is *Wachet auf* where the hymn tune " Sleepers, wake " appears and re-appears ; in which, for one moment, we can watch Bach's mind at work as the chorale melody gives rise to one of his own most noble melodies, which is thereupon combined with the chorale itself, at once an accompaniment and a profound commentary upon the whole expressive, poetic, and religious content of the cantata. No composer before had delved so deeply into the fundamental spiritual meaning of a religious text ; few since then have gone as far.

BACH TO-DAY

No sooner had Bach died than his music entered a period of almost complete oblivion, as far as any wide popularity or knowledge was concerned, and this neglect lasted for three-quarters of a century. It was partly occasioned by the character of the music that he left behind him. Handel appealed to Gluck as a great, even though by then extinguished, opera composer, to Haydn as a powerful writer of oratorios ; with them his fame was assured. Bach could count on no such support in those two imposing types of composition. In so far as his cantatas, his orchestral works and his chamber music appealed to the people of his day and place —manifestly a minority audience—that style of writing belonged, in general estimation, to a past age, and as such it quickly faded from men's memories.

If Bach was remembered at all, it was as a writer of keyboard fugues, themselves hardly known outside a small circle of the more scientifically-minded. It was such a circle that Baron van Swieten entered when he went from Vienna to Berlin in 1782 and was persuaded by Frederick the Great to interest himself in Bach (Swieten thought he referred to one of Bach's sons) and so came in contact with the *Well-Tempered Clavier* and the *Art of Fugue*, and eventually made them available to Mozart. Meanwhile Bach's other music lay unperformed, and it is significant that Mozart had to decipher a Bach motet from the separate parts, no score being available, when with astonishment he heard Bach's unaccompanied vocal music during his visit to Leipzig in 1787.

The first sign of a revival of interest came in 1829 when Zelter, the friend and musical mentor of Goethe, having for some years been a knowledgeable enthusiast for Bach's music, persuaded his pupil Mendelssohn to give a performance of the St. Matthew Passion in a version which, though badly truncated and in other ways mishandled, did in fact arouse the enthusiasm of musicians. From that performance the revival may be said to date. It was as swift as had been the eclipse in 1750. The German Bach Society was founded in 1850, and work was begun on collecting, collating, editing, and printing the Bach Society edition. (Handel's works had already been collected. Arnold's edition, the one sent to the dying Beethoven, had begun to appear in 1786, and the German Handel Society was started in 1843.)

The influence of Bach cannot be precisely indicated, but he enriched composers of later times as diverse as Mendelssohn, Wagner, Brahms, and Bruckner. To which may be added the fact that when Igor Stravinsky began to turn from the rich harmonic textures of his *Rite of Spring* and to thin out his music in a more contrapuntal perspective, he was said to be writing in a " neo-Bach " style. The label was only partly applicable, but the phrase was symptomatic of a climate of opinion in which Bach's primacy and the wide extent of his influence were for the first time fully acknowledged.

THE SONS OF J. S. BACH

Bach's sons carried on the family tradition of music, but in ways quite different from those pursued by their father. They owed him a musical education for which posterity has envied them and an example of dedicated labour such as few musicians have had ; but his style of elaborate contrapuntal composition was already becoming outmoded during the latter part of his career. While he stayed at his post in Leipzig, they went farther afield, came into contact with new ideas, submitted to the fascination of new and enlivening doctrines, and worked their way to the forefront of musical life.

Two of these younger Bach musicians are historically significant. Bach's second son, Carl Philipp Emanuel (1714–88), is known to posterity as the Berlin Bach. His intellectual gifts apart from music were such as to suggest a career other than the normal Bach tradition of music ; and in fact he went to the university to study law. Nevertheless his grounding in music, such as was natural and probably inescapable in his family surroundings, was thorough and absorbing, and eventually it proved paramount. He became *Kapellmeister* to Frederick the Great at Potsdam, and it was to visit him that Johann Sebastian went there and had the famous encounter with Frederick that resulted in the *Musical Offering*. As a composer C. P. E. Bach was to become an impressive musician. We see him to-day as the link between the creative style of his father and that of the new generation, whose most brilliant example was to be Haydn. His influence was most strongly exercised through his keyboard sonatas, where he shows a lively imagination and inventiveness which made a great impression on the young Haydn.

Johann Sebastian's youngest son, Johann Christian (1735–82), is the other outstanding musician of that family whose work has had lasting effect. If his elder brother can be linked with Haydn, Johann Christian, who eventually found his whole activity to be centred on England and became known as the London Bach, forged a link with Mozart, who was brought to London as an infant prodigy, was taken to see Bach in Soho, and from his example learned something of the possibilities inherent in the early flowering of symphonic form—possibilities that Mozart was to explore deeply. Unlike his elder brother, Johann Christian took to the composition of operas, a fact which places him still more firmly in the succession leading to Mozart.

VIII

HANDEL

GEORGE FRIDERIC HANDEL was born in 1685 at Halle in Germany, a town lying between Berlin and Weimar. The name Handel is found in a number of forms, all derived from an original term meaning trader, a singularly apt derivative for the name of a musician who was to prove an expert businessman. Unlike his exact contemporary Bach, and their other contemporary Domenico Scarlatti who was the son of one of the supreme creative musicians of his day, he had no notable musical ancestry. Halle was, at the time of Handel's birth, a quiet provincial town which had recently declined from the position of court residence of the Dukes of Saxony.

Handel's father was a barber-surgeon who became personal surgeon to Duke Augustus of Saxony, and appears to have continued to serve the new Duke when he moved to Weissenfels. He married twice, and George Frideric was the child of his second wife. The family went on living in Halle, and it was on one of his occasional visits to the court at Weissenfels that the father took with him the child, whom the Duke heard by chance playing the organ. It seems that the elder Handel disliked music, or, more likely, that he mistrusted musicians, subscribing to the opinion that they were vagabonds and rogues. He was a man of integrity who valued the court position he had won through his own exertions and intellectual ability, and he looked to something more solid than art as a basis for his son's career. Whatever musical gifts Handel enjoyed by birth were inherited from his mother's side. It will have been she who saw the trend of her young son's thought ; her husband had other visions. She it was who had a clavichord installed in an attic for the child to play, without her husband being told ; the child could have his wish and indulge his dear passion, and he was always grateful to his mother.

When the Duke heard him play at Weissenfels he urged the father to promote this gift for music. But the older Handel, subservient though he might be to his employer, was not easily to be moved. The boy was sent to school with the idea that he should eventually go to the University of Halle to study law. Fortunate as he was in his mother, he was thus hardly less so in his father, who saw to it that he received the grounding of a good education.

THE YOUNG TALENT

Handel's father died in 1697. In 1702, three days before his seventeenth birthday, Handel matriculated as a student of law at Halle University. In so doing he honoured his father's memory, though by then he was steadily and with irresistible force drawn towards music and was, in fact, already a practising musician and a composer too. Years later Handel, then in England, was shown what purported to be an early work of his, written at ten. He acknowledged it as a true document, a set of trios for oboes and bass, refined work of which it has been said that " even Mozart wrote nothing at that age that can be compared with them for freshness of melody and maturity of musicianship ".

When at length Handel's father had given in to the wish of the Duke to the extent of putting his boy to the serious study of music, an excellent teacher was found for him in Friedrich Zachow, organist of the Lutheran church in Halle. Zachow was not only a good practical musician ; he possessed a large music library and set his pupil to copy out the works of the composers represented there, a valuable training in style and method. This made Handel a well-read musician even before he had gone out into the world and heard music unknown in Halle. In the same year that he entered the University, he became organist of the Cathedral in Halle. Try as he might to fulfil his father's behest and become a lawyer, he was by now steadily set on the course of music.

He had by then met Telemann, who was to become his friend and mentor. To Handel the visit of Telemann must have seemed like the opening of a new vista. Telemann was only four years older than he, but belonged to the great outside world of art ; and to the young organist in Halle he brought news of Berlin and Hamburg, of the operatic world of which Handel was just beginning to be aware. In the early summer of 1703 Handel arrived in Hamburg, which was called " the Venice of the north" not, like Amsterdam, because of its canals, but because of the opera, with its echoes of Italian manners and methods under the vigorous though erratic management of Reinhold Keiser, himself a fluent operatic composer.

At Hamburg Handel had the opportunity of seeing opera for the first time, and with his quick mind to discover for himself the fundamental elements of operatic style. He met Mattheson, an alert, bombastic, highly talented musician who is said to have taken the young man from Halle under his wing and introduced him to the musical life of Hamburg. Handel was a willing pupil, up to a point ; but his naturally stubborn individuality was already strong. The following appears to be a true Handel tale. Mattheson, singer as well as composer, took a chief part in one of his own operas, called *Cleopatra*. When not singing in the character of Anthony, Mattheson would come down into the orchestra and take over the harpsichord from Handel. But this irritated the young man after a time, and eventually he refused to leave the keyboard. The tale goes that the infuriated singer-composer-conductor challenged him to a duel, that by chance his sword broke on a button on Handel's coat, that honour was satisfied and the two were friends again. Handel had shown his mettle.

HANDEL IN ITALY

By then he was having his own operas produced in Hamburg. It was not long before he left Germany for Italy, then the centre of all opera.

He had reached Italy by 1707 ; how he compassed the long, expensive journey from Hamburg is not known. What is known is that in Hamburg he met Prince Gian Gastone de' Medici, son of the Grand Duke of Tuscany, who invited him to Italy, but that Handel travelled there independently.

Handel spent three years going from city to city in Italy, playing the organ and harpsichord and writing operas. He was excellently received by the Italian intelligentsia who, musically at least, were accepted as the most cultured in Europe. Manifestly he came with powerful credentials, probably from Gian Gastone and the Grand Duke of Tuscany, and his splendid keyboard technique will have helped. He soon became " il caro Sassone " (" the beloved Saxon "), known as an expert player in the palaces of great musical patrons such as Cardinal Ottoboni in Rome. After Innocent XI and his successor Innocent XII banned opera on grounds of public morality, Ottoboni turned to chamber music and to oratorio for his private parties, at which Handel shone. It was in such surroundings that he came into contact with Corelli, and the story goes that he once rated the older man for not playing his music as he wished. Taking the instrument out of Corelli's hands to show him how some passage should be played, Handel was answered by that great violinist and gentle, cultured man with a tentative " But . . ."—and there followed an explanation of the difference between the two styles of performance, Corelli excusing himself on the grounds that he had not understood Handel's demands. It is a revealing tale, and we see the eager young Handel at that moment clearly, and realise what there was already there that would take England by storm and win the battle against philistinism by sheer brute persistence.

Handel succeeded in impressing by his gifts not only Roman society but the larger public of Florence and Venice, where his operas were produced. It was in Venice that he met the Earl of Manchester (the English ambassador to the Republic of Venice), Prince Ernst Augustus of Hanover (younger brother of the Elector George who was to become King of England), and Baron Kielmansegg, who was to be a standby later. Manchester is said to have given him a pressing invitation to come to England and write Italian opera for the entertainment of the aristocracy. So when in June 1710 Handel took up the position of *Kapellmeister* in Hanover—probably as a result of the influence of Prince Ernst and of the court musician Steffani, whom Handel had met earlier—within a few months he had applied for leave of absence to visit the court of the Elector-Palatine in Düsseldorf and then, remembering Lord Manchester's invitation, travelled by way of Holland to England.

FIRST VISIT TO ENGLAND

It remains curious that he should have left his new appointment in Hanover so soon after having taken it up, but it has been suggested that the Elector of Hanover always intended that he should spend some time abroad, presumably to broaden his mind, before taking up regular duties at the Hanoverian court. Evidently Manchester had given him an agreeable picture of the condition of music in England and the opportunities available to a young opera composer. Handel must also have furnished himself with letters of introduction to people with strong social influence, for he was well received from the start.

It was not long before London had the opportunity of assessing his worth more directly than by reports from Hamburg, where his opera *Almira* had achieved considerable success, or from Venice, where the more impressionable but more critical Italians had hailed his *Agrippina* with shouts of " Viva il caro Sassone ! " Once in London, Handel appears to have got very quickly in touch with operatic circles and was taken up by the manager Heidegger, a Swiss impresario, generally considered an adventurer. Italian opera in England, the product of admiration for Italian music and a snobbery based on the air of culture assumed by those who understood a foreign tongue, was then still a very young, tender plant. From 1705 there had been works by Italian composers translated into English (*e.g.* Bononcini's *Camilla*), whose success had led English writers to copy Italian models ; Clayton's *Rosamond*, however, to a libretto by Addison, was a dismal failure. Italian actors were thus introduced into performances, who sang in their own language while their English colleagues continued to sing in English ; among works played in this way was Alessandro Scarlatti's *Pyrrhus and Demetrius*. The final step, to opera entirely in Italian, was taken in 1710, the year before Handel's first London opera, with Bononcini's *Almahide*.

At this time Vanbrugh was in correspondence with Lord Manchester in Venice about the possibilities of Italian opera in London, and it was not long before this that Handel had met him in Venice and heard from him how things were going in London. The outcome was the production of a new opera at the Queen's Theatre in the Haymarket, Handel's first work for the London stage, the opera *Rinaldo*, with a libretto based on Tasso's *Jerusalem Delivered*.

" RINALDO "

Rinaldo was written in a fortnight, not an unusual feat for Handel who, when he was in good health, came to the actual physical labour of getting notes down on paper with his mind clearly possessed of the general scheme of the work, the main features of the music and all but the finest details of the various numbers. Writing was not merely the last but the least labour. The opera was produced in February 1711, and had fifteen performances that season.

It aroused much popular acclaim and inevitably as much jealousy. Addison, his self-esteem bitterly hurt over the failure of his *Rosamond*, lampooned Handel's successful opera in the *Spectator*, while Steele attacked it in the *Tatler*. Alert readers would have realised that personal bias lay behind all this, for Steele was financially interested in theatrical production and Addison in the writing of opera libretti. Nevertheless, the public would have savoured Addison's concern about the sparrows released to accompany the aria *Augeletto che cantando vai*. " Instead of perching on the Trees and performing their parts," he wrote, " these young actors either get into the Galleries or put out the Candles." He feared " that in other plays they may make their Entrances in very wrong and improper Scenes, so as to be seen flying in a Lady's Bed-Chamber or perching upon a King's Throne, besides the Inconveniences which the Heads of the Audience may sometimes suffer from them ". Had Addison lived on until the days of *The Ring* he would have been as much interested in Brünnhilde's horse and Wotan's ravens as in the sparrows of his day.

The opera season ending in June, Handel left for Germany. Once again he stayed at Düsseldorf, a welcome guest of the Elector-Palatine, who wrote to Hanover to explain Handel's absence from the court to which he had been appointed and to excuse, as between one prince and another, his delay in presenting himself there again. Undoubtedly Düsseldorf was a more lively court than Hanover and Handel was quite ready to delay his departure. In November 1711 we hear of him in his native Halle standing godfather to his niece and seeing his mother. For her his affection remained undiminished in spite of being parted from her continually for long spells while he pursued his fortunes in London.

" LADY SEATED AT THE VIRGINALS " (*circa* 1671) BY VERMEER

THE SECOND VISIT TO ENGLAND

Handel lived on in Hanover until the autumn of 1712, when he again asked for and was accorded permission to go to London, on condition that he engaged to return " within a reasonable time ", which was certainly an arrangement vague enough to suit all tastes. Handel's situation becomes increasingly strange and his position mysteriously interesting. What was in the mind of the Elector, who was already looking to the throne of England should Anne die and the Stuart line fail ? His agents will have been busy under the surface in England, testing the political winds and jockeying for position, while not a few members of the aristocracy, Marlborough among them, played with both parties, the Electoral court in Hanover and the Pretender in Paris. Did Handel have his finger in this pie, and if so, was he officially backed, if not during his first, then during his second visit to England ? It is an intriguing supposition, but there is as yet no proof.

He rapidly increased his hold on the esteem of the operatic faction in London. The young Lord Burlington gave him patronage, and at his house in Piccadilly Handel, who is said to have stayed there for as long as three years, met such leaders of English culture as Pope, Gray, and Arbuthnot. He would go from time to time to St. Paul's Cathedral to play the organ with young Maurice Greene (with whom he afterwards fell out), and repair with him after an organ session to the Queen's Arms, a tavern near the cathedral, where they could drink and talk. Handel was beginning to know, through first-hand contact, the character of English life, and he made his way with remarkable ease. Queen Anne, probably at the request of Lady Burlington (who was one of her Ladies of the Bedchamber), took an interest in him. Unusually for a foreigner, Handel was commissioned to write royal occasional music such as the Birthday Ode for the Queen and the *Te Deum* to celebrate the Peace of Utrecht in 1713, thus becoming a court musician to the Queen of England while in Hanover his master had to be content to wait for two events, Handel's return (his leave now long over-spent) and the death of Anne, which would leave his way open to the throne. In the meantime Handel stayed on, receiving a pension of £200 a year from the Queen.

CANNONS

Queen Anne died on August 1, 1714, and the Elector became George the First of Great Britain. When Handel's master, whom he had forsaken in Hanover, arrived in London, a piquant situation was created which, though amusing for posterity, must have been embarrassing for Handel, who had been given a blank cheque, as it were, and had overdrawn it. He was beginning to be well established in England ; his opera *Teseo* had been a success in 1713. But this could hardly be expected to influence the new king, who was even-tempered when in a contented frame of mind but easily irritable when his self-esteem was threatened.

What exactly happened between the King and Handel is not clear. It is known that George went to see Handel's new opera *Amadigi* late in the 1715 season. Eventually a reconciliation was brought about, though precisely how that happened we do not know. There are two stories. Mainwaring, Handel's first biographer (his book is dated 1760, a year after the composer's death), tells the tale of a water party on the Thames arranged by Baron Kielmansegg, Handel's friend from the Venice days and now (as husband of one of George's mistresses) Master of the Horse. Handel's music for this occasion charmed the King, who is said thereupon to have pardoned his erring court musician. But Mainwaring seems to have got his dates mixed ; he appears to suggest 1715 for this water party, but later research places it, or one of its kind, in 1717. The Envoy of Brandenburg reported to his government a notice in the London *Daily Courant* about a royal water party given by Kielmansegg with music by Handel, music that so pleased the King that he had it repeated after supper. The second story is less complicated and quite credible. It is that Geminiani, the violinist, having to play before George I and being notoriously difficult to please in the matter of accompanists, demanded that Handel should play on that occasion. Again, the King is said to have been impressed to the extent of pardoning Handel.

At all events, the quarrel, if it ever existed, was safely interred. The King confirmed Handel's £200 pension from Queen Anne. He went further, adding a further £200 a year of his own, and a few years afterwards Handel netted still another £200 pension, making the respectable total of £600 a year for life. This was a large sum for those days, and it must be taken into account when discussing Handel's reputed bankruptcies.

In July 1716 the king went back to Hanover and Handel accompanied him ; so that we can be sure that the quarrel was patched up by that time. Handel was free to go about in Germany. He visited his friend Mattheson in Hamburg and his mother in Halle, where he found his old teacher's widow, Frau Zachow, in straitened circumstances and helped her. Back in London, where the opera was in a state of collapse, Handel took service with the Duke of Chandos. This flamboyant man, immensely rich (he had used his position of Paymaster to the Forces to his own advantage) and recently ennobled, had built a renaissance palace at Cannons near Edgware, and Handel was his resident composer from 1718 for just over a year. Chandos was not interested in music other than superficially, but his name has been immortalised by the splendid " Chandos Anthems " that Handel wrote for his private chapel at Cannons.

" THE HARMONIOUS BLACKSMITH "

With Cannons also is connected a diverting and quite spurious piece of Handelian gossip invented in the next century, the tale of the blacksmith at Edgware heard singing the tune that Handel, handily within earshot, thereupon used for his clavier variations. Another Cannons tale, that Handel " composed " *Esther* on the organ in the church at Whitchurch, is demonstrably unhistorical. Cannons, however, can be remembered not only for anthems but for the English *Acis and Galatea* (not a revision of a serenade of the same name he had written in Naples, but a new work), and for the masque *Esther* which was to reappear later as an oratorio at a crisis in Handel's career.

THE NEW OPERA COMPANY

At the beginning of 1719 Handel went abroad to seek singers for a new opera venture that had been started by the nobility. Opera in London had languished, inevitably since it relied on a fickle public of wealth and fashion who were willing to pay only so long as they were amused. Opera is not, by its nature, wholly amusing, but Burlington manifestly thought it a worthy artistic adventure and Chandos probably considered it an adornment to his person ; Handel, who was brought in as chief musician, took it to heart and hoped to take it into his purse. The noble patrons of this Academy of Music, as it was called in imitation of the French Opéra, called in the popular Giovanni Bononcini (1670-1755) from Rome and Ariosti from Berlin, and a sum of £50,000 was got together ; shares were £100 each, and the King subscribed £1000.

The first great success of the new company was Handel's *Radamisto* in 1720. Handel became the fashion with Society, and his music was enjoyed as the latest type of expensive entertainment. Society was ready to support him and as ready to drop him. Young Burlington, his first patron, brought Bononcini from Italy, partly from artistic considerations, partly for the malicious amusement of watching the effect on a musician who had enjoyed his patronage but had now become bigger than Burlington House wanted. So the spirit of rivalry was fostered. It spelt ruin to the patrons of the

Royal Academy and almost to Handel himself. Opera after opera was produced by Handel at how much expense of energy and intense thought few realised or cared. *Floridante* appeared in 1721, the exquisite *Ottone* at the beginning of 1723. In that opera a prima donna appeared, Cuzzoni, who was to give Handel much trouble by her tantrums and got as good as she gave when, making trouble at rehearsal, she was told by this mere composer, " Madam, you may be a devil but I would have you know that I am the prince of devils and ", seizing her round the waist, " if you don't behave, I'll throw you through the window."

In February 1724 Handel provided the splendid *Giulio Cesare* for his patrons. Then more trouble was made by the arrival of Faustina Bordoni who was brought in, certainly not on Handel's advice, as a rival to Cuzzoni, a situation that produced much trouble for the management and much amusement for the audience. Inevitably, with rival prima donnas and rival composers, opera became not so much the talk of the town, which might have increased its financial stability, but the laughing-stock of both intelligent and foolish. Furthermore, opera became a pawn in the game of politics, Handel being supported by the King's party, while Bononcini was backed by the powerful opposition which included the Dukes of Rutland, Queensberry, and Marlborough.

THE BEGGAR'S OPERA

The way was open for a clever mind to make capital out of a ludicrous situation, and the nail was driven home into the coffin of Handel's operatic ventures by John Gay's *The Beggar's Opera*, produced in 1728. This burlesque of Handelian opera with a highwayman as hero and two rival sluts as heroines—an allusion to the rival prima donnas, Bordoni and Cuzzoni, at the King's Theatre—has outlasted, as a viable stage-piece, the operas it guyed. Even the satire on Walpole's Administration, which Gay combined with his operatic burlesque, has not suffered the usual fate of topical humour.

At one stroke Gay, with the help of John Pepusch (1667–1752), a German musician settled in London, established a characteristically English form of operatic entertainment—the ballad opera. It consisted of a play with songs frequently interrupting the dialogue and such other music in the way of overture, dances, and so on as might be required. The distinguishing characteristic of the ballad-opera was that the lyrics were fitted to existing tunes. For *The Beggar's Opera* Gay drew upon various collections of traditional and popular melodies, besides borrowing from the works of known composers, including Purcell and Handel himself, whose march in *Rinaldo* was turned into the highwaymen's chorus, *Let us take the road.*

Pepusch, who arranged and harmonised the music and composed the overture, must have taken the more pleasure in guying Handel's work for the fact that he had been the Duke of Chandos's sole resident musician until Handel was brought in. The piece, no doubt, owed its enormous success to the piquant association of Gay's pungent, witty verses with familiar melodies. To a modern audience its attraction lies in the charm and beauty of those immortal tunes, and in a slightly less degree to Gay's considerable dramatic skill and vigorous language.

Gay's success let loose a flood of ballad-operas in the same vein, among them his own sequel to *The Beggar's Opera*, called *Polly*. But none came up to the level of the original. In a sense, the form once invented was easy enough to fill, but without the fire of Gay's imagination the results were too often insipid counterfeits. The fashion exhausted itself about 1735, but was revived in the 'sixties in the more genteel productions of Thomas Augustine Arne (1710–78) and Charles Dibdin (1745–1814).

DECLINE OF OPERA IN LONDON

But meantime George I had died in 1727, and the Academy collapsed; and though Handel was not financially involved, he had no opera-house for which to compose. After returning to Halle to see his mother—a visit of which Bach heard and sent his son Friedmann from Leipzig asking Handel to visit him, as he was too ill to go to him (but the meeting never took place)—Handel went into partnership with Heidegger, and with him leased the King's Theatre, by that means bringing himself into direct financial contact with opera in London. It was a risk that proved extremely hazardous, with the position already undermined by the popularity of *The Beggar's Opera*.

The Handel-Heidegger opera season opened in December 1729 with Handel's *Lotario*, only a moderate success. *Giulio Cesare* was then revived, and in the following February Handel produced another new opera, *Partenope*, also only a token success. The winter season of 1730 began with a revival of *Scipio* so that the famous male soprano Senesino, brought over to London again at great expense, could shine in one of his most popular parts and prove, it was hoped, a draw. Handel's consistently fine music, his scores lit with flashes of powerful dramatic intensity, seem to have been too serious for the fickle opera public in London. The affairs of his company began to deteriorate. His singers quarrelled among themselves and he with them. The aristocracy, which at first had cherished him, now lost interest. He was lampooned, caricatured, called "The Great Bear" for his independence—his integrity as a creative musician, we might call it—which his noble ex-patrons considered to be rough, " bearish " behaviour. A few constant friends he had, among them the Princess Royal, who greatly admired him. The new King (George II) and Queen supported him, and owing to the breach in the royal family this meant that Frederick, Prince of Wales and the young society around him automatically boycotted Handel's operas. The future progressively darkened.

FROM OPERA TO ORATORIO

Moments of comparative brightness there were, however. *Esther,* the Cannons masque, was revived in 1732 but fell under the Bishop of London's ban forbidding dramatic performances in the theatre of sacred subjects. The ecclesiastical ban in fact proved fortunate. Handel could hardly ignore this censorship, but he had a keen eye to the main chance and could turn a hindrance into an opportunity for further advance in another direction ; this he now did. *Esther* was announced for public performance in the King's Theatre, Haymarket, as " the sacred story of Esther ; an oratorio in English, formerly composed by Mr. Handel, and now revised by him with Several additions, and to be performed by a great number of voices and instruments. NB. There will be no acting on the stage, but the house will be fitted up in a decent manner for the audience. . . ."

Thus the ban was eluded, and a new way opened for Handel's genius which led him from opera towards oratorio, the beginning of a change from Italian to English. Handel was still, however, to have some years of thorny existence ahead of him as he struggled to impose his operas on a heedless public. The following July he had a pleasant interlude in Oxford for a series of performances of his works, and there he wrote the oratorio *Athaliah* ; but his operatic venture, despite masterpieces like *Orlando,* was foundering. The nobility started a rival company in an opera house in Lincoln's Inn Fields, and Handel found himself gradually deserted by his great and expensive singers, and eventually by his partner Heidegger also.

In 1734 his lease of the King's Theatre fell in, and instantly his rivals procured the theatre for themselves. Stubborn and undaunted, Handel went east to Lincoln's Inn Fields and opened his new season there with Rich, of *Beggar's Opera* fame ; later he moved to Covent Garden. Assiduously he provided new works for a listless public. In January 1735 it was *Ariodante* ; that April it was the delightful *Alcina,* which contained a good deal of ballet music. The next year brought *Atalanta,* and 1737 *Arminio* in January, *Giustino* in February, and the exquisite *Berenice* in March. But the venture was by then in ruins. Handel is said to have been bankrupt, by which is probably meant that his fortune was depleted to the point of his having to ask for time to pay his creditors.

What is certain is that his health was seriously impaired. In 1735 he had a serious illness which necessitated his going to Tunbridge Wells to be cured. Two years later he suffered a paralytic stroke, for which he had to take the drastic sulphur cure at Aix-la-Chapelle. Even after that severe blow he continued to write and produce operas, *Faramondo* in January 1738 (a work full of fine music), *Serse* (his only comic opera) that April. But in the next year, no operas ; he was busy with the oratorios *Saul* and *Israel in Egypt*. In 1740 he finished his last opera, *Deidamia*, produced in 1741 and given only three performances. For Handel, Italian opera in London, with all its excessive expense of energy, was over and done with. From now onward oratorio was to have his undivided attention. After *Deidamia* Handel paid a visit to Dublin ; and there, the following year, was given the first performance of the oratorio on which his fame now most securely rests, *Messiah*.

"ISRAEL IN EGYPT" AND "MESSIAH"

In many respects *Israel in Egypt* and *Messiah* may be considered Handel's finest oratorios. Certainly they are among the best known. The text for each was taken from the Bible and, whether or not Handel had an acute appreciation of English, he could hardly fail to distinguish between these words and the absurdities that had so often served for his librettos. Handel, like Purcell before him, had proved that musical genius could transcend literary doggerel although, with the possible exception of *The Occasional Oratorio*, he did not continue fortunate with his texts even after *Messiah*.

The grandeur of *Israel in Egypt* lies in its long succession of thrilling choruses and double choruses, which fact in itself impeded initial success with a London audience that had heard nothing of the kind before. The work depicts the fortunes of the Children of Israel in their delivery from bondage to freedom ; and the choruses form a dramatic narrative that loses nothing of intensity by being occasionally picturesque, as where the strings plainly indicate the hopping of frogs, or in the pastoral beauty of the words " He led them forth like sheep ". Handel set these words to a melody taken from a *Serenata* by Stradella from which, along with two other Italian works (which reminds us of Handel's Italian training before he finally left Germany to settle in England), he borrowed freely when writing *Israel in Egypt*. But this is not the place to be too concerned with the intricacies of eighteenth-century conventions in which Handel, neither more nor less than others, followed the custom of his time. That was a period when many musical ideas were common currency ; it is what the master achieves with those ideas that matters, and Handel often borrowed again from his own past works.

In *Israel*, then, Handel combines greatness and simplicity to achieve a monumental choral drama, one which he could produce without the added expense of costumes and scenery. In *Messiah* Handel dispenses with the operatic elements that inform *Israel*. There is no attempt to portray dramatically the life of the Saviour. Emotion takes the place of action, and soloists and chorus ponder over the facts that constitute the mystery of Redemption. It is a matter for some surpise that in *Messiah* (except in the one brief instance of *Lift up your heads*) Handel's choral writing never exceeds four parts. Here we do not have the splendour of the eight-part choruses in *Israel*, yet the style is always fitting and invariably impressive. The famous "Hallelujah" Chorus is a case in point. It has been pointed out that the two main themes echo the Advent chorale *Sleepers, wake !* and the opening of the canon *Non Nobis Domine*, both of which were known to Handel. Yet with these, and a few ordinary chords of the tonic, dominant, and subdominant, Handel gives us his vision as of " all Heaven opened before him," and we are amazed at the simple wonder of it. This, perhaps, is the secret of *Messiah* ; its economy and directness of appeal, its inspired majesty, its occasional moving pathos, and the universality of its theme.

Messiah was written at speed and first performed in Dublin in April 1742. At Covent Garden the following year it was coolly received ; but within a few years the annual Foundling Hospital performances had begun, directed by Handel himself, and from that time the success of the oratorio was assured. Its performance was a feature of the mammoth Handel Commemorations held in Westminster Abbey towards the end of the eighteenth century, and of the Handel Festivals begun in Crystal Palace in 1857. Almost all choral societies now perform it at least once a year. There have also been many recent attempts to produce the work on a smaller scale, in style and intent much nearer to the conditions of Handel's own day.

It must be realised that these modern attempts to reproduce Handel and Bach as they were performed in their own time do not necessarily mean that the works are being performed as the composer wished to hear them. Handel has been described as the Berlioz of his day. Contemporaries wrote of him as " that noisy composer who always wants an orchestra twice as big as anyone else ". His orchestrations in the score were often mere outlines, to be filled in by the organ or harpsichord (played by himself or under his direction). At performances of his oratorios in London, where the King's trombone-players were available, he wrote special parts for them. His orchestras for the " Fireworks " and " Water " music were huge. In fact he added instruments whenever they became available. At the Foundling Hospital there still exist accounts of money paid to five horn-players for an oratorio performance, although they do not appear in the score and the parts have been lost.

Chorally the situation was difficult, since there were no large choirs. The only professional singers were at the Opera House or in the churches. The best that Handel could do for his first performance of *Messiah*—a work conceived on a gigantic scale—was to assemble three small church choirs in Dublin. He had hoped to supplement these with amateur singers from England, but he could find none capable of singing this elaborate music. At later performances in England he had to help out his weak soprano line by adding twelve oboes. Many of our modern " re-creations " of first performances are fascinating as museum examples, but do a doubtful service to the composer's original intentions.

SUCCESSES AND REVERSES

Back in London from Dublin, Handel—now sufficiently detached from opera to be able to laugh at its absurdities, as he reveals in a letter—was encouraged by the success of his new oratorio *Samson* ; but *Messiah* did not fare well, although George II was so overcome by the " Hallelujah " chorus that he instinctively rose to his feet—thereby setting a fashion which persists to this day. Despite further ill-health, Handel produced a *Te Deum* to celebrate the victory of the English troops at Dettingen, and this was received with enthusiasm. The following year saw the production of *Joseph* and *Semele*, the latter a reversion to the masque type, and an oddly profane story (as was disapprovingly noted at the time) to choose for Lent. *Hercules* and the barbaric *Belshazzar* failed to make much impression on a restive public, to Handel's " great loss, and the nation's disgrace " ; and at the end of 1745 he was again in financial straits and broken in health.

It was the Jacobite rising of 1745 which was to put him back on his feet. Handel wrote an *Occasional Oratorio* in honour of the Duke of Cumberland, in charge of the royal forces ; this was a popular move, and in its approval of the work's bellicose spirit the public seems not to have noticed the extent to which Handel had plundered his own works (chiefly *Israel in Egypt*). When the Pretender was finally routed at Culloden in April 1746, Handel commemorated the event in *Judas Maccabaeus* (produced a year later), which was an instant success ; in it Handel discovered that he had interested a new section of the public—the Jews, who were " attracted by the glorification of a national hero of their own ".

THE FINAL YEARS

Handel saw which way the wind was blowing, and his next oratorio was *Alexander Balus*, which was written in 1747 and produced with another new oratorio, *Joshua*, at Covent Garden the next spring. A year later both

Susanna and *Solomon* were given at Handel's Lenten concerts, and in that year (1749), the Peace of Aix-la-Chapelle being celebrated with fireworks in the Green Park in the presence of the King, it was Handel who was commissioned to write appropriate music for the occasion.

That occasion is forgotten, and all that remains in the memory of posterity is Handel's music. By then he had overcome the antagonism of his London public. He was a man of sixty-four and had become very much a public figure in English life. He was regarded as a kind of musical Laureate, the composer to whom the State would turn for the provision of suitable occasional music, such as he had provided on his own instigation for the defeat of the Pretender.

The Fireworks Music created a sensation. A public rehearsal was given a few days before the event, and the crowd on the south side of the river at Vauxhall was immense, twelve thousand people and traffic on London Bridge jammed for three hours. The Green Park celebration was marred by the collapse of the central pavilion, an outbreak of fire and a consequent disturbance ; but the music was admired and Handel, realising what a draw he had created, at once offered a performance at the Foundling Hospital. That name brings in a notable episode in his life and throws light on his nature. Like many another bachelor, he felt affection mingled with an apprehensive pity for other men's children, and *Messiah* was part of his gift to this Hospital, founded by Captain Coram in Bloomsbury in 1740. His performance there of *Messiah* brought in some £7000. He was made a Governor, and to the end his concerts in the Hospital, where he would play his concertos on the organ even when his eyesight had gone, were enthusiastically patronised by the public.

HIS END

With age and with failing sight Handel's inherited piety began to grow. He had not been a great churchman, though always profoundly religious. Now he attended St. George's, Hanover Square, the parish church to which he belonged as an inhabitant of Lower Brook Street. He had enjoyed popularity and had suffered its decline. He knew his English public thoroughly ; he realised their essential fickleness, as they his determination. A kind of respect had grown up between them and Handel, who had been naturalised in 1726 and had become as English as any of them. The noble façades of their Palladian mansions he had suggested in his music, as well as the sadness of the lives of the men and women whom Hogarth portrayed in " Gin Lane " : this was the world which existed as best it could behind that façade, the breeding-ground of the inmates of Coram's Foundling Hospital.

His sight became incurably bad and he underwent the hideous torment of an operation without anæsthesia to no lasting purpose. He died on April 11, 1759. Five days before, he had been led to the organ at the Foundling Hospital and had presided as usual over the performance of his *Messiah*. He was buried in Westminster Abbey, and three thousand people attended the funeral.

THE MAN AS HE WAS SEEN

Roubiliac's statue of Handel, set up at Vauxhall Gardens and later transferred to 160 Wardour Street (where customers of Messrs. Novello may see it to-day), represents him "in a loose robe, sweeping the lyre". Roubiliac was a good portraitist, and we may accept this as Handel in the flesh.[1] As was natural for a man leading a sedentary life at his desk, Handel became well fleshed. Nevertheless, his face never lost its sensitive look or, in later life, that lined awareness of sorrow that is the inescapable lot of the creative artist. The legend grew up that he was boorish in his habits and a gross eater, and the cruel caricature by Goupy (once his friend) entitled "The Charming Brute", shows him with the head of a pig, seated at the organ. Here we may see evidence, even clearer than Handel's own spiritual likeness, of the jealousy that his presence in England had by then aroused among those who discovered that he could not be browbeaten into submission. Burney says of him, "The figure of Handel was large, and he was somewhat corpulent and unwieldy in his motions ; but his countenance . . . was full of fire and dignity".

CHARACTERISTICS OF HANDELIAN OPERA

In his operatic writing Handel showed both consummate technical skill, sharpened by his experience of Italian models, and a natural instinct for dramatic music. In *Agrippina* there is, for instance, a short but very lively quartet in which, on a false report of Claudius's death, Nero is proclaimed Emperor. It is interrupted by a fanfare of brass off-stage announcing the approach of the supposedly dead Claudius. It is a parallel to the trumpet-signal in Beethoven's *Fidelio*, and Handel strikes home with a sureness that owes its force to perfect timing. Unfortunately the rich flow of melodies and the happy dramatic strokes are hopelessly handicapped by the ludicrous and complicated story, and the often undignified behaviour of the noble

[1] See illustration.

Roman personages. There is even one scene which seems to belong to French bedroom farce rather than to a serious dramatic entertainment. Like all dramatic composers of his day, Handel was further hampered by the strictly observed convention that at the end of every aria the character singing it must leave the stage. Such a convention inevitably produced a disjointed inconsequential movement of the dramatic action, which is one of the great obstacles to the revival of the serious operas of the period.

These disabilities, and the allocation of heroic rôles to castrato singers, stand in the way of our appreciation of the Italian operas Handel wrote for London after his arrival in 1710. The problem of casting is really insuperable, because the music written for the male sopranos cannot be effectively sung by the tenor voice an octave lower, while, appearance apart, the voice of a woman sounds ridiculous to modern ears in the character of Julius Caesar or Alexander. In order to understand Handelian opera—or for that matter any *opera seria* of the period—we must realise that it is concerned with an ideal world, where life always moves on a heroic plane and the ordinary sanctions of the material world do not apply. A parallel with contemporary art may assist our understanding. For Handel's *Cleopatra*, say, has much in common with Tiepolo's ; the elegance and charm are common to both. But Handel's Egyptian Queen moved in a more solid setting, one that might have been designed by William Kent. North German that he was, Handel rarely approached the Mediterranean sensuousness of the Venetian painter, though in his music for the Queen of Sheba (essentially an operatic character, for all that she appears in oratorio) he does come very close to it.

THE ORATORIOS AS DRAMAS

Indeed, Handel's most approachable dramatic works are the cantatas and oratorios with English texts, which, with one or two exceptions such as *Messiah*, can perfectly well be presented on the stage.

In recent years—a stage production of *Samson* at Covent Garden (1958) serves as an example—we have come to realise that Handel the oratorio-composer is simply Handel the opera-composer in another guise. The dramatic element in all the oratorios is strong ; and had it not been for the Bishop of London's ban, many of them might well have been seen in costume on the stage. Theatrical rather than religious, they are not a direct expression of devotional feeling, but epic or narrative, often making vivid use of local colour, and always with the most impressive use of the chorus as the most important medium of expression. In this, Handel the oratorio composer was in no wise different from Handel the opera composer; he had merely found a new outlet for his creative genius.

HANDEL'S INFLUENCE

To Gluck, Handel was the inspired master of the art of music ; to Beethoven he was the greatest composer that ever lived. When the latter declared, on examining one of Handel's oratorios, "Therein is the truth", he had already given proof not only of his esteem, but of his close observation of Handel's technique, the form and spirit of which music can be seen in his overture *The Consecration of the House*—which, he let it be known, was a Handelian overture apt for the opening of a theatre. To some ears it seems, in the slow introduction, to have an echo of Handel's *Saul*.

Beethoven was not the first Viennese genius to undergo that influence. Haydn had been in London some thirty years before. It was during his first visit that he went in May 1791 to a Handel Commemoration festival in Westminster Abbey, and for the first time was assailed by the full force of Handel's choral music. He was profoundly affected ; the "Hallelujah" chorus in *Messiah* disturbed his outward composure and led him to exclaim that Handel was "the master of us all". Haydn saw at that moment the possibilities that lay in the Handelian chorus and its attendant arias ; the immediate result was a quickening of his thought, and *The Creation* was produced six years later.

Gradually it was to become clear what it was in Handel's conception of choral music that was to produce its most lasting value for posterity, as exemplified first in Haydn, then in Beethoven : its monumental stability and its dramatic brilliance. Berlioz's monster effects in the *Grande Messe des Morts* owe to the example of Handel, whose music he professed to find distasteful, their essential character of dramatic intensity, that ability to seize upon the right type of expression for a given moment of impressive grandeur. Without Handel it is unthinkable that nineteenth-century choral music could have taken the path it followed, notably in the work of Mendelssohn. The choral portion of the *Hymn of Praise*, the whole conception of *St. Paul* and that above all of *Elijah*, owe their being to the Handelian idea of oratorio as a scheme that could include as effectively the events of a dramatic tale, the lyrical emotions aroused during the telling of that story, and the thoughts engendered by the contemplation of such events. It is hardly necessary to-day to draw further attention to the lasting effect of this aspect of Handel's wonderful art.

IN THE SHADOW OF HANDEL

In England, Handel's influence was all-pervasive, and native composers found it difficult to escape being overpowered by this colossus who had settled in the country. His popularity was such that, as we have seen, even in his lifetime his statue graced Vauxhall Gardens, one of the summer pleasure-grounds favoured by Londoners. The music of many lesser composers was also heard at these gardens (the chief others were at Marylebone and Ranelagh), with which is associated a characteristic type of English song, usually light in nature and very regular in its musical pattern, which flourished throughout the eighteenth century and even beyond. *The Lass of Richmond Hill* by James Hook (1746–1827), who was himself organist at Vauxhall Gardens, is a good late example. When J. S. Bach's youngest son settled in London and became known under the anglicised name of John Christian Bach, he too wrote songs for the pleasure gardens.

The English composers who flourished in the early and middle parts of the eighteenth century lived directly under Handel's shadow. English cathedral music, in the form of services and anthems, held fast to its own traditions. Among notable contributors to its store were William Croft (1678–1727), Maurice Greene (1695–1755), and William Boyce (c. 1710–79), who also compiled an important collection of such cathedral music. To Croft is ascribed the hymn tune *St. Anne* (" O God our help in ages past "). Boyce's other works include eight " symphonies " (more like suites of Handelian pieces than symphonies in the later sense), but he is now best known for the song *Heart of Oak*, written to commemorate the British victories against the French in " this wonderful year " of 1759 ; the melody as now sung is an improved version of what he originally wrote. Instrumental music for strings and for organ is the chief contribution of the blind organist John Stanley (1713–86). An older composer, Thomas Roseingrave (1690–1766), went to Italy, became friendly with Alessandro and Domenico Scarlatti, and wrote harpsichord pieces and Italian cantatas.

A principal occupation for eighteenth-century composers was provided by the stage. Boyce's *Heart of Oak* in fact comes from *Harlequin's Invasion* or *A Christmas Gambol*, to a text by David Garrick, presented at Drury Lane Theatre. It was that theatre which gave an engagement as resident composer to the greatest English-born musician of the time, Thomas Augustine Arne (1710–78), and it was there that his famous settings of Shakespeare songs were first heard, as incidental music for productions of the plays. There also Arne's *Comus*, perhaps his finest work, was presented in 1738 ; its text was an adaptation of Milton's masque, to which music had originally been set by Henry Lawes. The song *Rule Britannia* occurs in Arne's masque *Alfred*, originally presented privately in 1740 and brought to Drury Lane five years later. The version of this song which came into general use in the nineteenth century is corrupt, but recently the Promenade Concerts have happily brought Arne's superior original melody back into currency.

Arne has become somewhat oddly known as " Doctor Arne ", as if he were the only one to possess a title which, in fact, was quite general among English composers. In his own day it served at any rate to distinguish him from Michael Arne (1741–86), his illegitimate son, who wrote the song *The Lass with a Delicate Air*. A contemporary of Michael Arne's, Samuel Arnold (1740–1802), was the composer of much music of all types, including dozens of works for the stage. Many of these, as was the custom, were adaptations of works by earlier composers, or were the joint work of Arnold and one or more contemporaries. The English stage at that time was no place for opera in the unified sense in which we know it, and additions and alterations were the regular treatment even when Mozart's operas began to reach London.

IX

THE REFORM OF OPERA

ITALIAN *opera seria* represented only one type of musico-dramatic work, though one to which overwhelming importance was given in the eighteenth century. It is time, however, that we examined other currents in the operatic world.

THE BEGINNINGS OF COMIC OPERA

When Apostolo Zeno, under the influence of French tragedy, carried out reforms in the operatic libretto, this involved, as we have seen, the abolition of the comic scenes that were a feature of the Venetian and Roman operas of the seventeenth century. Zeno spent part of his career in Vienna as court poet (*Poeta Cesareo*) to the Emperor, and in the Viennese and German court opera houses, for which he was writing, low comedy in Italian was not likely to be appreciated. The Italian public, on the other hand, wanted to be amused as well as edified when they went to the theatre. As has been wittily observed, the comic scenes in later seventeenth-century opera had tended " to sink like sediment " to the end of the acts. Now that they were definitely extruded from the action of the opera, they reappeared as independent interludes or *intermezzi* between the acts of *opera seria*.

These *intermezzi* at first consisted of short scenes between two or three characters, usually the domestic servants who had fulfilled a comic function in the older operas from the days of Monteverdi's *Poppea*. They were often written in the local dialect of the city where they were played. They have a long ancestry, going back to the comedies of Plautus through the *Commedia dell'arte* or Comedy of Masks whose characters are stock comic types—the rascally valet, the rich old man who is fooled, the bragging captain, the pedantic doctor, the pert maidservant and the sentimental young lovers. The Comedy of Masks was an improvised entertainment and was therefore, as a form, at the opposite pole to opera. Yet the characters of the masks furnished admirable material for the composers of comic opera. Arlecchino, or Harlequin, becomes Figaro ; Doctor Bartolo is recognisably the Bolognese pedant ; Don Pasquale is one of a large family of Pantaloons bamboozled

WOLFGANG AMADEUS MOZART (1756–1791)

Silver-point drawing by Dora Stock, 1789. This is the last life-portrait of Mozart and clearly shows incipient disease

LUDWIG VAN BEETHOVEN (1770–1827)

Bust by Franz Klein, 1812, now in the Beethovenhaus, Bonn

by young lovers with Harlequin's help; and Colombina has a thousand reincarnations from Pergolesi's Serpina through Mozart's Susanna, Zerlina and Despina to the soubrettes of nineteenth-century operetta.

The *intermezzi* were originally played, as we have remarked, between the acts of an *opera seria*. As this normally had three acts, the *intermezzi* had two. Soon the incongruity of these interludes led to their being played together as a separate piece after the serious opera. But such is the influence of tradition in the theatre that the two-act form survived in comic opera long after the reason for it had ceased to exist and the *intermezzo* had achieved an independent existence as *opera buffa* in theatres of its own.

PERGOLESI

The first composer to make his name chiefly as a composer of *opera buffa* was Giovanni Battista Pergolesi (1710–36). In his brief career he produced five comic operas, of which the most famous is *La Serva Padrona* (" The Maid turned Mistress "), which was produced in 1733 at Naples as an *intermezzo* in Pergolesi's *opera seria*, *Il Prigionier Superbo* (" The Proud Prisoner "). Partly owing to the fact that it became the cause of one of the recurrent squabbles between the supporters of French and Italian opera in Paris, *La Serva Padrona* achieved for its composer a posthumous fame out of proportion to its actual importance. Yet the piece can still hold the stage, slight though it is, because the stock characters of the maid and her elderly employer are shown with a truth to life that includes a touch of real pathos in the comic action.

La Serva Padrona was not the first piece of its kind. Its theme was used in a piece called *Pimpinone* by Tommaso Albinoni (1671–1750), produced in 1708. In 1725 this *intermezzo* was performed in Hamburg in a version with German recitatives and some German songs by Telemann added to Albinoni's music. This appears to have been the first appearance of Italian comic opera in North Germany. The first independent piece in the form appears to be Hasse's *La Serva Scaltra ovvera La Moglie a Forza* (" The Clever Maid, or Forced to Marry "—the title sufficiently indicates the similarity to Pergolesi's *La Serva Padrona*), which was produced at Naples in 1729 with *Tigrane*. *Opera buffa* was, indeed, a Neapolitan product, and many of its early librettos were written in the Neapolitan dialect (*e.g.*, Pergolesi's *Lo Frate 'nnamorato*).

CHARACTER OF OPERA BUFFA

The popularity of these comic operas soon resulted in their attaining a status of their own, and small companies were formed to take them round the Italian cities and, eventually, abroad. At first they were rather low-class entertainments with a good deal of horse-play in the action, while the musical resources of the companies were modest and imposed narrow limits on what they could do. The chief merit of these pieces, and one which derived from the resourceful style of the improvising actors of the Comedy of Masks, was the vivacity of the declamation, which soon developed into a perfect musical vehicle for Italian comic dialogue and the exchange of quick repartee. In the arias, too, a distinctive style appeared, notably melodious songs in the popular manner and rapid patter-songs, usually for a bass, who played a more important part in *opera buffa* than in *opera seria*, where he was confined to the subsidiary rôles of old men, priests, sages, and so on. For the pathetic scenes, which were not always mock-pathetic, a new *cantabile* type of aria appeared, often in a minor key and with chromatic harmonies. From the first there was a tendency to burlesque the conventions of *opera seria*—an easy target, indeed.

VENETIAN COMEDIES

By the middle of the eighteenth century the comic operas began to achieve a greater refinement and artistic dignity, appealing to a better class of audience. This improvement was largely due to the collaboration in some twenty works of the Venetian playwright Carlo Goldoni with Baldassare Galuppi (1706–85), who composed about a hundred operas, many of them comic. Goldoni introduced new ideas into the stock plots, giving them more variety and substance, and raising them above the old farcical level on to the plane of comedy. Hand in hand with the improvement in taste went a better organisation of the dramatic structure. This was all the more necessary in view of the greater number of characters who now took part in the action.

From the musical point of view the most important development was the evolution of the concerted *ensemble*, especially at the end of the acts, in which all the characters on the stage take part. In *opera seria* it was unthinkable that two or more characters should sing at the same time, unless they were uttering the same words and the same notes. Even duets within these restricting limits were rare. The nearest that Alessandro Scarlatti approached to a concerted piece was to divide an aria between two or more voices, each taking up the music where the last dropped it. Only at the end do the voices sing together in a brief coda. It is significant that these pieces are not called quartet or trio, but *aria a quattro*, etc. They usually occur at the end of the act, but, unlike the comic finale, they make no pretence of carrying the dramatic action to a climax and a " curtain ".

THE COMIC FINALE

The dynamic character of the finale in *opera buffa*, which normally deals (at the end of the first act) with comic misunderstandings between the characters who are all at cross-purposes, and leads (at the end of the second) to a resolution of the discord in a happy ending for the young lovers, eventually had a profound and supremely important influence upon operatic form in both comedy and tragedy. One may say that this influence worked backwards until it assimilated the whole of the act, obliterating the formal distinctions between recitative and aria, and substituting a more homogeneous and flexible musical texture that could respond with greater subtlety to every movement of the action and every emotion of the characters. The great examples of this continuous style do not appear until late in the nineteenth century. And before that development could occur, the comic finale had to undergo the transformation of symphonic organisation at the hands of Mozart.

Even before Mozart's time the finale had reached a state of elaboration and complexity quite beyond the range of the simple buffooneries of 1720–30. Moreover, the crudities of those early *intermezzi* were softened by the spirit of " sensibility " that marked the middle years of the eighteenth century. Richardson's *Pamela, or Virtue Rewarded*, published in 1740, is one of the earliest manifestations of this spirit, in which sentiment is seasoned with salacity. This novel had a great vogue on the Continent, and Goldoni used it as the basis for his libretto for *La Cecchina ossia La Buona Figliuola* which was set by Niccola Piccinni (1728–1800). After enjoying a great success in Rome in 1760, *La Cecchina* was soon popular all over Europe. Historically, Piccinni's comic operas are important as being among the first in which the finales are carefully planned and have a unifying element in a recurrent musical theme, on the same principle as a rondo-theme in the finale of a symphony. Here was a definite step in the direction of the symphonic finale developed twenty-five years later by Mozart.

OPERA IN FRANCE

In France there was a gap after the death of Lully in 1687, when no operatic successor to him was apparent ; for Lully had made it impossible for any other composer to gain experience in opera. Marc-Antoine Charpentier was Lully's junior by only two years, but was nearly sixty when his *Médée* was produced in 1693. The most successful, eventually, of the younger composers was André Campra (1660–1744), whose opera-ballets, *L'Europe Galante* (1697), *Les Fêtes Vénitiennes* (1710), *Les Amours de Mars et Vénus* (1712), anticipate the lighter style of French lyric entertainment. There was in Campra's opera-ballets only the merest pretence of a consistent plot. The acts consisted of a string of barely related scenes, in which the pastoral, the fantastic, the humorous, and the exotic followed one another, rather after the manner of a modern revue. Campra was of Piedmontese descent, and his music reflected his Italian origins and so accorded with the taste for Italian music which was making headway even in Paris. The conflict between admirers of the Italian style and the supporters of French music raged intermittently throughout the eighteenth century.

During the minority of Louis XV, the change in artistic taste proceeded. The strict symmetry of seventeenth-century French architecture, furniture, and decoration gave place to the livelier fantasies of rococo, while the formal compositions of Claude, with their idealised classical landscapes, were followed by the more vibrant, sensuous *fêtes champêtres* of Antoine Watteau. Music, too, took on a livelier aspect through the introduction of fantastic, pastoral, and exotic scenes.

RAMEAU

Jean-Philippe Rameau (1683–1764), who made his tardy début as an opera-composer at the age of fifty, himself reacted against the frivolity of the opera-ballets of the Regency (1715–25). He was a serious and learned composer, who had begun his career as an organist and made a reputation as a theorist by the publication of the important *Traité d'harmonie* in 1722, the outcome of seven years' hard work in retirement at Clermont-Ferrand. Therein he established for the first time a systematic theory of the principles of music, and, in particular, justified in scientific terms (in so far as they were understood) the diatonic scale as the basis of the art. In all this he codified the existing practice of the leading composers of his time. Having thus worked out intellectually the technique of music, including the nature of melody, Rameau proceeded to put his principles into practice and achieved fame as a composer for, and performer on, the harpsichord.

Only then did he proceed to opera, but not to assume the mantle which Lully had laid down nearly forty years before, nor to follow the more frivolous direction taken by Campra's opera-ballets. Rameau accepted the Italian fashions, which had been adopted by French composers, while at the same time adhering to the dramatic principles of his great predecessor. *Hippolyte et Aricie*, composed in 1733 at the instance of his patron, the financier Jean Le Riche de la Pouplinière, was the outcome of much earnest thought. Yet, such was Rameau's genius, the result was not, as might have been expected, a pedantic embodiment of the theorist's " system ", but a potent work of art which had a lasting influence upon the development of French opera.

Hippolyte was based upon Racine's *Phèdre*, which adds to the severely restricted *dramatis personæ* of the Euripidean tragedy a young princess Aricie, with whom Hippolyte is in love. The theme of Phèdre's passion for her stepson is worked out to its tragic conclusion, but Hippolyte, though supposed dead at one point, survives to marry Aricie and bring the opera to a happy and triumphant close. For a genuinely tragic ending was unthinkable in an age which insisted that Cordelia (with the help of Nahum Tate) must survive to marry Edgar, and would have it that Othello saw the light before killing Desdemona, and not after. Throughout this period operas invariably ended, as films mostly do nowadays, with what the Italians called, with a nice respect for technical terms, the " matrimonial catastrophe ".

Yet, though Rameau's operas make no break with the conventions of the seventeenth century, there is a greater vitality and sense of movement in them. Listening, as we may now do with the help of the gramophone, to *Hippolyte* after Lully or Charpentier's *Médée*, which keeps close to the Lullian model, we are conscious of entering a different world closer to our own. Indeed, it would now be possible to claim with justification that the story of modern opera begins not with Gluck, as we are often told, but with Rameau, for all that he introduced no " reforms ".

Rameau's art was, in fact, of that rare kind in which an equilibrium is maintained between the past and the future ; and in this he resembles Mozart. By combining a thorough knowledge of the craft of dramatic composition as practised by Lully with a more highly developed feeling for expressive modulation and a mastery of the more progressive features of late baroque polyphony, Rameau forged a style of his own that was both solid and original. For this reason *Hippolyte* was acclaimed by the " advanced " musicians and connoisseurs as the symbol of a French musical renaissance, and strenuously condemned by the conservatives as a treasonable surrender to Italianate forms and German counterpoint. Rameau himself never supported the pro-Italian party and always claimed Lully as his artistic father.

Rameau's characters, however formal they may appear to us, are more human than Lully's, because they are represented in music which uses, almost for the first time, an emotional language recognisably similar to that of the familiar classics of two generations later. Their recitatives, though consciously modelled on Lully, are more supple, breaking out into expressive figurations on emotionally charged words, and supported by more freely flowing basses. Above all, the intervals of the seventh and the ninth come into their own as the means of emotional expression, while the minor is used to create a feeling of pathos.

RAMEAU'S ORCHESTRA

Perhaps the most striking change is in the constitution of orchestra and in Rameau's use of it. Even as late as 1713 the orchestra of the Opéra was still that of Lully's day—twelve violins, seven violas, eight violoncellos or viole da gamba, eight wood-winds (flutes, oboes, and bassoons), and one drummer. Composers still retained the archaic practice of writing for the strings in five parts, as Lully had done. Elsewhere the string-orchestra was settling down to the four-part system, supported by the double-bass, of later classical practice. Rameau naturally adopted the new system and enlarged the orchestra, which by 1751 had assumed more modern proportions —sixteen violins, six violas, twelve violoncellos with probably one or two double-basses, five flutes or oboes, four bassoons, one trumpet, and one drum. Oddly enough, although France was the land of the *cor de chasse*, the horns did not appear in the orchestra till 1754, when two were added. But they were in the *Concert Spirituel* orchestra earlier, and presumably the numbers of the players at the Opéra, quoted by the Almanach, were those of the permanent establishment and did not preclude extras.

Rameau used these more powerful and varied forces with a mastery which anticipates the orchestral virtuosity of the Mannheim school in the middle of the century. In his later years he may well have been influenced by the Mannheim composers, of whose work he can hardly have been ignorant. For Stamitz visited Paris in 1754 and stayed at the house of Rameau's patron, La Pouplinière, with whom he had been in correspondence six years earlier about the inclusion of horns in La Pouplinière's private orchestra. But already in *Hippolyte*, nearly a decade before the Elector Karl Theodor's famous orchestra at Mannheim came into being, Rameau composed the music for a monster who appears in a terrifying whirlwind of sound, breathing fire and slaughter. Such orchestral set-pieces, representing earthquakes, storms, and other natural phenomena, differ considerably from Lully's battle-pieces and divine interventions by a *deus ex machina* not only in degree, but in their imaginative realism. The earthquake in *Les Indes galantes* (1735–36), a grand *ballet-héroique* in four acts, is the most impressive of these orchestral "disasters", which are the musical embodiment of the then fashionable æsthetic theory that art was an ideal "imitation" of Nature.

Apart from the overtures, in which again Rameau keeps to the Lullian form while bringing the contents up to date with fugal entries and rococo ornaments, there are the dances, by which Rameau is best known to modern audiences. Here, indeed, he shows an inexhaustible invention, whether in the tender sentiment of his *sarabandes*, or in the livelier *rigaudons*, *tambourins*, *musettes*, and *contre-danses* (the Gallic form of the English country-dances), which retain the vigour of their rustic origins. In the *chaconnes*, with which the operas normally end, there is again a compromise between the ceremonial formality appropriate to the context and a freer and more dramatic treatment of the material.

During his extraordinary career as an opera-composer between the ages of fifty and eighty-one, Rameau produced seventeen major works as well as a large number of one-act pieces. He certainly re-established and enhanced the reputation of French opera, and were it not that his music, like Handel's operatic music, is allied to conventions which make its survival on the modern stage difficult if not impossible, Rameau might well take his place beside his great contemporary in popular estimation. His greatness is not to be found in his charming ballet-music, which corresponds exactly to the *galant* idylls of contemporary French painting, but in his choral movements, in his powerful descriptions of natural phenomena, and in his orchestration, which makes that of his Italian contemporaries look stereotyped and flimsy.

THE BEGINNINGS OF FRENCH COMIC OPERA

While *opera buffa* was finding its legs in Italy, corresponding indigenous forms appeared in France, England, and Germany as the *opéra-comique*, the *ballad-opera*, and the *Singspiel* respectively. All these differed from the Italian comic opera in that the action was carried on in spoken dialogue instead of *recitativo secco*, which is the musical embodiment of rapidly spoken Italian and therefore more or less unsuitable for other languages. They also tended, to a greater extent than the Italian operas, to make conscious use of traditional and folk melodies adapted to new words. The influence of folk-melody on Italian comic opera is largely confined to the musical style of the Neapolitan composers.

The German *Singspiel* assumed no artistic importance until it suddenly blossomed out under the sun of Mozart's genius at the end of the eighteenth century ; and the English ballad opera soon lost the raciness of *The Beggar's Opera* and became merely more polite and civilised, and consequently somewhat anæmic, in the hands of Arne and Dibdin. The French *opéra-comique*, on the other hand, grew from humble beginnings to be a leading form of opera in its own right, and exercised an important influence upon the course of operatic history in general.

The genealogy of *opéra-comique* is complex and its early history involved. Like *opera buffa* it derived ultimately from the *commedia dell'arte*. But no sooner had the Italian comedians invaded France in the latter years of the sixteenth century than the characters of the Comedy of Masks began to assume French names—Turlupin, Gros-Guillaume, Scaramouche, and so on —and to acquire French idiosyncrasies. In Paris the performances were given at the big fairs of Saint-Germain and Saint-Laurent, where they entertained the crowd with farcical pantomimes of a very " low " character. Music entered into their performances only in the form of snatches of well-known melodies, which acquired distinct meanings well understood by the audience, just as the music-hall comedian of yesterday had his musical japes and the radio performer of to-day has his signature tune. These rudimentary leading motives soon developed into little songs with a more distinct life of their own, consisting of a refrain sung in chorus and couplets for the individual singer. In this form they were known as *vaudevilles*, and the performances were called *comédies en vaudevilles*.

THE VAUDEVILLES

The etymology of the word *vaudeville* is obscure. It eventually developed several meanings, the most important from our point of view being that of a piece at the end of an opera, where each character comes forward in turn and sings the verse of a song, the others joining in the refrain. The final piece in Mozart's *Die Entführung aus dem Serail* (" The Rescue from the Seraglio ") is like a vaudeville, though it may be noted that Mozart cannot resist giving the infuriated Osmin individual music of his own—he, at least, remains fully " in character " to the end. The same happens in a more disguised form at the end of *Don Giovanni*—a passage which has caused much head-shaking among those who wish that the *dramma giocoso*, as Mozart styled it, had been instead a romantic tragedy and " wholly serious ".

The comedians of the Parisian fairs attracted, besides the common people, an audience drawn from royalty and the aristocracy, who found in their salacity and rough humour a refreshing change from the stately ceremonial of the court entertainments. No doubt with this section of the audience in view, the comedians began to burlesque the serious operas and *comédies-ballets*, as Gay was to do in the time of Handel. But they went too far when in a piece called *La Fausse Prude* (1697) they held up Mme. de Maintenon (who had secretly married Louis XIV in 1683) to ridicule—

a rash proceeding which enabled the King to suppress these licentious entertainments.

The prime movers in imposing the ban were the Comédie Française, established in 1680, and the Académie Royale de Musique, which held monopolies for the production of drama and opera respectively, and feared the rivalry of these popular entertainments which infringed their exclusive rights. The comedians soon reappeared, evading the ban by performing the action of their little pieces in dumb-show, while the actor's words were displayed on cards lowered from above. Accomplices stationed in the audience provided a chorus to sing the songs. Thus developed the characteristically French art of mime, as distinct from ballet. Mime played a large part in the performances of the *commedia dell' arte*, but the presentation of dramatic action exclusively in mime seems to be a French invention which has survived into our own day through the art of Deburau, creator of the pathetic love-sick Pierrot, and Jean-Louis Barrault, who perpetuated the type in the film *Les Enfants du Paradis*. Older readers may remember the charming mime-play *L'Enfant Prodigue*, with music by André Wormser (1851–1926), produced at the Cercle Funambulesque in Paris in 1890 and revived many times both in France and England.

THE PALAIS ROYAL OPERAS

After the death of Louis XIV licence returned during the years of the Regency, and the restrictions lapsed. The Regent even installed the comedians in the Palais Royal, which became for centuries the home of farce. In these more respectable surroundings *opéra-comique* was born. It was still rudimentary in form, and until the third decade of the century it remained a coarsely indecent entertainment. About 1730, frank libertinism gave place to a more refined sensuality and a tendency to moralise. The characters of these early comic operas are still recognisably related to the Comedy of Masks, but they have been transformed into French bourgeois types. The bragging Spanish captain is now a Gascon, the Bolognese " doctor " is a pedant from Lyons or Limoges. The eternal Arlequin, Colombine, and Pierrot remain barely disguised under such peasant names as Colin or Colette or Bastien. The songs are still simple *couplets*, but the orchestral resources, though still modest, were developed by the necessity of accompanying wordless pantomimes.

With the arrival on the scene in 1732 of Charles Simon Favart (1710–92) the comedies became " a decent and ingenious entertainment ", as Voltaire put it, concerned with light and gallant stories which never cut deep below the surface of passion but maintain an air of gay equivocation and ingenuous innocence. At first Favart, who was engaged by Jean Monnet, director of the Opéra Comique de la Foire Saint-Germain, to write for his theatre, followed the practice of using existing melodies for his pieces *en vaudeville*. But soon he began to employ composers to write music for him, among them Duni and Monsigny.

In 1758 Favart succeeded Monnet as director of the theatre which, it will be noted, maintained its connection with the great Parisian fair and was now definitely designated the Opéra Comique. Meanwhile Pergolesi's *La Serva Padrona* had been produced in Paris, and its impact was out of proportion to its intrinsic merits. It showed the Parisian public that comic opera could be something more artistic than the rather crude and naïve productions of the fairground. As the result of Italian competition, *opéra-comique* itself improved in quality, and by the end of the century had begun to take on those more serious characteristics which ended by making the title *opéra-comique* something of a contradiction in terms.

REASON AND SENSIBILITY

The eighteenth century saw the dawn of the Age of Sensibility ; it was also the Age of Reason. Indeed, Reason and Sensibility were two facets of the same phenomenon—the progress of European civilisation towards a more humane conduct of life based upon a rational philosophy. As might be expected, the nerve-centre of the Age of Reason was in France. Sensibility found expression equally in the novels of Richardson, which were translated into French by the author of *Manon Lescaut* ; of Rousseau, who imitated Clarissa Harlowe in his *La Nouvelle Héloise* (1762) ; in the middle-class *comédies larmoyantes* of Diderot ; and in Goethe's *The Sorrows of Young Werther*, which shook all Germany in 1774. Richardson's *Pamela*, as we have seen, travelled to Venice, where Goldoni turned it into a libretto for Piccinni's most successful comic opera. By the end of the century sensibility could afford to laugh at itself affectionately in Mozart's *Così fan tutte* and the novels of Jane Austen, where, both in opera and in books, satire is inextricably mingled with genuine feeling.

The most conspicuous monument of the Age of Reason is the *Encyclopédie ou Dictionnaire raisonné des Sciences, des Arts et des Métiers*, edited by Diderot and Jean D'Alembert, which sought to codify all human knowledge. The publication of this immense work occupied a quarter of a century from the appearance of its first volume in 1751. It embodied the philosophic spirit of the age, seeking to give a rational explanation of the universe, and its influence was commensurate with its size. The *Encyclopédie* affected the development of the arts no less than the course of history, for it publicised those ideas of freedom and of the rights of the individual, whose denial was leading to the Revolution. And it codified rational æsthetic principles, whose acceptance modified the practice of the arts, particularly of opera and ballet.

FRENCH THEORISTS AND THEIR PRACTICE

The *Encyclopédie*, however, was a symptom, not a cause, of the intellectual ferment. Its musical articles resumed theories which were already in the air ; they can hardly lay much claim to original thought. Jean-Jacques Rousseau, who also published a Dictionary of Music, Jean-François Marmontel, who wrote some of the articles, and Melchior Grimm, who played a prominent part in the subsequent controversies, were amateur musicologists and their actions were often at variance with the theories they set out. Their chief article of faith was that all art should imitate nature ; yet they preferred Italian opera, the most artificial product conceivable, to French. They pointed to Greek art as a model of ideal form and taste ; yet neither Rousseau's novel nor Diderot's comedies have any relationship, in form or feeling, to Greek literature. Nor did they show any great perspicacity of judgment in their enthusiasms where contemporary music was concerned. Grimm failed to recognise genius in the young Mozart ; Rousseau backed Italian *Bouffons* against Rameau; and Marmontel was among the foremost supporters of the talented Piccinni against the genius of Gluck in a much-publicised journalistic controversy, in which neither of the principals took any active part. When Piccinni, after Gluck's death, paid him a public tribute comparing him to Corneille, Grimm countered by likening Piccinni to the " inimitable " Racine, whose " purity, uninterrupted elegance of style, and exquisite sensibility . . . we do not find either in Gluck or in the great Corneille ". Similarly, Voltaire, in his preface to *Semiramide*, eulogised the librettos of Pietro Metastasio, the successor to Apostolo Zeno, as " worthy of Corneille, when Corneille is not declamatory, and of Racine, when Racine is not insipid ". It is difficult, indeed, to square such utterances with the æsthetics of the Encyclopædia.

ALGAROTTI AND TRAETTA

But though they showed little consistency save in the backing of wrong horses, the French intellectuals did promulgate æsthetic theories which were to dominate artistic practice during the next half-century. In 1755 Algarotti, a friend of Voltaire and Frederick the Great and artistic adviser to the court of Parma, published an essay on opera in which he advocated a simplification of the complex plots of *opera seria*, the introduction of choruses and ballets in the French style, a great use of accompanied recitative (with a view to breaking down the rigid demarcation between *recitativo secco* and the static formality of the aria), and an abandonment of stereotyped pauses on certain "expressive" words such as "father" or "son". He also suggested that the overture to an opera should have some definite connection with, or appropriateness to, the action of the drama, and urged a more imaginative use of orchestral colour.

These principles were, to a great extent, practised by the court composer at Parma, Tommaso Traetta (1727–79). He had already written *opera seria* for Naples, Rome, and Venice, but in his first Parma operas he consciously followed in the footsteps of Rameau. Not only were *Ippolito ed Aricia* and *I Tintaridi* ("The Sons of Tyndarus") based on translations of librettos used by Rameau, but the former practically quotes Rameau's music. Traetta might possibly have travelled further along this road but for the accident that his next work, an *opéra-ballet* composed for the wedding of the Duke's daughter Isabella to the Archduke Joseph of Austria (later the Emperor Joseph II), brought him to the favourable notice of the Austrian court. He was commissioned to compose an opera for Vienna, and produced an *Armida* with a libretto by a follower of Metastasio, which represented a return to the conventional style. In *Ifigenia in Tauride*, produced at Schönbrunn in 1763, the Euripidean subject of the libretto, which was written in the new style of directness and simplicity by a pupil of Calzabigi, offered one more opportunity for the composition of a "reform" opera. It was the best that he wrote, containing flashes of dramatic power not unworthy of Gluck himself. But he lacked the force of character to carry a great and radical reform in opera through to its logical conclusion.

JOMMELLI AT STUTTGART

Among the German courts which looked to France for their culture, Württemberg was at this time conspicuous. In Stuttgart, its capital, Noverre found a more favourable field for his activities as a ballet-master than in Paris. The Duke Charles Eugene took a personal interest in the ballets and operatic productions in the theatre, which he had reconstructed at enormous expense. In 1753 the Duke, on a visit to Italy, sought out Jommelli, at that time *maestro di cappella* at St. Peter's, and persuaded him to come to Stuttgart as his court-composer and director of music.

Niccolò Jommelli (1714–74) was, like Traetta, trained at Naples, and won his reputation with operas, both serious and comic, in the usual

Neapolitan style. He was by nature neither an intellectual nor an adventurous explorer. But he had studied counterpoint, and at Stuttgart he acquired from Noverre an insight into the principles of French opera, and must have discussed the new aesthetic ideas promulgated in Noverre's *Lettres sur la danse*, in which was advocated a return to Nature and to Greek ideals. Noverre abolished the masks and cumbersome dresses which had hampered the movements of dancers in the French ballet and limited their powers of expression. His ideas ran parallel with those of the operatic reformers, and like them he found in Gluck the composer who could best turn them to practical account.

At Stuttgart Jommelli also came into contact with the newly developed style of German orchestral music, and under its influence he enriched his operas with a more solid and complex instrumentation than was to be found in the typical Neapolitan score. He also enlarged the proportion of accompanied to *secco* recitative, thus following one of Algarotti's precepts. He did not, however, alter the form or manner of *opera seria* in any important respect. His vocal writing is as florid as any virtuoso could wish ; he adhered to the conventions of the *da capo* aria ; and he gave little prominence to the chorus.

Just as Traetta was in character too pliable, so Jommelli was too complacent and good-natured to effect a radical revolution. Such a change could only be made by a strong will and a forcible personality, coupled with a feeling for dramatic propriety and for literary as well as musical style. Christoph Willibald Gluck (1714-87) was endowed with these qualities, and coupled with them a high degree of obstinacy tempered by a peasant shrewdness which kept the main chance in view. Gluck was the son of a forester in the service of the Elector of Bavaria living on the borders of Bohemia (Czechoslovakia). His musical education was sketchy, and he never acquired the full technical command of harmony and counterpoint enjoyed by the other great masters, or indeed the multitude of lesser ones, among his contemporaries. His progress was empirical, rather than forwarded by academic learning. Like every other major operatic composer of the century, with the solitary exception of Rameau, he acquired such technical proficiency as he attained in Italy and fashioned his early works on the accepted Italian models. In this style he won a moderate success, which has been attributed to the energy and forcefulness of his melody.

METASTASIO AND HASSE

In order to appreciate the nature of Gluck's " reforms ", it is necessary to examine briefly the character of what he reformed. In 1750 Apostolo Zeno was succeeded in the office of *Poeta Cesareo* (Poet Laureate) at the

Viennese court by Pietro Metastasio, who had been living in the Austrian capital since 1730. Metastasio took his vocation as a poet more seriously than Zeno ; he was also a trained musician, having studied with Porpora, and was therefore better capable than most poets of understanding what composers wanted. Although he came to be regarded as the very embodiment of the old order which Gluck was to overthrow, he did much to improve the literary quality of opera-books, and his poetry is one of the major ornaments of eighteenth-century Italian literature. His verse is charming and melodious, a poetical counterpart of the current rococo style ; but it was lacking in strong dramatic contrasts and in any attempt at the realistic portrayal of violent passion. Since he wrote for the court opera, which existed to enhance the prestige of the dynasty, his librettos were almost invariably designed to portray benevolent despots in a favourable light and to culminate in some act of magnanimity. As dramas they seem to us unbearably monotonous and stilted, but in their own time they had an enormous vogue. They were set to music by all the leading Italian or Italianate composers of the century from Scarlatti and Handel to Gluck, Mozart, and Haydn. Some of them were set as many as forty times ; and the use of his libretti even persisted into the nineteenth century.

The poet found in Johann Adolph Hasse (1699–1783) a musician after his own heart and kind. Hasse, a pupil of Alessandro Scarlatti, not only set every one of Metastasio's twenty-seven librettos, but set some of them several times, as also did Jommelli. His genial temperament was reflected in his music, whose outstanding characteristics were sweetness and charm. A master of writing for the voice, he produced a copious flow of pleasing vocal melody supported by a bare minimum of instrumental accompaniment. But his very suavity led to monotony ; and such dramatic interest as his operas possess is concentrated in the arias, almost invariably in *da capo* form, occasionally diversified by a duet, more rarely by a trio, and with a simple chorus at the end. The nearest we are likely to approach to Metastasian opera in practical experience is in the rare performances of Mozart's *La Clemenza di Tito*, whose libretto is a remodelled version of one of Metastasio's characteristic essays in despotic benevolence. Yet Mozart's *opera seria*, archaic though it seems, is a long way in advance of Hasse in all that concerns dramatic propriety and the expression of genuine feeling.

It was against the conventions of the Metastasian drama with its involved intrigues, its pallid emotions and its tedious insistence on the goodness of the great, that the younger generation of intellectuals revolted. Even Frederick the Great, crusted conservative though he was in his musical tastes, evinced his impatience with the *da capo* ritual. For when in 1754 he himself wrote the French draft for his *Montezuma*, which was then translated into Italian and versified for Carl Heinrich Graun (1704–59) to set, he wrote to his sister that the majority of the arias were designed to be without repeats, *i.e.* they were *cavatinas*. " There should be repeats ", he declared, " only when the singers know how to vary the music ; otherwise it seems to me it is an abuse to repeat the same thing four times over." Thus did the *cavatina*, a short aria with no reprise of the opening part, come into fashion in Berlin, but that was as far as operatic reform went at Frederick's court. Graun's music differed little from Hasse's, save in being a little less elegant and cosmopolitan ; yet, largely owing to Frederick's own re-shaping, Graun attained a far greater dramatic power.

THE EARLY OPERAS OF GLUCK

Hasse provided the models for Gluck's early operas, but Gluck, the sturdy peasant, could never compete with his suave elegance of style, the embodiment of sensibility. Gluck's strength lay elsewhere, in the creation of an ideal opera distinguished by its harmonious proportions and statuesque grandeur. The *galant* style of Hasse and his kind reflects the rococo fashions of the mid-eighteenth century, whose counterparts in architecture are Cuvilliés's elegant gold-and-silver rooms in the Amalienburg at Munich and Neumann's Residenz for the Prince-Bishop of Mannheim, with its frescos by Tiepolo and its enchanting stucco statues. Gluck, on the other hand, embodied in his mature operas those principles of " noble simplicity and calm greatness " preached by Winckelmann, whose aesthetic had a powerful influence upon his contemporaries and the artists of the immediately succeeding generation. These included the Adam Brothers with their classical elegance of design, the sculptors Thorwaldsen and Canova ; and ultimately, to take an example familiar to Londoners, the architect of the Athenæum Club.

Gluck had signally failed to capture the London audience, used to Handel's mastery, with two operas of his, one of which celebrated the victory at Culloden. But on his return to Vienna he began to consider consciously those theories which he embodied in the operas of his last thirty years, largely owing to the stimulus he received from Count Durazzo, who was in charge of the Imperial Theatres in Vienna from 1754 until ten years later, when he was removed from his post owing to the unpopularity of his policy with the court.

Like the Florentine theorists of nearly two centuries earlier, Durazzo desired to return to the imaginary Greek ideal of a music-drama in which the music was to heighten the effect of the poetry and not stand between it and the audience. He saw in Gluck the musician who could give practical effect to this reaction against the Metastasian conventions. The first step in the new direction was taken in 1755, when Gluck collaborated with Durazzo as librettist in the production of *L'Innocenza giustificata*, an opera on the theme of the Vestal Virgins, which was to furnish the subject of Spontini's most famous opera fifty years later. Durazzo was still bound to the Roman historical scene favoured by Metastasio, which Gluck was to abandon later in favour of more warmly human subjects, drawn though they were from mythology and legend. But there is already none of the jealous intrigue or the political conspiracy which are the mainsprings of the Metastasian drama. Durazzo seems to have modelled himself upon Euripidean tragedy and infused his libretto with something of Euripidean passion.

GLUCK'S ACHIEVEMENT

Gluck was himself no intellectual theorist or fanatical reformer. He happened to find in the type of opera advocated by Algarotti and the other theorists of the day the best vehicle for his particular kind of musical genius ; and he possessed the strength of character to carry through to their logical conclusion the principles which had already been accepted in a half-hearted fashion by Traetta and Jommelli. His achievement is indeed to have re-established opera as a coherent art-form worthy of intellectual respect and admiration. At the same time, he was quite ready, after collaborating with Calzabigi in *Orfeo* and *Alceste*, to revert to conventional *opera seria* when that was demanded of him. Gluck's shrewd common sense led him to comply with the requirements of his patrons, even as he also complied—no doubt with greater enthusiasm because their ideas suited his own temperament and abilities—with the demands of Count Durazzo, and later François du Roullet, the attaché in the French Embassy in Vienna who negotiated Gluck's contract with the Paris Opéra.

It would be too much to say that Gluck's reforming zeal stemmed entirely from his librettists ; nevertheless it is true that Gluck's pronouncements on operatic theory were, if not composed for him by one or other of his literary associates, closely derived from the published writings of the theorists. The famous preface to *Alceste* bears a strong resemblance to the content of Algarotti's essay, while the statement of his aims issued by Gluck to a Parisian journal, the *Mercure de France*, as advance publicity for *Iphigénie en Aulide* echoes so many of the favourite dogmas of the Encyclopaedists that it is difficult to believe that it was not drafted for him by du Roullet, who was a disciple of Diderot.

GLUCK AS THEORIST

The preface to *Alceste* was, like many another pronouncement of historical importance, a statement of what had been accomplished and a summary of the principles upon which action had been taken, not a manifesto for future revolutionary policy. After the usual attack on the vanity of singers and the subservience of the music in the older operas to their technical exhibitionism, it sums up the central tenet of the new faith in a famous sentence :

I have endeavoured to restrict music to its true function of aiding poetry in the expression of the emotions and the situations of the story, without interrupting the action or smothering it under vain and superfluous ornaments ; and I believed that this could be done in the same way that the use of colour produces a correct and well-proportioned drawing by a carefully calculated contrast of light and shade, which seems to give life to the figures without altering their shape.

The letter to the *Mercure* displays a skill in flattering the French in general, and Rousseau in particular, that would do no discredit to a member of the *corps diplomatique*. In one passage the author of this epistle astutely echoes Diderot :

No matter how gifted a composer may be, he will produce only mediocre work if he is not inspired by the poet. . . . All arts must imitate Nature. That is the goal I try to achieve in my music, which I try to keep as simple and natural as possible, merely attempting to emphasise and lend greater expression to the poetic declamation.

The final statement of his aims is characteristically sensible :

We might succeed together . . . in producing a music which will appeal to men of every nation, and so in eliminating the ridiculous distinctions of national music.

GLUCK'S " ORFEO "

The first of Gluck's operas in the new manner, *Orfeo ed Euridice* (1762), is also the earliest opera to survive in the modern international repertory. It is not an antique to be taken off the shelf and given a performance or two as a matter of musicological interest, but a living masterpiece always sure of revival whenever a singer appears who is able to do justice to the part of Orpheus. In it neither poet nor composer broke completely with the past—an impossible feat—but Calzabigi's libretto provided Gluck with the basic structure he needed in order to fulfil himself in musical expression.

There are still frequent marks of Metastasian influence in the literary style of the libretto, in the inevitable similes and commonplace metaphors which abound in it. Structurally, too, the libretto makes no important break with the past, save that all the secondary intrigues and sub-plots are eliminated in favour of a plain, straightforward presentation of the story. This only emphasises the essentially static character of *opera seria*—an effect further reinforced by Calzabigi's glance at French models, which provided him with the opening scene at Eurydice's tomb. The statuesque character of the drama was precisely what Gluck's genius needed for its full realisation, hampered as it was by his technical shortcomings as a musician which put elaborate or complex movements outside his scope. His strength lay in the noble gesture, in simple pathos and angry defiance, and in grave choral reflections upon the events of the drama.

The melody of *Che farò*, Orpheus's lament for Eurydice after he has finally (so it seems) lost her, never fails to move us deeply, precisely because it does not indulge in any conventional expression of grief. The melody is in C major and, removed from its context, might even be supposed to express a happy mood. In its context, it transcends all expression, and must have done so all the more when it was sung by a *castrato*, whose emotionless voice, like a choir-boy's with the power of a man's, would accentuate its ideal quality. The transfer of the part to a tenor, as was done when the opera was performed in Paris in 1774, spoils this effect, and a contralto remains only the more satisfactory substitute. For Orpheus, it has been well said, "is not merely a plaintive human being, but also a symbol of the singer's most exalted art, transcending all that is personal". Gluck could attain such heights of expression by the most apparently simple of means ; yet he was less happy in handling, in musical terms, the dramatic conflict of the preceding scene where Eurydice, jealous because Orpheus will not look on her face, finally breaks down his will and causes him to disobey the edict of the infernal gods.

THE HAPPY ENDING

Nor did Gluck and Calzabigi throw overboard the conventional happy ending, whereby, in spite of everything, Orpheus and Eurydice are united. The excuse advanced in their favour has always been that *Orfeo* was produced to celebrate the name-day of the Emperor Francis. Yet, though Calzabigi himself protested in principle against the convention of the happy ending, it is extremely doubtful whether he would have had the courage of his convictions, whatever the occasion of the opera's production. Tragedy, as we understand it and as Æschylus and Shakespeare understood it, was outside the conceptions of eighteenth-century taste, according to which the conflict of passions, amorous or political, must always be happily resolved in the final act. So far as can be discovered, Dido is the only one of Metastasio's heroines who comes to her inevitable end, the idea of Æneas and the Carthaginian queen living happily ever after being too much even for eighteenth-century audiences to swallow. The best Metastasio could do, as Berlioz did after him, was to emphasise Æneas's nobility and sense of mission.

It is, at least, significant that after *Orfeo* Calzabigi avoided the difficulty by choosing themes which had no tragic ending. The whole point of the story of Alcestis is that in the end she is restored to life and to her husband, while the version of the tale of Paris and Helen used by Calzabigi, though serious in its treatment, has no suggestion of tragic feeling, and Helen is not even guilty of adultery, being affianced, but not yet married, to Menelaus. Gluck followed this precedent in his French operas, the two *Iphigénies*, and though Armide herself dies, she is the villainess of the piece and her downfall is the means of Renaud's salvation.

In setting the dialogues in *Orfeo*, Gluck abandoned the *secco* method and adopted the French style of accompanied recitative, thereby at a stroke giving his opera a more homogeneous texture throughout. This homogeneity is further heightened by the absence of the abundant florid ornaments which were a conspicuous feature of *opera seria*. Thus Gluck restored the balance between the narrative and the lyrical elements, the arias, which are mostly cast in the cavatina-form without *da capo* and arise naturally out of the emotionally heightened moments in the drama. *Orfeo* and its successors in the reformed style are, in the sense understood by Wagner, music-dramas.

THE TWO VERSIONS OF " ALCESTE "

Like *Orfeo*, *Alceste*, which was produced in Vienna in 1767, was also revised and translated into French for performance in Paris. Euripides presented the story as a glorification of the sacred duties of hospitality; but such a theme would hardly have interested an eighteenth-century audience, and Calzabigi transformed it into one of conjugal devotion, the happy dénouement being effected, not by Hercules's rescue of Alcestis from the lower world, but by the intervention of Apollo as *deus ex machina*. Du Roullet, author of the French version of 1776, restored Hercules to the story, but still retained the intervention of Apollo. The Paris version, which is the one usually performed, was further amplified by the addition of a large amount of choral and ballet music, with the result that the work was turned into a *tragédie-ballet* and the static character of the drama was further emphasised.

THE TWO "IPHIGÉNIES"

Although *Alceste*, with its preface setting out the new æsthetic of opera, is the consummation of the ideal opera as conceived by the reformers, it is not Gluck's masterpiece. In the two *Iphigénies* Gluck's dramatic powers were able to expand more grandly in response to the superior construction and imagination of the French librettists. Du Roullet's *Iphigénie en Aulide* (1774) and, still more, Guillard's *Iphigénie en Tauride* (1779), are more dynamic than Calzabigi's librettos. And although the first act of *Alceste* proceeds from its tragic overture (the first serious attempt to establish the mood of the subsequent drama) in a monumental *crescendo* through the great choruses of mourning and the oracle's pronouncement to the decision of Alcestis to sacrifice herself for Admetus and her grand defiance of the "Divinités du Styx" it is outclassed, both dramatically and musically, by the great scene in the first *Iphigénie* where Agamemnon, torn between his duty to the army and his love for his daughter, resolves to save Iphigenia's life. Nor is there anything in the earlier operas to match the deep pathos of Iphigenia's farewell, one of the most perfect emotional utterances of the eighteenth century.

Iphigénie en Aulide suffers, from the point of view of modern taste, from having been derived not directly from Euripides, but from the tragedy of Racine, who introduced the necessary love-interest into the story by making Iphigenia the betrothed of Achilles. It is in their love scenes that Gluck's limitations as a composer appear, for, confronted with the unheroic sentiments of a young man and woman, as distinct from the ideal love of Orpheus or the sensual passion of Paris and Helen, Gluck tends to become sententious and conventional. *Iphigénie en Tauride* was adapted by Guillard direct from Euripides, whose masterpiece, as a drama, it may well be reckoned. It is certainly superior in dramatic excitement and tension to the earlier *Iphigénie*, and its story has a greater appeal to a modern audience, which can better understand the predicament of Orestes caught by a tyrannical enemy than a tale of human sacrifice performed to secure a fair wind for the fleet.

In *Iphigénie en Tauride*, Gluck showed himself complete master of his world. He had freed himself from the theoretical notions which had tended to cramp the uninhibited expression of emotion in lyrical music, while at the same time adhering to the spirit of his æsthetic principles. The result is that in this opera he achieved a true balance between the music and the drama. He had destroyed the old domination of the music, or rather the singer, in *opera seria*, and could now afford to relax the rigid rules of dramatic propriety in the interest of musical expansion. Unlike *Iphigénie en Aulide*, which has a formal overture, the second *Iphigénie* has a prelude depicting the storm in which Orestes' ship is wrecked. The difference is that which distinguishes the overtures to, say, *Don Giovanni* or *Der Freischütz* from the storm-prelude which sets the scene for the opening of *Die Walküre*. One cannot say that it is necessarily a better thing to have done, but it is certainly a striking advance towards achieving a complete poetic coherence in the work as a whole. The prelude has become an integral part of the action, replacing the overture which served merely to put the audience in the right mood for the drama.

Because Guillard's libretto was based directly on Euripides, the chorus in the second *Iphigénie* maintains for the most part the rôle of commentator upon events, whereas in the former it had taken a much more active part in the drama. Yet, while it tends to stand apart, the chorus does serve in a remarkable way to intensify the vivid delineation of the characters. The noble, pathetic Iphigenia, the conscience-stricken Orestes, the sullen, tyrannical Thoas, even the conventional friend and confidant Pylades, are depicted as individual human beings with strong passions and distinctive personalities. Nothing had ever before been achieved in opera so powerful as the scene in which Orestes, haunted by remorse embodied in the terrible chorus of the Eumenides, sees the vision of the mother he had murdered. And in the recognition scene between the brother and sister, Gluck transforms that convention of the old Metastasian opera into a tense and pathetic dramatic action, which even all Richard Strauss's superior technical equipment could later only equal (in *Elektra*) but not surpass.

" ARMIDE "

Armide, produced in 1777, two years before *Iphigénie en Tauride*, presents an entirely different aspect of Gluck's genius. It was the direct outcome of the rivalry of Gluck and Piccinni, or rather of their respective supporters in Paris, who contrived that each composer should, unknown to the other, make a new setting of Quinault's libretto on *Roland* which had been written for Lully nearly a hundred years before. Gluck, however, got to hear of the scheme, abandoned *Roland* to Piccinni, and set *Armide et Renaud* instead. Inevitably the antiquated style and formalities of the five-act drama failed to inspire Gluck to a consistent level of achievement. Yet *Armide* contains some of his most beautiful music, and proves that he could portray the sensual love of the enchantress no less successfully than the ideal love of Alcestis or Orpheus. Moreover he responded to Quinault's formal nature-poetry with music of an idyllic and sensuous charm which reflects the nascent romanticism of the late eighteenth century.

GLUCK'S COMIC OPERAS

Gluck also composed a few comic operas in the French manner, a form for which he had little aptitude. The last and best of these pieces, *La Rencontre Imprévue* (" The Unforeseen Encounter "), is important as the effective link between the French *opéra-comique* and the German *Singspiel* as developed by Mozart. *La Rencontre Imprévue* (given later in German as *Die Pilger von Mekka*) was composed in 1763 for Durazzo, who wished to introduce *opéra-comique* to his Viennese audience. The Oriental setting of the piece, and certain of the incidents and characters (particularly the servant who resembles Pedrillo, and the Dervish, a comic bass in the style of Osmin), foreshadow Mozart's *Die Entführung aus dem Serail*. Mozart knew the opera well, for he made a set of variations on *Les hommes pieusement* (" Unser dummer Pöbel meint ") which he played at one of his concerts when Gluck was in the audience. But if Gluck's comedy seems ineffective beside Mozart's, it is accomplished, indeed, when compared with one of the models of this operetta form—Rousseau's *Le Devin du Village* (1752), which served as a source for another of Mozart's works, the juvenile *Bastien et Bastienne*. For Rousseau, the champion of *opera buffa*, paradoxically produced a little French piece which, for all the amateurishness of its music, did have a considerable influence in establishing a typically French style of comic opera.

THE CHARACTER OF GLUCK'S OPERATIC STYLE

Although Gluck's contribution to comic opera was unimportant, *opéra-comique* contributed something to the formation of his individual style. That style was a synthesis of the simple directness of French comic opera, the sensuous charm (without the vocal gymnastics) of *opera seria*, and the statuesque nobility of the *tragédie-lyrique*, supported by an orchestral texture based upon the contemporary symphonic music of Italy and Germany. Out of these ingredients Gluck fashioned an opera which, whatever the language used, was neither French nor Italian nor German, but genuinely cosmopolitan. He achieved, indeed, the aim propounded in his letter to the *Mercure de France*—the production of a music which would appeal to all nations. He himself said that when he composed an opera, he tried to forget that he was a musician. Perhaps so ; but he also never forgot that it was drama he was composing, and his operas survive not because of their poems, or of anyone's theories, but because of his essentially dramatic music.

Gluck's music is never superficially exciting ; but when the moment comes, it strikes with a tremendous force that never fails to astonish because its power seems so disproportionate to the means employed. It is especially in his dramatic use of orchestral colour that Gluck stands out above his contemporaries, many of whom were far more expert in craftsmanship. Like Racine, Gluck stands for an ideal style of drama, whose classical formality is at the opposite pole to the looser construction and all-inclusive humanity of English tragedy, even Shakespeare's, which to the countrymen of Racine often seems almost barbarous in its lack of form.

X

THE VIENNESE BACKGROUND AND HAYDN

A S the first half of the eighteenth century gave way to the second, so the age of Bach and Handel gave way to that of Haydn, Mozart, and Beethoven. The change was gradual, and to the people of that day no clear-cut division between the old and accepted and the new and untried was visible. The Thirty Years War had driven a breach into the defences of the old feudalism ; the French Revolution eventually disposed of it altogether and substituted another type of class domination. After the romanticism of Bach's cantatas, with their insistence on a blissful existence after death, and the very different romanticism of Handel's operatic vision, there was to be the classic coolness of Haydn's symphonies, and thereafter the spiritual fervour of Beethoven's, which seem to mirror the storm and stress of the contemporary poets Schiller and Goethe. This was a fertile ground where music could take root and exercise its peculiarly evocative and visionary powers of expression.

Compressed within the space of a paragraph, the change appears immense, and such as would demand vast fresh musical resources. The accent was to be increasingly upon harmonic values, upon what is called colour in music. Yet for the expression of these great new matters surprisingly little more was needed than already existed in the dramatic harmonisations that Bach had created for the chorale melodies which he set his Leipzig choirs to sing. It was in the enrichment of the form and texture of music that more exploratory thought was needed, and in which greater advances were made. Haydn, who at the time of Handel's death was a young musician still feeling his way by instinctive processes of trial and error, made a signal contribution to instrumental development with the string quartet, which he blended with the touch of a genius. But while blending the four instruments to new uses he was also providing the string quartet with a new stability and development of form. In this respect, among others, his work was to become equally fruitful, and his influence no less profound, in the domain of the orchestral symphony.

VIENNA

The great flowering of music in Vienna between 1750 and 1830 is one of those features of history that seem to have been almost spontaneous. The common belief in Vienna as a " city of song ", a musical centre of great vitality and influence, was as easily justified before 1750 as it is now, and for the same reasons ; Vienna was and is a city of music-lovers with a taste for playing and hearing a great deal of music. It produced its own composers in considerable numbers, but usually they were less in fame and influence than those who flocked from Italy and Germany into the city, owing to its status as an Imperial capital. Of the great masters who constitute the Viennese School, only Schubert was a true native of Vienna ; the capital became the centre of activities for Haydn, Mozart, and Beethoven because of its wealth, its cosmopolitanism and the Viennese appetite for music, which gave a composer wider opportunities than he was likely to obtain elsewhere.

Vienna's geographical position made it an Imperial centre exceptionally open to influences from Italy and South Germany. Between the earnest, Protestant north and the Austrian capital was a cultural and religious rift across which the masterpieces of Schütz, Bach, and Handel could not travel. As a choirboy at St. Stephen's Cathedral in 1740, Haydn learned the church music of the traditional Palestrina style, for the elaborate music of services for festival days came from Italy, or was based upon Italian models. His most cherished textbook was the *Gradus ad Parnassum* of Johann Jacob Fux (1660–1741), the Viennese court composer whose scholastic work followed the principles of strict Palestrina counterpoint.

The Austrian Empire was a great melting-pot of races, each of which contributed its own culture to the life of the whole ; so that apart from the music of the church, a huge reservoir of folk-song and dance was a common cultural heritage. The Viennese delight in *al fresco* music-making, the love of serenades and " cassations " (a term apparently meaning " back street music " and derived from the word *Gasse*—" alley " or " back street ") remained wedded to the popular musical tradition and was an inescapable influence upon any composer working in Vienna.

The emotional and spiritual deepening of instrumental music during the seventeenth century, which we associate with such composers as Purcell, Bach, and Handel, had made little impression on Austria, or upon the Italian masters whose ideas dominated Austrian music. In the Austria in which Haydn was born, entertainment music of the Italian type, natural, virile, graceful, and easy to listen to, was a social necessity not only in the streets but in the court of almost every nobleman, each of whom would, as a matter of course, employ as many musicians as his means allowed. The musical establishment of a great nobleman included not only a body of players and singers but also a *Kapellmeister* (or Musical Director) to train, conduct, and compose for them ; and he was expected to write for the chapel, the private theatre, the salon, and the ballroom. The music required was composed quickly, heard once, and then normally forgotten. An occasional work might capture the popular imagination and become part of the repertory for a time, but the great demand was for new music in familiar styles and idioms. Paradoxically, it may seem, the very popularity of the art discouraged experiment. Little was published of the great mass of music composed, and composers understood and accepted the ephemeral nature of their works.

It was from street music that one of the most notable musical changes originated. Polite music and the music of the church remained bound to seventeenth-century concerted style, with a keyboard instrument filling in the harmony from a figured bass; but the bands of street musicians responsible for serenades—which in Vienna were entertainments in several movements played by a group of instrumentalists—could not easily transport a harpsichord to play a *continuo* providing the harmonic backbone of the work. Serenades therefore (and music for *al fresco* entertainments, like Haydn's *Feldpartien*) had to evolve a new and fuller style of orchestration, and this style eventually made its presence felt in the court, opera house, and church. Whilst the church looked to the past for its musical style and the opera house was an entirely Italianate institution (as late as 1790 Mozart wrote *Così fan tutte* in Italian for an aristocratic audience), the new style of music, which we associate with Haydn and Mozart, seeped upwards from the popular street style into the salon before it affected either church or opera-house. Popular Viennese opera, as distinct from that of the court, was something quite different from the opera of the educated classes in such great commercial centres as Venice, Hamburg, and London. It used the German language and spoken dialogue and its music was in popular folk-song style, straightforward, catchy, and with practically no dramatic pretensions.

THE SYMPHONIC REVOLUTION

In the music of the seventeenth century, whose type Bach and Handel maintained until the middle of the eighteenth, a style had been evolved in which the basic harmony of the instrumental *continuo* supported a structure in which polyphonic writing had reached a compromise with harmonic thought. As the modern system of tonality developed, relationships and antipathies between keys became more apparent, as did the expressive effect of varying the tonality in a single work or movement. Tonality had given the aria, as Bach and Handel used it, its final form, and it had enabled Purcell to make musical and dramatic points by moving from key to key between sections or movements of an extended work. Nevertheless, apart from the aria, seventeenth-century music may have glanced at keys related to that in which it was written, but it rarely moved into them. Extended movements would be built by the elaboration of a single melodic line, whose motives and phrases would be treated in a manner often referred to as " spinning out ", and by the use of instrumental and dynamic contrast. The style was elaborate, powerful and often highly imaginative, but it was reaching the point of exhaustion. Bach brought up his sons, who were no mean composers, in his own complex and highly finished art ; but even before his death, as we have seen, they were leaders in the new style of composition.

What artists in general had come to require was a greater naturalness and simplicity, charm instead of grandeur, wit and brevity in place of the monumental nature of works of the past. In so far as the aspirations of the age can be summed up in a slogan, their motto was " Back to Nature ". Simplicity of style and sentiment began to be the composer's aim early in the eighteenth century, and in order to realise that aim the new harmonic technique of key-relationship and key-contrast was used in place of the harmonic-polyphonic liaison of the baroque era. Freedom of modulation —that is to say, the ease of passage between contrasted or related tonalities —was the basic principle of the music of the new age ; and it replaced the idea of the instrumental or dynamic contrasts on which so much of extended seventeenth-century music had been based. Notably, it took the hitherto vague terms *sonata* and *sinfonia* and turned them into definite forms, in which a formal discipline still permitted great freedom of expression and method. The special achievement of the " Viennese School " was the full development of the sonata principle.

SINFONIA AND SONATA

The title *sinfonia* began its career as a name for an orchestral interlude in an oratorio or opera—the " Pastoral " symphonies in *Messiah* and Bach's *Christmas Oratorio* are examples. From such interludes it passed, in Italian usage, to the operatic overture in three sections—quick, slow, and quick. *Sonata* originally implied no more than the converse of *cantata*—music played on instruments rather than vocal music. It was then applied to the types of multi-movement works known as the *sonata da chiesa* and the *sonata da camera* (which latter Bach preferred to call *partita*). These evolved into *trio sonatas*, consisting of an instrumental duet over a keyboard continuo which filled in the harmonies from a figured bass. The *sonata da chiesa* (or church sonata) was so called because it was performed between the Epistle and the Gospel at High Mass. It began with a slow introduction, continued with a fugue, and had two more movements. The movements of a *sonata da camera* (chamber sonata) were normally in dance forms, alternating between quick and slow tempos and treated with greater musical elaboration than was possible in the ballroom. The chamber sonata was distinct from the suite only in that it tended to treat dance forms as abstractions, whilst in the suite these remained tied to the purposes for which they had been evolved. The term *sonata* also came into use for solo works, as in the keyboard sonatas or " exercises " of Domenico Scarlatti, which are mostly single-movement works in a binary form which generally progresses from the tonic key to the dominant in its first half and returns to the tonic in its second.

Scarlatti's form may possibly be explained as an abbreviation of the form of the *da capo* aria established by his father, Alessandro. The aria, with its introductory *ritornello* leading to the vocal delivery of the main subject, its second section in the dominant key, and its final return to the first section, had provided the formal organisation for the first (and normally the most highly organised) movement of the *concerto grosso*, the younger Scarlatti's solo instrumental form with mixed timbres and varying expressive possibilities, which automatically implied expansion. It was itself influenced by the already popular aria and concerto, which introduced subsidiary melodic material as a matter of course.

This form, taken over by the Italian operatic composers, provided the formal structure of the first movement of the operatic overture or *sinfonia* ; and symphony and sonata developed on parallel lines. What is essential in the first movement of this early sonata form is an exposition beginning in the tonic key and ending in the dominant, and a working back from the dominant to a close in the tonic. As in Scarlatti's sonatas, this is a binary form. But the examples of aria and concerto often led to an intensification of the contrast in tonalities by introducing new material in the dominant when the exposition reached that key. Upon the return to the tonic it was necessary, for balance, to recapitulate in the main key of the movement all the material originally presented. We have, therefore, an *Exposition* of material in the two keys ; a *Development* working back from the dominant to the tonic ; and a *Recapitulation* in which all the material reappears in the main key of the movement. A *Coda* may then round off the movement.

In the early stages, the development was little more than a passage leading back to the tonic key : the essence of the form was the exposition of two contrasted keys and their eventual reconciliation. It was only at a more advanced stage that the movement's centre of gravity was shifted to the development section, and what was originally a bridge between the two tonalities thus became the most important section of a ternary form.

EARLY SONATA AND SYMPHONY

Both sonata and symphony were originally three-movement forms, and there was no special discipline for the composition of the slow movement. In early days it was lyrical and normally based upon aria (*i.e.* ternary) form ; the last movement, in its infancy, was a *presto* movement in the rhythmically restricted 3/8 time.

The solo sonata first established the form and the overture-sinfonia developed it, until in the 1730s and 40s Carl Philipp Emanuel Bach began his series of two- and three-movement piano sonatas in which the two contrasting groups of the exposition were used with real expressive force, and the development first began to be more than a mere chain of suspensions leading back to the original tonality. C. P. E. Bach's example naturally had its effect not only on pianoforte writing but also on orchestral practice, which in its turn began to influence chamber music. The attractiveness of the sonata idea, its contrast-in-unity, and its essentially expressive, dramatic structure, left no form of music uninfluenced.

NATIONAL AND LOCAL STYLES

As we have seen, the first impetus towards sonata and symphonic style came from Italy, and it was the Italian composers who turned the *sinfonia* from an operatic overture into an independent concert piece in which many theatrical elements survived. The early Italian and Austrian symphonies, especially in their finales, break out into the idiom of *opera buffa* with unmistakable hilarity. Their orchestral style continued to be based upon seventeenth-century practice. The bass line was played by violoncelli and double-basses, with bassoons added if available. The melodic line was given usually to the violins, with oboes and horns adding harmony. The bass line was " figured " for the convenience of the harpsichord player, who added the harmonies indicated, and conducted the rehearsals and perform-ances at the keyboard.

The native Viennese predecessors of Haydn, notably Georg Christoph Wagenseil (1715–77) and Georg Matthias Monn (1717–50), followed this lead. Symphonic style, and to a lesser extent solo sonata style, varied considerably from centre to centre throughout the eighteenth century, according to local traditions and the taste of the all-important patron. In Italy, operatic affiliations survived until the symphonic school died out in the last quarter of the century. In Austria its theatrical character was modified by a tendency to bring it into line with the serenade and the divertimento, with their popular-style melodies. At Salzburg, where the Archbishop's court dominated musical life, it became virtually a polite form of divertimento in the works of Mozart's father, Leopold, whose symphonies are for the most part deliberately and ingeniously "light" music. In Paris the symphonies of such composers as Gossec (1734–1829) inherited much of the grace and gravity of the great composers of Louis XIV's court, and demanded considerable orchestral virtuosity. The north Germans, C. P. E. Bach at Hamburg and his elder brother Wilhelm Friedemann (1710–84) at Dresden and Berlin, brought a deeper and more serious tone to the style, which in London, in the works of Karl Friedrich Abel (1723–87) and J. S. Bach's youngest son, Johann Christian, was combined with an elegance that tended to sentimentalise it.

THE MANNHEIM SCHOOL

The most important early symphonies, however, were written for the Electoral court at Mannheim by the group of composers who surrounded and followed Johann Stamitz (1717–57), who was court *Kapellmeister* for the last twelve years of his life. His influence—directly through his own work and indirectly through that of his followers—affected the formal growth of the symphony, and therefore of chamber music and the sonata, and the development of the orchestra. In Stamitz's works the second subject became more lyrically expansive and the development a more adventurous process ; the slow movement grew deeper and more emotional; and the use of a minuet and trio between the slow movement and the finale forced the latter out of its more or less trivial 3/8 mould. In the Mannheim symphonies, contrapuntal methods were often introduced into the development—a symphonic innovation that provided an infinite enrichment of the possibilities of the section.

In matters of orchestration Stamitz established an orchestra larger than the eighteenth-century norm. Whilst other composers used oboes, horns, strings, and a keyboard *continuo*, in Mannheim flutes and clarinets were already frequent members of the orchestra for symphonies, and trumpets augmented the horns. The need for a keyboard *continuo* vanished with skilled orchestration and the training of what was probably Europe's first virtuoso orchestra ; and the Mannheim composers were credited with the invention of the *crescendo* and the *diminuendo*, in themselves a sharp break from the contrasted alternate loud and soft "terraced dynamics" of baroque music. In 1777, the later days of Mannheim's glory, Mozart visited the court and wrote to his father commenting on the size and excellence of the orchestra—twenty violins, four each of cellos and violas, two each of flutes, clarinets, oboes, and horns as well as trumpets, drums, and four double basses.

Stamitz and his orchestra established a tradition that lasted until the end of the eighteenth century. Amongst the players collected by Stamitz were at least half a dozen notable composers who practised his teachings, including his sons Carl (1745–1801) and Anton (1754–c. 1800), the latter of whom settled in Paris. The new Mannheim style was exciting alike in its virtuosity, the unprecedented demands it made upon the discipline and teamwork of the orchestra, and in its emotionalism ; and there were few musical centres where the influence of Stamitz did not make itself felt during the 1760s and 70s. Among his pupils and successors, Anton Filtz, Ignaz Holzbauer (a Viennese who succeeded Stamitz as *Kapellmeister* at Mannheim), Franz Beck, and Christian Cannabich produced valuable work. Certain of the symphonies produced by Franz Beck in the 1750s and 60s have an emotional force and intensity unparalleled in orchestral writing until the mature work of Haydn and Mozart. The Mannheim decline, when it came, was the result of the drying-up of the original impetus towards greater emotional expressiveness, and a resultant dependence upon orchestral cleverness. The influence of Mannheim and its composers upon Haydn, Mozart, and Beethoven cannot be exaggerated, and many of the Mannheim works themselves are anything but museum pieces.

THE EIGHTEENTH-CENTURY COMPOSER'S STATUS

Such was the symphonic and sonata situation when Haydn came to it at the beginning of his career, though the special developments of the Mannheim School did not reach Vienna until Haydn had won an established place in Austrian music. Little that Monn and Wagenseil had done was technically novel ; and both depended upon melodic styles and a method of orchestration that looked back to the seventeenth century.

In other respects, too, Vienna was conservative. The duty of the eighteenth-century composer was to write the works demanded of him, in the appropriate styles, for a patron who might well be himself an educated amateur musician. He was not expected to develop a personal style but to write dance music, church music, salon music, or opera according to accepted conventions. His personality, in so far as he wished to express it, had to be contained within these forms and their implicit social limits. The attitude of mind is foreign to us, but Haydn's work shows that it is at least no more artistically stultifying to write for a cultured patron than to appeal to a mass audience. His greatness, and Mozart's, lies in the fact that having assimilated the various conventions they did, within clearly realised limitations, develop their own personal styles, and ended by overriding the conventions and carrying their audiences with them.

In the middle of the eighteenth century, a symphony was still regarded as entertainment music with no pretensions to emotional or intellectual depth ; and it was one of Haydn's great achievements to make it a vehicle for deep emotional and intellectual utterances without detracting from its immediate appeal. When the forms were used for serious purposes, which was rarely, it was not on account of the composer's belief in their intrinsic seriousness, but simply thanks to the occasion or to a private inspiration of the composer's. When Haydn began to handle the major instrumental forms in the 1750s, neither he nor his audiences accepted any essential difference between serenade, cassation, string quartet, or symphony ; and when his string quartets op. 2 were published in Paris in 1764, they were entitled " *Six Symphonies ou Quatuors Dialogués* ", the sixth work being one of his cassations. That what we regard as a serious chamber and orchestral form should thus appear so casually in close alliance with popular forms of light entertainment is sufficient demonstration of the status of the symphony and string quartet.

THE SPAN OF HAYDN'S LIFE

Because the work of Haydn differs so profoundly from that of Bach and Handel, the distance in time between them seems to be greater than it actually is ; and it may be as well to map out the chronology of Haydn's life in relation to the great events of European music.

Haydn, the son of a wheelwright, was born in 1732, the year before Bach began to compose his B minor Mass. He had been a choirboy at St. Stephen's Cathedral, Vienna, for two years before the production of *Messiah* in 1742. By the time of Bach's death in 1750, Haydn had probably written his first Mass (the *Missa Brevis* in F, which he liked throughout his life for its " youthfulness and fire "), and he was composing serenades and cassations for *al fresco* performances in Vienna. When Handel died in 1759 Mozart was three years old, and Haydn already had his first official post and was working on his earliest symphonies. When Mozart died in 1791 Haydn was the musical master of Europe, in the middle of his first sensational visit to England. His last Mass was composed in the year of Beethoven's second symphony, and he died in 1809, the year of the " Emperor " concerto, well after the " Pastoral " symphony. In the following year, the opera *Il Cambiale di Matrimonio* (" The Marriage Contract "), by the eighteen-year-old Rossini, was produced in Venice, while Schubert, a boy of twelve, was following in Haydn's footsteps as a chorister of the Imperial Chapel.

FRANZ SCHUBERT (1797–1828)

Drawing by Kupelwieser, 1821

ROBERT SCHUMANN (1810–1856)

Drawing by A. Menzel

Haydn's life spans one of the greatest periods of musical history, and his work, more than any other single factor, determined the direction in which music developed during that time.

HAYDN'S YOUTH

Joseph Haydn's birthplace, Rohrau, on the border of Austria and Hungary, was peopled by a mixture of Germans, Croats, and Hungarians, and it may well be that his musical education began with his knowledge of the mixed folk-song heritage of his home, a knowledge of inestimable value to him as a mature composer. As a boy at the Cathedral Choir School in Vienna he learnt the standard repertory of church music, and became aware of the latest secular works when the choir took part in social functions at court or in the houses of the aristocracy. Musical theory, not a part of the school curriculum, he taught himself, largely from Fux's *Gradus ad Parnassum*.

After leaving the choir school at the age of seventeen, he lived precariously for some six years as a teacher of the piano and a member of, and composer for, street serenading parties, and later as accompanist to the singing-teacher Porpora. Through the contacts he made there, he established a reputation amongst the aristocracy—a necessary step towards professional success. He became music master to the family of Baron von Fürnberg in 1755, and in 1759 was appointed *Kapellmeister* and composer to Count Morzin, at whose estates at Lukavec in Bohemia he spent the greater part of the next two years. When Morzin disbanded his orchestra in 1761 Prince Paul Anton Esterházy, who had heard Haydn at Lukavec, offered him the post of Assistant *Kapellmeister* at his own palace in Eisenstadt, with succession to the Kapellmeistership when its elderly occupant died. His acceptance of this post largely determined the course of his career.

THE EARLY WORKS

It is likely that the string quartets of op. 1 and op. 2 were composed for von Fürnberg, in whose quartet Haydn played the viola. Unlike the early *Missa Brevis*, these works did not meet with the mature Haydn's approval, and he later told his publishers that he wanted the collection of his string quartets to begin with his op. 9. These first attempts at the form are entertainment music, distinguished only by an energy and inventiveness that is too much for his sense of form. They were obviously written with an eye to orchestral performance, for the cello's habit of climbing into a high register leaves the bass so denuded that Haydn seems to have been counting on double-bass support.

Most of the first twenty symphonies were written at Lukaveč.[1] They are scored for strings, oboes, and horns, and require a keyboard *continuo* player (a requirement that persists throughout the first forty or so of the works) with a bassoon to reinforce the bass line. Their scoring is less ambitious than that of some of the divertimentos written at the same time, and most of them are in three movements; it is only in his avoidance of the conventionally trivial finale that Haydn shows any dissatisfaction with the symphony as he found it. The last movements of Nos. 3 and 4 (written before the composer went to Esterház) are fugues, and in other works of this period Haydn writes his finale on sonata-form lines.

In many respects the early piano sonatas are the most finished works of Haydn's earliest days, but they were restricted in scope by the fact that they were written for the instruction of the composer's pupils. Since the early 1750s, Haydn had known and admired the sonatas of C. P. E. Bach, in which he found a richness and freedom of expression coupled with the fullest development of sonata form that he had encountered; and however limited the purpose of his own sonatas, the example of the Hamburg Bach was a perpetual stimulus. In most respects, however, the conditions under which Haydn wrote at this time offered little stimulus to his ambition. He was expected to produce only conventionally acceptable music, and the development of a richer and more personal style would have brought him no reward.

ESTERHÁZ

Prince Paul Anton died soon after Haydn's appointment and was succeeded by his son, Prince Nicholas, nicknamed "the Magnificent", a keen musician for whose instrument, the baryton (a kind of viola da gamba), Haydn wrote a vast amount of chamber music. Prince Nicholas moved his court from Eisenstadt, where Haydn began his duties, to Esterház, a primarily Hungarian neighbourhood where he built a palace in imitation of Versailles and collected round him a court of intellectuals and artistic connoisseurs. "At Esterház", said Haydn, "I was forced to become original."

In 1762 Haydn was writing symphonies that demanded at least six

---

[1] The normal system of enumeration used for Haydn's symphonies is that worked out for the still incomplete Complete Edition of his work in 1907. Various mistakes of chronology in this system have been corrected by H. C. Robbins Landon in *The Symphonies of Joseph Haydn*, and this account is based upon the chronology established in Landon's book.

violins, a viola, two cellos and two double basses, two oboes, two horns, a bassoon and *continuo*. He also had at his disposal a flautist, the trumpeters and drummers of the Prince's military band, and the tiny string orchestra of the chapel. A year later his symphonies have virtuoso parts for four horns. A picture of an opera performance at Esterház (probably of the first performance of Haydn's *L'Incontro Improvviso*, in 1775) shows thirteen violins, two oboes, bassoon, and timpani, whilst other instruments demanded by the score are out of sight. Two clarinettists were added in 1778, and in 1785 the orchestra had twenty-four players. The singers of the Esterház opera were also the soloists of the chapel choir, and a chorus could be raised from amongst the servants and officials. The growth of the musical establishment in Haydn's time shows that his ambitions were at any rate partially encouraged by his patron. In addition, several of the performers were fine virtuosi, and from the early years at Esterház come most of Haydn's concertos, apparently written to ingratiate himself with his colleagues. The first Esterház symphonies, " Le Matin ", " Le Midi ", and " Le Soir " (Nos. 6, 7, and 8), have elaborate solo parts for two violins and a cello.

Later in his career, Haydn complained of social isolation at Esterház, but never of musical frustration, for Prince Nicholas rarely travelled ; even when he did, it was not to the social life of Vienna, where his orchestra would have accompanied him and his Assistant *Kapellmeister* (who succeeded to the senior position in 1766) could have mixed with his musical equals. It was these stay-at-home habits that were rebuked by the " Farewell " symphony (No. 45) in the finale of which the players depart one by one until only a couple of violinists are left. But by keeping him away from any of the real musical centres, the Prince compelled Haydn to develop his own resources and forced him into the originality of which he later spoke.

THE GROWTH OF THE SYMPHONY

During his years at Esterház, Haydn's most significant work was in the fields of the symphony and chamber music. Sonatas had to be written when they were required, but were necessarily governed by their recipient's taste. Nevertheless, in the piano sonata as well as in the larger forms, Haydn began an emotional, and with it an intellectual and formal, expansion of the medium. The piano sonatas for a time continued to explore the possibilities suggested by the work of C. P. E. Bach, so that a critic even accused Haydn of writing a deliberate parody, though this charge drew from the Hamburg master the statement that no one understood his work so well as Haydn. But it is only a few of the earlier sonatas, like No. 36

in C sharp minor and major, which reflect the emotional and technical vigour of the symphonies and chamber music.

It was some time before Haydn finally accepted four-movement form as the norm for concerted works. Most of the pre-Esterház symphonies have three movements; and among his first works for Prince Paul Anton, " Le Midi " has five movements, a recitative for solo violin intervening between the first and slow movements. Four-movement form, with the minuet and trio following the first movement, first appears regularly in the quartets of op. 3, a set of six works, the fifth of which contains as its slow movement the beautiful but now inescapable Serenade, with its violin melody accompanied by the other instruments *pizzicato*. This movement is typical of the domination of the ensemble by its leader which we find throughout these early quartets; and their nearness to conventional " entertainment " music is demonstrated by the way their finales look to the world of comic opera.

A few years later Haydn composed the quartets of op. 9, in which the claims of the lower parts to equality begin to make themselves heard and the composer first moves the centre of gravity of the first movement into the development section. To Haydn, sonata form was never a system of cut-and-dried regulations; and the perfection of form meant the adaptation of an elastic scheme to the material he was using. The earliest four-movement works treat the minuet as second movement; the sonata-form movement might follow a slow introduction or be the slow (second) movement. In the " Philosopher " symphony (No. 22), the first movement is a powerful chorale-prelude in sonata form, and is marked *adagio*, the second movement being an *allegro*. Other works of this period show the same indebtedness to the scheme of the old church sonata.

Certain aspects of the composer's personality appear almost at once. C major is a ceremonial key, demanding trumpets and drums over and above the standard orchestra. Movements begin to be determined by a powerful rhythmic drive that anticipates his later interest in a sonata form without a real second subject, and an isolated early example of this interest is No. 21. Similarly, we find from the start of the Esterház days the steady, firm-treading basses that hold the music together.

Haydn's search for emotional expression led to the dramatisation of sonata form, the attempt to achieve an effective sense of reconciliation between contrasting materials and keys. This involved expanding the development section to allow a fuller treatment of the potentialities of the themes. The number of keys through which the music passes therefore increases, and the sharper key contrasts become a vehicle of more intense drama, as the listener's expectation of the eventual recapitulation gains an element of suspense.

The composer seems quickly to have realised that a symmetrical type of melody containing separable motives was required by the kind of symphony he wished to write. At the same time he began to explore other possibilities, and Symphony No. 28 has a minuet, surprisingly marked *allegro molto*, in Hungarian gypsy style. Folk-music themes, still in Haydn's day essentially popular and plebeian, appear frequently in his work from this time. In the " Alleluia " symphony (No. 30), composed in 1765, and the " Lamentations " (No. 26) of 1766, Haydn returns to plainsong melodies adapted into tonality and regular metre. In the former the main theme of the first movement is derived from an Easter " alleluia," whilst " Lamentations " draws the material of its first movement from one of the chants for the Passion narrative during Holy Week, and the slow movement is based upon a chant to which the Lamentations of Jeremiah are sung. For some reason this work has also been nicknamed the " Christmas " symphony, though its mood is one of almost wild mourning.

From the beginning of his symphonic career, Haydn was conscious of the problem of the finale. The stronger the first movement became, emotionally, intellectually, and dramatically, and the richer the second, the more difficult it became to write a fourth movement that would neither overshadow its predecessors nor fall into complete triviality. In these symphonies of Haydn's development he adopted various procedures for closing his works. Apart from movements mainly contrapuntal in design, No. 12 (1763) ends with a movement in sonata form, and both the " Horn Signal " (No. 31) and No. 72 (composed at the same time) end with a set of variations in slow time leading to a *presto* coda.

HUMOUR IN HAYDN'S MUSIC

Haydn's humour has received a disproportionate amount of attention from popular writers, and it should be said at once that the picture of a brilliant composer devoting his talents to buffoonery bears no resemblance to the truth. Haydn could, and did, play the buffoon at times. " Il Distratto " (" The Absent-minded Man "), for instance, his 60th symphony, was written to introduce the first production in Vienna, in 1774, of a play of the same name. The first three movements are full of witty absent-mindedness ; developments are interrupted by instruments which forget their proper work and begin to sing folk-songs. Fanfares herald and punctuate the minuet, which is suddenly disturbed by a horn that sets off with a new and " incorrect " fanfare of its own. The finale in particular exploits absentmindedness to the point of sheer clowning ; it has hardly begun before it has to stop to allow the violinists to test the tuning of their strings.

The comic vision is no more common, and no less precious, than the tragic vision ; and Haydn was too great a man to keep half his personality out of his work, too packed with irrepressible vitality not to give way to thunderous high spirits when they took possession of him.

STORM AND STRESS

The 1760s were the chief decade of Haydn's experiment and his exploration of the ways in which the dynamics of sonata form could be used to express richness and variety of emotion. The "Lamentations" symphony marks the beginning of a new epoch in the symphony and its allied forms. Whilst an earlier symphony, like No. 34 (1765), might begin with a slow movement in the minor, the succeeding movements are set firmly in the major mode. The "Lamentations", with its unrestrained and angry passion, was the first symphony he composed throughout in the minor mode, and probably the first minor-mode symphony of importance. It marks the end of the days when symphonies were composed throughout in one key, and therefore the beginning of an extension of the composer's sense of tonality. In a major-mode symphony, from now on, the slow movements and the trios of his minuets will probably be in the dominant of his main key, in which the minuets themselves and the finales are set. In works in the minor key the relative major takes the place of the dominant. Again, as always with Haydn, new forms of expression were leading to a technical expansion. Naturally, Haydn's exploration of sonata-form possibilities did not end here ; but whilst the works of the 1760s reveal his search for the right means of expression, they left him with a wealth of experience that enabled him quickly to find the necessary modifications of formal style.

The 1760s and 70s were a period of extreme emotionalism in the literature and music of the German-speaking world, described by the historians as a period of *Sturm und Drang* (Storm and Stress). Contemporaries who probably had not encountered Haydn's work were writing in a similar mood of stormy passion ; Franz Beck, for example, wrote a number of minor-mode symphonies concentrating on emotional expressiveness. The emotional climate, therefore, may have had much to do with directing Haydn's energies towards deeper emotionalism. We know that his marriage was not happy and that the social conditions of life at Esterház irked him from time to time, but we cannot attribute the special qualities of works in any given period to what was a more or less permanent condition of his life.

We find the concentration on emotional expression affecting the string quartets of opp. 17 and 20. In both these sets the instruments are treated with the equality we expect in chamber music ; and the development sections, without suggesting that they are written for a miniature orchestra rather than a more intimate medium, become as actively dramatic as those of the symphonies. The op. 20 quartets (the " Sun " quartets, so-called from the symbol of a rising sun on the title page of an early edition) are marked by the composer's intention to leave nothing to chance in their performance. Dynamic markings are more frequent and carefully graded, whilst in addition to the conventional tempo directions—*allegro, adagio, presto*, and so on—Haydn adds instructions like *affettuoso, scherzando*, and *mancando*.

Formally, in the " Storm and Stress " works, Haydn wrote with an altogether new audacity. The development sections grow longer and more dramatic with the introduction of the " false recapitulation "—the interruption of the development by the appearance of the main theme in the main key, as though the recapitulation were reached. This became a favourite device of the composer's. Allied to it is the introduction of the main theme in a distant key during the development, a device that makes its first appearance in the 51st and 54th symphonies. Its effect is to intensify the expectation of the true recapitulation. The minuet of No. 44, the " Mourning " symphony, is a gaunt canon ; the recapitulation of No. 47 begins in the minor, though the resolute theme opens in the major, and we are given a tragic shock by the change ; the trio of the same symphony is a canon *al rovescio, i.e.* the theme reversing itself as it enters in alternate voices.

At the same time the desire to find the necessary contrast within a single theme was growing on the composer, so that in the " Farewell " symphony (No. 45) the main theme is developed before the second subject appears as a sort of epilogue to the development section. The " Farewell " is one of the most daring of symphonies, with its then outlandish key of F sharp minor and its gradually diminishing orchestra in the finale, a *presto* that turns into an *adagio* with the same atmosphere of noble sorrow as the slow movement of the " Mourning " symphony. The *adagio* finale of the " Farewell " begins in the relative major after the *presto* in the main key, but turns back to F sharp as the orchestra disbands.

The passionate expressiveness found in the works of this period makes the *Missa Sancta Cecilia*, composed between 1772 and 1774, Haydn's greatest church work up to this date. This is his first " Cantata Mass ", on the lines of Bach's Mass in B minor, with each section of the text treated as a separate movement and solo voices employed in elaborate arias. Without departing from the traditional style of church music, Haydn makes this a work of tense drama and jubilation.

A PERIOD OF RELAXATION

The intense adventurousness that had marked Haydn's symphonies up to 1774 seems to die out during the following decade. It may be that the uncourtly energy, passion, and occasional gloom of these works, with their plebeian folk-tunes and disregard of courtly manners, were more than his patron could stand. Possibly his energies were diverted from the symphony by the composition of two Masses, an oratorio, and five operas between 1774 and 1784 ; or the intense expressiveness of his instrumental works may have temporarily exhausted him. Whatever the explanation may be, the symphonies composed in this period, roughly Nos. 60–81, though they rapidly became highly popular and were published and performed all over Europe, offer perfection of form and grace of utterance in place of the exploratory genius of their predecessors.

The string quartets of op. 33, composed in 1781 and called the " Russian " quartets from their dedication to the Grand Duke Paul of Russia (or *Gli Scherzi*, from their substitution of a scherzo third movement for the minuet), are stronger than the symphonies, although they share their formal grace. According to the composer they were written in " an entirely new style ", and this means not only the substitution of the active scherzo for the minuet, but the dependence upon fully developed sonata form in their first movements. Although Haydn continued throughout his life to call his quartets *divertimenti*, in op. 33 he breaks entirely and irrevocably with *divertimento* style.

Though we cannot explain this period of relaxation from any of the facts at our disposal, Haydn's aim for a time seems to have been formal perfection and graceful lightness of expression. He seems to have been trying to become a sort of Boccherini ; for Luigi Boccherini (1743–1805), Haydn's greatest Italian contemporary, devoted his almost inexhaustible melodic gifts and rich harmonic sense to the creation of chamber and orchestral works of refined beauty, whilst avoiding the dramatic, adventurous style for which we chiefly love the works of Haydn.

Though these qualities are temporarily in abeyance in his symphonies, they are abundantly present in the operas of this period and in his religious music. The Italian oratorio *Il Ritorno di Tobia* (1775) is Italian in vocal style as well as language, and chiefly notable for five great choruses, two of them written for a revival in 1783 ; one of them, the " Storm " chorus, is known in English cathedrals to the Latin words "Insanae et vanae curae". The greatest church work of the period, however, in spite of the drama and humanity of "Tobias", is the Mariazeller Mass, or *Missa Cellensis*, of 1782. Written for the pilgrimage church at Mariazell, the work is inspired by truly popular devotion, and Haydn uses melodies of a folk-song type in much the same way as in the symphonies. In elevating popular style to serve the purposes of religion, Haydn sacrifices nothing of the formal strength and vigour of counterpoint and orchestration that had marked the *Missa Sancta Cecilia*; so that in addition to its moving beauty and hard-won simplicity, the work is an important step to the final integration of its composer's style.

OPERA AT ESTERHÁZ

When Haydn came finally to sum up his achievements, he decided that his operas were his finest works; and the Empress Maria Theresa, herself a musician, said, "When I want to hear good opera, I go to Esterház". At Esterház, however, operas were "occasional" works for some special celebration and, as Haydn explained in 1787 when refusing a commission from the Prague Opera, their scope was governed by the vocal and histrionic abilities of the Esterház company. They were also subject to his patron's taste and the conventions of courtly entertainment. Their subjects were conventional *opera seria* or *opera buffa* librettos, and though Haydn seized every opportunity of humanising the conventions, the richness of their music has not succeeded in keeping them alive.

Between his first extant opera *Acide e Galatea* in 1762, and *Armida*, his last Esterház opera, in 1783, Haydn had composed ten other operatic works. By the time he reached *Lo Speziale* ("The Apothecary"), in 1768, he had begun to dramatise aria form by breaking it into sections connected by recitative, so that for his characters the aria was a way of thinking out their problems, considering alternatives, changing their minds and coming to conclusions.

Perhaps the finest of Haydn's operas before his treatment of the Orpheus legend for a projected London production is *Il Mondo della Luna* ("The World on the Moon"), a beautifully designed work in which action and music reach complete unity. The comic element is set always in G major, a key that returns for all scenes of clowning and buffoonery; the moon itself, on which the principal character, an old eccentric, imagines he lives, is always expressed in the outlandish key of D flat. The finales, like those of Mozart's operas, are extensive movements developing to their climaxes through symphonic ranges of tonality. This work is probably the most important step before Mozart's *The Marriage of Figaro* in what we might call the "symphonisation" of opera. In *L'Isola Disabitata* ("The Uninhabited Island"), Haydn's imaginative portrayal of the austerities of the desert island is remarkable from a stay-at-home composer, and his use of characteristic themes to express leading ideas, returning as these ideas are brought to mind, is an early foreshadowing of the methods of Weber and the symphonically conceived opera of Wagner.

Haydn's virtual abandonment of opera after 1783, like his later abandonment of the symphony, suggests that in the type of theatre to which he was limited he had done all he had to do. The different operatic conditions of London brought a masterpiece from him in 1791. Moreover, after 1783 he knew the operas of Mozart, and in his letter of refusal to Prague, after discussing the limitations of his own operas, he added that " scarcely any man could stand comparison with the great Mozart ". It is as though the younger composer was doing in the theatre the things Haydn would have wished to do.

NEW STIMULUS

The inspiration Haydn needed to carry his instrumental work in form and emotion beyond the " Storm and Stress " period came in 1785. First, he was commissioned to write a series of orchestral meditations on " The Seven Last Words of the Saviour on the Cross " for the Good Friday devotions in Cadiz cathedral, with an overture and an epilogue depicting the earthquake at Christ's death. He composed the work as seven successive *adagios* in sonata form, later introducing each by a baritone recitative declaiming the " Word " with which it deals. Later in life he remarked on the difficulty of composing a succession of movements similar in form and tempo but with sufficient variety of expression to hold the listener's attention. Certainly the immense, concentrated effort which the task demanded, together with its appeal to his deep Christian devotion, produced music of great and masterful daring, intense in its emotion and originality. The popularity of *The Seven Last Words*, together with his own love of the work, led him to publish it as a set of string quartets (in which form it is now best known) in 1787, and as an oratorio for voices and orchestra in 1796.

In 1785 Mozart, whom Haydn had met first four years previously and had since consistently befriended, invited the older composer to listen to the six string quartets he had dedicated to him.[1] The friendship between the fifty-three-year-old Haydn and the twenty-nine-year-old Mozart is surprising enough, for Mozart was not the easiest friend for an established composer to make. What is even more surprising is that the older master, who had come to dominate European music from his seclusion at Esterház, should have had sufficient elasticity of mind to learn from a younger man at that time noted for the difficulty and obscurity of his instrumental works.

[1] K.387, 421, 428, 458, 464, and 465.

Haydn's influence upon Mozart we shall discuss later. The younger composer's influence upon Haydn showed itself in a greater richness of orchestration, a more tensely chromatic style of melody and harmony, and a more vigorous drama in development sections, as well as in a leaning towards free polyphony in place of the strict counterpoint of which Haydn was so notable a master.

THE PARIS SYMPHONIES

Haydn's position in the musical life of Europe in the 1780s is demonstrated by the wide range of his work. *The Seven Last Words* was composed for Cadiz in 1785 ; six symphonies for the Concerts de la Loge Olympique in Paris followed in 1786, together with five concertos for two *lire organizzate* (a kind of hurdy-gurdy) for the King of Naples, who then, in 1788, ordered a series of *Notturni* for a pair of his favourite instruments and small orchestra. When in 1790 Mozart advised him not to travel to England on account of his age and his ignorance of languages, Haydn justly replied, " My language is understood everywhere ".

The " Paris " symphonies (Nos. 82–87) were followed by three others aimed at performance in France, and all show him at his adventurous best. All except No. 82 have slow introductions (a feature of all except two of the symphonies that followed them) of great dignity, solemnity, and occasional pathos ; and these are linked with the following *allegros* or with the slow movements by thematic reference, in a way we might expect from a composer who had spent half a lifetime on the integration of symphonic forms. His inborn desire for unity led him to treat the second subject, in all of these works except Nos. 84 and 85 (which have single-subject first movements with their main themes repeated in the dominant), as an expansion or derivative of the main theme. In No. 88, Haydn's custom of repeating the first subject immediately after its initial statement led him to follow the first, quiet statement with an orchestral *tutti* in which the theme is accompanied by a semiquaver figure based on the notes of the tonic chord. In the development this accompanying figure provides two further motives for interplay with the main theme. Symphonic unity had come to mean to Haydn that everything in the exposition is developed, because there is nothing in the exposition which is not worthy of development.

In these works Haydn progressed beyond the tragic style of the early 1770s without losing anything of his formal and harmonic audacity or his melodic fertility. Pathos and poignancy are dissolved into serenity ; and the composer's wit marks the dancing-bear finale from which No. 82 (" The Bear ") takes its name, and the peck and cluck of violins and oboes in the second subject of No. 83 (" The Hen "). Now for the first time Haydn leaves the woodwind unsupported by strings and gains a new timbre from it. Perhaps it was the influence of Anton Kraft, the Esterház virtuoso for whom Haydn wrote his D major concerto, that led him to give the cellos more important melodic parts ; and whenever the symphonies' keys permit the use of trumpets in their outside movements, Haydn adds them to his orchestra. The finale problem is solved in all these works either by the use of sonata-rondos with eventful development sections or by movements in single-theme sonata form. His easy-going symphonies of 1775-85 had won him international fame ; but the " Paris " symphonies consolidated his position by their combination of formal freedom with formal perfection, emotional adventurousness and directness of utterance.

THE LAST YEARS AT ESTERHÁZ

Whilst Haydn obviously came to regard the symphony as he regarded opera—a form which involved a certain duty to his audience—his attitude to the string quartet came to be one of purely personal devotion. The special intimacy of the string quartet, its homogeneity of tone and its limitations of timbre and dynamics, drove him continually in the direction of a corresponding intimacy and unity of style. The " Prussian " quartets of op. 50 (dedicated to the King of Prussia) and the opp. 54, 55, and 64 quartets were all composed between 1786 and 1790. They develop single-theme principles ; but the derivatives and variants by which the minuet of op. 50, No. 4 grows out of its initial phrase, as its second subject has grown out of its first, and the trio of No. 5 (" The Dream ") evolves from its minuet, are revelations of the amazing variety that Haydn can find in his material. An interest in single-theme structure might suggest that the composer was short of material ; but throughout his career, as we have seen, Haydn was fascinated by the idea of diversity in unity, and at this point he provided it because of the superlative richness of the material he used. Perfection of form still demands that a work should take its own course and not one provided by blueprints, so the " Razor " quartet (op. 55, No. 2) begins with a slow movement in variation form, and puts its sonata-form movement second. (It takes its name from Haydn's promise to an English visitor of his best quartet in exchange for a good razor.) All Haydn's confident adventurousness and vast stock of experience mark the quartets of op. 64, of which No. 5 (" The Lark ") has always been one of the most popular of his works.

The works for *lira organizzata*, composed for the King of Naples, have already been mentioned. The lira was a type of hurdy-gurdy, with a wheel to sound its strings and at the same time to feed air into tiny organ pipes. Its weak voice and restricted possibilities compelled Haydn to provide works of the utmost delicacy of texture. The orchestra of these concertos consists of two horns and a string quartet, whilst the eight *Notturni* have, in addition to their two *liras*, two clarinets, two horns, two violas, and cello. Some of the concerto movements appear, rescored and amplified, in the symphonies composed immediately after them, whilst the *Notturni* were made available for performances in London in rearrangements for flute, oboe, and strings.

After a holiday in Vienna in 1785, Haydn found Esterház increasingly a place of exile, and one of his moods of depressed homesickness coincided with the death of Princess Maria Elizabeth, his patron's wife. This combination of events led to the piano sonata in E flat, No. 49, in which the social duties of sonata composition are forgotten. This entirely subjective work moves through extreme dramatic tension in the first movement to a solemn *adagio*, and concludes with a vigorously extrovert finale.

LONDON

The death of Prince Nicholas in 1790, and his successor's lack of interest in music, freed Haydn from his exile and left him comfortably off. From Prince Nicholas he had a comfortable pension, and his salary was continued though he was no longer needed. His prompt removal to Vienna was followed by the offer of several court positions, but Haydn accepted instead the contract offered to him by John Peter Salomon, a violinist-impresario from Bonn who had settled in London where, since 1786, he had presented annual seasons of subscription concerts. Haydn was to preside at the concerts of 1791–92, composing for them six new symphonies and a variety of smaller works, as well as an opera to be produced during his stay in London. The scheme was backed by a guarantee of generous payment, and it is probable that Salomon enticed the composer with an account of the excellence of his orchestra (highly praised by German critics who heard it during Haydn's stay). Moreover, his visit to London would not interfere with his newly-won freedom.

For all his international celebrity, Haydn had spent almost thirty years wearing livery, waiting morning after morning in an antechamber to receive his orders, and addressed like a servant. But his enormous personal, as well as musical, success in London did not go to his head. The efforts of a rival organisation, the "Professional Concerts", to destroy confidence in his ability to produce interesting new works were belied by the masterpieces that arrived as punctually as they were required ; and the importation in

1792 of Haydn's old pupil Ignaz Pleyel (1757–1831) as a rival attraction failed because of the friendship between the two composers. Haydn attended Pleyel's concerts and was lavish in his appreciation of his pupil's work, but London audiences understandably found it inferior to Haydn's. Pleyel, however, had brought with him so many old works new to London that his old master found it difficult to keep up an equal supply of novelties.

The usual intrigues that surrounded eighteenth-century opera prevented the promised production of Haydn's work on the Orpheus legend, *L'Anima del Filosofo* (" The Philosopher's Soul "); but Haydn became a protégé of the Prince of Wales and played for the Duke of York at his house at Oatlands in Surrey. Oxford awarded him a Doctorate of Music, in return for which Haydn offered the " Oxford " symphony (No. 92), which was composed before he came to England and substituted for a new work which could not be ready for performance in time for the ceremonies.

Haydn returned in July 1792 to Vienna, where the young Beethoven came to him for lessons in counterpoint ; but he found little to keep him in Austria and returned to England for a second triumphal season after a year's absence, even considering the possibility of spending the rest of his life in London. However, the death of Prince Paul Anton Esterházy and the succession of the second Prince Nicholas took him back to Esterház to reconstitute the musical establishment in his seven remaining years of active life.

THE LONDON SYMPHONIES

Discussing his revision of the 91st symphony for performance in London, Haydn said, " A good deal must be altered to suit English taste." In the works he wrote especially for English performance he aimed at depth of feeling, perfection of form, and brilliance of style, couched in an idiom that London would appreciate. As always with Haydn, perfection of form meant a precision arising from the individual characteristics of the materials with which he dealt. With his orchestral and melodic art at its richest and his melodic inventiveness as exuberant as ever, he returned to devices he had previously exploited, and linked them with every innovation that seemed necessary to express himself, in a way that makes the twelve final symphonies a summing-up of his life's work and experience. Several of them contain brilliant solo passages, the slow movements of 93 and 96 use *concerto grosso* technique, and 95, in C minor, returns to *Sturm und Drang* passion.

The minor-mode symphony is on the whole the least impressive of the twelve, for Haydn seemed to draw back from tragedy ; so that whilst minor episodes in major movements reach great expressive depths, they become reconciled in the end to the lively radiance of the major key. The legends of the " Surprise " and " Miracle " symphonies (94 and 96) deserve mention. The " surprise " crash that ends the repetition of the naïve little nursery rhyme of the slow movement of No. 94 is traditionally attributed to the composer's wish " to make the ladies jump " ; indeed, late in life, Haydn explained that the " surprise " was put into the symphony simply to produce a startling effect. The application of the title " Miracle " to No. 96 (actually the first of the " London " symphonies in order of composition) is one of music's mysteries. Before the performance of No. 102, in February 1795, the audience crowded to the front of the hall to see the composer, so that when a chandelier crashed to the ground no one was injured. Somehow, this event has become attached to a symphony written and performed two years earlier.

More important than mythology is the musical quality of these works, which include Haydn's greatest masterpieces in Nos. 102, 103, and 104, wide in emotional range, intensely concentrated in expression and rich in utterance. Their freedom of procedure is as marked as that of anything Haydn ever wrote. Only No. 95 is without a slow introduction integrally linked to the rest of the work—the legend that Haydn's slow introductions are irrelevant is as incomprehensible as the legend of the " Miracle " symphony—and though he is reconciled again to a two-subject sonata-form, his second subjects are largely and subtly derived from his first. The " Clock " symphony (No. 101) embarks upon a bridge passage of great length and turns it into a tense development of the main theme before the second subject is allowed to appear, and similar novelties of form mark all the symphonies. The codas of these movements are rarely mere perorations ; so much has happened to the themes in development that instead of rounding off the movement, the last word has to be a final definitive statement upon their true nature. Brilliant in polyphony (as in the finale of the " Clock ", the fugue of which calls to mind Mozart's " Jupiter " symphony) and in the remorseless, driving development of No. 102, richly romantic in harmony (as in the final apotheosis of the " Surprise " tune, really a greater surprise than any drum crash), masterly in orchestration, and ranging from almost savage strength to ebullient humour and to transparent delicacy of texture, these works are not only perfect in themselves but prophetic of the next development of symphonic style. In fact they are only separated by a decade from Beethoven's *Eroica*.

All Haydn's work of these years is affected by his concentration on the symphony. The last three piano sonatas, Nos. 50–52, are very far from educational utility music, and are as rich in expression and device as the symphonies. The six string quartets of opp. 71 and 74, composed in the Viennese interlude of 1793, achieve the power and drama Haydn had previously associated only with the orchestra. Like the symphonies, they have slow introductions which subtly determine much of the course of the work.

Haydn's later art seems to reconcile and dissolve tragedy and thus to be close to his last religious works. His London opera L'Anima del Filosofo is his greatest tragic opera and follows the story of Orpheus from his loss of Eurydice to his destruction by the Bacchantes. The orchestra is handled with symphonic force, and the choruses are strong, integral to the drama, and vividly expressive. The tragic, the savage, and the eerie are expressed with power and inescapable dramatic momentum, qualities owing little to the slow and conventional libretto.

HAYDN AND RELIGION

After his visit to London Haydn, although he continued to compose until 1802, never returned to the symphony. Other instrumental music—the finest of his piano trios, the trumpet concerto and the quartets of opp. 76 and 77—belong to his last years of activity ; so that his abandonment of the symphony, like his abandonment of opera in 1783, suggests that he felt all his symphonic problems to be solved and his last word in the form uttered.

The quartets of his late sixties held a place amongst his chamber music comparable to that of the " London " symphonies amongst his orchestral works, and they have a similar expansiveness of form that grows from their use in the development of every salient feature of the exposition. They adopt devices Haydn had handled in the past, and present them with new force and expressiveness. The " Fifths " quartet (op. 76, No. 2), so-called from its main theme which opens in falling fifths, is an example of this expansive unity of form ; for the four-note " fifths " motive dominates the entire movement, as a counterpoint to other material, both in its own shape and inverted. The minuet, often called the " Witches' Minuet ", returns to a style of two-part writing (violins in octaves against viola and cello in octaves) which he had used in early works when the quartet was hardly separated from open-air music ; and the finale is a late excursion into the world of Hungarian melody.

The last years of Haydn's career, however, are dominated by religious works—the oratorios The Creation and The Seasons and a series of six Masses which apply all the intellectual and emotional wealth of his late symphonic style to the service of religion.

Whilst critics have always considered it natural for Palestrina, Bach, and Handel to have composed religious works in the same style as that which they used for secular music, they have frequently condemned Haydn and

" LA BARRE AND OTHER MUSICIANS " BY ROBERT TOURNIÈRES

On the left is a viola da gamba, on the right a *flûte à bec* or recorder   The picture
is early 18th-century.

Mozart for the same practice. It is easy to divine in the later symphonies the religious cast of Haydn's thought ; and had he found it necessary to adopt a special idiom for religious works, it might well have meant that his religion was neither so deep nor so sincere as it was. The late Masses are, in a special sense, his religious testament. He declared that the thought of God made him happy, and when criticised for the gaiety with which he would close a Mass, he explained that in setting the *Agnus Dei,* he thought more of the words " Who taketh away " than he did of the word " sins ". His religion was one of joyful confidence confidently expressed.

Haydn had written no Masses for the fourteen years (1782–96) during which the use of orchestras in Austrian churches had been forbidden ; and the six final Masses return to the style of the *Mariazeller* Mass rather than that of the *Missa Sancta Cecilia,* with its elaborate arias. The solo voices are used most frequently in ensembles contrasted with the full choir. The text permits the composition of a series of movements at contrasted speeds ; and whilst, as in the earlier works, he observes the traditions, everything he writes is permeated by his mastery of the symphony. The opening *Kyrie eleisons* are planned like symphonic introductions, and the *Sanctus* and *Benedictus* have a similarly symphonic range of expression, whilst the fugal endings of the *Gloria* and the *Credo* anticipate the urgency and expansiveness of Beethoven's fugues in the Mass in D. The mysteries of the Incarnation and Crucifixion inspire him to music of great emotional power, usually expressed, as in the Mass of Saint Bernard of Offida or *Heiligmesse* (so-called from its quotation in the tenor part of the *Sanctus* of a German hymn, " Holy, holy, holy "), by means of symphonic treatment of themes and tonalities. In the *Heiligmesse,* the *Incarnatus* is a canon of touching simplicity for three trebles which plunges into minor-mode tragedy for the *Crucifixus* and achieves a startling austere power with the utmost economy. If depth of feeling and unshakable artistic integrity are trustworthy criteria, these works rank amongst the many masterpieces of Christian art.

THE ORATORIOS

The Masses are inspired equally by the Catholic tradition and the symphonic way of thought. The inspiration of the two oratorios is Nature as the manifestation of God, and the immediate stimulus was the deep effect on Haydn of the works by Handel which he had heard in England. Each of his oratorios has an engaging simplicity of style that conceals the subtlety of its harmonic language and the strength of its exquisite formal precision. Haydn's gaiety remains, in passages of imitation that demonstrate his delight in the world ; but few things in music are more powerful than the " Representation of Chaos ", which opens *The Creation* and struggles to build a definite tonality in the musical chaos where tonalities dissolve under bleak, inexpressibly sad fragments of melody. As the act of creation begins, we reach C, which turns into a great C major chord as light is created. The first sunrise grows from a single long-held D through intricate harmonies to a gloriously scored D major chord ; and God's command to His creatures to " be fruitful and multiply " has a polyphonic accompaniment that grows and proliferates upwards from divided cellos as though generating life. *The Creation* is a vision of the world before the Fall, and its apparent naïvety is an intrinsic aspect of its truth.

The Seasons, with a German libretto based on the poem by James Thomson, has individual scenes of vivid imagery finely realised, and its choruses range from the gently pastoral to the nobly grand. It lacks the continuous inspiration of the earlier oratorio because its text did not appeal to Haydn's imagination so strongly as that of *The Creation,* which was a third-hand recension of *Paradise Lost,* transformed into an oratorio for Handel (who rejected it) and then translated into German for Haydn. There is no slackening of the composer's power in *The Seasons.* Natural beauty and natural devotion delighted him ; but he admitted that he could not take much pleasure in the self-conscious and self-congratulatory passages in which the personages of the work applaud their simple industry.

THE MUSICAL ACHIEVEMENT

If, as has justly been claimed, Haydn was a great musical revolutionary, he was an unconscious one. He was not a theorist putting into practice his intellectual concepts, but a practical musician using available forms and materials in order to express his personal vision of life. To do this, he defined the categories of chamber and orchestral music and mastered their individual styles ; it is his work that draws the frontiers between them. He united the idioms of court, street, and church, taking human passion, joy, and aspiration into the Mass and the language of the multitude into the refined atmosphere of Society. Through his work instrumental music became a vehicle for the expression of deep emotions. In doing all this, and almost without noticing, he established the structure of the modern orchestra.

XI

MOZART

WE have already met the name of Wolfgang Amadeus Mozart (1756–91) as an important influence in Haydn's musical development. Any genius influences the future, and the human race has produced no creative mind more glorious than Mozart's. But his influence was not, like that of Haydn or Beethoven, in the direction of new techniques of expression. Where his works went beyond the normal boundaries of music in his day, it was into regions where only his personality could penetrate. He was not a reformer or an innovator ; but his work added to the common stock of his nation's music all the devices and expressive ideals he encountered in a cosmopolitan life, and reached unparalleled precision of utterance by uniting them.

A CHILD PRODIGY

The story of his childhood as a touring prodigy is well known, and it is easy to blame Leopold Mozart for the slavery to which he subjected his abnormally gifted children ; but Leopold was an educated man who knew that although infant prodigies are rare enough to be sensational, it is even more unusual for them to develop into mature geniuses, and he was playing for time. Wolfgang and his sister were both brilliant keyboard players, and the boy was more. He had a precocious instinct for improvisation and composition that chose good models and poured its own ideas into them.

In addition to the easy-going Salzburg style, with its old-fashioned prolongation of seventeenth-century manners, Mozart was from the first trained in two musical languages. Moreover, his early concert tours provided the models that he needed as a composer and, along with the models, the stimulus to compose. At the age of seven his tour of Germany and France, which also brought him to London, taught him a variety of musical styles—the poetic keyboard writing of France and the vivacity of Italian opera, as well as the dignity of the French theatre composers.

London music in 1764, the year Mozart arrived, was dominated by J. C. Bach and Karl Friedrich Abel. For Mozart, Abel's solid North German workmanship provided a firm stock. On to this was grafted the style of "London" Bach, who had been originally trained by his mighty father but had spent twenty years in Italy and had evolved a composite language designed to suit English taste. The elegance, fastidiousness, and poetry of J. C. Bach—in itself a synthesis of two traditions—taught Mozart how to write personally in a graceful, apparently extrovert style, and provided the sonata-form principles which, later modified and enlarged by works more powerful than J. C. Bach could conceive, never lost the Bachian fusion of grace and personal feeling. It is worth while remembering that more than half of Mozart's forty symphonies were written before he encountered the series of Haydn's masterpieces which appeared between 1768 and 1774.

The return to Salzburg provided new models in the work of Michael Haydn (1737–1806), the great composer's younger brother, who had become *Kapellmeister* in Salzburg in 1762, a master of counterpoint and an honest, sincere musician of the old-fashioned Viennese type.

Mozart's Italian tour of 1769–71 taught the boy the traditional polyphonic style which was the key to recognition by the academies of Bologna and Verona, which granted him their membership. But Italian polyphony in the strict style meant less to him than the livelier operatic manners which he exploited in his own Italian operas, *Mitridate*, *Rè di Ponto* and *Lucio Silla*, as well as the semi-dramatic "serenatas" *Ascanio in Alba* and *Il Sogno di Scipione* ("Scipio's Dream") written on his return to Salzburg.

THE INFLUENCE OF HAYDN

Three months in Vienna, between July and October 1773, brought Mozart into contact with the Haydn of the *Sturm und Drang* symphonies and the "Sun" quartets. Almost immediately the young man launched into a series of six quartets that show how his musical thinking was revolutionised by Haydn's example. The previous year had seen the production of two sets of string quartets—K.136–138 (more in the nature of string symphonies) and six entrancing Italianate works, K.155–160, composed in Italy and marked by lyrical warmth and fluency. The six Vienna quartets were so closely modelled on Haydn's op. 20 that we can almost see the younger composer trying to teach himself the essence of Haydn's art.

Haydn's symphonies produced a more immediately satisfactory reaction in the "little" G minor symphony (No. 25, K.183) of 1773 and the group of works that followed it. The G minor was modelled on Haydn's work in the same key (No. 39), but its melancholy and imaginative exuberance is pure Mozart, even to the second theme of the slow movement, where the

youth fails to find the right foil to the dark mood of the rest of the work
and lapses into triviality. It was through Haydn's symphonies that Mozart
reached artistic maturity ; and a young man's restless *Weltschmerz* has never
been more forcefully expressed than in the little G minor, in which the
stormy minuet and sonata-form finale maintain the passionate energy and
rebelliousness of the first movement. Whatever he learned from Haydn,
Mozart was the best of disciples—one who did not echo his master's voice
but enriched his own personality with what the master gave him. Critics
have often commented upon the parallel between Mozart's earlier and later
G minor symphonies, and it is a parallel close enough to show how mature
in technique and feeling the young composer was by 1773, whilst demonstrating the towering greatness of the later work.

The A major symphony (No. 29, K.201) was the last of a series which
worked out the Haydnesque form in Mozartian terms ; it was precisely
limited to Salzburg orchestral requirements, and sunny vitality and happiness
do not preclude tenseness of development, the use of contrapuntal devices,
or dramatic vigour. We begin in fact to see how different, for all his debt
to Haydn, the younger composer was from the elder. It was natural that
Haydn should be perhaps the greatest decisive influence in Mozart's development, for it was Haydn who defined the terms in which Mozart did much
of his greatest work. But whilst Haydn finds variety and contrast in a
single theme and his imagination leads him to fantastic, dramatic developments of diversity from unity, Mozart uses sharply contrasted themes and,
with an equally exciting dramatic tension, draws unity from diversity.
Haydn's development sections extend, whilst Mozart's tend to grow terse
and epigrammatic.

By the time he left Salzburg for good in 1781, Mozart had created his
own style from the varieties of musical speech that he had encountered. To
the influence of Haydn he added that of the Mannheim composers and the
French symphonists, with their emphasis upon orchestral virtuosity. His
imagination was always stimulated by the technical challenge of an imposed
discipline. Yet although he would handle materials in the most audacious
manner or juxtapose forms with an infallible sense of balance and progress,
he did not set out to create new ones for himself. His most dramatic surprises
and original inspirations were cast in forms learnt from other men.

MOZART IN VIENNA

It is easy to understand Mozart's dislike of Salzburg. The town was
provincial in atmosphere after the great cities Mozart had seen ; and it had
no opera. Ever since the production in Milan of *Mitridate* in 1770, his

ambitions had been focused on the theatre ; so that when, after the production of *La Finta Giardiniera* in Munich in 1774, no opera but *Il Re Pastore* was commissioned from him in six years, he went to the extreme of working upon the *Singspiel*, *Zaide*, without a commission. Salzburg wanted serenades, *divertimenti* and cheerful, unexacting, old-fashioned symphonies ; it did not want the intellectual and emotional disturbance of symphonies in G minor. Church music was in unfailing demand, and there is a handful of masterpieces amongst the amount that Mozart composed between 1774 and 1781.

The musical disadvantages of Salzburg might have been overcome by Mozart's genius for accommodation, had it not been for the attitude of the new Archbishop, Hieronymus Colloredo, who was enthroned in 1772. Colloredo was glad to have a musician of European eminence upon his staff ; but he believed that musicians, who ranked with the servants, were not entitled to privileges. Although Mozart's fame depended upon his work outside Salzburg, Colloredo made it as difficult as possible for the composer to escape the routine drudgery of his official post. To him, Mozart was a spoiled, conceited lackey whose self-importance needed to be punctured. Needless to say, the composer's early success, the petting and adulation of the great, had done nothing to make him amenable to Colloredo's discipline. The unsuccessful visit to Paris in 1778 may have shown Mozart that an infant prodigy is naturally more sensational an attraction than a full-grown genius, but it did nothing to shake his confidence in his powers. He had been a great man when he was a little boy ; he was incapable of submitting to the off-hand treatment of an employer who was incapable of understanding either his quality or his situation.

His effort to resign in 1781 led to his being ejected from the Archbishop's palace in Vienna, where he was in attendance on his patron ; but despite the humiliation of his dismissal, he could only rejoice in his freedom. The world seemed open to him ; better patronage would surely not be hard to find ; he could accept all the commissions that came to him, publish his works, give concerts in the greatest centre of the musical world. In the event, his optimism proved appallingly unfounded. The only official post that came to him in the last ten years of his life was that of Court Composer to the Emperor Joseph II, a post he gained in 1787 ; and, apart from *Così fan tutte*, all the Emperor commissioned from him was dance music for Court Balls. He was no longer an infant prodigy, but an adult whose instrumental music was considered too melancholy, too subjective, too complicated and too obscure for popularity. Haydn and a band of connoisseurs might acclaim his work, but it was above the heads of his audiences. Publishers could be found for it, but even Haydn at the height of his fame found that a little sharp practice with publishers (such as selling the same work to two or three of them) was a necessary adjunct to the profitable disposal of his manuscripts. In any case, publication ended a composer's hope of any financial gain from his work, and there was no copyright law to give him a reasonable return from its performance. As for the promotion of concerts, the public performance of suspiciously " modern " works has always been a financial risk, and there were showmen-pianists in Vienna more popular than Mozart. There are few stories more painful than that of the destruction of a supreme genius by overwork, continued disappointment, and gnawing poverty.

We should not, however, look in the music of Mozart's last ten years for a direct translation of his experience into art. Possibly without the drudgery of Salzburg, the " little " G minor symphony might have been a less angry work, but Mozart's music comes from areas of the spirit untouched by the turmoil of everyday experience. The D minor string quartet (K.421), with its ominous first movement and tragic apprehension of life, was composed while his eldest son, Raimund, was being born in the next room. In 1788 *Don Giovanni*'s failure in Vienna was immediately followed by the last three symphonies, and whilst the G minor accords with Mozart's tragic circumstances, the severities of the E flat and the " Jupiter " transcend them. The following year, in which *Così fan tutte* was written, was full of personal anxiety, debt, professional disappointment, and resignation to apparent failure. Mozart wrote often enough in a mood of painful anguish, just as he wrote in moods of savage irony and delighted contentment ; but these moods came from an apprehension of life itself, not from its accidental everyday changes and chances.

THE DISCOVERY OF HANDEL AND BACH

In 1782 Mozart became one of the musicians who met at the house of the Baron van Swieten, a diplomat who had served in London and Berlin and in these cities had developed a love of the works of Handel and J. S. Bach. Van Swieten's Handelian enthusiasm was to spur Haydn, twenty-five years later, to the composition of *The Creation* and *The Seasons*, for both of which he produced the German texts. His library contained a number of scores of Handel's oratorios which, for performance in his house (where no organ was available), needed rescoring to provide an instrumental realisation of the figured bass. Mozart provided the new arrangements of *Messiah*, *Acis and Galatea*, *Alexander's Feast*, and the *Ode for Saint Cecilia's Day* in 1788–90. The Baron's Bach collection contained the *Well-Tempered Clavier*, *The Art of Fugue*, and probably some of the organ works, but apparently none of the choral music, which was unavailable in print. When Mozart became acquainted with this music, its mastery of polyphonic style used for poetically expressive purposes, and its towering intellectual and imaginative force, fertilised everything that he had learnt in youth about academic counterpoint and gave him a new expressive resource to assimilate.

Just as Haydn's mature style was not easily taken into Mozart's personal language, Bachian polyphony was difficult to digest. In 1773 Mozart learned Haydn's secrets by writing works directly modelled on Haydn's; so now he taught himself Bach's art by the composition of preludes and fugues in which, for a time, his personality was subjugated to the new technique. Mastery of Bach's style did not appear in further directly Bachian works but in the growing polyphonic resource and vigour of, for example, the first movement of the " Haffner " and " Prague " symphonies, or the finale of the " Jupiter ".

It was not until he visited Leipzig in 1789 that Mozart encountered the unpublished choral works of Bach. In appreciation of Mozart's organ playing, Bach's aged successor had the great Cantor's motet *Sing to the Lord* performed for him, to his great delight. No score was available, so Mozart studied this and other motets then and there from the separate voice parts with the remark, " Here's something I can learn from ". What he learned appears at moments in *The Magic Flute* and the *Requiem*.

CATHOLICISM AND FREEMASONRY

Throughout his youth Mozart was a composer of church music, a sincere Catholic but, like his father, liberal in his interpretation of rules and dogmas. His church music, like his symphonies, contains great masterpieces of personal utterance, as well as beautifully written works that appeared when called for, with no special quality of personal feeling. In the *Missa Brevis* (K.192), for instance, his imagination takes fire and produces music in which the eighteenth-century idiom is used in a profoundly devotional manner. This work uses to the word " Credo " the four-note theme that became the opening of the " Jupiter " symphony's finale, as a means of providing his setting with musical unity. The *Litany of the Blessed Sacrament* (K.243), composed as a matter of personal devotion in 1776, on a scale too large for Salzburg, shows the genuine depth of Mozart's Catholicism.

As a thank-offering for his marriage in 1782, Mozart vowed to write the C minor Mass, which, however, he never completed. As it stands, it is the torso of a work of supreme grandeur, in which the severe majesty of the North German style is united with the warmth and melodiousness that Mozart never sacrificed ; and the composer's failure to complete the work has never been explained. It has been suggested that, though Mozart solemnly vowed to compose the work if he were able to marry, his vow probably contained a proviso stipulating that his wife should be accepted by his father and sister—who, as a matter of fact, treated her with considerable coolness. It was at this time, also, while the completion of the Mass was still occupying his mind, towards the end of 1784, that he became a Freemason. He had already composed his first Masonic work, the cantata *Dir, Seele des Weltalls* (" To Thee, Soul of the Universe "), K.429.

There was at this time no open conflict between Freemasonry and the Catholic Church ; but the fact that Masons accepted members of all creeds into their fellowship and thus implicitly encouraged a liberal attitude in matters of faith and behaviour brought the brotherhood into suspicion. Whilst Mozart's religion was sincere but conventional, his Freemasonry became a matter of urgent conviction. The liberal, humane idealism of the order, its devotion to human brotherhood and the service of mankind, its mystical search for a familiarity with death as the gate to greater knowledge and awareness, all moved Mozart deeply. It is as though, in the new Brotherhood, the composer found a creed that harmonised with his delight in human character and action, from the noble Pasha of *Die Entführung aus dem Serail* to the triumphant underlings of *The Marriage of Figaro*.

Mozart's Masonic works—a group of cantatas, the *Masonic Funeral Music* and *The Magic Flute*—all bear witness to the impact of Freemasonry upon his imagination. The *Funeral Music*, a masterpiece complete in sixty-nine tremendous bars, is a funeral march in the style of a chorale-prelude built upon plainsong psalm chants, introduced and dismissed by music of intense passion and mourning. Chorale-prelude form appears very rarely in Mozart's work, and then only at moments of immense solemnity, like the duet of the Two Armed Men in *The Magic Flute* and the *Hostias* of the *Requiem*. In the *Funeral Music* it gives character and shape to a work of amazing power and passion.

Mozart wrote no church works in Vienna until the *Requiem* was commissioned, because he had no church appointment, so that his greatest years are represented only by the C minor Mass. His instinct for worship, indeed, and his whole religious sense, express themselves through the sublime solemnities of the Masonic music ; and in the *Requiem* Catholic and Masonic sentiments about death meet as complementary aspects. Much of the music that has no overt connections with the brotherhood reaches into the world of Masonic idealism, which seems, at such moments as the introduction to the first movement of the E flat symphony, to inspire much that is deepest in his thought and personality.

PIANOFORTE AND CHAMBER MUSIC

Mozart was a keyboard virtuoso, and therefore little of his solo music for the keyboard is intended for teaching. He wrote music to play at his own concerts and, with the exception of the very early improvisations written down by his father, almost all his pianoforte music can be related to his own or his pupils' needs as performers.

If we consider Mozart's part in the evolution of a true piano style, we see that it shows the same progress, the same affiliation to ideas made plain by the operas, and the same combination of formal perfection and exploratory audacity of harmony, that we find in his other works. Of the sonatas of the 1780s, the C minor, K.457, a work accompanied by the disturbing Fantasia K.475, is the clearest indication we possess of Mozart's style of improvisation. In the D major, K.576, and the two still later movements in F (to which an earlier rondo was added to make up the sonata described as the " 18th " in Collected Editions), we have Mozart at his most personal and expressive, following trains of thought wherever they led him, and expressing them with a clarity of form that perfectly assimilated their novel harmonic and contrapuntal procedures.

In all the chamber music that includes a piano, the keyboard instrument dominates the ensemble. That it should do so in the sonatas for " piano with violin accompaniment " is common eighteenth-century practice ; but the piano trios and quartets are *concertante* works in which the piano is accompanied by subordinates, rather than true chamber music of equal partners. A similar relationship exists in the two flute quartets (K.285 and 298) and the oboe quartet (K.370) ; the distinctive woodwind tone dominates its partners, who deliberately act as a foil to its special characteristics. It is only in the radiant perfection of the clarinet quintet (K.581) that a woodwind instrument and strings achieve perfect equality. In this work it is almost as though the technical problems of creating such an equality have ceased to exist. The work is one of those which were written in a mood of resignation to earthly failure at the end of Mozart's life ; but instead of technical problems or music displaying mere virtuosity, it explores a rarely exalted emotional state.

For ten years after the six string quartets of 1773 Mozart did not attempt the form. The six quartets dedicated to Haydn were composed between 1782 and 1786, and in the remaining six years of his life only another four quartets were written. All ten are superbly mature works, and even the last three (K.575, 589, and 590), written for the cello-playing King of Prussia and giving him a specially elaborate part, maintain their intimacy and balance in spite of their special character. None of these later works, however, has the special intensity and exploratory passion of the "Haydn" quartets. The first (perhaps because imitation is the sincerest form of flattery) is the only one that is openly Haydnesque ; and the following works, in their harmonic daring and controlled passion, do much to explain Mozart's dubious reputation for writing excessively melancholy, subjective music in an age that preferred its emotions kept within conventional bounds. The dissonant slow introduction to the sixth of the set, in C major (K.465), sets free contrapuntal parts grinding against each other in remarkable false relations. In the D minor (K.421), the foreboding of the first move- ment leads to a slow movement of almost hectically intense beauty—a quality shared by the slow movements of the B flat "Hunt" quartet (K.458) and the C major. Minuets are emancipated from the ballroom by the breaking of their rhythmic patterns into unequal phrase-lengths and by the use of contrasting phrase-rhythms in the trios. Moreover, with incalculable significance for the future, Mozart at times places the centre of gravity of a work in a finale, which thus resolves the questions raised by the earlier movements. The A major quartet (K.464) does not reach a resolution but ends in a mood of troubled, anxious questioning that must have shocked its orginal hearers, who were used to receiving a happy ending.

To many musicians the four mature quintets for two violins, two violas, and cello mean even more than the later quartets. An early quintet in B flat (K.174), composed in 1773, exploits the contrast in tone between violin and viola, and ends with a display of contrapuntal fireworks that seems to exist in order that Mozart might enjoy his own ingenuity. Apart from the arrangement of the wind serenade in C minor for string quintet, the other four works were all composed in the last four years of his life. K.515 and K.516 were not composed to any specific commission, though they may have been written to attract the attention of the cello-playing Prussian King. The second of them, in G minor, is one of the most perfectly designed of all Mozart's works, a symphonic form that seems to have grown entirely out of the material, bitterly sorrowful, resigned, and pleading rather than combative. The additional viola gives all these works a texture of rich depth and beauty, and although the two later quintets do not explore the tragedies of the G minor, they are witty, brilliant, and introspective.

SERENADES AND SYMPHONIES

Although we may speak of Mozart's implicit acceptance of the forms he handled, he does not treat any of them as though they had their own special emotional connotations ; he was too near their origins for that. The Salzburg demand for light works meant that after the twenty-ninth symphony, in 1774, he produced only a handful more works in the form before he left the Archbishop's service, and one of those is the "Paris", (K.297), composed for his visit to France in 1778. This work is a brilliant but nearly impersonal exploitation of French styles and devices that meant little to him. He wrote in sardonic vein about it to his father and pointed out that the celebrated French unanimity in attack—the *premier coup d'archet*—to which he had pandered in the opening of the first movement was no cause for excitement ; French players simply began all together, like orchestras everywhere else. Even with such concessions, the original slow movement had to be replaced by a shorter and simpler one, and it is unlikely that the original audience made very much of the sparkling harmonic wit of the finale.

These works, written within the context of eighteenth-century entertainment music, developed Mozart's tendency to express a basically tragic view of life in terms of irony. To his contemporaries a melancholy composer, he was impelled by the social purpose of much that he wrote to express his mind through ambiguities of harmony and tonality. There is a case for regarding the "Haffner" serenade, written in 1776 for the marriage of the Salzburg Bürgermeister's daughter, as his first completely mature work, for part of the miracle of the "little" G minor symphony is that it embodies adolescent thought and experience. The "Haffner" underlines its external gaiety with subtle, sometimes sad, harmonies, and its sliding chromatic melodies present a world in which happiness and sorrow are inescapably companions. The "Posthorn" serenade (K.320), written three years later, makes no effort to disguise its emotional unrest ; its slow movement is a heartbroken good-bye to someone or something carried away in the flowing minuet, the trio of which, with its posthorn calls that give the work its name, makes the symbolism plain. The *Gran Partita* or Serenade (K.361) for thirteen wind instruments, begun at Munich whilst Mozart was working on *Idomeneo* and completed in Vienna after he had won his freedom from the Archbishop, exploits the sensuous qualities of woodwind tone through music in which gaiety is offset by sadness and longing by self-mockery. There is no suggestion that music must embody thought in any way inferior because cast in a conventionally cheerful form.

As Mozart's music deepened, he did not cast aside irony. He rarely uncovered his deepest emotions or wore his heart on his sleeve, but revealed himself through melodies and textures often coloured by shifting harmonies and tonalities. Grace, elegance, and perfection of form are all qualities of the music in which he spoke most profoundly, but these qualities were imposed by sheer technical mastery upon a world of often troubled emotion.

At times tragic drama is expressed directly, as in the minor-mode concertos and the second of the two Vienna serenades for wind octet in E flat and C minor respectively (K.375 and 388). The first has the solemn expansiveness which E flat (the key for Masonic rituals in Mozart's work) always arouses, whilst the C minor omits the serenade's customary first minuet and delivers music of the deepest tragic import, ending in a C major not triumphant but resolutely courageous. The composer arranged the work for string quintet, sacrificing the biting pungency of its original orchestration, although it did not really belong in the class of extrovert five-movement works. It is typical of Mozart that a work of great dramatic tension and tragic feeling should be written in the category conventionally reserved for cheerful entertainment music.

If we try to imagine the last six symphonies in the context of the late eighteenth century we shall easily understand contemporary objections to the complexity of his music. His technical mastery and perfection of concerto form demand more material in the exposition; and in the " Linz " symphony (No. 36, K.425) there are eight themes for development in its two subject groups. Conversely, developments become more terse and concentrated, for after his study of Bach, Mozart was able to display essential relationships with the greatest conciseness.

In the " Haffner " symphony (No. 35, K.385), originally a serenade to celebrate the enoblement of the Salzburg Bürgermeister but converted into a symphony by simply removing the first minuet, polyphony is an essential element of the music. The first movement is dominated by a main theme that strides into the dominant to become a counterpoint to the true second subject. In the " Prague " symphony (No. 38, K.504) the copious material is worked out with breath-taking polyphonic excitement. At the same time Mozart's harmonic daring functions freely along with this contrapuntal texture : the first movement of the " Linz " symphony in C opens its second group not in the " correct " G major but in E minor.

It is conventional to describe the three final symphonies as respectively gay, tragic, and serene, but like all Mozart's greatest works they comprehend and unite widely different emotional states. Only the G minor (K.550), unique among Mozart's work in leaving its struggle unresolved, concentrates upon a single aspect of experience. It begins like Cherubino's aria *Non so più* in *The Marriage of Figaro*, but with the rhythmic and melodic contour turned from adolescent longing for experience into an urgent grimness, unappeased by the classic grace of the slow movement. Only the trio of the minuet offers a momentary peace before the finale ironically applies the old *opera buffa* style finale to desperate tragic ends. The E flat (K.543), like the " Linz ", opens with a slow introduction (rare in Mozart's symphonies and found in only two of his mature works) that moves through spacious solemnities into remarkable dissonances as it passes into the unusually lyrical first movement. The slow movement is troubled, and relieved by a pastoral trio after a stately minuet : the ending is happy.

In Mozart's last symphonic work, the "Jupiter" (K.551), the first movement strides relentlessly, despite a main theme that conventionally represented the suppliant pleading to the tyrant in contemporary *opera seria* and a second subject that was originally a comic aria interpolated into another composer's opera. Nostalgia and regret in the slow movement lead to a minuet that droops into pathos. In the last movement the first subject group opens with the four-note theme that had served for the *Credo* in the early *Missa Brevis* and had functioned as a motto theme in many other lesser works. Both groups contain a multitude of themes notable for their polyphonic utility. This, we may say, is the final vision of the dance of life. All sorts and conditions of themes contribute to a total richness of existence and move with enormous power to their consummation in the stretto of the coda, where they spin in order round the revolving axis of the four-note theme in music of supreme intellectual ecstasy.

THE CONCERTO

Miraculous as are the symphonies and great chamber works, it is from the concertos and operas that they draw their significance and to which, usually, they refer in their greatest moments. Even the expansion of subject matter in sonata-form movements—Mozart's greatest gift to symphonic form—follows from his elaboration of the concerto scheme.

When Mozart started to write, the structure of the concerto was still uninfluenced by the growth of the symphony. The first movement was similar in form to an extended aria, and its exposition provided a theme for the orchestral *tutti* which framed the special contribution of the soloist, who entered when the tonality was carried to the dominant. Both the soloist's and the orchestra's contributions would be discussed and developed, first by the soloist and then by the soloist with the orchestra, and they finally returned to the tonic for a shortened recapitulation, which ended in the orchestra's holding a conventional chord as a signal for the soloist's cadenza, before the two combined forces again in the coda. This was virtually an expansion of the instrumental *ritornello* and the singer's part in an aria ; and so it has elementary affinities with the two subject groups of sonata form, although the relationship between what is said by the orchestra and the soloist is hard to define explicitly even in the earliest concertos. The slow movement is lyrical and thus dominated by the soloist ; and the last movement, as in a symphony, is lighter in tone and usually cast in rondo form, dividing the material of its episodes between soloist and orchestra.

Mozart's earliest concertos were arranged from the sonatas of J. C. Bach and other composers for his concert tours in 1765 and '67. His earliest original work in the form was a lost work for trumpet composed in 1768. The Salzburg years first produced the concerto for bassoon, which exploits the instrument's nature and resources with felicity but does not seek to be more than entertaining light music. A year later, in 1775, came the five violin concertos, which Mozart wrote for his own use ; these exploit all his range of style and a youthful emotionalism that is specially moving and free in its profusion of melody. Each of the works gains in certainty and depth upon its predecessors, and it seems as though the composer cared for nothing but the production of aurally satisfying music. The richness of melody forces the form to expand without, however, developing its special characteristics. The woodwind *Sinfonia Concertante*, composed in Paris for virtuosi from the Mannheim Orchestra, is planned on a grand scale to reveal the accomplishments of its four soloists—oboe, clarinet, bassoon, and horn— and the slow movement is marked by an appearance of Mozart's favourite four-note theme, which we usually associate with the finale of the "Jupiter" symphony. The flute and harp concerto which followed is written with tactful regard for the limitations of the aristocratic amateurs who commissioned it, and is salon music at its most ingratiating. The flute concerto (K.313) and the oboe concerto (K.314) followed ; in the former the slow movement had to be replaced because it was too personal to be comprehensible to the Dutch amateur who commissioned the work.

The *Sinfonia Concertante* for violin and viola, composed in 1779, is the supreme masterpiece amongst these works. Its themes are fully symphonic and owe nothing to earlier concerto principles. The orchestra is large and treated with eloquence, whilst the two soloists are involved throughout in dialogue and duet of the deepest intimacy. The four horn concertos do not —indeed, in view of the solo instrument's limitations, could not—rise to this height : they are delightful works in popular style exploiting to the full the solo instrument's capacity for nobility of utterance, rich singing tone and lively hunting music. Three were written for the Salzburg horn-player Leutgeb, who followed Mozart to Vienna and seems to have aroused the composer's sense of humour. The autographed scores of these works are full of Mozartian jokes, but they reflect admirably on Leutgeb's virtuosity.

The first original piano concerto (D major, K.175) is a brilliant and dramatic work with a vigorously contrapuntal finale that combines learning with elegance ; but it is the E flat concerto (K. 271), completed in 1777, that provides the first masterpiece in the form. Mozart brings the soloist into the second bar of the work, almost dispensing with the *ritornello*, and delivers the exposition more or less in dialogue between soloist and orchestra. The exposition provides six themes, all of which are used in the development: none of them belongs exclusively either to soloist or to orchestra. The slow movement drops into a dark C minor that grows increasingly troubled until the soloist breaks out into a recitative, as though giving a semi-verbal statement of his attitude. Throughout the movement he pours out a stream of increasingly poignant melody, under which the orchestra provides stability by concentration upon the principal melody ; the two are partners in a close intimacy. The finale is a racy, elegantly capricious rondo, in which the troubles of the slow movement are not forgotten but transcended, and which includes a symphonically expanded minuet as an episode.

This work is the point of departure for the great series of concertos written in Vienna. The later works maintain the extreme intimacy of orchestra and soloist whilst exploring the possible affinities between concerto and symphony. In the later works Mozart does not disregard the *ritornello*, but uses it to frame a sonata-form movement in which the soloist takes the lead. In the great collection of twelve concertos written between 1784 and 1786, years filled with a mass of other compositions besides *The Marriage of Figaro*, every variety of symphonic procedure is accommodated within the concerto framework, from the Haydnesque concentration on a single theme shown by the D minor concerto (K.466) to the development of processions of themes in two subject groups strongly contrasted. The *ritornello* itself is not a single theme or melody, but a chain of themes of great inner unity and closely related to everything that follows.

Mozart is not, however, writing symphonies with obbligato piano parts. The piano is the friend and partner of the orchestra, but it is a virtuoso instrument with enormous expressive powers to be exploited, and we should never forget that these works were written for performance by Mozart the virtuoso. The symphonies show the inner unity of apparently contrasted themes, but in the concertos the piano and the orchestra are beings of different natures whose unity of purpose is achieved by art. The piano may open the exposition by taking over material that has been heard in the *ritornello*, to show that its full nature cannot be appreciated only from orchestral statement, but usually the exposition opens with new material from the soloist.

It would be impracticable to lead the reader through all these works. Even to touch upon their relationship with the operas—the prophecies of *Figaro* in the E flat, B flat, and F concertos (K.449, 456, and 459), written before the opera, or of the unearthly justice of Don Giovanni's downfall and the Queen of Night's supernatural malignancy in the D minor—would entail an elaborate study of the essential unity of all Mozart's work. But

FRÉDÉRIC CHOPIN (1810–1849)

Drawing by Winterhalter

FELIX MENDELSSOHN (1809–1847)

Oil painting by Schadow, 1835

it is in the piano concertos that the essence of everything Mozartian is distilled and presented with the most subtle perfection of form.

The passionate drama of the D minor and C minor (K.491) concertos not only complements the tragic drama of the chamber and orchestral works in the minor mode ; it also foreshadows the nineteenth-century concerto idea of the heroic soloist opposed by the orchestral mass which he eventually dominates, and thus symbolises the later belief in the artist as an isolated individual struggling against, suffering for and eventually dominating the vast inarticulate mass. The last two concertos, the B flat (K.595) for piano, and the clarinet concerto (K.622), both belong to Mozart's shadowed musical autumn, the brief period of resignation where, with his hopes finally crushed, he said his farewell in music of unalloyed beauty, at times almost unbearable in its painful sense of loss.

THE OPERAS

In childhood Mozart had taken to music as to his natural element. At the age of twenty he already showed a complete grasp of the potentialities of symphonic form (including the special requirements of the solo concerto). Confronted at twenty-four with the already antiquated style of the libretto for *Idomeneo*, he acted with determination and sound judgment to reduce its sententious verbosity to manageable proportions. He could not transform a bad libretto into a good one, but he did turn an unpractical one into a piece which is still viable in the theatre.

Mozart was not given to theorising about music in general, or opera in particular. As we know from his letters to his father, when he was working on *Idomeneo* and *Die Entführung*, he held decided views about operatic composition, but he had arrived at these views intuitively rather than by any process of reasoning. They were, moreover, the views of a musician who conceived drama entirely in terms of music. In contrast to Gluck, he regarded the words of a libretto as the servants, not the masters, of the composer. Yet such was his dramatic genius that he never failed in his major operas to give the most powerful imaginable expression to the words. He achieved, indeed, that perfect equilibrium between music and drama which has always been the aim of thoughtful operatic composers but so few have been able to attain.

It has been said that Mozart, unlike Purcell, was fortunate in the moment of his birth, which fell at a time when all the material was at hand for a musician of genius to fashion into a new and original style. So far as symphony, concerto, and chamber music are concerned, this may be true enough ; but in opera Mozart laboured under considerable handicaps. There existed in the eighteenth century no genuine tragic drama. Schiller, three years younger than Mozart, produced his first important tragedy, *Don Carlos*, in 1787, the year of *Don Giovanni*, and did not fully mature as a tragic poet until the end of the century. It is interesting to speculate what Mozart's reaction to Schiller's dramas might have been, had he been given a normal span of life. As it was, his only outlets for serious dramatic music were in *Idomeneo*, a hybrid of *opera seria* and *tragédie-lyrique* ; certain scenes in the Italian comedies, particularly in *Don Giovanni* ; and *The Magic Flute*, where by some miracle of alchemy Mozart transmuted Schickaneder's leaden libretto into gold. There was also *La Clemenza di Tito*, which is only a tragedy in the sense that Mozart should have had to waste precious weeks in his last year upon setting Metastasio's libretto and so producing the last specimen of the already out-of-date " dynastic " opera for the glorification of his unappreciative Emperor.

" IDOMENEO "

How much Mozart might have achieved in tragedy may be deduced from *Idomeneo*, where he gives musical life to his librettist Varesco's card-board figures. The pathos of Ilia and, still more, the jealous fury of Elettra are wonderfully depicted ; and it is one of the good points of the story that it involves these two well-contrasted feminine types, who are the mainstay of so much opera in the nineteenth century, culminating in the splendid conflict of Aida and Amneris. In her first aria, *Padre, germani, addio !*, Ilia gives expression to exactly the same emotional conflict between love and patriotism as Aida does in *Ritorna vincitor !* Idomeneo, too, comes to life as a genuinely tragic figure, for all the absurdity of his predicament. And nothing shows more clearly Mozart's instinctive grasp of operatic principles than the quartet in which the central dramatic crisis is summed up.

It was unusual, if not quite unprecedented, for the singers in *opera seria* to join in a concerted piece, and the tenor who sang the part of Idomeneo tried to persuade Mozart to replace the quartet with an aria (for himself, needless to say). But what is so remarkable is not the mere originality of the proceeding, but the dramatic power of the quartet, which makes it a landmark in operatic history. Here for the first time are four characters giving expression each to his or her own emotional reaction to the dramatic situation, in music that is distinctly individualised in each part yet entirely homogeneous as a composition.

Mozart naturally benefited by Gluck's reforms, though Gluck's influence is only indirect in those of Mozart's operas which we know best. The

Italian essays of his boyhood may be disregarded as mere exercises in an outmoded style. For *Idomeneo* (1781) Mozart obviously took Gluck as his model. But even at the age of twenty-four he showed a remarkable independence and a mastery of symphonic resources, which he used to build up his climaxes in a manner quite beyond the capacity of the older composer's comparatively slender musical technique. His resourcefulness, which included a nice appreciation of the use of contrasts between forceful diatonic harmonies and a chromaticism expressive of suffering, enabled him to depict the jealous fury of the thwarted Elettra with a truthfulness and power far beyond Gluck's imagination.

THE ITALIAN COMEDIES

Nevertheless, daring and original as was much of *Idomeneo*, it was to comic opera that Mozart made his greatest contribution. In *Le Nozze di Figaro* (" The Marriage of Figaro ") (1786), *Don Giovanni* (1787), and *Così fan tutte* (" Women are all the same ") (1790), ably assisted by his librettist, Lorenzo da Ponte, he raised the conventional farce of Italian *opera buffa* to the level of high and subtle comedy, in which laughter may be dissolved in tears. In his creation of character Mozart rises to the level of Shakespeare. His characters are no longer the types derived from the old *commedia dell' arte* who persist in the operas of his contemporaries ; they are individuals conceived in the round, and cannot be mistaken one for another. Susanna and Zerlina were designed for the same type of voice ; Figaro and Leporello actually for the same singer. Yet each is a distinct individual whose music is an inseparable, indeed the vital, part of his or her personality. Susanna and Figaro are portrayed at the very rise of the curtain as witty and worldly-wise—the lady's maid and the " gentleman's gentleman ". Zerlina and Leporello are less sophisticated, humorous rather than witty, peasant-types and, especially Leporello, coarser in grain.

Even the minor characters have a life of their own ; they are as carefully drawn as the principals, and contribute their full share to the drama. Basilio, Antonio the gardener, and, tiniest part of all, little Barbarina in *Figaro* are excellent examples. Of all Mozart's characters only Don Ottavio is a failure, a lay-figure from *opera seria*, whose lack of personality is thrown into relief by the immense vitality of all the rest, from Don Giovanni, Elvira, and Anna down to the surly Masetto and the dignified and ultimately awe-inspiring Commendatore.

Così fan tutte presents a rather different type of comedy, completely artificial and unreal, at times even parodying the conventions both of comic and tragic opera. Yet within its artificial conventions are presented a set of perfectly drawn human characters ; and though we cannot—indeed, are never required to—believe in their actions, we do believe in and are moved by the emotions that actuate them. Here Mozart's music attains the zenith of delicate and subtle wit, even as *Don Giovanni* manifests his immense dramatic power and *Figaro* his command of comic force.

THE MOZARTIAN FINALE

Mozart's greatest contribution to the development of opera was unquestionably his enlargement of the part played by the concerted ensembles. The proportion of duets, trios, and so on in his comic operas is much greater than in the operas of his contemporaries, and he developed the concerted finale to immense symphonic proportions with a skill that has never been equalled. It is here that his mastery of musical characterisation is most evident. In these elaborate compositions each character retains his dramatic individuality by virtue of the distinctive music he has to sing ; and even when the same melody is passed from voice to voice it is nearly always given some twist which fits it to the particular personality of the singer. Only in the final *tutti*, where all sing together, is there a relaxation of this dramatic and musical tension between the characters.

The dynamic character of the *opera buffa* finale has already been noted. In the second act of *Le Nozze di Figaro*, da Ponte provided Mozart with an exceptionally well-constructed example of the form, beginning with Susanna's unexpected entrance from the cabinet where the Count and Countess believe Cherubino to be hiding, through the successive entries of Figaro and the gardener, each bringing his own entanglements to the complex situation, and culminating in Marcellina's arrival with her two "witnesses". Mozart brought all his skill as a symphonic composer and his genius for musical characterisation to the creation of this supreme masterpiece of high comedy in music. Nothing remotely like it had ever been achieved before in the farcical *opera buffa* of his predecessors and contemporaries, whose finales rarely contained music of any real interest, but consisted of noisy clichés and opportunities for the broadest comedy.

RECITATIVE AND ARIA

Though he retained the convention of *recitativo secco*, an admirable vehicle for the quick exchanges of Italian comedy, for the dialogue, Mozart broke some other operatic " rules ", more from dramatic instinct than on principle. Even in *Idomeneo* the characters do not always leave the stage at the end of their arias ; in the comedies, where a relaxation of strict etiquette was more natural, they never do so unless the dramatic situation demands it. More important, though perhaps less obvious, is the new relationship which Mozart established between voice and orchestra in the aria. Here again his experience as a symphonic composer, coupled with the natural bias of a German towards instrumental music, influenced his operatic practice and enabled him to achieve a musical texture of unprecedented beauty and richness, as well as a perfect equipoise between voices and orchestra. We are inclined to think of Mozart's operas as the repositories of the finest examples of vocal melody. So, indeed, they are. But their abiding musical interest—the cause of their survival in the theatre when the operas of Mozart's contemporaries, hardly less rich in similar vocal melody, are forgotten—rests upon the fascinating interplay of voice and instruments.

VOICE AND ORCHESTRA

Sometimes the melodic interest of an aria is actually found to be not in the voice-part, but in the orchestral "accompaniment". Susanna's aria in the second act of Figaro, *Venite, inginocchiatevi*, is a good example. In the middle of this aria the orchestra takes over the melodic burden of the piece entirely, while the voice supplies what is in effect an obbligato consisting of little phrases which reflect with absolute accuracy the normal inflections of the Italian words, as in a recitative. Here Mozart approaches very closely to the ideal of later German composers, anticipating Wagner's method of setting words in an orchestral texture which is all-important, instead of applying, in the Italian manner, a suitable accompaniment to a vocal melody.

Moreover, even when the vocal part is paramount, Mozart's arias frequently make a radical departure not merely from the *da capo* convention (which, as we have seen, had already been abandoned by many composers) but also in their freedom from the old melodic formalities. The melody tends to proceed in one unbroken line without any repetitions even of individual musical phrases. Pamina's sorrow-laden G minor aria *Ach ! Ich fühl's* in *The Magic Flute* is the latest and most striking example of this new development. Here the music reflects perfectly the emotion of the words, flowering at moments of special poignancy into an expressive coloratura far removed from the type of ostentatious floridity inserted merely to show off the singer's voice.

Every now and again he also broke with the convention of the formal close, as in Guglielmo's aria *Non siate ritrosi* in *Così fan tutte*, which simply breaks off in a volley of laughter when the two girls, to whom he is pointing out the beauty of his personal appearance, indignantly flounce out of the room. So the aria has no ending, but proceeds straight into the subsequent recitative, even as the *Idomeneo* and *Don Giovanni* overtures lead straight into the opening scenes of the operas. In this, as in the poetic (as distinct from the thematic) relationship he established between his overtures and the subsequent action of the operas, Mozart was following and improving upon Gluck's example. On two occasions, in the overtures to *Così fan tutte* and *The Magic Flute*, he also quotes salient motto-themes which appear in the course of the opera, but without utilising these motto-themes in conjunction with the main material of the overtures or developing them in any way. He was far from turning the overture into a pot-pourri of melodies from the opera, perceiving that the proper function of the overture is to establish the right mood for what is to follow, not to anticipate it. Beethoven appreciated the point when he removed his magnificent symphonic poem, "Leonora No. 3", from the score of his opera and substituted the simple *Fidelio* overture.

THE SYMPHONIC ELEMENT

It is the symphonic character of Mozart's operas that sets them above the productions of his contemporaries. Paisiello and Cimarosa were equally capable of writing melodies, but they had neither his dramatic imagination nor his ability to invent melody that illuminates character, *e.g.*, the melody allotted to Basilio when he excuses himself to the Count for his indiscreet remarks about the page (*Ah, del paggio*). Mozart's operas survive, while those of his contemporaries are forgotten, by virtue of their musical construction and texture. He applied to opera his mastery of symphonic form, which means not a rigid structure built upon two themes, but the ability to work out an interesting musical drama based upon the conflict of tonalities. Even though these tonalities must be embodied in themes which themselves have some intrinsic interest, it is Mozart's unfailing invention of new turns of harmony, of fresh ways of handling often stereotyped material, that gives life to his symphonic music. So too the tonal structure of his operas, each of which is "in" this or that key almost as strictly as any symphony, contributes enormously to their abiding vitality.

MOZART'S GERMAN OPERAS

Besides raising Italian *opera buffa* to the level of high comedy, Mozart may be said to have created German opera. For he did more than lay the foundations on which later generations of German composers were to build.

He had himself little enough in the way of foundation for his structure. After an aspiring start at Hamburg under Keiser's régime, German opera sank to a low level. It was hardly more than a coarse entertainment for a booth in a country fair. Yet in his last year Mozart composed an opera which contains all the typical characteristics of German art—the fantasy of fairyland, the romanticism, the broad humour, and the high moral purpose. Beethoven, Weber, Wagner, and Richard Strauss were to use these ingredients in varying proportions. Sometimes one or the other of them is omitted, but together they remain the basic elements of German opera.

Apart from *Bastien und Bastienne*, composed at the age of twelve and closely modelled on Rousseau's *Le Devin du Village*, Mozart wrote two German operas in *Singspiel* form, that is, with spoken dialogue—*Die Entführung aus dem Serail* (" The Rescue from the Seraglio ") in 1782, just after his arrival in Vienna as a free man, and *The Magic Flute* in 1791, shortly before his death. *Die Entführung* is a curious hotch-potch of styles, with an *opera seria* heroine, who sings a tremendous aria with obbligato instrumental accompaniment in the style of a concerto-movement ; a pair of comic servants from *opera buffa* ; and a comic bass whose humour is most nearly German. These disparate styles are successfully combined into a sublime masterpiece, if not into a consistent drama, in *The Magic Flute*, which started life as a fairy pantomime and ended by presenting, with comic interludes, the ultimate problems of human life and love and death in the form of an allegory derived from the ritual of the Freemasons. *The Magic Flute* is the first truly German opera, a synthesis of the Italian serious opera (with elements derived from Gluck) with a new German style, which appears both in the traditional popular humour of Papageno and in the solemn ritual scenes, whose music often owes its nobility to Mozart's study of J. S. Bach.

MOZART'S CONTEMPORARIES

Among Mozart's contemporaries there were numerous opera composers who were far more successful with the public in Vienna and elsewhere, precisely because they did not complicate their operas with the subtleties of characterisation and orchestral ingenuity that delighted Mozart. There are plenty of individual passages in the operas of Domenico Cimarosa (1749–1801), of Giovanni Paisiello (1740–1816), of Antonio Salieri (1750–1825), of Giuseppe Sarti (1729–1802), and the Spaniard, Martín y Soler (1754–1806), which might pass for, and even be rated as good as, Mozart. But when we hear a whole opera, or even a whole act, by one of them, we soon become aware of a poverty of invention, a thinness of texture, and a lack of individuality in the characters, who remain merely stock musical types. There was plenty of good craftsmanship and of delightful music, but no genius, and insufficient dramatic power to give the operas lasting life.

MOZARTIAN TIMES IN ENGLAND

Though Mozart never returned to England after his visit as a child prodigy, he frequently thought of doing so, and as late as 1787 was seriously contemplating settling in this country. He had friends here, such as the singer Nancy Storace (the original Susanna in *Figaro*), to whom he was greatly attracted, and the tenor Michael Kelly ; in Italy he had struck up a close personal friendship with the gifted Thomas Linley, junior (1756–78), who was drowned in a boating accident at the age of twenty-two. Linley collaborated with his father, the elder Thomas Linley (1733–95), in writing incidental music for *The Duenna* by Sheridan, who had become the elder composer's son-in-law. The well-known song *Here's to the Maiden* comes from the elder Linley's contribution to *School for Scandal*. Two other English musicans were pupils of Mozart : Nancy Storace's brother Stephen (1763–96) and Thomas Attwood (1765–1838), who was to write anthems for the coronation of three British sovereigns. Storace's operas *No Song, No Supper* and *The Pirates* are superior examples of the current type of English musical entertainment. Though Attwood is now hardly known except for a little church music, he is of particular interest in having been, apparently, the first English composer to write what we may think of as modern songs—that is, with fully written out piano accompaniments, instead of a mere bass-line, figured or unfigured, from which the player had himself to fill in the harmonies. Attwood had doubtless been stimulated by the examples of Haydn, who twice visited London, and whose works include twelve English " canzonets " (a common term of the period for songs not drawn from stage works). Among these the over-popularity of *My Mother bids me bind my hair* hardly compensates for the neglect of such a superior specimen as *The Spirit's Song*.

The piano was everywhere gradually replacing the harpsichord. The harp was becoming a popular drawing-room instrument, especially for accompanying songs. The " German flute " (that is, the ordinary side-blown flute, as distinct from the " English flute " or recorder) had become a much-favoured instrument by the end of the eighteenth century. The modern orchestra was becoming established and standardised, so that London provided Haydn with about sixty players, a force larger than he had ever had before. But forces a good deal larger than this had already been summoned for the Handel Commemoration Festivals which were given in Westminster Abbey from 1784. The orchestra then included ninety-five violins and (note the proportion) twenty-six oboes and twenty-six bassoons. The English type of massed performance had in fact begun—a type of performance which much impressed such illustrious visitors as Haydn and, later, Berlioz. From this period also dates the very idea of a " festival " of music, the very word originating in English and later spreading else-where. The Three Choirs Festival, based on the choral forces of Worcester, Gloucester, and Hereford Cathedrals, dates from at least 1724, and later in the century became especially associated with Handel's oratorios.

Many long-lived popular songs had their origin in the early eighteenth century—among them *The Vicar of Bray*, *The British Grenadiers*, *Down Among the Dead Men*, and *The Roast Beef of Old England*. The last named is by Richard Leveridge, a composer and noted singer whose long life (*c.* 1670–1758) spanned the era of both Purcell and Handel. Another successful composer of popular songs was Henry Carey (*c.* 1687–1743) who wrote the words of *Sally in our Alley*, and also its original tune, although the tune to which these words became popular is by another (and unknown) hand.

Convivial male gatherings, where solo-and-refrain songs like *Down among the dead men* (celebrating both liquor and patriotism) would have been welcomed, also provided a market for sociable part-songs of which the " glee " is a characteristic English form—usually for three or four male voices. The glee chiefly flourished in the late eighteenth and early nineteenth centuries, and a notable glee-composer was Samuel Webbe (1740–1816). It was common for convivial songs to make allusions to Bacchus and other propitious figures of classical mythology, and one of them managed to combine economically the notion of a Greek poet with that of a Christian saint :

> To Anacreon in heaven, as he sat in full glee,
> A few sons of harmony made a petition
> That he their inspirer and patron would be,
> When this answer came down from that jolly old Grecian. . . .

The probable composer of the tune to these words was John Stafford Smith (1750–1836) ; and it was this tune which, with other words fitted in America in 1814, became one of the best known of the world's songs, *The Star-Spangled Banner*. It was not, incidentally, declared the official anthem of the United States until 1931.

XII

BEETHOVEN

IN the nineteenth century, Ludwig van Beethoven (1770–1827) was
normally regarded as the revolutionary who shattered the world of
courtly restraint in which, it was thought, Haydn and Mozart had lived
at ease. Modern critics are more inclined to see everything that Beethoven
did as the work of a traditionalist who did not simply follow precedents,
but expanded the tradition in which he took his place.

The man Beethoven was as intransigent as Mozart ; he felt that he was
set by his genius above his fellows, and he had none of Mozart's social sense.
The unamiable characteristics of a young man driven by relentless genius
and incapable of social compromise were intensified by the tragedy of his
deafness and the misery of isolation and ill-health. Even his consistency
was a largely musical consistency. For all his parade of republican principles,
he was ready to accept court employment if it were offered ; and despite
his high moral protestations he was prepared to sell his work to several
publishers at once. The intense sensibility of the music he wrote seems to
have been coupled with an almost total incapacity to divine the feelings of
others.

The riddle of Beethoven's personality and the legends that sprang up
about him during his lifetime all point to the special qualities of his music.
Despite the fact that music can be great only as music—not as an expression
of philosophy or as ethics—writers have more often attempted to discuss
his works in terms of extra-musical meaning than to consider precisely
what he did and where his greatness lies. But what makes Beethoven so
supremely popular a composer is that his music embodies something of
universal human experience, and his triumph (for he is always ultimately
triumphant) is the final hope of men.

THE ROAD TO VIENNA

Ludwig van Beethoven was born at Bonn, where his father was a tenor
singer in the Archbishop Elector's court. The family originally came from
Antwerp, and the composer's grandfather had joined the Electoral musicians

in 1733, eventually rising to the post of *Kapellmeister*. The tenor Beethoven, an ill-tempered drunkard, decided that his musically gifted son should be, like Mozart, an infant prodigy. He bullied him through a strict course of training as a pianist and violinist that did not produce anything so phenomenal as another Mozart, although young Ludwig's first published music appeared in 1783 and was given out by his father to be the work of a child of ten. Prodigy or not, from the age of eleven the child occasionally deputised for the court organist, Neefe, who gave him the first constructive teaching he received and set him to play *The Well-Tempered Clavier*, the work upon which his later success as a piano virtuoso was founded. Young Beethoven became deputy harpsichord player to the court theatre in 1783, was officially appointed deputy court organist in the following year, and subsequently played the viola in the theatre orchestra.

His compositions of this period, all of which precede the piano trios published as Opus 1 in 1795, have none of the finesse that marks Mozart's earliest productions. But a virtuoso pianist of those days was expected to extemporise, and it was Beethoven's power of extemporisation that aroused Mozart's interest when the boy first visited Vienna in 1787. " He'll make a great noise in the world some ", day was Mozart's comment—a considerable compliment from one whose attitude to possible rivals was rarely cordial.

Beethoven's brief meeting with Haydn, as the old master made his way to London in 1791, led him to Vienna when Haydn returned, to study at the fountain-head of what was then modern music. The elderly Haydn, however, made a poor teacher of elementary musical grammar, which was what Beethoven sought. But he seems to have treated the young man with friendliness and, despite his inadequacy as a teacher, charged him a ludicrously small fee and introduced him into Esterház society. Beethoven's crude self-assurance seems not to have disturbed their relationship, and though Haydn's advice about the publication of the op. 1 trios displeased the young man—Haydn tried to persuade him to withhold the most original of the works—Beethoven revered his personality and genius.

A second journey to Vienna was made with the help of his patron the Elector, and his friendships amongst the nobility of the Electorate won him a position in Viennese musical life which persuaded him to settle there. The Viennese aristocracy took him to their hearts despite his rudeness, quickness of temper, and refusal to concede their social superiority. Where Mozart's personality, utterly concentrated on music, had no effect, Beethoven's enormous vitality, impressive appearance, and air of complete self-confidence won the day, and the friends he made were for life. Despite much that reads unpleasantly in his social behaviour, his personality contained something irresistible.

LIFE IN VIENNA

Beethoven originally made his name as a pianist. The neat, crisp style of Mozart, a pianist who grew up at the harpsichord, did not exhaust the possibilities of the piano, as the works of, for instance, Muzio Clementi showed. Clementi (1752–1832) explored the dynamic resources of the instrument, exploiting its powers of *crescendo* and *diminuendo* and its sustaining qualities more freely than Mozart ; his influence upon Beethoven can be seen in the singing tone at which Beethoven always aimed, and in matters of instrumental lay-out. To Beethoven he was anything but a negligible composer. Beethoven's " Pathetic " sonata, op. 13, is directly based upon the sonata op. 34, No. 2 which Clementi had composed in 1788, ten years before Beethoven's work. This contains a sombre, dotted-note introduction to the dramatic first movement, and repeats the introduction, as Beethoven does at the beginning of the recapitulation. Clementi, however, never achieved either the long sustained cantabile tone that Beethoven demanded, or the younger composer's range of semi-orchestral effects.

Because he was accepted as a virtuoso, Beethoven never lacked an audience or the opportunity to publish his works. He was, in fact, the first composer to make an adequate income from publication. In spite of the usual criticisms aimed at highly original work, Beethoven's fame, as the number of contemporary stories about him shows, spread rapidly. It was only his unreadiness either to give time to the management of his affairs or to trust anyone else to manage them for him that prevented him from living comfortably, and the notorious squalor of his lodgings coincided with the time of his greatest financial success.

From 1794 on and off until 1806 Beethoven lived in the house of Prince Lichnowsky, leaving his lodgings when he refused with physical violence the Prince's suggestion that he should play to officers of Napoleon's occupying army. Despite his detestation of Napoleon, he was almost tempted in 1808 to accept the Court Kapellmeistership of the puppet kingdom which the French had created in Westphalia. It was the promise of an annual subsidy from four aristocratic friends that dissuaded him, though the deaths of two of his patrons and the depreciation of Austrian currency through the war made the offer less valuable than it appeared.

His popularity continued to grow until in 1814 it reached a peak from which it never declined. As his later music became more complex, his earlier works became more widely known and enhanced his reputation.

THE FIRST PERIOD

Commentators often divide the work of any creative artist into three periods. In the first he develops a personal style and wins an audience; in the second he addresses his audience with full authority; and in the third he works for his own satisfaction. Such a division is particularly applicable to Beethoven's work. The music of his early years, up to about 1800, is work of unbounded ambition, written by one who felt himself to be one of nature's overlords. "I'm not interested in your morality", he wrote to a friend. "Power is the morality of outstanding men, and it is mine, too." It was through music that he would gain and exercise power.

The music that to Beethoven most clearly represented contemporary preoccupations and offered a technical challenge was that of Mozart. Temperamentally, however, as his works soon began to show, Beethoven was closer to Haydn. He was no ironist, for issues appeared to him in black and white. The serious was never a laughing matter, and the comic was not an individual aspect of the sad. What Beethoven had to say demanded expansive utterance, not Mozartian compression. Nevertheless, the challenge of Mozartian harmony and form lies behind the piano trios of op. 1 and the early sonatas, even though the latter are dedicated to Haydn. Mozart, too, is recalled in the early septet for wind instruments and the quintet for piano and wind. It is not that Beethoven wanted to write like Mozart, but that he had to master everything external in Mozart's style.

Of the juvenile compositions, the first really important works are piano quartets composed when Beethoven was fifteen; they are typical of the composer in that he launched out into an almost unpractised form, for the boy can hardly have known Mozart's piano quartets of the 1780s. (His quartets later provided some material for the first and third of his piano sonatas.) Typical of Beethoven, too, is the discovery in these childish works of one of his greatest expressive innovations—the fact that a series of free modulations leading towards remote tonalities can be logically effective and moving, provided the listener's ear can relate them to the main tonality. His struggles with this new idea in the juvenilia enable him to use it with complete certainty in the works of op. 1 and op. 2.

The first two piano concertos (the so-called No. 1 belonging to 1797 and No. 2 to 1795, but revised in 1798) and the first symphony all came before the "Pathetic" sonata. By this time Beethoven was using Mozartian and Haydnesque forms in a completely personal manner. The concertos frame their first movements inside a *ritornello*, but use fewer themes than

Mozart's and develop these more extensively. The slow movement of the second concerto is the first of many in which Beethoven produces a broad *sostenuto* melody, broken by rests, which is sufficient material for the entire movement to elaborate. The first symphony declares his affinity with Haydn, not through its mastery of Haydn's forms but in its open, unhesitating declaration of emotions and plainspoken vitality of utterance. There is no question of Beethoven finding a way to convey his mind beneath the surface of politely social music. The first traditional rule of large-scale music, that the main tonality should be impressed upon the listener at the outset of a work, is completely ignored in a slow introduction that begins upon a dominant seventh chord leading away from the main key, C major—which appears only at the opening of the *Allegro con brio*. The two subjects are strongly contrasted, and there is no sign of Haydn's love of presenting two aspects of the same material or Mozart's way of presenting themes diversified within themselves. The minuet is a forerunner of the later scherzos, its harmony expansively dramatic ; the trio is enigmatically elusive. The finale is boisterously good-humoured ; the violins try repeatedly, with pretended faint-heartedness, to announce the main theme before they pluck up courage and dance away with it, and after the coda has said what appears to be the last word, a new march tune appears to dismiss the work.

The six string quartets of op. 18, composed between 1798 and 1800, show the same mastery over a much wider range of emotion. The first opens with an insignificant melodic tag in which it finds a whole world of expression. Here, too, Beethoven anticipates his latest idea of development as the drawing-out of germinal themes into powerfully impressive statements. The second movement, said to be based upon the closing scene of *Romeo and Juliet*, achieves great intensity and depth without straining the intimacy of its medium. The second quartet is graceful and friendly ; the fourth, in C minor, takes its point of departure from the throbbing, repeated quaver bass which Mozart had first used, and builds a moving lyrical movement over it.

The string quartet and the piano sonata were henceforward to be the vehicles of the composer's deepest and most personal utterances. Works for many players and singers proclaimed what he desired to tell the world ; works for the piano were his own deepest thought because he was a great pianist, and string quartets rank with them because of the special intimacy which they demand. He could use these early quartets and such sonatas as the " Pathetic " and the so-called " Moonlight ", with its sustained rapture and ultimate vehemence, to embody a music that was quintessentially his own. From this point onwards, if expression clashed with form, form must give way ; it was not in Beethoven's nature to struggle towards the balance of the two elements. If there was any struggle, it resulted in the discovery of a significant, expressive, formal innovation.

The third piano concerto, of 1800, departs from Mozartian precedents and announces all its material in a quasi-symphonic orchestral exposition before the solo instrument is heard. The main key, C minor, is lost during the treatment of the second subject, and the piano establishes its primacy by entering *fortissimo* in the tonic after the orchestral *ritornello*-exposition. The slow movement is in the distant key of E major, and Beethoven explains its presence in the work by demonstrating that E flat is the relative major of the tonic C minor, and therefore in evidence in a C minor sonata-form movement : E flat, on a piano, is also D sharp, the leading note of the E major scale, and it can therefore lead us into the remote key without difficulty. Therefore an E major episode in the C minor rondo finale becomes a completely logical enrichment. Beethoven's extensive tonality is planned over the work as a whole, not over its individual movements.

THE SKETCH BOOKS

Throughout his life, Beethoven noted down themes as they occurred to him, carrying pencil and paper for this purpose when he went out. Rough notes were later transferred to the sketch books in which he moulded them into the shapes he desired.

No other composer left a comparable account of his rough work. Mozart left notes of such things as the polyphonic development of the " Prague " symphony, but no body of work comparable to the struggles of Beethoven to produce exactly the themes he imagined from their first intimations. We cannot say that they show him to have worked more than his predecessors, but only that they show how he worked. Beethoven evolved his themes in such a way as to produce subject-matter that would be responsive to sonata-style development ; that is to say, themes that would be memorable in their first skeletal essential form and grow into their full significance as the movement develops them. Usually his finished themes are far less elaborate than the first outlines of them found in the sketches.

We see the genesis of Beethoven's greatest works in a special sort of thematic material rather than in richness of melody or powerful strokes of drama. Fiery, dramatic harmonies, compelling eloquence and effective orchestration rise from the theme itself. What the sketches aim at is usually some quality of rhythm coupled with a striking rise or fall in pitch, as though the conception were already in his head and had to be reached through moulding the rough material. Decoration and sensuous beauty were swept away, often with obvious reluctance, because a strong theme would develop its own elaborations and sensuous beauty as it grew. One of the melodies over which Beethoven worked most hard is that of the Funeral March in the *Eroica* symphony, and his final version is remarkably austere in comparison with the basic idea from which it was chiselled. In some sketches, like that of the slow movement of the fifth symphony, we even find spontaneity abandoned in favour of classic strength and gravity.

THE CRISIS

Beethoven first found cause to worry about his hearing in 1798 ; by 1800 he knew that he was becoming deaf and that further medical treatment was useless. The social success of a lionised virtuoso crumbled away at once ; for although he could play in public without betraying his secret, in conversation his deafness was becoming painfully obvious. Driven into neurotic introspection, for a time he isolated himself, unwilling to become an object of his friends' pity. At the village of Heiligenstadt, where he had taken refuge, he wrote to his brothers the almost incoherent letter which biographers have called the " Heiligenstadt Testament ". In it he explains his growing isolation, his sense of irretrievable defeat, the consequent harshness of his manner and his rejection of suicide as a solution for his problems because he feels himself to be possessed by a genius to which he is responsible. He must live, however unbearable life becomes, in order to write the music which his genius compels him to write.

The works of the " second period " which follow this tragic crisis were specially directed to the listener. His personal tragedy had given the composer a special insight into experience, and he had to declare this to the world with all the clarity that he could achieve. From the composer's determination to voice the message that had been entrusted to him arose the growth and eloquence of form, the expansion of the time-scale of sonata-form works, the instrumental largeness of the music that follows—for an orchestra large enough for Haydn's " London " symphonies and Mozart's final masterpieces could not do justice to Beethoven's *Eroica* or C minor symphonies.

In the " Heiligenstadt Testament ", Beethoven had begged for a " day of pure joy ", and it seems that such a day is enshrined in the second symphony, composed during his stay in the village. The reverent love of its introduction and the sense of ecstasy that gives its joy a special radiance are, perhaps, the fruits of his determination to fulfil his destiny in spite of hardship and tragedy. In the *Eroica*, composed a year later, Beethoven expounds one of his favourite texts—the power of the human will. The story of its dedication to Napoleon the democratic hero, cancelled when Napoleon became emperor, is well known. The careers of Lord Abercrombie and Nelson were also in the composer's mind, but martial heroism is only his symbol for the Hero who triumphs through the power of Will.

To say that the *Eroica* embodied Beethoven's experience as well as his thought about heroism is dangerous. No less a lover of the work than Berlioz, who wanted to expound the idea behind the work in terms of programme music, decided that the order of movements must have an actual narrative significance, and felt himself bound to explain away the fact that the Hero dies and is buried before the symphony is half over. But the Funeral March is an angrily rebellious statement about loss and suffering, whilst the scherzo that follows it leaps to a continuing action. The finale is a set of variations on a melody and its bass that Beethoven had used previously in the finale of his ballet *The Creatures of Prometheus*, where it celebrated the apotheosis of his hero, the bringer of freedom, as well as in a *Contredanse* composed in the same year (1801), and as the theme of his piano variations op. 35. A theme used so frequently and springing from so explicit a context must have had some special meaning for the composer, and it suggests that the Hero is, like Prometheus, a bringer of freedom and creative action. Beethoven exhausts the potentialities of the striding bass in a series of contrapuntal variations before the melody takes control and the two are worked out together. The climax comes in a final *poco andante* variation of soaring ecstasy. One other point about the composer's view of tonality is made plain by the symphony ; the anger and rebelliousness of the Funeral March leads to a consoling trio, the theme of which is no more than a statement of the notes of the common chord but which is, in its context, amongst the most sublimely consoling passages in music. The harmonic adventures of the March itself are startling, audacious, and suitably novel for so forceful a conception as the great lament to which they belong, but the trio simply states the eternal musical law as Beethoven saw it ; the law of nature is, as it were, all the consolation there need be.

BEETHOVEN AND THE WORLD OF IDEAS

Whatever the inspiration offered by Napoleon, Nelson, and Abercrombie to the composer of the *Eroica*, the story of its destroyed dedication to Napoleon is well attested ; and it introduces the point at which we must consider Beethoven's attitude to the world. Despite his semi-literate letters, the composer was widely read in literature and the classics, interested in philosophy and fascinated by Eastern mysticism. To all his interests he brought enthusiasm rather than learning, for his education had been seized here and there as opportunity offered, and those extra-musical interests were important to him rather as stimulants to his imagination than as ends in themselves.

His attitude to society was unambiguous. Mozart had challenged it and been crushed, but Beethoven set out to conquer it. Most of his closest friends were aristocrats, perhaps because amongst the aristocracy he could find more men with the breadth of outlook needed to understand his work than he could in other classes. But from the start he was a fervent liberal in the historical, revolutionary sense of the word. Amongst his friends he was the leader, and those who refused his leadership were not his friends. He knew the value of his own gifts, and in his ideal society they would have given him a privileged position. His criticisms of the established order were made loudly and publicly ; that they never led him into trouble was probably thanks to his aristocratic friends.

This political attitude lies behind much of his work. *Egmont*, like *Fidelio*, is music dedicated to the idea of human freedom, and even the choral setting of Schiller's *Ode to Joy*, which had been present in his mind since 1798, though it eventually became the finale of the Choral Symphony, had a liberal political significance. The word " Joy " (*Freude*) in both the title and its stanzas replaced, as Beethoven knew well, the dangerous word " Freedom " (*Freiheit*). Even Goethe's greatness was marred, according to Beethoven, by his courtly deference to his social superiors, just as, according to Goethe, Beethoven's was flawed by his exceptional and gratuitous ill-manners towards the nobility. It is Goethe who tells the story of how at Teplitz, in 1812, the composer rammed his hat firmly on his head and strode forward as he saw the Emperor approach. To Beethoven, men were worth the quality of their gifts, therefore he himself was a superior being ; in his own world of human values he was king among men who should have been free.

The great human brotherhood has its divine father. There was little conventional piety in Beethoven, and in his Masses he worked out the implications of the text to his own way of thought without reference to the ecclesiastical tradition—though on his death-bed he received the Catholic last rites with gratitude. His indifference to conventional religion, however, did not exclude an intense belief in God as the Father and Companion of men. The " Joy " of human brotherhood in the ninth symphony is consummated in an ecstasy of worship.

In other matters he was a man of strict morality except in the composer's then traditional occupation of cheating publishers. His extreme censoriousness in matters of sexual behaviour points to psychological tensions which found their sole relief in his music. He never married, and his affairs of the heart seem to have been frustrated to a great extent by his own, doubtless unconscious, wishes.

To Beethoven, the artist had a special responsibility both in his work and in matters of conduct because of his duty to voice an attitude to life. He was never aware of the irony of Mozart's aristocratic operas, and could not forgive them for their " frivolity " and innocence of all explicit moral judgments. It was thus inevitable that he should adore *The Magic Flute* and dismiss the rest. As a composer he existed, he believed, to convey in music what he had learned from life.

THE MIDDLE PERIOD

The *Eroica* marked a turning point in the composer's development, both musically and as a man. After it, he no longer hid his growing deafness, but plunged again into professional and social life ; and he was able to perform in public intermittently until 1814. The huge scale of the *Eroica* is not always maintained, but in music greatness is not the same as physical size, and there is no " greater " music than the finale of the " Jupiter " symphony. To a musician a daring harmonic progress to remote keys can be as spiritually and intellectually satisfying as the long struggle of the *Eroica*'s first movement.

In the year after the *Eroica* symphony came the " Waldstein " (op. 53) and " Appassionata " (op. 57) piano sonatas. The former grows so vastly in the development of its first movement and its triumphant rondo finale that Beethoven eventually replaced its original slow movement (the *Andante Favori* in F) with twenty-eight bars of hushed, solemn introduction to the finale. The F major tonality essential to the structure remains, but it is a base for a wonderful expansion of tonalities that leaves the rondo dominating the whole of musical space and provides a rationale for all its excursions out of the main key. The " Appassionata " is abundantly lyrical, its second subject a great full-throated song which expands the form by its mere character ; and the challenging, tragic first movement paves the way for a slow movement in variation form that gives way to the whirlwind of the finale. Its activity is " creative ", not simply because the composer created it, but because it establishes and defines new musical relationships.

Beethoven returned to the piano sonata in 1809 with a group of works which often fall into only two movements ; the *Lebewohl* (" Farewell ") sonata, op. 81a, is the exception because its poetical idea—Departure, Absence, and Return—demands three movements, but the sonatas op. 78 and op. 79 telescope three into two contrasted and widely ranging movements. Op. 78, in F sharp major, belongs to the world of fantasy and rapture better known from the "Moonlight" sonata, whilst the "Farewell", with its motto theme in the first movements, is as heroic and large in stature as the "Waldstein" or "Appassionata". Two-movement form is, after the "Waldstein", an economy. The range and emotional content of two movements can say all that is to be said, and to separate them would require a slow movement that repeats the first or anticipates the second without offering anything essentially its own.

Chamber music, too, was a sporadic activity. The "Razumovsky" quartets, op. 59, composed in 1806, contained Russian themes in honour of the Russian ambassador who commissioned them—overtly in the first and second, by implication in the third. They are amongst the greatest of Beethoven's works, their far-reaching harmonies arising from a single expressive impulse, their lyrical freedom unhampered by their precision of form. Beethoven countered the incomprehension of some of his friends at a first hearing by declaring that they were written for the future. The first is lordly and expansive, the second full of wonder and awe, set entirely in E minor and major, as though concentrating upon a single aspect of life's mystery. The third opens with a misty, indeterminate introduction which somehow generates an *Allegro* of magnificent energy, and its finale is a fugue of splendid fire and pace. The three works do for chamber music what the *Eroica* and C minor symphonies do for the symphony—they define a seriousness and intensity of aim which has coloured the attitude of almost all later composers to quartet form. The "Harp" quartet, op. 74, of 1809, which takes its name from the *pizzicato* passages of the first movement, is graciously lyrical but unadventurous. The F minor quartet, op. 95, of the following year, rough yet shot with tenderness, is more characteristic ; it ranges over a wide experience of life to dismiss its problems in a gay finale, enigmatic in its rejection of everything that has gone before.

The later piano concertos, like the third, completely telescope *ritornello* and exposition. The fourth, however, launches the soloist on its main theme at the outset. If there is no formal lead-up to his entry, and the work is gentle, his domination has to be established in this way. The "Emperor" concerto has a *ritornello*-exposition similar to the third, but the pianist introduces it with a magnificent flourish across orchestral chords. The violin concerto has a first movement whose exposition seems to be self-sufficiently symphonic until it is mysteriously subdued to allow the soloist's entry.

Like the concertos, the middle-period symphonies reflect their composer's invincibly buoyant optimism in the face of adversity. The most famous, and perhaps the most compelling, is the fifth in C minor, which leads through the grimmest of Beethoven's tragedies to the most tumultuous of his triumphs, for which the normal orchestra needs the extra weight and solemnity of trombones. Its only exordium is "the knock of Fate at the door", and it plunges into a main theme of which the knock itself is the germ, but which grows and develops additional contours and meanings as the movement progresses. The slow movement is restrained and statuesque, though it rises like a hymn of hope and is cast down and perpetually thwarted. The scherzo has a power equivalent to that of the first movement; it is a nightmare, from which the music is released by the long transition of drum-taps beating for the announcement of the finale's hymn of triumph. This is again interrupted by the spectral menace of the scherzo, but terror and tragedy have been overcome. Beethoven may have been conscious of the special musical unity of these four movements. The rhythm of Fate's knock provides the staple material of the scherzo, just as it combines with the triad of C minor to make the melodic substance of the first movement. The C minor triad appears again as the ghostly arpeggio which haunts the scherzo, and the main theme of the finale is based upon a C major triad. For technical as well as spiritual reasons, the C minor symphony is the work to which the nineteenth century owed most.

The unity of the seventh symphony, which marks in its relentless vigour and determination the vindication of the composer's decision to face the world with courage, is achieved by the extended slow introduction, in which the music lays down the pattern of keys through which the work is to travel. Its second movement, marked *Allegretto*, is march-like in rhythm but impressively solemn in character, and is cast in a combination of rondo with variation form; perhaps no other single movement has had such a wide and overt influence upon later composers.

Whilst the fourth, sixth, and eighth symphonies are overshadowed by the gigantic third, fifth, seventh, and ninth, they are not less splendid in drama and logic, although the dramatist tends to turn in them to relaxation. It is as though his aim in the lesser symphonies was simply to write beautiful music after the prophecies and violences of the odd-numbered works. The "Pastoral" provided a justification for the composers of programme music in the succeeding age, for whom the descriptive titles which Beethoven gave to the music carried more weight than his declaration that the symphony is "an expression of feeling rather than an illustration". The composer's delight in nature, another aspect of his longing for unity with God, needed expression in music as logical as the account of his spiritual struggles and triumphs in its predecessor. Even the openly picturesque storm is a movement of the most precise formal accuracy, framed within the apprehensive quaver figure which opens it, and which itself is derived from the dance-like theme of the countryfolks' merrymaking. The finale of the entirely gracious eighth symphony is an extended harmonic joke worthy of Haydn or Mozart, based upon the interruption of the F major main theme by an inexplicable C sharp which is forgotten until the coda, where it proves itself to be a much more rational D flat.

" FIDELIO "

There was one more musical form that Beethoven tackled in this period, in which he achieved only a qualified success—opera.   Although perpetually in search of a libretto to suit his taste, he was only once satisfied.   *Fidelio, or Conjugal Love* had as its text a German version of Bouilly's *Lénore, ou L'Amour Conjugal.*   The first version of Beethoven's opera, in three acts, was heard in Vienna late in 1805.   In the following year it was revised and reduced to two acts, though in this form it was perhaps even less successful, and further revision took place before the final version, which was not heard until 1814.   Beethoven wrote four overtures for this much altered work.   At the first production the " Leonore No. 2 " was played, in 1806 " Leonore No. 3 ".   The present *Fidelio* overture was played at the revival in 1814 and the " Leonore No. 1 " was written for a performance at Prague which never took place.

The third " Leonore " overture is such an outstanding masterpiece that many conductors feel that it cannot be omitted from a performance of the opera.   Unfortunately its triumphant ending is a bad introduction to the opening action, and Beethoven was undoubtedly right in replacing it by a less overwhelming prelude.   " Leonore No. 3 " is now often played as an entr'acte in the opera.

If *Fidelio* had a chequered career in the opera-house, this is less surprising than the character of the work itself, which needs some explanation.   There is at first no obvious connection between Beethoven and the light, at first only semi-musical, *opéra-comique* of France, but it was to this world that he turned for inspiration.   We will discuss the matter in the next chapter so as to keep it in its historical perspective.

THE SECOND TRAGEDY

The seventh and eighth symphonies were performed in 1812 ; in the following year came *Wellington's Victory, or the Battle of Vittoria,* a piece of blatant popular music in which the English army is represented by *Rule, Britannia* and the French by *Malbrouck s'en va-t-en guerre.*   Popular opposition to Napoleon made the work fantastically popular, and with the acclaim won by the final revision of *Fidelio* Beethoven reached the height of his success, artistic and financial.   In the next five years, however, his production all but completely dried up. The years 1816–22 brought five great piano sonatas and the overture *The Dedication of the House*, but little else, although 1817 saw the beginning of work on the ninth symphony and 1818 that on the *Missa Solemnis*.

In 1815 Beethoven's brother Karl died, leaving the composer the care of his nine-year-old son, a second Karl. Beethoven determined to interpret this trust in the widest terms, and, disapproving of his sister-in-law's moral character, contrived after a couple of lawsuits to win complete control over the boy. For a time he sent him away to school; but, tugged to and fro between his uncle and his mother, the boy failed to settle there and returned to his uncle, to be subjected to a terrifying devotion and domination. Biographers have on the whole been unfair to Karl, who was only twenty-one when his uncle died and was subjected to the possessive love with which the composer tried to compensate for his inescapable loneliness. To win his uncle's favour, Karl had to abuse his mother, insult the servants, and assume an intensity of devotion one cannot believe a child in those circumstances to have been capable of possessing. Beethoven's demands, his censoriousness, his invincible belief in his own rectitude and wisdom in determining the boy's life, made existence impossible for them both ; and their life together drove Karl to attempt suicide in 1826. It also embittered and finally killed his uncle, for it was his rush to the injured Karl that brought on the pneumonia which led to his death in March 1827. Between 1816 and 1818, the composer was too occupied in winning his nephew to be able to work ; the worries and anxieties of trying to form an unsuitable character in the mould he thought proper wore him out ; worries and anxieties, not the least of which rose from his determination to preserve his savings as a legacy for Karl, added to his normal discomforts.

But the works Beethoven composed during this time are not a direct reflection of this destructive relationship ; the experiences of the last ten years of Beethoven's life added their own depth to his later works, and it may well be that bitter human disappointment did much to turn his attention to the religious themes overtly expressed in the Mass in D (*Missa Solemnis*) and implicit in the ninth symphony. But there is no music about Karl, about thwarted love, possessiveness, and loss ; they are only part of the life to which Beethoven voiced an attitude of heroic determination, hope, and reconciliation.

THE LAST PERIOD

The silence of the struggle for Karl was brought to an end with the production of the " Hammerklavier " sonata (op. 106). Its title is simply a German name, which Beethoven apparently wished to popularise, for the piano, for both this work and its predecessor, composed two years before, were given the same name. Similarly, he used German instead of Italian directions for tempo and expression in these works. The two together mark a new development of Beethoven's style ; the conquering lyricism of his second period combines with a passionate attempt to marry the expressive qualities of the fugue—a different matter from Mozart's free polyphony—with sonata forms. There are those artists who, in struggling with their medium, find that the actual struggle for expression adds to the power and profundity of their work. Such was the case of the masterpieces of Beethoven's second period, and it applies no less aptly to the works of the third.

The enormous length and furious energy of the " Hammerklavier " sonata, its intellectual force and emotional ecstasy, are unique revelations of human greatness, coming from a world of feeling and thought too vast for many to endure. The op. 109 and op. 110 sonatas, which followed it, are relaxing, human, and lovable ; but it is the " Hammerklavier " which establishes Beethoven's mastery over a fugal sonata style. Its successors carry these achievements into the everyday world, while the new style enables the composer to return, in the final sonata, op. 111, to a theme he had sketched some twenty years before, and to build from it the last of his combative tragedy-and-triumph sonatas. The overture *The Dedication of the House*, which belongs to 1822, the same year, uses the new style with a mellow, humane wisdom.

The ninth symphony and the Mass in D, both of which had occupied much of the composer's time since 1817, appeared in 1823. The symphony has never ceased to disturb many musicians by its choral finale ; for though it was not the first symphony to demand voices, none of its predecessors has survived, and the sheer length of the finale, after three movements of great intellectual and emotional power, strains the sense of proportion. It is as well to remember, however, that like Mozart's "Jupiter", Beethoven's odd-numbered symphonies balance the intensity of their first movements with equal power in their last. German critics write with accuracy when they describe such works as " finale symphonies". Furthermore, the setting of Schiller's *Ode to Joy* with which the symphony closes was not Beethoven's first intention for the work but was, apparently, forced upon him by the emotional compulsions of the preceding movements.

The symphony opens with tremolo fifths, which imply neither tonality nor mode, and the descending, cataclysmic theme jerks through three tonalities before it settles in D minor. The movement is itself an act of creation, tragic and catastrophic, as though the composer were suggesting that any creation contains potential evil as well as good, terror as well as beauty. Scherzo and slow movement exchange their normal positions—

perhaps because the first movement is really more moderate in tempo than any of the composer's earlier openings—and Beethoven works with explosive energy and gaiety to a slow movement of intense reflectiveness. This is a set of variations on two themes, the second of which is in the mood of the " Pastoral " slow movement, as though the composer were dwelling upon the memory of past happiness. The opening struggle to gain the right tonality colours the slow movement, in that twice its modulations pass through D minor and recall the whole world of tragedy. The introduction to the finale takes the themes of the preceding movements one by one and dismisses each with savage outbursts of cacophony : the problems of human life can be solved only by the joy of human brotherhood, which Beethoven celebrates in a choral rondo that for all its splendour and ecstatic vision is essentially popular in melodic style.

The intensity of emotion, and Beethoven's determination to speak his mind clearly and explicitly in music, lead to the use of a main theme that is every man's music, and also, in the finale's introduction, to the recitative of cellos and double basses which anticipates the opening cry of the bass soloist. Instrumental recitative for Mozart was a means of dismissing emotions that were beyond expression. To Beethoven, in whose later sonatas it revealingly appears, it is a way of lifting up the music of instruments to a new sort of meaning, of preparing a definite, quasi-verbal statement.

The choral finale is music that defies singers by the demands it makes upon them, and the Mass in D is equally merciless, stretching voices beyond their natural limits and at the same time asking for a supreme fierceness and vigour of attack in regions beyond the normal.

Beethoven's earlier Mass in C, composed in 1807 for Prince Esterházy, had only slowly won popularity. Here Beethoven, intent on liturgical purposes, showed a strict concentration on the text rather than on the formal conventions followed by Haydn and Mozart. The first three and the last movements are in C, but each uses C as a starting point for different harmonic explorations, whilst the *Sanctus* and *Benedictus* are radiant C major movements ; the music of the opening *Kyrie* returns to conclude the work symmetrically in the *Dona nobis pacem*. The work's close-knit symbolism and dramatic energy are remarkable, but the later Mass overshadows them completely.

The *Missa Solemnis*, or Mass in D, intended for the enthronement of Beethoven's friend and pupil, the Archduke Rudolph, as Archbishop of Olmütz, despite its size followed liturgical custom in that each section of the rite is a single movement and that it includes a " Prelude " to be played during the Elevation. Beethoven returned to a close study of the text before he began the composition, and he approached it as a fervent believer in God who found in the words of the Mass a symbolism valid for his own beliefs rather than as a conventional Catholic. The work prays for and celebrates man's relation to a divine Father. In some matters Beethoven's attitude had changed considerably since 1807 ; in the earlier Mass, the words " And was incarnate " are a descent into misery ; in the second they are carried in on a flood of radiant major harmony. The *Dona nobis pacem* with its terror of drums and trumpets uses war to symbolise all the misery and pain of man's condition. In addition the Mass exemplifies Beethoven's preoccupation with fugue in his closing years. Conventionally, the *Gloria* and *Credo* of a Mass ended with fugues, and Beethoven always accepted conventions when they were meaningful to him. In the Mass in D, the huge fugues on the words " In the glory of God the Father " and " The life of the world to come " are his symbol of eternal life—not the ecstasy of contemplation we find in the *Benedictus*. To Beethoven, the one seems to be a human condition, a glorious consolation for deafness, disappointment, and loneliness ; the others represent an eternal life of creative action in which new and vital relationships are set up. Sensuous musical beauty has almost disappeared ; creative energy, directness of statement and power of meaning are all that matter.

THE LAST QUARTETS

If Karl Beethoven had been either completely submissive or completely hypocritical ; if he had been great enough to understand his uncle ; if he had not wanted to be a soldier and had passed his exams as his uncle wished ; if he had not made debts of which he was afraid to tell his loving tyrant ; if he had not attempted suicide—then the five quartets which close his uncle's work would perhaps appear to us as the bridge between all that he had previously done and another group of masterpieces, possibly mainly choral and predominantly contrapuntal. The whole of what we know as his third period might well appear, if he had lived longer, as a transition to the numerous works he was planning when he died. To write this does not imply that the five quartets are not great music, but only to suggest that their numerous difficulties might well have been resolved by their unwritten successors.

The choice of the string quartet medium for these works is easily understood. They are mainly polyphonic in character, to which the homogeneity of the string quartet is well suited. They are entirely intimate, and intimacy demands the union of minds rather than the domination of a soloist. Their principle is that of expansion and development from single germinal phrases, so that they fulfil the methods that Beethoven had been perfecting ever since the time of the *Eroica*. It has even been suggested that all the last three works are expansions of the four-note phrase that opens op. 132, the first of the works to be finished—a rise of a sixth preceded and followed by a rise of semitone. Certainly, most of the thematic material of the works includes the rising sixth or its inversion, a falling third.

Although no other medium than the string quartet is possible for these works—even the " Great Fugue " that was originally intended as the finale of the op. 130 quartet does not demand other instruments—they torture their instruments, as the Mass and the ninth symphony torture their singers, not because Beethoven misjudged his medium but because what he had to say stretched them almost beyond the reach of humanity.

The composer's studies for the Mass had led him to Palestrina and the counterpoint of old church music, so that the harmonic strangeness and poignancy of modal music (which makes a momentary appearance in the *Resurrexit* of the Mass) had a greater influence in these works. The second of the five movements of op. 132 is a " Convalescent's song of thanksgiving for his recovery, in the Dorian mode ". Beethoven's Dorian mode is not beyond dispute, and the modal hymn is framed in passages of normal tonality which link it with the other four movements of this work. The finale of the six-movement op. 130 is the " Great Fugue " which Beethoven subsequently replaced because of its length and difficulty (both of performing and understanding). The last quartet, a seven-movement work, has over its finale the title " The difficult resolution ", and its main theme is given the words, " Must it be ? It must be." The movements develop with enormous subtlety one from another.

The last quartets, in their expansion of the idea of development, underlie much of the music of the nineteenth century, *e.g.*, Liszt's treatment of the thematic material of his symphonic poems and Wagner's symphonic operatic processes. Their novelty, however, is a matter of outlook and content rather than of technique, and they are still to be understood only after study and concentrated attention.

BEETHOVEN, THE KEY TO THE FUTURE

A genius exhausts his own style, and those who set out from where he left off usually end by creating inferior copies of what he did ; for if it is true to say that the style is the man, it is equally true to say that the man evolves the style to express his own ideas, and that for creative purposes it dies with him. This is as true of Beethoven as of any other artist. All the nineteenth-century masters traced their descent from him, but none of them was at his best when he deliberately wrote in the mood of Beethoven.

However, Beethoven, like any other genius, opened paths into the future. He closed those along which he travelled, but his determination to make music the language of his attitude and faith was the real inspiration of the nineteenth-century composers, and his technique of thematic development and transmutation provided them with a technique. Furthermore, he had appealed to the millions, not only in the sentiments he voiced in such works as the ninth symphony, but in his expansion of forms and means. His work demanded larger orchestras, larger halls, and therefore larger audiences. It had left the church and the palace, it had left the small coteries of music lovers, and was addressed to the world. It led to the modern concert-hall, the mass audience and the virtuoso players and conductors who are the modern heroes of music.

Finally, and no less influentially, Beethoven was a composer who gave broad, lyrical melody an immense weight of meaning, and expanded the forms he used to make the meaning explicit. Even before he died, others, the greatest amongst them Schubert, had learned that freedom of melodic life had to be the governing principle of their music, rather than the dramatic architecture which had once been the determining factor in sonata form and all its offshoots.

XIII

GERMAN OPERA AND ITS FRENCH ORIGINS

THE French Revolution, and the wars that followed it, produced a social upheaval that powerfully affected human thought and activities in every sphere. The Revolution was not, however, a prime cause but rather a symptom—an exceptionally violent one, inflamed by economic causes and the intolerable oppression of an obstinate régime—of a movement that had been gathering impetus for half a century, and was by no means confined to France or to the world of politicians. This movement, called "Romantic", manifested itself in a great upsurge of humanitarian feeling.

As most great movements have trivial beginnings, so one of the first signs here was the play-acting of the French nobles disguised as shepherds and shepherdesses in the park at Versailles—whence all those pastoral comedies, among which Rousseau's *Le Devin du Village* is a landmark of importance in musical history, though not an important work of art. The movement went on to discover in the beauty and the terrors of Nature the widest possible sources of artistic inspiration. These had hitherto been, if not disregarded altogether, either regarded with aversion or taken for granted as a mere background to human activities.

Romanticism was not a new invention of the eighteenth-century philosophers. It is, indeed, one pole of the world of art, and has always existed. As we have seen, Gluck's reform was away from the domination of music in *opera seria* towards a more reasoned attention to the drama, so that, despite the apparent classicism of his operas, Gluck was moving in the direction of romanticism. For all that, *Armide* was the only one of his operas to which the term, in its ordinary meaning, could be rightly attached. And it is significant that *Armide* had a seventeenth-century libretto ; for opera in the seventeenth century had at least some of the characteristics of romanticism which reappear in the nineteenth century—one being a preoccupation with natural phenomena and their dramatic use as symbols.

It was Mozart who achieved a perfect equilibrium between the poles of classicism and romanticism, balancing his music on the hair-line between them. Classical in his handling of form, he is yet romantic in his imaginative power and passionate expression of feeling. In his mature operas the characters cease to be types of humanity and take on the realism of individual personalities, except where, in *The Magic Flute*, they are transformed further into symbols (not types) of human aspirations and weaknesses in an environment that is romantic in feeling, even while the structure remains classical.

Under the impulsion of political events, art swung strongly towards the romantic pole during the years immediately following Mozart's death. Beethoven put his genius at the service of humanitarian and libertarian ideals, and though in his symphonies (the ninth excepted) he continued to subordinate theme to form, his solitary opera *Fidelio* is the first great romantic opera in the full sense of the term.

GRÉTRY AND THE OPÉRA-COMIQUE

It is necessary at this point to retrace our steps and examine the development of *opéra-comique* during the latter half of the eighteenth century. For *opéra-comique* provided the necessary catalyst that changed the character of serious opera in the following century. The discreetly licentious *comédies à ariettes* of Favart, which have been compared with the art of François Boucher, made no claim to any musical importance. Their artificial world, peopled by pretty and ingenuous shepherdesses, was the object of the Encyclopaedists' attacks. Boucher's dimpled Venuses gave place to the more "natural" girls of Greuze, who were at once more sentimental in appearance and less overtly sensual. And, as a contemporary remarked, Greuze had a musical counterpart in André Ernest Grétry (1741–1813).

Grétry, who was born in what is now Belgium, was a theorist as well as a composer, and it may be that his theoretical writings surpass his actual achievements as a composer, since he lacked the power to put his ideas fully into practice. Although he sometimes echoes Gluck, he also anticipates Wagner. His pronouncements are unexceptionable, if sometimes naïve and superficial. Yet he clearly understood the basic principles of opera, and had he been endowed with sufficient force of character and subjected to a more thorough musical training to enlarge and perfect his technique, he might well be something more than a name in the histories of music and a link between the eighteenth and nineteenth centuries.

In Grétry's view vocal music was the highest form of art, and vocal music, to be good, must faithfully follow the accentuation of the words. In just declamation lay the whole secret, and the highest achievement of the composer was to transform declamation into melody. We are reminded of Lully modelling his style upon the speech of the actors of his day. To both might be applied the words Wagner wrote of Gluck : " In his music he took pains to speak correctly and intelligently." The core of Grétry's æsthetic philosophy is contained in the pronouncement :

Music is a mistake if, by its noisy orchestration, it prevents the words reaching the listener's ear in an intelligible form ; it is a mistake if it makes a vain display of technique ; it is a mistake if, in repeating words, it prolongs an emotional situation beyond reason ; it is a mistake if it does not give to each character in the drama the appropriate idiom ; it is again a mistake, if it serves to make a character shine above his station in the dramatic scheme ; it is finally a mistake when it is not so closely in accord with the poem that one hardly knows how to distinguish the composer's contribution.

As a composer Grétry had a quality that marked him out from his often more accomplished rivals, Philidor and Monsigny—the gift of poetic feeling. It may be slender in range and gentle in its expression, whether he is retelling the story of Beauty and the Beast in *Zémire et Azor* (1771) or depicting the faithful Blondel outside his royal master's prison in *Richard Cœur de Lion* (1784). It is often undeniably sentimental, like Greuze's simpering girls. But it is certainly not lacking in a charm which saves the comic scenes from lapsing into triviality and makes the pathos genuinely moving. Under Grétry's influence *opéra-comique* moved out of the realm of farce into that of comedy, even if not on to the high plane achieved by Mozart. Grétry's comedy is tenderer, with less bite in it.

When the Revolution came, Grétry was not the man to provide the heroic and epic pieces that the new régime required, though he conformed to republican ideology in *Denys le tyran* and *La Rosière Republicaine*. He had none the less created, notably in *Richard Cœur de Lion*, a type of *opéra-comique* that could serve the demand for romantic, historical opera, and whose range could be extended by more forceful composers beyond the narrow boundaries of Grétry's art.

DEFINITION OF "OPÉRA-COMIQUE"

Thus did *opéra-comique* attain those characteristics that will now be described. In the first place, it should be observed that *comédie* is a more inclusive word than our *comedy*. The *Comédie Française* is the French National Theatre, where Racine is played as well as Molière, and a *comédien* is an actor. So *opéra-comique* is not confined to the limits of comic opera, as we understand the term. Its limits are, indeed, difficult to mark precisely, because they are drawn by style and feeling rather than by dramatic form. It is therefore easier to describe what it is not than to frame a positive definition which will cover all examples. Thus one may say that, in contradistinction to grand opera, it is not heroic in character nor built on the scale suited to a large theatre. It is more modest in its use of chorus, orchestra, and ballet, while it normally, though not invariably, employs the spoken word rather than recitative to carry on the action. For the same reason, spectacle plays a comparatively small part in it ; and, just because its themes are not heroic, it inclines to realism, and its characters are usually ordinary people drawn life-size. That is about as far as one can go in definition of a *genre* which embraces, besides the operas of Auber and Boieldieu, Thomas's *Hamlet* and Gounod's *Faust* in its original version, *Carmen, Manon Lescaut* and *Louise, Pelléas et Mélisande* (which shows how little comedy need enter into it) and, though it bursts the bounds of form, *Fidelio.*

REVOLUTIONARY OPERA

During the revolutionary period, as before it, French opera maintained its customary individuality, its isolation from the cosmopolitan style. As usual, it owed much to foreign sources and was often written by foreign composers. Yet what it borrowed was absorbed into its system, and made to serve the main purpose of the French operatic ideal—the clear presentation of the drama. The influence of Gluck still persisted in the *Médée* of Luigi Cherubini (1760–1842), produced in 1797, and *Joseph* by Etienne Méhul (1763–1817), which treats the Biblical story with a broad and simple dignity that contrasts strongly with the inflated nobility of Spontini's *La Vestale* produced in the same year (1807).

The most characteristic product of the years immediately after the Revolution is a type of *opéra-comique* with a serious story involving a rescue from injustice in the nick of time, such as might have happened to many individuals during the upheavals of the French Revolution. These operas were usually topical rather than ideological, and attained a considerable popularity. German writers, with their passion for categories, have coined for them a term, *Rettungstücke* or "rescue-pieces". One of the most successful practitioners in the new style was Henri Berton, who found in its excitements a more sympathetic medium than the old *comédies mêlées d'ariettes*. His *Les Rigueurs du Cloître* (1790), which comprised an attack on the religious orders, is an early example of a "rescue-piece". Another example of the *genre*, *La Caverne* by Jean François Lesueur, was produced in 1793 during the worst excesses of the Reign of Terror. Others of importance are Pierre Gaveaux's *Léonore, ou l'Amour conjugal* (1798) and Cherubini's *Les Deux Journées* (1800), though the importance of the first-named rests solely upon its book having been adapted by Beethoven's librettist, Ferdinand Sonnleithner, for *Fidelio*, of which the first version was produced in 1805.

HECTOR BERLIOZ (1803–1869)

RICHARD WAGNER (1813–1883)

GIUSEPPE VERDI (1813–1901)

Les Deux Journées, or *The Water-carrier*, as it was known in both the English and German versions, exercised a direct influence on Beethoven's solitary opera. Cherubini's opera, in which there is a remarkable change from the classicism of his *Médée* three years previously to a more homely and more realistic *opéra-comique* style, embodies just those admirable sentiments about the ideals of loyalty and kindness to fellow human beings which found so deep a response in Beethoven's heart. The ballad-like songs in the tradition of Grétry's *Richard* and the choruses whose melodies sound like folk-tunes established precedents, if not for Beethoven, for Weber and for Wagner. Senta's ballad and Wolfram's "romance" *O Star of Eve* derive ultimately from such things as Blondel's song in *Richard* and Anton's *Un pauvre petit Savoyard*, with its refrain "Bon Français, Dieu te récompense, Un bienfait n'est jamais perdu", in *Les Deux Journées*. That refrain well indicates the rather smug moral tone of the librettos of Jean Bouilly, who wrote the books for *Léonore* and *Les Deux Journées*.

BEETHOVEN'S "FIDELIO"

Beethoven was concerned, however, with something more than amiable sentiments, and when he took over Bouilly's *Léonore* he transformed her into a heroic character larger than life-size—a symbol of all that is noblest in human loyalty and love. Such a theme could hardly be adequately treated in the idiom of *opéra-comique*, and although Beethoven opens his opera with an effort to present the lovers' quarrel of Marzellina and Jacquino in a suitably light vein, directly Fidelio (Leonora in her boy's disguise) enters the scene the whole mood of the music is at once lifted to the higher plane of heroic tragedy. It is true that Beethoven wrote for the gaoler Rocco a song about the importance of money, in which he strives for a light and humorous touch, only to achieve a cumbrous jocosity. Thereafter we lose sight of the *opéra-comique* style, Beethoven having become absorbed in the grand drama of Leonora's heroism.

Fidelio is, indeed, the classic example of an operatic masterpiece which achieves greatness in defiance of theory. It breaks almost every rule. Stylistically it is freakish, beginning as *opéra-comique* and ending in cantata. The vocal writing is often so ungrateful that few singers can make it sound convincing. It was not that Beethoven did not give deep thought to the problems of opera. He spent years on fashioning and refashioning *Fidelio*, whose definitive version in two acts with a revised libretto appeared in 1814, nine years after the original three-act version. Subsequently he spent a great deal of time and energy in a fruitless search for another suitable operatic subject. It is evident that his gifts did not fit him for comedy, in which sphere he might have found well-constructed librettos, and he regarded the type of comedy set by Mozart as immoral. There was no one who could provide him with the idealistic drama he required for the embodiment of his musical thought, and he had, perforce, to fall back on Bouilly's ill-constructed book. Yet paradoxically *Fidelio* rises above its patent weaknesses, standing as a great monument to the ideals of human freedom and of the true partnership of man and woman in marriage, and as a moving musico-dramatic experience for all to see.

Fidelio is, in the nature of the case, a unique phenomenon, and could not serve as a model to later composers. Its form derives, as we have seen, from the French original, but in spirit it is nearer to *The Magic Flute*, though the ideal figures of Tamino and Pamina have been replaced by actual human beings, Florestan and Fidelio-Leonora, to whom the events depicted in the story had happened in real life. For Bouilly based his book on a similar case of wrongful imprisonment at Tours during the Revolution, the prisoner's escape having been effected by his devoted wife.

In the homely melodramas, of which Bouilly's *Léonore* and *Les Deux Journées* are typical examples, the peasant-characters have lost all the equivocal naïvety or the earthy humour that were turned to comic account by earlier composers. They are presented rather as noble products of the brave new world supposedly created by the Revolution, and the sentiments they utter are unexceptionable and often priggish. Such pieces did not suffice when the First Consul, still following Roman precedent, emerged from his republican chrysalis and crowned himself Emperor in 1804. An Empire demanded grander entertainments to bolster up its new-found pride.

NAPOLEONIC GRAND OPERA

This want was supplied by Gasparo Spontini (1774–1851), whose *La Vestale* was at first condemned by the authorities at the Paris Opera as "bizarre and noisy", but was nevertheless produced, through the personal intervention of the Empress Josephine, and achieved a brilliant success. *La Vestale* (1807) is the first example of a new kind of opera that was to dominate the French scene during the greater part of the nineteenth century —grand opera with spectacular pageants, realistic and complicated scenery, elaborate ballets, a large chorus supplemented by a host of supers and supported by a big orchestra with a supernumerary band on the stage, all demanding a vast stage and principal singers with stentorian voices. The ensembles of *La Vestale* made their novel and overpowering effect by sheer volume. But, as their musical content was insufficiently substantial, it needed only some other composer, Meyerbeer for example, to increase the number of performers and the weight of sound for *La Vestale* to become, in its turn, thin and old-fashioned.

La Vestale was followed in 1809 by a more typical " grand " opera, *Fernand Cortez*, whose historico-political story, chosen in this instance to enhance the prestige of the Empire, which was involved in the Peninsular War, became a recognised type. This attained its highest level in Verdi's *Don Carlos* and *Aida*. After 1819 Spontini transferred his activities to Berlin as director of the royal theatre. There he composed German operas, adapting his last Parisian work *Olympie* to that language with the help of the poet E. T. A. Hoffmann. During his latter years Spontini occupied himself in the composition and revision of an immense and ponderous opera on a subject from German medieval history, *Agnes von Hohenstaufen*, first produced in 1829.

THE RISE OF GERMAN NATIONALISM

The long hegemony of Italy in the opera-houses of Central Europe was now at an end. Under the influence of romanticism there developed among the peoples of Europe a growing consciousness of national identity and aspirations—a consciousness fully awakened under the impact of Napoleon's attempt to impose a New Order under his own dictatorship upon the whole continent. The costly failure of that attempt impoverished the old aristocratic rulers, who formed a supra-national caste with cosmopolitan tastes. Their subjects, especially the middle classes, who had acquired some of the wealth their rulers lost, began to aspire to a greater share in the government and to an assertion of their nationhood. People became more conscious of the old legends and past history of their native land. The demands made upon Beethoven and other composers for arrangements of Scottish and Irish traditional melodies were straws in the wind.

This social revolution inevitably affected opera, whose manner and subject-matter have always been determined by the social conditions in which it has been created. Hitherto opera had been, in the main, an entertainment for the aristocracy and a prop to the régime. It used the fashionable Italian language and Italian musical style as a universal tongue. Now the awakening of national consciousness and the arrival of a new middle-class audience gave a strong impetus to such sporadic attempts as had been made to write opera in the vernacular.

It is not surprising that the first important manifestations of this movement came from Germany where, under the integrating pressure of war, the ferment of nationalism was working most strongly in the agglomeration of petty states of which that country consisted. Goethe, whose intellectual influence was enormous, was, it is true, no patriot. From his seclusion at Weimar he viewed with indifference the strife of nations and, indeed, regretted the ultimate defeat of Napoleon, whose genius he admired. But his massive achievements in verse and prose freed Germany once and for all from subservience to French literary models. Deriving his inspiration not from the work of his mediocre German predecessors, but rather from Shakespeare and the classical literature of Europe and the East, Goethe purged German literature of its chief vices—its tedious pedantry and its obscurity of expression. If he had no immediate and direct effect upon the musical life of his time—though Beethoven wrote music for his *Egmont* and some of Schubert's finest masterpieces are settings of his lyrics—he did more than any other man to create the atmosphere of the Germany that emerged from the Napoleonic ideal, not yet a political entity but a people conscious of a common ideal. One of the striking features of the decade after 1815 is the emergence of a fully equipped German operatic style.

In Austria Mozart had shown the way with *The Magic Flute*. Beethoven was patriotically substituting cumbrous German equivalents for the Italian musical terms in common use, and had composed in *Fidelio* not merely a typical opera of the Revolutionary period but an authentic German masterpiece.

WEBER'S " DER FREISCHÜTZ "

Although Mozart's *Magic Flute* (1791) and Ludwig Spohr's *Faust* (1816) have some claim to be considered the first German romantic operas, the true initiator here was Carl Maria von Weber (1786–1826). Spohr was one of the leading violinists of his day and the composer of much instrumental music—including fifteen violin concertos—once famous but now mostly forgotten. Weber, though brought up in the theatre and belonging wholly to it by temperament, is also remembered for a number of instrumental works. Chief among these are four piano sonatas, written between 1812 and 1822 in the " brilliant " style fashionable during the Congress of Vienna, which was not without its influence on Beethoven and Schubert and was to serve as a model for the young Mendelssohn. His *Concertstück* for piano and orchestra shows this style used for the purposes of a romantic " programme ", and his *Invitation to the Dance* (1819) is a waltz which was to be given orchestral form by Berlioz and to be adopted as a ballet. Other instrumental works of Weber's include concertos for clarinet and for bassoon and concertinos for clarinet and for horn. But it was Weber's period of service as Music Director at the Dresden Opera that was most fruitful for German opera, which he found despised and subordinate to the Italian repertory and which he left richer by at least two major works.

His first great success was *Der Freischütz* ("The Wild Huntsman"), produced at Berlin in 1821. In this the chief characters are humble foresters and huntsmen. Its story is a melodramatic tale of magic derived from German folk-lore. Technically, the work is a *Singspiel* with spoken dialogue. The homely melodies and Weber's remarkable, and at the time unprecedented, power of creating in his music a sense of romantic horror have gained for the opera a wide popularity. But only a German audience appreciates to the full its melodies, derived from traditional patterns, and the national customs which play so large a part in the action. This provincialism of outlook is at once the strength at home and the weakness abroad of the new kind of national opera which came into being in the nineteenth century. The choruses of huntsmen and bridesmaids, which are apt to sound naïvely hearty and cosily arch to English ears, have especially endeared the opera to sentimental German audiences who cherish the memory of the simple customs these choruses embody.

But Weber could rise above this parochial charm. Agathe's air *Leise, leise* ("Softly sighs") has a breadth and grandeur not to be matched, in its period, outside Beethoven's *Fidelio*. And although the characterisation of the persons is not particularly subtle, it is effectively done. Agathe and her maid Aennchen are differentiated by the kind of music they have to sing, and though Kaspar is something of a "ham" villain, his *faux bonhomme* nature is well presented in the drinking song. And, "ham" or not, his villainy is wonderfully drawn in the music which accompanies the casting of the magic bullets in the Wolf's Glen.

MELODRAMA

The peculiarity of this Wolf's Glen scene is that it uses, with a rare success, the device of *melodrama, i.e.* spoken dialogue supported by an orchestral accompaniment. *Melodrama* seems to be of Bohemian origin, one of the earliest references to it being in a letter of Mozart's from Mannheim in 1778, where he mentions two pieces by Georg Benda, the *Kapellmeister* at Gotha. "There is no singing in it," he explains, "only recitation, to which the music is like a sort of obbligato accompaniment to a recitative." Mozart was sufficiently interested to contemplate the composition of a *Semiramis* in this style. Indeed, he went so far as to say that "most operatic recitatives should be treated in this way—and only occasionally sung when the words *can be perfectly expressed in music.*" But his enthusiasm seems to have evaporated, and nothing more was heard of *Semiramis*. He used *melodrama* in the incidental music for *Thamos, König in Ägypten* ("Thamos, King of Egypt") which he composed in 1779, and also in the opera *Zaïde*, which he never finished. For the rest, he abandoned it. Even the spoken part of the Pasha in *Seraglio* has no musical accompaniment, nor is *melodrama* used in *The Magic Flute*, where it might have seemed appropriate in the Temple scenes. Beethoven, on the other hand, made striking use of it in the grave-digging scene in *Fidelio* and again in his music for Goethe's *Egmont*. It was no doubt his example that inspired Weber.

Mozart's idea that " most operatic recitatives should be treated in this way " comes strangely from the most musical of composers, and it was evidently only a fleeting notion based on a novel experience, for *melodrama* represents an abandonment of the central principle of opera. Yet, despite this, it can be used with powerful dramatic effect as a contrast to the sung word. In situations of great emotional intensity its employment creates the feeling that the potentialities of vocal music, normally the vehicle *par excellence* of emotional effect, have become exhausted, and that we have passed on to a plane where the spoken word takes on an even greater intensity than the sung. It is obviously a device that must be used sparingly, and the purely musical interest of the orchestral accompaniment cannot be more than slight. For the human ear, which can readily assimilate words and music when the words are sung, finds it difficult to take in the meaning both of a recitation and of the music accompanying it.

Melodrama is essentially a romantic device adapted for use in romantic situations. Indeed, the most successful instances of its use are the pathetic scene in *Fidelio*, where the spoken word seems to indicate the matter-of-fact nature of the task on which Rocco and his apprentice are engaged, while the music underlines the agony of Leonora's mind as she helps prepare the grave for her husband ; and the horrific scene in *Der Freischütz* where the music depicts the supernatural phenomena accompanying Kaspar's invocation of Samiel and the sinister ritual of casting the magic bullets.

Here it may be remarked that short passages of spoken text, sometimes without musical accompaniment, are found in later nineteenth-century operas, particularly where a character reads a letter or a message. The spoken word serves to differentiate what is read from the normal dialogue or soliloquy and, in a strange way, heightens the pathos of the situation. Violetta's reading of Alfredo's letter in the last act of Verdi's *La Traviata* is the most moving of these scenes, the pathetic effect being intensified by the appearance in the orchestra of the memorable phrases of the music to which Alfredo had first confessed his love.

" EURYANTHE "

The success of *Der Freischütz* brought Weber an invitation from Domenico Barbaia to compose an opera for one of his theatres in Vienna. This event is, in itself, significant of the changed circumstances under which opera was now produced. The change had begun towards the end of Mozart's life. His most successful opera—immediately successful, that is—*The Magic Flute*, was composed for Emanuel Schikaneder, a travelling showman who had become director of a suburban theatre in Vienna, the Freihaus-Theater auf der Wieden. This theatre had nothing to do with the Court and catered for a popular audience, much as the Old Vic used to do in Lilian Baylis's day. A generation later the commercial theatre aspired to higher rank, and Barbaia, the resourceful impresario-director of the Scala Theatre in Milan and the San Carlo in Naples, had in 1821 taken over the Kärntnerthor Theatre in Vienna. Here Weber's *Euryanthe* was produced in 1823, as a change from the operas of Rossini which Barbaia had been introducing to the Austrian capital.

Euryanthe represents another facet of the Romantic movement. Based on an episode in the *Roman de la Violette* which reappears in Boccaccio's *Decameron* and was borrowed thence by Shakespeare for incorporation in *Cymbeline*, the story combines supernatural events with medieval pageantry. It is a characteristic product of the Gothic revival, which took a long time to reach the opera-house. For it had begun to make its influence felt in the days of Horace Walpole, who began to build at Twickenham his " little Gothic castle " in 1747. His novel, the *Castle of Otranto*, came out in 1764, while Tetbury church, the first ecclesiastical example of the style, was rebuilt in elegant Gothic taste in 1771. The influence of the " Gothick " novel, compounded of supernatural horror and romantic medievalism, soon spread through Mrs. Radcliffe and " Monk " Lewis, and degenerated into the obscene fantasies of the Marquis de Sade on the one hand and the donnish satirical fables of Thomas Love Peacock on the other.

Helmine von Chézy, the librettist of *Euryanthe*, was a sorry example of the " Gothick " authoress, novelettish and ingenuous. Insufficiently equipped for the difficult task of fashioning a good drama from her chosen subject, she was able to provide what Weber wanted only after much revision under his guidance. The result, if far from satisfactory, is not so feeble as some critics have maintained. What has militated against the survival of *Euryanthe* in the repertory is the fact that it is the first opera of its kind—unless we count Spohr's *Jessonda*, produced three months earlier —and that it has been excelled at many points by more expertly written successors.

Euryanthe has not the homely, popular atmosphere of *Der Freischütz*. It is a " grand " opera, without the spoken dialogue which Weber used in his other operas. It comprises all the elements which Wagner was to turn to better use in *Tannhäuser* and particularly in *Lohengrin*. For Euryanthe herself is the model for Wagner's Elsa, even as the powerfully drawn villain and villainess are the prototypes of Telramund and Ortrud. Yet outmoded though it is, *Euryanthe* can still hold an audience by its charm and its effective handling of the dramatic situations. As a conscious attempt to compose a work on a combination of poetic drama, scenic art, and music, in anticipation of the theory formulated at such length by Wagner, *Euryanthe* deserves respect and occasional revival.

" OBERON "

Oberon, Weber's third and last important opera, again differed from its predecessors. It was commissioned by Charles Kemble for production at Covent Garden, where it was first performed in April 1826. The English libretto was written by J. R. Planché, who produced a curious farrago that may best be described as a grand pantomime in the manner of *The Magic Flute*. There are the fairy-tale atmosphere, the original setting, the serious love-allegory of the hero and heroine, their comic servants in the vein of Papageno, and, as an additional ingredient, the chivalric properties which had already been used in *Euryanthe*. Hampered by its stilted dialogue and by the costly nature of the production it requires, owing to its frequent elaborate changes of scene, *Oberon* is hardly a practical proposition nowadays. Yet it contains some of Weber's loveliest music, which sometimes captures the authentic note of the Shakespearian fairyland, even as young Felix Mendelssohn was simultaneously, and quite independently, doing in Berlin. It should, however, be remarked that Planché's libretto, though its personages include characters named Oberon and Puck, has no connection with *A Midsummer Night's Dream*.

THE DRESDEN OPERA

It may be that Weber's greatest service to the cause of German opera, to which he was so devoted that he regarded his friend Meyerbeer's defection to Italy as something akin to treason, was his establishment at Dresden of a theatre devoted to the performance of opera in German. This he accomplished in the teeth of opposition from the Court and of the long-established Italian Opera over which Hasse, in the previous century, had presided for nearly thirty years. Thus he not only provided models of what German opera should be, but also created a tradition of performance that made the Dresden Opera one of the most famous in the world for over a century. Here was the stage on which Wagner, who became its director in 1843, could spread his wings, and where all but two of Richard Strauss's operas were produced between 1900 and 1938.

Of Weber's immediate successors the most important was Heinrich

Marschner (1795–1861), and he is important only as a contributor to the ideas which were to be taken up and transmuted by the genius of Wagner. Both *Der Vampyr* (1828) and *Hans Heiling* (1833) have as their central characters a damned and haunted figure of melodramatic wickedness, who is nevertheless presented, unlike Kaspar in *Der Freischütz*, in a partially sympathetic light. Here are the models for the tragic Dutchman of *The Flying Dutchman*. Again, the central situation in *Der Templer und die Jüdin* ("The Templar and the Jewess"), one of the many operas of the period derived from Scott's novels, closely resembles that in *Lohengrin*. For the rest, German composers during the first half of the century produced either still-born works like Schumann's worthy, but undramatic, *Genoveva* (1850) or gay pieces in the *Singspiel* tradition such as Conradin Kreutzer's *Nachtlager in Granada* (1834) ("Night Camp in Granada") and Albert Lortzing's *Zar und Zimmermann* (1837) ("Tsar and Carpenter"), which can still pass an evening pleasantly.

XIV

SCHUBERT

WHILE opera continued to engage the attention of the majority of composers in all countries, it was not the main preoccupation of the greatest, as we have seen in the cases of Haydn and Beethoven. For their worthiest immediate successor in Vienna it brought nothing but disappointment.

Franz Peter Schubert was born in Vienna in 1797. His father, in whose footsteps he for a short time followed, was a schoolmaster who had left Silesia to settle in the capital. The older Schubert, despite his poverty, was a man of real, if narrow, culture, and a devoted cellist.

To the twentieth century there are specifically "Viennese" musical qualities which did not, as special entities, exist until Schubert defined them. They are sometimes suggested in Mozart's more relaxed moments; but it was Schubert who made them into the nostalgic, affectionate music we know. This is not to say that the Viennese style comprehends everything Schubert wrote. Much as he loved his native city, he had many un-Viennese characteristics—a sense of tragedy, a love of things on the epic scale, a searching vigour of mind. He was a Viennese of provincial descent who found a home in the atmosphere and musicality of the capital, rather than a native whose outlook was circumscribed by its tastes and tendencies.

As a boy he became, like Haydn before him, a chorister of the Imperial Chapel, and was educated with the rest of the choir at the Royal Imperial Municipal Seminary, known as the "Konvikt", where, like any promising pupil, he was allowed to remain until he was seventeen. His musical training, wider than Haydn's, included lessons in piano, organ, and violin as well as thorough-bass. His masters, all accomplished musicians, found him quick in learning. In addition, the school prided itself upon an orchestra of sufficient strength to play the symphonies of Haydn and Mozart; Schubert was for a time its leader and, in the absence of the master in charge, its conductor.

On leaving the Konvikt in 1813 he received lessons from the Court composer, Antonio Salieri (1750–1825). The legend of Schubert as an uncultivated, instinctive genius dies hard, and is encouraged by the fact that shortly before his death he was planning to take counterpoint lessons;

but all his masters were accomplished musicians, and Salieri was great enough to be considered a rival to Mozart. For a year Schubert underwent an elementary schoolmaster's training ; but after two years of this profession he escaped, and for the rest of his life led a hand-to-mouth existence amongst his numerous friends, who provided for him when he could not provide for himself ; he did the same for them.

Unlike his predecessors, Schubert was not a brilliant performer, but simply a composer who had to earn his living by publication ; and it was not until 1821, when his friends subsidised the publication of a volume of his songs, that any particular attention was paid to him. In 1816 he applied for the musical directorship of the training college at Laibach (Ljubljana), but was refused, just as ten years later he was refused the post of Assistant *Kapellmeister* at the Austrian court. Apart from short spells spent as music master to the Esterházy family in 1818 and 1824, he refused to consider teaching as a means of livelihood. His friends were the music-lovers, poets, and amateur players of the city, rather than professional musicians, so that he received few commissions. His "occasional" works were for small private or family occasions. He wrote a great deal—operas, an oratorio, church music, designed to carry his name to the fore, but his gregariousness and his ability to lose himself in work were not qualities to accompany the compulsive demands of ambition.

THE GENESIS OF A STYLE

Schubert's earliest surviving music dates from 1810, and by 1815 his music has its own unmistakable character. The legend of the untutored genius has its accompaniment in the story that Schubert's music was a spontaneous outpouring never worked out intellectually in advance and never revised. But numerous sketches and numerous revisions preceded many of his works, even if his shorter pieces (and particularly songs) were often composed in that flash of inspiration known only to genius. Schubert was beyond question a thorough and conscientious musician : he knew what he was trying to do, and in those works that he could base upon his own musical experience—the songs, chamber music, and early orchestral compositions—his training and craftsmanship show plainly. In the "Unfinished" and "Great C major" symphonies, he was doing something for which no precedent existed, and he never heard the result of his work, but there is nothing that strikes the listener as incompletely or clumsily expressed.

As a boy Schubert wrote beautiful melodies and had a fine feeling for orchestral and chamber music combinations and a disturbingly original harmonic sense, which he had too little experience to order into convincing form. Throughout his early work his sonata-form tonalities are unorthodox from a mixture of daring and inexperience. Recapitulations sometimes begin in the dominant, as though he finds it hard to escape from the key of the development ; but more often they open in the sub-dominant, a tone lower. This procedure means that the second subject will automatically reach the desired tonic key simply by transposing the entire recapitulation down a fifth. If this was originally an easy way of avoiding the problems of the recapitulation, by the time he was eighteen Schubert had made it a valid expressive device.

In addition, another sort of ambition was present even in the earliest works—the ambition to use all the traditional devices for the sake of their expressive power. His somewhat disorganised harmonic adventurousness was coupled with a knowledge of technical means before he had the experience with which to make full use of them. From the beginning, Schubert realised the power and effectiveness of counterpoint, and many of his earliest works show him determined to write contrapuntally. The amateurishness of Schubert's earliest music is due, at least in considerable part, to his originality, his adventurous decision to work in lyrical melodies rather than themes and formulae, and to follow them wherever they lead him. The harmonic potentialities of a fully developed melody are often greater than those of a theme which has perhaps, like a theme by Beethoven, simplified its melodic form. A greater weakness, and one that Schubert found harder to overcome than his imaginative luxuriance of harmony, was an inconsistency of style in a work of several movements ; music of great emotional tension and directness sometimes found itself cheek by jowl with café or street-song styles.

Schubert was a torch-bearer at Beethoven's funeral, but Schubert himself said that they never met. The younger composer survived the elder by a little more than a year, and the greatest of Beethoven's works did not, perhaps, ever become sufficiently familiar to Schubert to influence him deeply. As a boy he was a doubtful admirer, and an entry in his diary when he was nineteen speaks of Beethoven, for all his personal genius, as the cause of a great deal of eccentric " modernism " in composers who tried to copy him. But Schubert's later works, and remarks, show how he absorbed Beethoven's command of epic scale and drama. Beethoven's second symphony and the *Allegretto* of the seventh seem specially to have haunted Schubert's imagination.

While Schubert was a boy in his teens, Rossini's operas became the rage of Vienna, and he was sufficiently impressed by them to imitate and even to parody them. The parodies were not unkind, but Schubert realised that many of the Italian operatic conventions needed only a gentle push to topple them over into absurdity. He assimilated a great deal from Rossini, but it is the great tradition of Haydn, Mozart, and Beethoven that inspires his work.

His spirit did not occupy the regions of intense moral effort in which Beethoven's was at home, and he did not involve himself with the ethical conceptions which were so decisive in Beethoven's work and influence. What he gives us is the music of his own direct experience of life, as time and experience deepened his personality. How great that personality is can be seen in the later chamber music or the " Great C major " symphony ; and it can be seen in almost any random collection of his songs, which give us the same insight into an imagination of unsurpassed vividness and versatility. In their range and imaginative power, it is the songs that are the key to most of what is greatest in his work.

DEVELOPMENT

Schubert was determined not to be a schoolmaster. His short period as a teacher was filled with works on the largest scale designed to build his reputation up to the point at which he could confidently expect a worthy position. Between 1814 and 1816 he composed five operas, three of them full-length works, and sketched another. Their librettos were all chosen with an eye to what was most popular on the Viennese stage, but none of them achieved performance. Church music offered another hope of escape, and it was on the whole easier to secure performances of uncommissioned Masses. Three were composed between 1814 and 1815, and a fourth in the following year ; all these were accompanied by a considerable quantity of other church music.

Before we begin to explore the other music of these and later years, we need, perhaps, to point out that no greater chaos exists than that of Schubert's opus numbers. The works that he himself published were numbered by whoever brought them out according to their dates of publication, so that, for example, the A minor string quartet composed in 1824 is op. 29, No. 1 whilst that in B flat composed ten years earlier is op. 168. We shall use opus numbers here because they still represent a handy means of identification for those works to which they have been affixed, but shall add for purposes of chronological accuracy the numbers given to the works in the catalogue compiled by Otto Erich Deutsch, in which Schubert's music is accurately dated.

Apart from songs, which we shall consider later, the years from 1814 to 1820 (when it is possible to say that Schubert reached complete maturity as an instrumental composer) produced innumerable small works for piano ;

the first thirteen piano sonatas, several of them incomplete in one way or another ; a good deal of work for piano duet, including the first of the two duet sonatas ; the three sonatas for violin and piano, which the publishers issued as "sonatinas", and the first six symphonies, as well as four quartets. The eighth quartet, op. 168 (D.112) in B flat, is perhaps the first of the chamber works to combine Schubert's lyrical and harmonic freedom with the precision of form that he had looked for in the earlier pieces. The piano sonatas aim more than anything else at beauty of sound, richness of texture, and harmonic fullness. Accepting the tradition that the place for lyrical statement is in the second subject, they allow the second group to grow to an unusual extent. After a more or less tersely melodic main theme comes an extended exposition of new material with its own key changes, and usually including passages of dance-like rhythm ; the extra tonalities exert their own pressure on the form. Many of these early sonatas, though they are overshadowed by the nine he was to write after 1823, have passages of power and eloquence that anticipate his later greatness.

The first five symphonies were composed between 1813 and 1816. Only the fourth tries to be more than entertainment music. If the first three remind us of Mozart and Haydn, this is because the style of the two older masters was still the style of the day, but in melodic content and harmonic extensiveness they are pure Schubert. The main theme of the third's first movement, for example, foretells the "Great C major" symphony, and its last movement is a study in pure speed that owes nothing to any of his predecessors. Probably Beethoven was the inspirer of the fourth, for Schubert later decided to call it the "Tragic", and it is in the Beethovenish key of C minor. For a nineteen-year-old composer it is a work of astonishing ability. Its slow introduction is based upon a single figure which moves with restless pathos from key to key, generating imitations in the bass and melodic counterpoints in the wood-wind, and the first movement has a fine, compelling drive that tends to spend itself in the development. The second movement, perhaps modelled on that of Beethoven's seventh symphony, may concentrate too entirely upon a single rhythmic figure, but the minuet has a speed, a rhythmic ambiguity and an intensity of expression that owe much to both Mozart and Beethoven. The drive of the finale seems to dissipate itself in modulations too diverse to be significant, but the recapitulation pulls it together through Schubert's device of starting outside the tonic key and moving into it only as the second subject is reached.

The fifth is the most popular of these early symphonies. Composed immediately after the "Tragic", it is almost chamber music in its lightness of texture, with a single flute and neither drums nor trumpets. There is no slow introduction, but four bars of a quiet phrase leading to a main theme that for once is less a melody than a rhythmical presentation of the notes of the tonic chord. The quiet introduction is used in the development, but disappears before the recapitulation, which begins in the sub-dominant but modifies all its opening material in such a way that the second subject is seen to be the movement's real hero.

If the composer was remembering Mozart's G minor symphony in his slow movement and minuet, he was in no sense copying it. The unrest and melancholy of the slow movement, moreover, are different from the bitterness of Mozart's masterpiece, and are achieved in a purely Schubertian way. The movement is based upon two themes, each varied in its second statement, and the whole rounded off by the reappearance of the first in its original form. The first theme stands four-square in a secure major tonality (E flat), whilst the second moves restlessly through minor keys. The minuet is in a rebellious G minor, but is square-cut where Mozart's is bitingly contrapuntal. The exuberant finale has a bridge-passage that hints at the minor and its melancholy, so that the second subject has a similar tendency to glance off from the lighthearted major ; but everything is worked out to a happy ending with unfailing craftsmanship.

The sixth symphony was begun in 1817 and completed early in the following year. Schubert headed his manuscript "Grand Symphony", and apparently set to work with an ambition that he unselfconsciously sacrificed to vitality, gaiety, and naturalness. In this work he shows the influence of Rossini in the world of the classical symphony, and it is impossible to understand why the work has not achieved a popularity equal to its predecessor's. It was preceded by three "concert overtures", to the second and third of which the title "Italian" has been applied. These are the results of Schubert's interest in and admiration for Rossini, and in them he makes Rossini's style a part of his own.

In 1817, a year of songs and piano sonatas, Schubert was rapidly developing into the rich maturity by which we know him best ; 1818, bringing his first spell of duty with the Esterházy family, caused him to return to the piano duet, probably to provide concerted music for his pupils. Amongst smaller works for duet, mostly groups of dances and marches, are two sets of variations and the sonata in B flat, op. 30 (D.617). A new symphony, in D, was sketched but never completed, and 1819 saw the production of his "Trout" quintet (so called from the fourth of its five movements, a set of variations upon his song The Trout) during a holiday in the Austrian Alps. The work was composed for violin, viola, cello, double-bass, and piano, more in the style of a serenade than with the seriousness which Beethoven had imposed upon chamber music ; and even the agitated scherzo remains frankly popular in style. On the surface the variations are old-fashioned and decorative, rather than the sort of melodic analysis which Beethoven had practised and from which he had made new melodic compounds. But its harmonic scope and wide-ranging modulations belie the idea of superficial conservatism; it is not until the finale of the variations that the song melody, originally presented in a simplified form, appears in all its naïve charm.

One of the many unfinished masterpieces belongs to a group of works written in the hope of a permanent appointment in 1820. The two completed parts of the cantata *Lazarus* contain more developed and personal work than most of the operas Schubert had written up to this date, perhaps because he was not so directly concerned with the conventions of popular taste. The vocal writing has the eloquence that he had already achieved by the fusion of melody with declamation in the songs, while the orchestral writing is so richly descriptive and packed with thematic interest that it anticipates the mature Wagner. The work's incompleteness is one of the many Schubert tragedies.

THE GERMAN SONG

The liveliest and most ingratiating, as well as the most important, music that Schubert heard as a boy was instrumental. But Haydn, Mozart, and Beethoven had all written attractive songs. Haydn's best were written in London to English words; Mozart set a poem by Goethe, "The Violet", in the style of a miniature operatic *scena* and others, amongst them the beautiful *Abendempfindung* ("Evening Feelings"), might well belong to his chamber works. Beethoven's songs are more impressive. At their best, they use poems that reflect either his longing for love or his sense of worship; and it was Beethoven who in his set of six songs *To the Distant Beloved* first composed a song-cycle in which each of the component numbers leads unmistakably to the next. Beethoven's songs are strongly constructed, but even the finest of them are offshoots from his major preoccupations, and they often contain, in their free, arioso-like melodies, more feeling than the form is able to contain.

North German composers had, on the whole, paid more attention to song form, and it is their precedents that Schubert, as a boy, tended to observe. Notable amongst them were Johann Friedrich Reichardt (1752–1814), Carl Friedrich Zelter (1758–1832), and Johann Rudolf Zumsteeg (1760–1802), the composer of long, cantata-like works in several sections linked by recitative, which provided the model for pieces like *Hagar's Lament*, which Schubert composed in 1811, and numerous other lengthy ballad or cantata songs stretching over twenty or thirty manuscript pages.

Schubert's admired teacher, Salieri, regarded such compositions as boyish indiscretions and dismissed the whole field of German song as a barbarous vulgarity, trying to cure his unfortunate addiction by setting him Italian texts to compose. We may say that in all the important senses—in the development of songs that are not strophically constructed but which develop throughout in obedience to their texts; in the modification of simple strophic songs so that not every verse has the same music; in the exploration through harmony and a symphonically developing accompaniment of the emotional implications of a poem; and, above all, in the creation of an equal partnership between voice and piano—Schubert's songs are a new creation.

Besides the long, cantata-like effusions of his apprenticeship, Schubert composed numerous simpler songs of an ingratiatingly lyrical type where there was no time for meanderings from key to key or for a collapse into formlessness; but there was nothing to prepare for the sudden blaze of genius with which, at the age of seventeen, he set the lament of Gretchen after Faust has deserted her. She sits and remembers him as she spins, and the whirr of her spinning wheel provides a restless, chromatically expressive accompaniment to her voice. Her first stanza, repeated continually as a refrain, provides the forms from which the later stanzas derive their music, and she grows increasingly agitated, spinning more swiftly and driving the music up in tonality at the beginning of each new stanza, always falling back to the original D minor for the refrain. Only as she remembers his kiss does she lose herself in her memories and cease to spin. That a seventeen-year-old ex-choirboy, less than a year out of boarding school, should have the imaginative insight to accomplish all this is one of music's miracles.

The style and perfection of *Gretchen at the Spinning Wheel* presents us with the essentials of Schubert the song-writer. All the music, accompaniment as well as melody, arises directly from the poem, so that the one is as important a part of the composer's expression as the other. He uses richly complex harmony, in a sense entirely dramatic, for it is not a song *about* Gretchen but the song *of* Gretchen, with whom the composer identifies himself. Amongst later songs there are many narratives, like *The Erl King*, and they tell their stories with intense dramatic force; but even Schubert's meditative songs are similar to *Gretchen* in their expression of a unique personality facing a unique situation.

Enough drafts and sketches remain to show that Schubert's songs were no more haphazard compositions than his orchestral works. Moreover, despite the legends, he was not a composer without literary taste, setting any and every poem that came to hand. The qualities he wanted from a poem are plain—clarity, concreteness of imagery, grace of form, and intensity of expression. The words of the two great song-cycles, *The Maid of the*

Mill and *The Winter Journey*, are not great poetry, but they were enough to fire the composer's genius, and in so far as they present the required qualities, they became masterpieces when he handled them. We know the poems he refused to set because they gave him nothing he needed. The truth is that the field of choice was small, for German lyric poetry was a new art. Its greatest masters, Goethe and Schiller, were born in 1749 and 1759 respectively, and it was their work which inspired the poets with whom Schubert dealt.

The best songs always provide some musical phrase of great significance immediately referable to the poem, even when, like *The Wanderer*, they extend through several linked sections. Gretchen's spinning wheel, the thundering horse of *The Erl King*, the obsessive rhythm of *Du liebst mich nicht* (" You do not love me "), or the tolling chords of *Der Doppelgänger* (" The Wraith "), are all typical of Schubert's method. Song forms depend entirely upon their texts. Often they are strophic, repeating the same melody for all the stanzas of a poem, but Schubert more often varied strophic compositions as they developed in accordance with the emotional development of the poem. Many songs are freely declamatory, with eloquent, arioso-like vocal lines. Much has been said about instances of faulty declamation in the songs, where insignificant words fall on the accented first beat of a bar ; but these can more often than not be traced to the musical necessity which springs directly from the poem, and a capable singer can easily remove the stress from the words. Wherever the words lead, Schubert's music follows with entire integrity, and often its salient theme is developed, as in *Prometheus* or *The Young Nun*, with symphonic breadth and power.

The songs, too, explain the poetic, exploratory tendencies of Schubert's harmony. *Du liebst mich nicht* is a short song, but it involves a wider range of tonality than most symphonic movements existing in 1822, when it was written ; and the involved tonalities circle round to their starting point with complete naturalness, implicit in a melody that is Schubert's instinctive reaction to the poem. *The Erl King*, like Gretchen's spinning wheel, drives upwards tone by tone as the child's terror grows, interrupted only by the allurements of the spectre, which are immovably rooted in the main key, G minor, in which the song opens and closes. This is the starting and finishing point of the circle round which the music moves.

The sense of major and minor tonality in Schubert's music is something that stamped itself upon his Viennese successors. When Mozart resolved a minor mode into its own major, he did so with the manner of making a courageous decision. Beethoven made the turn from minor to major into blazing triumph ; but when Schubert, in the songs and instrumental works—for instance, in *The Signpost*, late in *The Winter Journey*, or in the

Andante con moto of the "Great C major" symphony—evolved a major tonality from a minor, he was resolving distress and agitation in a tragic acceptance.

The richness and subtlety of Schubert's harmonic language commands many varieties of procedure, and equally varied is his command of melody —as frank and easy as folk-song in *The Trout*, *The Hedge Rose*, and the early songs of *The Maid of the Mill* ; powerfully dramatic in *Prometheus*, *Atlas*, *Der Doppelgänger*, and many others ; sometimes richly Italianate, as in the central melody of *The Wanderer*.

To speak of development after such songs as *Gretchen at the Spinning Wheel* and *The Erl King* sounds like impertinence, but nevertheless the songs gain increasing concentration without any sacrifice of the other, and lovable, Schubertian qualities.

THE TURNING POINT

The single movement of an abandoned quartet in C minor, which the Germans call the *Quartettsatz* (" Quartet movement "), is the first instrumental work to rise to the same level as the songs. Composed in 1820, it begins with a sombre theme in triplets that haunted the nineteenth century, and its elaborate tonal structure, with four keys used as main dramatic points, leads to the use of an inverted recapitulation in which the tragic music of the opening brings back the main key. Schubert's brooding poetry initiates these adventures, and the movement's depth of expression marks something new in Schubert's instrumental work. A completed quartet of such quality would have ranked amongst the world's supreme masterpieces, but an incomplete *Andante* is all that Schubert left as continuation.

The first of two unfinished symphonies, in E minor and major, was sketched out in 1821, and marks a step forwards from the unassuming style of the earlier symphonies, a transition stage between the sixth and the great " Unfinished " symphony. Schubert left the first movement of the symphony in E completely scored up to the entry of the second subject, and from then on noted only its melodies, with salient points of harmony and occasional detailed scoring of climaxes. For the first time, Schubert added trombones to his symphony orchestra and used them more lyrically than earlier composers had done, with a special love of their voices as a quiet harmonic support.

In the autumn of the following year Schubert fell seriously ill, and his health for the rest of his life remained precarious ; he was unable to resume his normal activities until 1823. This crisis in his life is reflected in the new depth and power of his music, for in the autumn of 1822 came the two completed movements of the " Unfinished " symphony in B minor. The composer's sketches carry the work to the end of the scherzo, but the two orchestrated movements, with a single page of the third, were handed to the composer's friend Anselm Hüttenbrenner, to be presented to the Styrian Music Society, which had made Schubert an honorary member. The manuscript remained in Hüttenbrenner's possession until 1865, when he handed it over to the Viennese conductor Herbeck, who performed it for the first time in Vienna.

Endless attempts have been made to explain the symphony's incompleteness. Before the piano sketches were found in 1883, musicians were inclined to believe that Schubert, influenced by many of Beethoven's later sonatas, had planned a work in only two movements, although the second is not in the main tonality. The discovery of the scherzo sketch led to the theory that, as the scherzo is music on a lower plane than the earlier movements, the composer abandoned the work rather than complete it with music of less power. This presupposes self-criticism of a degree Schubert did not always exhibit, and it has been suggested with somewhat greater plausibility that Hüttenbrenner's silence about a masterpiece entrusted to him was due not to its incompleteness, but to the fact that he had lost the manuscript of the last two movements, for the surviving page of the fully-scored scherzo ends with tied notes to be carried over into the next bar, suggesting that whatever was intended to follow it was already in existence. However, in November 1822, the more immediately profitable *Wanderer* Fantasy for piano was required urgently ; the surviving sketches for the " Unfinished " do not reach to a finale ; and the manuscript of two movements in orchestral score, if they were on any scale comparable to that of the opening movements, would not easily be lost. The survival of the sketches therefore suggests that Schubert intended to return to the work but found no opportunity.

What is new in the " Unfinished " symphony is its combination of lyrical feeling with grandeur of structure, and its permeation by an urgently compelling poetic mood. B minor is the key for some of Schubert's most dark, awesome, tragic songs, of elegies and unappeasable sorrows. The ominous atmosphere of the first movement, generated by the theme of the introduction (which, though not openly related to the first subject announced by the woodwind, is the impetus behind the great battle of the development), is alleviated but not dispelled by the G major second subject, a melody of infinite charm that is almost a *Ländler*. In the development, the second subject is represented by its syncopated accompaniment rather than its melody ; there are few dynamic shades, only alternations of *fortissimo* with *piano*, and a framework that involves a startlingly wide tonal area. Not only is the unorthodox G major an odd key for the second subject (Schubert oved to juxtapose keys a third away from each other), but the stroke by which it is reached, through a single held note from a B minor chord on which the whole harmonic structure swings round, is one of Schubert's most supremely poetical moments—a wonderful dispelling of clouds. The recapitulation opens in the relative major, D; we notice that Schubert is really beginning to use keys in the modern way, as centres of tonality rather than closed areas, so that a composition in B minor really involves, to some extent, all the keys that are related to his home tonic.

The E major of the second movement is also related to many of his songs, those dealing with the comforts offered by nature to the sorrowful, with resigned serenity and with daydreams. The movement has two alternating sections, its second back in B minor to link it with the opening movement, and entered through a long, sighing figure in the woodwind. The sensuous beauty of this music and its rich iridescence of harmony are matched, as is the epic drama of the *Allegro moderato*, by the composer's firm intellectual grip on all that happens. Schubert's music has many false starts, great openings that were either uncompleted or completed by music unworthy of them, but none of them has a greater splendour than the B minor symphony. Unlike most immediately accessible works that have won immense popularity, it shares the undying appeal of the Beethoven symphonies because here the composer's intellect is as strong and as keen as his emotions are immense and universal.

OPERATIC FAILURES AND THE GERMAN OPERA

As we have seen, Schubert regarded success in the opera-house as the most effective way of consolidating his position, and between his first attempt on the theatre in 1814, *Des Teufels Luftschloss* (" The Devil's Castle in the Air "), and his first opera to achieve production, *Die Zwillingsbrüder* (" The Twin Brothers ") of 1819, lay three complete and three incomplete efforts. The incidental music for the play *Die Zauberharfe* (" The Magic Harp ") followed the year after *Die Zwillingsbrüder*. Neither of these two was particularly successful in the theatre. All his operas, so far, had used spoken dialogue ; their music invariably begins with an effective overture and contains fine arias.

Alfonso and Estrella, which followed in 1822, and *Fierabras* in 1823, were more ambitious works. *Alfonso and Estrella* is Schubert's only " grand " opera without speech, and its libretto, by Schubert's friend Franz von Schober, was designed to allow the composer every opportunity to write lyrically, so that action is sacrificed to musical beauty. The libretto of *Fierabras* is better in so far as it contains more action ; but both these works are full of conventional romantic extravagance which makes their characters and situations quite unreal, mistakes high-flown improbability for fantasy, and creates an atmosphere so far from any normal humanity that it becomes trivial. The only one of Schubert's libretti to attain complete humanity is that of *Der häusliche Krieg* ("Domestic Strife"). This is the story of Aristophanes' *Lysistrata*, in which women refuse to allow their husbands any matrimonial privileges until they abandon warfare. Set in Vienna at the time of the Crusades, the work was originally called *The Conspirators*, but the political censorship insisted upon the change of name.

Although he was a song composer accustomed to small vocal forms, the number and variety of ensembles he almost forces into his operas show the instinct of a true dramatic composer. The colour and vitality of their orchestration are often effective ; and the thematic, developing accompaniment of recitatives and ariosos is advanced beyond anything composed until Wagner's mature operas. The wealth and splendour of their melodies goes without saying, and with a librettist worthy of him Schubert might well have altered the whole course of German music.

In 1823 the failure of the play *Rosamunde*, for which Schubert's incidental music is still very popular, apparently dashed his hopes of stage success until, on his death bed, he returned to *Der Graf von Gleichen* ("The Count of Gleichen"), on which he had been working intermittently for over a year, and began to plan the remaining parts.

THE LATER WORKS

Between the "Unfinished" symphony and the "Great C major", completed six months before his death in 1828, Schubert wrote no orchestral music except the problematic symphony which he is believed to have composed during a holiday at Gmunden and Gastein in 1825. There are sufficient references in the letters of his friends to encourage belief that a Gmunden-Gastein symphony was written or sketched, and many authorities suggest that it was subsequently lost. It has been suggested, however, that much or all of a symphony sketched in 1825 lay unscored and probably uncompleted until 1828, when it became the C major work we know as the last symphony Schubert composed.

As we have seen, work on the "Unfinished" symphony was interrupted by the *Wanderer* Fantasy for piano, a massive four-movement work, unusually brilliant in style. Its main theme is drawn from the central section of the song *The Wanderer*. As a theme for variations, this melody is stated explicitly in the slow movement, but it is presented in the rest of the work in various disguises and through its derivatives. It is an imposing work, not only in brilliance of treatment, but in the powerful imaginativeness of its harmony, and it shows in the composer's piano style new trends that he continued to develop throughout the remainder of his life. There is an orchestral quality about the writing, a suggestion of string tremolandos and of characteristic instrumental phrases that is never far from any of Schubert's later piano music. It was this quality that led Liszt to arrange the work for piano and orchestra.

The greatest of the piano duet works—the *Grand Duo* in C (D.812), given its name by the publishers because Schubert's title, " Sonata ", was not at the time very popular—came in 1824. It is so large and so orchestral in its style that many commentators have suggested it to be an arrangement of a symphony, possibly the missing Gmunden-Gastein work. But efforts to score the music as it stands have been made by musicians having the greatest sympathy with Schubert's style, and none of them is convincing. Nevertheless, it seems obvious that from time to time Schubert turned to the piano duet as the largest practicable form because of the difficulty of finding performances for any of his full-scale orchestral works. In the *Grand Duo* and the two sonatas for piano—the A minor, op. 42 (D.845) and the C major (D.846) left unfinished and published posthumously under the title *Reliquie*—the sonata-form subjects are different versions of the same essential themes. The *Reliquie*, like the " Unfinished " symphony, to all intents and purposes ends with the slow movement, but the completed music is on Schubert's most expansive scale.

Of his last three string quartets, the A minor, op. 29, No. 1 (D.804) and the D minor (D.810) were written in 1824. The A minor is as closely connected with the songs as is its successor. The opening of its Minuet is a quotation from Schubert's setting of Schiller's poem " The Gods of Greece " (" Beautiful world, where have you gone ? "). Like the 1824 piano sonatas, it derives the second subject of its opening movement from the main theme, but viewed from an entirely different emotional outlook. The slow movement is based on the first Entr'acte (in B flat) from the *Rosamunde* music, as though the composer were eager to salvage as much as he could of his music written for an unsatisfactory play. The whole quartet is a great lyrical outpouring, sombre, melancholy, resolute, and eventually happy, expressed in most consummate musicianship.

The next quartet, the D minor (D.810), takes its name from its second-movement variations on the song *Death and the Maiden*. Commentators have often seen the whole work as a meditation upon death, with the variations advancing from an impassioned revulsion through sombre resignation to the noble consolation which Death brings in the song. This is the greatest of Schubert's quartets, intensely dramatic, fearful at times, with a wonderful eloquence drawn from the use of the plangent upper register of the cello against high string chords. In the finale Schubert exploits wild tarantella rhythms, sometimes savage, sometimes almost panic-stricken, but leading away from the despairing grief of its opening into a cheerful acceptance of life.

The final string quartet, in G major (D.887), was composed in 1826 and published after the composer's death as op. 161. As in the previous work, themes are developed in the exposition before being used in the development section. The main theme is a G major chord that jerks into G minor, followed by a tonally ambiguous figure ; and the whole work oscillates between major and minor modes. The sad, lyrical E minor slow movement is twice shattered by a passage that destroys all sense of tonality and security, but the movement ends in the hard-won contentment of E major. The scherzo and trio cynically abandon the struggle, but the rondo shares the frenzied tarantella energy of the finale to " Death and the Maiden." Finally, the composer turns his back on his problems and sails away, perhaps a little disappointingly, in a serene G major.

The two piano trios, in B flat, op. 99 (D.898), and E flat, op. 100 (D.929), followed at the end of 1827. The first, though not a masterpiece on the level of the last quartets, is an endearing work of considerable happiness broken only by wistful regret. Together with its lovable qualities goes, however, a somewhat dubious handling of its medium, with the piano too often dominating where it should only accompany.

THE LAST YEAR

By 1828 Schubert had begun to pin his hopes of success on the idea of a public concert in which he should present music other than the songs by which he was almost exclusively known. The concert took place in March of that year, and contained choral music, songs, the first movement of a quartet (probably the G major), and the E flat piano trio. The event made little impact on the Viennese critics, though correspondents of other journals were greatly impressed.

The year was crowded with work ; the C major symphony, the sixth and last of Schubert's Masses, the string quintet in C major (D.956), and the last three piano sonatas, in C minor, A, and B flat (D.958, 959, and 960), as well as numerous other piano works and songs, for it was in 1828 that he first came upon the poems of Heine. His health deteriorated under the strain of work and disappointment, and in October he caught typhoid fever. On November 19 he died. His last completed work was the song with clarinet obbligato, *Der Hirt auf dem Felsen* (" The Shepherd on the Rock ").

In many respects Schubert's work grew more combative towards the end of his life. The last three piano sonatas, for example, range widely. The C minor has a stern, Beethovenesque challenge. The A major begins in solemnity and ends in lyrical gaiety. The B flat major is a work of great grandeur of structure and theme, enriched with all the colour and movement of Schubert's harmonic sense.

The quintet, like the last quartets, is one of the supreme masterpieces of chamber music. C major is usually regarded as the key of frank and confident action; but in the opening of this work Schubert discovers its sombre, combative side, and climbs from that through the meditation of one of his most lyrically beautiful slow movements and the ebullience of the scherzo to an easily gay, relaxed finale. The development of the first movement is based, after a developing exposition, on the music of the codetta, and it is held together by a roughly forceful counterpoint. Schubert wrote nothing more gripping, and the music's quality is the sum of the composer's lyrical expressiveness and intellectual mastery. The richness of texture in this work, with two cellos in place of the two violas which Mozart had preferred, is never less than exquisite, and the tension in the first movement is echoed in the work's final cadence.

The "Great C major" symphony is an epic conception throughout, as unified in atmosphere and method as the "Unfinished". In atmosphere it is akin to the music that Schubert gave to many of the songs of wandering, particularly the bleak masterpieces of *The Winter Journey*, which he had completed in 1827. All his themes in the symphony use the interval of a third as their main structural unit, and every movement has a powerfully rhythmic theme of ascending and descending notes. The *Andante con moto* of the symphony is another of Schubert's movements that looks back to the *Allegretto* of Beethoven's seventh symphony, but it does so through the *Winter Journey* songs, whose shuffling, reluctant rhythms underlie the symphony's slow march, which is twice interrupted by a lyrical, chorale-like interlude. The first reappearance of the march produces a battle of themes and tonalities as savage as any in music, and it subsides into the reappearance of the interlude music in the main key of the movement, A (major), as though it were a second subject. There is no hope for this theme, and its last appearance, as it marches away, is in broken fragments. The scherzo is a peasant's dance designed for giants, on *Ländler* and primitive waltz themes and rhythms; and the finale, unlike most of Schubert's concluding movements, is not a relaxation but an urgent sonata movement based on three themes which expand in rhythm.

The E flat is the finest of Schubert's six Masses. All of them contain moments of great beauty, but Schubert was not a practising believer. His correspondence makes it plain that his attitude to life was largely fatalistic, and this explains the sense of dogged endurance that haunts his most tragic music. In the earlier Masses he is moved by the portions of the text that can be dramatised. He can imagine human penitence, and write splendidly in the central section of the *Gloria* and in the *Agnus Dei* ; the centre of the *Credo—Incarnatus*, *Crucifixus*, and *Resurrexit*—again inspires him ; but he is less successful in the glories of the *Sanctus* and *Benedictus*. The fifth Mass, in A flat, composed between 1819 and 1822, uses all Schubert's harmonic and melodic resources to present a humanistic and sentimental conception of the text ; it is very beautiful, but shows no profound understanding of the liturgical words. In the E flat work, however, Schubert has found a personal symbolism in the text. Here the composer seems to celebrate the life of Christ, with whom he rejoices and suffers, though there is little in it that can be called worship. Orchestrally, it is amongst the richest of the composer's works, and its drama and sorrow are deeply moving. The *Incarnatus* is a lyrical outpouring of great beauty, the *Crucifixus* shudders with horror, the *Sanctus* presents a heaven of limitless horizons of tonality, whilst the *Agnus Dei* piles up great mountains of choral and orchestral supplication which die away in muted pleas for mercy.

THE SCHUBERT WORLD

Little of this music spread outside the circle of Schubert's friends. Not all the greatest songs were published, and the instrumental music was barely known. It was Schumann who discovered the " Great C major " symphony when he visited the composer's brother in 1839 and sent a copy of the score to Mendelssohn, who gave the first performance three months later. The " Unfinished " symphony remained unheard for forty-three years, and other Schubert works appeared intermittently throughout the nineteenth century. In 1865 the first complete study of the composer could draw attention to the number of works still unknown.

Schubert's marriage of lyrical melody and dramatic sonata form was not immediately seen as a great enrichment of symphonic style, and critics haunted by the greatness of Beethoven still fail to do justice to Schubert as a large-scale composer, as though his greatest works came off only by accident. Schubert's innovations, however—the enlargement and architectural use of tonality, the codettas that have their own key, the irregular recapitulations and the expositions that develop their themes as they present them—are not out of keeping with sonata form, whose legalisms are the deductions of scholars rather than the discipline of the masters. They accord with the principle of opposed tonalities reconciled in a development, and we have noticed, for example, that Haydn's variety of form included the use of a developing exposition. The world of Schubert's tonality is that of the modern composer, who regards any tonality as a centre to which all the related keys are more or less closely connected. It is perhaps significant that the composers most deeply influenced by Schubert's methods, Bruckner and Mahler, are composers whose work has been slow to gain recognition.

With Schubert it is melody that ultimately determines everything. A melody's transformation will demand ever varying and expanding harmonies and fresh eloquence of orchestration, but it is always clear and precise in its direction and purpose. To look at the two great symphonies, the last three quartets, the last eight or nine sonatas, the *Winter Journey* songs —a cycle entirely indivisible, with component parts that cannot be studied except in their relationship to each other—is to confront genius as certain of its operations and as sure of its direction as any in music. It is, in many respects, an earthbound genius for all its vitality and human richness. Schubert never looks beyond the limits of human experience ; but within those limits, as the songs alone show, few composers have shown a wider imaginative apprehension of human life.

XV

THE ROMANTIC MOVEMENT

WITH the death of Schubert in 1828 Vienna ceased to be the creative centre of music in Europe. The great composers of the following generations visited what was still a great musical capital, but lived their lives elsewhere, and it was not until the later years of the nineteenth century that Vienna was again in the forefront of musical history. Schumann, Chopin, Mendelssohn, and Berlioz were all born in the first decade of the nineteenth century, and spent their formative years in the era of reaction and disillusionment which followed the collapse of the Napoleonic Empire. They were men of a different type from Haydn, Mozart, Beethoven, and Schubert—of middle-class background and education, more articulate, more sophisticated, more self-conscious. Schumann, Mendelssohn, and Berlioz were steeped in the literature of romanticism, which coloured the outlook of the sensitive spirits of their generation, a literature which did not seek, as did the classical Goethe, to see life steadily and whole, but rather to lose itself in, and draw poetry from, life's suffering and mystery. Although less literary-minded, Chopin too was deeply affected by this spirit.

As the spirit was different, so were the musical idiom and form. Beethoven the " Romantic Classic " and Schubert the " Classic Romantic " had already struck new paths. We have already met these terms in discussing opera, but some further definition may not be amiss. Goethe distinguished "classical " as meaning healthy, and " romantic " as meaning diseased or unbalanced. That is no doubt far too simple, but we shall not be far wrong in thinking of the classical artist as one for whom emotion is subordinate to intellect, colour to line, and atmosphere to structure. The romantic artist in his exaggerated moods glories in a subjective view of the world, cultivates extreme and extraordinary emotional states, and values intensity of expression higher than intellectual balance.

The irruption of the romantic spirit into music coincided with a strong pressure of literature upon the sister art. From the orchestra and from the piano new shades of expressive sonority had been drawn, and from the language of harmony new worlds of sensuousness and passion. The classical design of sonata form had been rendered more fluid and elastic. The character of the classical sonata as a whole—and of the symphony, concerto, and quartet—had undergone a change : what had been an aggregate of conventionally contrasted movements, together forming a balanced whole, was becoming (above all in the great sonatas and symphonies of Beethoven) the medium of a spiritual experience, informing each of the movements and determining their course and relationship to one another.

Robert Schumann (1810–56) was steeped in the literature of romanticism. His father, August Schumann, was a man with a passion for literature, who had written novels and translated Byron's *Beppo* and *Childe Harold*. The son of a needy clergyman, he had made good as a publisher and bookseller in the town of Zwickau in Saxony, where he had reared a family of five, of whom Robert was the youngest. Although not musical, August valued music and encouraged the gifts which Robert revealed at an early age by arranging piano lessons for him, acquiring scores and throwing open the house to amateur music-making. But Robert had also inherited his father's literary gifts, and here August could intervene directly by stimulating his enthusiasm, influencing his reading, and drawing him into editorial work.

SCHUMANN'S LITERARY TASTES

Romantic literature attracted the boy : Byron, Schulze, Franz von Sonnenburg, above all the novels of Jean-Paul Richter. It is no exaggeration to say that the youthful Schumann's very conception of himself was drawn from this German romantic writer whose works seem to-day a bizarre mixture of sentimentality, morbidity, and forced humour, redeemed by occasional flashes of eloquence and self-insight. In a diary which he kept at the age of eighteen Schumann observes that " Jean-Paul is all the time portraying himself in his works, but always in the form of two persons " ; that " the contrasts are very harsh sometimes, not to say extreme " ; that " Jean-Paul always enchants ", but that " through the enchantment there is a feeling of dissatisfaction, an eternal sadness ". Schumann continues : " I often ask myself what would have become of me if I had never known Jean-Paul . . . He must have some affinity with me because I foresaw him. Perhaps I should have written the same kind of poetry "—Schumann thought of himself as a poet at that time—" but I should have withdrawn myself less from other people and dreamt less. I cannot decide, really, what would have become of me, the problem is impossible to work out."

The versatile youth was torn between literature and music. At the age of fifteen he tried his hand at a love-story in the gushing Jean-Paul manner, but already, before he was ten, he had composed and improvised at the piano, delighting his hearers by his knack of inventing figures which hit off their various mannerisms and characteristics. From the age of eleven he had frequently performed at school concerts ; and by the time he was fifteen his teacher, a local worthy of modest attainments but a discerning lover not only of Mozart and Haydn but of Beethoven, whose works in those days were a novelty, declared that the boy had outstripped him.

SCHUMANN'S UNIVERSITIES

The problem was complicated by his father's death when Schumann was sixteen. His mother was a woman of limited outlook and anxious disposition. Robert was dreamy, introspective, unstable. But he was affectionate and impressionable, and to allay her fears he agreed to take the safe course and embark on the uncongenial career of lawyer. In 1828 he enrolled as a student at the university of Leipzig and spent a year there, and another at Heidelberg, failing to apply himself and fortified by a mounting pile of evidence that his destiny lay elsewhere. Gottlob Wiedebein, a song composer of note to whom he had sent some songs, had written an encouraging letter. Leipzig's leading piano teacher, Frederick Wieck, from whom he took lessons, formed a high opinion of him. At Heidelberg he cut a considerable figure as a pianist. In 1830 the inevitable happened. At Schumann's request his mother put the issue to Wieck, who wrote to her that in three years he could turn Robert into " one of the greatest pianists now living ".

The story of Schumann's early years is remarkable compared with those of earlier composers, in that his background was middle-class and cultured and in that he took so long to decide upon a musical career. It is made still more remarkable by the fact that before the fateful decision of 1830 Schumann, without having gone through the mill of an academic training, had *already* formed himself as a composer. " My piano tells me all the deep sentiments which I cannot express ", the solitary, unsettled student had written to his mother from Leipzig in 1828. At Zwickau and throughout the years of abortive legal study he had been teaching himself to compose ; had copied Bach preludes and fugues and works of Beethoven ; had made sketches of ideas improvised at the keyboard—" urgent ideas, often short passages of pianoforte texture, which if not straightway fixed in writing were irretrievably lost "—and laboured to perfect them. In 1829 he had begun a masterpiece, no less : *Papillons*, the forerunner of *Carnaval* and all those other collections of piano miniatures, gay, tender, and poetic, which Schumann was to pour out in the eighteen-thirties, and upon which his fame chiefly rests.

Nevertheless it was with Wieck's " one of the greatest pianists now living " ringing in his ears that Schumann settled again in Leipzig. Not that Wieck's promise had been unqualified : it depended upon whether " our dear Robert " was prepared to curb his " unbridled fancy " and practise patiently—and again upon whether he could bring himself to study " dry, cold " harmony and counterpoint, mastery of which Wieck deemed essential to the building of a great pianist. Wieck's first doubt was soon justified. In 1832, impatient to make up for lost time, Schumann invented a contraption which clamped the fourth finger of his right hand while he practised with the other fingers, and in consequence maimed himself for life. Disaster though this was, it left him free to concentrate all his energies upon composition. After a year's lessons in harmony and counterpoint with Heinrich Dorn, the conductor at the opera house, he left him and continued the self-education which had led to *Papillons*, the *Abegg* Variations, the *Toccata*, the *Allegro*, op. 8, the *Intermezzi*, op. 4, the Studies on Caprices by Paganini. These he published during 1831 and 1832, attracting attention as a composer of force and originality.

Gratifying though this was, it did not solve the problem of how to achieve independence of his mother's and elder brothers' support, now that he had ruined his career as a pianist. In 1833 a solution began to present itself. Two years previously he had sent to the *Allgemeine Musikalische Zeitung*, the leading musical periodical in Germany, an article on an early work of Chopin, the *Là ci darem* Variations, in which he had employed his literary gifts to convey his delight in the fresh, poetic, romantic quality of Chopin's genius. The difficulty which he experienced in getting the article accepted prompted the thought of founding a journal of his own. The narrow, pedantic outlook of the *Allgemeine Musikalische Zeitung* was typical. A journal was needed to create a body of opinion capable of appreciating the romantic spirit which animated Chopin's music and his own ; to attack the exclusive enthusiasm for Rossini's operas and for the trivial garish concertos, variations, fantasias, galops, and pot-pourris concocted by such composer-pianists as Herz and Hünten in order to display their virtuosity. On the positive side Schumann hoped to arouse enthusiasm for Bach, Haydn, and Mozart, and above all for the recently deceased Beethoven and Schubert, whose works were not only masterpieces of form, but models of poetic expression, pointing to a future in which " the poetry of our art " might come to be honoured again.

THE NEW MUSICAL JOURNAL

With the co-operation of a number of like-minded spirits Schumann brought out the first number of *Die Neue Zeitschrift für Musik* (The New Musical Journal) in 1834 and edited it for the following ten years. His contributions reveal a young man of rare nobility of character and richness of mind. Only very seldom did he mention his own compositions, and he never allowed the idiosyncracies of his own style to affect his judgments. He preferred to praise rather than to blame, to kindle enthusiasm rather than entertain with witty polemics or overawe with display of learning. In order to draw his readers into an atmosphere of warm-hearted companionship he adopted the device employed by E. T. A. Hoffmann in *Die Serapionsbrüder* ("The Serapion Brothers"), in which a collection of romantic tales was presented as the proceedings of an imaginary club whose members read stories to each other. Schumann's club was a band of choice spirits, the "Davidsbündler", or David's Leaguers, pledged to wage war against the Philistines of Pedantry, Triviality, and Virtuosity. Congregated round a piano, they judge, speechify, coin epigrams, express different points of view, at heart united and inflaming each other with their zeal. Each contributor wrote under a fanciful pseudonym, Schumann himself under more than one. When expressing the tender, susceptible side of his nature he signed himself "Eusebius", when appearing as the impetuous outspoken critic and champion of new causes, "Florestan". Like characters in a Jean-Paul novel, the two represented contrasting aspects of his personality. But the self-portrait did not end there; the opposites were reconciled in a third figure, who represented, Schumann said, "the man into whom I should like to see them moulded". This was Raro, the mature master, whose judgments, though still informed by feeling, were tempered by the wisdom of experience.

As editor of a progressive musical journal Schumann not only achieved financial independence; he also became a notable figure in the musical world of Leipzig. He could contemplate putting an end to his unsettled bachelor existence. He fell in love with Ernestine von Fricken in 1834, the year in which he began to compose the *Études Symphoniques* and *Carnaval*, a collection of pieces based on four notes whose letters spelt the name of the town (ASCH) where she lived. He proposed and was accepted, but after a few months broke off the engagement. Towards the end of 1835 he became aware of his love for Wieck's daughter Clara, who, when he first took lessons from her father, had been an infant prodigy, and was now a girl of sixteen on the threshold of a career as one of the greatest pianists of the age. Wieck's love for his daughter was fiercely possessive, and he still continued to regard Schumann as a wayward, unstable character. He refused his consent, and it was not until 1840, after legal proceedings had been taken to have his refusal set aside, that the lovers were united. On Schumann the long-drawn frustration acted as a stimulus to composition. Into the *Fantasie*, op. 17, he wove a quotation from Beethoven's song cycle, *To the distant Beloved*. He told his former teacher Dorn that it was Clara

ANTONÍN DVOŘÁK (1841–1904)

JOHANNES BRAHMS (1833–1897)

who had inspired his piano sonatas, the *Davidsbündlertanze* ("Dances of the David's Leaguers"), the *Kreisleriana*, the *Noveletten*. "I have found that nothing sharpens one's imagination so much as to be expecting and longing for something", he wrote to her in 1838. "I have been waiting for your letter and consequently composed whole bookfuls of things." And in another letter to Clara during that period we find : "It is very curious, but if I write much to you, as I am doing now, I cannot compose. The music all goes to you."

MARRIAGE

The year of Schumann's marriage, 1840, was a turning-point in his life. Hitherto all his music, except for a symphony (believed to have been written as an exercise set by his teacher Dorn) and some songs, had been piano-music. He had written a few large-scale works, but his output had consisted mainly of collections of romantic miniatures. For some time past he had aspired to higher things. Schubert's *Impromptus, Moments Musicaux*, and dance music had been the chief inspiration of the miniatures ; but in 1838, during a stay in Vienna, he had visited Schubert's brother Ferdinand, inspected a pile of unpublished scores and found among them the "Great C major" symphony. He had sent it to Mendelssohn, at that time the director of the Leipzig Gewandhaus orchestra ; it had been performed, and the performance had left Schumann "tingling to compose a symphony himself". The example of Mendelssohn was another inspiration. Here was a "Davids-bündler" who not only waged lusty war on the "Philistines", but revived in his compositions the heritage of the past while infusing classical sonata form with a romantic poetic spirit. Of Mendelssohn, Schumann wrote in *Die Neue Zeitschrift* that he was

the Mozart of the nineteenth century ; the most brilliant among musicians ; the one who has most clearly recognised the contradictions of the time, and the first to reconcile them. . . . Nor will he be the last composer. After Mozart came Beethoven ; this modern Mozart will be followed by a newer Beethoven. Indeed, he may already have been born. . . .

In the light of Schumann's career after 1840 we cannot but suppose that subconsciously he had himself in mind when he penned those words. In 1840 he wrote only songs—all his greatest were written in that year, under the inspiration of Clara's love—but thereafter his main occupation in life was the task of playing Beethoven to Mendelssohn's Mozart. From time to time he still wrote songs and piano miniatures, but henceforth his energies were given mainly to the composition of large-scale works.

During the first two years of his marriage Schumann enjoyed a happiness and peace of mind such as he had never known. In 1841 he composed the B flat and D minor symphonies and the *Phantasie* in A minor for piano and orchestra, which he was later to convert into the first movement of the piano concerto. In 1842 followed the three string quartets and the piano quintet and quartet. Thereafter his life was clouded by mental illness. He had never been mentally stable, and in 1833 the successive deaths of a sister-in-law and brother had precipitated a severe nervous breakdown. The intense creative activity of the first years of his marriage brought about another in 1843, and although Schumann recovered, it was only to plunge into renewed activity and to be stricken by a still severer breakdown in 1844. This unhappy story continued until 1854, when the sufferer threw himself into the Rhine and was rescued, only to spend the last two years of his life in an asylum.

During his later years Schumann occupied some important positions. He taught piano and composition at the Leipzig Conservatory of Music; conducted a men's choral society in Dresden; became director of the Düsseldorf orchestra, although his illness made him too introspective and unaware to discharge his duties effectively. His output was never so large and varied as in this period, but much of it is of little interest now save to the specialist. Much of it, but by no means all; the divine fire sometimes failed when Schumann was composing instrumental music, but often it burned. In 1845 he completed the piano concerto and in 1845–46 composed the C major symphony. In 1847 he composed the D minor and F major piano trios, in 1850 the " Rhenish " symphony and the cello concerto; as late as 1851 the G minor trio and the violin sonatas. In the field of dramatic and choral music, in which Schumann's genius was not at home, the flame was much feebler and more fitful.

THE PIANO MINIATURIST

It is upon the early products of his genius, the piano miniatures of the 1830s, of which *Papillons* was the forerunner, that Schumann's fame chiefly rests. Like *Papillons*, each collection was given an evocative title, not hinting at any programme, but designed to attune the listener to its mood. Only *Carnaval* had a programme. As a child Schumann used to improvise musical portraits, and the pieces of this collection were portraits of personages, some real, some fanciful, supposed to be attending a carnival : Pierrot, Arlequin and Coquette, Florestan and Eusebius, Chiarina and Estrella (Schumann's nicknames for Clara and Ernestine von Fricken), Pantaloon and Columbine, Chopin and Paganini. In the *Davidsbündlertanze* Schumann also allowed his romantic fantasy some play. He signed each piece according to its mood, " F " for Florestan, " E " for Eusebius, and in the last piece but one, " F and E ". Above the last piece of all, a tranquil waltz, half-humorous and half-wistful, he could not resist writing : " Quite superfluously Eusebius added the following—but with a look of bliss in his eyes. . . ." Of the other titles—*Kreisleriana, Fantasiestücke, Novelletten, Scenes from Childhood, Humoreske*—the only one which calls for comment here is *Kreisleriana*. Schumann borrowed this title from a collection of quasi-autobiographical sketches by E. T. A. Hoffmann, who presented them as the work of a fictitious musician named Kreisler, a romantic misfit, in love with the " poetry of art ", whose ways were so eccentric that his friends believed him to be mad.

What were the qualities of this music which determined this mode of presentation ? Perhaps the most obvious is the sheer wealth of Schumann's invention. When the mood was on him, when the image of Clara evoked a riot of romantic images and longings, Schumann could not wait to elaborate his miniatures. They tumbled out pell-mell—not related structurally, and only " belonging together " in the sense that they expressed a series of passing moods, reflecting different facets of his personality.

Miniatures do not in any case lend themselves to elaboration. Beethoven's great sonata-form structures had been built upon rhythmically clear-cut, concise, triadic motives, which could serve as foundation stones, supporting a massive weight of development. Schumann's miniatures were finished articles, not foundation stones. They were square-cut symmetrical structures, built out of four-bar stanzas balancing each other like lines of poetry, but containing some complicating element which gave point and character to the simple pattern. The complicating element might be provided by syncopation or by the tug of a two-against-three rhythm. It might be provided by the humorously accented weak beat of *Arlequin* in *Carnaval* or above all it might be provided by chromaticism, either in the accompaniment or in the melody.

Another factor determining Schumann's miniature style was his individual treatment of the piano. It was in the third decade of the nineteenth century that the instrument first assumed its modern form, with " double-escapement " action making for speed and responsiveness, metal bracing for power and volume, hammer-heads of felt for rich cantabile tone. Eusebius revelled in the evocative beauty of rich cantabile tone—especially when the tone was deepened by pedal-sustained bass notes (as in the seventeenth *Davidsbündlertanz*, over which Schumann wrote : " as though from a distance ")—or tinged by a delicately chromatic accompaniment (as in the fourteenth *Davidsbündlertanz*, marked " tender and singing ")— or when the melody was drifting into a mysterious " remote " key.

Romantic effects such as these, immediate in their potency, demanded no elaboration. They revealed a whole world in a grain of sand.

Schumann, as we have seen, attacked the Philistines who exploited the speed and power of the modern instrument for the sake of vulgar display. Florestan exulted in speed and power, but not as ends in themselves. Speedy, powerful scale and arpeggio figures, however extended, embroidered and ramified, were so much acrobatic machinery ; in his hands a figure was an expressive idea, a complex of notes to be employed throughout a piece or section of a piece, varied in different registers and harmonic contexts, but preserving its identity, stamping the whole with a specific character.

SYMPHONIC VARIATIONS

During the eighteen-thirties Schumann composed not only collections of miniatures, but also a number of large-scale works for the piano ; three sonatas in F sharp minor, F minor, and G minor, the set of variations which he entitled *Études Symphoniques*, and the *Fantasie*, op. 17. By far the finest of these works are the *Études Symphoniques* and the *Fantasie*. Of the sonatas the F sharp minor and F minor are superior in respect of content, the G minor in respect of structure. The style of Schumann's lyric miniatures did not lend itself to the requirements of classical sonata form. Not only was his idiom charged with complicating elements which precluded further elaboration, but his habit of thinking in terms of square-cut phrases creates an effect of short-windedness and monotony. Again, in an extended movement, the breathless urgent onrush of Florestan was liable to create a compulsive effect, as though the composer were in the grip of an idea he could not shake off. But in the first movement of the G minor sonata Schumann re-orientated himself successfully. The phrase-lengths are sufficiently varied ; the first subject has a clear-cut rhythmic drive ; the bridge passage performs its function of acting as a springboard to the second subject ; the second subject brings a touch, if only a touch, of needed contrast, and the development section a moment, if only a moment, of genuine climax. The movement is not a masterpiece—the first subject is dominated by a slightly commonplace motive, which in the event tends to overweight the whole—but it is superior to the first movements of the other two sonatas, both of which after an eloquent beginning lose their grip, the eventual impression being less that of a movement in sonata form than of a series of miniatures arbitrarily tacked on to each other.

The *Études Symphoniques*, a set of variations, posed different problems : the composing of miniatures based on a common theme, yet stamped with individual character, and rounded off by an effective finale. Schumann solved the first problem triumphantly. As for the second, the finale tends to fall into the rut of a compulsive dotted rhythm, but here the compulsive effect is turned to account. Just when the need is most urgent, the situation is saved by an electrifying modulation leading to one of the most thrilling perorations in the whole literature of the keyboard. In the *Fantasie* one can point to structural defects. The title notwithstanding, it was designed as a sonata in three movements, and Schumann originally planned to call it one. The impassioned first movement sprawls, and the jubilant martial middle movement and the unconventional slow finale both lean heavily on the Schubertian device of repetition *en bloc* in different keys. But these defects count for little in the total effect of this work, of which Schumann told Clara that it was " the most passionate thing I have ever composed . . . a deep lament for you ". Together the three movements create the effect of a single unfolding experience. Schumann created this effect not by riding roughshod over the classical sonata structure—the movements are separated and the first is in sonata form—but by modifying it to meet the needs of romantic expression : to convey passion giving way to jubilation, and jubilation to a mood of yearning, sorrowful, yet touched with romantic ecstasy.

SCHUMANN AS SONG-WRITER

Early in 1840 the piano miniaturist, who had been bred up in the literature of romanticism, turned to song-writing, and in that one year produced nearly the half, and nearly all the most celebrated, of his 250-odd songs. Schumann's feeling for verbal values surpassed Schubert's and matches Wolf's. His ability to compose music convincing in its own right yet reflecting the sense of the poem surpass Wolf's, matching Schubert's. Schubert's range, though, was wider than Schumann's. His nature was less complex, his emotion more homogeneous, more full-blooded ; the brook and the flowers and the racing mill-wheel of *The Maid of the Mill* promise utter happiness, the snow and ice of *The Winter Journey* convey utter desolation. In Schumann's emotional world joy and sorrow are subtly commingled. It is characteristic that his greatest landscape picture should have been moonlit and that the climax of *Mondnacht* (that breath-taking moment when the slender semiquaver chords, gently pulsating through the first two stanzas, broaden out to a crescendo) should have been evoked by the poet's

> My soul now upward soaring
> Hath found a home at last.

Schumann was less at home in the normal daytime world. The Rhine resplendent on a Sunday morning inspired one masterpiece (*Sonntags am Rhein*), but as a rule there is a touch of artificiality in his treatment of obvious earthly emotions. The greatest of his song cycles is not Chamisso's *Frauenliebe und Leben* (" Woman's Love and Life "), telling of the joys and trials of wedded love, but Heine's *Dichterliebe* (" Poet's Love ") telling of love lonely and poisoned by secret sorrow. Thus in *Ich hab' im Traum geweinet* (" I wept in my dreams ") the poet wakes weeping from a dream in which his beloved was in her tomb, and from another in which she had abandoned him. A third time he dreams that she is true, but still he wakes weeping.

It is worth studying some of the details of this great song. Schumann's conception is not that of a melody-plus-evocative-accompaniment in the manner of Schubert, but of an utterance in which the piano combines with the voice on equal terms. The first two stanzas are declaimed by the singer unaccompanied, the piano rounding off each phrase ; at the stanza in which the words tell of the third dream, voice and piano unite, the piano pointing the anguish of the poet's mysterious confession with a harshly chromatic progression. Schumann closes this stanza on a discord, which the piano then resolves, rounding off the whole song. It is as though the emotion of the poem were beyond words, even Heine's.

Ich hab' im Traum geweinet is an example of the Schumann song at its most individual. One or other of its features—the subtle interplay of voice and piano, the telling chromaticism, the piano postlude—are to be found in (for example) *Wenn ich in deine Augen seh* (" When I look into your eyes "), *Erstes Grün* (" First Green "), or *Am leuchtenden Sommermorgen* (" On a shining summer morning ") where the exquisite piano postlude covers nearly a whole page. But Schumann also wrote great songs in Schubert's more straightforward manner : *Ich grolle nicht* (" I bear no grudge "), *Die Lotusblume* (" The Lotus Flower "), *Die beiden Grenadiere* (" The two Grenadiers "). When writing below his best, his feelings for emotional chromatic effects tend to run away with him : the vocal line is registering the sense and stress of the words, but the piano's harmonies betray that the words are less a source of inspiration than an outlet for sentimental indulgence in emotion for emotion's sake.

The songs of 1840 form the climax of Schumann's career in smaller forms. Besides many more songs, he wrote folk-song settings, duets, part-songs, and from time to time piano pieces, notably the *Album für die Jugend* (" Album for Youth "), *Waldscenen* (" Woodland Scenes "), and *Gesänge der Frühe* (" Morning Songs "), but he seldom if ever matched the achievements of the past. Henceforth Florestan and Eusebius give way to the mature master Raro, into whom Schumann had hoped to see them moulded.

How impressive is this Raro? To regard Schumann only as a miniaturist is a dangerous simplification. It is also a tempting one. The cap so
perfectly fits the youthful Schumann, a figure dreamy, ardent, impulsive,
typically romantic, more vivid and comprehensible than the psychopath of
the later years. Certainly the platitude can be safely applied to Schumann's
neglected dramatic and choral works (the opera *Genoveva*, the incidental
music to *Faust* and *Manfred*, the oratorio *Paradise and Peri*, the Mass and
Requiem). These all contain beauties, but the hyper-sensitive, highly
wrought miniaturist lacked the necessary objectivity and breadth of style.

SCHUMANN THE SYMPHONIST

Of Schumann's four symphonies, the fourth in D minor (so called
because, although it was the second to be written, after its unsuccessful first
performance in 1841 he revised it ten years later) occupies a precarious
place in the standard repertory, while the others lie off the beaten track.
The most obvious reason for this neglect of works which contain many
characteristic beauties is their scoring, in particular Schumann's strange habit
of duplicating wholesale instead of scoring for individual solo instruments,
and thus producing a continuous web of undifferentiated sound. Schumann
did not fall into this habit because he was insensitive to the possibilities of
the orchestra. He could on occasion score beautifully (for example in the
piano concerto), but it would seem that in the less romantic world of
symphonic form it was not second nature to him to invent the appropriate
variegated texture, calling for a constant thrust and parry of different
instruments. The weakness is most apparent in the fast " outside " movements in full-scale sonata form. We have seen what problems sonata form
set, and to what extent Schumann overcame them at the monochromatic
piano. We have also seen that in Florestan's fast pieces, original ideas were
liable to become overworked and create a compulsive effect. Bearing in
mind that it is the outside movements which demand the fullest possible
exploitation of the orchestral canvas, one can understand how difficult it
was for Schumann to solve the architectural problem here. He took the
line of least resistance and continued to think in terms of the piano. This
accounts for the thick texture and the tendency of subjects to take a
compulsive hold, precluding those really " big " developments which are
the *sine qua non* of a successful large-scale orchestral movement in sonata
form.

Another radical weakness of the symphonies is that their movements
too often fail to create a sense of belonging together. The quality of
invention and orchestration is too uneven, tending to fall in the outer

movements and rise in the smaller-scale *andantes* and *scherzos*. It varies somewhat less in the B flat symphony, which was inspired, Schumann said, " by the spirit of Spring ", and is pervaded throughout by the appropriate joyous lyrical warmth. It varies greatly in the C major symphony, of which the slow movement is a masterpiece, composed in a truly orchestral style, rising to a passionate climax worthy of Wagner or Tchaikovsky. It varies again in the " Rhenish " symphony, which contains two slow movements, the first less remarkable, the second a movement unique in Schumann's output. Early in the 1840s he had resumed his studies of Bach, and inspired by a visit to Cologne cathedral, he turned them to account in a polyphonic movement in which a stately ascending theme infiltrates the whole texture, its interweaving wonderfully evoking the intricate ornament of a Gothic cathedral.

The one symphony against which the reproach of movements not belonging together cannot be levelled is the D minor. Beethoven had shown how a unifying effect could be induced by running movements into each other (in the " Emperor " concerto) and by recalling a theme from a previous movement (in the fifth and the ninth symphonies). Weber, Spohr, and Mendelssohn had taken one or other, or both, of these hints. Schubert (in the *Wanderer* Fantasy) had not only recalled but re-worked a theme from a previous movement. In his D minor symphony Schumann went still further : he ran all four movements into each other and based them on material common to each. Thus in the nature of the case the quality of invention is consistent, and this no doubt makes the D minor the most convincing of the symphonies, although the scoring is often pianistic, and Schumann nowhere reaches the heights of the slow movement of the C major and the " cathedral " movement of the " Rhenish ". From the historical point of view, too, this is the most significant symphony. Schumann's striving to create an effect of totality more explicit than that attained by the separate movements of the classical symphony was typically romantic. He did not, indeed, attempt to make the effect still more explicit by attaching a programme ; but played without a break, its themes transformed from movement to movement, expressing now one mood, now another, this symphony belongs to the same world as the programme-symphonies of Berlioz and the symphonic poems of Liszt and Richard Strauss.

The *Manfred* overture is another piece unique in Schumann's output. He could vividly see himself in the hero of Byron's poem, tormented by fears of madness (" I never devoted myself to any composition with such lavish love and power as to *Manfred*", he is reported to have said). The scoring is still pianistic ; but here the compulsive onrush of a basic figure does not preclude " big " developments.

CHAMBER MUSIC

Amongst the post-1840 compositions there are two which warn us still more forcibly against regarding Schumann as a mere miniaturist : the piano concerto and the piano quintet. Moreover, we must guard against the impression that these two, together with the *Manfred* overture, are in the nature of glorious flukes. There is architectural mastery—not to mention music of searching beauty, of a kind unmatched in Schumann's whole output—in some comparatively neglected works.

Schumann wrote nothing comparable to the first movement of the A major quartet, for example. Like the first movement of Beethoven's piano sonata in E flat, op. 31, No. 3, it is based on a wistful phrase of a falling fifth ; but Schumann's handling of it creates a sense of intimate abandon, of thoughts being voiced which are not meant to be overheard. There is no attempt to be grand or profound : it is simply " shapely " music in the dexterous manner of Mendelssohn, as are also the other two quartets in A minor and F major. All three were thrown off in less than two months, and this speed and ease are reflected in the music. The familiar Schumann is there too in the lyrical slow movements, in the syncopated lilt of the first movement of the A minor, and in the whirling semiquavers of the finale of the F major.

At the end of those two months Schumann returned to the keyboard and proceeded to write the quintet and quartet for strings and piano. Before him only Schubert had composed a piano quintet (the "Trout"), but whereas Schubert had added a double-bass, Schumann added a second violin. For here the architectural problem was to be solved by playing off the piano against the strings, and if the piano was to be given its head, a second violin was needed to prevent the strings being overweighted. In the development section of the first movement the piano comes to the fore with a Florestan-like *perpetuum mobile*, in which a coiling quaver figure, derived from the first subject, is allowed to run on for some sixty bars. But here the effect is not compulsive, for the flow of quavers and the elusive coiling figure cunningly offset the crotchet stride and clear-cut presentation of the first part of the movement. In the development section of the finale the strings come to the fore with a ringing lyrical theme. But it is in the coda of the finale that Schumann scores his crowning triumph : the joy of combining strings and piano inspires two fugatos, the second a double fugato, harnessing the striding first subject of the finale to the exuberant opening theme of the first movement.

In the piano quartet in E flat major Schumann missed the second violin which had served him so well in the quintet. Some critics have complained that the finale rambles and that the scherzo is clumsy, but the slow movement is exquisite and the development section of the first movement masterly. Similarly the three piano trios in D minor, F major, and G minor are unequal. The most striking success is the first movement of the D minor, whose impassioned first-subject melody—winding chromatically upwards to a surge of pianoforte arpeggios—matches the eloquence of the *Fantasie*, op. 17.

Schumann gave that melody to his violin, not to his cello. He loved the dark lyricism of the violin's lower register—indeed, in his two sonatas in A minor and D minor for the violin he neglected its brilliant upper range (which perhaps explains why they are less often heard than they deserve). The first movement of the A minor is truly powerful, dominated throughout by a single theme (a shift to a new key does duty for second subject), in the development section lashed by chromatic harmonies to a climax of vivid intensity.

Perhaps Schumann's delight in the violin's G string explains why in 1850 he wrote a concerto for the dark-toned cello rather than for the violin itself. (In 1853, inspired by the playing of Joachim, he did write a violin concerto, but by that time his powers were failing.) In the first two movements Schumann grasped the opportunity with both hands, creating a cellist's paradise of warm rhapsodic melody. But a concerto must have a lively finale, and this created difficulty ; liveliness is not easily attained in performance, and the cadenza is ungrateful.

SCHUMANN'S PIANO CONCERTO

Combining the low tones of the cello with orchestra raised problems of balance which Schumann successfully solved. A piano concerto raised no such problem, although there was no question of using the orchestra merely as a foil to a display of keyboard virtuosity. Thus Schumann telescoped the conventional " double exposition " (in which the *tutti* go over the ground before the soloist's entry) into a single one, in which the orchestra participates with the soloist on equal terms. He left it to the orchestra—not to the piano, as Beethoven had done in the " Emperor "—to run the slow movement into the finale. He reduced the soloist's cadenza to a lyrical episode in keeping with the romantic character of the concerto as a whole.

Throughout there is a perpetual give-and-take. The soloist heralds the woodwind's quiet delivery of the first subject with a passage of ringing dotted chords, echoes the first subject, sets up a ripple of supporting accompaniment, takes the second subject into his hands, dialogues with the oboe.

There is no trace of the heavy-handed scoring of the symphonies. Surveying the possibilities of the orchestra from the vantage point of the piano, his home ground, Schumann's imagination took wings.

CHOPIN

Compared with Schumann, Frédéric Chopin (1810–49) is an elusive, enigmatic figure. Jean-Paul and Heine reflect the inner world of Schumann's emotional life. He composed significant songs, attached evocative titles to his instrumental music, edited the *Neue Zeitschrift*, wrote revealingly to his family and to Clara. Chopin was not literary-minded, composed only a handful of songs and attached no significant titles to his instrumental music. His letters to his mistress, George Sand, have not been preserved and those to his family are not revealing. He presents an elusive, enigmatic figure in his emotional relationships with Constantia Gladkowska, Maria Wodzinska, and George Sand. Slight and delicate, he was irritable, jealous, withdrawn, subject to strange fits of melancholy and indecision.

It is important to draw attention at the outset to these aspects of Chopin's personality, since "the man in the music" cannot be perceived unless we form a picture which offsets other impressions. He was a dandy in Paris, a fascinating companion, ironical, a born mimic, a gifted caricaturist. We meet the dandy in his letters to his family, before whom he wore a mask. When not discussing his own affairs or matters of immediate moment, he tended to regale them with superficial chatter—gossip about mutual friends, light talk about current musical events.

CHILDHOOD IN POLAND

Chopin's father, like Schumann's, was a man of parts. Nicolas Chopin was a Frenchman of humble origin, who in his youth had emigrated to Poland. At the time of the composer's birth in 1810 he was tutor to the Laczynskis, a noble family; and shortly afterwards he obtained the post of professor of French at the High School in Warsaw. Chopin was deeply attached to his father, his mother (the daughter of an impoverished nobleman), and his two sisters. After he settled in Paris in 1831 he corresponded regularly; his father's death was a terrible shock; when he himself lay dying, he wrote to his sister Louise begging her to come from Warsaw to his bedside.

Chopin's childhood and boyhood appear to have been happy and uncomplicated. He was an infant prodigy with amazing technical facility and powers of improvisation. After doing well at school—his father insisted on a normal general education—he spent three years at Warsaw's principal musical academy undergoing a thorough all-round training. In 1829 he paid a visit to Vienna, and his success there, as pianist and composer, put the seal on the triumphs he had enjoyed in his native city. It was evident that if he was to cultivate his powers to the full and reap the rewards they deserved, he must establish himself in one of the great cities of Europe ; but he was in love with Constantia Gladkowska, a soprano at the Warsaw opera, and could not bring himself to leave Poland. Nor could he bring himself to declare his love. "How hateful when something weighs on you and there's nowhere to lay it down. . . . I often tell my pianoforte what I want to tell you", runs one of the many enigmatic passages in Chopin's letters to his friend Titus Wojciechowski at this time. In another he writes : "I wish I could throw off the thoughts which poison my happiness, and yet I love to indulge in them." He eventually tore himself from Warsaw and, Titus travelling with him, returned to Vienna at the end of 1830 in order to consolidate his previous success there.

In Vienna Chopin suffered further trials. Poland was at that time a Russian province, and shortly after his arrival revolt broke out in Warsaw. Chopin, whose art was steeped in Polish folk music, who had scored many triumphs with fantasias and improvisations based on Polish tunes, was deeply perturbed. Should he follow the example of Titus and return to take part in the revolt, or listen to his father and friends who urged him to consider his career ? Would his career be better served by remaining in Vienna or by seeking his fortune in Paris, where the Polish cause was popular ? In the event he stayed in Vienna for some months, giving only one not very brilliant concert and seeking escape from worry in a round of parties. To his parents he wrote cheerfully, but the cheerfulness was forced, as a letter to another friend reveals :

> I laugh, and in my heart as I write this some horrible presentiment torments me. I keep thinking that it's a dream . . . that I am with all of you ; the voices I hear, to which my soul is not accustomed, make no other impression . . . than the rattling of carriages in the street.

PARIS

In July 1831 Chopin left Vienna, and travelling via Munich and Stuttgart reached Paris. He was already a master. The *Là ci darem* variations, the *Krakowiak*, the *Fantasia on Polish Airs* and other works, with which he had scored his early triumphs, were bravura pieces touched with genius. But he had also composed the piano concertos in F and E minor, several characteristic mazurkas, waltzes, polonaises, and nocturnes, (among them the celebrated E flat Nocturne of op. 9), and the first set of Études, op. 10, (among them the celebrated "Revolution" Étude, said to have been written in Stuttgart, where the terrible news reached him of the collapse of the Warsaw revolt). Last, not least, his portfolio contained sketches of two large-scale works drafted in Vienna; the B minor Scherzo and the G minor Ballade.

In Paris Chopin's triumph was immediate and enduring. The previous year revolution had toppled the régime of Charles X. In the city of Victor Hugo, Chateaubriand, George Sand, and Delacroix, revolutionary fervour had also swept art, promoting a cult of romantic originality. An exile from oppressed Poland, whose art was nothing if not romantically original, was *persona grata*. Letters of introduction carried Chopin into the highest musical circles, where he won the friendship and esteem of Liszt, Berlioz, Hiller, the pianist Kalkbrenner, and other luminaries. Furthermore, in the summer of 1832 Prince Valentin Radziwill introduced him to the Rothschilds, and this introduction proved momentous. Early that year Chopin had given a brilliantly successful concert, but the success was not repeated; he lacked the exhibitionism of a great executant, withdrew into himself, played too softly. He was at his best in a salon, and the introduction to the Rothschilds gave him the run of the fashionable salons of Paris, where he could earn large sums by playing, and still larger ones by teaching. Hitherto his father had supported him, but soon Chopin found himself independent, even affluent. His head was not turned: "I know how much I still lack to reach perfection: I see it more clearly now that I live only among first-rank artists and know what each one of them lacks", runs a letter to Titus. He was not happy: "Inside something gnaws at me: some presentiment, anxiety, dreams—or sleeplessness—desire for life and the next instant desire for death". But it meant much to be able to live in style in a handsome apartment and still more to win the reputation of a genius in a class apart, only to be heard behind closed doors, too rare and exquisite for the plebeian concert world.

And so the pattern of Chopin's subsequent mode of life was established. In the summers of 1834–6, it was varied by visits to Germany, where he met Schumann and played him the first Étude of the second set, op. 25, the famous piece in A flat in which a melody is heard through a mist of harp-like accompaniment. ("Imagine an Aeolian harp possessing all the scales and an artist's hand combining these with all kinds of fantastic embellishments, but always with an audible deep ground bass, and in the treble a softly flowing cantilena—and you will have some idea of his playing", wrote Schumann). In Dresden in 1835 he fell in love with Maria Wodzinska, the daughter of a noble Polish family known since childhood.

The following year he proposed marriage and was accepted ; but in the winter of 1835 the first signs had appeared of the consumption which was to bring Chopin to a premature grave, and when in the winter of 1836 he fell ill a second time, Maria's parents withdrew their consent. Chopin did not persist, but the rejection was a bitter blow.

GEORGE SAND

In 1836, however, Chopin met George Sand. The free-thinking, free-living novelist, seven years older than he, loved music and was fascinated by his genius and by the charm of his personality. He inspired in her a protective maternal love, whereas she knew how to kindle in him a passion deeper than he had ever known before. Furthermore, she was able to provide the ailing genius with the home and the affectionate care he needed if he was to maintain his life of teaching and composing. They spent some disastrous months in Majorca in the winter of 1838–9, but thereafter life was uneventful. The winter was spent teaching in the city, the summer composing at Nohant, George Sand's country estate. In 1841, and again in 1842, he gave a recital.

Chopin's previous concerts in Paris, Vienna, and Warsaw had been the typical mixed programmes which the public of those days expected. Chopin would play with the orchestra or join forces with Liszt, Hiller, and other fashionable virtuosi in works for more than one piano ; we read of a *Grand Polonaise with Introduction and March* by Kalkbrenner employing as many as six. The orchestra would contribute an overture or two and stars from the opera add their lustre. The recitals of 1841 and 1842 were arranged by Chopin's publisher, Pleyel, and took place before a select gathering of patrons, friends, and pupils. Some singers contributed ; but in effect Chopin, playing the F major and A flat Ballades, the A major Polonaise, the C sharp minor Scherzo, and various impromptus, nocturnes, études, and preludes, had the field to himself. What an impression he created may be gathered in the panegyrics in the Press. Liszt, who was present at the 1841 concert, wrote afterwards :

For new ideas he has adopted a new style. The hint of a wild and fiery nature, which is part of his inheritance, finds expression in strange harmonies and deliberate discords, while all his delicacy and grace is shown in a thousand touches, the thousand tiny details of an incomparable phantasy.

Not until early in 1848 did Chopin give another recital. It took place under the same auspices, the impression was no less marvellous ; but by now his world was collapsing. He had not saved, and the revolution which broke out a week after the concert was to put an end to the teaching which had been his chief source of income. The previous year he had broken with George Sand after their relationship had been poisoned by jealousies and misunderstandings provoked by her son and daughter. In the atmosphere of loving solicitude which she had created for him during those summers at Nohant, masterpieces had poured from his pen. Now, thrown upon his own resources and with his health deteriorating, the stream had dried up. How was he to live, where should he go ?

A Scottish pupil, Jane Stirling, suggested that he should spend the season in London and then visit her in Scotland. Chopin clutched at this straw. He had a reputation in London, was entertained in society, gave two successful *matinées*, took a few pupils ; but whereas in Paris he had been idolised as a being apart, here, to all save the discerning few, he was no more than an object of fashionable curiosity. At the end of the season he accepted the hospitality of Jane Stirling and her friends and drifted from house-party to house-party, sometimes diverted, more often bored, at heart forlorn. Jane Stirling, good soul, was no George Sand. To earn needed money he steeled himself to play before a large audience in Manchester and smaller ones in Glasgow and Edinburgh. He returned to London in a horrible November and, ill though he was, dragged himself to play at a charity ball for Polish refugees. That was his last public appearance. At the end of the month he returned to Paris, where he lingered for nearly a year, confined to his room, suffering and worried, never quite giving up hope, sketching only a couple of mazurkas, sustained by the affection of friends and, towards the end, by his sister Louise. He died in the autumn of 1849.

A NEW STYLE

" For new ideas he has adopted a new style " : Liszt might have said " new styles ". Chopin confined himself almost entirely to the keyboard, whereas Schumann ranged far and wide over the whole field of composition ; nevertheless, Chopin was by far the more eclectic and versatile. His first teacher had loved Bach and the Viennese classics, and Bach and Mozart especially became life-long influences. But Chopin did not share the earnest Davidsbündler's rather priggish aversion to Italian opera. Like Eusebius, he revelled in the delicate poetry of *cantabile* melody, but the bold flowing line and sparkling ornamentation of operatic *bel canto* was also a source of inspiration. The loveliness of the square-cut melodies of Schumann's miniatures is bound up with the complicated texture of their setting ; Chopin's melodies are more free in structure, more independent, more vital. Above all, he knew how to sublimate the ornamentation of *bel canto*, how to exploit the melodic range and rhythmic impetus provided by the interpolated notes of lesser time-value which constitute an ornament.

VIRTUOSITY

Chopin, who had been an infant prodigy and throughout his boyhood had delighted Warsaw by his technical prowess, did not share the earnest Davidsbündler's aversion to virtuosity either. As he sublimated the coloratura of Italian *bel canto*, so he sublimated the dazzling figuration of Thalberg, Hummel, Ries, Kalkbrenner, Field, and other popular pianist-composers of the day. His two youthful concertos in F minor and E minor are typical virtuoso-concertos, in which the orchestra is a mere accompaniment to the soloist. He regaled his listeners with unheard-of brilliance and elaboration —intricate chromatic runs sweeping the entire compass of the keyboard, passages of rushing double-notes, broken-chord figures spanning the sensuously beautiful interval of the tenth instead of the conventional octave. In the études, which he designed as exercises in the technical problems created by his virtuosic style, Chopin's sublimation went still further. In the manner of Florestan he employed virtuosic figures as structural ideas, and employed them even more resourcefully and powerfully than Schumann.

Chopin had in common with Schumann a genius for exploiting the romantic expressiveness of chromatic harmony ; but he also had in his blood the modal melodies of Polish folk-songs, implying progressions different from those of the Italo-German major-minor system. He was a most imaginative harmonist ; indeed, he has well been cited as one of the forces responsible for the eventual collapse of the major-minor system at the end of the nineteenth century.

LARGE-SCALE WORKS

Schumann wrote only one really great large-scale work for solo piano, the *Fantasie*, op. 17. Chopin wrote several. His eclectic keyboard idiom contained classical, operatic, virtuosic, imaginative harmonic elements, and limitless potentialities. The sections of a large-scale work must dovetail, must provide grand contrasts and point of sweeping climax. Already in the B flat minor Nocturne of op. 9, a miniature in ABA form, Chopin, with an art concealing art, steals out of his B section into his A by means of a beautifully managed chromaticism. And already in the third Étude of op. 10, the famous one in E major, he revealed his ability to provide grand contrasts and points of sweeping climax in the cascade of spectacular chords which crowns its middle section. We find him employing these resources on a large scale in the early G minor Ballade, sketched before he reached Paris. The tranquil entry of the lyrical second subject (the piece bears sufficient resemblance to a movement in sonata form to justify this terminology) is floated by a beautiful chromaticism ; in the development section virtuosic chords and octaves transform the lyrical second subject into a passionate outburst. The passion spent, an episode of sparkling finger-work conveys a passing mood of hectic gaiety ; and at the coda the ultimate of violence is expressed by a climactic scale in contrary motion delivered by both hands in octaves.

The G minor Ballade was the greatest of Chopin's early works, but he did not therefore regard it as marking a new stage in his development. To Schumann, after the achievements of 1841, the composition of miniatures was henceforth merely a sideline, but Chopin remained faithful to the miniature, and in the *Variations Brillantes*, op. 12, and the *Allegro de Concert* (composed as late as 1840–41), reverted to the bravura style of his early triumphs. With the years his texture grew more contrapuntal, his harmony more subtle, his architecture bolder ; but in essence the idiom of the Chopin who took Paris by storm in 1831 remained unchanged.

ASPECTS OF CHOPIN'S STYLE

At the risk of appearing pedantic, we can broadly distinguish the various aspects of Chopin's eclectic style : the operatic lyricist, the virtuoso, the architect, the Pole, the imaginative harmonist, the improviser, the salon composer. The first three we have encountered in the nocturnes, études, and G minor Ballade. In the mazurkas we meet the Pole who transfigured Polish folk-music. The mazurka is a dance in 3/4 time, the accent falling on the " weak " third beat. The form is sectional, the melody often modal and built out on tiny one-bar motives. The melodies were nearly always Chopin's own, for the most part unadorned, and constructed upon a basis of simple rhythmic accompaniment. The operatic lyricist and the virtuoso had little scope ; but the architect is sometimes in evidence. In each of the C sharp minor mazurkas (op. 41, No. 1 and op. 50, No. 3) there is finely wrought structure, with sections dovetailed, harmony highly charged, inspiration reaching its highest tension on the final page. Moreover, the imaginative harmonist's idiom was never so flavoured with strange modal spices as in the mazurkas.

In the polonaises Chopin was transfiguring not folk-music but an aristocratic dance performed in traditional splendid costume to a ringing martial rhythem. The transfiguration was another triumph of melodic invention and imaginative harmony; but here the architect is less in evidence. The form of the polonaise, like that of the mazurka, is sectional, and Chopin respected this structure, relying upon the eloquence of each individual section and upon the force of the contrasts they generated. He wrote six great polonaises; and in the last two the virtuoso came into his own, the ringing chords and octaves imparting to the music the character of a tone-poem evoking the historic splendours of ancient Poland.

Beside the polonaises stands the *Polonaise-Fantasie*, one of Chopin's greatest works. Here the architect came to the fore, the form being not sectional but continuous and cumulative. And yet Chopin had good reason to call this work a *Fantasie*, for despite the careful structure, the overriding effect is one of glorious abandonment, of ideas flung off in the heat of the moment, leading the composer he does not know where, of the whole improvised in a single session at the keyboard in one prolonged burst of inspiration.

Chopin the improviser is paramount in the great F minor *Fantasie* and in the four impromptus. Here ideas were poured out without regard to the eventual form they would take. If an idea was short and homogeneous, then to create a presentable form it sufficed merely to repeat the first section in accordance with the simple ternary principles. But this expedient was less effective when Chopin's idea was neither short nor homogeneous, as in the F minor *Fantasie*. The player, when he comes to repeat this marvellous section, is hard put to it to avoid an effect of anti-climax.

The improviser was in his element when he concentrated upon a single idea—as in the *Berceuse*, in which a tender melody, set above a lullaby *ostinato* bass, dreams itself into an enchanted world of virtuosic figuration; and in the twenty-five wonderfully diverse miniatures, some covering no more than a page, to which he gave the anomalous title of Preludes. In these inspired pieces, uninhibited by architectural problems, Chopin reveals the whole wealth of his mind.

In the waltzes we meet the fashionable salon composer, the Chopin who, though he shrank from the public exhibition of a concert, enjoyed giving pleasure by turning and embellishing a pretty tune. Here the harmony is generally straightforward, the figuration brilliant yet plain-sailing, the architecture unpretentious. Not always, though; towards the close of the *Grande Valse Brillante* op. 18 in E flat, and of the two great waltzes in A flat major, Chopin rounds off with a burst of exuberant development. And in the two *lento* waltzes—op. 34, No. 2 in A minor and the familiar A flat, op. 69, No. 1—Chopin shows his heart. Although composed in 1836, only six years after he had left Poland, this A flat Waltz is touched by that poignant homesickness of the last mazurka composed in the year of his death.

Chopin's four scherzos are rapid, violent, and rhythmic, and contain contrasting trios in which the tension is relaxed. But Chopin's trios push the contrast much further. Beethoven relaxes, as it were, on his feet, his ears cocked to the pulse of the movement as a whole. Chopin stretches himself on the ground and dreams of other things—in the B minor Scherzo of a Polish folk-lullaby, in the E major of a tender lyrical melody, in the C sharp minor of a fantasy-chorale, embellished by strains of Aeolian-harp-like figuration. In the most celebrated of the scherzos, the B flat minor, Chopin provides a closer resemblance to Beethoven ; in the course of the main body of the scherzo a new lyrical theme—a sort of second subject—takes charge, and the trio, at first a dream-like interlude like the others, becomes in the event a sort of development section, raising the music to fresh heights of tension and excitement.

CHOPIN'S FORMS

Chopin the architect is at his greatest and most original in the four ballades, the *Barcarolle* and the sonatas in B minor and B flat minor. Chopin drastically modified sonata form. But we shall misunderstand the essential originality of Chopin's architecture if we content ourselves with analysis in terms of first and second subjects and the like. In the classical sonata the creation of a fundamental sense of balance between the sections of a movement is paramount. Chopin's modifications destroyed this balance and set in its place another controlling principle : a logic, akin to that which governs the telling of a story, of *cumulative* effect, driving the music continuously forward to a final dramatic climax. Already in the early G minor Ballade we meet this logic. It is above all the recapitulation which safeguards the balance of a movement in classical sonata form but, since it repeats what has already been stated, this is a stumbling-block to the logical unfolding of a story. The recapitulation of the G minor Ballade is in the nature of a transfiguration. What was originally delivered *sotto voce* to an accompaniment of quiet crotchets becomes a passage delivered *fortissimo* to an accompaniment of surging quavers. Although it is a true recapitulation, since the same melody is being set in the same key, the effect it creates is that of a new chapter in the story.

A purely musical logic such as this lent itself to a romantic programme, but Chopin did not care for such things. Only once in his letters do we find a passage divulging the " meaning " of a work, that in which he says that the *Adagio* of the E minor concerto " should give the impression of gazing tenderly at a place which brings to mind a thousand dear memories ... a sort of meditation in beautiful spring weather, but by moonlight ".

However, we have Schumann's word for it that, during the visit he paid to Leipzig, Chopin said that the F major Ballade was inspired by " some poems " of his compatriot, the poet Mickiewicz, and this has led to the probably mistaken connection with the story of a village engulfed by an enchanted lake. Chopin's idyllic first subject is duly engulfed by a torrential second subject. In the development section the first subject drifts out of F major, mourning over its shattered idyll. But then he allows classical musical logic to take charge, driving out whatever thoughts he may have had of a programme. The development section is engulfed by an exact recapitulation—as it were, a second inundation—of the torrential second subject. At the close of the ballade, though, the programme seems to assert itself again, and Chopin gives his idyllic first subject a final pathetic word in A minor.

In Chopin's two greatest Ballades in A flat and F minor, composed in the early 1840s when he was at the height of his powers, he preserved the pattern of the G minor Ballade and developed it further. Thus in the A flat major it is the recapitulation itself which constitutes the dramatic climax of the piece. In the development section the music fights its way back to A flat major across a quagmire of shifting keys, in the teeth of a growling gale of left-hand figuration. When at last the home key is reached and we hear the tenuous, wistful first subject transfigured by brilliant chords and octaves, it is as though we have mounted a sunlit plateau.

The F minor Ballade is perhaps the greatest piece Chopin ever wrote. It has the glorious improvisatory abandonment of the *Polonaise-Fantasie*, and yet the overriding effect is architectural. Beginning like a nocturne, it ends in a furious majesty which demands of the player the utmost energy and passion, coupled with the utmost dexterity and control.

Its title notwithstanding, the *Barcarolle* is a work of the same genre as the ballades. Chopin composed it in 1845–46 during the last two of those fruitful summers at Nohant. Its intricate texture and daring harmony are characteristic of many of his late works of the 1840s. But Chopin never wrote anything more richly involved than its transfigured recapitulation, in which above a tonic pedal-note, sustained by a rocking barcarolle figure, a thematic phrase is put into canon and steered through a succession of impassioned chromatic harmonies—until suddenly, after a magical coloratura passage, passion is forgotten and the peaceful gondola atmosphere of the opening restored.

THE SONATAS

As important as a fundamental sense of balance between the sections of a movement is the creation of a sense of balance between the movements themselves. Of Chopin's two sonatas, certainly the B minor meets this latter requirement. The characters of its four movements are conventional : an extended opening *Allegro* (whose coherence is attacked by a destructive flood of virtuosic figuration before the main ideas have had time to establish themselves), an exquisite slow movement, a high-spirited scherzo, and a superbly dynamic finale ; together they form a satisfactorily balanced whole.

Concerning the total effect of the B flat minor sonata, opinions differ. In the opening *Allegro* Chopin succeeded, as he did not in that of the B minor, in reconciling virtuosity with the demands of a balanced classical design. But the scherzo contains a dream-like trio, the slow movement is the celebrated Funeral March, and the finale a brief ghostly *perpetuum mobile*, played throughout in bare unison or octaves. The fact that the Funeral March was composed long before the other movements lends a certain plausibility to the view that as a whole the sonata does not cohere. In fact the total effect of the sonata, comparable to that of Schumann's great *Fantasie*, op. 17, presents a single unfolding experience of a kind precluding expression in terms of the balanced classical design. Chopin in that ghostly last movement looks beyond the romantic ecstasy that Schumann achieved. He was a romantic, Schumann's contemporary ; yet that last movement has less in common with Schumann's than with the finale of Vaughan Williams's sixth symphony. In both there is the sense of an ultimate desolation, of existence bereft of humanity, of an eternal barren meaninglessness.

XVI

MENDELSSOHN AND THE CLASSICAL IDEAL

VERY different in character, upbringing, and gifts was Chopin's almost exact contemporary, Felix Mendelssohn-Bartholdy (1809–47). Mendelssohn admired Chopin, though he seemed to him " to toil rather too much in the Parisian spasmodic and impassioned style . . . often losing sight of time and sobriety and true music. I, on the other hand, do so perhaps too little. . . ." So Mendelssohn wrote his mother after a meeting with Chopin in Germany in 1834. With a touch of rueful humour he added that his effect on Chopin was to make the latter feel rather like a trivial Parisian dandy, whereas Chopin made him feel " rather like a schoolmaster ".

Mendelssohn was only a year older than Chopin, but he had matured even more rapidly. The twenty-one-year-old Chopin who in 1831 took Paris by storm was already the Chopin that we know, although he had not yet developed his full powers. By 1831 Mendelssohn had already written some of the vintage works by which he is remembered : the octet and the overture to *A Midsummer Night's Dream* (composed before he was eighteen), and the *Hebrides* and *Calm Sea and Prosperous Voyage* overtures. Others— the *Reformation*, *Italian*, and *Scottish* symphonies, for example—were already being sketched. Perhaps it lay in the nature of Mendelssohn's genius to mature rapidly. Certainly when we consider his formative years—his parents and their milieu, his family life, his education—we form the impression that extraordinary circumstances partly account for his extraordinary precocity.

HIS BACKGROUND

Mendelssohn's parents, Abraham and Lea, were not only wealthy, high-principled and cultured, but distinguished. Thus Abraham's father was Moses Mendelssohn, the famous Jewish philosopher and friend of Lessing ; his brother was the friend and patron of Alexander von Humboldt, the famous philosopher, botanist, and traveller ; his sister the wife of Friedrich Schlegel, the famous poet, scholar, and translator of Shakespeare. Among those who visited Abraham and Lea in their spacious Berlin home were the philosopher Hegel, the sculptor Schadow ; Heine, Spohr, Moscheles, Kalkbrenner, Paganini, and other musical and literary celebrities.

Abraham Mendelssohn applied himself with patriarchal zeal to the task of educating Felix, Felix's elder sister Fanny (who was also a musical prodigy), Rebecca, and Paul. Though not a professing Jew (he adopted the Evangelical faith, changing his name to Mendelssohn-Bartholdy), Abraham was deeply religious, instilling an exacting code of self-discipline and exalted ideal of service to humanity. Every morning at five o'clock (except Sunday, to which Felix accordingly looked forward) the children rose in order to garner the cultural riches which their father, the head of an eminent banking firm, was in a position to provide. At first Abraham himself and Lea taught the children. She played and sang with expression and grace, drew exquisitely, and besides knowing French, English, and Italian, could read Homer in the original. Later Karl Heyse (subsequently a famous philologist and father of the poet Paul Heyse) was employed as resident tutor. There was also a drawing master, not to mention instruction in gymnastics and riding. As for music, Felix learnt the piano from one of the most esteemed teachers of his time, Ludwig Berger, a pupil of Clementi, and composition from Karl Zelter, the director of the Sing-akademie and friend of Goethe (to whom he duly introduced his prize pupil). On alternate Sunday mornings an orchestra, specially engaged for the purpose, assembled in the large dining-room in order to perform under Felix's baton the symphonies, concertos, operettas, and other works which poured from his pen. Thus it is not to be wondered at that Mendelssohn's precocity was extraordinary, and that in the company of Chopin the repository of so much learning and culture should have felt " rather like a schoolmaster ".

If Mendelssohn's father's code of life seems to have inhibited the subsequent development of his son's genius, it obliged him to form a habit of composing whether in the mood or not (" doing his duty ", he called it) ; and he wore himself out writing a great deal of inferior music. The exalted ideal prevented him from drawing the hard-and-fast line, which a creative genius must learn to draw, between obligations to others and duty to his art ; so that in his later years, when he became famous as a conductor and administrator, he wore himself out fulfilling engagements and coping with the manifold responsibilities heaped upon him. Worse still, the exalted ideal ran counter to his romantic bent. According to Abraham, the rich resources of the modern orchestra would go to waste if they were not harnessed to subjects of moral significance (" an object must be found for music . . . which by its fervour, its universal sufficiency and perspicuity may take the place of the pious emotions of former days ").

He accordingly advised Felix to "hang on a nail" the romanticism of his youthful overtures and "proceed to graver works"; and Felix all too dutifully followed this advice.

He did so partly because he loved his father, as he did his mother, brother, and sisters, above all Fanny. To read their published letters, that rare testament of family affection binding into happy unity a group of gifted kindred spirits, is to suspect that perhaps in the last resort it was the sheer happiness of Mendelssohn's early years which inhibited his subsequent development. He could not move out of the family orbit, could not, like Schumann and Chopin, re-orientate his emotional life and draw richness from the depths of acknowledged longing and passion. His muse was at home in the shallows of happy domestic affection and a comfortable, superficial piety, touched at times by melancholy and passion but at its characteristic best conveying a happy adolescent's romantic vision of the beauty and wonder of the world.

MUSICAL TRAINING

The composition of the octet and the overture to *A Midsummer Night's Dream* are the first important events in Mendelssohn's career. The next important one occurred in 1829 when, due principally to his enthusiasm, the first performance of Bach's *St. Matthew Passion* took place under his baton at the Singakademie.

Bach too was part of Mendelssohn's cultural heritage. Not only his composition teacher Zelter, but also his maternal grandmother and both his parents loved this composer, at that time esteemed by a comparatively few enthusiasts and connoisseurs. (When Fanny was born, Lea observed that she had "Bach fugue fingers".) Zelter had for years been collecting manuscripts of Bach's choral works, among them the *St. Matthew Passion*. In the winter of 1827, with a choir of sixteen voices, meeting regularly to perform rarely heard works, Mendelssohn began to study it. "He . . . mastered its difficulties so completely", wrote Devrient, who sang the part of Jesus, "that what had hitherto seemed mysterious complication, only for the initiated, became to us natural and familiar." The epoch-making first performance, bringing about the first public realisation of Bach's greatness, was the climax of Mendelssohn's early career. For the next three years, at his father's behest, he travelled. This was partly in order to round off his education by seeing the world and learning to fend for himself; and partly, since in Berlin he was regarded as a wealthy amateur upstart, to choose where to settle and lead a socially useful life as an active professional composer and conductor. He went to London, where he enjoyed the first of his many musical and social triumphs. He went on a walking-tour of the Highlands. ("There is little corn, much heather brown and red, precipices, passes, beautiful green everywhere, deep-blue water—but all stern, dark, very lonely.") He made the trip to Fingal's Cave on Staffa, where the opening bars of the *Hebrides* overture occurred to him. (He jotted them down in a letter.) He went to Weimar and spent some weeks sitting at the feet of Goethe. He went to Vienna, to Rome, to Naples, to Paris ; but in these places the son of Abraham Mendelssohn, the pupil of Zelter, the devotee of Goethe, found much that displeased him. In Vienna " not one of the best pianists . . . ever played a note of Beethoven, and when I hinted that he and Mozart were not to be despised, they said ' so you are an admirer of classical music ? ' ' Yes,' said I." The Italian operas he heard were " mean and low " and standards of performance disgraceful. Paris was a Babylon of superficiality and self-seeking. As for the French romantics, we have seen how Mendelssohn (who at Weimar had heard Goethe inveighing against " the universal yearning of the young men who are so melancholy ") disapproved of Chopin's " Parisian spasmodic and impassioned style ". In Rome he had met another exponent of this style, Berlioz, in himself charming and interesting, but " without a spark of talent " and withal monstrously vain, superficial, and affected. (" I cannot stand his obtrusive enthusiasm and the gloomy despondency he assumes before ladies.")

PROFESSIONAL CAREER

At the end of the three years Mendelssohn decided to settle in Germany. His professional career began in 1833, when he accepted the position of general music director at Düsseldorf. More than filial piety was involved. Mendelssohn was animated by a Davidsbündlerish zeal to raise standards and, unlike Schumann, he was a born conductor and orchestral trainer. He was furthermore a man of great charm, with a gift for friendship, ready to put himself out to please and help others. The record of his brief career—he died in 1847—is breath-taking. After 1835, when he exchanged his position at Düsseldorf for that of conductor of the Gewandhaus concerts at Leipzig, the main fields of his activity were Leipzig and Berlin, where despite official hostility various dazzling (though in the event unsatisfying) positions were offered by his admirer Frederick William IV. His range as a conductor was wide. Besides his own enormously popular compositions, he brought forward works by Schumann, Gade, Macfarren, Sterndale Bennett, and other contemporaries. He ran an enterprising historical series, and conducted Bach cantatas, Handel oratorios, and Beethoven's Ninth. Six more times he crossed the Channel in order to conduct, not only in London, where Queen Victoria and the Prince Consort entertained him and played and sang his music, but in Birmingham, Liverpool, and Manchester. He played concertos ; his favourite was Beethoven's in G major, at that time a rarity. He gave organ recitals. He edited *Israel in Egypt* for the Handel Society. At Leipzig he founded and directed a conservatory and organised the erection of a monument to Bach. And all the time he was composing.

In 1846 his health began to fail, but though he talked of retiring, he continued to direct the Gewandhaus concerts and to attend with scrupulous care to his duties at the Conservatory. " The habit of constant occupation instilled by his mother made rest intolerable to him ", says Devrient. Since he was not only highly strung and irritable, but liable to be thrown off his balance by the manifold frictions to which he was exposed, the wonder is that his health did not fail sooner.

EARLY DEATH

His death in 1847 was precipitated by the shock of his sister Fanny's six months previously. His father's death in 1835 had plunged him into a depression which had caused concern. Shortly afterwards he had married, and even this step seems partly to have been an act of filial piety. Abraham had wanted him to marry, and Fanny, alarmed by his " solitary, almost desperate mood ", persuaded him to seek a wife. He fell in love with Cécile Jeanrenaud but, though his age made it no longer necessary, he would not act without his mother's consent. The marriage seems to have been happy, though their correspondence was destroyed and we have no intimate particulars. They had children, yet when Mendelssohn talked of retiring, his thoughts turned to his brother and remaining sister in Berlin. " My plan is that we should form all together one pleasant united household such as we have not seen for long, and live happily together." It went without saying that the seat of this household should be the home of his parents, in which after their mother's death Fanny and, from time to time, Felix himself and other members of the family had continued to live.

To his early masterpieces Mendelssohn subsequently added only five comparable works : the *Melusine* and *Ruy Blas* overtures, composed in 1833 and 1839, the incidental music to *A Midsummer Night's Dream*, produced in 1843, the violin concerto in 1844, and *Elijah* in 1846.

THE CHILD PRODIGY

Before the octet we at first stand tongue-tied. Granted the extraordinary circumstances, it is incredible that a boy of sixteen could have composed this large-scale work in four movements, three in convincing sonata form, scored with the skill of a Weber, and in places revealing a command of counterpoint almost comparable to that of Mozart in the finale of the *Jupiter*. It is still more incredible to find this miraculous technical expertise employed not imitatively, but as the medium of a personal expression, if not as profound, at any rate as fresh and original as the masterpieces of Schubert's 'teens. The sheer happiness of Mendelssohn's early years was partly responsible for his subsequent failure to mature, but the octet positively exudes happiness. The opening arpeggio theme, besides being an admirable vehicle for development, is alive with the buoyant spirit of youth : the quiet three-bar phrase of the second subject not only provides the necessary touch of contrast, but expresses a characteristically Mendelssohnian mood of happy relaxation. And the technical coup—the harnessing of his opening figure to an arresting fresh idea—which the sixteen-year-old brings off towards the close of the exposition creates an effect of sheer rejoicing.

The happiness of the octet is streaked with romanticism. Romanticism, it has been said, meant a " new relationship " to " the most direct and perceptible element of music, its sound. The most immediate expression of this new relationship was the development of the orchestra." An octet for strings lent itself to quasi-orchestral effects, and on his manuscript Mendelssohn actually wrote that " this octet must be played by all instruments in symphonic orchestral style ".

In the scherzo the archetype of Mendelssohn's many inspired scherzos (though the *presto* of the *Rondo Capriccioso*, op. 14, written the previous year, forestalls it), romanticism is explicit. Lines from the *Walpurgisnacht* scene in Goethe's *Faust* ran through his mind as he composed it, he told Fanny :

> Floating cloud and trailing mist
> bright'ning o'er us hover :
> Airs stir the brake, the rushes shake,
> and all their pomp is over.

Tiny motives repeated through a rustle of staccato semiquavers have the quality of an incantation. Mendelssohn employs the typical romantic device of sustaining for some bars a chromatic common chord (here a D major triad, the key of the piece being B flat). Heard as a chromaticism, the euphony of the familiar common chord acquires a delicious faraway quality. But the scherzo also reveals the influence of Bach. One can understand that the " 48 " and *The Art of Fugue* meant much to the sixteen-year-old who could shake out of his sleeve the canonic entries (at one point as many as seven) of the development section. The finale, in which all eight voices enter one by one in the manner of an eight-part fugue and dialogue in passages of brilliant counterpoint, reveals Bach's influence still more strongly. One can understand that it could have seemed natural to Mendelssohn, with this effortless command of learned counterpoint in his blood, to follow his father's advice to " hang on a nail " the romanticism of his early masterpieces and " proceed to graver works ".

The slow movement, as one might expect of a sixteen-year-old boy, is comparatively light-weight. Even so, it contains promising touches : an emotional veering into the key of the flattened supertonic in the opening paragraph, a melody soaring to a climax of highly charged dissonance. The movement seems to strengthen the assumption that Mendelssohn's subsequent failure to write a significant slow movement—those of the *Italian* symphony and the violin concerto are exceptions proving the rule —was due to some flaw in his emotional development ; that, other things being equal, he might have attained a mastery of romantic pathos matching his mastery of romantic orchestration.

The celebrated opening chords of the overture to *A Midsummer Night's Dream* beautifully illustrate Mendelssohn's mastery of romantic orchestration. The first chord is delivered by flutes, and thereafter the orchestration grows progressively richer : at the second chord, clarinets are added ; at the third, horns and bassoons ; at the fourth, oboes. It is as though we are being gently lured into the slumbering fairy-world of Shakespeare's play. And when the cushioned horn-and-woodwind chord of the last two bars of the introduction has faded away, Mendelssohn divides his upper strings and proceeds to make music of a kind never heard before : fifty-four bars of pianissimo violin sound, *sempre staccato*, gossamer-light. Yet this tone poem is firmly riveted—how firmly, we see if we compare it to another celebrated piece of romantic orchestration, Weber's *Oberon* overture, composed the same year. Weber starts with a mysterious horn call and shreds of gossamer figuration, but very soon he dismisses the fairies and settles down to the composition of a full-blooded operatic overture, containing only at one point a perfunctory reminder of his preliminary spellbinding. Mendelssohn's first thoughts, on the other hand, are firmly integrated in the design as a whole. The development section, after an animated start, loses momentum, gradually re-creating the atmosphere of hushed stillness of the opening—and then we hear those chords announcing that the wheel has come full circle and the recapitulation is about to begin. Later it is the coda which re-creates the atmosphere of hushed stillness. A delicately poignant phrase steals across, and in its wake those chords, uttering the final word, bringing the whole movement to a peaceful close.

CONCERT OVERTURES

The *Calm Sea and Prosperous Voyage* overture, which was inspired by two poems of Goethe, is a disconcertingly unequal work. The introductory *Calm Sea* is an evocative seascape—indeed, one passage (an upper pedal-note held for eight bars above slowly shifting harmonies) has an almost Debussyan quality. But the main body of the work, the *Prosperous Voyage*, has the busy, cheerful pointlessness of Mendelssohn below his best. The harmonic scheme is too obvious, the thematic argument too slight to justify the orchestral commotion. Similarly the *Beautiful Melusine* and the *Ruy Blas* overtures make an unequal impression. The tale of the beautiful mermaid inspires a delightfully watery arpeggio-theme, forestalling that of Wagner's Rhinemaidens, but nothing significant happens to it.

On Mendelssohn's other overture Wagner delivered the verdict of posterity when he declared that Mendelssohn was a landscape artist of the first order and the *Hebrides* one of his masterpieces. Here there is no busy cheerful pointlessness. Mendelssohn had sailed across the Minch to Fingal's Cave, felt the tang of Highland wind, seen the misty Hebridean coast. He had been exhilarated, but he had been also filled with a sense of the sea's restlessness and violence. A restless sea is in the figure which beats through the first subject to a continuous murmur of trickling figuration. It is a leaden sea, for the key is minor, and though not stormy it is swept by gusty chromatic scales. When the music modulates into the major for the second subject, the sun comes out and Mendelssohn welcomes it with a trumpet. But the sun is a Highland sun, windswept and fitful. In the development section the music is buffeted from key to key; chromatic scales sweep by more violently; the first-subject figure contracts into a staccato fragment tossed between strings and woodwind. At the coda the figuration churns, but the violence is not catastrophic. His first-subject figure safely rides out the tempest.

SYMPHONIES

It is significant that of Mendelssohn's four published symphonies—the early C minor (composed in 1824), the *Reformation* (written in 1830 to commemorate the tercentenary of the Augsburg Confession), the *Italian* (1833), and the *Scottish* (1841–42)—it is the two latter, which bear the imprint of local tone-colour, that have held the boards. The *Italian* was composed during Mendelssohn's stay in Italy. The stately modal tune of the slow movement was inspired by the spectacle of a religious procession witnessed in Naples, and the high-spirited last movement, which Mendelssohn called a *Saltarello*, by the leaping rhythm of a popular Roman dance. Not that the other movements are inferior. The opening *Allegro vivace* has the youthful exuberance and architectural sweep of the octet ; the scherzo flows charmingly ; the trio recaptures the fairy-atmosphere of the overture to the *Midsummer Night's Dream*. In the *Scottish* the quality of inspiration is less consistent. It was conceived during Mendelssohn's Scottish tour and elaborated during his stay in Italy, but he did not add finishing touches until as late as 1842. For Mendelssohn was intensely self-critical, and even when a work was published he would want to revise it. (So self-critical was he even with the *Italian* symphony that during his lifetime it remained unpublished.) The *Andante* is a typical Mendelssohn slow movement *manqué*, and the lively finale fired by characteristic " Scotch snap " dotted rhythm. But the scherzo cuts delightful capers, and the first movement has an evocative beauty comparable to that of the *Hebrides*. It was inspired by the spectacle of the ruined chapel at Holyrood ("everything around is broken and mouldering and the bright sky shines in ", runs the relevant passage in Mendelssohn's letters). The movement has great atmosphere and range. The melancholy introduction ; the agitated first subject ; the exquisite tune (very like Brahms in the first movement of his second symphony) which holds the tonality in E minor at the close of the exposition ; the quiet surge of the first subject at the beginning of the development section, as the music drifts out of E minor into the twilight of C sharp minor —the whole is absolutely personal and well conceived.

THE VIOLIN CONCERTO

The violin concerto, ideas for which had been running in Mendelssohn's head for six years, was composed during a happy summer holiday with Cécile and the children in 1844. The previous year had proved that, although he was wearing himself out by overwork, he could still on occasion match the quality of his early masterpieces. Commissioned to write incidental music for a performance of *A Midsummer Night's Dream* at the Court Theatre of Potsdam, he had continued in the inspired vein of the overture ; he composed a delicate *Scherzo*, an *Intermezzo* vividly depicting the plight of the lovers wandering at cross-purposes through the forest, a *Notturno* with magical scoring for the horn, and the famous *Wedding March*. The youthful Mendelssohn is still there in the first movement and finale of the violin concerto, and in the slow movement, on the other hand, a Mendelssohn all too rarely encountered. The inspired youth might have written the chastely lyrical melody of the opening section—but not the lament that follows, not those bars where, goaded by the soloist's octaves, the music rises to a moment of passionate outburst, imparting to the movement the character of mature expression.

The violin concerto is an illuminating example of Mendelssohn's powers as an architect. He came into the world "a little Conservative", endowed with a faculty for writing movements in convincing sonata form. This faculty was more than a gift for applying a well-tried formula. A Mendelssohn neo-classical movement in sonata form has individual fingerprints. Towards the close of an exposition he will give a fresh twist to material lifted from the first subject. A recapitulation he will cut short or vary, yet leave in a form which balances the exposition ; not for Mendelssohn the transfigured recapitulations of Chopin's "Parisian spasmodic and impassioned style".

In his concertos he employed romantic innovations similar to those of Schumann. He telescoped the "double exposition" into one, ran movements into each other. In his piano concertos he went further even than Schumann and dispensed with a cadenza altogether. Into the first movement of the violin concerto he admitted one—not, however, as a parting blaze of fireworks let off just before the final *tutti*, but into the development section, where it plays a vital part in the structure of the movement. Mendelssohn starts the section animatedly and then interrupts it, this time not for the re-entry of the first subject but for the cadenza. The soloist duly lets off his fireworks and then settles upon a quiet arpeggio, waiting for the orchestra to re-enter with the first subject and put an end to the thematic vacuum he has been creating. The moment when the orchestra at last brings in the overdue first subject is one of the most arresting in the whole literature of the violin concerto.

" ELIJAH "

Mendelssohn's violin concerto has never lost its hold. His *Elijah*, in public appeal, has. In the nineteenth and early twentieth century its prestige and popularity in this country, if not elsewhere, were second only to Handel's *Messiah*.

Elijah is the nearest Mendelssohn came to writing a serious opera. In his early youth he wrote operettas and a comic opera (*The Wedding of Camacho*, produced unsuccessfully in Berlin). Throughout his life he searched for a suitable libretto, giving himself and others enormous trouble, all to no end. He was too domesticated, too gentle, too high-souled to warm to the theatrically effective subject-matter of a viable opera. With *Elijah* he could feel at home. The resurrector of the *St. Matthew Passion*, who had found Italian opera " mean and low " and Paris a modern Babylon, who throughout his life had striven to raise standards and spread enlightenment, could find inspiration in the story of the prophet who revealed the ways of God to the children of Israel and delivered them from the priests of Baal.

Mendelssohn's correspondence with his librettist, Pastor Schubring, shows that he was eager to exploit the dramatic possibilities of the story. The pivotal scene of the Baal choruses (the priests' fatuous confidence—Elijah's mocking interjections—the priests' urgent *Baal ! Hear and answer !* —Elijah's *Draw near, all ye people*) is a musical and dramatic masterpiece. His choruses, it has been pointed out, fall into two classes, those which are Handelian in outline and those which, looking to the future, envisage a choral-orchestral amalgam. In his youth Mendelssohn had studied Handel and learnt how to write " through-composed " choruses in fugal style, flowing and grateful to sing. *Be not afraid* is a typical example, and the cumulative effect has something of the authentic Handelian sweep and breadth. The Baal choruses look to the future (even as far as Walton's *Belshazzar's Feast*), since their effect is bound up with orchestral dynamics and tone-colour. Thus throughout the *andante e grave maestoso* of the opening *Baal, we cry to thee,* the upper strings are silent in order that the rush of their entry at the *allegro non troppo* of *Hear us, Baal, hear, mighty God,* should build the desired effect of gathering urgency. *He that watcheth over Israel* is another choral-orchestral amalgam ; it owes much of its charm to the rippling accompaniment of the strings, and to the woodwind, colouring and rounding off the choral melody. In *Behold, the Lord passed by,* the orchestra's surging *tutti* before the verses describing the tempest, earthquake, and fire—swelling in five bars to a richly scored fortissimo—looks forward to the *Ring,* and the ethereal upper register of the strings and woodwind at " And in that still small voice onward came the Lord " echoes the contemporary *Lohengrin.* The inspiration of this music, as of Wagner's, is bound up with the romantic magic of its orchestration.

DOMESTIC PIANO MUSIC

It would be unfair to judge Mendelssohn's powers as a lyricist only on the strength of his performance in *Elijah* and in the other pieces we have discussed. To do him justice we must take into consideration another work : not a masterpiece, but nevertheless a delightful body of music, which only Mendelssohn could have written—the *Songs Without Words.*

The charm of the *Songs Without Words* lies partly in their unpretentiousness. Mendelssohn was a fine pianist, but the piano was not for him, as

MODEST PETROVICH MUSSORGSKY (1839–1881)

Oil painting by Ilya Repin

GIACOMO PUCCINI (1858–1924)

it was for Schumann and Chopin, a confessional in which to pour out the heart. Schumann wrote impassioned " songs without words " to Clara, but Mendelssohn's were pleasant party pieces, which he sent as presents to his sister Fanny. With the significant exception of the charming evocative *Venetian Boat Songs* of Books I, II, and IV—significant because here, as in the symphonies, romantic local colour brought out the best in Mendelssohn —he was content to operate with conventional clichés of keyboard figuration. But these unpretentious pieces contain a number of delightful lyrical melodies. One should not complain of the *Andante espressivo* of Book I that it fobs us off with pretty phrases ; the melody is an organism, beautifully wrought and integrated. The *Andante con moto* of Book I and *Andante espressivo* of Book V have pathetic chromatic inflections which bring them close to Schumann. At times the invention sags—the *andantes* turn insipid and the *allegros* and *prestos* lose their zest and sparkle—but there is charm in the restraint and modesty of this music.

It remains to single out from Mendelssohn's vast varied output—of orchestral, chamber, organ, and piano music, religious works, choral pieces, songs, part-songs, operettas—certain works which, if not vintage Mendelssohn, nevertheless (unlike the bulk of the others) still have some flavour and sparkle.

PIANO CONCERTOS

Thus the G minor piano concerto is a work of charm and character. The pounding rhythm of the opening theme bears the stamp of Beethoven. The contrasting lyrical second subject is like a pleasure-boat riding prettily in shallow water, but the movement regains its stature in the *tutti* leading into the *Andante*. After a re-statement of the Beethovenian theme in G minor, the trumpet startles us with a resounding B natural, impressively heralding a change of key and mood. The *Andante* is a pleasant dream, enhanced by virtuosic figuration, albeit of a conventional kind ; and as in a Beethoven concerto, we are brusquely wakened by the onset of the finale, heralded (an original stroke, this) by that same trumpet, sounding its B natural, which had heralded the *Andante*. The finale itself recalls Weber rather than Beethoven : a gay, racy movement, demanding of the soloist no more than ability to cover the ground with the utmost speed and *esprit*.

CHAMBER MUSIC

There is charm and character too in the piano trios in D minor and C minor. True, the piano clatters too obtrusively ; second subjects are pretty-pretty ; the *Andante* of the C minor fails to emulate that of Beethoven's

" Archduke " trio. But the coiling arpeggio-theme which opens the C minor is a fascinating gloss on the first bars of Beethoven's violin sonata in that key, while the opening theme of the D minor has a fine lyrical sweep which looks forward to Brahms. Nor is the promise of that fine lyrical opening disappointed—indeed, its first two movements contain touches worthy of Mendelssohn at his best. The gem of the first movement occurs (as so often) at the beginning of the recapitulation. The first theme has borne the brunt of the development section and is in danger of sounding over-worked. Mendelssohn beautifully avoids the danger : while the cello is bringing back the theme, the violin blankets the re-entry with a phrase of eloquent pathos. A passing inspiration this seems to be, until in the *Andante* we reach the affecting middle section and find it dominated by this very phrase.

Perhaps it could also be said of Mendelssohn's *Variations Sérieuses* for piano that they look forward to Brahms. The undistinguished theme has a Brahmsian earnest purposefulness, which stamps the character of the whole. The sober forcefulness of the variations and their powerful cumulative effect must have provided a valuable model.

Last, not least, must be singled out the piece which has always been regarded as standing in a class by itself among Mendelssohn's compositions for the piano : the E minor Prelude and Fugue from the set of six Preludes and Fugues, op. 35. The prelude flashes past in one swoop, a superbly integrated melody, riding an accompaniment of demi-semiquaver arpeggios which never alter their shape nor relax their momentum. The fugue starts as an example of Mendelssohn's neo-Bachian keyboard manner. The sinuously chromatic subject winds its way slowly through a mesh of counter-point, elaborate yet austere, recalling the contemplative minor fugues of the " 48 ". Though not really memorable, the subject and the counterpoint it generates have enough character to escape the charge of being a mere pastiche : and this is also true of other fugues of Mendelssohn's, especially of the B minor Fugue of op. 35 and that of the third organ sonata in A major of op. 65. In any case, once the fugue is under way Mendelssohn takes the law into his own hands, gives the un-Bachlike direction *cresc. ed accel. sempre*, and relaxes his counterpoint to include some pianistic chords and octaves. Later the direction runs *accelerando poco e poco all' Allegro con fuoco* ; counterpoint is abandoned and the subject is unharnessed and left to race forward to an accompaniment of excited quavers. Towards the close the virtuoso in Mendelssohn takes charge. Arpeggios delivered by the left hand in thundering octaves dramatically retard the tempo in preparation for a stroke of romantic showmanship worthy of Berlioz, a ringing climactic chorale melody delivered above a thunder of left-hand octaves. The epilogue which follows is something of an anti-climax. Mendelssohn atones for his lapse from " sobriety and true music " by rounding off his fugue with a reminder of its not really memorable subject in its original form.

MENDELSSOHN'S OPERATIC CONTEMPORARIES

If Chopin never attempted an opera, and both Schumann and Mendelssohn made only abortive attempts in that field, it was largely due to the preponderance in their day of operatic ideals in direct opposition to their seriousness, and their gift for intimate communication. Italy was still dominant in this field, and her position was only later disputed by the composers of French " grand " opera, which was in many ways the very negation of all that Schumann, Chopin, and Mendelssohn stood for.

The impact of nationalist sentiment on opera in Italy was at first less obvious than in the rest of Europe, if only because hitherto opera had everywhere been Italian. Even in France the chief composers of serious opera, with the signal exception of Rameau, were Italians, like Lully, Spontini, and Cherubini, or Italian-trained, like Gluck and Meyerbeer. Yet in fact the roots of Italian opera always had struck down into and drawn sustenance from the fertile soil of native melody. There was no other source on which Alessandro Scarlatti and his followers could draw than the popular songs of Naples, whose nostalgic sweetness flavours the operas of Hasse no less than of Pergolesi. The appearance in the nineteenth century of a more obviously Italian style may well be due to the fact that Italian was now no longer the supra-national common language of the European opera-houses, but took its place as one among a number of distinct and independent musical styles.

Between the operas of the older generation that was dying out in 1800 and those of the three composers who dominated Italian opera during the next four decades there was, indeed, a striking change. It was a change rather than a transition, because at the beginning of the century there occurred a curious gap of ten years during which Italian opera almost ceased to exist so far as history is concerned. The composers of established reputation had either retired, like Paisiello, or were working abroad, as were Spontini and Cherubini in Paris, and Salieri, whom the Viennese preferred to Mozart.

SIMON MAYR

The gap was bridged only by the exertions of a Bavarian priest who combined the duties of organist in Bergamo with a successful career as an opera-composer in Milan and Venice. Simon Mayr (1763-1845) earned his modest niche in operatic history not merely as the teacher of Donizetti, but as a composer in his own right. In *Ginevra di Scozia* (1801) he anticipated the fashion for the " grand " treatment of quasi-historical subjects in opera, whose invention is usually credited to Spontini. Mayr also seems to have been the first to exploit the dramatic use of *crescendo* in the manner we associate with Rossini, and, as Professor Grout observes, " he was able to do what Jommelli had vainly attempted, namely, persuade Italian audiences to accept more flexibility of form in serious opera as well as a greater participation of the orchestra in the whole scheme ".

The title of Mayr's opera, *Ginevra di Scozia* (" Guinevere of Scotland ") is significant, for all that the libretto is derived from Ariosto. Italy too was smitten with the romantic fever ; among the chief causes for the rise of temperature were the novels of Walter Scott, whose immense vogue equalled that of Byron and influenced men as diverse as Schiller and Berlioz, Donizetti and Victor Hugo.

THE RISE OF THE MIDDLE-CLASS AUDIENCE

The Waverley Novels had a more immediate and potent influence on musical history than the august utterances of Goethe, whose thought took time to filter down through cultivated minds before it reached the consciousness of the ordinary man. And it was the ordinary man who now set the pace for artistic endeavour and ordained the style of creative activity. For the ordinary man belonging to the newly enriched and emancipated middle class had begun to take his place beside the princes and nobles as a patron of the arts—and was soon to supersede them. If the ordinary man received as his reward the paintings of an Ingres, a Delacroix, or a Wilkie, the music of the young Mendelssohn and Rossini, and the novels of Dickens and Thackeray, of Balzac and Manzoni, he was indeed fortunate, though he probably, in his heart, preferred the more insipid products of Landseer or the more vulgar ones of Meyerbeer and Offenbach.

In Italy the rise of the middle class was especially rapid. For the princely courts were already in the last stages of decay, and their ruin was completed by the wars which left the peninsula torn and impoverished. The northern provinces were under Austrian rule, and that influence was extended farther south by the presence of an Austrian duchess in Parma and an Austrian duke in Florence. For the rest, Italy consisted of two ramshackle kingdoms (of which the Neapolitan and Sicilian was ruled by the least admirable of the surviving Bourbons, with Austrian support) ; a couple of minor dukedoms ; and the Papacy, which retained only the insubstantial shadow of the old temporal power. Here was a field ripe for a national resurgence stimulated by the hopes and desires of ordinary men.

Patriotism did not, however, at once play any conspicuous part in opera during the first decades of the century. That came later, when Verdi focused in his music the aspirations of his countrymen and became, despite the Austrian censorship, a powerful force in the Risorgimento. It is true that in *L'Italiana in Algeri* Rossini did once give surprisingly strong expression to his patriotic feelings in Isabella's rondo *Pensa alla patria* (" Think of your fatherland "); but that is an exceptional utterance from a composer too indolent to concern himself with politics and too timorous to run his head into trouble. In *Guillaume Tell*, which was composed for the Paris Opéra, he also treated a subject in which the idea of national independence was paramount.

ROSSINI

For the new middle-class audience, opera was no longer provided by the princely families or merchant-nobles (as in Venice), but by the new tribe of commercial impresarios, of whom Mozart's friend Schikaneder was an early specimen. The most successful and powerful of the early nineteenth-century impresarios was Domenico Barbaia, a café waiter who became director of the two foremost opera-houses in Italy, the Scala in Milan and the San Carlo in Naples, besides controlling two theatres in Vienna.

This remarkable man found in Gioacchino Rossini (1792–1868) the ideal purveyor of opera for the new type of audience. Extraordinarily gifted, Rossini had a meteoric career, beginning in Venice at the age of eighteen and ending, his musical genius prematurely burnt out, in Paris in 1829, nearly forty years before he died. During the nineteen years of his activity as an opera composer he produced some thirty-five operas, ranging from one-act pieces of a trivial character to tragedies on the grand scale. We think of Rossini nowadays as essentially a comic genius, but it should not be overlooked that to his contemporaries he was, first and foremost, the composer of *Tancredi* (1813), *Otello* (1816), *Mosè in Egitto* (" Moses in Egypt ") (1818), *Semiramide* (1823), and above all, *Guillaume Tell* (1829).

By 1810, when Rossini first had an opera produced, the old *opera seria* was dead. Few of its conventions survived the turn of the century, though a small number of *castrati* lingered on, the most famous being Velluti, for whom Rossini wrote the principal rôle in *Aureliano in Palmira* (1813) (whose overture is familiar enough, since it was transferred to *The Barber of Seville*). In some of his later operas Rossini still wrote male rôles for high voices ; thus Malcolm Graeme, Ellen's lover in his version of *The Lady of the Lake* (1819), is a mezzo-soprano, the part being played by a female singer *en travesti*. Arsace, the Assyrian general in *Semiramide*, is likewise cast for a contralto.

ROSSINI'S REFORMS

The formal conventions of Metastasian opera had by this time completely disappeared. Rossini's librettists were free to construct their dramas on more rational lines. Unfortunately, for the very reason that opera sufficed to satisfy the theatrical needs of the Italian public, there was no strong dramatic tradition such as existed in England, France, and Spain, and such as was being created in Germany. Felice Romani, the most distinguished Italian theatre-poet between Metastasio and Boito, wrote only three of Rossini's librettos, and for the rest Rossini had to rely on the wretched poetry and incompetent dramatic technique of hacks.

Even so, Rossini contrived to achieve a greater homogeneity and continuity in his dramas, both by the elimination of the *secco* recitatives accompanied by a harpsichord, and by the transfer to his serious operas of the ensembles for several voices and the finales that had long been a feature of Italian comic opera. From Mozart, a special object of his veneration, he learned the value of a cumulative movement to carry an act through to an exciting climax.

Rossini also curbed the liberty of the singers to improvise (often to an extent that made the music unrecognisable) upon what the composer had written for them. It was on this account that he quarrelled with Velluti, who, like all his kind, regarded the musical text as a starting-point for the exercise of his virtuosity. Hence arose the appearance of greater floridity in Rossini's vocal writing as compared with the unornamented scores of eighteenth-century composers. He wrote down exactly what the singers were to sing, whereas early composers left the ornamentation to the discretion of the singers. He also followed Simon Mayr in giving greater prominence to the orchestra, so much so that singers complained that they could not make themselves heard, and Lord Mount Edgecumbe, an old-fashioned connoisseur of opera, inveighed against the noisiness of his orchestration, even as later critics were to attack Wagner for the same fault. Rossini's orchestration is brilliant even to the point sometimes of being blatant, especially in the comic operas which are most familiar to us. But he can also achieve a delicacy worthy of Berlioz, for instance in the Prelude to *Mosè*, while his feeling for atmosphere is well represented in the familiar overture to *Guillaume Tell* and in the introduction to Mathilde's aria *Sombres forêts* in the second act. His sparkling wit is self-evident.

Like his contemporaries, Rossini gave great prominence to the chorus, which in the Italian operas of the eighteenth century had played an insignificant part. Here his example was provided by Gluck and his French successors. In *Mosè* the chorus has an importance that lends weight and dignity to the opera, which has something of the grandeur of Handelian oratorio, even though Rossini's incorrigible cheerfulness breaks in from time to time.

ROSSINI'S COMEDIES

In comedy Rossini's output ranged from the little one-act pieces, composed for Venice at the beginning of his career, to the more extended operas which followed his success with *L'Italiana in Algeri* in 1813. Of them, *The Barber of Seville* is deservedly the most popular. Beaumarchais's *Le Barbier de Séville* was designed in the first instance as a comedy interspersed with songs, and the play with its admirably drawn characters was easily adaptable to the musical stage. Rossini's Latin vivacity and his copious gift of melody —which did not, however, prevent his transplanting music from one opera to another—sufficed to make *The Barber* the most successful of all Italian comic operas.

Although Rossini commonly composed according to a small number of formulas, he could respond to the stimulus of a dramatic situation with music that is entirely individual and appropriate. Amid the buffooneries of Don Magnifico and Dandini in *La Cenerentola* (" Cinderella ") (1817), Cinderella herself stands out as a genuinely pathetic character, very different from the conventional soubrettes of *opera buffa* ; and Isabella, the heroine of *L'Italiana in Algeri*, is an extremely forceful personality as well as an engaging minx. In *Il Turco in Italia* Rossini, the least theoretic of composers, even anticipated Richard Strauss in representing the action as being in process of creation by the poet, who is one of the characters. Unfortunately in modern performances, including the existing recording of the opera, this aspect of Rossini's amusing libretto is almost wholly eliminated.

THE FRENCH OPERAS

After settling in Paris in 1823 Rossini, like Lully before him, set himself to master the French declamatory style and to accommodate his music to Parisian tastes. The results were seen in *Le Comte Ory* (1828) and *Guillaume Tell* (1829). The first represents a modified form of *opera buffa* and served as a model for the development of the characteristically French type of operetta which became popular during the middle years of the century— a gay, witty, nonsensical burlesque with lively and melodious music.

Guillaume Tell was an altogether more important work, of large dimensions and composed with far more thought than Rossini had hitherto given to his work. It is the culmination of a development whose stages were marked by *Otello*, *Mosè*, *Semiramide*, and *Le Siège de Corinthe* (1826). Based upon Schiller's drama *Wilhelm Tell*, Rossini's opera set forth in the grandest terms the liberal aspirations for national freedom that were agitating so much of Europe.

With its historical subject, its bourgeois characters—significantly, the only aristocrat is the oppressive alien Governor—and its picturesque setting in an Alpine valley, *Guillaume Tell* was a typical product of Franco-Italian culture in the 1820s. Musically it combined Italianate vocal melody and the sharp characterisation of *opera buffa* with the solid choral style of French grand opera derived ultimately from Gluck, and with a novel use of orchestral harmony and colour to substantiate the emotional situations in the drama. It established a model for the grand opera of the succeeding period, and its influence appears no less in the early works of Wagner than, as one would expect, in those of Meyerbeer and Verdi.

GAETANO DONIZETTI

Guillaume Tell was a French grand opera conceived on the largest scale. The typical Italian tragic opera of the period was less spacious and more economical in its demands on the finances of the impresarios. In the years after Rossini's settlement in Paris and his retirement from operatic composition in 1829, it was supplied by two greatly talented men, Gaetano Donizetti (1797–1848) and Vincenzo Bellini (1801–35). Donizetti, born in Bergamo, acquired from Simon Mayr and from a period of study at the Liceo in Bologna a musical technique adequate to supply a simple harmonic support to the copious flow of lyrical melody which he could turn on at will. During the twenty-five years of his working career he composed sixty-five operas. Even though some of these were slight pieces in one act, such rapidity of creation could not make for depth of expression, for elaborate workmanship or subtle harmonic invention. Yet such was his gift of melody that, combined with a very real dramatic sense, it afforded an effective means of presenting the characters in pathetic situations, whether tragic or comic. His tragic heroines, of whom Lucy of Lammermoor is the most familiar, often find in madness an escape from the predicament in which fate has placed them. Though they became stereotyped, their " mad scenes " (which Sheridan had already burlesqued in *The Critic*) provided a perfect dramatic excuse for an elaborate display of vocal fireworks.

Donizetti possessed exactly the amount of musical technique he required for his purpose. That this purpose was by no means always so elementary as is sometimes suggested is shown by the great sextet in *Lucia di Lammermoor* (1835), with its assured command of counterpoint and its dynamic use of voices in concert to create a sense of extreme dramatic tension. Donizetti had also considerable literary gifts. He partly wrote his own libretto for the most successful of his comic operas, *Don Pasquale* (1843), and also provided his own text for the last act of *La Favorite* (1840), which is the finest single act in any of his operas.

The amiable character of this singularly attractive and modest composer makes itself felt especially in the charm of his comic operas, especially *L'Elisir d'Amore* (" The Love Potion ") (1832), with its very likeable country bumpkin lover who doses himself with love-potions supplied by that splendidly observed comic character, the egregious quack Dr. Dulcamara. The heroine of this work is no less attractive in personality than the roguish Norina in *Don Pasquale*, who can show genuine sorrow for the sorry plight to which she has reduced her poor old " husband " by the trick she plays on him. There is a touch of sentiment in these operas that rarely makes itself felt in Rossini's comedies, and this compensates for a comparative lack of strength and brilliance. Donizetti is amusing rather than uproariously funny.

VINCENZO BELLINI

Bellini's brief career and sensitive nature present an even more complete contrast with Rossini's. Between 1827, when his first important opera, *Il Pirata*, was produced in Milan, and his death six weeks before his thirty-fourth birthday in 1835, he composed eight operas, most of them to librettos by Felice Romani. Of them *Norma* (1831) is his masterpiece, a work that combines the classic grandeur of the French style with a wonderfully sensitive and intimate expression of pathos embodied in long and flexible melodies. At its best, in such arias as Norma's *Casta diva* (" Chaste goddess "), Bellini's melody attains an ideal beauty, at once sensuous and pure, that has hardly been surpassed. It is purely vocal melody, though it bears a family resemblance to Chopin's *cantabile* themes for the pianoforte. Indeed, the two composers, who were friends, seem to have had a mutual influence on one another.

Bellini's musical resources were as limited as Donizetti's. His accompaniments have not unjustly been called guitar-like, and his harmony is conventional and uncomplicated by any counterpoint. Yet by the simplest means he can subtly reinforce the emotional effect of his melody to a degree that is wholly unexpected. His nearest approach to comic opera is the semi-serious *La Sonnambula* (" The Sleep Walker ") (1831), in which the heroine's sleep-walking scene is a variant of Donizetti's mad scenes. Any other composer would have treated the subject as comic, but Bellini is wholly sentimental about it. He incidentally shows an ability to suggest the Swiss environment with sure strokes of orchestral colour, if with less than Rossini's forcefulness in *Guillaume Tell*.

XVII

HECTOR BERLIOZ

ITALIAN opera maintained its hold on the public largely by the appeal
of great individual performers. Pasta, Malibran, Mario, and Lablache
combined the appeal exercised to-day by film stars and great conductors,
and to them were rapidly being added the great instrumental virtuosos—
Paganini among violinists and Liszt, Chopin, Thalberg, Herz, Hünten, and
Kalkbrenner among pianists. The orchestra as an instrument of virtuosity
and the conductor as its director had not yet emerged, and this next step
in the development of European music was taken by a single man—a
Frenchman whose musical training was belated and sporadic and one who
could himself play no instrument but the guitar. This was Hector Berlioz
(1803–69).

Mendelssohn, as we saw, had a low opinion of Berlioz's talent, and so
had Chopin, who is reported to have said that Berlioz's music justified any
man breaking with him. Schumann, on the other hand, hailed him in the
Neue Zeitschrift, though he too had his doubts. Berlioz was wonderfully
talented and original, but his trend was eccentric and much of his music was
unusual and so repellent to a German-trained ear. It was hard to decide
whether to term him a genius or a musical adventurer.

To this day Berlioz still presents a problem. In recent years his
champions have claimed that he is one of the great composers of all time,
and if not all would agree with this, few will now agree with Mendelssohn
and Chopin. After all these years the majority regard him, as Schumann
did, with mixed feelings. The author of the classic *Treatise on Instrumentation*,
the master-orchestrator, who unlocked new riches of expression, was a
great seminal force, whose widespread influence can be traced in the works
of Wagner, Liszt, Tchaikovsky, Dvořák, Verdi, Mussorgsky, Strauss,
Sibelius, and Stravinsky. But his own works, even the *Damnation of Faust*,
the most famous, seem strangely unequal. In this country only the *Symphonie
Fantastique* is firmly established in the standard repertory, and performances
of *Harold in Italy*, the *Messe des Morts*, the *Te Deum*, the *Childhood of Christ*,
even of the *Damnation*, have the air of departures from the beaten track,
welcome but unlikely to be repeated in the near future. Of his three operas,
Benvenuto Cellini, *Beatrice and Benedict*, and *The Trojans*, only *The Trojans*

is regarded as significant, and it did not reach Covent Garden until 1957. An acknowledged genius, Berlioz has nevertheless remained a perpetual stranger in our midst, from time to time admitted over the threshold, but never into the family circle of composers intimately known and loved.

At least one particularly damaging allegation should at the outset be ruled out : namely, that Berlioz's idiosyncratic harmony, generally felt to be one of the principal causes of his unpopularity, can be attributed to a defective harmonic sense or to inadequate training. In the first place, Berlioz's harmony is by no means invariably idiosyncratic ; when he chose he could employ orthodox progressions, indeed with wonderful effect. Rather than regard him as a genius who happened to be a bungler in this vital branch of his art, it would seem more sensible to assume that his harmonic sense was original, and to look for factors that could have contributed to its originality. Unlike Mendelssohn, Schumann, and Chopin, Berlioz was not influenced in boyhood by a teacher familiar with the great German masters. He was not brought up on the piano, and his exceptional ear for orchestral tone-colour affected his handling of chords. The exaggerating romantic temperament displayed in Berlioz's celebrated Memoirs—that temperament which led to actions of which Schumann, Chopin, and Mendelssohn would have been incapable—reflected itself in his harmony, as it did in other aspects of his art.

YOUTH AND STUDIES

Berlioz was born in 1803 in the " outlandish " (so he called it in his Memoirs) little town of La Côte-Saint-André, near Grenoble. His father, Louis, was a doctor, who took it for granted that Hector, the only son among his six children, would adopt his profession. Not that he discouraged his early musical leanings ; there was no piano in the house, but the boy was given lessons on the flageolet, the flute, and the guitar, and managed to teach himself some harmony from a textbook. At the age of twelve he began composing songs and pieces of chamber music modelled on quartets of Haydn or Pleyel, performed at amateur gatherings. These did not compare with the compositions of Mendelssohn in his 'teens ; but when we learn that a melody from an early quintet became the principal subject of the *Francs-Juges* Overture and a song the basis of the introductory *Largo* of the *Symphonie Fantastique*, we wonder whether Berlioz, had he enjoyed Mendelssohn's advantages, might not have been just as great a prodigy.

In 1821 Berlioz went to Paris in order to study medicine, in much the same spirit that Schumann went to Leipzig to study law, torn between love for music and sense of duty to a parent. But the young tyro had at hand no Wieck to convince the parent of his genius. In any case, for one such as Berlioz a musical career in Paris was bound to mean a hard and bitter struggle. Throughout the Napoleonic Wars and their aftermath of exhaustion and disillusion, music in the capital had stood at a low ebb. It was scarcely ever contemporary music, for it rarely showed any trace of having assimilated the life of its own day, and remained unaffected by the hot young Romantic blood that in the second and third decades of the century was transforming both French poetry and French painting. The poets and the musicians seemed to inhabit different worlds of thought. In this world the masterpieces of the Viennese classics had as yet made little impact. The representative composers were opera composers : Boieldieu, Auber, Adam. To make his way in the sphere of instrumental music, a composer needed to be a virtuoso like Chopin or Liszt ; in the sphere of opera, to be a wealthy careerist like Meyerbeer, able to purchase backing and prepared to pander to the box-office demand for spectacle and sensation.

" What was the good God thinking of when He dropped me down in this pleasant land of France ? ", the Memoirs exclaim. The young Berlioz had already been thrilled by literature—by Chateaubriand, and by Virgil's tragic tale of Dido (which decades later inspired *The Trojans*). And already at the age of twelve his " hot young Romantic blood " had been stirred by love for a girl of eighteen. Under the influence of this love he had started to compose, and it was this that had inspired the song —a setting of verses from Florian's " Estelle et Némorin "—which found its way into the *Fantastique*.

Loyalty to his father—an anxious parent, and a man of liberal views and lovable character—kept Berlioz for some time at the École de Médecine. But it did not prevent him from studying harmony with Lesueur, a teacher at the Conservatoire, from haunting the Opéra, from poring over scores of Gluck and Spontini and teaching himself the secrets of orchestration. In 1824 he left the École and in 1826 was admitted to the Conservatoire as a regular pupil. Throughout these and the following years he had to endure many trials and discouragements, his father's concern and his mother's anger (she was a conventional woman of her class who regarded the career of a musician as a disgrace to the family). Matters were not made easier by repeated failures to obtain the coveted distinction of the *Prix de Rome*, which would have entitled him to study for two years in Rome and another year in Germany ; nor by his father cutting off his allowance, with the resulting humiliation of having to support himself by singing in the chorus of the Théâtre des Nouveautés.

FIRST ACQUAINTANCE WITH SHAKESPEARE

Nevertheless during these years of painful apprenticeship Berlioz under-went the great formative experiences of his life. In 1827 Paris for the first time heard Shakespeare, performed by an English company headed by Charles Kemble. The performances inspired Victor Hugo's famous preface to *Cromwell*, proclaiming a new ideal of romantic drama. Their effect on Berlioz he thus describes in the Memoirs :

Shakespeare, coming upon me unawares, struck me down as with a thunder-bolt. His lightning spirit, descending upon me with transcendent power from the starry heights, opened to me the highest heaven of Art, lit up the deepest depths and revealed the best and greatest and truest that earth can show. . . . The scales fell from my eyes, I saw, felt, understood : I arose and walked !

Mendelssohn would have sniffed at the " obtrusive enthusiasm " of this characteristic passage, but the enthusiasm was genuine : Berlioz even went to the length of falling violently and hopelessly in love with the Ophelia of the company, Harriet Smithson. It was during this period, too, that he discovered Goethe. *Faust* set him composing the *Eight Scenes from Faust* upon which, years later, he was to base the *Damnation* ; and Weber's *Der Freischütz*, when he heard its first performance at the Opéra, revealed fresh worlds of romantic orchestration. Last, not least, there was the mighty stimulus of Beethoven—the first performance by the Conservatoire orchestra of the great C minor symphony.

In the summer of 1830 Berlioz at long last won the *Prix de Rome* ; but now he had no desire to go abroad. Trials and discouragements notwith-standing, he had been making headway in Paris. In 1825 a Mass had been successfully performed ; and in 1828 he had taken the unprecedented step of giving a concert devoted entirely to his own works, and the venture had attracted favourable notice. Early in 1830 he had composed a huge programme-symphony in five movements, the *Symphonie Fantastique*, whose performance later in the year created a sensation and won him the friendship of Liszt. The programme-symphony had been associated with Harriet ; its composition had the effect of purging him for the time being of his passion for the English actress and leaving him free to transfer his affections to a more accessible object, Camille Moke, a charming and talented young pianist, to whom he became engaged to be married.

ROMAN INTERLUDE

But the conditions of the award obliged Berlioz to go to Rome. He went early in 1831 and, although he shared Mendelssohn's view of Italian music and disliked the atmosphere of the French Academy and the company of his fellow-students, he would have found life tolerable if only letters from Camille had been forthcoming. He decided to give the authorities the slip and return to France ; but it so happened that he was delayed at Florence and that a letter was forwarded there from Camille's mother, announcing his fiancée's marriage to Camille Pleyel, the pianoforte maker. In the Memoirs Berlioz describes his reaction to this bombshell with a gusto which conceals its earnestness. He decided to go to Paris, enter the Moke household disguised as a lady's maid, and shoot Camille, her mother and himself. He had been revising the *Symphonie Fantastique* : he wrote a note regarding an alteration to the second movement and

. . . threw it into a valise with a few clothes, loaded my pistols, and put into my pockets two little bottles, one of strychnine, the other of laudanum (in case the pistols should misfire), then, conscience-clear with regard to my arsenal, spent the rest of the time raging up and down the streets of Florence like a mad dog.

Travelling along the coastal road to Nice he began to have second thoughts :

. . . the stupendous majesty of Nature burst upon me with greater force than ever before and woke anew the tempest in my heart—the awful wrestling of Life and Death. Holding with both hands on to my seat, I let out a wild " Ha ! " so hoarse, so savage, so diabolic, that the startled driver bounced aside as if he indeed had a demon for his fellow-traveller.

At Nice, after an unsuccessful attempt to drown himself (this the Memoirs do not mention), he not only recovered his sanity, but passed the " twenty happiest days " of his life, bathing, sleeping and—as he had purged himself of Harriet by composing the *Symphonie Fantastique*—purging himself of the faithless Camille by composing the *King Lear* overture.

He returned to Rome and after a year persuaded the authorities to permit him to resume his interrupted career in Paris. One of his first undertakings was a performance of the revised *Symphonie Fantastique*. It was attended by Harriet, who had fallen on evil days and was by no means displeased to learn that Berlioz had associated his sensational programme-symphony with her. Berlioz called on her the next day ; she received him graciously ; his passion was rekindled. After sundry quarrels and mis-understandings, and in the teeth of the bitter opposition of their families, Berlioz married her in 1833.

It is not possible here to do justice to the subsequent events of Berlioz's crowded and chequered life. Throughout most of it his only regular income was drawn from musical journalism, for which he had a brilliant flair, but which he bitterly resented for the time and energy that it took from composition. Even so, by 1840 he had gained the position of an important composer, commissioned to write ceremonial works for public occasions : the *Messe des Morts*, performed in 1837, the *Symphonie funèbre et triomphale* in 1840. Another programme-symphony, *Harold in Italy*, was successfully performed in 1834, and still another, *Romeo and Juliet*, in 1839. But their success was ephemeral ; there was no place for such works in the musical life of Paris. There might have been one for the opera, *Benvenuto Cellini*, upon which Berlioz worked for three years ; but its production in 1838 was a failure, and there was no escape from the treadmill of musical journalism. The only hope was a lucrative official position, and this was denied him by his mordant pen and his refusal to compromise when artistic issues were at stake.

A EUROPEAN CELEBRITY

From 1842 dates Berlioz's career as a European celebrity. His music was thrillingly novel, he was a magnificent conductor, and his personality was fascinating. We read of visits to German cities (among them Leipzig, where the editor of the *Neue Zeitschrift* welcomed him warmly, and the conductor of the Gewandhaus concerts courteously), to Brussels, to London, to St. Petersburg and Moscow, to Budapest, to Vienna. In Vienna he was offered the position of director of the Imperial chapel, but he refused. Notwithstanding his triumphs abroad and the disappointments Paris continued to bring—above all the ruinous failure of the first performance of *The Damnation of Faust*—his hopes were still centred there.

In time his fame grew, and he added to his list of compositions—in 1844 the *Carnaval Romain* overture, in 1849 the *Te Deum*, in 1854 the *Childhood of Christ*. In 1856 he was offered a chair at the French Academy, to which was attached a salary bringing comparative freedom to devote himself to the composition of a gigantic opera, *Les Troyens* (" The Trojans "), to a libretto of his own. The task took two years, not because the music did not flow, but because he was stricken with a painful intestinal complaint which ultimately proved fatal. Negotiations for the production of the opera, which Berlioz regarded as his crowning masterpiece, hung fire for many years, and the work did not reach the stage until 1863, and then only in a truncated version and with a success which again was ephemeral.

" LES TROYENS "

With his strong sense of dramatic effect Berlioz unfortunately did not combine a comparable feeling for dramatic structure. His uncertainty of aim is evident in *The Damnation of Faust*, described as an *opéra de concert*, which was originally produced as a cantata and since 1893 has frequently been performed as an opera. Conversely *Les Troyens* lapsed from time to time into the static choral manner of a cantata.

It is also a monument to the composer's lack of practical understanding. Rather long for a single evening's entertainment (though it can be so given if some cuts are made), its two parts, *The Capture of Troy* and *The Trojans at Carthage*, are not long enough to fill two evenings, even if the French public of his day would have accepted such a scheme. It also involves a very large cast of singers and a lavish expenditure on production. It is not surprising that in the heyday of Meyerbeer this strange, austere masterpiece, compounded on the literary side of Shakespeare and Virgil, and on the musical of Gluck's classicism and Berlioz's own flaming romanticism, should have failed to achieve a performance at the Paris Opéra. The second part was produced in 1863 at the Théâtre Lyrique, while *The Capture of Troy* was not performed until 1890, at Karlsruhe and in German.

Yet no account of individual operatic characters and scenes of outstanding quality could omit the figures of Cassandra and Dido, the infinite pathos of the *tableau vivant* in which Andromache and her son appear as the representatives of all bereaved in war, and the love-duet in *The Trojans at Carthage*, in which extreme sensuousness of expression is held in restraint, and so given an added intensity, by the classic poise Berlioz maintains. For this duet Berlioz, his own librettist, put into the mouths of Dido and Æneas the words of Jessica and Lorenzo from the last act of *The Merchant of Venice*. During the very years in which Berlioz was working on *Les Troyens*, Wagner was engaged on the composition of *Tristan und Isolde*, and there could hardly be a stronger or more instructive contrast with Berlioz's duet than Wagner's philosophical disquisitions on love set to music that knows no emotional restraint. As a musical representation of the great figures of antiquity, *Les Troyens* surpasses even Gluck in its sense of authenticity.

THE LAST PERIOD

After completing *Les Troyens* Berlioz composed a lightweight comic opera, *Beatrice and Benedict*, based on Shakespeare's *Much Ado About Nothing*, fresh and youthful in character and full of exquisite detail, which was produced in 1862 in Germany with success. As a Grand Old Man, he was fêted whenever he went abroad, and sometimes even in Paris ; but he was ill, disillusioned, and lonely. He had composed many religious texts, but he had no religious faith : life to him was " a tale told by an idiot, full of sound and fury, signifying nothing ". Harriet had died in 1854. They had loved each other, but had for many years lived apart, owing to her possessiveness and extreme jealousy. He had lived with, and after Harriet's

" CONCERT " (*circa* 1782) BY GUARDI

The picture shows a concert being held in one of the four Venetian hospices of
the period. These were originally charitable institutions which gradually assumed
the position of conservatories.

death married, Marie Recio, a singer with whom he found little happiness. She died in 1862, and his son Louis, to whom he was deeply attached, in 1867. Yet Berlioz preserved his characteristic humour and warmth and freshness of heart. Five years before his death in 1869 he had sought out, and thereafter remained in contact with, his first love, Estelle, now an elderly widow. In his account in the Memoirs of his visit to her at the house near La Côte-Saint-André, where he had first adored her, the old note of " obtrusive enthusiasm " still rings :

. . . ah ! how changed her face ! Her complexion darkened, her hair silvered. Yet my heart went out to my idol as though she had been in all the freshness of her early beauty.

FANTASTIC SYMPHONY

In the forefront of Berlioz's compositions stands the *Symphonie Fantastique*, of all his large-scale works the most consistently inspired, the most convincing in its total effect.

We have seen that Harriet Smithson was intimately associated with this programme-symphony, and that through its composition Berlioz purged himself of his passion for her. But the actual idea of composing a symphony had been inspired by Beethoven, and the idea of composing a programme-symphony had been inspired by Beethoven's " Pastoral ", not to mention the example of Berlioz's master, Lesueur, who attached descriptive notes to his instrumental works in order to recommend them to a public habituated to the descriptive music of opera and ballet. Nor does Harriet seem to have inspired the material of the music, much of which was taken from previous works, unfinished or unpublished (a life-long habit of Berlioz). Thus the introductory *Largo* was drawn from the early song inspired by Estelle ; the exposition of the first movement from the cantata, *Herminia*, which won the *Prix de Rome* ; the fourth and possibly the third movements from portions of an early rejected opera, *Les Francs-Juges*. And it seems likely that the fifth movement, which bore the Goethean title *Dream of a Witches' Sabbath*, was drawn from a Faust ballet which Berlioz planned to compose shortly after he discovered Goethe.

In a letter of 1829 Berlioz spoke of writing a " descriptive symphony of Faust ". But early in 1830 scandal concerning Harriet reached his ears, and it is assumed that his violent reaction—how violent can be guessed from his reaction to Camille Moke's infidelity—was the fuse which sparked his imagination and inspired the design of a programme-symphony in five movements. In the first, *Rêveries, Passions*, a " young musician of abnormal sensibility " takes opium and dreams that he is undergoing the paroxysms of unfulfilled love. *A Ball* depicts a dream-meeting in a ballroom. In *Scenes in the Country* he finds peace, though haunted by thoughts of her. Then dream becomes nightmare. In *March to the Gallows* he has killed her and is being led to execution ; and in *Dream of a Witches' Sabbath* he is the centre of a demoniacal orgy attended by a degraded incarnation of the beloved. A melodramatic *March to the Gallows* and *Witches' Sabbath* must have struck Berlioz, with his penchant for sardonic laughter, as ideal final chapters of a programme describing the history of a frustrated passion.

In order to relate his five movements Berlioz employed the romantic device which Schubert had already employed in his *Wanderer* Fantasy and Schumann exploited in his fourth symphony, of lifting and transforming a theme from movement to movement. Berlioz's *idée fixe* is supposed to represent the thought of the beloved, and it haunts the music from beginning to end of the work.

Berlioz subsequently withdrew the programme, leaving only the titles, in the hope that, thus presented, the music would speak for itself. It is a question whether all of it does. The symphony never descends to the level of mere *rapportage* ; but it does contain passages which, eloquent though they are in themselves, are only fully intelligible in the light of the programme. Thus *A Ball* swings steadily along for some time to a pleasant waltz tune ; suddenly it lurches out of key and the cellos slither down the chromatic scale, and the transformed *idée fixe* is heard resuming the waltz. The passage is fully intelligible only if felt to convey the shuddering " There she is ! " of the lover encountering the beloved. Without the programme, even the eloquent middle section of *Scenes in the Country* would seem arbitrary. After the long-drawn idyllic melody of the first section—one of those sculptural melodies of Berlioz which (as Schumann observed) seem like folk-songs, demanding no accompaniment—the music's passionate outburst catches us unawares.

Of the *March to the Gallows* and the *Witches' Sabbath*, on the other hand, one could say that the programme is what a programme ideally should be : an analogy giving imaginative point to an already existent purely musical logic. The *March* ceases to march only in the penultimate bars, when the *idée fixe* has its decapitated recitative, a piece of symbolism admirably expressing the psychology of the Berlioz who planned to murder Camille Moke. From the purely musical point of view this recitative performs the function of providing a breathing space—the space Berlioz needed before winding up his macabre G minor movement with nine electrifying chords in G major.

In the *Witches' Sabbath* the programme and the music play magnificently into each other's hands. From an orchestra of unprecedented size—violins divided into six parts ; four horns ; four bassoons ; trumpets reinforced by cornets-à-pistons, trombones, tubas—Berlioz starts by drawing effects out-doing the Weber of the horrific Wolf's Glen scene of *Der Freischütz*. The music creaks, bumps, groans—indeed sounds mad, and madder still when the E flat clarinet begins its cackling dance burlesquing the *idée fixe*. But there is method in the madness. These preliminaries are an admirable foil to the stately next phase of the movement, in which strains of a *Dies Irae* are heard, burlesqued by a ghostly bell and snatches of tripping melody. And this phase in its turn serves as an admirable foil to the next : the *Witches' Sabbath* itself, a wild and whirling fugue, of which the subject undergoes breath-taking transformations, yet never loses its control, and towards the end is combined by tearing strings with the *Dies Irae* delivered in blatant unison by the full force of Berlioz's colossal battery of brass and woodwind.

Rêveries, Passions depict no event, but merely subjective states of mind ("indefinable longing ", " sombre melancholy ", " objectless joys ") and so leave the symphonist a freer hand. The introductory *Largo* leads to an *Allegro* which, although it contains some unruly passages, starts like a movement in sonata form. But the classical principle, of conducting a development section in keys *other* than the tonic, Berlioz throws to the winds. " A young musician of abnormal sensibility ", he called himself, but exploiting the structural functions of key-change did not express his temperament. This found expression instead in the infectious rhetorical effect of key-change *as such*, or rather—since with the abnormal sensibility went an abnormal ear for instrumental tone-colour—the effect of key-change heightened by excited orchestration.

But Berlioz had another remarkable gift, already mentioned : a power to invent melodies of such vitality as to seem independent of an accompaniment. They are not square-cut like Schumann's, but asymmetrically phrased, gathering momentum and significance as they unfold. The first subject of *Rêveries, Passions* is such a melody : it lasts for forty bars and is repeated entire in the middle of the movement (in the key of the dominant) and again at the end. Like pier-props, the three repetitions support a structure standing amid a raging sea of orchestral rhetoric in which there is no pretence of development, where Berlioz is revelling in the sheer excitement of setting, say, his strings stamping in unison up and down the chromatic scale against a wailing two-note phrase delivered by his horns and woodwind.

The chronic excitability of this movement is eloquently expressive of its programme, needless to say. It indicates why Berlioz, who had at his finger-tips the techniques of symphonic writing, and in the *Witches' Sabbath* brought off an architectural *tour de force*, never composed a great abstract symphonic piece. Of his overtures only the evergreen *Carnaval Romain* (extracted from the opera *Benvenuto Cellini*) is truly architectural, resembling in structure *Rêveries, Passions*. Each of Mendelssohn's overtures has its own unmistakable atmosphere, but Berlioz, although inspired by such widely different topics as the sea (*The Corsair*), *Benvenuto Cellini*, a novel of Scott's (*Waverley*), plays of Shakespeare (*King Lear, Beatrice and Benedict*), still makes all his overtures sound strangely alike. They are vital and they have splendid melodies, even if in the last resort they do not bite on the mind.

"HAROLD IN ITALY"

Berlioz's overtures may be regarded as a side-track lying off the main path of his development after the *Fantastique*. The path first led to an unsuccessful sequel to the *Fantastique*. This was *Lélio, ou le Retour à la Vie*, in which a collection of songs and choral pieces was linked to a bombastic narrative declaimed by an actor. Then it led to *Harold in Italy*. Thereafter the path forked, leading on the one hand to what proved to be the blind alley of *Romeo and Juliet*, and on the other to the " choral-orchestral amalgam " of the *Messe des Morts*, the *Te Deum*, the *Childhood of Christ* and *The Damnation of Faust*. Finally it led to *The Trojans*.

Harold in Italy is richly inspired, but lacks the unity of the *Fantastique*, the fruit of a single overwhelming experience. Paganini, who had greatly admired the *Fantastique*, commissioned a viola concerto. Berlioz's initial sketches were not brilliant enough for the virtuoso, but writing a concerto for the dark-toned viola stirred his memories of wandering in the Italian countryside, attracted by picturesque scenes but at heart melancholy, like the Childe Harold of Byron's poem. And so Berlioz formed the plan of a programme-symphony in four movements : *Harold in the Mountains, March of the Pilgrims, Serenade*, and *Orgy of the Brigands*. Into the *Orgy* he introduced fragments from previous movements, as Beethoven had done in the finale of the Ninth. Unlike Beethoven, though, he brought them not only into the finale's introduction, but also into its coda. Up to the coda Berlioz's finale is wild and fierce, if not orgiastic. Just before the end the peaceful strains of the *Pilgrims' March* cause the brigands to run amok. The *Allegro* of *Harold in the Mountains* is an unruly movement in sonata form, in which the solo viola is hard put to it to hold its own in the orchestral *mêlée*. The whole work is perfectly characteristic of Berlioz—the wandering brooding fugato, which opens the long introduction to *Harold in the Mountains* ; the *Harold* theme, shrouded in a mist of violin tremolo, cello semiquavers, and trombone chords before it emerges, noble and simple ; the *Pilgrims' March*, interrupted by a quivering pianissimo phrase evoking the image of a whispered *Pater Noster* ; the limpid counterpoint of the

Harold theme threading its way through the marching pilgrims and the merry-making of the *Serenade*. It is music such as this, original yet free of eccentricity, evocative yet perfectly rounded, which precludes the idea that Berlioz's harmonic equipment was defective.

"ROMEO AND JULIET"

Of the *Romeo and Juliet* symphony the only movements which have frequent performances are the *Queen Mab* scherzo and the *Love Scene* which, Wagner declared, contained the loveliest theme of the century. This vast work, to which Berlioz gave the sub-title of "dramatic symphony", is interspersed with choruses, arias, and snatches of recitative. But this attempt by Berlioz to employ the sung word (instead of a mere programme-note) to formulate the content of a symphony falls between two stools. The cantata numbers, formulating the programme, are uninteresting in themselves ; but they encourage Berlioz in the symphonic portions to extremes, compared to which the most over-excited passages of the *Fantastique* are staid. The passages of purely musical inspiration—the *Queen Mab* scherzo, (a sparkling exercise in fairy-orchestration à la Mendelssohn) and the exquisite *Love Scene*—are gems buried in a welter of orchestral rhetoric pushing fidelity to programme to extreme lengths. Berlioz himself seems to have realised his mistake ; for above the score of the moment depicting Romeo's frenzied despair at the discovery of Juliet in her tomb, he inscribed a note, advising the conductor to omit this movement unless the symphony were being performed before an audience familiar with the tragedy. Wagner drew the moral that symphonic-programme music must be wedded to a revolutionary art of music drama. The moral which Berlioz drew can be gathered from the fact that after *Romeo and Juliet* he turned in his tracks and, following the course which he had taken with the composition of the *Messe des Morts*, sought to satisfy his instinct for literal expression within the framework of classical choral and operatic forms.

The romanticism of Schumann and Chopin was reflected in their harmony, but whereas theirs was an imaginative development of romantic possibilities already latent in the idiom of Beethoven and Schubert, Berlioz's harmony is peculiar to himself. He arranges and spaces chords in unorthodox ways, and when handling common chords exercises a strange preference for triads in "root position" (which, it has been suggested, may have been partly due to his early training on the guitar). When leaving a key he disdains to smooth his passage with a cushioning modulating chord ; moreover he moves into extreme keys with little or no transitional apparatus. Probably these two latter idiosyncracies are responsible for the sense of estrangement which his harmony arouses. The programme sometimes justifies such extraordinary passages, but it is a different matter when such progressions are employed as though they were normal. Berlioz does this most frequently in his later works, where his harmony became increasingly bizarre. Had his idiosyncracies been due, as Berlioz's detractors allege, to defective training, they would have diminished, not increased, with the lessons of experience.

REQUIEM MASS

In the case of the *Messe des Morts* and *Te Deum* an unevenness of inspiration may be due, perhaps, to a certain inconsistency in Berlioz's attitude towards religion. If he had no religious faith, religion was still part of his being. His mother was a devout Catholic, his earliest musical impressions had been experienced in church, and one of his earliest successes had been a Mass. He could compose music expressing the *spirit* of a faith whose dogmas his mind rejected, even a simple unclouded faith such as we find in the seraphic calm of the organ voluntary which leads into the *Tibi omnes* of the *Te Deum*. But the aspect of faith which was the greatest inspiration to this atheistic religious composer was that which presents God in the guise of a dread Judge, visiting punishment upon those who deny Him. In Italy Berlioz had projected a colossal oratorio, entitled *Le Dernier Jour du Monde*, in which amid *Witches' Sabbath*-like scenes, mankind under the rule of an anti-Christ is doomed at the Day of Judgment. A colossal apocalyptic vision formed the centrepiece of the *Messe des Morts* and the climax of the *Te Deum*. In the days of the First Republic and the Napoleonic Empire vast forces had been assembled on occasions of public celebrations, and Berlioz followed this precedent, demanding for the *Messe* a chorus of 210 and an orchestra of which the first violins alone numbered 50. In the *Te Deum* he asked for three choirs, one a children's choir of 600 voices, the others each 100 strong. In the *Tuba Mirum* of the *Messe*, Berlioz employed four brass bands, posted at the four corners of the orchestra. But in the *Judex crederis* of the *Te Deum* Berlioz struck the apocalyptic note with awe-inspiring power. His "Judex crederis esse venturus", delivered to a hieratic chanting phrase intoned by different sections of the vast choir, is built up to a stupendous climax and marvellously conveys the obeisance of a multitude to the dread will of an almighty judge. It is no exaggeration to say that this stupendous chorus, which Berlioz regarded as his "most grandiose creation", is one of the supreme masterpieces of choral music.

The *Te Deum* also contains choruses eloquently voicing a faith which does not shudder before God's fearfulness, but praises His grandeur and

His mercy. Mendelssohn's choruses of praise are Handelian in outline, couched in a flowing fugal style with the orchestra playing a comparatively subordinate part ; but the *Te Deum laudamus*, *Tibi omnes* and *Christi, Rex gloriae* of Berlioz's *Te Deum* are sumptuous " choral-orchestral amalgams ", daringly combining elaborate polyphony with grandiose effects of mass-sonority. At the words " omnis terra veneratur", the elaborate fugue of the *Te Deum laudamus* merges into a hushed succession of plain triads, conveying a sense of awe. At the word " Sanctus ", the *Tibi omnes* becomes a tone-poem of long-held chords and ethereal woodwind fluttering. But when Berlioz turns from the objective to the subjective—from God the worshipped to Man the worshipper—his touch in the *Te Deum* is less certain. The *Dignare, Domine*, a chorus of supplication, is laboured, and the solo tenor's prayer *Te ergo quaesumus* is delivered to a jejune accompaniment of syncopated quavers. In a Requiem the note of supplication is inevitably sounded more often than in a *Te Deum*, a hymn of rejoicing in which the sinister majesty of Berlioz's *Judex crederis* is, strictly speaking, out of place. Furthermore, in a Requiem the supplication is more urgent, more charged with dread, and this may partly explain why what had failed to inspire Berlioz in a *Te Deum* could inspire him here. His *Messe des Morts* contains many beauties—the dark translucent counterpoint of the lamenting *Requiem et Kyrie* ; the *Offertorium* (which Schumann admired), through which the chorus intones a single swaying two-note phrase ; the melting melody and ethereal orchestration of the solo tenor's *Sanctus*. Even so, the total impression is of a work strangely inchoate, restless, disorientated. The big " objective " choruses such as *Tuba mirum*, *Rex tremendae*, and *Hosanna* lack the majestic dignity of those of the *Te Deum*. And sometimes we find Berlioz, as we never find Mendelssohn, employing orchestral effects as ends in themselves, even making strange experiments. Thus in the *Lacrymosa* the chorus is whipped by a recurring rhythm delivered *fortissimo* by the brass, and in the *Hostias* the phrases are punctuated by hollow chords delivered by trombones and flute.

" THE CHILDHOOD OF CHRIST "

The *Messe des Morts* and the *Te Deum* were conceived as *pièces d'occasion*, performed by specific forces in a specific building—the one in the Chapel of the Invalides, the other in the Church of St. Eustache. It was in relation to these that all effects, delicate (of which there were many) as well as grandiose, were carefully calculated. The case is otherwise with *The Childhood of Christ*, an oratorio scored for a normal choir and orchestra. Its libretto, beautifully designed by the composer, presents the Massacre of the Innocents and the flight of the Holy Family into Egypt, thus providing an admirable opportunity to exploit his taste for the horrific in an objectively dramatic context. The early scenes are dominated by Herod, visited by evil dreams (Herod's great aria, *O misère des rois*, looks forward to *Boris Godunov*), consulting soothsayers (whose bizarre " évocation cabalistique " Berlioz depicts with characteristic skill), and joining with them in a chorus which closes the first part. A few gently syncopated bars in A flat major transport us at once to a scene in which Mary and Joseph sing an idyllic duet, and a chorus of angels counsels the flight to Egypt. Berlioz had written in a pastoral idyllic vein in the *Scenes in the Country* of the *Fantastique* and the *Serenade* of *Harold in Italy*. Throughout the whole of the second part of the *Childhood* he does so again, lightening his orchestra, simplifying his melody, at times employing archaic modes to provide a framework for the unorthodox harmonies which were second nature to him. There is no hint of the *faux-naïf*: the delicate modal fugue depicting the flight across the desert, the lullaby of the *Shepherds' Farewell*, above all the mingled pathos and tranquillity of the *Repose of the Holy Family*, are unforced inspirations.

" THE DAMNATION OF FAUST "

There is no excuse of illness to account for the glaring unevenness of Berlioz's most famous work, *The Damnation of Faust*, composed in his middle years. On the basis of his early *Eight Scenes from Faust* Berlioz concocted a highly subjective version of Goethe's poem, in which the hero is not a rejuvenated old man in search of the meaning of life, committing many sins from which he is ultimately redeemed, but a young and melancholy " Harold in Italy " in search of the meaning of love, committing one sin for which he is damned. The instrument of his damnation is a Mephistopheles who expresses himself (apart from a pleasantly sinister *Song of the Flea* and *Serenade*) in theatrical recitative, punctuated by melodramatic brass flourishes, and commanding a train of sylphs and will-o'-the-wisps that might have stepped straight out of Mendelssohn's *Midsummer Night's Dream*.

Yet there is no denying the effectiveness of the work. The familiar Faust legend is made the subject-matter of an imaginary opera, in which the orchestra scene-shifts and tone-paints a panorama almost impossible to stage (although attempts have been made). As in Goethe's play *Faust*, Marguérite and Mephistopheles appear before a background of peasants making merry and singing Easter hymns, soldiers marching, students carousing and blaspheming. At the *Ride to the Abyss* we realise that it is just this panorama of a normal, everyday world, from which the orchestra's pounding rhythm is carrying Faust, which heightens the magnificent horror of the passage, and raises its stature to that of the climax towards which the whole of the previous action has been moving. So overwhelming is the effect that it cannot be spoilt even by Berlioz's ridiculous anti-climax of demons greeting Faust in a banal chorus, mouthed in Swedenborgian gibberish. That lapse is redeemed by the calm of *Marguérite's Apotheosis*, the chorus simple and processional, the orchestra weaving the figure of a lullaby through every bar, creating a sense of eternal rest.

The Damnation of Faust contains many other beauties—the brilliant Rákóczy March, an arrangement of a famous traditional Hungarian march which Berlioz made during a visit to Budapest and subsequently incorporated ; the windswept orchestration of Faust's *Invocation to Nature* ; the stark, exquisite simplicity of Marguérite's quasi-archaic ballad *The King of Thule*. Most beautiful of all, perhaps, is the forlorn, broken melody (at its first delivery by the cor anglais each phrase dying away in a *fermata*) of Marguérite's *Romance*, conveying the sadness of a voice crying in the wilderness—a melody comparable to that of the cor anglais in the introduction to the *Scenes in the Country* and to that of Berlioz's famous song *L'Absence*, inspired by Gautier's

> Reviens, ma bien-aimée !
> Comme une fleur loin du soleil
> La fleur de ma vie est fermée,
> Loin de ton sourire vermeil.

Lonely, forsaken love plays a vital part in *The Trojans*, Berlioz's last great work for the opera-house. Here he returned to the tale of Dido and Æneas, over which he had wept as a boy, and attempted to carry into the intensely commercialised world of Parisian opera a grandiose vision of ideal love and devotion to duty. In order to gauge the boldness of such a project we must go back a little and trace the story of French opera during Berlioz's lifetime.

FRENCH GRAND OPERA

So far as Paris is concerned, the period between Rossini's retirement from the opera-house and the fall of the Second Empire in 1870 is dominated by the large, though hollow, figure of Giacomo Meyerbeer (1791–1864), the son of a wealthy Berlin merchant-banker, who was regarded by many contemporary musicians (including Bizet and the young Richard Wagner) as the peer of the greatest composers of the past. Meyerbeer began his operatic career as the chief hope of the German nationalists headed by

Weber. A sojourn in Italy turned him into an Italianate composer (he significantly translated his first name, Jakob, into Giacomo), and he produced a series of operas that successfully reproduced the manner of Rossini but not his genius. Of them *Il Crociato in Egitto* (" The Crusade in Egypt ") (1824), an *azione teatrale* or dramatic oratorio in the style of Rossini's *Mosè*, is the most important, since its production at Rossini's instance in Paris a year later introduced Meyerbeer to the French capital and afforded him a new field for the exploitation of his extraordinary powers, in collaboration with Eugène Scribe.

THE NINETEENTH-CENTURY LIBRETTO

Scribe was the chief purveyor of librettos in Paris from 1823 until his death in 1861. All the major composers, and some minor ones, who wrote for the Parisian theatres were supplied by Scribe who, single-handed or with an assistant, could turn out to order a grand " Gothick " tragedy, a romantic drama or a trivial comedy. Among his opera-books were those for Auber's *La Muette de Portici* (" The Dumb Girl of Portici "—also known as *Masaniello*) which in some respects served as a model for *Guillaume Tell*; Rossini's *Le Comte Ory*; Donizetti's *La Favorite*; and Verdi's *Les Vêpres Siciliennes* (" The Sicilian Vespers "). His literary integrity may be assessed from the fact that the last-named piece was a transference to thirteenth-century Sicily, with hardly any alteration, of a drama originally placed in Flanders during the reign of Philip II and set by Donizetti as *Il Duca d'Alba* (" The Duke of Alba "). Of all the products of the " Scribe factory ", the librettos for Meyerbeer's grand operas are the most characteristic.

MEYERBEER

Meyerbeer represents a return to the baroque idea of combining every possible ingredient in a work of art. He demanded of Scribe dramas in which each scene was to provide the greatest possible contrast with the next. He demanded of the Opéra the most elaborate and spectacular scenery and costumes, and months of rehearsal during which he refashioned what he had composed. (" I never know what I have written ", he confessed, " till I actually hear it performed.") Being an immensely rich man he got his way. The results were immense, unwieldy spectacles in five acts, which contained, as Mendelssohn said, " something for everyone ", adding, " but there is nothing for the heart in them ".

In his search for sensational effect Meyerbeer incorporated such artistically questionable scenes as a ballet of nuns who had broken their vows, raised from the dead by Robert the Devil ; a ballet of women bathing in the Loire ; and a skating ballet, which, delightful as it may be torn from its context, seems out of place in an opera dealing with John of Leyden. There were orgies at court, scenes in church, and, above all, the solemn taking of an oath by a band of conspirators—an effect Meyerbeer had used already in *Il Crociato*. Alternating with these grand set-pieces for chorus and orchestra were lyrical love-scenes and airs with straightforward melodies.

Unhappily Meyerbeer's musical invention was unequal to the support of these immense structures. His melodies, which often begin well, have a way of disappearing like water into the desert sand of commonplace. And there is no substance behind the majority of his grand tableaux, which have been likened to stage-scenery, producing the illusion of grandeur without the reality to sustain it. And nothing becomes shabby more quickly than scenery after a little use.

If that were all there is to Meyerbeer, he would hardly be worth more than a bare record of his operas—*Robert le Diable* (" Robert the Devil ") (1831), *Les Huguenots* (1836), *Le Prophète* (1849), and the posthumous *L'Africaine* (1865) being the most important. Yet, though these operas to-day may seem a compendium of dramatic and musical clichés, he was a genuine originator. It is his misfortune that the new operatic formulas which he devised were put to much better use by the greater composers of the next generation, foremost among them Verdi and Wagner. There is more than a grain of truth in the joke that Wagner's *Rienzi* is Meyerbeer's best opera, and it is impossible to imagine Verdi creating in the manner he did such scenes as the conspiracy in *Ernani*, the *auto-da-fé* in *Don Carlos* or the triumph scene in *Aida* without the " Blessing of the Daggers " in *Les Huguenots* or the coronation in *Le Prophète* as models. Moreover, Meyerbeer invented, sometimes with a glance at the practice of his former friend Weber, a great many of the orchestral effects which were to be employed by Gounod and Bizet as well as Verdi, to produce sensations of romantic horror or sinister foreboding.

HALÉVY AND OFFENBACH

Another successful practitioner in the same line was Jacques Fromental Halévy (1799–1862), whose *La Juive* (" The Jewess ") (1835) has had a longer life even than *Les Huguenots*, the best of Meyerbeer's operas. *La Juive*, whose libretto is also by Scribe, contains all the usual ingredients of grand opera, among them a setting of *Te Deum* with organ which furnished a model for many subsequent adaptions of church music to theatrical use.

Halévy also composed a number of comic operas, but in this sphere he was outclassed by Jacques Offenbach (1819–80), who became the chief purveyor of gay entertainment to the Paris of the Second Empire. Bright, blatant, and garish, Offenbach's music has a tremendous verve which has ensured the survival of his best pieces, never intended as more than topical entertainments in the Parisian theatres. *Orphée aux enfers* (" Orpheus in the Underworld ") (1858), *La Belle Hélène* (1864), and *La Grande Duchesse de Gerolstein* (1867) hold up a distorting mirror to a vanished social and political scene, but the wit of the verses and animal vitality of the music give them an immortal place in the history of light opera. They stand beside the more sentimental operettas of the Viennese, Johann Strauss (1825–99), whose *Die Fledermaus* (" The Bat ") (1874) has a universal appeal, and the more parochial humour of W. S. Gilbert's " Savoy Operas " which survive by virtue of the melodious and witty music of Arthur Sullivan (1842–1900).

At the end of his life Offenbach, like the clown who hankered after the part of Hamlet, turned his attention to a more serious theme, and in the romantic *The Tales of Hoffmann*, produced after the composer's death in 1881, contributed a work of unique character to the lyric stage.

CHARLES GOUNOD (1818–93)

The disaster of 1870 and the collapse of the Second Empire made a break in the artistic, no less than in the political, life of France. The world in which Meyerbeer could be acclaimed as the greatest of operatic composers was destroyed, and a strong impetus was given to a movement, already in existence, towards a less pretentious and more truly Gallic style of opera. The first important manifestation of this new spirit had been the production in 1859 of Gounod's *Faust* at the Théâtre Lyrique. Furnished with a libretto which concentrated on the Gretchen incident in Goethe's drama, Gounod produced a more viable work for the theatre than Berlioz's highly original *Damnation of Faust*. The lyrical charm of Gounod's opera won it a merited success that was never wholly spoiled by its lapses into sentimentality. Its success resulted in its transfer to the Opéra in 1869, when Gounod transformed the work into a " grand " opera by composing music for the previously spoken dialogue and adding a ballet, whose ingenuous dance-movements are singularly at variance with the orgies of the Walpurgisnacht or Witches' Sabbath they pretend to represent.

In its original form *Faust* represented an important phase in the development of *opéra-comique*, which now moved away from the merely amusing romantic world of Auber's *Fra Diavolo* (1830) and *Les Diamants de la Couronne* (" The Crown Diamonds ") (1841) into one where sighs and tears were more prominent than laughter. Some of the ingredients in

Faust, especially the character of Mephistopheles as presented by Gounod, and the Church scene which is the most impressive thing in the opera, are modelled on Meyerbeer; but *Faust* avoids any attempt to vie with the grandiose spectacular effects of the German composer. He had already attempted a melodramatic grand opera in the manner of *Robert le Diable* when he wrote *La Nonne Sanglante* ("The Bleeding Nun") (1854), which failed completely. Indeed, although Gounod scored another success with *Roméo et Juliette* when it was produced in 1867, it may be suggested that his true bent lay in the direction of comedy and the lighter sentimental themes. His witty setting of Molière's *Le Médecin malgré lui* (1858) and the charming lyricism of *Philémon et Baucis* (1860) show how elegant he could be when he was not straining his powers of expression beyond their strength. *Faust* in its *opéra-comique* version represents his powers stretched to their utmost. His later essays in the grand manner, *Cinq-Mars* (1877), *Polyeucte* (1878), and *Le Tribut de Zamora* (1881) were still-born. *Faust* served as an example to Ambroise Thomas (1811–96), who also drew on Goethe for *Mignon* and followed it with *Hamlet* (1868), in which Ophelia has an effective mad scene in the manner of Donizetti's Lucia.

XVIII

WAGNER AND VERDI

AMONG the galaxy of composers born at the end of the first decade of the nineteenth century, two of the greatest have as yet been mentioned only in passing. In the world of opera Richard Wagner (1813–83) and Giuseppe Verdi (1813–1901) were to dominate the century, and Wagner's influence on the whole history of music was to be second only to that of Beethoven.

Wagner was born into the family of a police official, whose widow married an actor (who was possibly the boy's real father). From an early age he was close to the theatre, and both his mother and step-father were cultivated and intelligent, while the previous generations of his family included a church musician and an author. His own education, though sporadic, followed the classical curriculum, his favourite subject being Greek. He was fortunate in that his step-father was acting at the Dresden Theatre when Weber was in charge of the Opera. On the other hand, Giuseppe Verdi came of peasant stock, his birthplace a humble cottage in a village near Parma. His education was meagre, but his early display of a talent for music won him the attention of a wealthy amateur who obtained a musical education for him in Milan, while Wagner was completing his studies at Leipzig.

Wagner approached opera in the first place by way of the drama, the Greek drama in particular, on which he modelled some juvenile essays in play-writing ; and in the second, by conducting opera, of which he had experience in several theatres before he succeeded to Weber's former post as the musical director of the Dresden Court Opera. Meanwhile he had completed in 1840 his first important opera, *Rienzi*, a grand historical drama whose successful production at Dresden secured him the directorship in 1843.

" THE FLYING DUTCHMAN "

He had also completed the far more original *Der Fliegende Holländer* (" The Flying Dutchman "), which was produced at Dresden in 1843. Throughout his career Wagner was his own librettist, and he looked on opera as a form in which the music was the medium for the presentation of the drama. Dissatisfied with the conventional operatic formulas of the day, especially those employed by the Italian composers, and also with the important part allowed to mere vocal virtuosity in the music, without regard to dramatic truth, Wagner reverted to the principles of the first creators of opera and of Gluck and Calzabigi. *The Flying Dutchman* represents only a first step towards his ideal of a complete integration of drama, music, and spectacle. In subject it follows the example of Weber and of Marschner's macabre *Der Vampyr* and *Hans Heiling*. The set aria is not yet wholly eliminated, and Senta, the heroine, has a strophic *ballade* quite in the French style. But there is a new and unprecedented power in the nature-music surpassing anything Weber had achieved, while the macabre element is lifted to the higher plane of the supernatural by being linked with the noble theme of man's redemption through the love of a self-sacrificing woman.

" TANNHÄUSER " AND " LOHENGRIN "

In *Tannhäuser* (produced in 1845), whose theme is the conflict between love sacred and profane, Wagner advanced further towards the emancipation of opera from set forms and of vocal music from the strict metres of classical convention. But he had not yet evolved, as he did later, a free melodic declamation backed by an orchestral texture woven of motifs that by their character or association serve to illuminate and comment upon the text. In *Lohengrin*, produced in 1850, he did achieve a greater musical continuity. As he wrote himself, " I have been at pains . . . to indicate the spoken accent of the words with such sharpness and certainty that the singer has only to sing in the tempo prescribed, giving each note its proper value, to have the speaking expression completely under his control."

Wagner's achievement in *Tannhäuser* and *Lohengrin* was, however, sufficiently remarkable. In great parts of *Tannhäuser* his imaginative grasp and intensity of expression lift the hearer above the atmosphere of rather stuffy grand opera, while the story of *Lohengrin* is given a timelessness and a symbolic significance without depriving the characters of their humanity.

Lohengrin is the highest peak and the last example of German romantic opera in the tradition of Weber. After it was completed in 1848, and before its first performance at Weimar two years later, there came a break in Wagner's career, for, owing to his implication in the abortive revolution of 1848, he had to leave Dresden and go into exile. It was seventeen years before his next opera, *Tristan und Isolde* (1865), was produced. In the meantime he worked on his greatest project, *The Ring of the Nibelung*, in preparation for which he elaborated his æsthetic and philosophical ideas in a huge quantity of books and pamphlets. It will be convenient at this point to examine the achievement of his Italian contemporary.

VERDI'S EARLY OPERAS

As with Wagner, we may leave aside Verdi's first two operas. His career really began with *Nabucodonosor* (" Nebuchadnezzar "), usually called *Nabucco* (1842), a semi-biblical opera in the style of Rossini's *Mosè*, which at once proclaimed that a new and vigorous personality had arrived at the Scala Theatre. The strong melodies and vehement expression of passion, carried sometimes over the borderline of vulgarity, made Donizetti and Bellini seem pale indeed. Incidentally, Verdi's arrival coincided with the resurgence of Italian patriotism that was to effect the liberation of the northern provinces from Austrian rule and the unification of the nation under Victor Emmanuel in the 1860s. Verdi gave expression to these aspirations in opera after opera, whose stories, though medieval in setting like *I Lombardi alla prima crociata* (" The Lombards at the First Crusade ") (1843), *Ernani* (1844), *Giovanna d'Arco* (" Joan of Arc ") (1845), *Attila* (1846), and *La Battaglia di Legnano* (" The Battle of Legnano ") (1849), gave opportunity for the more or less overt expression of hatred for the oppression of a foreign ruler.

But if Verdi's popularity in his own country to some extent derived from his being the mouthpiece of Italian aspirations, his growing reputation abroad rested on more lasting, less topical foundations. To the sheer vigour of his music must be added his uncanny strength in the delineation of character, which gives to the persons in his operas a roundness and a humanity for which we may look to Donizetti or Rossini in vain. In particular, Verdi's baritones, though usually cast for the villains of the story, are more than mere personifications of the malice that provokes the dramatic conflict (a type to which Sir Henry Ashton in Donizetti's *Lucia di Lammermoor* belongs). *Nabucco* is far from being wholly wicked, and, within the limitations of the conventions to which Verdi subscribed, he is drawn as a human being with whom we can sympathise.

Verdi's early operas conform to the accepted pattern of arias and duets, trios, etc., linked by recitative, each act culminating in a concerted finale for as many of the singers on the stage as the plot could justify, supported by the chorus. Within the limits of this convention Verdi was able to create such a striking, though uneven, masterpiece as *Macbeth* (1847), and nothing is more remarkable in this first period of his activity than the greatness of his response to a genuine tragic drama as compared with the

PETER ILYICH TCHAIKOVSKY (1840–1893)

Oil painting by Kuznetsov, 1893

CLAUDE DEBUSSY (1862–1918)

mere forcefulness evoked, for instance, by the romantic melodrama of Victor Hugo's *Ernani*. Although the version of *Macbeth* performed nowadays is the result of a revision made for Paris in 1865, some of the finest pages in it belong to the original version. The sleep-walking scene, for example, which is set as it stands in Shakespeare's drama, including the comments of the doctor and the lady-in-waiting, is an astonishing essay in supple *arioso* responding to the inflexions of the words, without a trace of the old formalities of aria-construction. The scene stands as a prophetic indication of the musical dramaturgy Verdi was to apply to whole operas in his later years. There is nothing quite comparable with it in any of his works before *Don Carlos*, twenty years later.

Among the operas composed at this time *Luisa Miller* (1849) is important in that its subject, derived from a drama by Schiller, called for music of a less heroic, more intimate type than the historical themes Verdi had hitherto used. Luisa's tragedy cannot be called " realistic " in the manner of Carmen : she belongs rather to the world of the peasant characters in *Guillaume Tell*, and her sufferings evoke music of a tender pathos foreshadowing the style of *La Traviata* (1853).

THREE POPULAR MASTERPIECES

Meanwhile Verdi had created in *Rigoletto* (1851) and *Il Trovatore* (1853) two other popular masterpieces. In *Rigoletto* the excellent characterisation, which includes the precise thumbnail sketch of the cut-throat Sparafucile, is embodied in a novel structure. As Verdi himself remarked, *Rigoletto* was conceived as a series of duets, and though there are notable solos it is in the duets (the great quartet of the last act is in the nature of a double-duet) that the clash of characters is revealed and the dramatic action carried forward. There is also a real attempt to give the music the continuity at which Wagner was simultaneously aiming. In the last act, above all, the new-found flexibility and continuity of Verdi's music gives a complete coherence to the dramatic action, which moves forward to its tragic climax unfalteringly. The Duke's song *La donna è mobile* is the only formal piece, and it is so easily memorised that the dullest member of the audience will recognise it when its repetition, off-stage, brings about the horrible dénouement.

By contrast, *Il Trovatore* is a cruder melodrama and its libretto, a byword for obscure complication, uncovers one weakness in Verdi's dramatic sense which he never entirely overcame. He was interested, at any rate during the greater part of his career, in " strong " dramatic situations, and he did not trouble always to ensure that his librettists made it clear how these situations came about. When, as happens in *Il Trovatore*, the situations are forced and improbable, derived from theatrical convention rather than from actual human experience, the effect is apt to be unconvincing and even ludicrous. Nevertheless, the copious succession of strong and beautiful melodies and the finely drawn figure of the crazed gypsy, Azucena, redeem the obscurities of the story.

In *La Traviata*, the third of the masterpieces of his first maturity, Verdi adjusted his style to the intimate character of Dumas's play. In place of heroics there is tender passion embodied in exquisite lyrical melody, supported by a more sensitive use of orchestral colour.

THE MIDDLE YEARS

For the better understanding of the parallel growth of the two composers after they had reached maturity it may be helpful to set out in tabular form the dates of their activities :

Wagner		*Verdi*
1848–52	Text of *Der Ring des Nibe-lungen* written	
		1853 *Il Trovatore & La Traviata*
1854	Score of *Rheingold* completed	
		1855 *Les Vêpres Siciliennes*
1856	*Die Walküre* completed	
1857	*Siegfried* completed up to the middle of Act II	1857 *Simone Boccanegra*
1857–59	*Tristan und Isolde* composed	1859 *Un Ballo in Maschera* ("A Masked Ball ")
1862–67	*Die Meistersinger von Nürnberg* composed	1862 *La Forza del Destino* (" The Force of Destiny ")
1865	*Tristan* produced at Munich	
		1867 *Don Carlos*
1868	*Die Meistersinger* produced at Munich. Resumption of composition of *Siegfried*	
1869–70	*Rheingold* and *Die Walküre* produced at Munich	
		1871 *Aida*
1869–74	*Götterdämmerung* composed	
1876	*Der Ring* produced complete at Bayreuth	
1877–82	*Parsifal* composed and produced at Bayreuth	
1883	Death of Wagner	

While in the years up to 1853 Verdi had been producing, on an average, one opera a year, after *La Traviata* (which was composed in the space of three months) the intervals between his operas progressively increased. Opera composition had ceased, indeed, to be the uncomplicated business it was in the days of Donizetti, who could compose a whole work within three weeks of receiving the libretto. Each work now had to be given its individual character, and the growing complexity of orchestration alone involved a great increase in the composer's work.

Moreover, of the operas by Verdi listed above up to *Aida*, only two (*A Masked Ball* and *Simone Boccanegra*) after 1853 were composed for Italian theatres. The others were commissioned by the Paris Opéra or by theatres (St. Petersburg and Cairo) which were under French influence. The operas had to conform to the requirements of these theatres, which demanded long spectacular operas on the Meyerbeerian scale. Verdi, an artist of the utmost integrity, groaned under the burden of the five-acts-and-a-ballet imposed by the Opéra, but he was a conscientious craftsman and faithfully fulfilled his contracts. He was no æsthetic theorist, but he had learned by experience how to make the most of a dramatic situation in his music. When the text was feeble or the situation unconvincing, his music did not always disguise the weakness. Nor was he at first successful in handling scenes of social gaiety, which failed to stir his imagination. His progress in this direction may be observed in *A Masked Ball*, where the " court " music is superior to that in *Rigoletto*, through the more plebeian humours of the camp and of Melitone in *The Force of Destiny*, to the subtly observed court scene in *Don Carlos*. But Verdi was essentially a tragic composer in whom grief evoked a noble compassion. It is in dark-hued works like *Simone Boccanegra* and *Don Carlos* that his genius is most finely manifested in these middle years, which culminate in the splendid outpouring of great melody in *Aida*.

Throughout these operas there is a steady advance towards that continuity of texture which was so astonishingly achieved in Lady Macbeth's sleep-walking scene. The distinction between recitative and aria diminishes, and the free interplay of characters in dialogue is faithfully mirrored in the music, nowhere better than in the scenes between the King and Posa and with the Grand Inquisitor in *Don Carlos*. The dramatic use of orchestral colour has also increased in subtlety along with the greater richness in texture. One need only cite the marvellous evocation of the Egyptian night in the third act of *Aida*.

THE TEXT OF " THE RING "

Wagner meantime had set himself problems of an intellectual character that far exceeded anything undertaken by Verdi. Having chosen as his next subject the mythological saga of the Nibelung's Ring, he found that when he had composed the drama *Siegfried's Death* (which we know as *Götterdämmerung*), he needed a further drama to explain how the situations arose, and then still more explanations to precede that. In this way, what had been conceived as one opera became three (*Die Walküre*, *Siegfried* and *Götterdämmerung*), with a " *Vorabend* " or introductory piece, *Das Rheingold*, as prelude. The mere task of organising the immense quantity of poetic and musical material into a series of coherent dramas, each developing into its successor and culminating in the vast spaces and final cataclysm of *Götterdämmerung*, still seems daunting, even a century after its inception. That Wagner succeeded, after an occasionally hesitant start in *Das Rheingold* (which is apt to sound episodic), in filling every bar of his enormous composition with music that is continuously alive and characteristic, and that sustains the hearer's interest through the least promising scenes, is a staggering achievement.

Three elements contributed to his success. The first was his adoption of short, irregular verses on the pattern of medieval poetry, in which assonance and alliteration take the place of rhyme. The text of *The Ring* makes tiresome reading and is easy to burlesque, but it provided an admirable basis for a flexible music, free from the constraints of regular metre.

THE FUNCTION OF LEADING-MOTIVES

Secondly, Wagner developed the system of " leading-motives ", already used by Weber in *Euryanthe* and by himself in *Tannhäuser* and *Lohengrin*, into a means of constructing what are, in effect, huge symphonic movements. His motives are usually terse, generally two bars and rarely more than four in length. Consisting both of melodic and harmonic elements, they are susceptible to change and symphonic development, and to combination in step with changes in the dramatic situation or developments in the characters or ideas they represent. They are much more than musical tags or labels ; they have a symbolic meaning and the vitality of a living organism capable of growth. By this device Wagner is able to clothe long scenes of narrative and dialogue with music of continuously developing interest, culminating at the dramatic climax in a lyrical outpouring of emotion, which corresponds to the aria of Italian opera though lacking its formal shape.

THE WAGNERIAN ORCHESTRA

In the third place, Wagner developed the resources of the orchestra beyond anything that had hitherto been achieved even by Berlioz, whose example was not without its effect on him. His highly developed sense of instrumental colouring had already been shown in *Lohengrin*, where the characterisation is achieved partly by the association of Lohengrin with string-tone, Elsa with woodwinds and so on. *The Ring*, with its array of gods and supermen and sub-human creatures, its natural phenomena and supernatural events, called for larger resources. Wagner not only increased the number of players, balancing his additional woodwinds with a large body of strings ; he also wrote parts for a set of four extra brass instruments, the so-called " Wagner tubas ", which had to be specially made, in order to give the right tone of majestic colour to the music associated with Wotan and Valhalla.

This huge orchestral apparatus was not used merely to produce a greater effect of grandiloquence and volume than had been achieved, by, say, Meyerbeer. Wagner's orchestration shows restraint and sensibility. There is a great stretch of *Götterdämmerung* in which the violins do not have a note to play, the result being an ominous and sombre musical texture exactly in keeping with the dark character of the Gibichungs. Only with his enlarged and varied palette could Wagner have achieved such memorable themes as that of the sword with its flashing trumpet-tone, the growl of Wotan's anger, the bitter tang of the Nibelung's hate, and the dissolving harmonies associated with the Tarnhelm or with the magic potion that destroys Siegfried's memory. Nor could the full splendour of the " Entry of the Gods into Valhalla " or the finales of *Die Walküre* and *Götterdämmerung* have been realised otherwise.

The composition of the *Ring* dramas in reverse order resulted in some inconsistencies in the story and in a considerable amount of repetition, which has been the subject of criticism. The repetitions, however, may be justified on the ground that they afforded the composer the opportunity for musical recapitulations which give shape and coherence to the architectural design. For despite the immensity of the scale, Wagner did not allow himself to become too involved in detail, and so succeeded in creating an over-all muscial form which can be comprehended despite its unusual magnitude.

" TRISTAN "

As will be seen from the table on page 310, Wagner abandoned the composition of *The Ring* half-way through its course. The diversion was due in part to an emotional experience in his private life, in part to the realisation that *The Ring* was not a practical proposition for the opera-houses of the day. He turned his attention to the tragedy of Tristan and Isolde, embodying in his text his philosophy of love. Again his music redeemed the verbose text. For the music explores with an unprecedented subtlety and minuteness the innermost springs of action in the characters. As drama *Tristan* is, by ordinary standards, extremely static. Nothing *happens* on the stage through long stretches, and when action does come it is short and sharp. But the characters *live* before our eyes with a fullness exceptional in opera (Verdi achieved the same kind of effect in certain scenes in *Simone Boccanegra* and *Don Carlos*, but never consistently throughout an opera). *Tristan* is, indeed, more like a novel of the kind written by Henry James than a drama in the usual sense. As a musical composition it is, with *The Mastersingers*, Wagner's masterpiece and the vindication of his system. The themes, while thoroughly characteristic, are completely assimilated into the texture of the continuously flowing music, which takes the form of a huge symphony in three movements, in which the third movement is a tragic recapitulation of the first.

This is not the place to discuss the harmonic consequences of the idiom adopted by Wagner for *Tristan*, in which the use of chromatic intervals tends to confuse the firm sense of tonality usual in classical music. But this idiom gave the work a character of its own quite distinct from Wagner's other operas. It was at the time so original that even a musician of Berlioz's stature confessed that he could make nothing of the Prelude.

" THE MASTERSINGERS " AND AFTER

When he was finishing *Tannhäuser*, in which there is a song-contest, Wagner contemplated following it with a companion-piece, a comedy on the analogy of the Greek satiric plays. The idea recurred to him after *Tristan* was finished, and he set to work on an opera about Hans Sachs and the Guild of Master Singers in medieval Nuremberg. Again the work was on the largest scale, yet the structure never sags. And once more the music has its own character, more simply diatonic in harmony and with frequent allusions to Bach-like counterpoint. In this medium Wagner invented burly themes for the worthy Masters, crabbed ones for the pedantic Beckmesser (a burlesque of the Viennese critic Hanslick, whose attacks had irritated him), and genially lyrical ones for Sachs and Eva and Walther.

Eventually, even though *Das Rheingold* and *Die Walküre* received isolated performances at Munich, thanks to the interest of King Ludwig, Wagner came to realise that only in a specially designed theatre could the whole cycle be properly presented in accordance with his ideas. So this amazing man undertook, over and above the work of completing the composition, the task of designing and building the Festival Theatre at Bayreuth as the temple of his art. The gigantic scheme materialised in 1876, and by good fortune—for even now the science of acoustics achieves as many misses as hits—*The Ring* was produced in a theatre worthy of it. Nowhere else but at Bayreuth can the majesty of its music be so fully realised.

It is small wonder that these efforts left Wagner an exhausted man. *Parsifal* contains some of the most beautiful and serene music Wagner wrote, although its mixture of Christian ritual with erotic symbolism and ideas drawn from Buddhism, Freemasonry, and other sources does not commend itself to all tastes. After its production in 1882 Wagner's overstrained heart gave out, and he died while on a visit to Venice in January 1883.

VERDI'S OLD AGE

In contrast with Wagner, Verdi's old age was green and vigorous. He went from strength to strength, and at seventy-seven produced, with his librettist, Arrigo Boito (1842–1918), the greatest of Italian tragic operas, *Otello*, followed six years later by a supreme comedy, *Falstaff*. Boito was a distinguished poet and a composer of exceptional seriousness and integrity. His *Mefistofele* (1868) may claim to be the best of the operas inspired by Goethe's *Faust*, and, though the posthumous *Nerone*, which occupied him for forty years and was still unfinished when he died, suffered from being overworked, it was a marvel of historical reconstruction. For Verdi's most formidable rival, Amilcare Ponchielli (1834–86), he wrote the libretto of *La Gioconda* (1876), a powerful melodrama with an Iago-like villain based on a drama by Victor Hugo. The opening crowd scene in *Gioconda* seems to have served as a model for that in Verdi's *Otello*.

Shakespeare, in whom Verdi saw the supreme dramatist rather than the greatest of poets, always evoked the finest response from the composer's genius, and in *Otello* he attained the highest peak of noble passion and pathos. This mood finds beautiful expression in the love-duet, even more poignant in the superb last act, in whose dramatic construction Verdi himself had a large share. Othello's rages are embodied in harsh and violent outbursts from the brass, which also in quieter euphony shows forth the greatness of his soul.

If *Otello* is Verdi's masterpiece, *Falstaff*, produced in his eightieth year, is an even more surprising achievement. That a composer who had touched comedy only incidentally since the disastrous production of his *opera buffa Un Giorno di Regno* (" King for a day ") (1840) half a century before should have produced music of such quicksilver mobility, so witty and so youthfully fresh, is nothing less than a miracle.

In the musical continuity and flexibility of his last operas (from *Simone Boccanegra* onwards) Verdi achieved, no less than Wagner, the means of

315

presenting his drama through music, which has been the aim of all great opera-composers. He attained his aim without reference to his great contemporary and never resorted to the symphonic use of leading-motives. Indeed, as he told Puccini, he disapproved of symphonic music in opera. He made dramatic use of recurrent melodies, as many Italian composers had done before him. Violetta on her deathbed remembers early ecstasies of love ; Othello " dying on a kiss " recalls his passionate embrace of Desdemona in the love duet ; and through the grosser humours of Falstaff and the Merry Wives runs the silver thread of the melody associated with Nanetta and Fenton, the music of the young heart's rapture made audible.

Although Verdi's influence was still paramount in Italy at the time of his death, and Wagner cast a shadow even over France, there emerged both there and in Russia and Eastern Europe, as we shall see, schools of opera that owed much to one or both of these giants and yet contrived to be original.

BIZET

The early death of Georges Bizet (1838–75) was a great disaster, for only in the last four years of his life did he find the subjects which brought out the full brilliance of his genius. Before 1870 Bizet composed several operas, of which the most successful is *Les Pêcheurs de perles* (" The Pearl Fishers ") (1863). The romantic Oriental setting does not successfully conceal the stereotyped character of the story, in which two sworn friends are rivals for the love of a priestess sworn to chastity. All Bizet could do was to provide lyrical melody in the manner of Gounod and use his imagination as a colourist to suggest the exotic background.

La Jolie Fille de Perth (" The Fair Maid of Perth ") (1866), based on Scott's novel, has an inept libretto, which bristles with improbabilities and introduces a " mad scene " for the soprano for which there is no warrant in the original novel. Bizet started work on various other operatic projects, only to abandon them as unsuitable, before the Franco-Prussian War interrupted his activities.

REALISM—" CARMEN "

One may suspect that Bizet was affected, whether consciously or not, by the new reaction against romanticism. In 1856 Flaubert's *Madame Bovary* was published and was the subject of an unsuccessful prosecution. The Salon, which accepted innumerable nudes so long as they were called

" L'Enlèvement de Psyché" or "Les Sabines", rejected Manet's "Le Déjeuner sur l'herbe" in 1863, and in the following year his masterpiece, "Olympia", was subjected to violent abuse. In 1867 Zola published *Thérèse Raquin* and soon after 1870 began his great series of realistic novels, *Les Rougon-Macquart*.

This was the atmosphere in which Bizet found his feet as a composer in 1872, when he composed the incidental music for Alphonse Daudet's *L'Arlésienne* (" The Girl of Arles "), a drama about life on a Provençal farm. Then came *Carmen*, which aroused in the audience of the Opéra Comique in 1875 a reaction similar to that aroused by Manet, the painter of contemporary life, who was labelled "the apostle of the ugly and the repulsive".

The hostile reception of *Carmen* seems the more extraordinary when it is recalled that there had been a Spanish vogue in Paris for many years, even before the arrival of Napoleon III's Spanish Empress Eugénie in 1853 gave it added impetus. In the 1860s a troupe of Spanish dancers visited Paris. Manet painted them and also an imaginary scene in the bull-ring. Bizet can hardly have been unaware of these events, and they almost certainly influenced the choice of Prosper Merimée's novel, one of the earliest manifestations of the Spanish vogue, as the subject of his masterpiece.

Had Carmen been represented not as the lover of a deserter from the army but, like Donizetti's *Favorite*, as the mistress of a medieval Spanish king, her lack of morals would no doubt have been acceptable. But the time was past when (to quote Zola) " the reader was kept in suspense by a complicated but improbable story ". Now the sole object was " to register human facts, to lay bare the mechanism of body and soul. The plot is simplified, the first man one comes across will do as hero ; examine him and you are sure to find a straightforward drama which allows full play to all the machinery of emotion and passion." Such a creed could, and sometimes did, lead to drab stories drably told. But Zola also allowed for the poetic side of life, and it is that element that redeems the masterpieces of the realist school, among which *Carmen* occupies a high and important place. For, notwithstanding the prior claims of Verdi's *La Traviata* (1853), whose heroine at least moves in a polite society and whose contemporaneity was at first disguised in costumes of the seventeenth century, *Carmen* is the first unromantic realist opera.

Its realism is underlined by the Gallic lucidity of Bizet's music, whose texture had attained both here and in *L'Arlésienne* a marvellous transparency. It matters very little that the melodies and the rhythms of *Carmen* rarely achieve an authentic Spanishness ; they are certainly Mediterranean in their sensuous beauty and strong passion.

SAINT-SAËNS

Bizet's early death was a calamity for French opera. There was no one to carry on as an interpreter in music of the contemporary scene, after the style of Manet in painting. The leaders of the next generation were Camille Saint-Saëns (1835–1921) and Jules Massenet (1842–1912), who produced their first important operas, *La Princesse Jaune* (" The Yellow Princess ") and *Don César de Bazan* respectively, in 1872. Saint-Saëns was endowed, in the words of Gounod, "with one of the most astonishing musical organisations ". As a craftsman he was without an equal, but he lacked both real originality of invention and genuine dramatic feeling. *La Princesse Jaune* was a failure and caused the Opéra to reject *Samson et Dalila*, which was ultimately produced by Liszt at Weimar in 1877. Of Saint-Saëns' twelve operas *Samson* alone has survived, by virtue of its coherence as a work and the success with which the composer for once created a consistent musical atmosphere. The heroic Samson is well drawn, and Dalila's music is voluptuous yet restrained (as was Berlioz's love-music) by a classical sense of proportion. Like Berlioz, too, Saint-Saëns tended to present static *tableaux* with choruses in the style of oratorio, rather than dynamic action.

MASSENET

Massenet's *Don César* was a conventional comic opera, and it was not until he composed *Hérodiade* (1881) that he introduced into the opera-house the particular brand of " discreet and quasi-religious eroticism " (as Vincent d'Indy called it) which he had exploited in his oratorio *Marie Magdaleine* (1873). The erotic mysticism of the story of Salome was clothed with delicately sensual melody. In his next opera, *Manon* (1884), Massenet created his masterpiece, for here was a story of amorous intrigue which he was eminently fitted to compose. The fragile Manon required of the musician a tender response to her charms, not a heart-searching depth of feeling. The music of *Manon* is captivating in its prettiness and facile lyricism ; but the same gifts applied to a grand, heroic subject like *Le Cid* (1885) proved inadequate. Nor was Massenet successful in adapting himself to the realistic style of his pupil Alfred Bruneau (1857–1934), who drew his subjects from the novels of his friend Zola ; and *La Navarraise* (" The Woman of Navarre ") (1894) and *Sapho* (1897), based on Daudet's novel, show Massenet attempting this naturalistic style. *Werther* (1892) and *Thaïs* (1894) were subjects better suited to his talent, though the sentimentality of the one and the religious eroticism (in this case not even discreet) of the other, embodied in saccharine music, are not to everyone's taste.

Among other composers who made worthy contributions to the French operatic repertory of the period were Edouard Lalo (1823–92), Léo Delibes (1836–91), and Emmanuel Chabrier (1841–94). In *Lakmé* (1883) Delibes followed the example of Bizet's *Les Pêcheurs de perles* and *Djamileh* in choosing an Oriental setting for a vivacious and charming score. Lalo's single opera to be produced, *Le Roi d'Ys* (1888), is based on the Breton legend of a city beneath the sea. The music is powerful and original, and bears evidence of attention to Wagner's achievements, while maintaining its independent character and French lucidity. Rather surprisingly, Chabrier, the author of the brilliant and popular rhapsody *España*, was more completely under the Wagnerian spell when he composed *Gwendoline* (1886), and the composer admitted that the music was too concentrated, "like a meat-extract requiring dilution with water to be palatable". *Le Roi malgré lui* (1887), though still Wagnerian in its orchestration, is far more representative of the Chabrier we know from his vivacious and piquant orchestral rhapsody. The other repercussions on French music of the Wagnerian revolution in Germany may be deferred for later consideration.

XIX

NATIONAL MOVEMENTS

SO far the history of music has been confined to the chief countries of Western Europe—Italy, Germany, Austria, England, and France. The concept of nationality has hardly done more than colour the lines of the picture, and there has been no question of composers deliberately cultivating a local dialect for political or any other reasons. Those who were not born in one of the great musical countries made all haste to learn what was still virtually a universal language and to forget their native dialect. With the appearance of racial consciousness and political aspirations to self-government and independence the picture changed.

The political map of Europe in 1815, after the Napoleonic Wars, discloses no Italy and no Germany, but only a group of several separate states. The Austrian Empire stretched not only over Northern Italy but also over Hungary ; the Turkish Empire held sway over the Balkans ; the Russian Empire included Poland and Finland. After this, a century of change, much of it accompanied by fighting, culminated in the major upheaval of the 1914–18 war and a radical alteration in the map—to the establishment of what we recognise as modern Europe, based on the " national " state. Political historians speak of " nationalism " as one of the impelling ideals of the nineteenth century, and what are called " national movements " in music and in literature bear an evident relationship to the political processes of the period.

The " nationalism " of such music is often plain to see in the titles of works, such as Dvořák's *Slavonic Dances* and Grieg's *Norwegian Dances*. Often there is a deliberate use of the folk-music of oral tradition, carrying strong national associations for the composer's countrymen, for the exaltation of folk-music was the most remarkable phenomenon of musical nationalism. Moreover, just as nationalism in the political field is thought of as a movement of protest or revolt, so in musical history nationalism also carries the idea of revolt against a dominant convention, especially against a " foreign " type of musical expression. Yet, needless to say, an exact correspondence between political and musical nationalism is impossible to establish. It remains a curiosity, for instance, that Greece, with a history of turbulent political nationalism throughout the nineteenth century, produced no composer to cause even the mildest international ripple until a little post-humous notice was taken of Nikos Skalkottas (1904-49), a pupil of Schoenberg.

Because a "national movement" in music carries something of the notion of protest, it is impossible to apply the term to the course of evolution of music in France, Germany, Austria, and Italy, which already had a living and continuing tradition of music-making of first-class European importance. So Wagner, though he theorised about the rôle of "the people" and pro-pounded an anti-semitism which later won him favour with the Nazis, cannot be said to have written "national" music—if this is taken to imply that his contemporaries who observed different æsthetic principles, such as Brahms, were in some way less "national". Nor was the foundation in France of the Société Nationale de Musique in 1871 (including Massenet, Franck, Saint-Saëns, and Fauré) a sign of artistic nationalism so much as a patriotic and fraternal gesture in time of national crisis by composers not united in their æsthetic doctrines.

The same is true of Italy. Italian nineteenth-century opera is full of references to political nationalism, but we do not speak of such opera (which never ceased to capture the world market, and often had first performances in Paris, London, and St. Petersburg) as a "national" musical movement. Still, Rossini and Verdi knew their countrymen's feelings. Thus we have seen a song of serious patriotic appeal in Rossini's comic opera *The Italian Girl in Algiers*, and the chorus of the exiled Israelites in Verdi's *Nabucco* was understood as referring to the longing for a free, unified, national Italy. When Verdi painted a reigning duke as a seducer in *Rigoletto* or made the priests the villains of *Don Carlos* and *Aida*, he was making a gesture that would not be mistaken in Italy where nationalism, hostility to petty princes, and anti-clericalism went together.

This, however, was music of a long-developing tradition merely making a gesture towards current political passions. For something that we may call a genuine nationalism in music we must look elsewhere ; and first of all, to the Slav countries.

CZECHOSLOVAKIA

In the region we now know as Czechoslovakia (then corresponding approximately to Bohemia and Moravia) musical nationalism in the nine-teenth century contrasted with the internationalism of Czech musicians of a previous generation. Such earlier musicians had assimilated them-selves to the dominant German tradition, using German versions of their names. Thus in the so-called "Mannheim School"[1] of composers in the

[1] See page 146.

mid-eighteenth century (notable forerunners of the Haydn-Mozart type of symphonic writing) we find a number of Bohemian composers—among them Jan Václav Stamic (1717–57), who used the German form Johann Wenzel Stamitz. Another composer, who played string quartets with Haydn and Mozart themselves and was known to them as Johann Baptist Wanhall, was a Bohemian christened Jan Křtitel Vaňhal (1739–1813) ; and a successful pianist and composer called Jan Ladislav Dusik or Dušek (1760–1812) used the Germanised surname Dussek.

A quite different musical outlook is seen in Bedřich [1] Smetana (1824–84), who is regarded as the patriarchal figure of Czech musical nationalism. He openly expressed his sympathy with the abortive Czech revolt against the Austrian Empire in 1848, the year of revolution. For five years he accepted a post abroad, at Göteborg in Sweden ; and when he returned in 1861 the Austrian repression of Czech cultural aspirations had been a little relaxed. A national Czech theatre, for plays and operas, was opened in 1862 ; and in 1866 the production there of Smetana's opera *The Bartered Bride* gave to the world an operatic treasure which it has never ceased to value. In its dance-rhythms and the lilt of its melodies it borrows from Czech folk-music and Czech speech ; but Smetana did not found his style on the mere borrowing or the mere imitation of folk-music. Indeed, he specifically declared such a method inadequate, and the truly " national " character of his music is made clear not by musicological evidence but by his country-men's instinctive acceptance of it as national.

The Bartered Bride, with its gay rustic story, is only one of eight operas which Smetana completed. The others, some of which are of serious and partly political content, have never matched its success, though they are still performed in Czechoslovakia—*Dalibor* and *Libuše* on heroic, national themes and the more light-hearted *Two Widows*, *The Secret*, and *The Devil's Wall*. However, *The Kiss* (1876), a romantic tale, is not without its moments of darker passion. By the time it was written Smetana was already suffering from the deafness and nervous trouble which later grew worse and which left music one of its most pathetic and curious autobiographical documents : Smetana's first string quartet headed " From my life ", in which a long-held high note in the finale represents " the fatal whistling in my ear . . . which in 1874 announced my deafness ".

Smetana also composed much piano music, now rarely heard, most of it in the form of dances or " characteristic pieces " under various titles. For the orchestra he composed in 1874–79 the cycle of six symphonic poems called *Má Vlast* (" My Country "). The cycle consists of : (1) *Vyšehrad* (the ancient citadel of Prague) ; (2) *Vltava* (The river Moldau) ; (3) *Šárka* (a Bohemian Amazon leader) ; (4) *From Bohemia's Fields and Groves* ;

[1] The Czech form of Frederick.

(5) *Tabor* (a city associated with the Hussites) ; (6) *Blaník* (the legendary sleeping-place of dead Hussite heroes).

In cultivating the symphonic poem Smetana learned from Liszt's example, but fashioned something that expressed his own personality. In *Vltava* particularly, the integration of the main tune with its wide-sweeping melody into the constant movement of the whole piece is masterly. It is a minor curiosity, sometimes remarked on, that this " big " tune is remarkably like a traditional Jewish hymn which has become the first national anthem of the State of Israel. Jewish hymns of this type have, however, no particular claim to antiquity, and it is more likely that Smetana's tune was borrowed (perhaps at one or two removes) by the Jews of Central Europe than the other way round.

Czech music-lovers have awarded high status as a symphonist to Zdeněk Fibich (1850-1900), who wrote three symphonies as well as seven operas and various works for "speech against music" (*melodrama* in the old technical sense, considerably cultivated by Czech composers). But for the wider world Czech symphonies begin with Antonín Dvořák (1841-1904). He wrote music with a conscious and explicit national pride in being a Czech. But it is notable that Dvořák, the Czech, was encouraged and helped by Brahms, the German ; and his "nationalism", far from confining his appeal, made instant friends for him in England, where he conducted the first performance of his Symphony in G, and in America, which inspired his Symphony in E minor (" From the New World ").

In the nineteenth century there was still—as in earlier periods of musical history—an interest among ordinary audiences in hearing *new* music ; if specially commissioned for the occasion, so much the better. This attitude partly explains the confusion in the numbering of Dvořák's works, many of which bear later opus numbers than they should because the publishers wanted to make them appear new. Since Dvořák's symphonies were not published in their order of composition, there is some confusion in their numbering. The following table may clearly explain the matter.

Chronological numbering	Key	Title, if any	Date	Conventional numbering
1	C minor	The Bells of Zlonice	1865	—
2	B flat	—	1865	—
3	E flat	—	1873	—
4	D minor	—	1874	—
5	F	—	1875 revised 1887	3
6	D	—	1880	1
7	D minor	—	1885	2
8	G	—	1889	4
9	E minor	From the New World	1893	5

It is accordingly safest to refer to the symphonies by their keys, using "the early D minor" for the chronological No. 4. Dvořák's symphonies show, within a structure recognisably related to that of Schumann and Brahms, a remarkably personal feeling in melody, harmony, and orchestral colouring. He evinces a special liking for bird-song—a taste shared by a later Czechoslovak composer, Janáček. It has been said that the "New World" symphony owes some of its extreme popularity to having a title. Some, maybe ; but the appeal of the music itself is of a particularly direct kind, even if it is possible on better acquaintance to prefer one of the others, perhaps the D minor, miscalled No. 2. Much ink has been spilt discussing whether, and to what extent, Dvořák borrowed Negro, or American Indian, melodies for the "New World", and it is indeed tempting to find *Swing low, sweet chariot* in the first movement ; but if he borrowed melodies (which he denied doing) he at any rate transmuted them into pure Dvořák.

The same comment applies to the string quartet in F, op. 96, known to earlier generations as the "Nigger" Quartet but now often called the "Negro" or "American". In his favourite field of chamber music Dvořák's most obvious borrowing is from nearer home—in the *dumka*, a Slav lament in which fast and slow tempos alternate (the plural is *dumky*), and the *furiant*, a quick Czech dance which has nothing to do with fury. Two orchestral masterpieces, less known than they should be, are the *Symphonic Variations* (twenty-seven of them, on a short theme) and the *Scherzo Capriccioso*. The cello concerto, one of only three or four master-pieces for cello and orchestra, roused Dvořák's heroic as well as his medita-tive soul, and is a more important work than the violin or piano concertos. Five symphonic poems, written towards the end of his life, do not come off as well as Smetana's. Dvořák's nine published operas show inadequate dramatic sense, though *Rusalka* (1900) occasionally pleases on revival : the title signifies a water-nymph in Slavonic legend. Dvořák's songs, despite the success of *Songs My Mother Taught Me*, have not had the universal appeal of his instrumental works, and his choral works (including *The Spectre's Bride*, composed for England) are now also rarely heard, though the *Stabat Mater*, *Requiem*, and *Te Deum* contain much fine and characteristic music.

The text of *The Spectre's Bride* was also set to music by Vítězslav Novák (1870–1949). If Novák was a pupil of Dvořák, Josef Suk (1874–1935) was not only a pupil but also became his son-in-law, and these two composers continued, with modifications, the traditions of Dvořák.

RUSSIA

Whereas musical nationalism in Czechoslovakia can be linked with the contemporary political movement against the overlordship of a foreign power, the same cannot be said of the similar movement in Russia. Indeed, the Russians were, to such other nations as the Poles, themselves the hated foreign overlords. Yet the Russian musical nationalists were more than tinged with the ideas of social protest, and it can be no mere coincidence that they flourished when a Russian liberal intelligentsia was developing, and that the poet who chiefly inspired them was a man who resembled Byron in combining romanticism with social criticism, the poet Alexander Pushkin.

The cult of collecting folk-songs, or of composing in the manner of folk-song, or some other deliberate vernacular, is scarcely conceivable in an aristocratic society without a social sympathy for " the people " ; and such a sympathy is not in fact hard to find among Russian nineteenth-century composers. Mikhail Glinka (1804–57), told that his opera *Ruslan and Ludmilla* was only fit for coachmen, replied : " And why not, since the men are better than their masters ? " In an absolutely matter-of-fact tone, Modest Mussorgsky (1839–81) wrote in a letter : " I have little else to tell you, no impressions of this place, which I know inside out with its smug, sanctimonious landlords. One thing I must say : the peasants are far fitter for self-administration than the landlords. At meetings they come straight to the point and show that they understand their own interests. Whereas the landowners are forever wrangling and giving themselves airs."

The term " nationalism " is often applied indiscriminately to the significant Russian music of the nineteenth century, though some prefer to distinguish the so-called " Mighty Five " group (Balakirev, Cui, Mussorgsky, Rimsky-Korsakov, Borodin) as nationalist, and to speak of such a composer as Tchaikovsky as an " anti-nationalist " or " westerniser ". In the context of the personal and professional friendships and rivalries of the time, that is accurate enough. But to-day as we look back on the field as a whole, Tchaikovsky seems to represent his country's voice no less than any of the Mighty Five. Incidentally, if he did not make a cult of folk-music as they did, he was not averse from quoting it lovingly (as in the second and fourth symphonies), and he was no less a devotee of Pushkin. Glinka was the patriarchal figure for Tchaikovsky as well as of the " Mighty Five " ; for them it was the Glinka of *Ruslan and Ludmilla* (1842), whereas for Tchaikovsky the inspiration came from Glinka's more cosmopolitan opera, *A Life for the Tsar* (1836), also known as *Ivan Susanin*.

Ruslan and Ludmilla has a supernatural element in its plot and an Oriental strain in parts of its music, two features that recur again and again in later Russian opera. Use is also made (particularly in one principal character) of the declamatory style of vocal writing, by which is meant a style which is based on the natural spoken intonation, heightened in music but not artificially cut into predetermined metrical pattern. This feature was adopted by Glinka's disciple, Alexander Dargomyzhsky (1813–69), in *The Stone Guest* (produced posthumously in 1872)—a historically important but now little-heard opera, based on Pushkin's version of the Don Juan story. This declamatory style reaches its height in the work of Mussorgsky (1839–81), especially in his masterpiece *Boris Godunov*, where, though the texture is not "symphonic" in the way that it is in Wagner's operas, there is a closely worked system of musical leading-motives which bears a relationship to Wagner's.

MUSSORGSKY, BALAKIREV, AND CUI

In his youth Mussorgsky was an army officer, and he later became a civil servant. Temperamentally unstable, he declined into dipsomania, which caused his early death. He left a number of works unfinished, including the operas *The Khovansky Plot* ("Khovanshchina"), *Sorochintsy Fair*, and *The Marriage* ; in the years following his death hitherto unpublished works of Mussorgsky appeared, edited by his friend Rimsky-Korsakov. The latter went far beyond what would now be conceived as the functions of a musical editor, altering Mussorgsky's scores in the belief that he was making them sound less crude and more "correct". For, though he admired Mussorgsky's burning vitality and originality, Rimsky-Korsakov considered that his manuscripts showed "absurd, disconnected harmony, ugly part-writing, sometimes strikingly illogical modulation, sometimes a depressing lack of modulation, unsuccessful scoring. . . ."

Nowadays these "crudities" no longer offend our ears, but are relished as part of the essential Mussorgsky. Yet it was Rimsky-Korsakov's bowdlerised edition of *Boris Godunov* that first came into the Western European repertory (when Chaliapin made the title rôle famous). Mussorgsky's own original version of the opera (1869) had been rejected by the Maryinsky Theatre in St. Petersburg (Leningrad) ; and even a revised version (1872), made in order to accommodate criticisms, was itself rejected at first. But eventually a modified version of this revised text was produced at the theatre in 1874, and published. The 1869 version was not published until a complete collected scholarly edition of Mussorgsky had been initiated by the Soviet government, and it was not performed until 1928 in Leningrad (1935 in London, at Sadler's Wells).

To-day *Boris Godunov* is recognised as among the great operatic works of its century. There may be room for argument as to whether Mussorgsky's first version should be used (it has no love interest, as the act introducing the Polish princess Marina is a later addition) or his second version, or (as is a common but dubious practice) a mixture of the two. There is no excuse, however, for the retention of Rimsky-Korsakov's glosses, despite the unwillingness of many singers to re-learn rôles already in their repertory. It is in any case (and despite Chaliapin) quite mistaken to think of *Boris Godunov* as merely a showpiece for a particular singer. The hero is not only Boris but the Russian people—a point most clearly shown in the 1874 version, in which the final curtain descends not on the death of the conscience-stricken Tsar, but on the solitary lament of a simple-minded Russian peasant for his unhappy countrymen.

The Khovansky Plot (completed by Rimsky-Korsakov) and *Sorochintsy Fair* (of which five different composers have made completed versions) are occasionally revived, but have been felt to lack dramatic force. Mussorgsky's most notable works, apart from *Boris Godunov*, are his songs with piano (some lyrical, but others written in sharply characterised declamatory style, like *The Seminarist* and *You Drunken Sot*) and his *Pictures from an Exhibition*. This last work, with vivid characterisations in music linked by a " walking-round " theme, was originally written for piano solo, but is now much better known in the orchestration made by Ravel.

The piece which on concert programmes is usually described as Mussorgsky's *Night on the Bare Mountain* (or, in America, *Night on Bald Mountain*) needs a comment. The proper title should be *St. John's Night on the Bare Mountain*; and the work, describing a witches' sabbath, took various forms, originating in 1867 as a separate piece and ending as an introduction to Act III of the opera *Sorochintsy Fair*. Though an authentic Mussorgsky score has been performed at concerts since 1933, the version generally performed and recorded is one considerably altered by Rimsky-Korsakov, and it is misleading to pass this off as Mussorgsky's own.

The man to whom Mussorgsky looked as his mentor was only two years older than himself : Mily Balakirev (1837–1910). Balakirev was also the musical mentor of Borodin and Rimsky-Korsakov, and his disciples accepted from him not only general musical ideas but detailed participation in their work of composition. He would suggest a folk-theme for treatment, and would even suggest the keys to be used in a composition. It would not indeed have been inapposite had the name of " the Balakirev group " been bestowed instead of the nickname of the " Mighty Five " or " Mighty Handful "; but this nickname, bestowed by the critic Stassov in doubtless sarcastic vein, has remained the historical label for Balakirev, Cui, Borodin, Rimsky-Korsakov, and Mussorgsky.

Balakirev himself was of an unstable temperament. After a nervous breakdown he retired from musical life from 1871 to 1876, for a time becoming a railway official; he was first an atheist, later a devout and even superstitious adherent of Russian Orthodoxy. As a composer he sympathised with Schumann, Berlioz, and Liszt. His own chief works are two symphonies showing folk-song influence, a symphonic poem called

Tamara, and an "Oriental fantasy" for piano solo called *Islamey*. (The last-named, boldly written and exceedingly difficult to perform, is also known in an orchestration by Casella.) Balakirev was also prominent in running the Free School of Music in St. Petersburg, largely founded to propagate his ideas and in opposition to the official Conservatory.

César Cui (1853–1918), who was of French descent, composed ten operas and various other works, none of which have survived in the general repertory. Like Mussorgsky, Cui was an army officer. The fact that the Russian nationalist composers walked in and out of other professions indicates a dilettante strain in their musicianship, though it also reflects the difficulty of earning a living as a composer outside narrow channels of official preferment. Alexander Borodin (1833–87) was a professor of chemistry whose duties left him comparatively little time for music. Nikolai Rimsky-Korsakov (1844–1908) was at first a naval officer, and later admitted that he had picked up much of his musical technique *after* being appointed to a professorship at the St. Petersburg Conservatory in 1871.

BORODIN AND RIMSKY-KORSAKOV

Borodin's output, small though it is, bears the stamp of genius—especially the second symphony, the symphonic poem *In Central Asia* describing the approach and passing of a caravan, the two string quartets, and the opera *Prince Igor* with its fine contrast of Russian and Oriental elements. Yet Borodin's creative originality, so notable in his strong melodies and piquant harmonisations, would probably be even more in evidence if we had access to his original intentions. As it is, his unfinished works had to be helped on to paper after his death by others. In particular, much work was left to be done by Rimsky-Korsakov and Glazunov on *Prince Igor* before it could be posthumously staged in 1890. The brilliant overture to *Prince Igor* was scored by Rimsky-Korsakov from hearing the composer play it at the piano. This has prompted some critics to infer that it is "mostly Rimsky-Korsakov"; a mistaken conclusion, in that the form of the overture is easy to memorise, and its orchestration, melodic and harmonic structure very clear-cut.

Apart from his work as a musical editor and as a teacher, Rimsky-Korsakov was a prolific composer for the opera-house and the concert-hall. In his music he makes free use of themes taken from, or modelled on, folk-song, and also of those Oriental effects such as had delighted Russian musicians from Glinka's time onward. In addition, Rimsky-Korsakov had his own individual mastery of brilliant orchestral colouring. A combination of these musical elements led to the perennially successful symphonic poem

Scheherazade. This is a musical illustration of episodes from the Arabian Nights, and the characterisation of the wily and charming story-teller herself by means of a solo violin has an effectiveness that even Richard Strauss could not surpass. The highly coloured *Spanish Caprice* and *Russian Easter Festival* overture are also relished in concert programmes.

Rimsky-Korsakov recognised the suitability of the operatic form for showing the mutual impact of the human and the supernatural. The use of the supernatural element is seen in the tragic fairy-tale of *The Snow Maiden* (1881), the mystic vision of *The Invisible City of Kitezh* (1905), and the satirical fantasy of *The Golden Cockerel*, which was at first banned by censorship and produced only in 1909 after the composer's death. The rarely performed *Invisible City of Kitezh* has an intense and a peculiar power ; but his most puzzling and fascinating work is *The Golden Cockerel*, at the end of which the Astrologer tells the audience that all the characters were imaginary except the Queen and himself—and the audience is left wondering what significance the exceptions have. *The Maid of Pskov* (1872, later revised), also known as *Ivan the Terrible*, is a straightforward human chronicle ; *Sadko* (1896) concerns its hero's legendary adventures in an under-sea kingdom—and here the composer, partly basing himself on the singing of a traditional Russian bard whom he had heard, employed a broadly heroic type of declamatory utterance. This expansive conception of opera makes a strange contrast with the curious little " conversational " opera of Rimsky-Korsakov's, *Mozart and Salieri* (1897), a setting of a dramatic poem by Pushkin postulating the false idea that Mozart was poisoned by his fellow-musician.

Ranged against the " Mighty Five ", with their insistence on a specifically Russian musical art, was Alexander Serov (1820–71), who championed Wagner (without, however, producing music-dramas in Wagner's sense). Even his most famous works, the operas *Judith* and *The Power of Evil*, are of now merely historical interest. Similarly an " anti-nationalist " was the pianist and composer, Anton Rubinstein (1829–94), whose long list of works is mocked by the fact that only the trifling piano piece *Melody in F* is now remembered. But his opera *The Demon* is not negligible, and its heroine seems to be a musical ancestor of the heroine of one of the great works of nineteenth-century Russian music, Tchaikovsky's opera *Eugene Onegin*.

POLAND

The Polish national movement in music is linked with the name of Fryderyk Franciszek Chopin (1810–49), or, to give him the French form which he adopted in public life, Frédéric François Chopin. We have already considered him as one of the leading composers of the Romantic movement, and it is only the "national" element in his music that concerns us here. In what sense can this music be said to have Polish national characteristics? Firstly, in its raising of the Polish dance forms and characteristic rhythms, the mazurka and polonaise, to the status of conscious and refined art. Secondly, in certain subtler musical flavours which Poles recognise as being linked to their country's traditional music. Thirdly, in Chopin's own declared attitude of patriotism. This patriotic outlook is no less a fact because of certain misguided legends that the four Ballades are programmatic illustrations of four poems by the Polish poet Mickiewicz (which they are not). We do not need, however, to dismiss as legend the story that the so-called "Revolutionary" Study owes its name to Chopin's anger on hearing of the Russian capture of Warsaw after the abortive Polish revolt in 1831.

Chopin wrote no music for the theatre, and it was another composer who wrote what came to be regarded by the Poles as their national opera. This was *Halka* by Stanislaw Moniuszko (1819–72), which in 1848 was first produced at Vilna (Lithuanian territory under Russian rule) but arrived in Warsaw in 1858. Its heroine is a lowly-born girl deserted by her aristocratic lover. Moniuszko wrote over twenty other operas (not all complete)—of which perhaps the most notable is *The Haunted Manor* (1865)—much church music, and some songs which succeeded in their aim of being widely sung by his countrymen in their homes.

The link between Polish musical nationalism and political nationalism is most obviously shown in the career of Ignacy Jan Paderewski (1860–1941), a pianist and composer whose prestige was such that he assumed for ten months the position of Prime Minister of the newly created Polish state in 1919. As a performer, Paderewski was among the greatest of his time; as a composer (his works include a symphony, a piano concerto, and operas) he is now barely remembered, except by a once-famous *Minuet in G* for piano solo.

HUNGARY

Hungary lies almost at Vienna's back door. In fact it is much nearer from Vienna to the Hungarian border than to Salzburg or Innsbruck; and so it was natural that Viennese composers in the nineteenth century should occasionally borrow the local colour of Hungarian music. Thus Schubert wrote a *Divertissement in Hungarian Style* for piano duet—an inferior work, though formerly widely known. Thus also the younger Johann Strauss not only made the disguised Rosalinda sing a Hungarian *csárdás* in *Die Fledermaus*, but also borrowed more extensively from Hungary in another splendid operetta, *The Gipsy Baron*.

But the man who is felt to be the first real Hungarian national composer is a man who, by one of those ironies of which musical history is full, spoke German better than he did Hungarian, and whose whole artistic treatment of traditional Hungarian music has come under suspicion since his day. This is Franz Liszt (1811–86). (It is notable that we know him by the Germanised name Franz, not Ferencz, as in Hungarian.) Liszt's musical enthusiasms, and indeed his entire career, developed logically from the cradle. Son and grandson of stewards to the Esterházy princes in Hungary, he was brought up on a vast feudal estate with great houses and a court establishment, for which Joseph Haydn had made music for thirty years. Little Franz was taught the rudiments of music by his father, Adam Liszt, an amateur of some talent. Instantly the child showed extraordinary aptitude. He gave his first piano recital in one of the towns on the Esterház estate at the age of nine, conquered Vienna three years later, and is said to have been publicly embraced by Beethoven for the brilliance of his playing. From the beginning he extemporised on well-known tunes or themes picked at short notice by others.

Liszt seems to have had a certain amount of musical science from a tender age. Eighteen months after meeting Beethoven he played in a concerto at Drury Lane. The concerto over, he asked for an improvisation subject. A lady in the stalls suggested a tune from Rossini's *Cinderella*. On this Franz extemporised " in the manner of a fugue, to the great delight of his audience", according to one who was there. The operetta *Don Sanche*, which he wrote at the age of fourteen, seems to have been of no artistic account. But the *Studies in the Form of Twelve Exercises for Piano*, which he published in his sixteenth year, are a different matter. These contain the germ at least of the famous *Transcendental Studies* which appeared in their final form (after an interim revision in 1838) in 1851. At sixteen Liszt was technically under the influence of Czerny, who had been his teacher for a while in Vienna, and artistically under that of Weber, whose power and originality as a piano composer have, incidentally, been consistently underrated. Already, however, he was developing an accent of his own. As transformed and expanded in the 1838 revision, the twelve " exercises " of 1827 contain almost the entire Lisztian gamut as reflected in the output of half a century. *Mazeppa*, *Vision*, *Eroica*, and *Wild Hunt*, together with the *Preludio*, represented the sinister, romantic, and virile swashbuckler in Liszt. Such items, on the other hand, as the *Paysages*, *Feux Follets*, and *Chasse-Neige* were the first full flowering of very different gifts. Here we note Liszt's unique strain of nostalgia ; his swift, aerial fancy ; his exceptional harmonic vision ; and his devising of new pianistic textures. In these matters he has an obvious though limited affinity with Schumann, as well as with Weber. In many ways, however, he was even more closely allied to Chopin and Berlioz and had as great an effect on later French and Russian composers—among them Rimsky-Korsakov, Debussy, and Ravel —as upon fellow Central-Europeans.

VIRTUOSO AND VAGABOND

Liszt's early musical training in Vienna was overwhelmingly Germanic. The years from 1827 to the late 1840s were spent either in Paris or as a touring virtuoso pianist, with a touch of genial vagabondage thrown in.

During the period of his ten-year liaison with the Countess Marie d'Agoult, mother of his three children (one of whom, Cosima, became the wife of Richard Wagner), the Germanic element in Liszt was overlaid by a French-flavoured cosmopolitanism. From this period date the *Petrarch Sonnets* (written originally as songs, but transferred to the piano), the great *Dante Sonata* (better known in this country as music to a ballet than as a recital piece) and, grouped with this sonata, a score or so of other pieces which were published in two volumes under the general title *Years of Pilgrimage*. The titles given to individual numbers in the *Pilgrimage* volumes sufficiently indicate Liszt's æsthetic trend. *By the Spring*, *On the Lake of Wallenstadt*, *Storm*, and *The Bells of Geneva* were an incursion of landscape painting into music.

BEETHOVEN'S EXAMPLE

For this there was some precedent, though a limited one, in Beethoven's "Pastoral" symphony. But Beethoven was no title-maker. In the main he was content to let his music speak for itself. Both the leaders and camp-followers of the New German School, on the other hand, were voluble theorists to a man. It was proclaimed to the four corners of the earth that Liszt and Wagner alike believed in the "fertilisation of music by poetry".

Liszt's doctrines found their ultimate expression in more than a dozen symphonic poems, mostly written during his Weimar period. Their titles include *Tasso*, *Les Préludes*, *Mazeppa*, *Hungaria*, *Prometheus*, *Festal Sounds*, *Orpheus*, *The Battle of the Huns*, and *Hamlet*. It is worth noting that the term "symphonic poem", in itself an affront to all strict Brahmins, was devised by Liszt himself, a fertile inventor of titles. In each of the symphonic poems the music, as well as being satisfying in itself (according to Lisztians, at least), purports to have some inner affinity with the poetic or dramatic idea that inspired it. The *Faust Symphony*, with its choral finale based on a Goethe text, reveals a power and breadth of musical conception not usually suspected by the ordinary concert-goer in Liszt. In *Faust* can be seen a precursor of Mahler's vast Symphony No. 8 (the "Symphony of a Thousand"), which likewise ends with a choral setting of Goethe.

That some of Liszt's piano music is trivial and showy is generally accepted. During his virtuoso years he was undoubtedly in the habit of stunning musically unsophisticated audiences with a maximum of keyboard technique allied to a minimum of musical ideas. This fact has been unduly held against him. As a serious composer Liszt not only created music valid in its own right, but also, as an innovator, inspired other men of genius, and thus widened music's boundaries.

WAGNER'S DEBT

As early as 1859 Richard Wagner confided to Hans von Bülow, " Since my acquaintance with Liszt's compositions, my treatment of harmony has become very different from what it was formerly." Liszt's last works (*e.g.* *La Lugubre Gondola*, *Nuages gris*, and the third *Mephisto Waltz*) look forward harmonically to Debussy and even Bartók.

Liszt's Weimar period was artistically the most fruitful decade of his life. Moreover, under Liszt's influence as conductor and impresario Weimar became a great musical centre. It was in 1844 that Liszt, at the suggestion of the Grand Duchess Marie-Pavlovna of Russia, became court conductor to her son, the Grand Duke Karl Alexander of Saxe-Weimar. The original arrangement was that he should spend three months a year in Weimar, directing opera and concerts. After a few years he found it more convenient to settle in Weimar and make his home there at the Altenburg with his new love, the Princess Carolyne of Sayn-Wittgenstein. Liszt, who had already broken with Marie d'Agoult, met Carolyne, wife of a Russian nobleman and herself of Polish blood, while on a concert tour of Russia in 1847. Carolyne, then twenty-eight, fell irrevocably in love with him, left her husband and stayed at Liszt's side until 1860, worshipping, counselling, and intellectually cosseting him. Very much the blue-stocking, she read voraciously into the small hours, smoked strong black cigars, and concerned herself intimately with Liszt's artistic projects. When, in 1847, Liszt was planning his *Dante Symphony*, to be illustrated in performance by magic lantern on the diorama principle, Carolyne, who was still a woman of means—her estates in Russia had not yet been sequestrated by the Tsarist government—enthusiastically offered to back the venture to the tune of £3000. Although this idea never materialised, the Princess never ceased to surround Liszt with evidences of her intense devotion both to himself and to his work. Far from finding such adoration disagreeable, Liszt flourished on it both as man and artist. Yet, with a selflessness and vision which are perhaps without parallel in music, he gave most of his thoughts and energies while at Weimar to the music of other men. He came to the rescue of Wagner and Berlioz in times of exile and discouragement by producing respectively *Lohengrin* and *Benvenuto Cellini* in the opera-house. To Berlioz's music, indeed, he devoted an entire week in theatre and concert-room, conducting in addition to *Cellini* three works of signal originality, towards which French concert promoters had shown glacial indifference : *Romeo and Juliet, The Damnation of Faust,* and *Harold in Italy.*

FRIEND AND PUBLICIST

In an age when musicians were ranged in hostile parties, Liszt rode high above the conflict, uniquely catholic in his tastes and activities. As a conductor he gave himself as fully to Rossini's *Comte Ory* and *Italian Girl in Algiers* as to Handel's *Samson* and *Messiah*, Bethoven's Choral Symphony and *Fidelio*, Mozart's *Don Juan* and *Magic Flute*, and Gluck's operas. Although a champion and the complete master of Wagner's music, he could appreciate very different or even opposed schools, producing both the great operatic spectacles of Meyerbeer and two early pieces of Verdi—*Ernani* and *The Foscari Brothers.*

In short, his Weimar activities were (Brahms's music apart) a synthesis of all that was established or emerging in the musical Europe of the 1850s. His capacity for work was prodigious. In addition to producing, conducting, and composing he was for ever transcribing other men's music for the piano, or making it the springboard for pianoforte fantasias, paraphrases, or " reminiscences ". The latter were based for the most part on operas or specific operatic numbers in current vogue.

One of the most remarkable of these productions is the organ Fantasia and Fugue on *Ad nos*, the chorale which is sung by the three Anabaptists in Meyerbeer's *The Prophet*. Most of Liszt's transcriptions and arrangements, although technically brilliant, were of a more utilitarian and less creative character. He arranged imaginatively the Beethoven symphonies for two hands and edited three of Beethoven's piano concertos for two pianos. His transcription of Berlioz's *Fantastic Symphony*, published at a time when few musicians had come to grips with that disturbingly original score, is still regarded as an outstanding feat of musical " transubstantiation ".

It was from this sort of activity that Liszt derived most of his income, an exceedingly modest one, after settling at Weimar with Carolyne. As a touring pianist he had earned thousands of pounds a year, as well as the sort of public homage usually reserved for princes. In 1849 his financial prospects were unlimited, and he could have continued earning his thousands for another thirty or forty years. Instead, he withdrew from the market-place and made do at Weimar with £200 a year. From then until his death, his annual income never exceeded the equivalent of £300 or £400. His renouncing of wealth and the adulation of vast and glittering audiences represents a turning point for which few careers offer a parallel.

On the strength of his Weimar withdrawal and the generosity with which he succoured rival talents and championed controversial causes, Liszt has been depicted by certain sentimentalists as a kind of secular saint. In fact he was a flamboyant mixture of good and bad. There can be no doubt as to the sincerity of his religious views and professions. It was his ardent wish as a youth to take vows and enter a religious order. From this ambition he was diverted by other passions. His father on his deathbed told him that the one thing he feared in his son's regard was the part women would play in his life.

Adam Liszt's premonitions were amply borne out. There were many more women in Liszt's life than the Countess Marie and the Princess Carolyne : his susceptibilities and conquests were legendary in his own lifetime. But against these impulses and predilections his nature constantly swung back like a pendulum towards the religious vocation which had always been his ideal. When the liaison with Carolyne came to an end, after she had failed to secure the dissolution of her marriage, Liszt took minor orders and lived for a while in the cloister of the Church of Santa Maria del Rosario in Rome. At the same time he contrived to see a good deal of fashionable society, and led a triangular existence between Rome, Budapest (where he became honorary director of the Conservatoire), and Weimar, where he instituted piano classes which became historic.

RELIGIOUS MUSIC

It was during this period that he completed and produced two of his four outstanding devotional scores—the *Mass of Gran*, written for the consecration of Gran (Esztergom) cathedral in Hungary ; the setting for tenor solo, chorus, and orchestra of the Thirteenth Psalm ; *The Legend of St. Elizabeth*, which commemorates Hungary's patron saint ; and the vast *Christus* oratorio which takes four and a half hours to perform.

As to the worth of Liszt's religious music, there are diverse views. When the *Mass of Gran* was performed at the church of St. Eustache in Paris, Berlioz, although an old comrade and beneficiary of Liszt, walked out before the end, declaring that it was " the negation of art ". Undoubtedly the weaker aspects are there, and not only in the religious scores. But when

Liszt died in 1886, soon after listening with radiant face to a *Tristan* performance at Bayreuth, the world lost a mind and a vision which, as well as creating new beauty, had given music a vital and essential leadership.

AFTER LISZT

A brilliant and popular performer of Hungarian music (in the "gypsy" style) was the Hungarian-Jewish violinist Eduard Reményi (1830–98). He toured, in company with Brahms as pianist, in 1852–53, and to him we owe the inspiration for Brahms's *Hungarian Dances*. These were originally written for piano duet, but Brahms later arranged some of them for piano solo, and made orchestral versions of three. Reményi also introduced Brahms to another Hungarian-Jewish violinist of a very different stamp and notably earnest character—Joseph Joachim (1831–1907). The "Hungarian" flavour in the finale of Brahms's violin concerto probably represents a compliment to Joachim, to whom the concerto was dedicated, and who had by then become Brahms's close friend. Joachim himself, though entirely Germanised in musical outlook, borrowed the Hungarian gypsy colouring in several of his own works—which formerly enjoyed considerable esteem, particularly the *Hungarian Concerto* for violin and orchestra.

NORWAY

In the autumn of 1869 a young Norwegian composer brought a sonata for violin and piano, and a piano concerto, to Liszt in Rome. And Liszt not only played them over with tremendous effect on the piano ("I think I laughed—laughed like an idiot", wrote the overwhelmed young composer to his mother), but jumped up with enthusiasm at the ending to what was to become one of the most popular of all concertos. The young composer was Edvard Grieg, and it is with Grieg (1843–1907) that the national movement in Scandinavian music really begins. His compatriot Johan Svendsen (1840–1911) is a much lesser figure, and the Danish composer Niels Vilhelm Gade (1817–90) may be fairly accurately pinned down as a follower of Mendelssohn. A famous Norwegian violinist, Ole Bull (1810–1880), an enthusiast for his country's folk-music, is to-day remembered for the encouragement he gave to Grieg and not for the music he himself composed.

Germany was the recognised centre to which musicians from Scandinavia gravitated for study, and Grieg went for his training to Leipzig. But he retained and developed certain individual traits which may have owed something to the Norwegian folk-music which he loved and of which he made several arrangements. Such a distinctive trait, for instance, produced that flattened seventh at the end of the piano concerto (G natural instead of G sharp, in the key of A major) which so stirred Liszt's enthusiasm. Grieg also showed a piquant individuality of harmony, especially with falling chromatic phrases, which had their influence on both Debussy and Delius.

Norway, previously under Danish rule, passed into Swedish possession in 1814 and did not become independent until 1905. Though Norway had its own parliament, of limited power, there was a growth of nationalistic anti-Swedish feeling which expressed itself not only in political activity but in a Norwegian literary revival headed by Henrik Ibsen and Bjørnstjerne Bjørnson. In this intellectual climate Grieg came to maturity, and the connection between musical and political nationalism is again evident. Ibsen's and Bjørnson's verse figured prominently in Grieg's song-settings, and it was a commission to provide music for the production of Ibsen's *Peer Gynt* in 1876 that first established Grieg's authority as a national composer.

It is of pieces from *Peer Gynt* and of the piano concerto that most music-lovers still think when Grieg is mentioned. Ironically, however, in Norway itself it has of recent years been felt to be too " romantic " for Ibsen's bitterly satirical play, and new music by Harald Saeverud was introduced in the theatre in 1948. The music of *Peer Gynt*, the salutes to old styles in the *Holberg Suite*, the *Lyric Suite* (for orchestra, arranged from piano originals), and the songs, make clear Grieg's distinction as a miniaturist ; but the piano concerto shows that he was something more too. The *Symphonic Dances* are worth more hearings than they receive.

SWEDEN

Sweden, politically a " contented " and not a protesting country, produced no nineteenth-century musical nationalism comparable to that of Grieg in Norway. The Swedes look on Johan Helmich Roman (1694–1758), who was influenced by Handel, as the " father " of their music, and they have a romantic composer of some charm in Franz Berwald (1796–1868), whose *Symphonie Sérieuse* was the only one of his six symphonies to be publicly performed in his lifetime. Sweden has a rich store of folk-music, much of it based on fiddle-playing, but it has produced little of importance in the concert-hall. Of the well-scored but somewhat long-winded *Swedish Rhapsodies* by Hugo Alfvén (b. 1872), some fame has been won by No. 1 (" Midsummer Vigil "), one of its tunes even penetrating the commercialised world of American popular music.

XX

THE END OF THE GREAT GERMAN TRADITION

WE have described in some detail what amounted to a revolt against the Central Powers of music which swept over the hitherto musically less developed countries from the middle years of the nineteenth century onwards. We must now consider the final years of the German leadership, enormously rich and productive even in decline.

The spread and enjoyment of German music were favoured by material circumstances. The Victorian age was, among other things, the age of the piano. Most households owned, or aspired to, a " cottage " piano at least. Three or four generations of music-lovers picked up their basic knowledge of the German classics mainly from two-hand or four-hand piano transcriptions.

At his Austrian boarding school during the 1870s, the thirteen-year-old Hugo Wolf, future song-writer, played transcriptions of the Beethoven symphonies with fanatical zeal. Some of his schoolfellows were so imprudent as to gibe at him for this. He used his fists on them, we are told. At Linz in the 1860s, a budding symphonist called Anton Bruckner played Beethoven four-handed with the wife of an official at the Austrian Imperial court. Instances could be multiplied. Up to a point, piano transcriptions served the purposes that radio and the gramophone serve to-day. Without this agency, Germany's musical supremacy could not have been half as effective.

NEW ORCHESTRAS

Gradually opportunities increased also for hearing full-scale performances. Throughout Europe, as urban populations expanded in size and wealth, great concert halls were built and symphony orchestras founded. In consequence the Beethoven cult in particular became more accessible and widespread. Not long before this, " third-period " Beethoven had been something of a puzzle even to musicians of learning and taste. After hearing her famous brother Felix conduct Beethoven's Choral Symphony at Düsseldorf in 1836, Fanny Mendelssohn wrote that it was in parts abominable and that the concluding section was " the height of burlesque ". By the 1870s, however, the Ninth Symphony was being taken up and revered by provincial choral societies even in England, where musical culture—unsustained by court orchestras and theatres on the pattern of the German principalities—was relatively backward.

At the same time Mozart's music, which had made relatively slow headway, began to be prized at its true worth. Weber was if anything a degree more popular than he is to-day. Schubert's music widened its place in the repertory from toe-hold to niche. In 1844 his " Great C major " symphony had been laughed out of a London Philharmonic Society rehearsal because the violinists found their reiterated triplets in the finale funny. But now even the " Great C major " began to be taken seriously.

SEVEN NEW MEN

Old as well as new German music added to Germany's domination. Led by men of such diverse ideas and genius as Mendelssohn and Liszt, the Bach revival of the mid-nineteenth century proliferated in Bach societies and, little by little, introduced the plain concert-goer to the grandeur and beauty of polyphony, i.e. the simultaneous pitting of voice against voice, melody against melody on different levels.

Then came the new men—Brahms, Liszt, Bruckner, Hugo Wolf, Mahler, Max Reger, Richard Strauss. These composers took over the German heritage and immensely expanded it in bulk and variety. Some of them were predominantly conservative, and these expressed their individualities in the forms and styles that had served their great predecessors since J. S. Bach. Others were innovators. In the fields of harmony and orchestral colour they struck out new paths, which later composers of many different nationalities were to follow with striking and sometimes startling results.

BRAHMS AND " MUSIC OF THE FUTURE "

Between the conservative and innovatory parties differences of theory and practice developed which bred much rancour. Reference will be made later in this chapter to the feud which divided upholders of the " Music of the Future ", headed by Wagner and Liszt, from the traditionalists, whose champion was Brahms. Looked back upon from our own time, these battles, like so many others, seem to have been unnecessary. The music of Brahms did not, as it were, refute or disprove the music of Liszt, nor vice versa : the two men supplemented each other. The art of each was a

facet of music considered as a wider reality. But while the quarrel lasted
—and it went on for most of the half-century with which this chapter is
concerned—it made a great stir. Far from undermining Germany's musical
supremacy, the quarrel cemented it through sheer excitement and publicity.

Let us take a closer look at the personalities involved in the conflict,
starting with Johannes Brahms (1833–97). No composer of outstanding
mastery and eminence had so adverse an upbringing. His father played
the horn in military bands, the double-bass in Hamburg's waterfront taverns
and dance halls. When ageing, he joined the Hamburg Municipal Theatre
Orchestra and at various times played in light music ensembles at polite
parties. But the keynotes both of his life and that of his wife, Christiane,
a former domestic servant and seventeen years her husband's senior, were
poverty, struggle, and squalor. Young Johannes grew up in Hamburg's
" Gängeviertel ", a district of crooked, narrow streets and decaying old
houses, with dirt, disease, and disorder on all hands. Miraculously his
parents contrived to send him to a tolerably good school which taught
Latin, French, and English among other subjects.

THE YOUNG BRAHMS

At seven he was put to the piano. Like the infant Mozart and Schubert,
he seems to have known music and its basic laws intuitively. Music lessons
were a drawing-out of something which had been born in him. His first
and only teacher of theory and composition was the Hamburg composer
and pianist Eduard Marxsen, certain of whose works are considered by some
to foreshadow Brahms's own maturity. Throughout his life Brahms remained grateful for the technical grounding that Marxsen gave him. In
1882 he dedicated his second piano concerto to his old master, and the
following year, to celebrate Marxsen's fiftieth anniversary in music, had
printed at his own expense Marxsen's *Hundred Variations on a Folksong*.

After leaving this teacher Brahms taught himself. At twenty-two he
studied counterpoint anew, regularly exchanging contrapuntal exercises for
mutual criticism with his new—and lifelong—friend Joseph Joachim who,
in addition to being one of the century's greatest violinists, wrote music
copiously. Already, in the *Variations on a Theme by Robert Schumann*, op. 9,
young Brahms had—in variations 8, 10, 14, and 15—achieved marvels of
contrapuntal art.

Not all his training had been academic, however. At the age of thirteen
he began to play the piano in the same type of lowly, even disreputable,
waterfront haunts that had employed his father. He got little pay, saw
much that was ill-suited to young eyes, and was allowed as much drink

SIR EDWARD ELGAR (1857–1934)

RALPH VAUGHAN WILLIAMS
(1872–1958)

BENJAMIN BRITTEN

as he wanted. Often he was called out of bed late at night for some dance-hall stint, getting to bed at dawn or later. The strain of all this so weakened him, he told a friend years afterwards, that " he could only walk along an avenue by staggering from tree to tree ; otherwise he would have fallen ". From the waterfront he graduated to theatre bands. For a local publisher he arranged dance numbers and wrote popular drawing-room numbers under an assumed name. Whatever spare time he had was devoted to composing music after his own heart. When Schumann visited Hamburg to give concerts, Johannes sent the Master a sheaf of his own compositions for criticism. Schumann, a busy man, returned the parcel unopened. Brahms was cast down.

THE MIDDLE-AGED BACHELOR

From fifteen onwards he enjoyed consistently sturdy health until his last years, but his adolescence and youth held bitter memories, none the less. It has been suggested that influential fellow-townsmen looked down their noses at the man who had been reared in the Hamburg slums. It is certain that he was twice passed over, at the age of twenty-nine, and again at thirty-four, for the vacant directorship of the Hamburg Philharmonic Orchestra. By the age of thirty-four he was established and beginning to prosper in Vienna, then the musical capital of the world. But Vienna was no solace to Brahms. " I am altogether an old-fashioned person ", he once wrote : " I am not a cosmopolitan, but love my native town as I love my mother". To direct Hamburg's orchestra was one of the abiding ambitions of his life. When finally offered the Philharmonic Orchestra at the age of sixty-one, he replied that it was too late and remarked to a friend, " Had I been elected at the right time, I might still have become a respectable citizen. I could have married and lived like other men. Now I am a vagabond."

There have been other surmises as to the reasons for Brahms's obstinate and cautious bachelorhood. If the published correspondence between them is reliable evidence, he was passionately in love with Clara Schumann both before and after her husband's mental collapse and fatal illness in the 1850s.

When the opportunity for marriage presented itself he appears to have run away from Clara Schumann, just as, a few years later, he ran away from the Göttingen professor's daughter, Agathe von Siebold, to whom he was all but engaged. The view has been advanced by at least one of his biographers that Brahms deliberately renounced marital fulfilment and happiness because he considered that renunciation, with all the pain that it entailed, would bring his art to a finer bloom. Other writers incline to the view that Brahms's attitude to women was warped for all time by his youthful experiences and disillusionment in Hamburg's dockland dives. Neither hypothesis is convincing. What is certain is that Brahms had an odd and divided nature, often at war with itself. He was an attentive and loyal son, loved children and always had sweets in his pocket for them, and he readily helped the old and needy. But from his youth there was a sardonic strain in him which he indulged increasingly with the years.

In his middle fifties, with honours and celebrity thick upon him, he was asked one night at the house of his friend Billroth, a renowned surgeon, to play some of his latest pieces for his fellow guests. He declined in such sarcastic, even hostile, terms that Billroth never invited him to his house again. Nor was his nature sweetened by religious faith. The composer of *A German Requiem* prided himself on his biblical knowledge and selected many scriptural texts for musical settings ; but from the Psalms he chose what he called " godless " or " heathenish " passages. Nothing, indeed, made him angrier than to be taken for an orthodox church composer on the strength of his sacred composition.

BRAHMS IN HIS MUSIC

Whether his task happened to be ecclesiastical or, as was more often the case, secular, the best of Brahms went into his music. On this subject there is a revealing sentence in one of his letters, written when he was in his mid-forties. He has been staying with close friends, a married couple, both musical. On his return to Vienna he writes to say how delightful his visit has been. " The memory ", he goes on, " is still warm, and I feel I want to keep it snugly buttoned up for a long time. But these things are easier to express in music."

This feeling of rather cosy affection is easily read into much of Brahms's work ; there is something of it in his slow movements and in many of the songs. But cosiness is only one side of Brahms. There are many other sides, the whole adding up to one of the richest musical natures the world has seen. The three piano sonatas which he wrote when twenty or younger already disclose the essential Brahms. The influence of the later Beethoven sonatas is evident, as well as that of Haydn and Mozart. The strong surge of romantic feeling is backed by strong polyphony and thematic science. The youngster's fancy is so fertile, his musical logic so far-ranging, that sometimes a movement gets out of hand. The enormous first movement of his B major piano trio, op. 8, ran in its original form to 800 bars and had a secondary development section inserted into its recapitulation.

Thirty-six years later Brahms revised the score, cutting its length by one-third. Many critics consider that he did not achieve maturity combined with economy and flawless proportion until the string quartets in C minor and A minor, which came out in 1873.

As evidence of his development the piano quartet in C minor, op. 60, which was completed in 1875, is of special significance. The first movement dates from 1855, the period of Brahms's self-torturing and futile devotion to Clara Schumann. Of this movement Brahms is reported to have said to a friend : " Now imagine a man who is going to blow his brains out because there is nothing else he can do ". This phase in Brahms's life has often been labelled his *Sturm und Drang*—his time of storm and stress. It links him in terms of musical ideology with the " wild men " of the century —Wagner, Berlioz, Liszt. The finale of this same piano quartet, composed eighteen or nineteen years later, reflects very different purposes and procedures. By this time his ideal had become a perfect balance between feeling and form. There was not to be a waste note. We are told, in fact, that Brahms overdid conciseness, and that the final version of the movement included an interpolation of thirty-three bars that do not appear in the first draft.

Brahms wrote music ceaselessly from his boyhood in the Hamburg slums until the age of fifty-seven when, fearing that inspiration might soon be sapped by age, he made his will, laid down his pen and, although still in excellent health, began to reflect upon his latter end. It was his resolve to compose no more.

In fact, however, he relented, and the following year brought forth notable chamber music for clarinet, including the noble quintet in B minor for clarinet and strings, op. 115. On his sixty-third birthday he completed the *Four Serious Songs* for contralto, with scriptural texts culminating in the Epistle to the Corinthians. This was Brahms's true farewell to his art and to the world.

THE SYMPHONIST

His output had been nobly comprehensive. It included four great symphonies—in C minor, D major, F major, and E minor, which were composed in that order. The C minor begins in menace and gloom and ends in a mood of sturdy hope. He had completed the draft of the first movement, apart from the slow introduction as we know it to-day, by 1862. The remaining movements were not added until 1874-76, when he was in his early forties. Altogether he meditated and worked on the C minor symphony intermittently for twenty years. That is a measure of the caution and awe with which he approached the form which had been handled with such power by Beethoven.

Of the remaining symphonies, the D major was completed in 1877, the F major in 1883, and the E minor in 1885. They were all written with relative ease and swiftness, although when it came to rehearsal Brahms sometimes had doubts about their effectiveness. To his confidante Elisabeth von Herzogenberg he wrote about the No. 4, not altogether in jest, "I doubt whether you will have patience to sit through the finale". The movement referred to is the majestic *passacaglia*, variations on a simple theme of eight bars repeated thirty-one times without a single modulation or transitional passage. Brahms's fears, which do not appear to have been simulated, were without foundation. Ever since the première of No. 4 at Meiningen under von Bülow in 1885, this *passacaglia* has been one of Brahms's most admired creations. (It is interesting to note that the first criticisms in England complained of the "poor orchestration" of the Brahms symphonies, and that G. B. Shaw gave them not more than ten years of life!)

Among Brahms's purely orchestral works there is only one other, the superb set of *Variations on a Theme by Haydn* (1873), which shares the popularity of the symphonies ; but the *Academic Festival* and *Tragic* overtures are also favoured in the concert hall. Of the two piano concertos (in D minor, op. 15, and B flat major, op. 83), the first has long been acknowledged as one of the mightier products of Brahms's *Sturm und Drang*. But it went clean over the heads of the Leipzig public, who were still attuned to the gentler strains of Mendelssohn, when the twenty-five-year-old Brahms played it there in 1859. To Clara Schumann he wrote, "It was a complete fiasco. At the rehearsal there was complete silence. At the performance, where hardly three people raised their hands to clap, it was actually hissed." He added stoically, though probably untruthfully : "But all this made no impression on me".

This seems to have been the only set-back of any moment in Brahms's career. A few people found his music over-cerebral and learned for learning's sake. "Music hath charms, except when it's Brahms" was a typical Philistine comment. But by the great mass of concert-goers throughout Europe, and gradually in the United States, his music was loved for its warmth and its rich, strong craftsmanship. Most of his big works were quickly taken up.

The *German Requiem*, on which he worked for eleven years, had twenty German performances in its first year and was soon heard in London, St. Petersburg, and Paris. This remains Brahms's most widely sung choral work. Next in favour come the *Rhapsody*, op. 53, for contralto, male chorus, and orchestra, and the *Song of Destiny*, op. 54, both written in the late 1860s. The violin concerto in D major, written for Joachim and with Joachim's technical advice, came out on New Year's Day 1879, and, notwithstanding its exacting demands on fingers and brain, soon found many champions in many countries.

Brahms's piano music is dominated by two works which he composed in his late twenties—the *Variations and Fugue on a Theme by Handel*, op. 24, and the *Variations on a Theme by Paganini*, op. 35, which couple keyboard virtuosity with polyphonic science to a degree previously unimagined. The Capriccios, Intermezzi, and Rhapsodies of the later years are, on the whole, of a more warmly intimate character.

CHAMBER MUSIC AND SONGS

The chamber music, although linked in form with his symphonies, displays yet another aspect of Brahms's creative personality. Including, among other things, three string quartets, four quintets, two string sextets, five piano trios, and three piano quartets, it is intensely characteristic of its period both emotionally and technically, yet remains valid for later generations. As a song-writer, too, Brahms occupies a permanent niche. He published in all 380 songs, nearly three-quarters of them for solo voice and piano. In the typical Brahms *lied*, part-writing, harmony, and piano rhythms, although finely fashioned, are always subordinate to the voice and its essentially melodic function. Although on so much smaller a scale than the *German Requiem* and the fourth symphony, such things as *Mainacht*, *Vergebliches Ständchen*, *Feldeinsamkeit*, *Der Schmied* and *Von ewiger Liebe* are equally characteristic of their composer.

RECOGNITION

No music was more saluted in its composer's lifetime. Britain was especially fervent. Cambridge University offered him the honorary degree of Doctor of Music when he was but forty-three. (To accept would have meant coming to England, and having a morbid disinclination to being lionised and to sea travel, Brahms refused this honour.) In the same year Novello's, the publishers, offered him 15,000 marks for an oratorio on the same scale as Mendelssohn's *Elijah*. A year later the Philharmonic Society of London awarded him its gold medal. A wealthy English admirer left him £1000 in his will; Cardiff asked him to write a festival cantata, and a Bradford choral society proposed renaming itself the Brahms Society as a "living monument" to his genius.

From this fame and congratulation there were relatively few dissentients. Generally speaking, Wagner's extreme supporters abused Brahms simply because the " Brahmins ", as they were called, abused Wagner. It was largely a matter of retaliation. In his Vienna *Salonblatt* articles on music the young Hugo Wolf, later to be saluted as a song-writer of the highest genius, derided Brahms as a mediocrity whose music consisted of " nullity, emptiness, and hypocrisy ". Of the Fourth Symphony he wrote that it exemplified the art of composing without ideas. Wolf's real complaint against Brahms was that he did not compose in the Wagnerian manner.

Wagner's own attitude to Brahms was variable. After hearing Brahms play his Handel variations at a private party in 1864, he civilly remarked, " One sees what can still be done with the old forms by one who knows how to handle them ". Later, on the strength of such works as the waltzes for piano duet and the *Hungarian Dances* for two pianos, he sneered at Brahms as a " street singer ", a " Jewish csardas player ", etc. On another occasion he is said to have remarked of Brahms's music generally, " This is music for people who, for preference, would rather have no music at all ".

Brahms himself was a good deal more level-headed than the more extreme " Brahmins " in his attitude towards Wagner. He visited Munich for early performances of *Rheingold* and *Die Walküre* in 1870. In 1882 he would have attended the première of *Parsifal* had it not been that he went in dread of the Wagnerians, " who would spoil my pleasure in the best of Wagner ". He added playfully that he might after all risk a trip to Bayreuth because of his beard, " which still allows me to trot about anonymously ".

BRAHMS MEETS LISZT

During his recital tour of Germany with the Hungarian violinist Eduard Reményi in 1853, Brahms, then twenty, had been introduced to Liszt at his villa in Weimar. The villa was adorned with medallions of Wagner and Berlioz, swords of honour which had been presented to Liszt in Hungary, Russia, and Turkey, the Broadwood piano on which Beethoven last played, a small early piano which had belonged to Mozart, and a giant piano made to Liszt's own design, with three keyboards, sixteen registers and stops that imitated all the woodwind instruments of the orchestra.

Fresh from slum and struggle in Hamburg, young Brahms must have been overcome by Liszt's grand manner and the luxury in which he lived. Liszt's music was equally alien to him, and there is little doubt that the beginner and the celebrity intuitively realised that they belonged for ever to different artistic camps.

Seven years later, with his friend Joachim, Brahms published in a Berlin newspaper a manifesto against the "New German School" which has generally been interpreted as an attack upon Liszt's works. The productions of the school were dismissed in the manifesto as "contrary to the innermost spirit of music".

Ill-conceived and clumsily managed, the attack was shrugged off by Liszt and made little impression in musical circles. The last recorded contact between the two men was in 1882, when Liszt politely asked for a copy of Brahms's newly published second piano concerto. Brahms duly sent him one. In his letter of thanks, Liszt addressed Brahms as "honoured master". "Frankly speaking", he added, "at the first reading this work seemed to me a little grey in tone. I have, however, gradually come to understand it. It possesses the pregnant character of a distinguished work of art, in which thought and feeling move in noble harmony."

HUGO WOLF

Among Liszt's followers was the song-writer Hugo Wolf (1860–1903). Reference has already been made in this chapter to Wolf's attacks on Brahms's music in the fashionable Viennese *Salonblatt*. Wolf contributed a weekly musical article to the *Salonblatt* over a period of three years while a needy and struggling beginner. At that time he wrote fiery and often wrong-headed prose. Manuscript paper on knee, he would dash off *lieder* while sitting in parks and public gardens.

When Liszt came to Vienna, Wolf played some of his songs over to him. Liszt was very charming and said they delighted him. Kissing Wolf on the brow, he said he hoped to hear a work from him in one of the "larger forms". Accordingly Wolf set to work on a tone-poem, *Penthesilea*. This was accepted for trial performance, with several other new scores, by the Vienna Philharmonic Orchestra. By a strict rule composers were barred from attending trial performances, but on the appointed day Wolf bribed an attendant and got a gallery seat where he could hear without being seen. What he heard enraged him. Conducted by Hans Richter, the performance, he later alleged, was an unholy discord, a Babel. All this, he implied, was Richter's deliberate doing.

At the end the players laughed resoundingly, and Richter, laying down his baton, said to them, " Gentlemen, I should not have let the piece be played to the end, but I wanted to hear for myself the man who writes in such a way about Meister Brahms." Wolf assured his friends that he would make those responsible for the fiasco roast in hell's brimstone and drown in dragon's poison. " I will publish an article against Richter ", he added, " that shall make the devil himself grow pale."

About the rights and wrongs of the *Penthesilea* episode there is more than one view. Richter later denied having sabotaged the trial, but one thing is beyond doubt. As a journalistic champion of the New German School, Wolf aroused enmities which stood in his way as a composer and so caused him bitter disappointments. One example of the spirit that prevailed is the contemptuous rejection note that he received from the celebrated Rosé Quartet of Vienna after another trial performance. This read as follows : " We have attentively played through your D major quartet and unanimously resolved to leave your work for you with the doorkeeper of the Court Opera House. Will you have the kindness to send for it as soon as possible ? He could easily mislay it." The man who drafted and wrote this note, down to the signatures of his three colleagues, was one Sigismund Bachrich, viola player in the Quartet, who was also a composer. Wolf had slated his compositions in the *Salonblatt*, and the trial of Wolf's piece enabled Bachrich to get his own back.

Apart from his articles, Wolf gave offence in many quarters by his streak of impatient arrogance. This trait made his already thorny path thornier still. There is no more sorrowful life story in the history of music. Wolf was another of music's great " intuitives ". Born of predominantly German stock in an Austrian border village, he began to play the piano and mastered the first position on the violin at the age of four or five. His teacher was his father, a tanner and leather merchant, whose hobby was music and who played with fair proficiency the piano, flute, violin, harp, and guitar. As second violin, young Hugo played with his father, brothers, an uncle, and the village schoolmaster in a household orchestra. Against his inclination, his father, who knew how precarious the musical profession was, let Hugo enter the Vienna Conservatory at fifteen. There he stayed for two years, urged to unlearn what technical knowledge he had picked up, preparatory to relearning it. All this was irksome to him, and he finally walked out of the Conservatory, informing the principal that he was deriving no benefit from tuition there. The principal responded by formally expelling him.

It is probable that Wolf got most of his really formative training during his early Vienna years by queueing for the gallery at the Vienna Opera and saving up for cheap seats at Philharmonic concerts. He heard his first Beethoven on the orchestra two months before his sixteenth birthday. The piece was the " Pastoral " symphony. Already he was a fanatical Wagnerian. During Wagner's visit to Vienna in 1875 he used to hang about in the lobby of the Master's hotel for the privilege of opening the cab door when Wagner left for rehearsals at the Opera, and he would run ahead of the cab in the hope of opening the door again at the artists' entrance. In November he heard a performance of *Tannhäuser* which Wagner supervised in person. The following day Hugo wrote to his parents, " The overture was wonderful and then the opera ! . . . I can find no words to describe it."

A YEAR OF SONGS

Wolf installed himself at Perchtoldsdorf, some twenty miles from Vienna, in the freezing early months of 1888. His combined bedroom-sitting-room-study was a tower-like chamber at the head of a winding stone stair, with windows facing in four directions. The place was deserted as well as chilly, the old tiled stove worked imperfectly, and water had to be fetched from outside.

In these quelling circumstances Wolf experienced ecstasies of self-realisation which recall stories of the great mystics. He took with him to Perchtoldsdorf a sheaf of manuscript paper and a volume or two of Eduard Mörike, the nineteenth-century German poet. Once the frenzy of composition gripped him, Wolf worked at his piano and writing desk " incessantly, with a thousand candle power, from dawn until late at night ", setting at least one poem a day and often two or even three. In twelve weeks he set forty-three Mörike texts, most of the settings being of deathless quality. His letters to friends, both at this time and later, are unparalleled in their exultation. Here are typical passages : " I have just written down a new song. A divine song, I tell you. Quite divinely marvellous. By God ! it will soon be over for ever with me. My cleverness increases from day to day. . . . I feel my cheeks glow like molten iron with excitement. This condition of inspiration is . . . exquisite torment, not pure happiness. . . ." " I have just written my masterpiece, *A Maiden's First Lovesong*. This music . . . would lacerate a block of marble. . . ." Of another song, *Journey on Foot* : " When you have heard this you can have only one wish—to die ".

Some years later, when at work on his opera *The Corregidor* (whose story, like that of Falla's famous ballet, is based on Alarcón's *Three Cornered Hat*), he wrote, " I cannot play this music often enough—candidly, I revel in it. God, how fortunate I am that it is in my power to give myself such pleasure ! If somebody else had written this music it certainly would not please me any less, but as nobody else has rendered me that service I must do it myself ; and God knows, I do it truly only for my own pleasure, for to write for humanity would never occur to me in a dream. I like it, and that's sufficient."

349

A MAN POSSESSED

In the autumn of 1888 he took up Goethe. In three and a half months fifty Goethe songs were composed. The forty-four poems which constitute the *Spanish Song Book* (settings of German translations from the Spanish by Paul Heyse and Emanuel Geibel) were written in two spells totalling three months. A corresponding selection, the *Italian Song Book*, was completed at equal speed, one batch of twenty-four songs being written in little over a month. On the three acts of *Der Corregidor* he spent fourteen weeks like a man possessed.

But the barren interludes were torturing, as we gather from the letters. To a friend he wrote in 1891, "I am the most unhappy creature on this earth. . . . I live through the days, stupid and insensible, like a brute beast. . . . It's all over with composing. I cannot any longer conceive what harmony, what melody is, and begin already to doubt whether the compositions bearing my name are really by me." This is typical of many passages which reflect an agony of despair. The creative hiatus of 1891 lasted for eleven months. It suddenly ended with the composition pell-mell of fifteen of the *Italian Song Book* numbers. The urge and fire of Wolf's genius came and went in this way until the end.

MADNESS

The last years were heartrending. His first mental collapse occurred in the autumn of 1897. He went around telling his friends that he had been appointed director of the Vienna State Opera in place of his boyhood friend Gustav Mahler and invited some of them to take office under him. For all this there was no foundation whatever; he was in the grip of madness and its delusions. At times he was violent. In the lunatic asylum where he spent his last four and a half years he was at times confined in a bed with railed sides like a cage. His handwriting and speech alike disintegrated; occasionally he went completely dumb. He even began to be muddled about his own identity. "If only I were Hugo Wolf!" he would mutter. He died after torturing paralytic convulsions.

The day of his funeral was Carnival Tuesday, and the hearse passed through streets crowded with masked revellers, an ironical and macabre touch of the kind which Wolf illustrated so subtly in music. Hugo Wolf's name would have meant nothing to the revellers had they known it. But already his art had a fervent minority of admirers both in Austria and Germany. His fame became unshakably established throughout the world.

PSYCHOLOGICAL INSIGHT

Wolf's procedures as a song-writer were markedly different from those of Brahms, in that the piano, instead of being in the main subordinate to the voice and its melodic purpose, often fills the rôle of independent commentator. Although fascinating and individual in purely musical terms, Hugo's piano " accompaniments "—piano " collaborations " would perhaps be a better term—have strong psychological overtones. His rhythms, harmonies, and figurations open a window into the poet's mind and heart. With all these refinements and rarities go gaiety, rousing declamation, and —especially in the *Spanish Song Book*—a gift of character delineation, both humorous and tragic, that matches the achievements of Wagner and Verdi in the theatre. In writing about the Mörike songs, Frank Walker speaks of Wolf's " symphonic style, in which the voice delivers the poem in a sort of fine melodic rhapsody over an elaborate pianoforte part built up out of one or more themes, somewhat in the manner of a symphonic development ".

Whether, if he had lived longer, Wolf would have re-directed his thoughts towards symphonic composition is an interesting speculation. Nothing much came of his youthful essays in this field. The manuscript of one symphony he left behind him in the railway station waiting-room at Graz and, despite anxious telegraphic enquiries, he never saw it again. Of Wolf's non-vocal works, the only one which has found a lasting place in the repertory is the delightful *Italian Serenade* for string quartet, later for small orchestra. This was to have been the first movement of a larger work which Wolf had in mind. Like the rarely heard *Penthesilea* tone-poem, it is evidence of quasi-symphonic talents in Wolf whose full realisation was barred by disease and death.

ANTON BRUCKNER

In a sense Wolf's career was the reverse of Anton Bruckner's. Honoured mainly as a symphonist, Bruckner (1824–96) spent the first thirteen years of his grown-up life as a schoolmaster in Austrian villages, where he " doubled " as local church organist. He was uncertain and unconfident about his vocation until well into his thirties. Even when he had fifty compositions to his credit—they were mostly church pieces—he still thought in terms of teaching appointments, brushed up his Latin, took training courses in non-musical subjects and regarded music as an expendable sideline. About his gifts as a composer he for long had misgivings. So had certain others. One of the leading Vienna pundits to whom he submitted his latest composition, a setting of Psalm 114, frankly advised him to renounce music altogether. Bruckner was so discouraged that he thought for a while of becoming a civil servant. Happily he was persuaded by more discerning friends to continue composing.

With another famous Viennese theorist, Simon Sechter, he re-learned the elements of music (in which he had been well grounded in boyhood) and later set himself arduous exercises in counterpoint. He wrote a " trial " symphony in F minor when nearly forty, and the following year the first symphony he later acknowledged. This work in D minor, later became known as the " Zero " Symphony, or Symphony No. o.

Symphony No. 1 (in C minor) was not completed until 1866. At forty-two, an age at which Hugo Wolf's creative life was long over, Bruckner had launched upon his essential life mission. He continued to write symphonies for thirty years or more. On the day he died in 1896, he was working on the finale of his Symphony No. 9.

Most critics are agreed as to the intensely " Austrian " quality of Bruckner's symphonies and their affinity, from this point of view, with the music of another great Austrian, Franz Schubert. Certainly, Bruckner was very much the product of his native soil and its culture. He came of a family who had been peasant smallholders in the same region for seven centuries. Like Wolf, he had his first music lessons from his father, himself a schoolmaster-cum-organist, the vocation his son was to adopt. Anton's first post as assistant master was at Windhaag, a village near the Bohemian frontier. Here the eighteen-year-old had to get up at 4 a.m. in summer and 5 a.m. in winter and teach the three R's all day long on insufficient food. He and a friend used to break away at night and at week-ends to play the violin at peasant fêtes and weddings, along with a hard-bitten old dance musician who was good at trumpet and clarinet alike. Into these primitive musical activities Bruckner put his heart and soul, and they helped to form him as an artist, so that we find typical Upper Austrian dance rhythms and tunes in the scherzos of his maturity. But the deepest strain in Bruckner was his staunch Catholic piety. Bruckner's religious music, which culminated in the great *Te Deum* (written between 1881 and 1884), reflects a personal faith which remained unclouded to the end of his life.

It was his appointment to the Linz post that enabled him to drop school-teaching. His external life had only one other milestone, when in 1868 he became professor of harmony, counterpoint, and organ at the Vienna Conservatory, as well as Court organist, in succession to his former tutor. In other words, he did not cast off small-town influences, which had certainly begun to oppress him, until his middle forties.

CIRCLE OF DISCIPLES

It cannot be said that Vienna treated him cordially. For years he lived on academic pittances and was constantly petitioning the Conservatory, Court, and University authorities for better pay so that he could devote more time to composition. Not that teaching was in itself irksome to him. Both at the Conservatory and at Vienna University, where he became lecturer in musical theory in 1875, he gathered round him a circle of students (among them the composer Gustav Mahler) who became his ardent followers and disciples, though not his pupils. Hugo Wolf was one of his champions. In the *Salonblatt* he lashed the Vienna Philharmonic management for their neglect of Bruckner's symphonies and, as usual, took the opportunity of slating Brahms's symphonies.

Needless to say, Bruckner was drawn into the maelstrom of the " New German School " controversy. He openly and naïvely expressed his admiration for Wagner's music and suffered accordingly at the hands of the Brahmins. That is to say his symphonies, in so far as they were played there at all, made their way in Vienna only against a strong opposition which was headed by Eduard Hanslick, the influential pro-Brahms critic.

Bruckner had become a confirmed Wagnerian during his years at Linz, where he first heard the *Flying Dutchman* and *Tannhäuser*. Later came *Tristan*—first in piano transcription and then in the theatre, and friendship with Wagner himself.

" BIG AS BEETHOVEN "

Wagner made much of the simple-hearted organist. After reading through Bruckner's third symphony he pronounced that Anton was the only living symphonist " as big as Beethoven ". In its original form this symphony incorporated several motifs borrowed from the Wagner operas, but these were suppressed by common agreement between the two composers when the symphony appeared in a definitive version dedicated to Wagner.

Bruckner first broached the matter of the dedication at a meeting with Wagner in Bayreuth. He had been undergoing a cure at Marienbad, and arrived at Wahnfried in a frail state. Out of sheer cordiality, Wagner insisted on his drinking glass after glass of beer. As a result Bruckner became fuddled and next morning could not remember for the life of him which symphony Wagner had agreed to have dedicated to him—the second or the third. He hastened to Wahnfried again. Wagner cleared up the point. No. 3 it was.

Bruckner's dedication was affectionate and glowing. It earned for him in Vienna the doubtful nickname of " the Wagnerian symphonist ". Actually there is little in Bruckner's music which derives from that of the Bayreuth master or, for that matter, bears much affinity with it. But in their malignity the extremer opponents of the New German School were not concerned with the facts of the matter. In their view No. 3 and all the symphonies that followed it were Wagnerian to the core.

After various delays and evasions the symphony was produced at a Vienna Philharmonic concert in December 1877. It was received with open raillery, the hall emptying gradually as the performance went on so that at the end only ten persons were left in the stalls. Outside the hall a group of Bruckner's pupils waited with consolatory words. With them was a certain Herr Rattig, who offered to publish the score. Bruckner could hardly believe his ears. Certainly the proposition seemed fantastic. Herr Rattig was as good as his word, however.

Hanslick's notice described the symphony as a compound of Beethoven's Ninth and Wagner's *Walküre*. He insinuated that, as many people considered Bruckner to be a madman, it would perhaps be a good thing if the University authorities deprived Bruckner of his chair. Some nine years later the tide showed signs of turning. When the seventh symphony was played by the Philharmonic in 1886, it received a great ovation from a new and fervent Bruckner public. Hanslick was obliged to confess that he had never previously seen a composer recalled to the platform four or five times after each movement of a symphony. He added, as a matter of course, that the symphony was, none the less, " unhealthy ", " artificial ", and more in the same vein. Another critic said it was "the triumph of Chaos over Cosmos ". A third critic said Bruckner wrote as though he were drunk.

As well as public abuse of this type there was a good deal of animosity and derision behind the scenes. In her cosy intellectual intimacy with Brahms, Elisabeth von Herzogenberg wrote tartly about the seventh symphony, which she had been hearing in Leipzig. She told Brahms how she and her circle rebelled against having Bruckner's music thrust upon them " like a compulsory vaccination ". " There are ", she added, " so many people in this world of so-called culture ready to be imposed upon by an inflated windbag. . . . One or two quite impossible motifs like grease swimming on the top of weak soup—and there we have ' Meister ' Bruckner's whole stock-in-trade. I should just like to know who started the Bruckner crusade, how it came about, and whether there is not some sort of freemasonry among the Wagnerians." Brahms was delighted : " Your delightful letter expresses most lucidly all that can be said—all that one has said oneself or would like to have said—so nicely. Hanslick shares your opinion and read your letter with pious joy."

POSTERITY'S REPLY

Posterity, however, has repudiated this judgment. Some of his symphonies were played with success in London, New York, Chicago, Boston, Amsterdam, The Hague, and most of the principal cities of Germany. The *Te Deum*, too, was quickly saluted as a masterpiece. In Cincinnati five years before Bruckner's death it was sung by a choir of 800 with an orchestra of 120 before an audience of 7000.

Bruckner's last decade was consoled by various ovations and official acknowledgments. The Austrian Emperor gave him a medal and contributed towards the printing costs of his No. 3 (revised version). In 1892 the Vienna Philharmonic produced his No. 8 : conducted by Richter, the symphony was jubilantly received. Even Brahms sent him good wishes on his seventieth birthday. The only adversary whom he failed to win over was Hanslick, whose criticism of the eighth symphony was characteristically sour.

In his quarter-of-a-century's battling with the musical "establishment" of Vienna, Bruckner was handicapped by a streak of naïvety that amounted almost to simple-mindedness. His appearance had more than a touch of the grotesque. A brilliant organist, he habitually appeared in wide, floppy trousers cut specially short to give his legs more freedom on the organ pedals. His massive head, with Roman emperor's profile, rose from an outsize collar that might have been worn by a circus clown. His flurries were comical and touching. For a Vienna concert in 1882 at which the Adagio and Scherzo of his sixth symphony were performed, he turned up long before the start wearing odd boots. After the last rehearsal of another of his symphonies he rushed up to Hans Richter, the conductor, a man of great consequence on the European musical scene, and overflowing with gratitude, slipped a *thaler* into his hand and said, " Take that and drink my health in a glass of beer." Richter is said to have been moved to tears at the memory of this. After Bruckner's death he wore the thaler on his watch-chain.

Bruckner's sentimental life had an oddity all its own. From youth to old age he was for ever losing his heart and vainly proposing marriage to young women, usually of inferior social condition to himself. The last of these frustrated idylls began when he was sixty-one and lasted until within a year of his death.

The young person in this case was a servant girl named Ida who worked in an hotel where he happened to stay in Berlin. The marriage which Bruckner sought would almost certainly have taken place had she not been a Protestant and averse to changing her faith.

SANCTA SIMPLICITAS

It may be argued that Bruckner's almost rustic naïvety is reflected to some extent in the cut of his melodies, especially those which occur in the trio sections of his scherzos and as subordinate subjects in his outer movements. These elements have an obvious affinity with certain aspects of Schubert. But with Bruckner as with Schubert (especially the latter's "Great C major" symphony), simplicity led to grandeur. His major movements have a weight, breadth, and splendour which compensate for their exceptional length.

Bruckner's æsthetic status is still a matter for controversy. Many critics find his symphonies meandering, but few deny his sense of climax, especially in the finales. One point of caution. The newcomer to Bruckner should be alive to the different versions of the symphonies which are extant. During his lifetime Bruckner, at the suggestion of eminent conductors, devoted pupils, and helpful friends, made extensive cuts and changes in instrumentation in the hope of obtaining a quicker and wider acceptance for his symphonies. It was in these mutilated versions that the symphonies were first published. The degree to which these versions depart from Bruckner's first thoughts became apparent with the publication, starting in 1932, of the symphonies according to Bruckner's original manuscripts, as bequeathed by him to the National Library in Vienna.

Reference was made earlier to Bruckner's prowess as an organist. It is probable that his prestige in this field helped to smooth the way in some quarters for his symphonic music. Like the piano, the organ was caught up in the maelstrom of nineteenth-century Romanticism, and for a brief period became one of Romanticism's prime agents. This was brought about in part by the improvements in organ mechanism which were effected during the first half of the century. Without these the organ would have been hard put to it to promote "the fertilisation of music by poetry".

Liszt wrote for the instrument, revelling in its thunders and the range of its tone and colours. He also extemporised on it. We read of an occasion during his Swiss "pilgrimage" (1835) when he entered the Church of St. Nicholas, Fribourg, attended by Countess Marie, the novelist George Sand and their combined families. The St. Nicholas organ was of some repute. Upon it Liszt improvised a wild fantasia upon a theme which has had a recurring fascination for Romantics down to Rachmaninov, that of the liturgical *Dies Irae*. On this occasion he seems to have frightened even his friends.

356

THE B-A-C-H THEME

As well as the *Ad Nos* Fantasia and Fugue, Liszt wrote an immensely elaborate organ fugue based on the letters B-A-C-H, which are the German names for the notes B flat, A, C, and B natural. Some consider this even more important than the B minor piano sonata, itself a key work. In this field, again, Liszt is to be judged not only by his own achievements but also by the spark he kindled in others.

Among his pupils was a boy of incredibly precocious genius. Son of a noted organ-builder, Julius Reubke (1834–58) died at the age of twenty-four. Among the handful of pieces that he left behind, mostly for pianoforte or voice and pianoforte, is the *Sonata on the Ninety-Fourth Psalm*, one of the most admired—and feared—items in the modern organ repertory. What makes it feared is the combined technical and emotional demands its complex and visionary writing makes upon the player. The *Ninety-Fourth Psalm* has been aptly described as depicting a descent into hell. The affinity with Liszt and Liszt's "literary" outlook is obvious. It must be added, however, that young Reubke handled Lisztian ideas, both musical and literary, with a compact power which his master rarely achieved. The entire musical fabric falls into three sections, one of them a free fugue, but is based on one theme, which has Wagnerian as well as Lisztian echoes. Young Reubke was undoubtedly a child of his time and school, yet such is the power of this sonata that his death must be counted a serious loss to music and particularly to the literature of the organ.

MAX REGER

Another career which started in the organ loft and was, in some measure, always conditioned by it was that of Max Reger (1873–1916). From thirteen to sixteen, Reger was a local church organist and later, under the tutelage of the celebrated Hugo Riemann, he immersed himself in the study of Bach and Beethoven. Later he turned his back on Riemann's rigid traditionalism, devoting himself to freer ideals and methods. By the age of twenty-five he was writing music with a copiousness for which that period and our own offer few parallels. Music in many forms continued to pour from his pen; sonatas, string quartets, preludes and fugues, variations, overtures, tone-poems, cantatas, songs by the score, *pièces pittoresques* for piano duet, psalm settings, miscellaneous choruses. He attempted a sinfonietta but never got as far as a symphony or an oratorio, although at the time of his death he was thinking of tackling both forms.

His opus numbers run to 146, on top of which he left a great mass of music without opus numbers. Works for organ solo or organ accompaniment account for a good fifth of his output. In his lavish way, he would put out ten or a dozen organ pieces as a single opus. Under op. 79 are comprised twelve *volumes* of pieces for organ, piano, voice, and various instrumental combinations. Among the most commanding of his organ works are a *Fantasy and Fugue on* B-A-C-H (op. 46) and the *Variations and Fugue on an Original Theme* (op. 73), both written by the turn of the century.

How Reger contrived to turn out such quantities of music while doing professorial work is a mystery. After a brief spell of teaching at the Munich musical academy, where he dispensed composition, theory, and organ, he became for a short time head of the music faculty at the University of Leipzig, and taught composition there for the rest of his life, also contriving to put in two concurrent years as director of the Meiningen Court Orchestra under Duke Georg.

Out of Reger's immense *œuvre* only one work may be said to have established itself in this country. That is the orchestral *Variations on a Theme by Mozart*, a learned yet adroit and genial score. Reger is in any case significant historically as a man who sought to apply new tints and flavourings to basic German classicism. In the orchestral pieces which he wrote during his Meiningen period (1911–13) Reger's harmonic progressions are often unorthodox and surprising—even disconcerting.

GUSTAV MAHLER

Two composers who, although they differed markedly in temperament and achievement, are inevitably allied as the great rounders-off and legatees of a century's Romanticism, are Gustav Mahler (1860–1911) and Richard Strauss (1864–1949).

Son of a Jewish shopkeeper, Mahler was drawn to music as the needle is drawn to the lodestone. As a student in Vienna he sat worshipping at the feet of Anton Bruckner in the late 1870s, and was chosen by Bruckner to make the piano transcription of his third symphony. The two of them used to foregather at Bruckner's lodgings. The arrangement was that Bruckner should provide the beer and that Mahler should bring along his own rolls and butter. As we gather from the biography by Alma Mahler, his widow, Gustav was so poor that he usually arrived empty-handed. As a budding symphonist he derived much from Bruckner, including vastness of scale and conception, coupled with the miniaturist's touch in lighter movements or interludes.

Again from Alma Mahler we gather that when, towards the end of his life, Mahler's own symphonies began to show signs of making a profit, he diverted their prospective yield to his publisher so that the latter could take over the Bruckner symphonies and advertise them at considerable expense.

" AN ODD PAIR "

This action was all the more noble in that his devotion to Bruckner's music, as distinct from Bruckner's memory, seems to have declined during his last decade. There is a letter of 1904 which after dealing disdainfully with the chamber music of Brahms—" a puny little dwarf with a narrow chest "—couples him with Bruckner and dismisses both as " an odd pair of second-raters ".

Hugo Wolf was another of Mahler's early friends. For a while the two of them shared a cheap one-room lodging in Vienna. Already Mahler had worked out the plan of his career. His main purpose was to create grandiose new music. If he found himself eventually committed to the career of a conductor, it was partly because only through conducting could he accumulate the money and secure the ultimate leisure that were necessary for creative work. He obtained his first post, in a small Austrian town, at the age of twenty. In the next eleven years he flitted from one conducting post to another in many parts of Austria and Germany, as well as Prague and Budapest, spending a year here, a couple of years there, six months in another post.

His first longish halt was at Hamburg, where he acted as first *Kapell-meister* in the municipal opera house from 1891 to 1897. It was in Hamburg that Mahler's tireless and dæmonic executive talent made its mark. He moulded and directed operatic productions down to the smallest detail. At rehearsal he would often put down the baton and climb on to the stage, using a double-bass fiddler's stool as his ladder, and coach the chorus or some leading singer in gesture and facial expression. To these tasks he brought a whirlwind energy that led to paralysing attacks of sick headaches. When these attacks came on he lay still for hours as if in a coma, all the strength drained from him.

From Hamburg Mahler was summoned to Vienna, where he became artistic director of the Court Opera in 1897 for a historic ten-year term of office. Here again he flung himself into the battle with fierce passion and conviction. As a result, Vienna opera productions reached standards of musical grandeur and finesse which, by common consent, have never been surpassed. Mahler's decade at the Court Opera was a golden age whose afterglow is still with us.

In pursuit of his artistic aims Mahler could be both rude and ruthless. It was in part because of the friction and animosities which his own tactics had aroused that he decided to quit his Vienna post in 1907. The brief remainder of his public career was devoted to guest conducting, mainly in America, where his annual visits became an institution. His death at the age of fifty was tragically premature. His energies were so volcanic, however, his spirit so questing and restless, that he seems to have burned himself out.

HOLIDAY COMPOSER

The abiding miracle is the quantity of music Mahler contrived to compose among his conducting and administrative burdens. Among the great figures of the German supremacy he is the only one whose status corresponds roughly to that of the " Sunday painter ". Mahler's " Sundays " —rather long ones, to be sure—were his summer holidays. As early as the Hamburg days he had a tumbledown waterside cottage at Steinbach-am-Attersee. Even his first symphony, written in the late 1880s, shows what were to be permanent features of Mahler's symphonic style. The brusque changes from idyllic nature-music to strident emotional rhetoric, the sinister dance movements and night pieces, the close juxtaposition of the heroic and the deliberately banal are to be found in at least seven of his nine symphonies. Symphonies Nos. 4, 5, 6, 7, and 8 were all composed in full sketch during Mahler's Vienna tenure at a second lakeside retreat, Maiernigg, on the fringe of the Austrian Alps. At the edge of the lake stood the Mahlers' house, gay with children's voices. Up the hillside among the trees stood a stone-built hut containing a piano and bookshelves with nothing on them but the music of J. S. Bach, the poetry of Goethe, and the philosophical works of Kant.

Wearing old clothes that made him almost unrecognisable to his town friends, Mahler worked daily in his hut from breakfast to noon or later. Sometimes he composed while on solitary walks, halting from time to time to jot down ideas in a notebook ruled for music.

At the end of the summer, yet another symphony completed, he would play it over at the piano to intimates. Alma Mahler remembers especially the playing of Symphony No. 6, with its intimations and forebodings of tragedy : " On that day ", she records, " we both wept." When the symphony was first performed—at Essen in 1906—Mahler walked up and down the artists' room after the final rehearsal sobbing and wringing his hands. Such was the sway which his own creations had over him. The summer holiday over, Mahler would return to Vienna with his latest symphony sketch. The instrumentation and the finishing touches occupied odd hours, half-hours, and week-ends throughout the winter.

As well as being a symphonist, Mahler was a prolific writer of songs and song-cycles. *Lieder eines fahrenden Gesellen* (" Songs of a Wayfarer "), songs from *Des Knaben Wunderhorn* (" Youth's Magic Horn "), and the *Kindertotenlieder* (" Songs on the Death of Children ") represent the intimate, miniature side of his art and illustrate its dependence upon literary and philosophical values. Song enters, indeed, into the very structure of the symphonies themselves and is often an actual ingredient. Nos. 2, 3, 4 and 8 include incidental verse texts and have important parts for women soloists and mixed choruses.

SONG-SYMPHONY

Das Lied von der Erde (" The Song of the Earth "), although a setting for mezzo-soprano, tenor, and orchestra of poems translated from the Chinese, was actually defined by Mahler not as a song-cycle but as a symphony. He would have named this his ninth symphony outright but was superstitiously deterred from doing so because, in the cases of Beethoven and Bruckner, the ninth symphony had been their last. Mahler did in fact survive not only to write a Symphony No. 9—when he had completed it he exclaimed, " Now the danger is past ! "—but also to begin a No. 10, of which only sketches remained at the time of his death.

Mahler was the last representative of the Viennese classical school, and his symphonies are a synthesis of previous symphonic practice, from Mozart to Bruckner, carried out by an original and intensely emotional genius of marked literary tastes. Certain of Mahler's symphonic subjects are disconcertingly blatant, others almost painfully naïve in character. But all that he wrote is consciously and deliberately planned, and the product of a highly individual sensibility. Mahler is, in fact, one of the most personal of composers. It is easy to find fault with individual traits or movements of his symphonies, but these faults are easily forgiven by those who find the strong personality of the composer sympathetic. Others will remain unconvinced.

MARATHON SYMPHONY

Certainly the extreme diversity of Mahler's thematic material is a factor to which the newcomer with a grounding in the German classics has to adjust his taste. Another unusual factor, as in the case of Bruckner, is the extreme length of Mahler's symphonies. The first movement of No. 3 lasts forty-five minutes, and there are five movements to follow !

A third factor is the intellectual background and conditioning from which Mahler s music sprang. Generally speaking his symphonies have " programmes ". That is to say, they are based primarily on Mahler's experiences and meditations as a complete human being, not merely as a musician. Some of these " programmes " are avowed. That of the second symphony, for example, opens beside the bier of a man beloved. . . . What is Life ? What is Death ? Have these things a meaning ? . . . Such is the initial challenge of No. 2, which takes us in its successive movements through negation, unbelief, and apocalypse before reaching its goal of universal light and love.

From the days when, as a youngster in Vienna, he followed university courses in philosophy and general history as well as studying music, Mahler retained a voracious appetite for things of the mind. He was immersed from early manhood in Goethe, Schopenhauer, Nietzsche, Jean-Paul Richter, E. T. A. Hoffmann as well as a wide range of foreign writers, from Dostoievsky to Laurence Sterne. The many-sidedness of his intellectual interests almost matched that of Richard Wagner.

MAHLER'S RELIGIOUS ASPIRATIONS

Of his artistic affinity with Wagner he was well aware. In one of his letters to Alma Mahler he wrote that Wagner and Beethoven were supreme. " After them ", he adds, " there is nobody. Mark that ! "

Some, at least, of his professional contemporaries regarded Mahler's music with as little cordiality as he did theirs. Three eminent French composers of the day—Debussy, Dukas, and Pierné—got up and walked out of the Châtelet Theatre, Paris, during the second movement of his second symphony when he conducted it there in 1910. They later explained that the symphony was too Schubertian for them—too " foreign ", Viennese and Slavonic.

The part that religion, or religious aspirations, played in Mahler's creative life is a fascinating theme. Of his conversion to Catholicism in 1897, Alma Mahler comments that, born of Jewish blood, " he had to be baptised before he could aspire to such a high position under the Royal and Imperial exchequer [as the directorship of the Vienna Court Opera]." She adds that he had in any case a strong leaning to Catholic mysticism, and that he could never pass a church without going in ; he loved the smell of incense and the strains of Gregorian chant ! It is evident from his letters, however, that Mahler was no orthodox believer. Looking back on his second symphony towards the end of his life, he saw in the funeral-march episode and in the storm scene that follows it "a flaming indictment of the Creator".

Bruno Walter, to whom this comment was made, has written, " In view of his inability to enjoy the lasting possession of spiritual gains, I feel unable to call him actually believing and devout. And this in spite of his religious inclinations and exaltations." The great problem for Mahler, adds Walter, was how to reconcile world-sorrow and world-evil with divine goodness and omnipotence. " At the bottom of his soul lay a profound world-sorrow whose rising cold waves would seize him in an icy grip."

RICHARD STRAUSS

Externally, at any rate, there was no corresponding streak of philosophic pessimism in Mahler's contemporary, Richard Strauss. To all outward appearance, the only world problems which preoccupied Strauss, who early became known as a keen businessman, concerned the success of his music in the two hemispheres. Protégé of the renowned Hans von Bülow and, at the age of twenty-one, his successor as conductor of the famous Meiningen Orchestra, Strauss became a master of modern orchestral techniques at an age when most musicians are hardly out of their apprenticeship. At twenty-four he was writing music which combined audacious energy with technical assurance and polish to a degree that has never been paralleled. Nearly three-quarters of a century after it first came out, the symphonic poem *Don Juan* still commands admiration for these qualities.

Mahler was early among Strauss's admirers. But in his case admiration was mixed with second thoughts, even with a touch of revulsion, as we gather from his letters to his wife. " I had a serious talk with Strauss in Berlin and tried to show him the blind alley he had got into. Unfortunately he did not follow what I meant. I can mean nothing to him, for, whereas I see over his head, he sees only up to my knees " (1901). " His [Strauss's] being will always remain alien to me. That way of thinking and feeling is worlds apart from mine. I wonder whether one of these days we shall meet on the same star " (1906). Again : " Strauss sheds such a blight—you feel estranged from your very self. If these are the fruits, how is one to love the tree ? . . . Better by far to eat the bread of poverty and follow one's star than sell one's soul like that. The time will come when the chaff shall be winnowed from the grain—and my day will be when his is ended " (1901). Of Strauss's opera *Salome* : " It is emphatically a work of genius. . . . A Vulcan lives and labours under a heap of slag, a subterranean fire—not merely a firework. It is exactly the same with Strauss's whole personality. That is why it is so difficult in his case to sift the chaff from the grain " (1907).

Although Mahler's metaphors are mixed, the point is clear. Strauss, he is telling us in effect, lacks moral sincerity and, what is more, he puts down on paper everything that comes into his head, bad and good music alike. Ironically enough, the identical reproach of lack of discrimination is often brought against Mahler himself. Mahler lived long enough to see Strauss internationally established as an operatic composer—on the strength of *Salome* and *Elektra*. The fact remains that at the beginning of this century Strauss was known mainly as a composer of symphonic poems. He had taken over the genre devised (or at least baptised) by Liszt and given it a quite new vitality.

As a youth newly out of Munich University, he wrote music in a cautiously neo-Brahmsian vein. His meeting with von Bülow and his circle at the age of nineteen expanded his ideas and made the seed of genius that was undoubtedly in him suddenly sprout. He committed himself whole-heartedly, in his own words, " to the development of the poetic and expressive in music, as exemplified by the works of Liszt, Wagner, and Berlioz". The main series of symphonic poems which followed began with *Macbeth* (1886–90) and ended with *A Hero's Life* (1898). Excluding the immature *Aus Italien* (1886), they comprise seven works written between the ages of twenty-two and thirty-four. They established Strauss as one of the commanding figures of the nineteenth century and, by virtue of their harmonic and other innovations, as a prophet of the twentieth.

Looking back upon the symphonic poems from the vantage point of our own day, we see very plainly something that was not evident to the mass of concert-goers in the 'nineties and early 1900s, namely, the extent to which Strauss assimilated and reflected the music of his Romantic precursors. Even the most daring of his scores carries flavours of Mozart and Weber. The technical influences of Berlioz and Wagner, which he avowed himself, are obvious. Even Brahms puts in a vicarious appearance now and then.

LEVITIES AND BRUTALITIES

These affinities were, generally speaking, overlooked by our fathers and grandfathers, simply because they had ears only for Strauss's levities and " brutalities ". In *Don Quixote* (1897) they were offended by the muted brass effects which suggest the bleating of a flock of sheep charged by the hero in one episode. (Considered purely from the angle of orchestral textures, this is a passage of extraordinary beauty and originality.) In *Till Eulenspiegel* (1894–95), the market-place and its brawlings pained many ears, and *A Hero's Life* was a twofold scandal. Not only did Strauss write woodwind music of unprecedented acidity in the " Critics " section and mount a full-scale battle-scene that left the contemporary hearer dazed and protesting ; he also made it clear that the piece was autobiographical—that the Critics were *his* critics ; that the " works of peace " section had reference to *his* works ; that the hero of *Ein Heldenleben*, in short, was Richard Strauss himself and no other.

A third piece which set the world at loggerheads was *Thus Spake Zarathustra*, with a " programme " based on Nietzsche's conception of the superman. This was heard for the first time in 1896. Old Sir George Grove in a private letter asked, " What can have happened to drag music from the high level of beauty, interest, sense, force, grace, coherence and any other good quality which it rises to in Beethoven, and also (not so high) in Mendelssohn, down to the low level of ugliness and want of interest we had in Strauss's absurd *farrago* . . . ? Noise and *effect* seems to be so much the aim now." As opposed to this we have Ernest Newman's judgment of *Zarathustra*—" A marvellous work ; no such overwhelming picture of man and the universe has ever been unfolded to our eyes in music ; it almost makes the world philosophy of Wagner seem in comparison like the bleat of evangelical orthodoxy." This view, it must not be forgotten, dates from 1905 and must not be taken as committing its author in perpetuity. *Zarathustra* is generally regarded nowadays as one of Strauss's more unequal and less successful essays. Strauss's music in general, the operas included, suffered a marked decline in favour between the wars. More extreme and astringent fashions made the music of the one-time firebrand seem almost cloying. We now appear to be on the way to a more balanced judgment.

Outside what has been described as the main series of symphonic poems must be reckoned the *Symphonia Domestica* (1902–03) and the *Alpine Symphony* (1911–15). Like *A Hero's Life*, the former is autobiographical. The " hero " is now depicted in slippered bourgeois ease. We hear the baby being bathed and having a fugal romp before breakfast. (These are actual " programme " details.) The most remarkable thing about the *Domestica* and the *Alpine Symphony* is their technical facility and exuberance. In musical content they cannot be considered to live up to the earlier tone-poems.

STRAUSS'S OPERAS

After an initial operatic essay in the Wagnerian manner, *Guntram* (1894), Strauss turned to the orchestra as a means of portraying character in music, as we have seen. In maturity he returned to opera by way of the symphonic poem. His first important operas, *Salome* (1905) and *Elektra* (produced 1909), each in one act, are huge symphonic poems with voices and visible action. In this way Strauss was able to escape from the Wagnerian model, while retaining and developing the symphonic structure of his operas. He used leading-motives as the basis of his musical structures and, as in Wagner, they are far from being mere labels attached to characters or ideas.

Strauss was more interested in the voice for its own sake, and especially in the soprano-voice, than Wagner ever was. Consequently, even in *Elektra*, which was once regarded as " unsingable ", the voices dominate the scene. In his next opera, *Der Rosenkavalier* (produced in 1911), a comedy in three acts, Strauss's vocal style was able to blossom out with magnificent effect, the three women's voices (one of them, the mezzo-soprano, being the adolescent lover) soaring over the rich orchestral texture in seemingly endless melodic strains. The character of Baron Ochs, the lecherous nobleman, is splendidly drawn, but Strauss seems to have taken little interest in the delineation of the secondary characters. We do not recognise Faninal as a personality in his music as we immediately recognise Mozart's Dr. Bartolo or Wagner's Fasolt or David.

With Hugo von Hofmannsthal, his librettist for *Elektra* and *Der Rosen-kavalier*, Strauss next wrote an opera, *Ariadne auf Naxos*, for performance before M. Jourdain and his guests in a production of Molière's *Le Bourgeois Gentilhomme*. In this form *Ariadne* was produced in 1912. The circumstances of its performance necessitated the reduction of the orchestra, and instead of the hundred or so players required for *Elektra* Strauss scored for a chamber-ensemble. Apart from the fact that he was composing a *pastiche* of Lullian opera, combined with a Comedy of Masks (anticipating both Busoni's and Puccini's interest in this form), Strauss inevitably refined his orchestral style in writing for the small orchestra. *Ariadne*, which was subsequently supplied with a new introductory act so that it could be performed independently of Molière's comedy, marks a turning point in Strauss's development. Before the effect of this experience was fully felt Strauss, again in collaboration with Hofmannsthal, composed *Die Frau ohne Schatten* in 1914–17, a huge allegorical drama, whose symbolism is often obscure and sometimes tasteless. The work contains some of the most luxurious passages of rich musical sound ever created, but, like Puccini, Strauss was always defeated by the sublime. Puccini generally managed to avoid the encounter, but Strauss, more ambitious, only achieved bombastic commonplace.

Intermezzo, an autobiographical conversation-piece produced in 1924, for which Strauss wrote the text, inevitably failed to travel abroad. *Arabella* (1933), the last product of Strauss's collaboration with von Hofmannsthal, has won wider popularity after an initial undeserved neglect. This admirable comedy of impoverished aristocracy in nineteenth-century Vienna is set to racy music, the witty dialogue being carried on in a light and natural style worthy of the best Italian recitative. Moreover, besides the beautifully drawn character of Arabella herself, her " rough diamond " of a suitor from the country is wonderfully well observed, and, as an exception to the rule, the lesser characters, especially Arabella's pathetically ridiculous parents and her aristocratic suitors, are distinctly characterised.

Strauss wrote five more operas after *Arabella*—*Die schweigsame Frau* (" The Silent Woman "), *Friedenstag*, *Daphne*, *Die liebe der Danae* (" Danae's Love "), and finally *Capriccio*. This last, produced in 1942, is of special interest as an exploration of the fundamental principles of operatic form. It is based on an eighteenth-century burlesque, *Prima la musica e poi le parole* (" First Music, then Words ") set to music by Salieri (1786), which Strauss had tentatively discussed in the first act of the revised version of *Ariadne auf Naxos*. In *Capriccio* the affections of the heroine are torn between the composer and the poet who are collaborating in an opera, and the action turns on the relative importance of the two contributors to the finished work of art. Though Strauss, represented by the soprano, does not come out definitely on one side or the other, we are given shrewdly to understand in the orchestral postlude that it is the musician who wins. The Wagnerian wheel had turned full circle.

During the long sunset of his life, Strauss, while still preoccupied with operatic problems and projects, turned again to concert music. The second horn concerto (1942) and the oboe concerto (1945–46) break no new ground, but reveal intact craftsmanship allied to good taste and modest æsthetic aim. More striking are the *Metamorphoses for Twenty-Three Solo String Instruments*, written during the last years of the war, while the Nazi tyranny was floundering. With its quotation from the funeral march in Beethoven's *Eroica* symphony, this score is Strauss's final salute to the age that bred him, an age of which he will surely remain one of the symbols and ornaments.

CARL ORFF

In a limited and slightly paradoxical sense, Carl Orff, born in Munich in 1895, may be considered a natural heir to the operatic traditions of Wagner and Strauss, against which he has strongly reacted. In his stage works (none are actually called operas) *Der Mond* (" The Moon ") and *Die Kluge* (" The Clever Girl ") there is a whittling down, in the interest of clear presentation, of all complexities of expression to the ultimate point of toleration—perhaps, indeed, sometimes beyond. Similar simplicity and repetitiousness are marked features of another substantial work by him of a dramatic character yet not specifically intended for the stage : the triptych *Trionfi*, consisting of *Carmina Burana*, *Catulli Carmina*, and *Il Trionfo di Afrodite*. To this vocal music there is something of an instrumental parallel in that of Orff's compatriot Werner Egk (*b.* 1901).

XXI

AFTER WAGNER—ITALY, RUSSIA, AND FRANCE

DURING the last decades of the nineteenth century the colossal shadow of Wagner lay dark upon Germany and, as the sun declined, stretched out over other lands. There was no one of the intellectual calibre or musical imagination needed for handling the new style with its vast resources.

The most successful among Wagner's immediate circle was Engelbert Humperdinck (1854–1921), who had assisted with the production of *Parsifal*. In *Hänsel und Gretel* (1893) he applied the Wagnerian apparatus, including the large orchestra, to Grimm's fairy tale and to folk-like melody. There is some disproportion here between the means and the end, but sufficient charm and melodiousness to maintain the opera's popularity. Humperdinck failed to repeat this success in *Königskinder* (" Royal Children ") (1910), the story of the Goose-girl, which was originally produced as a play with music and then turned into an opera. He also composed the music for a Passion play, *The Miracle*, produced by Reinhardt in 1911 in London. Somewhat similar in idiom was *Der Evangelimann* (" The Gospel Man ") (1895) by Wilhelm Kienzl (1857–1941), who also wrote a *Don Quixote* (1898) using the Wagnerian method lightly and without resort to its grander heroic gestures.

ITALIAN REALISM

In Italy, as we have seen, the evolution towards a more continuous style and a greater feeling for dramatic propriety had been gradual, though hardly less striking than the Wagnerian revolution. Verdi's junior contemporaries were confronted with a less formidable task, even though among them there was no one of his stature. Ponchielli produced nothing of the same quality as *La Gioconda*. Alfredo Catalani (1854–93) under the influence of German romanticism came nearer than most Italians to adopting the Wagnerian manner. But his music, though noble in intention and possessing a real lyrical charm, was not strong enough to compete with the rising tide of realism or *verismo* that now poured with such violence into the Italian theatre.

Pietro Mascagni (1863–1945) was the first exponent of the new style, which exploited the brutality of *Carmen* while ignoring all the refinement that makes Bizet's opera a great work of art. *Cavalleria Rusticana* (1890), a piece in two scenes joined by an orchestral intermezzo, soon found a suitable partner for an evening's entertainment in *I Pagliacci* (1892) by Ruggiero Leoncavallo (1858–1919). For all their enormous success in these operas, neither composer added anything to his reputation in later years, though Mascagni achieved some success with his *L'Amico Fritz* (1891) and *Iris* (1898). But the native instinct for theatrical effect and the gift of writing catchy and commonplace melody availed neither composer in their more serious works.

GIACOMO PUCCINI

In his search for a successor to Verdi, Giulio Ricordi, head of the Milanese firm of music publishers, lighted on Giacomo Puccini (1858–1924) as the most likely candidate. Puccini had entered a one-act opera, *Le Villi*, based on a Germanic legend, for a competition sponsored by the rival firm of Sonzogno. The work was rejected, but Ricordi obtained a hearing for it at one of the smaller theatres in Milan in 1884. Later the same year the opera was given in a revised form, expanded to two acts, at Turin. The music combines elements derived from Verdi's middle years, especially *Rigoletto*, with a Wagnerian treatment of the orchestra, leading Verdi to warn the young composer against confusing opera with symphony.

Though Ricordi's judgment was not vindicated by *Edgar* (1889), which suffered from a poor libretto imposed upon Puccini by his publisher, *Manon Lescaut* (1893) proved that he had been right, initiating a series of successes that made the composer's fortune. In *Manon Lescaut*, which skilfully avoided most of the ground covered by Massenet in his version of Prévost's story, Puccini established his special type of operatic heroine—a young woman, usually frail in physique, who is the victim of masculine passion. She is not so much immoral as amoral. Mimi in *La Bohème* (1896) and Cio-Cio-San in *Madama Butterfly* (1904) are her most typical incarnations. In *Tosca* (1900) and *La Fanciulla del West* (1910) she is, though suffering, a tougher, more positive character.

Puccini resorted for his subjects to the popular theatrical successes of the day, and his taste, or lack of it, is exemplified in his choice of plays by David Belasco for two of his operas. Sardou's *La Tosca* is, at least, a well-made melodrama with a political background that is convincingly sketched in, though it is almost completely eliminated from the opera. Belasco's *Madama Butterfly* and *The Girl of the Golden West* are novelettish and completely unconvincing in their characterisation and action. It says much for Puccini's craftsmanship as a composer that he was able to make such themes acceptable.

Puccini was fully aware of the developments that were going on in the music of his day, and he took from them whatever seemed to serve his purpose. Yet his music never sounds imitative or even eclectic, because he was able to absorb external influences, including the oriental idioms he used in *Madama Butterfly* and *Turandot* (produced posthumously in 1926), into his own musical personality.

If he was incapable of expressing sublime ideas or noble characters (especially men), Puccini could sustain emotional tension, whether activated by love or terror, over whole acts with an extraordinary intensity of expression embodied in poignant vocal melody. His appeal is direct to the hearer's emotions, which are unable to resist such earnest utterances. This power is heightened by Puccini's extraordinary flair for theatrical effect. He knew exactly how to extract the last drop of sensation out of a given situation. And he was adroit in his placing of touches of comic relief, for he had a considerable gift for comedy, which he exploited fully only once —in *Gianni Schicchi*, the third of three one-act pieces (1918), the others being the brilliantly effective melodrama, *Il Tabarro* (" The Cloak ") and the contrasting sentimental *Suor Angelica*.

PUCCINI'S CONTEMPORARIES

Among Puccini's contemporaries Umberto Giordano (1867–1948) made his mark with *Andrea Chénier* (1896), a melodramatic opera set in the French Revolution. The subject probably influenced Puccini's choice of *Tosca*, which in turn influenced Francesco Cilea (1866–1950) to write *Adriana Lecouvreur* (1902), an opera about an actress in the time of Louis XV. Riccardo Zandonai (1883–1944) showed in *Francesca da Rimini* (1914) a reaction against the realism of the previous generation and a reversion towards a more romantic type of opera, to which also belongs the more original *L'Amore dei tre Re* (1913) by Italo Montemezzi (1875–1952), one of the few operas which successfully used Debussy's idiom enriched with a fuller Wagnerian warmth of colour and combined with an Italianate lyricism. His *La Nave* (1918) foundered under the weight of imagery in the text of Gabriele d'Annunzio adapted by Tito Ricordi.

Rather apart from the rest stand Ferruccio Busoni (1866–1924) and Ermanno Wolf-Ferrari (1876–1948), both men of mixed German and Italian blood. Busoni, one of the greatest virtuoso pianists, was also a distinguished composer with individual views on operatic form. In particular he sought

in *Arlecchino* (1916) and *Turandot* (1917)—which is based on Gozzi's play
and adheres to it more closely than Puccini did—to bring back to the theatre,
and give new life to, the characters of the Italian Comedy of Masks. His
Doktor Faust, which was completed after his death by his pupil Philipp
Jarnach, is a more ambitious work based not on Goethe, but on the old
German puppet plays and, in part, on Marlowe's tragedy.

With the exception of one sensational excursion into realism, *I Gioielli
della Madonna* (" The Jewels of the Madonna ") (1911), Wolf-Ferrari concerned himself mainly with comedy. He went to Goldoni for the texts of
Le Donne Curiose (" The Inquisitive Women ") (1903) and *I Quattro
Rusteghi* (1906), which is given in England as " The School for Fathers ".
His best-known piece is *Il Segreto di Susanna* (" Susanna's Secret ") (1909),
a one-act *intermezzo*. In all these the composer cleverly contrived to
combine Italian melodic charm and gracefulness with something of the
robustness of German harmony and orchestration. Ildebrando Pizzetti
(*b*. 1880) has shown that the Italian lyric theatre possesses a continued vitality
in fields quite different from those explored by Puccini and his followers
or by the neo-classicists. Of his early operas *Fedra* (written in 1905, but
not performed until ten years later) was based on d'Annunzio, but for
Debora e Jaele (1922) and *Fra Gherardo* (1928) the composer wrote his own
librettos. Most remarkable of all is his *Murder in the Cathedral* (1958), a
skilful and effective setting of T. S. Eliot's verse-drama. The inevitable
reaction against Italy's exclusive interest in opera during the nineteenth
century was led by three composers. Ottorino Respighi (1879–1936) was
a string-player who became a pupil of Rimsky-Korsakov and wrote a
number of luxuriant orchestral works in which his master's brilliant instrumental colours are combined with Italian sensuousness and the bold, somewhat coarse late Romantic style of Richard Strauss. The best known of
these are the Roman tone-poems *Fontane di Roma* (1917) and *Pini di Roma*
(1924), but another and more original side of Respighi's musical character
is to be found in the *Trittico Boticelliano* (1927), in his concertos and chamber
music based on Gregorian themes, and the one-act " mystery " *Maria
Egiziaca* (1932). More revolutionary in style and temperament were
Alfredo Casella (1883–1947) and Gian Francesco Malipiero (*b*. 1882).
Casella studied, and for nearly twenty years lived, in Paris, where he
assimilated a number of influences—ranging from Debussy to Mahler—
which were all but unknown in Italy at the time. His orchestral and piano
music show a firm grasp of classical forms and a skilful grasp of neo-classical
idiom, both well suited to his cool, witty, and speculative nature. Like
Casella, Malipiero returned to the past, and especially to the Italian past,
in order to find a new point of departure for his own music. A member
of an old Venetian family, he showed particular interest in Monteverdi and

the seventeenth- and eighteenth-century Venetian masters. He has written a great deal in almost all the traditional forms and has been a strong educational force in his country's musical life.

RUSSIA

When Wagner died in 1883 he had, as we have seen, left his mark on the whole of musical Europe. No composer in France, where his influence was greatest outside Germany, in isolationist England, or even in Italy with its strong native operatic tradition, could afford to ignore Wagner's overwhelming impact. But Russia was not yet a part of musical Europe. Russian composers had travelled to Europe, the music of Wagner was known to them, but it meant almost nothing to them. A month before Wagner's death Tchaikovsky heard *Tristan* in Berlin and he recorded that " he had never been so bored in his life ". It seems strange to us that the composer of such unashamedly emotional music as *Romeo and Juliet* and the " Pathetic " symphony should have been so impervious to music in which, as in his own, the senses and the emotions are so mercilessly assailed. The reason was that Tchaikovsky, for all his wide popularity to-day, was very much the expression of an entirely new musical civilisation, the self-sufficient but highly sophisticated civilisation of aristocratic Russia, where Western ideas had never really taken root.

TCHAIKOVSKY

We have already considered Russian music in its more narrowly national context, but it is now time to trace its impact upon Western Europe. The Russian composers, and Tchaikovsky chief among them, were the discoverers of a musical universe, the novelty of which may nowadays elude us. Folk-music was one of the sources of their inspiration—and in turning to the spontaneous music of the people they were followed years later by Vaughan Williams in England, Bartók in Hungary, and Falla in Spain. But more than this, the new Russian music was an expression of the exuberant Russian temperament—exuberant yet at the same time pathetic, and somehow humorous, sensitive to sham, and altogether childlike in its sudden impulses. These, briefly, are the qualities underlying the irresistible appeal of Russian music.

Peter Tchaikovsky (1840–93) was not altogether unsympathetic to the nationalism of the " Mighty Five ". His own *Romeo and Juliet*, the orchestral " overture-fantasia " now deservedly so well known, was not only dedicated

ARNOLD SCHÖNBERG (1874–1951)

Archiv für Kunst und Geschichte, Berlin

Fot. Internationales, Bonn

ALBAN BERG (1885–1935)

ANTON VON WEBERN (1883–1945)

Archiv für Kunst und Geschichte, Berlin

IGOR STRAVINSKY

The Mansell Collection

BELA BARTÓK (1881–1945)

The Mansell Collection

to Balakirev but written under his guidance in 1869 (it was later revised). If he became critical of the " Mighty Five " in after years, it was not because he was enamoured of Wagner or Brahms, whom they too rejected. It is rather that Tchaikovsky was a solitary, whose music is shot through with a dark passion which it is hard not to relate to his private struggles. In an attempt to do violence to his homosexual nature he married a girl whom he did not love and left her immediately, and he never met face to face the woman who afterwards became his financial benefactress and "pen friend", Nadezhda von Meck.

He was greatly attracted to the lithe, sensuous music of Bizet and the polished grace of Saint-Saëns, though it is evident enough that the spirit of those composers was boldly transformed in his own more deeply coloured music. He was also blessed with a gift for the most generous form of melody, a gift which his detractors frequently refuse him on the ground that he was a gushing sentimentalist, an exhibitionist with no ideal of restraint. It is here that Tchaikovsky can easily be misjudged. There is a big heart in his music, but he was not gross or insensitive. Mozart, another of his few links with the West, was his ideal—as also of other seemingly un-Mozartian composers, among them Gounod and Richard Strauss. And, in fact, there is many a passage in Tchaikovsky which is exquisitely Mozartian in detail and subtlety. Nevertheless, Bernard Shaw in his days as music critic wrote that Tchaikovsky " had a thoroughly Byronic power of being tragic, momentous, romantic about nothing at all . . . like Childe Harold, who was more tragic when there was nothing whatever the matter with him than an ordinary Englishman is when he is going to be executed. . . ." We may or may not agree with the implication that the emotional climaxes of Tchaikovsky's music are too contrived ; but the comparison of his work with Byron's is not inept. Byron's *Manfred*, a highly self-centred adventurer of the soul, was the inspiration of Tchaikovsky's *Manfred* Symphony, an unjustly neglected work which is not included in the six numbered symphonies. Of these six, No. 2, the so-called *Little Russian* symphony, would be better named Ukrainian, which means the same thing and explains the origin of the folk-song utilised in the last movement. No. 3 is somewhat absurdly called—not by the composer— the " Polish ", merely because it uses a polonaise rhythm in the finale. The remaining symphonies, the most popular, are all intensely personal in expression, full of high-pitched emotionalism and a brooding sense of fatality. This is, indeed, explicit in the fourth symphony, which opens with an ominous fanfare which later reappears, with sinister insistence, not only in the first movement but during the merry-making of the finale. The fifth, even more, derives its whole atmosphere (except for the contrasting valse movement) from the introspective, melancholy introductory theme in the clarinets' lowest register, though the music (especially in the second move-ment) rises to almost hysterically passionate climaxes. It is again the introductory passage to the sixth—a dejected phrase on low bassoons—which sets the prevailing mood of the work, which is known as the "Pathétique", a nickname authorised by Tchaikovsky and justified by the emotional impact of the last movement. It is regrettable that the third movement is so often in programme notes referred to as a march : it is definitely a scherzo in character, and its metronomed fast tempo would make marching impossible.

Of the two piano concertos the first, in B flat minor, continues to enthral audiences and to baffle critics ; for it seems hardly possible that Tchaikovsky can have planned that the opening big theme of the concerto should never come back in the rest of the work. That Nicholas Rubinstein (Anton's brother), to whom it was originally dedicated, refused to give the first performance is well known ; not so well known is the fact that the version familiar to-day is a later revision of the composer's, showing that he must himself have seen defects in the original version which Rubinstein rejected.

For the two successes among his ten operas, Tchaikovsky went to Pushkin as his literary source. *Eugene Onegin* (1879) has intimate yet strong music, beautifully fitted to the theatrical action, which centres on the character of the passionate Tatiana (one of the most memorable heroines of opera) and the love which she offers but which is refused. *The Queen of Spades* is less intimate, musically more variegated and less strongly unified ; but the decaying old Countess, caught up in the mystery of the three fateful cards, is a fine creation. More remarkable than Tchaikovsky's operas, and fully deserving their great popularity by the freshness and beauty of their in-vention, are his three full-length ballets, *Swan Lake*, *The Sleeping Beauty*, and *Casse-Noisette* (" The Nutcracker "). Like Delibes in France, he justified the participation in ballet of a leading composer instead of the hacks whom it had been customary to employ.

AFTER TCHAIKOVSKY

Tchaikovsky's influence in Russia was twofold. It spread on the academic plane to his pupil Sergei Taneiev (1856–1915), and to Alexander Glazunov (1865–1936). Little of the former's music is heard nowadays ; but besides being a renowned teacher, he appears to have been a most endearing personality, an incorrigible humorist who wrote (but never published) a series of *Quartets of Government Officials*, toy symphonies, a ballet guying the style of Tchaikovsky, and songs on Esperanto texts. Glazunov, too, is now only known by a handful of works, chief among them the symphonic poem *Stenka Razin*, the ballet *The Seasons*, and a violin concerto. A highly accomplished symphonist, he was affected by German influences (which were never successfully assimilated by the Russians), with the result that his music soon lost its national flavour and became merely academic. We may also pass with hardly more than a mention such minor late-romantic composers as Tchaikovsky's pupil Sergei Lyapunov (1859–1924), and Anatol Lyadov (1855–1914), the composer of *The Enchanted Lake* for orchestra.

On the emotional plane, Tchaikovsky's influence is seen in the work of another late-Romantic, by whose side these lesser figures fade away. This was Sergei Rachmaninov (1873–1943), whose most famous works are for piano with orchestra—the second and third piano concertos and the *Rhapsody on a Theme of Paganini*, a magnificent set of variations. His sweeping, intense, emotional, often melancholy music evokes much the same responses as Tchaikovsky's. Rachmaninov's second and third symphonies, also works of substance and musicianship, are occasionally played; his cantata *The Bells* is unjustifiably neglected. Rachmaninov was, of course, a great pianist as well as a conductor and composer, something of a Lisztian figure, an aristocrat in bearing and thought. His music is often misrepresented in unworthy, sentimental performances. When he played his own works they became transported to an unexpected level of purity and cool beauty, far removed from " sweetness " or sentimentality.

SCRIABIN

With Alexander Scriabin (1872–1915) we enter a different world. A brilliant pianist, and at first a composer chiefly of neo-Chopinesque works for the piano, he later concentrated on large-scale orchestral compositions (including *The Divine Poem*, *The Poem of Ecstasy*, and *Prometheus, the Poem of Fire*) prompted by theosophical beliefs and incorporating a highly charged emotional style. Scriabin's harmony is luxurious and diffused in a kind of rainbow iridescence. The metaphor is appropriate, since Scriabin dreamed of a unification of the arts of sound and colour, smell and taste. Sensually indulgent and over-stimulated, he was a voluptuary; and the streak of self-delusion which led him to embrace wild philosophical and æsthetic theories sapped the purely musical character of his work. What impressed Scriabin's followers was not so much his sensationalism as the technical intricacies of his harmonic system; he invented, as the basis of his harmony, a so-called " mystic chord " built on fourths (instead of thirds and fifths, as in classical diatonic harmony). By one of the unfeeling ironies of history, these big " visionary " works are now all but forgotten, while pianists continue to cherish Scriabin's earlier and more traditional solo compositions and some of the later and more original sonatas ; but in *The Poem of Ecstasy* may be seen the origin of certain passages in *The Firebird*, the successful early work of Stravinsky, who was soon to undermine Scriabin's temporary hold.

FRANCE TO THE FORE

The main highways in the Russian musical scene of this period are recognisable enough. French music of this period presents a much less simple picture. It seems almost incredible that a mere thirty years separate the urbane charms of Delibes's *Lakmé* and Massenet's *Manon* from the audacities of Debussy's *Jeux* and Stravinsky's *Sacre du Printemps*, bewildering works in their time and not exactly repertory works even to-day.

This is a turbulent period, but one also offering some of the most delectable works in the whole history of French music, chiefly in the work of Gabriel Fauré, Maurice Ravel, and Claude Debussy. No single epithet can describe each of their worlds, but for the moment we may think of Fauré (1845–1924) as the discreet yet secure traditionalist, Ravel (1875–1937) as the consummate stylist, and Debussy (1862–1918) as the fearless explorer. In the background is Saint-Saëns, the arch-traditionalist, perpetuating the musical craftsmanship of the eighteenth century though without its underlying spirit, his mind set against the ravages made in French music by Wagner, and of great inspiration to Fauré. The finest works of César Franck (1822–90) were composed in the last ten years of his life, but the powerful spirit of this Franco-Belgian composer, the one truly Romantic figure of the period, long persisted in disguised forms in the work of his devoted pupils, among them Vincent d'Indy, Chausson, and Duparc. Equally pervasive was the irresistible charm of Jules Massenet (1842–1912), all *couleur de rose*, of which we find many a reflection in Debussy and even in French composers of the present day. Finally, in this bird's-eye view, there was the rumbustious Emmanuel Chabrier (1841–94), one of the most original of the French musical humorists, of whom there was to be a trace, later on, in the quaint music of Erik Satie.

IMPRESSIONISM

Music in France has always been closely integrated in the contemporary intellectual and artistic life, and cross-currents between literature, painting, and music were particularly evident at the close of the last century. This was the period of the great Impressionist painters, who themselves often aspired to a musical ideal—the very terms used by Impressionist painters,

" tones ", " scales of colours ", " harmonies ", suggest this—just as the musicians aspired to a visual ideal, borrowing terms of painting to describe their novel harmonies and orchestral sonorities. Both Chabrier and Debussy had originally intended to be painters ; and though we cannot be quite sure of direct parallels as between a particular score and a particular canvas, such works as Chabrier's *España*, in which the composer sought the equivalent of " red rather than pearl grey or canary yellow ", and Debussy's *Nocturnes*, intended to convey the effect of " the various combinations of colour in a study in grey ", do reveal a close artistic communion. Similarly, the music of this period has frequently a purely literary inspiration. Here again there are many cross-currents, often ignored by musical people, though they are highly illuminating. Many of the Symbolist poets thought primarily of the musical significance of poetry—they aspired to " a state of music "—and it was only natural that this aim should finally be attained in music itself. Mallarmé greatly admired Debussy's setting of his *L'Après-midi d'un faune*, but not without a twinge of envy. His comment, " I thought my poem was itself music ", shows immediately the extent to which ideals and even methods in the arts had become strangely intertwined.

WAGNER'S SHADOW

On the musical plane loomed the overwhelming figure of Wagner, an influence felt also as a menace. Wagner was the idol of this whole French era, though not an undisputed idol ; and indeed the impression is sometimes given that large sections of musical opinion were positively hostile to Wagner. As it turned out, it was in France that the fate of Wagner's theories on the unification of the art was decided, though not in the way he expected. It is easy enough to see now that the controversies that raged on this subject all sprang not from the merits or demerits of his music, but from a genuine fear of his stature. The result was that those French composers who professed to ignore the impact that Wagner was making did so at their peril.

Yet Wagner's influence on French music was at first unfortunate in its effects. *Fervaal* by Vincent d'Indy (1851–1931), produced in 1897, was a pallid reflection of *Parsifal*. *Louise* (1900), a Galsworthy-like play with a social message, set to music by Gustave Charpentier (1860–1956), owed its success to the skilful evocation of the Parisian setting (an achievement surpassed by Puccini in *Il Tabarro*) rather than to the musical interest of its main ideas, for its leading motives were banal and not susceptible of development.

In Debussy, however, the Wagnerian fever, to which he succumbed on a visit to Bayreuth in his youth, set up a strong reaction. Debussy found in Maeterlinck's poetic drama, *Pelléas et Mélisande*, the ideal vehicle for his music. He spent ten years on the composition of this, his only opera, which was produced at the Opéra Comique in 1902. Mussorgsky's songs and *Boris Godunov* provided a model for the rediscovery of a French musical idiom, with which Debussy had already experimented in his songs before bringing it to perfection in the opera. In its negation of all emphasis and violent movement, save at certain crucial moments in the action, Maeterlinck's play is a typical product of the *fin de siècle*. Debussy perfectly matched its mood in his music, which by its sheer beauty and poignancy raises the drama to the status of a masterpiece. Paradoxically, *Pelléas et Mélisande* fulfils more completely even than *Tristan und Isolde* the Wagnerian ideal of music-drama.

CÉSAR FRANCK

We cannot possibly bring all the figures of this time into sharp relief, nor follow the many intriguing lanes and by-paths of this active scene. Not all the composers of this period were wedded to literary or pictorial ideals. Even though César Franck wrote symphonic poems such as *Le Chasseur Maudit* (" The Accursed Huntsman "), the bulk of his output shows him fascinated by problems of purely musical construction, which he often solved in novel ways. His *Variations Symphoniques* for piano and orchestra, which reveal a high order of skill allied with poetic feeling, set the variations in the framework of a dramatic fantasia ; and the sonata for violin and piano (the finale of which has the main theme in canon between the two instruments) has a highly original scheme, the first movement being a kind of preamble to the second, which carries the main weight, and which is followed by a " Recitative-Fantasia ". The movements of the sonata are also connected thematically, a device carried still further in such works as his symphony. Franck's music is decidedly uneven in quality, but common features in much of it are a fondness for hesitant interrupted phrases (deriving from habits connected with changing registration at the organ, Franck's chosen instrument, for which he wrote a great deal) and a sometimes rather cloying chromaticism, which owes as much to his constant organ improvisation as to Wagnerian influence.

GABRIEL FAURÉ

Throughout this period, Gabriel Fauré established the distinctive French style of chamber music. His chamber works include two each of piano and violin sonatas, piano and cello sonatas, piano quartets and piano quintets. The size alone of this output entitles Fauré to be considered as a chamber-music composer in the class of Schumann and Brahms. But he is so defined not only because of this particular corpus of works. His *Requiem*, his stage works, his incidental music for *Shylock* and *Pelléas et Mélisande* were all conceived in the intimate spirit of chamber music. Hence the welcome afforded his music in recent years, particularly in England where, away from the hurly-burly of musical politics, it has been refreshing to discover this satisfying composer, subtle yet unprovocative. Fauré was an organist before he became director of the Paris Conservatoire, though curiously enough he wrote not a single work for the organ ; nor was he at any time attracted to the orchestra.

FAURÉ'S SONGS

He wrote beautifully for the voice and for the piano. But even here his imagination was never excited by vocal texture or the character of piano writing as such. The poetry in his music is of a more interior kind, springing from his finely spun-out melodies and from his remarkable harmonic modulations. It is the poetry of pure music. The chamber works are uneven, exhaling their full period charm in isolated movements (the last movement of the first piano and violin sonata, the scherzo of the first quartet and the first movement of the second cello sonata), though occasionally he is surprisingly nondescript for a composer who made such a personal contribution. While other composers were exploring and even undermining the harmonic language, Fauré could still refine the older usages of harmony. His many piano works—Nocturnes, Barcarolles, and Impromptus—contain, at their best, music of a warm, rose-tinted sentiment, kept severely from sentimentality. His most lasting music is probably to be found in the gentle *Requiem* and in his songs, particularly his settings of Verlaine. His response to the imagery of Verlaine's poetry was less acute than the response of Debussy though musically richer than that of Reynaldo Hahn ; all of them were inspired by certain of the same poems. By his nature Fauré was attracted, in *La Bonne Chanson*, *Green*, and *C'est l'extase*, to the lyrical rather than the sensuous aspects of Verlaine's poetry, and his Verlaine settings are rightly considered the supreme examples of his lyrical gifts. His remarkably consistent style became more sophisticated in the course of his long life, his early music having been written before the birth of Debussy and his last works when a new spirit was breaking through in the work of " Les Six ".

RAVEL'S STYLE

Fauré's pupil Ravel was a stylist too, but of an altogether different order
—perhaps the greatest stylist French music has ever produced. He was
unique among the composers of his time in that he introduced into the
swiftly changing musical scene of the end of the nineteenth century a clear-
cut, original idiom, created already in his early song *Sainte* and maintained
unchanged until his last works. It is as if the spirit of Couperin or Mozart
had somehow found itself by mistake in the *fin de siècle*, where it might
well feel superior but at the same time self-conscious and artificial. This
seems to have been the position of Ravel, aware of the superior, aristocratic
craftsmanship that came so naturally to him and aware also that, for all
the modernity of his music, its underlying spirit belonged to another age.

To-day, however, there is nothing whatever mystifying about Ravel's
art ; it seems to us, on the contrary, crystal clear. We are dazzled by its
jewel-like brilliance, we rejoice in it as an antidote to Brahms or Strauss,
and occasionally, in *Le Tombeau de Couperin* for instance, we are reminded
of Ravel's remote ancestry. True, there is something a little inhuman
about his stylistic perfection, something a little unnatural about his faultless
taste ; and people who are reluctant to consider elegance as an end in itself
are doubly conscious of Ravel's limitations, feeling more at ease with music
where these qualities are conspicuously lacking—Berlioz, for instance, and
Mahler. Alone in Jules Renard and in Colette, who respectively inspired
his *Histoires Naturelles* and *L'Enfant et les sortilèges*, do we find any literary
counterpart ; and there because the heart of these writers, like the tender
heart of Ravel himself, went out less to human beings than to animals and
children and the quaint fantasies associated with them. Ravel was unaffected
by Wagner, but not by another figure destined to shake the French musical
world almost as profoundly, Richard Strauss. When Strauss's *Salome* was
given in Paris at the beginning of the century, a hostility was aroused in
musical circles of which we can hardly imagine the intensity. It was the
desperate fear of Wagner all over again, though this time there was a
psychological factor. Strauss's great friend and champion, Romain Rolland,
perceived that the reasons for this hostility were moral as well as musical,
and he found in Ravel one of the few ardent admirers of *Salome*. Ravel
made no attempt to conceal an admiration for Strauss's stupendous sense
of the orchestra. At the outbreak of the First World War he was engaged
on a work originally entitled *Wien*, later changed to *La Valse*. One of the
finest of Ravel's virtuoso pastiches, this is inspired not by Richard, but by
Johann, Strauss ; yet the spirit of the composer of *Salome* was drawn into
Ravel's circle too.

There was a tragedy in the life of Ravel in the form of an obscure mental disturbance, our knowledge of which, scanty though it is, must be brought into any account of the psychology of his musical mind. Shrinkage of the brain was the official diagnosis after the operation from which he died. But years before, there is evidence to show that he might have been suffering from a psychological rather than a physical disturbance. Something had in any case snapped, and his last years were silent. It is not too fanciful to imagine that he was unable to bear the tensions of his ideals ; that he was aware that, in a world where time was moving against him, the ideals that he was cultivating with such beautiful artificiality could no longer be maintained.

Ravel excelled in his works for piano and for the orchestra. (Several of the latter were originally conceived in piano versions.) The *Rapsodie Espagnole*, the *Mother Goose* Suite and particularly *Daphnis et Chloé* display the full delights of Ravel's orchestral sense with its glinting colours and its love of often ravishing detail. It was a sense of the orchestra more sophisticated than that of either Rimsky-Korsakov or Saint-Saëns, from which it derives ; more subtle than that of Strauss ; less evocative and noticeably more superficial than that of Debussy. Few other composers of this period, apart from Debussy, show an orchestral sense so innate. Stravinsky was to be his equal in *The Firebird* and *Petrushka*, as certainly Chabrier had been in the *Marche Joyeuse* and *España*. Others are Dukas in *L'Apprenti Sorcier* and, to a lesser extent, in *La Péri*, and, one must add, Lalo in his overture *Le Roi d'Ys*, one of the most inspired of all the French overtures.

CLAUDE DEBUSSY

The soul of this generation is reached in the work of Debussy, whose short career is precisely contained in this period. A questioning, solitary figure, Debussy believed that the mind of a composer, like the mind of a poet, should be aware of its unconscious layers, and this is the explanation of his well-known preoccupation with dreams. *L'Après-midi d'un faune* and *Pelléas et Mélisande* are the works in which he was best able to project this dream state, and significantly they derive from the strong impact made on his mind by Mallarmé and Maeterlinck. Debussy was a poetic musician in a literal sense, and Liszt's description of Schubert as " le musicien le plus poète que jamais " would be more appropriately applied to this composer. He was an instinctive man, a man of the senses, relishing physical values in the arts, unafraid of the indulgent weakness in his musical character and of its violence. While a student he boldly challenged, in theory, the foundations of tonal harmony ; and though tonality is never banished from his music, he brought harmony to a point from which it was only a step to the non-tonal music of his successors.

EXPERIMENT

Debussy was not, however, a theorist. He proceeded by experiment. The inspiration that he derived from Wagner was twofold ; Wagner was an example of harmonic freedom, and he stood for a largely hedonistic art related to Debussy's ideal. Harmonically Debussy was more adventurous than Wagner had been, reviving the Gregorian modes, incorporating Oriental elements, and challenging the principle of tonality. On the emotional plane, the relationship is less evident. Wagner assaults ; the art of Debussy insinuates. For this reason the Wagnerian influence in Debussy is obscure. Nevertheless it can be traced ; and listening to *Pelléas et Mélisande* Richard Strauss was struck by its resemblance to *Parsifal*, which had inspired the earlier cantata *La Damoiselle élue*, and was still haunting Debussy in his last and most daring orchestral work, *Jeux*. (*Parsifal* was his model here in, as he put it, " effects as if the orchestra were illuminated from behind ".)

There are many views on Debussy's music, but no single one reveals the whole of his art. Having studied with a pupil of Chopin, he created a new style of piano writing in which the piano should seem to be an instrument " without hammers " : a technique of illusion in which the piano is not a piano. He replaced formal development by a continuity of musical thought that should produce the impression of improvisation. In passages like the opening flute solo in *L'Après-midi d'un faune*, his melodic ideal was what he called the arabesque. He wrote for the voice with a keen understanding of both poetic and vocal inflections, disdaining vocal traditions, and informing the cast about to sing *Pelléas* that they must forget that they were ever operatic singers at all. His orchestral works, notably *La Mer* and the *Images*, where almost each instrument has a voice of its own, have the texture of vast chamber ensembles. These two evocative works in particular represent, as no other music of this period, the counterpart of the Impressionist genius in painting.

DEBUSSY'S INFLUENCE

The influence of Debussy was wide, noticeably on Stravinsky (whose *Firebird* and *Petrushka* he greatly admired, though not *Le Sacre du Printemps*), and on Bartók. It is also true that Debussy, a shrewd critic and sometimes alarmingly prophetic, was aware that the evolution of music had been moving, through Wagner and himself, to a point where the future filled him with the greatest apprehension. The early works of Roussel were heard during Debussy's later years, and after the 1914 war a new spirit was to break through in the work of "Les Six". When Debussy died in the last months of the First World War, Romain Rolland, whose sympathies were with German music and who could muster little faith in his French contemporaries, recorded the composer's death in his diary, and revealingly added: "The last creator of beauty in music". It was beginning to look as if Debussy's dictum about Wagner, "a beautiful sunset that was mistaken for a dawn", was likely to prove even truer of himself.

XXII

GREAT BRITAIN

BEFORE we speak of the belated appearance of musical nationalism in Great Britain, it will be well to cast our eyes back over the earlier years of the nineteenth century, which were creatively a desert in this country, and a desert ruled by a succession of foreign masters who never became acclimatised like Handel, but easily imposed their music on a passive public.

Change came swiftly in Britain in the nineteenth century. To quote only the most obvious of social statistics, the population increased from 10·5 million to 37 million, and by 1851 half the population (excluding Ireland's) was urban—" a situation that had probably not existed before, in a great country, at any time in the world's history" (Clapham, *Economic History of Great Britain*). The concentration of industrial population supported the growth of countless choral societies devoted chiefly to oratorio and cantata. The brass band movement, emerging about 1840, was the result of the working man's desire for personal music-making. The artisan's rough hands can be expert on the valves of the brass, but would be hopelessly clumsy on strings or woodwind.

CONCERTS

Concert organisation in London assumed a broader basis. The Philharmonic (now Royal Philharmonic) Society of London, founded in 1813, was a select organisation giving only six to eight concerts a year and appealing to those referred to in advertisements as " the nobility and gentry". But the Crystal Palace, erected in Hyde Park in 1851, was removed next year to Sydenham in south-east London and there became the site of a notable series of popular concerts at cheap prices ; and in 1895 the establishment of Promenade Concerts organised by Robert Newman and conducted by Henry (later Sir Henry) Wood already constitutes a direct link with our own day. The term " Promenade Concerts " itself is more than half a century older.

In the provinces the relative decline of older centres such as Norwich and Bath, and the rise of newly important cities like Manchester and Birmingham, are observable in the musical as in economic activity. It was no coincidence that the Hallé Orchestra, the *Manchester Guardian*, and the Manchester Grammar School first flourished in the time of the city's economic ascendancy. With the spread of general popular education went a spread of musical education. The Tonic Sol-Fa movement, emerging in the middle of the century, was specifically designed as educational. Already a wave of enthusiasm for singing-classes had appeared through the activity of the German-born Joseph Mainzer (1801–51), whose book published in 1842 bore the modern-sounding title of *Singing for the Million*.

Mainzer's Musical Times and Singing Circular was indeed the journal which in 1844 became the present *Musical Times*, issued by the publishing house of Novello. That firm pioneered the circulation of " cheap music " —the word " cheap " being a matter for boasting in those days, not something to be ashamed of. In 1846 Novello offered Handel's *Messiah* for sale in twelve monthly instalments at 6d. each, and in 1854 he published a pocket vocal score of the work for 1s. 4d. (later reduced to 1s.). Nor were publishers backward in issuing songs and piano music (including quadrilles and other dances) to fit the taste of an age which was conscious of music as a social accomplishment and which thought of the art chiefly as a home pastime.

BALLADS

It is easy to-day to make fun of the Victorian (and pre-Victorian) drawing-room and its stream of genteelly sentimental ballads and piano pieces. In our own times, however, when the business of providing for informal and popular music-making has been abandoned to people with almost no connection with, or feeling for, " serious " music, we may be ill-advised to laugh at the generation which brought into its drawing-rooms piano arrangements of Donizetti's operas or the public for which Mendelssohn expressly wrote his *Songs Without Words*.

By the 1820s the piano had all but driven out the harpsichord. Among the earliest musicians to exploit the specific sound-qualities of the piano, in what we should now call Romantic style, was the Irish pianist-composer John Field (1782–1837), whose work was admired by Schumann and Liszt and from whom Chopin borrowed the name and the idea of the Nocturne. Field, however, settled in St. Petersburg, toured from there, and died in Moscow. His career concerns British music-making only remotely, and his influence on style in piano-writing in Britain was much less than that of the Italian-born Muzio Clementi (1752–1832), who settled here, or of Johann Nepomuk Hummel (1778–1837), whose work was widely known.

The writing of " ballads " (a word used, in this sense, to denote a straight-forward song of " drawing-room " type), further provided an income for composers who could no more expect to live on symphonies and serious opera than composers do to-day. But in the early part of the nineteenth century, as throughout the eighteenth, the stage could still prove lucrative. Sir Henry Bishop (1786–1855) wrote *Lo, here the gentle lark* and *Should he upbraid* for the botched versions of Shakespeare plays then popular ; and his *Home Sweet Home* itself, which became almost a second national anthem in Victorian England, appeared in his opera *Clari, or the Maid of Milan* after having first emerged, in a slightly different musical version and with different words, as a pretended " Sicilian air " in a collection of national melodies.

OPERA

There was, indeed, a two-way traffic between the realm of ballads and of English opera. In 1843 and 1845 were produced *The Bohemian Girl* by Michael Balfe (1808–70) and *Maritana* by William Vincent Wallace (1812–65), the two most famous operas of their type. And doubtless both composers inserted ballad-like items into these works partly because they would appeal, in the theatre, to the familiar taste of the audiences, and partly because they would be sung (and bought) separately afterwards. Similarly with another popular work of the period, *The Lily of Killarney* (1862) by a German pupil of Weber, Julius Benedict, who settled in Britain. The contemporaries of these composers included John Hullah, who had Charles Dickens as his librettist in his opera *The Village Coquettes*, but who achieved wider fame with such songs as *O that we two were maying* and *Three Fishers* ; and John Hatton, composer of the songs *To Anthea* and *Simon the Cellarer*.

The chief element besides ballads in the opera of Balfe and Wallace was the type of melody found in the fashionable Italian opera of the time. But Italian opera, though it remained a part of the London social " season " and patronised by Royalty, like the Derby, was not always approved of in more lofty-minded circles. The early and not-so-early Verdi was treated contemptuously by the London critics, and the operatic stage itself was suspected, probably with some justification, of being something less than strict in matters of sexual morality. This moral revulsion from opera can be clearly observed in the career of Jenny Lind, whose Swedish birth did not prevent her from becoming a typical Victorian Englishwoman. After triumphing on the stage in London and elsewhere, she renounced it and settled down to a blameless and non-theatrical life as a teacher and as the wife of the founder of the London Bach Choir.

In general we may observe in England a strictly musical turning-away from Italy and the opera towards Germany and the symphony. Having received Haydn in person, London took gradually to Beethoven's works, and was repeatedly visited by Spohr and Mendelssohn. (Spohr's claim to have introduced the practice of conducting with a baton at a London concert has, however, been shown to be based on faulty memory.) English composers in the eighteenth century—and indeed afterwards, as in the case of Balfe—had gone to study in Italy ; but nearly all those who won distinction later in the nineteenth century chose to study in Germany instead. William Sterndale Bennett (1816–75) studied in Leipzig, becoming a pupil of Mendelssohn and a friend of Schumann ; and his works, including four piano concertos, songs in German as well as English, and a still appealing overture called *The Naiad*, well show the direction of the new English style. So does the career of H. H. Pearson (1815–73) who, changing the spelling of his surname to Pierson, decided that residence in Germany offered greater scope for a creative musical life.

SULLIVAN

To Leipzig for study, on a scholarship, came the young Arthur Sullivan (1842–1900). His father was of Irish, his mother partly of Italian, descent. (Statements that he had Jewish ancestry are unsupported by any evidence.) One of his enthusiasms was for Schubert, and he and George Grove (the founder and first editor of the great *Dictionary of Music and Musicians* which bears his name) were responsible for unearthing in Vienna some of Schubert's lost *Rosamunde* music. Sullivan's own song *Orpheus with his lute* shows Schubertian influence, as his symphony and other orchestral works exemplify academic Germanic forms. In addition, Sullivan composed a serious opera, *Ivanhoe*, and had a number of large-scale biblical cantatas such as were expected of leading English composers and were also specially commissioned from figures abroad like Spohr, Gounod, and Mendelssohn.

Sullivan was indeed a serious-minded composer and is supposed to have been hurt when Dame Ethel Smyth (1858–1944) told him that his masterpiece was *The Mikado*. But she was right in seeing that Sullivan's operettas (as the " Savoy Operas " should properly be called) are full of distinguished musical workmanship as well as of theatrical effectiveness. Sullivan's stage collaboration with Gilbert began with *Thespis* (now lost), and first found success with *Trial by Jury* (1875), a one-act work, entirely sung and without dialogue. Then, by a decision which has never been given the consideration it deserves, Sullivan abandoned the all-sung pattern and embarked on the well-known series with spoken dialogue from *The Sorcerer* (1877) to *The Gondoliers* (1889). All were in varying degrees successful ; but the two works written afterwards, *Utopia Limited* and *The Grand Duke*, were not.

The mature Sullivan operettas show a greater harmonic subtlety and, on the whole, a greater complexity of structure. But this should not be exaggerated. It has often been pointed out that Sullivan used a little musical tag in *The Yeomen of the Guard* (1888) apparently to represent the Tower of London, as though he were attempting a Wagnerian leading-motive. Very much the same kind of recurring motive is found, however, in connection with the Lord Chancellor in *Iolanthe* (1882), while Sullivan's pet device of contrapuntally combining two apparently dissimilar tunes was never better displayed than in *How beautifully blue the sky* in *The Pirates of Penzance* (1879). The operettas have an element of burlesque and topical wit which they share with French operettas of Offenbach and others, popular in England at that time. But Sullivan sounds " solid " compared with Offenbach (" churchy " was Bernard Shaw's word), and Gilbert, by deliberately avoiding the " naughtiness " of contemporary French fare, won the lasting allegiance of a *Punch*-loving middle-class. Sullivan was knighted in 1883.

PARRY AND STANFORD

To the Scottish composer William Wallace (1860–1940—no relation of William Vincent Wallace) belongs the distinction of having written, in 1892, what is apparently the first British symphonic poem—*The Passing of Beatrice*. But the influence of Liszt, the inventor of this form, and of Wagner was slow to show itself in British music. As Mendelssohn had been the idol reigning in the era of Sterndale Bennett, so later it was Brahms who was worshipped in the era dominated by Sir Hubert Parry (1848–1918) and the Anglo-Irish Sir Charles Villiers Stanford (1852–1924). These two, with the Scottish Sir Alexander Mackenzie (1847–1935), were the architects of what is sometimes referred to by older historians as " the English renaissance ". Parry's unison song *Jerusalem* and his eight-part cantata *Blest Pair of Sirens* remain in the repertory, but other works by him and Stanford—save for a few fine songs—are but rarely heard.

The " renaissance " (if indeed we allow ourselves to use such a term at all) may be much more aptly dated from the emergence of Sir Edward Elgar (1857–1934) and Frederick Delius (1862–1934). These two men were dissimilar in so many ways, yet alike in owing almost nothing to formal instruction and in finding much early encouragement not in England but in Germany. The *Enigma Variations* (1899) and *The Dream of Gerontius* (1900) were the works that established Elgar. The former was dedicated to the great German conductor Hans Richter, "true artist and true friend", and the latter, after a disastrous first performance at Birmingham, found success at Düsseldorf. Of Elgar's later works, we may list his two symphonies (1908, 1911), his violin concerto (1910, dedicated to Kreisler), his "symphonic study" entitled *Falstaff* (1913), and (almost his only work of importance after the 1914–18 War) his cello concerto (1919).

In *The Dream of Gerontius* Elgar not only assimilated the power of Wagnerian scoring but also attempted the technique of Wagnerian construction—with themes recurring, combining, and being transformed. In *Falstaff* he showed himself the equal of Richard Strauss in the musical depiction of narrative and feeling, though the material reveals Elgar's own unmistakable fingerprints. His lyrically expansive violin concerto has remained in the international repertory. These works are heroic, the expression of a splendidly whole personality. It could be no surprise to learn that their composer also wrote the five *Pomp and Circumstance* Marches, from the first of which comes the tune to which the words "Land of Hope and Glory" were later added. Even though the cello concerto is superficially "intimate", it owes its peculiarly strong character to the heroic and spiritual elements which occasionally burst out in it.

Elgar's other works have not found such public acclamation. He embarked on a trilogy of oratorios, but finished only two, *The Apostles* and *The Kingdom*. These works contain much music of great beauty, but their episodic form has made them less easily acceptable to the general public, and they have not found favour with most critics. Work on a third symphony and an opera (based on Ben Jonson's play *The Devil is an Ass*) was interrupted by his death.

DELIUS

The career of Delius also crosses the century's boundary. Indeed, his first opera, *Irmelin* (composed 1890–92), never reached the stage until presented at Oxford in 1953 by Delius's never-failing champion, Sir Thomas Beecham. Neither this nor Delius's other operas have held the stage, though the popular *Walk to the Paradise Garden* is an orchestral excerpt from the opera *A Village Romeo and Juliet* (1900–01). Delius's popularity, now chiefly confined to England and certain parts of the Commonwealth, rests on his impressionistic orchestral pieces, capturing the most intimate of moods with a harmonic language and an instrumentation completely Delius's own. These include *Brigg Fair*, two *Dance Rhapsodies*, *On hearing the first cuckoo in spring*, *Summer night on the river*, and the *Irmelin* prelude (distinct from the opera)—all written after 1900. As early as 1896, however, he composed the original version for orchestra alone of *Appalachia : Variations on an Old Slave Song* (afterwards issued with chorus added). His chief choral works are *Sea Drift* (1903) and *A Mass of Life* (1905). Among his songs (in five languages) some show the influence of Grieg.

FOLK-SONG REVIVAL

The publication of Scottish, Irish, and (to a lesser degree) Welsh traditional songs had continued throughout the nineteenth century. George Thomson, an enterprising Edinburgh publisher, had persuaded Haydn and Beethoven to compose accompaniments for such songs ; and a Dublin publisher, George Power, embarked on a similar project, with Sir Henry Bishop and Sir John Stevenson in charge of musical arrangements and with Thomas Moore (1799–1852) to provide apposite words to the tunes collected. But Moore was himself a composer too, who wrote both the words and the music of *The Last Rose of Summer*—a song quoted and re-quoted in Flotow's opera *Martha* (1847).

Between 1855 and 1859 appeared two volumes called *Old English Popular Music*, edited by William Chappell. It was an antiquarian's work, concerned with discovering and collating written and printed sources. But in 1843, in a private edition, a country clergyman named John Broadwood had published traditional songs sung in Surrey and Sussex by farm-hands and others. Fifty years later his niece, Lucy Broadwood, collaborated with the musicologist J. A. Fuller-Maitland in publishing a volume of English County Songs. It is from the 1890s that the modern movement in the scholarly collecting and editing of English folk-song may be said to date, a movement immensely stimulated by the activity, from the early years of the new century, of Cecil Sharp (1859–1924). Approximately the same period saw the pioneering work of Arnold Dolmetsch (1858–1940), who established in England the practicability of reconstructing obsolete instruments such as the harpsichord, viols, and recorders, and of recovering the instrumental technique and musicological knowledge necessary to play the original music as the composers intended. The modern folk-music movement and the modern rehabilitation of " old music " are both to be related to a newly fashionable historicism in philosophical thinking, as distinct from an earlier idea of " progress " in music. Both are of fundamental importance in the next century's music-making in Britain.

About 1900, there arose a wave of enthusiasm for the scientific collection of folk-song (in which Cecil Sharp was a prime mover). There was a renewal of interest, too, in Purcell and in the madrigals and other music of the Elizabethan era.

TWO PIONEERS—VAUGHAN WILLIAMS AND HOLST

Ralph Vaughan Williams (1872–1958) was an assiduous collector of English folk-music in his younger days, and explicitly declared the indebtedness of his own music to the sense of liberation which he found in the rediscovery of English folk-music. This was the vital impulse to oppose to the basically Germanic ideas of form and melody which had all but captured English music. Yet his close associate Gustav Holst (1874–1934) managed to experience just the same kind of liberation without cultivating folk-music in Vaughan Williams's way.

Holst (he was of Swedish descent) was intellectually the more adventurous of the two. He mastered Sanskrit enough to make his own translations from the Hindu scriptures for songs, choral works, and the opera *Savitri* (composed 1908, produced 1916). *The Planets* (1914–16), an orchestral suite, had something quite new in English music in its use of irregular rhythms and its peculiar integration of pure musical content with orchestral colouring. Holst was a " fey " character and one who never seemed quite attached to this world. He was greatly attracted by the poetry and philosophy of the East, and much of his music gives direct and revealing expression to their characteristic unworldliness. His *Rig Veda* songs and the opera *Savitri* are eloquent examples of this refined emotion, and his *Ode to Death* breathes an ineffable comfort and longing. The choral *Hymn of Jesus* is one of the most striking expressions in music of the mystery of God made Man.

The Planets is Holst's greatest orchestral work. Written for a large orchestra—including bass-oboe, euphonium, and an enormous battery of percussion instruments—the music is nevertheless scored with meticulous clarity. The seven movements range from the brutal, insistent rhythms of *Mars* to the whispered ecstasy of *Neptune*. *Venus* is all tender serenity, *Mercury* the exhilaration of speed, *Jupiter* good-humoured merry-making, *Saturn* a poignant picture of old age and *Uranus* a brilliant magician's portrait. Towards the end of his life Holst adopted a much more austere idiom, best seen in his orchestral piece *Egdon Heath*. Ill-health may largely account for his failure quite to bridge the gap between originality of conception and effectiveness in performance, a gap which largely accounts for the fact that only three of his works retain their place in the general British repertory—*The Planets*, the *St. Paul's Suite*, and the ballet music from the opera *The Perfect Fool*.

Vaughan Williams's music captured a far greater place in the affections of the Anglo-Saxon public. (Elsewhere only his *Fantasia on a Theme of Tallis* (1910) has achieved regular performance.) His succession of nine symphonies, the last of them finished at the age of eighty-five, constitute a truly remarkable body of musical thought. *A Sea Symphony* (1910) is in effect a four-movement cantata on poetry by Whitman ; *A London Symphony* (1914) and *A Pastoral Symphony* (1922) have something of impressionism in them, and the latter shows the melodic "liberation" afforded by folk-song. The fourth symphony (1935) was new in its harsh urgency, a mood recaptured and intensified in the very successful sixth symphony (1947). The fifth (1943) shows the composer in a very characteristic mood of meditation, and much of the material belongs to the same austere vein as that explored in the subsequent morality *The Pilgrim's Progress*. The sixth reflects the spiritual and emotional upheavals of the war years, while the exquisitely beautiful finale suggests an enigmatic mood of desolation. The seventh (*Sinfonia Antartica*), eighth, and ninth were all works of substance, though they did not show any new side in the composer's music. The seventh was largely based on the music which Vaughan Williams had written to the film *Scott of the Antarctic* (1949), and the fact that he took up film music at the age of nearly seventy, as a contribution to the patriotic effort of the 1939–45 war, is some sign of the catholic use to which he put his musical gifts. The *Antartica* is the least "symphonic" of the nine, and some musicians regret its inclusion in this series, feeling it to be more justly regarded as a tone-poem. For the mouth-organ he composed a *Romance* with strings and piano accompaniment, and for the tuba a concerto. He wrote a distinguished ballet score in *Job* (1931), but his persistent attempt to earn professional success on the opera stage failed. Nevertheless, *Riders to the Sea*—in which he set Synge's play almost word for word in a "conversational" idiom comparable to Mussorgsky's in *Boris Godunov* or Debussy's in *Pelléas et Mélisande*—maintains a hold, chiefly among amateurs, on both sides of the Atlantic. Vaughan Williams was a late developing artist, earning his chief fame after he was fifty ; but it is worth remembering that the songs *Linden Lea* and *Silent Noon*, showing complete assurance in an earlier but still fresh-seeming style, both date from before 1910.

BROADCASTING

The character of Vaughan Williams's output reflected certain changes in the demand for music. The commissioning of scores for ballet, and even more for films, brought a new factor into composers' lives from the mid-1930s. A yet bigger change resulted from the establishment of the British

Broadcasting Company (later Corporation) in 1922, and with the wide circulation of gramophone records. At the same time, home music-making declined, and the writing of popular " ballads " by serious composers became less as Tin Pan Alley established the domination of American commercial popular music in the " light " field.

The popularity of symphonic performances grew steadily between the two world wars. The B.B.C. Symphony Orchestra (1930) and the London Philharmonic Orchestra (1932) were the first British orchestras to engage their players on a salaried basis, as distinct from an arrangement of paying by the concert. The B.B.C. not only familiarised a wide public with the existing repertory, but conscientiously encouraged new works. The gramophone industry explored a narrower repertory (considerably less narrow after the coming of long-playing records in 1950) but was equally important in popularising the actual sound of orchestral music. During World War II, a commercial impresario actually found it worth while to send the London Philharmonic Orchestra on tour as part of a twice-nightly entertainment, playing nothing but serious music.

The twentieth century thus altered the outlook for British musicians. At no previous time could even minor composers have become known primarily by their orchestral music. Those cultivating an expansive late-Romantic idiom included Sir Granville Bantock (1868–1946), with such works as the overture *Pierrot of the Minute* and the tone-poem *Fifine at the Fair*, and Sir Arnold Bax (1883–1953), whose shorter works (notably *Tintagel* and the *Overture to a Picaresque Comedy*) won a popularity denied to his seven symphonies. It would be interesting to know whether Samuel Coleridge-Taylor (1875–1912), the son of an English mother and a West African father, would have developed as an orchestral composer but for his early death. The monument he did leave is the popular choral trilogy *Hiawatha*, a work of considerable stature, both as a setting of words with a ceaseless melodic flow and as a model in the difficult art of providing an effective orchestral accompaniment to large choral forces. Another composer struck by early death (he was killed in action) was George Butterworth (1885–1916) ; his poetic gifts and the influence of the folk-song movement are apparent in his orchestral works *The Banks of Green Willow* and *A Shropshire Lad*, the latter based on material from a song-cycle. Housman was the favourite poet for this, as Tennyson had been of an earlier, generation of composers.

SONG WRITERS

John Ireland (*b.* 1879) has been a reticent composer (no symphony, no opera, no ballet), but notable for a personal romantic idiom often suggesting a tender nostalgia. His piano concerto strikes an individual note, and he is one of the few British composers of his generation to write a distinguished body of solo piano music. His numerous songs include *Sea Fever* (1913), the last song by a " serious " British composer to become genuinely popular; but other songs by Ireland are less extrovert in appeal. In a remarkable cycle *We'll to the woods no more* the songs are followed by a meditative piano solo which closes the work. Rutland Boughton (1878–1960) made a gallant but unsuccessful attempt to establish a home for English opera at Glastonbury in Somerset ; and his own chief work, the opera *The Immortal Hour* (based on Celtic legend), achieved an astonishing London run of 216 continuous performances in 1922. The songs and piano music of Cyril Scott (*b.* 1879) once earned him the unhelpful nickname of " the English Debussy " ; and although at present out of fashion, his work has a strikingly individual power of capturing a mood in music.

Roger Quilter (1877–1953) was the composer of that neat orchestral diversion on nursery rhymes entitled *A Children's Overture*, but his work was chiefly in songs—many to words by Shakespeare and by Herrick. He had a remarkable genius for melodic beauty in the setting of words, but was not driven by necessity fully to exercise his great talent.

Schubert and Parry were perhaps the chief influences on a composer who tilled a fine but rather narrow garden of English song, Ivor Gurney (1890–1937). The apparently diverse influences of Elizabethan song and the music of Delius nourished the gifts of Peter Warlock (1894–1930), who also wrote about music under his real name, Philip Heseltine. His songs are sometimes delicately intimate, like *Sleep* ; or, like *The Countryman*, have an honest vulgar jollity that links them with the genuinely popular art of the music-hall.

E. J. Moeran (1894–1950), not Irish but attracted by Irish lore, showed a lyrical gift in songs to poems by Seumas O'Sullivan and others. The traditional English type of festival cantata, which had proliferated in the nineteenth century, was now becoming much rarer ; but two post-1945 examples by workmanlike composers were *Hymnus Paradisi* by Herbert Howells (*b.* 1892), who has written much sensitive religious music, of simple and direct appeal but couched in a vocal style which is not easy to perform, and *The Hound of Heaven*, a setting of Francis Thompson's poem by Maurice Jacobson (*b.* 1896).

XXIII

THE TWENTIETH-CENTURY REVOLUTION

W E have already noted the purely French reaction against the music of the nineteenth century, and especially Wagner, whose music was felt as an overwhelming burden of orchestral volume and philosophical pretension. But there was a much more violent and far-reaching reaction to come in Central Europe, and one in which technical, musical change reflected much wider and deeper changes—psychological, sociological, and political. The enigmatic course of music in this century is often explained away as a series of technical developments ; but these are only a part of the complete picture. The reasons for the growth and decline of any form of art are manifold. Social, political, and economic factors, the composer's attitude to society, the stable or fluid state of compositional techniques, all these are only some of the forces which have governed the results of creative thought at any given moment of musical history.

THE COMPOSER AND SOCIETY

The chaotic state of Europe in the twentieth century has had its repercussions on music. The rise of Communism and Fascism, the race campaign against the Jews, two catastrophic wars, the menace of world-wide death from atomic " fall-out "—these are some of the exterior forces which have shaped our music. The composer's attitude to society has also been uneasy. Not content to be mere servants of the church or humble lackeys to patrons, composers have developed their own personalities to such an extreme of super-individualism that they have lost contact with to-day's mass audiences. Many accept as a fact that, for the time being, their music can be significant only to a small group of musical intellectuals, and that if it is ever universally accepted, it will be long after they are dead.

The situation became critical at the beginning of this century because of the extremes reached by the two great nineteenth-century musical forms —the symphony and the symphonic poem. Not only did the huge proportions of these forms under Mahler and Strauss suggest the obesity of decadence, but the basis of these enormous structures—tonal logic and clarity—was being gradually undermined. The late romantics found their ideal expression in melodies and harmonies which contained ever-increasing proportions of chromatic elements. As long ago as 1865, Wagner's *Tristan* had begun the movement towards chromaticism which through Wolf, Mahler, Reger, and Strauss reached the force of an avalanche, threatening to sweep away in chaos the then-known foundation of musical form—tonality.

SCHOENBERG'S EARLY WORKS

This was the situation when Arnold Schoenberg (1874–1951) began writing music in his native city of Vienna. His early works such as *Verklärte Nacht*, op. 4 (1899), and the symphonic poem *Pelleas and Melisande*, op. 5 (1903), follow the mainstream of late romanticism, but here and there is a presage of things to come—the tendency to obscure harmonic progressions with notes which no amount of theorising could justify, and which he called "roving harmonies". The stage was set for one of the most extraordinary revolutions man has made in the art of music—that of *pantonality*, or as it is usually miscalled, atonality. The word "atonal", meaning "nontonal", was at first coined as a condemnatory term, equivalent to "nonmusic". However, among musicians, "atonal" is by now synonymous with "pantonal", and it is used in the following chapters in this sense : a tonality which includes the whole of chromatic "space". "Atonality" is in fact a complete misnomer. Whenever two or more sounds are combined and woven together, harmonic relationships are formed ; and whether they can be classified in the terms of traditional harmony or no, those harmonic relationships exist. There is a world of super-tonality, an all-inclusive "pantonality", which spans the enormous space between diatonic harmony on the one hand and sheer chaos on the other.

"ATONALITY"

Schoenberg, and others such as Scriabin and Hauer, divined the presence of this pantonal world, but Schoenberg's approach must not be regarded from a merely technical angle. (Josef Hauer (1883–1959) developed his own "atonal" system independently of Schoenberg.) Pantonality would never have been used, perhaps not even discovered, without the propelling force of some artistic movement which demanded such new, revolutionary means. During the first years of the century, Schoenberg associated more and more with the German *avant-garde* of writers and painters (Kandinsky, Klee, and Marc among them) who created the Expressionist movement, which became the preponderant artistic tendency in Germany until about 1925 and has remained one of the two major artistic movements of the century. The expressionist refuses to express himself in objective, realistic terms. His is an introvert art, for he is in revolt against the outer world. His art is the expression of his own unique inner world, his elemental self, in terms which bear little or no relation to exteriorities. In music and painting this usually means that the artist expresses his inner world through abstractions which are outward manifestations of his psychological states. Inasmuch as these abstractions bear no resemblance to the " realistic " shapes and sounds which have been previously experienced, expressionism represents a direct revolution against tradition.

It will be seen now how the composer, establishing himself as a super-individualist in revolt against an industrialised, collectivist society, found in the expressionist movement those æsthetic principles most in accordance with his ideals, and how the new pantonal world furnished him with the very language that he needed. Schoenberg's penetration into the realm of pantonality, however, was not achieved overnight. It was a gradual process spread over the first decade of this century, beginning in *Pelleas and Melisande* with the occasional construction of chords built in fourths rather than by the traditional superimposition of thirds. In his *Chamber Symphony*, op. 9 for fifteen solo instruments (1906), Schoenberg begins the work with a chord built up in fourths, and immediately follows it with a melodic form of the same construction. Both these vertical and horizontal forms play predominant rôles in the whole work, and this use of material in vertical and horizontal forms anticipates a unifying principle of his " serial " music of almost twenty years later.

This *Chamber Symphony* was a deliberate reaction against the titanic orchestral forms of the post-Wagnerians. The large orchestra is reduced to a group of solo instruments, and an entire symphonic conception is compressed into one movement of only moderate proportions. Schoenberg's reaction against the enormous orchestral forces of his predecessors was so acute that, with one exception, he never wrote a work for large orchestra for the next twenty years. This exception was the *Five Pieces for Orchestra*, op. 16 (1908), but in this solo instruments predominate and the volume of orchestral sound is never excessive. In fact, the third piece rarely exceeds *pianissimo*.

Schoenberg's exploration of pantonal space, continued in the mono-drama *Erwartung* and the musical drama *Die glückliche Hand*, reached full fruition in 1911 with his *Six Small Piano Pieces*, op. 19. These small piano pieces form such an excellent introduction to Schoenberg's music, and illustrate so many facets of his expressionist style, that they are recommended to any piano player of medium ability.

Each piece is very brief. There are mere fragments of melody, brief episodes, silences, phrases which are no sooner formed than abandoned. There is little of a traditional character in these expressionistic melodic shapes. They have an unfamiliar, almost " abstract " design. To increase this " abstract " quality, the composer has adopted a principle of " perpetual variation " which prevents the repetition of any melody or rhythm. As the music progresses, everything is newly created and then discarded, never to be used again. Only in the second and sixth pieces is there any form of repetition, in the former a rhythm, in the latter a ghostly, echoing chord. The final bars of the sixth piece are characteristic : an " abstract " melodic shape, with a typically Schoenbergian leap of over two octaves, betrays his striving for intense expression, and rhythmic displacements destroy an obvious metre.

THE DANGER OF CHAOS

The absolute freedom with which such pieces were written, the elimination of any traditional discourse or form, is a result of Schoenberg's obedience to the expressionist postulate—" nothing must hinder the free expression of the subjective ego ". It was therefore, one might say, blindfolded and following only his creative instinct that Schoenberg entered an unexplored world in which sounds obeyed laws which were still unknown. There was the risk of falling into an abyss of absolute chaos. Without any firm principle of construction it was extremely difficult, if not impossible, to compose an extended piece. Schoenberg was aware of this, and he admitted that for this reason he was led to base most of his compositions of this period on a poetic text. In fact, of the eighteen works composed between *Pelleas and Melisande* (1903) and the year 1914 (the period of his style of absolutely *free* atonalism), there are as many as thirteen which depend on a literary text for their formal organisation—*Gurrelieder* ; *Eight songs*, op. 6 ; *Six orchestral songs*, op. 8 ; *String Quartet* No. 2 (with soprano solo), op. 10 ; *Two Ballads*, op. 12 ; the choral *Friede auf Erden*, op. 13 ; *Two Lieder*, op. 14 ; *Das Buch der hängenden Gärten*, op. 15 ; *Erwartung*, op. 17 ; *Die glückliche Hand*, op. 18 ; *Herzgewächse*, op. 20 ; *Pierrot Lunaire*, op. 21 ; *Four orchestral songs*, op. 22.

The most typical, and at the same time most disconcerting, of these works is *Pierrot Lunaire*, composed in 1912. This work and Stravinsky's *Rite of Spring* (written about the same time) have probably engendered more discussion, more upheaval in musical thinking, than any other compositions. But *Pierrot Lunaire* can now be seen in its right perspective and accepted as a classic of its period.

" PIERROT LUNAIRE "

It is a " melodrama ", a setting of twenty-one poems for female voice, piano, flute (doubling piccolo), clarinet (doubling bass clarinet), violin (doubling viola), and violoncello. The complete instrumental group is used only in six pieces ; in the others sometimes only one or two instruments are used.

The most disturbing factor in *Pierrot Lunaire* is the atmosphere of intense unreality, the expressionistic creation of a nightmare world where, in a climate of acute tension, the composer expresses the most naked sense of solitude and human desperation that a musician has ever achieved. This atmosphere is suggested not only by the instrumental background (a tracery of free atonal writing of great beauty), but by means of a new means of expression that Schoenberg created for the vocalist. This was *Sprechgesang* or " speech-song ". The score indicates a definite pitch and rhythm for each syllable, but the actual note indicated must be merely touched and not held by the singer. The intonation fluctuates between notes, with continuous crescendos and diminutions of volume, so that an equilibrium between singing and natural speech is maintained.

Though the instrumental accompaniment largely consists of atonal free writing in " abstract " patterns, according to the expressionist principle of perpetual variation, some movements are written in highly organised polyphony. For example, No. 17 (*Parody*) has complex inverted canons, No. 8 (*Night*) is a passacaglia, and No. 18 (*The Moonspot*) consists of a mirror canon (half-way through, the canon turns backward to end in a reversal of its beginning) combined with a two-part fugue and the same fugue in augmentation.

This revival of renaissance and baroque contrapuntal forms, which later became such a characteristic feature of the Schoenberg school, was probably not so much Schoenberg's free choice as some would have us think. Realising that music written with a sort of Freudian " free association " could not have a satisfactory formal structure, he had to look for forms which would help him construct pieces of adequate proportions. As eighteenth- and nineteenth-century forms depended on tonal and thematic clarity, they were of no use to him, and his only alternative was to revive the old contrapuntal forms which could be used in an atonal setting. Even so, this formal solution was not completely satisfactory, since contrapuntal forms were opposed to the stylistic freedom which was the expressionist artist's first aim.

" COMPOSITION WITH TWELVE NOTES "

Soon after *Pierrot Lunaire* Schoenberg's activity as a composer ceased for almost ten years. During the 1914–18 war he served in the Austrian army, and it was not until 1923 that new compositions were forthcoming. In these years he searched for a new principle which would serve to organise twelve-note space, a principle which would replace the classic unifying function of tonality, and serve in formal, melodic, and harmonic organisation. Realising that in his own works before 1914 he had tended to make consistent use of the total chromatic spectrum (*i.e.* all twelve notes of the chromatic scale were kept in perpetual movement) and that in his more contrapuntal writing he tended to use definite sequences of intervals which remained unchanged however much they were transposed, he devised a " method of composition with twelve notes ". In this method, frequently called " serial composition " or " dodecaphony ", the whole of the composition is derived from a series of twelve different notes which thus include the total chromatic scale. Used horizontally, the series forms *melody*, vertically it forms *harmony* ; or used in two or more horizontal streams, melody and harmony may result simultaneously. But the important function of the series is that, by ensuring a constant flow of all components of twelve-tone space, it guarantees a perpetual *pantonal equilibrium*. The twelve-tone method is a simplification, clarification, and logical culmination of Schoenberg's pre-1914 style of free dissonance.

Schoenberg was not the first to use all twelve notes of the chromatic scale melodically. Mozart, Liszt, and Strauss had all done so before him. But he was the first to evolve a method of composition by which *all* the material of a work was derived from a series of twelve notes. He first did this in the last movement of his *Five Pieces for piano*, op. 23 (1923). In the *Waltz* from these pieces the right-hand part plays the series in the first four bars, while at the same time the left hand divides the twelve notes into two groups—notes 6 to 12 are first grouped together, and then notes 1 to 5.

After his op. 23, almost all Schoenberg's works were written according to this serial method. The new form of composition seems at first to have produced results which are not always of great musical value. A certain cold academic quality is felt in some of his early twelve-note works, and Schoenberg seems to have ignored the possibilities of unifying the atonal resultants of serialism with the traditional tonal language. But serial composition does not in fact necessarily imply "atonal chaos", and certain tonal elements can easily be included in the sound patterns, as is evident from the beginning of the *Adagio* in Schoenberg's third string quartet. Here, apart from a few roving harmonies (which in any case can be logically explained away), the music easily fits into tonal components, and the result is not very different from that obtained by using a system of traditional chromatic harmony.

By the time Schoenberg wrote his vast *Variations for Orchestra*, op. 31 (1927–28), he had brought his method of twelve-note composition to a state of absolute completion. In only four years he was able to write a work of large proportions which explored a great variety of technical procedures. This was indeed a remarkable feat, even though the music is often heavily mechanical and sometimes betrays a pedagogic train of thought rather than fantasy and inspiration.

TEACHING AND EXILE

From 1925 to 1933 Schoenberg taught at the Prussian Academy of Arts in Berlin, but the Nazi campaign against the Jews forced him to fly for safety to America. After a period in New York and Boston, he went to California University in 1935, remaining in Los Angeles till his death in 1951.

Like other composers who have found refuge in America (Bartók, Hindemith, Stravinsky, Milhaud, etc.), Schoenberg soon discovered how necessary it was to write music which would be more easily understood by the American public. The days of a public of European intelligentsia were gone, and with his first American music—a *Suite in G* for string orchestra, designed specially for students, and comprising an *overture, adagio, minuet, gavotte,* and *jig*—he made an inconspicuous beginning.

From this moment, Schoenberg's artistic outlook changed. Up to 1930 he had striven with all his power to create a new musical language in which all traditional influences were apparently rejected. But after his arrival in America, he seems to have changed course completely and to have sought a means of uniting his new language with tradition.

His first major American work, the violin concerto, op. 36 (1936), thus begins a new epoch of "reconstruction". Schoenberg, faced at the age of sixty-two with the necessity of making contact with a less cultivated public, set about bridging the gulf between his twelve-note manner and the nineteenth-century traditional language which his new listeners could understand. In this concerto we therefore find lyrical melodies of more classical shape, harmonies which are less astringently atonal and more mellifluously consonant, and rhythmic configurations of classic clarity and simplicity.

But the work is highly virtuosic, and Schoenberg did not abandon for one moment his principle of " composition with twelve notes ".

This American period saw the composition of many other works which appeal to a much wider public than his European works. Typical examples are the piano concerto, op. 42, the string trio, op. 45, and the *Survivor from Warsaw*, op. 46. Some critics see in this more accessible Schoenberg a falling-off of his powers of invention. But perhaps the truth is that in America Schoenberg found a new equilibrium, the equilibrium of complete maturity, in which the great revolutionist at last reconciled his urge for innovation with an inner need for human communication.

His two biggest works, the opera *Moses und Aron* and the oratorio *Jacob's Ladder*, were still incomplete when he died in Los Angeles in 1951. The opera had its first stage performance at Zurich in 1957 ; the oratorio, completed by his pupil Winfried Zillig, was performed in Vienna in 1961.

SCHOENBERG'S PUPILS

The enormous revolution in music which Schoenberg initiated was furthered by two of his pupils, Berg and Webern, who in many ways reveal no less originality than their teacher. It is an extraordinary coincidence not only that they were all three born in Vienna within a short span of years, but that they were born with the exact artistic temperament and intelligence necessary to complete and bring to fruition just those aspects of Schoenberg's art which he himself did not develop fully. Each expanded Schoenberg's innovations in his own way, and in this manner the " Viennese School " accomplished an artistic task of unusual importance.

Both Berg and Webern began studying with Schoenberg about 1904, that is, at the beginning of his exploration of pantonality. From then on, as Schoenberg made each discovery, Berg undertook the task of associating the new development with tradition, while Webern examined it with a view to carrying the new revolutionary idea to its furthest conclusions. It might be very roughly said that Webern was a radical, and Berg a conservative ; and each developed Schoenberg's innovations along completely divergent lines.

ALBAN BERG

Alban Berg (1885–1935) was intensely human. His music lives by the strength and depth of its emotional content. He was an expressionist, and his music expresses a more neurotic personality than Webern's or Schoenberg's. His art is filled with dark melancholy and lacerating anguish, and is deeply coloured by the heavy, brooding atmosphere of late romanticism.

But Berg's expressionism is couched in less abstract terms than Schoenberg's. The shape of phrases and the rhythmic configurations are often late romantic in style, and therefore easily comprehensible to the average listener. The harmonic content too is less unfamiliar. Even when Berg used the twelve-note method of composition, he frequently designed the note patterns so that tonal elements were predominant.

" WOZZECK "

Berg did not produce a large number of works, but each was of singular artistic worth. His most famous is the opera *Wozzeck*, written between 1917 and 1921—a work of extraordinary importance in the modern theatre. The subject of *Wozzeck* is sordid, but Berg brings deep compassion to this study of a mentally under-developed soldier, victimised by the society he serves and betrayed by the woman he loves. He murders her and then drowns himself in a pond while their child plays innocently at the water's edge. There is no happy ending, no ray of hope even, for *Wozzeck* portrays the plight of the down-trodden waifs of humanity. Instead of following the Wagnerian concept of a " through-composed " opera, Berg chose to set each of the fifteen scenes in a distinct and separate musical form. He thus re-introduced the fashion for operas composed of a succession of different numbers (which tends to interrupt the dramatic flow) ; but the success of *Wozzeck* depends on an entirely different factor. In this opera the various forms for each scene (scherzo, rondo, pavane, gavotte, etc.) are so skilfully fused and unified in style that the listener is never aware of them. They exist only on paper. The success of *Wozzeck* derives instead from the way the music, moment by moment, intensifies the action, without imposing its own presence. In Berg's words—" I had no other intention . . . than to design music which would be aware, at every instant, of its duty of serving the drama."

Berg wrote little chamber music, but his *Lyric Suite* for string quartet has a passionate, dramatic quality which again reflects his intense humanity. The impressiveness of this music lies not only in its emotive values but also in the extremely highly organised forms through which this emotion is expressed. The *Lyric Suite*, written in 1925–26, belongs to the period when Berg was making the transition to serial composition. Only about half of the work is written in the twelve-note method, but there is no stylistic difference between the parts of the work written by serial methods and those which were not. For in his " free " style Berg was already exploring the possibilities of total chromaticism, and his adoption of the twelve-note method was natural and apparently effortless.

Contrary to his usual practice, Berg wrote his violin concerto (1935) with feverish haste. The work was dedicated to the memory of Manon Gropius, Mahler's step-daughter. But perhaps Berg was aware too that in writing this great lyrical vision with its religious apotheosis (his other works have no touch of mysticism) he was also writing his own requiem. Soon after its completion he was to die from blood poisoning at the tragically early age of fifty. Berg's violin concerto is considered by many to be one of the masterpieces of this century. It is one enormous arch of lyrical melody in which Berg reveals a new maturity. The music is less dense, simpler and clearer than any of his other works, and through his mastery of the twelve-note method Berg seems to establish what has been called a new tonal order. Certainly this work represents a remarkable reconciliation between the old tonality and the new pantonality or "atonality" in a most remarkable way. It should be noted that at its most emotional moment Berg quotes a Bach chorale; the light-shedding effect of each entrance of the chorale has undoubtedly made Berg's expression clearer to most listeners than he could have done in his own musical language.

ANTON VON WEBERN

Anton von Webern (1883–1945) was the antithesis of Berg. His mind was exploratory, analytical, lucidly exact. Like Berg's, his artistic approach was subjective, but he strove towards a degree of absolute interiorisation which was without precedent in music. From the beginning of his studies with Schoenberg, he took a more extremist attitude towards his master's innovations than Schoenberg himself. Webern's renunciation of traditional articulation and forms was dramatically thorough, and his full acceptance of atonality complete and permanent. His work touches the extreme of absolute abstraction. Furthermore, his life's work is remarkably consistent, and he never showed the slightest tendency, as did Berg and Schoenberg, to turn back and incorporate traditional elements into his style.

Only Webern's op. 1, a *Passacaglia* (1908), is comparatively traditional. After this, he began the drive towards those radical ideals—supreme economy, absolute brevity commensurate with maximum expression, and stylistic rarification—which are permanent characteristics of all his work.

His abandonment of tonality was so complete, his creation of an abstract art so absolute, that his instrumental works soon reached the ultimate point of brevity. Thus *Three Small Pieces* for cello and piano, op. 11 (1914), are so concise that the second movement lasts only ten seconds, the third is only ten bars long and has only eight notes for the cello and twelve for the piano. This extreme brevity reflected the complete lack of tonal and formal

FRANÇOIS POULENC

Houston Rogers

ARTHUR HONEGGER
(1892–1955)

Barratt's Photo Press Ltd.

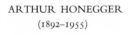

SERGEI PROKOFIEV
(1891–1953)

DMITRY SHOSTAKOVICH

structures which caused Webern to abandon instrumental music for the next thirteen years—until after his adoption of the twelve-tone technique. During these years all Webern's works were for voice and instruments, with the text functioning as a unifying factor and facilitating more extended compositions.

Even after Webern began composing with the twelve-note method in 1924, his output was still predominantly vocal; but he is known almost exclusively for his instrumental works. His writing for the voice presents formidable difficulties and few attractions for a singer, which has meant that over half of Webern's work is neglected.

Of the instrumental works, the symphony for small orchestra, op. 21 (1928), is best known. Webern wrote very few pieces for full orchestra. His æsthetic demanded quiet, subdued sounds, and he preferred solo instrumental colours to a mixed palette. The symphony requires only a clarinet, bass clarinet, two horns, harp, and a small group of strings without double bass. The work has only two movements, lasts only ten minutes, and the score has fewer notes per page than any other symphony ever written. This last is a notable feature of Webern, who attached great value to silence. Sounds are poised sparsely, often in isolation. Like Mallarmé before a virgin sheet of paper, Webern felt respect, even awe, at the thought of breaking silence.

In the symphony the discourse is extremely fragmentary, and melodic phrases are seldom more than a tiny group of two or three notes. Webern puts immense value on the single sound, be it a cello *pizzicato*, a violin harmonic or a horn *sforzando*. The thread of sound passes from one instrument to another, creating a " melody of timbres " (*Klangfarbenmelodie*) which assumes as much importance as any other composed factor. The first movement is a highly complex combination of two canons. The second, comprising a theme, seven variations and coda, is a miracle of economy. The theme is a mere eleven bars, but so constructed that the last half mirrors the rhythmic configuration of the first. Each variation and the coda, also, is only eleven bars long, and in every case consists of only five and a half bars of music with their " mirror ". The ninety bars of this movement contain the maximum of variation within the minimum space.

Construction by mirror patterns and perpetual variation are Webern's favourite procedures. His Variations for piano, op. 27 (1936), use this technique in the most extreme degree. The opening bars of this work give some idea of the way Webern composed by the application of logic with mathematical exactitude. First the right hand plays notes 1 to 6 of the series, and the left hand notes 7 to 12. In the following bars the construction is reflected as in a mirror; the music turns backwards and ends as it began. But notice too the note groupings. In the first half the right hand plays two notes together followed by one, and then the " mirror " of this plan—one note followed by two. The left hand, on the contrary, turns this design inside out—1:2 followed by 2:1. The whole of the first movement of the composition continues on this pattern, with successions of mirror forms constructed equally logically.

This cerebral approach to creation may seem execrable, this rationalist æsthetic the very negation of the spirit of abandon and artistic freedom with which the public associates the idea of artistic creation. But it may be argued that all great art results from the imaginative manipulation of certain basic factors which have probably been conceived in moments of extreme illumination. If we take, for instance, that miracle of lyric beauty, the first movement of Beethoven's " Pastoral " symphony, we find it to consist of an ingenious manipulation of the three melodic " cells " which compose its opening phrase. One of these " cells " is repeated no less than 113 times during the movement. The " cerebral " quality of Webern's workmanship means no more than that, like Beethoven, he knew what artistic results he wanted, and how to arrive at it in the most precise way. He was a musician of most profound sensibility ; the sound-world he created has a unique delicacy and other-worldliness. If he could create such a world, and at the same time establish such remarkable abstract note-patterns, we must not condemn the result because of the system. Nor, on the other hand, must we let the admirable logic of the system prejudice our appreciation of the music in its favour. Webern himself stressed that it is the music which matters, and not how it is written. Those who are not convinced that a great work of art can result from cerebral manipulation will argue that in Beethoven's case his repetitions and manipulations of small phrases were mentally unconscious, whereas Webern could not have achieved the mathematical exactness of his art-form without conscious calculation.

Webern's most important works include two cantatas, the Variations for orchestra, op. 30, and *Das Augenlicht* for chorus and orchestra. Although performances are rare, his music has been a very potent influence on post-war composers. During the Nazi régime he suffered years of artistic isolation, and when he died in 1945 it was as the victim of a tragic error—after the war was over, he was shot by an American sentry while smoking a last cigarette in the cool of the evening.

IGOR STRAVINSKY

The work of Igor Stravinsky (*b.* 1882) is in complete contrast to that of the Viennese School. Schoenberg, Berg, and Webern followed a straight path to a definite goal, with little deviation from their course. In comparison with this unswerving progress, Stravinsky's career appears to have lacked direction, his stylistic chopping and changing to have been the product of a grasshopper mind. But if the Viennese School had been less inflexible, we might have been the richer for it ; and Stravinsky's reckless, headlong pursuit of stylistic novelty has given us an enormously rich catalogue of works, each wonderfully individual and fresh. We are indeed fortunate that Stravinsky has possessed the " power to renounce ". His *Firebird* (1910) was an enormous success. He could have written a dozen similar works and reaped a big reward, but he renounced such an easy future, leaving the rôle of imitation to lesser composers, and moving on himself to new pastures. Stravinsky's is a mind extremely sensitive to every new artistic possibility and each new æsthetic environment, and if his frequent changes of style have often been frustrating, they have hindered rather than helped his career. It has even been tempting to attribute them to a deliberate attempt on his part to achieve notoriety, to make each work a *succès de scandale*. Viewed in retrospect, however, it seems certain that Stravinsky has been quite genuinely susceptible to the many different national, social, and artistic influences which have impinged on his sensibility. His fertile imagination has reacted as spontaneously to New York's Broadway and the negro jazz band as to his native Russian tradition. Pagan rites, Greek myths, Orthodoxy and Catholicism, Japanese lore, European fables, French impressionism—these are only a small selection of subjects and styles which have fascinated him and stimulated his creative mind. He is a man who has lived to the full all the main æsthetic experiences of this century. No wonder the story of his career reads like a compendium of all the stylistic and technical developments of the epoch.

Stravinsky was born near St. Petersburg in 1882. His father, who sang at the Imperial Opera there, made him study law, and it was only at the age of twenty that he definitely decided to be a musician. His only composition studies were with Rimsky-Korsakov, during the two years prior to the latter's death in 1908. His first big work, the Symphony in E flat, though modelled on the style of Glazunov reveals a preponderant influence of Wagner. The song cycle *Le Faune et la Bergère*, and the orchestral *Fantastic Scherzo* and *Fireworks* reflect the influence of the new French impressionistic school of Dukas, Debussy, and Ravel. But in *Fireworks* Stravinsky's personality emerges for the first time. Themes are cut with crystal clarity, the rhythm has an explosive exuberance, accents are displaced, bar-lines irregular, and the whole work reveals an exciting dynamic turbulence.

DIAGHILEV AND " FIREBIRD "

A single performance of the *Fantastic Scherzo* and *Fireworks* at St. Petersburg in 1909 convinced Diaghilev that he had found talent ; he then commissioned Stravinsky to write a new ballet. This was *Firebird*, and its first performance in Paris during June 1910 raised Stravinsky overnight to the rank of a celebrity. From then on Stravinsky became absorbed into Western society. During the following years his association with Diaghilev's Russian Ballet produced amazingly rich results, but in reality this " Russian " ballet ceased to be parochially Russian and developed a predominantly Western outlook. Stravinsky was cut off from Russia for the rest of his life and only returned for a brief visit in 1914.

But though *Firebird* is probably Stravinsky's best-known music, it is not really a typically Stravinskian work. It is an action ballet, but the music is mostly descriptive, and in the more veiled atmospheres one can trace the influence of Debussy and Ravel. Harmonic and melodic structures have sometimes the voluptuous chromaticism of Scriabin, the melody of the *Ronde des princesses* has a Tchaikovskian pathos, and the grand finale is in the manner of the Russian nationalist school. *Kashchey's Infernal Dance*, on the other hand, is true Stravinsky. Themes are concise, lugubrious yet energetic ; the musical discourse is formed of sharply defined blocks, sculptured with powerful lines ; the brass interject stabbing rhythms ; and the whole movement careers forward on a wildly pulsating rhythm, which is more vital than any other musical factor—melodic, harmonic, or contrapuntal. The orchestration shuns romantic sensuality in favour of crude, pungent timbres.

" PETRUSHKA " AND " THE RITE OF SPRING "

It was the Stravinsky of the *Infernal Dance* who wrote the next great ballets—*Petrushka* (1911) and *The Rite of Spring* (1913). The latter is one of the milestones of this century, and its first performance in Paris produced one of the greatest scandals in musical history. The whistles and cat-calls were so loud that even the orchestra was drowned—an extraordinary feat, for no musician had ever conjured such a volume of sound from an orchestra before! Expecting a Spring as sweet as so many composers have made it, the audience was horrified by Stravinsky's objective vision of reality—of a season violent and savage, as if the bowels of the earth were in the torturing pains of birth. The beauty of Spring is superficial, the reality is brutal and agonising. This is the Spring which Stravinsky depicted, through a ballet representing the barbarous rites and sacrifices with which the pagan Russians greeted the reawakening of Nature's forces.

To express this volcanic energy, Stravinsky amassed a colossal orchestra which speaks with unprecedented dissonance and force. Massive, complex chords are beaten out in orgiastic paroxysms. One aggressive chord is violently beaten out for eight, then nine, and finally for thirty-five bars, each of which has a different metre from that of the bar which precedes or that which follows, creating metrical successions such as : 9/8, 5/8, 3/8, 2/4, 7/4, 3/4, etc. These insistent rhythms are typical of Stravinsky's works of this period. In another ballet, *Les Noces* (" The Wedding "), begun in 1914 but orchestrated (for chorus, four pianos, and percussion) only in 1923, he used percussive rhythms so insistently that the effect is almost hypnotic. The work has a barbaric, primitive dynamism which runs counter to all our Western traditions of music as a refined, highly spiritual art.

In *Petrushka*, *The Rite of Spring*, and *Les Noces*, Stravinsky seems to have delved deep into his subconscious and released the more elemental, barbaric substratum of his nature. Though the primitivism is rendered with a certain sophistication, this music is of the flesh and not of the mind. It belongs to the dark world of superstition and instinct rather than the illuminated one of high human intellect.

Stravinsky himself realised this, and after *Les Noces* set about curbing what he called his " Dionysian " impulses and subordinating them to " Apollonian " principles. In other words, the flesh was in future to be subordinated to the spirit, instinct must bow to reason. But this was a process which took him years to complete.

WAR YEARS

During the war years, Stravinsky lived in Switzerland. The 1917 revolution in Russia deprived him of all income from his property, and the war prevented performances of his ballets, so that income from that source also disappeared. In an effort to earn money, Stravinsky wrote a number of works which required few performers and which he believed to be adapted to war-time economy conditions. These included the " burlesque tale " *Renard* ; *Ragtime* for ten instruments and percussion ; and *The Soldier's Tale*, an " entertainment " consisting of mimed narration and music. *The Soldier's Tale* required only seven instrumentalists, a narrator, and a minimum of actors, the idea being to go round from village to village as a travelling company. Although it was performed only once during the war, the music of *The Soldier's Tale* has become famous. The instrumental group is made up of an incongruous combination—clarinet, bassoon, cornet, trombone, violin, double bass, and percussion—treated with miraculous technique, in a succession of pieces which are as fascinating as they are varied. There is here a wonderful combination of simple buffoonery, melancholy and tragic spirituality which makes *The Soldier's Tale* one of Stravinsky's finest works.

During the war years, Stravinsky wrote a considerable amount of vocal music, some of it distinctly Russian in character, even if, like *Les Noces*, the nationalistic element is interpreted through a sophisticated primitivism. He also wrote a quantity of small instrumental works, some of which reveal his interest in jazz—for example, the *Piano Rag-Music* and *Ragtime*.

Stravinsky's " Russian period " ends with the opera *Mavra*, written in 1921–22. This is not a particularly strong work, but it is of particular importance as marking Stravinsky's final farewell to his Russian past. The musical discourse is closely related to the Russo-Italian *bel canto* operatic style begun by Glinka and continued by Tchaikovsky ; but the sweetness of the vocal line is often in contrast with an orchestral accompaniment of deliberately acid sourness. The effect is of a melancholy, bitter humour, which is characteristically Russian.

A NEW WORLD

Like Schoenberg, Stravinsky was acutely aware of the crisis in tonality. Some of his work reveals a deliberate attempt to establish an atonal language, especially after he heard Schoenberg's *Pierrot Lunaire* in Berlin in 1912. But for the ten years following 1910, his departure from a diatonic idiom usually assumed the form of bitonality or at most polytonality. (Bitonality means the simultaneous use of two keys, usually maintained quite distinct and on separate planes. Polytonality is an extension of this scheme, so that more than two keys are used at once.) The motive which opens the third scene of *Petrushka* is often quoted as Stravinsky's first consistent use of bitonality. Played by two clarinets, this is clearly composed of a C major chord in root position in the upper part, and an inversion of the chord of F sharp major in the lower—an exact repetition of the cadenza of Ravel's *Jeux d'eau* (1901). For bitonality is by no means new. Bach made passing use of it in the first Brandenburg Concerto, and Mozart in his Divertimento K.522. But it was only with such a work as *Petrushka* that bitonality achieved structural value on a large scale, as it does especially in *The Rite of Spring*.

The cantata *The King of the Stars*, which Stravinsky wrote soon after *Petrushka*, contains examples of polytonality pushed to such an extreme degree that harmonic coherence disintegrates into something approaching atonality. In this cantata and the *Japanese Lyrics* (1913) Stravinsky came very near to the pitch of atonality which Schoenberg had reached very little previously. If he had continued this tendency, his work would have been along the same road as Schoenberg's. But it was only forty years later that he took up the atonal style where he left it with the *Japanese Lyrics*. Instead, from this point his music is gradually clarified harmonically, so that by the 'twenties he had become the chief representative of a diatonic language which was in every way the antithesis of Schoenberg's atonal idiom.

A work which well illustrates Stravinsky's stylistic and harmonic development between 1909 and 1914 is the opera *The Nightingale*. Only the first act was completed when work had to be put aside to write *Firebird*. In 1913 Stravinsky was invited to complete the opera by a Moscow theatre, but in the intervening years he had developed a completely different style and could no longer return to the mellifluous Debussyan manner of 1908. The opening of the first act contains thirty-five bars of undulating successions of alternating fifths and thirds in a manner distinctly suggestive of Debussy's first nocturne, *Nuages*. But coming after the experience of *The Rite of Spring*, *The King of the Stars* and the *Japanese Lyrics*, the second and third acts of *The Nightingale* were couched in a polytonal or atonal idiom of an altogether different order.

Stravinsky resumed relations with Diaghilev after the war, and accepted a commission to adapt a number of fragments of Pergolesi for a new ballet, *Pulcinella*. This almost accidental contact with eighteenth century music set off a new train of thought in Stravinsky's mind. Though he was still in his " Russian period ", he was gradually shedding Russian influences. In *The Rite of Spring* and *Les Noces*, he had touched the extreme of barbaric primitivism : nothing could be done further in that direction. He was moving towards ideals of tonal and formal clarity, shedding his " Dionysian " urgings and searching for some means of applying his " Apollonian " principles. This contact with old music of the West showed him what he was searching for—a simple, clear style, spiritually elevated and yet novel. For there is no doubt that *Pulcinella* struck a very new note in the ballet theatre of 1920 and inaugurated Stravinsky's " neo-classical " period, which was to last for the next thirty years.

NEO-CLASSICISM

The neo-classical movement in music was not originated solely by Stravinsky, though he played a preponderant rôle in its development. Rather was it " in the air " at that time, for others such as Busoni, Casella, and Hindemith were thinking along similar lines. Neo-classical composers sought to recover the past—not the immediate past of sensual romanticism, but that of the Italian and German baroque and rococo periods, which with such grace and profundity typify the true " classical " spirit. Such a " return to the past " is not absolutely without precedent in music—Mozart and Mendelssohn turned to Bach, and Mozart and Beethoven to Handel—yet it is difficult to justify æsthetically, since the composer must justify his imitation of another's style by expressing in it something that is new and presumably better than before. Art should move ever forwards, and this enormous step backwards was brought about only by the peculiar artistic situation after the 1918 armistice. The spirit of disillusion at that time led to a reaction against romanticism, and consequently against nineteenth-century music. The "anti-romantics", in search of a musical style, were not yet prepared to accept Schoenberg's atonalism. They could see no other way into the future, and so their only alternative was to reincarnate the musical styles of the pre-romantic period. Time has proved the neo-classical style to have been a temporary phase, but it produced some beautiful music, and, in the case of Stravinsky, a number of major works from the years of his maturity.

After *Pulcinella* Stravinsky threw himself with fervour into the exploration of baroque music, but eventually his neo-classic stylistic " borrowings " ranged from the Middle Ages to Tchaikovsky. Space forbids a detailed examination of his various neo-classic manners, but briefly, Bach's influence is seen clearly in the octet, the *Concertino* for string quartet, and the concerto for piano and wind instruments ; Handel's oratorio manner on *Œdipus Rex* ; Mozart in the *Serenade* for piano ; Rossini in some parts of the ballet *Jeu de cartes* ; Weber and Mendelssohn in the *Capriccio* for piano and orchestra ; Tchaikovsky in the ballet *The Fairy's Kiss* ; and even Beethoven in the Symphony in C.

It must be emphasised that though Stravinsky borrowed the styles, and often even the themes, of earlier composers, he did much more than slavishly copy or imitate. His work was a genuine re-creation. Every style he touched was transmuted in his hands and became essentially his own, with his highly personal rhythmic buoyancy and energy, his astringent orchestral sonorities, his piquant dissonances and droll humour.

The neo-classic works can be very roughly divided as follows :

1. The instrumental works of the early 'twenties—the *Concertino* and *Symphonies for wind instruments* ; octet for wind instruments ; concerto for piano and wind instruments ; sonata and *Serenade* for piano. (Note in these works the typical anti-romantic insistence on wind instruments, and the refusal to use the more emotion-laden strings.)

2. The Greek ballets and dramatic works—*Œdipus Rex* (1927) and *Apollo Musagetes* : *Persephone* (1934) and *Orpheus* (1947).

3. " Concerto " works for the 'thirties—Violin concerto ; *Duo concertant* (violin and piano) ; concerto for two pianos ; the *Dumbarton Oaks* concerto (for fifteen instruments).

4. The " American Period "—*Danses Concertantes* ; *Norwegian Moods* ; sonata for two pianos.
5. Symphonic works of the 'forties—Symphony in C ; Symphony in three movements ; Concerto in D for strings.
6. Religious works—the *Symphony of Psalms* (1930), the cantata *Babel* (1944), the *Mass* (1948).

Stravinsky's neo-classic period ended suddenly with the opera *The Rake's Progress* (1948–51). This work, inspired by a series of narrative drawings by Hogarth, is planned as an *opera giocosa* in the Mozartian manner, with arias, recitatives, duos, quartets, etc., all conceived as separate numbers and without musical continuity. The scene is set in eighteenth-century London, and Stravinsky uses the musical styles of that period and the early nineteenth century, with strong references to Mozart and Gluck, and occasional touches of Rossini and Donizetti. Often accompanying figures are deliberately " old-fashioned " and banal, so that only slight dissonances and a certain perverse distortion of the verbal accentuation can be said to bestow a sense of " modernity " on such passages.

THE END OF NEO-CLASSICISM

The Rake's Progress seemed to mark the end of Stravinsky's resources. Other neo-classic composers too had given evidence that their idiom was exhausted. But at this point, at over seventy years of age, Stravinsky sprang on the world the biggest surprise of his surprising career. He abandoned neo-classicism and turned his attention to a style which for over thirty years had been the antithesis of his own—Schoenberg's serialism. For three decades Stravinsky had represented diatonicism, formal clarity, and a " backward-looking " alliance with the past. Now he swung round and joined with " forward-looking ", atonal serialism. In turning towards the future rather than the past, he for once played the rôle of follower rather than of innovator. Between 1933 and 1945, serialism seemed to languish and to have no future ; but with the end of World War II, many composers showed a new interest in atonalism and serial technique. By 1951, Schoenberg's methods were common practice with many formerly " neo-classic " composers, and Stravinsky's change to serialism was only part of a fairly universal movement.

SERIALISM

Since 1952, Stravinsky's adoption of serial methods has been gradual : each new composition has showed an increasing proportion of serial procedures. In the *Cantata* Stravinsky uses short series of diatonic scales in direct, inverted and retrograde forms. But the harmonic resultant is as diatonic as *The Rake's Progress*, and there is even a slightly archaic flavour. The *Septet* caused considerable hubbub in the musical world when it was first played, for it revealed for the first time Stravinsky's sympathy with Webern's music. Though the series is here only a group of six notes in the Aeolian mode, the rhythmic configuration of the *passacaglia*, the expressionist use of large intervals and the *Klangfarbenmelodie* (melody of timbres) all have clear associations with Webern. In fact, all Stravinsky's serial works are closer to Webern than to Schoenberg.

The *Three Songs from William Shakespeare*, *In Memoriam Dylan Thomas*, *Canticum Sacrum*, and the ballet *Agon* all reveal a partial use of serialism. In both the *Canticum* and *Agon* serial movements are mixed with others of traditional and even archaic character. It is only with the big cantata *Threni* that Stravinsky has produced an entire work in the twelve-note style. *Threni*, based on the Lamentations of Jeremiah, is sombre and lacks the rhythmic buoyancy and geniality of manner that we usually find even in his most abstruse works. In it Stravinsky seems to have stripped himself of all superficialities and exteriorities. He has set the Lamentations impersonally and with manifest sincerity, as a self-denying intermediary between God and man.

BELA BARTÓK

If, in the future, the thread of a true classicism is traced through the stylistic mazes of this century, it will probably be found that Bartók (1881–1945) is the one great composer who most nearly follows its path. Bartók, it will probably be found, was the one artist who created a true equilibrium between East and West, between the classic tradition and the new technical and formal forces of this century.

True, Bartók frequently introduces a very strong element of East European folk-music into his works, but usually this is so perfectly absorbed into a Western " classic " style that it does not obtrude excessively. Bartók was extremely alive to new influences, but he allowed none of them to overwhelm him. " I do not wish to subscribe to any of the accepted tendencies ", he said. " My ideal is a measured balance of these elements."

Bartók's music is not easy to assimilate. It neither seduces the listener with easy sentiment, nor sweeps him away on the tide of a mighty passion. But under its reticent exterior there are enormous riches of emotional, spiritual, and intellectual experience to reward the more persevering listener. This music may have less glamour than that of Stravinsky or Debussy and less stylistic novelty than Schoenberg or Webern, but it is possible that the future will hold it to be of greater value and of more lasting interest.

Bartók was born in Hungary, though his birthplace was assigned to Rumania after the 1918 armistice, and later to Yugoslavia. All his life he suffered from ill-health, particularly lung trouble, and his childhood was a continuous succession of illnesses. His mother, a schoolteacher, divined his talents very early, and in spite of financial difficulties, managed to get him a proper conservatoire training at Pozsony (Bratislava) and Budapest. At first his composition remained much inferior to his pianistic ability, and for many years he pursued the career of a piano virtuoso.

FIRST INTEREST IN FOLK-MUSIC

About 1905 Bartók began to take a great interest in Magyar music, realising that the Hungarian gypsies' flamboyant music which had been universally accepted was not truly Hungarian. His investigation of folk-music in general became an immense labour of love, forcing him, in spite of ill-health, to travel extensively in the Balkans and Asia Minor, listening to and transcribing peasant songs and recording them on his primitive wax cylinders. His publications of folk-music fill many volumes, and one of his last acts, during a period of extreme ill-health, was to transcribe literally thousands of recorded folk-songs for Columbia University.

Bartók said that Strauss's *Thus spake Zarathustra* was the musical experience which first gave him the urge to compose ; but he evidently had little lasting sympathy with the Straussian style, for most of his early work seems to stem from Brahms or the later Beethoven. But by 1911, in his *Allegro barbaro* for piano, the Magyar influence is strongly evident. This does not mean that from then on his music is exclusively orientated towards folk-music, which remains as a substratum to much of his work, only occasionally achieving preponderance.

Nevertheless, Bartók's melody and its rhythmic configuration are regularly marked by certain characteristics. Its shape is usually determined either by some form of modal scale, or by considerable use of chromatic notes in the manner of certain kinds of East European instrumental music. The intervals are usually small—semitones, tones, or minor thirds—and if a leap of as much as a minor third is made, the melody returns within the leap by steps of a semitone. Some Bartók melodies resemble *táragató* improvisations (the *táragató* is a Hungarian reed instrument, like a clarinet), with a brooding pastoral atmosphere. An essentially simple, almost static melodic outline is embellished with florid chromatic arabesques and insistent repetitions of small groups of notes. Other melodies are based on complex Bulgarian rhythms, in which the bar is divided into irregular groups (*e.g.*, 3+2+2+3) producing vivid, exciting atmospheres.

Bartók's rhythm can vary from a placid, almost imperceptible move-ment, as in his "night music", to machine-like percussive beats which have the elemental surge of barbaric primitivism. Most commonly both rhythmic complexity and taut vitality characterise his work. Harmonically Bartók's works are fundamentally chromatic, with the part-writing obscur-ing tonal centres, and much use of bitonality and polytonality. Atonality is, in fact, frequently achieved, but though Bartók was at one time attracted to serialism, at no time did he adopt a serial technique. Frequently his harmonisation of diatonic themes is highly discordant, for he believed that the more simple and tonal the melody, the more unusual can the accompany-ing harmony be made. This attitude results in the raw, virile flavour of all Bartók's music.

ARRANGEMENTS

Bartók's most characteristic compositions fall into three groups—folk-song arrangements, piano music (including the three piano concertos), and music for string instruments (string quartets, violin sonatas, etc.). He seems to have been little attracted by wind instruments. The only work calling for a solo wind instrument—*Contrasts*—was the result of a commission by Benny Goodman, the jazz clarinettist. Bartók's works include opera (*Bluebeard's Castle*), ballet (*The Miraculous Mandarin*), and orchestral music, but the real quality of his genius is most fully expressed in the smaller mediums of keyboard and strings.

Bartók's folk-song arrangements are numerous, and vary from groups of peasant songs with a simple piano accompaniment to works (such as the *Cantata Profana*) where the original melodic material is reorganised and extended into an art-form on a completely different æsthetic plane. In some original compositions, such as the *Dance Suite* for orchestra, it is difficult to distinguish which material is the result of Bartók's creative thought and which is directly derived from folk-songs. But in all Bartók's folk-song arrangements, and in his use of folk-music in original compositions, we find a unique fusion of his own creative thought with the native material. His is no superficial adaptation of native music to higher art forms, but a thorough process of re-creation in which the composer is spiritually at one with the peasant art.

BARTÓK AS PIANIST

Throughout his career, one of Bartók's main sources of income lay in his work as a concert pianist, and many of his piano works were written for inclusion in his own programmes. Consequently some works are prodigiously difficult, especially as Bartók's expanding technique of composition called for a corresponding expansion in keyboard technique. On the other hand, much of Bartók's piano music is very approachable, especially among the eighty-five pieces *For Children*, the *Rumanian Christmas Songs*, and *Fifteen Hungarian Peasant Songs*. His *Mikrokosmos*, a group of 153 piano pieces of progressive difficulty, sums up Bartók's researches into piano technique, and is a wonderful revelation of his exploration of the highways and byways of various modern techniques of composition. Many pieces are quite simple, yet they provide the clue to techniques of composition which appear elsewhere in more complex form. Other pieces in *Mikrokosmos* are of greater artistic value, and Bartók included them in his own concert programmes.

In both the *Allegro Barbaro* (1911) and the sonata (1926) we find Bartók emphasising the percussive characteristics of the piano. These works are packed with emphatic dynamics, and barbaric chords are beaten out with great rhythmic violence ; and as the harmonic idiom is singularly uncompromising, one is drawn to an inevitable comparison between this cultured savagery and the "Dionysian" primitivism of Stravinsky's *Rite of Spring* and *Les Noces*.

Bartók's second wife, also a concert pianist, joined him on the concert platform, and so gave occasion for the composition of one of the most singular pieces of contemporary chamber music—the *Sonata for two pianos and percussion* (1937). Especially in the second and third movements, the pianos cease to be treated separately from the varied battery of percussion instruments. They shed their conventional melodic and contrapuntal rôles and merge with the percussion as creators of sound effects and colours of remarkable ingenuity. This work is largely experimental, like much of Bartók's chamber music, but it is always the result of constructive, reasoned, artistic experiment.

Bartók's first piano concerto (1926) reveals his strong interest at that time in Western music of the German and Italian pre-Bach periods, and is largely based on the *concerto grosso* principle of fusing the solo and orchestral rôles in a unified, contrapuntal discourse. The second concerto is again designed on baroque lines, but approaches nearer to the early classic concerto in the *rapport* between soloist and orchestra. Both these works are remarkable for the fusion of Magyar-inspired material (usually short, fragmentary themes of vigorous, clear outlines) with a contrapuntal discourse of early eighteenth-century type, the two factors uniting into a completely twentieth-century style.

This use of the baroque (especially contrapuntal forms) is not infrequent in Bartók ; and one might be tempted to regard him as a "neo-classic" composer, were it not for the fact that the neo-classicists aimed at merely re-evoking the past in a new dress, but in a still recognisable form, whereas Bartók transmuted baroque forms into something completely new and seemingly unrelated to the original.

The third piano concerto, though more frequently heard, contains less distinguished material than the previous two. Still not quite finished when Bartók died in New York in 1945, this work is regarded as a result of the composer's desire to write a milder work which would more easily find approval in America.

Bartók was obliged to find refuge in the U.S.A. during World War II. His intense love for his country would not allow him to stand by in silence while Hungary was occupied by the Germans; but he was to find little happiness in America. His letters from America are filled with his pre-occupation with providing the most elementary necessities for himself and his wife. While enduring increasing illness (leucæmia) which doctors could do little to alleviate, his only regular source of income was a somewhat uncertain grant from Columbia University for the investigation and tran-scription of thousands of East European folk-songs. His music proved too austere for American audiences, and it was entirely natural that in his straitened circumstances he, like Schoenberg, should try to produce a series of works which would prove more accessible and agreeable to his new public. For this reason his third piano concerto, and such works as the *Concerto for Orchestra* and the viola concerto are more simple, direct, and emotional than his previous works. There is less introspection, and especially in the *Concerto for Orchestra*, more humour and exuberance than Bartók had ever previously demonstrated. Some regard such traits as a falling-off of his powers, others assert that Bartók's " American period " represents a mellowed and maturer outlook. It certainly seems probable that, but for his emigration to America, Bartók would never have written these more accessible works, and would have continued to exploit the medium of string quartet and string ensemble which had become nearest his heart.

It is remarkable that Bartók, essentially a pianist, should have developed the most resourceful string technique of any contemporary composer. His sonata for solo violin (commissioned by Szigeti) is a veritable sum total of all that the modern virtuoso can accomplish. His string quartets reveal the most intimate knowledge of the medium, and every movement is packed with ingenious effects which have since become the stock-in-trade of less imaginative composers.

THE STRING QUARTETS

Bartók's six string quartets represent the most significant contribution to chamber music since the death of Beethoven. Not only does his skill in using the medium amount to genius, but the content of these works alone is sufficient to win him immortality. The quartets cover a period from 1908 to the beginning of the Second World War, that is, almost his entire European career. They are Bartók's "purest" music. The folk element is present, but in a sublimated form, influencing the rhythmic and melodic shapes, infusing the more classic outlines with vigour and strength.

String quartet music is the most refined form of instrumental art, and there is no doubt that Bartók's quartets are his greatest music. Ever since Haydn's wonderfully delicate works the quartet medium has been regarded as one which should retain slight, fastidious textures. In short, the quartet must not compete with the orchestra. According to this ideal, Bartók's quartets are not quartets, for they are so robust, so packed with vital substance, and often so thick and dense in texture that they seem to have burst through the limits of the medium in an effort to become orchestral. But Bartók's expansion of the quartet medium is quite legitimate, because it is accomplished not only by an expansion in the technique of composition and by an enlargement of the instrumental possibilities of the four players, but by an increase in the spiritual and emotional expression of the music. With Bartók the quartet grew enormously in stature; its emotional range became something which Haydn could never have conceived, and the only standard of measurement is Beethoven.

The first quartet (1908), though written in a highly chromatic idiom, is not far removed from the late Beethoven quartets. It is an amazingly mature work; indeed in the string quartet medium it is almost impossible to conceive an immature Bartók. The second quartet (1917) is already the work of a master. Both the third and fourth quartets, like the two sonatas for violin and piano of the late 'twenties, belong to Bartók's most experimental period. The idiom of these works is uncomprising, the content highly introspective; and, especially in the fourth, the composer reaches a more extreme degree of atonalism than in any other of his works. The fifth and sixth quartets, covering the period 1934–39, show a return towards a more expressive idiom, and especially in the sixth he returns to the late Beethoven manner of his first quartet.

Within the space of the present chapter, a detailed analysis of Bartók's quartet writing is not practicable. It is only possible to hint at the most salient factors—his highly ingenious use of canon and other contrapuntal devices, and the marvellous technique of thematic expansion, whereby a small thematic cell is gradually expanded throughout the movements in a continually growing metamorphosis. The rhythm is always vital, metrical complexities abound, and the dynamic range is enormous. The use of double, triple, and quadruple stoppings is frequent, and Bartók delights in such devices as *glissando*, *col legno*, *ponticello*, *tremolo*, and *pizzicato* in order to produce colouristic effects.

The string orchestra was also one of Bartók's favourite mediums, and two of his most beautiful works are the *Music for Strings, Percussion and Celesta* (1936) and the *Divertimento* (1939). The latter is an easily accessible work, exuberant, stylistically uncomplex, and full of vital melody. The *Music for Strings, Percussion and Celesta* (which in reality includes also the piano and harp) is more complex, and is comparable only with the latter quartets. There is more stylistic variety between the movements, however, as the first movement (*Ricercare*) is based entirely on baroque counterpoint. The second is homophonic and makes considerable use of *ostinato*. The third movement is impressionistic, using a counterpoint of tone colours— timpani *glissandos*, trills on the strings, xylophone interjections, and arpeggio passages on the celesta and harp—which evoke the transfigured quietude, the nostalgic nocturnal landscape of Bartók's "Hungarian" manner, simple and direct and rhythmically exuberant.

OPERA AND BALLET

Little mention has been made here of Bartók's opera and ballet, principally because they occupy a comparatively small place in his output. The opera *Duke Bluebeard's Castle* (1911) is an early work inspired by French impressionism, and has justly been criticised as being too static to be wholly successful as an opera. The moral character of his ballet *The Miraculous Mandarin* (1919) has been severely censored, but it is a work of exceptional force. Written in a period of disillusionment, this work is not only highly erotic, but has an expressionistic brutality which is foreign to Bartók's style. Here there is less Hungarian influence than in any of his music. This ballet is typical of the general unease in post-war Central Europe, and one can only assume that this was the chief factor which induced Bartók to indulge in such a crude and violent form of artistic expression.

The real core of Bartók's music—the string music in general, and the quartets in particular—is strikingly devoid of any emotional crudity. His expression seems rather the sublimation of all the higher human emotions, and it is for this elevated spirituality that his music will be remembered. The best of his work represents the most stable equilibrium between this century's stylistic and technical developments; and there is little doubt that in the future he will be regarded as the central figure in European music in the first half of the century.

Keystone Press Agency

TEATRO ALLA SCALA, MILAN

Opened in 1778 with Salieri's *L'Europa Riconosciuta*. Damaged extensively by bombs
in 1943, it was re-opened in May, 1946. One of the most famous opera houses in the
world and famous for the standard of its singing.

ROYAL OPERA HOUSE, COVENT GARDEN

The present building, the third to stand on the site, was opened in 1858 with Meyerbeer's
Les Huguenots, and has been a national theatre for opera and ballet since 1946.

Associated Press Ltd.

METROPOLITAN OPERA HOUSE, NEW YORK

Opened in 1883 with Gounod's *Faust*. It shares with La Scala and Covent Garden a
reputation as the mecca of all operatic singers in search of an international reputation.

COLOGNE OPERA HOUSE

One of the most ambitious and successful of the new German opera houses. Opened on 8th June, 1957, with Wolfgang Fortner's *Die Bluthochzeit*.

PAUL HINDEMITH

Hindemith was born in Germany in 1895 and therefore belongs to a later generation than Schoenberg, Stravinsky, and Bartók. Unlike them, he took no part in the turbulent revolutionary artistic period which preceded the First World War. He left home at the age of eleven to make his own way as a musician, and by 1915 was already leader of the orchestra of the Frankfurt Opera ; but his definitive work as a composer began only after the war had ended.

Hindemith's creative work was therefore conditioned from the outset by artistic and social factors in post-war Germany which were far from ideal for the production of valid, well-balanced works of art. Disillusionment was universal and false artistic creeds abounded. The desperation of misery drove the youth of Germany into a delirium of false gaiety. This was a period of unprecedented artistic silliness, determined inevitably by the artist's own uncertainty of purpose and, in default of purpose, his willingness to fall in with society's most stupid whims.

"UTILITY MUSIC"

Hindemith, having something of the apostle in his nature, set himself to create order in this state of artistic chaos. He first defined the position of an artist in society, and then determined what kind of music should be provided for that society. In the 'twenties he regarded himself as a craftsman, with a duty to compose not as he himself wished, or for his own satisfaction, but strictly according to demand, as society determined. The Romantic ideal of "art for art's sake" was ruthlessly swept aside. For Hindemith, the composer was only an artisan with a utilitarian, functional duty to perform. He must write *Gebrauchsmusik*—"utility" music, for a large, enlightened public.

It is easy to be wise after the event and to pour scorn on such concepts, but many critics overlook the fact that, whatever his artistic creed at this time, Hindemith produced valid works of art. It should also be borne in mind that "utility music", at least before the Romantic period, had always been in great demand. The church continually demanded new Masses and new cantatas, while aristocratic patrons insisted on new concertos and symphonies by the hundreds, new operas by the dozen. There was an unceasing demand for something contemporary and something new, without pretending to eternal value. The principles of Hindemith's *Gebrauchsmusik* were, in fact, far from new.

If "utility music" succeeded so well in the past, why did Hindemith's fail ? Because Hindemith grossly miscalculated the needs of society. His lay public of enlightened music lovers was perhaps a fine ideal, but completely illusory. The general public, however enlightened, does not want to hear merely craftsmanlike contemporary music. There is hardly room for even the very best contemporary music in our concert programmes, and certainly none for a " utility " music which claims only limited artistic worth. The very nature of Hindemith's musical idiom was enough to isolate his art from the public, for it was anti-romantic and conformed to the current neo-classical fashion, which favoured baroque patterns. Hindemith's counterpoint is Bachian—at least he aims at Bach's brilliance in a horizontal sense. But vertically he avoids the grandiose harmonic results which Bach's counterpoint achieved. His harmony is dissonant, often polytonal, and results in music of a dry, almost bitter flavour. True, Hindemith sometimes indulged in " democratic " moments of humour and even uninhibited jazzy buffoonery, but such gestures are not typical of his most valid work.

Hindemith has always been an extremely prolific composer. He is a brilliant viola player, and his profound understanding of instrumental techniques has led him to produce a mass of works for every variety of instrument and combinations, even exploiting unusual instruments in such works as the trio for heckelphone, viola, and piano, and the concertino for trautonium and strings.

His *Gebrauchsmusik* therefore comprises a large mass of instrumental works, the finest pieces being his six sets of *Kammermusik* for soloists and chamber orchestra, various pieces of orchestral *Konzertmusik*, and several concertos. Six operas were also written during this period, and in these he generally exploited topical situations, or satirised various aspects of modern life. But satirical art can soon date, and though *News of the Day* (1929) and *Cardillac* (1926) are revived now and then, they show little signs of enduring.

The year the Nazis came into power, 1933, marked not only a big change in Hindemith's fortunes but a shifting of his artistic attitude. It was clear that a democratic public of enlightened music lovers no longer existed (if indeed it had ever existed except in his imagination) and that under the new régime the public would have very little to say in the matter of their musical preferences. Under Hitler, politicians directed artistic affairs, and Hindemith was soon condemned as a " cultural bolshevik ".

NEW SPIRITUALITY

At about the same period that the Nazis came to power, Hindemith's music began to show a new spirituality, and in such works as the *Philharmonic*

Concerto (1932) and the second string trio (1933) the idiom became less harsh and uncompromising. He was beginning that reversal of policy which was to turn him from a craftsman into a creative artist, from a self-avowed servant of society into a composer only concerned with art for its own sake. This crisis, both within himself and in his surroundings (Hindemith was teaching at the Berlin High School for Music when the Nazis came into power), urged him to the composition of his greatest work, the opera *Mathis der Maler* (" Mathis the Painter "), in which the unsatisfactory relations of the artist to society and politics are exposed. Though the hero is Mathias Grünewald, a painter at the time of the sixteenth-century Peasants' Revolt, it is clear that the opera refers to Hindemith and the Nazi régime. The Nazis banned the opera on the grounds that it challenged the right of political bodies to control the creative artist, but this was not Hindemith's only theme. There is considerable philosophic reflection on the general position of the artist in society, and particularly on the question whether, in times of national emergency, he is justified in retiring within the shell of his art. It seems that Hindemith reached no completely satisfactory solution of these problems, but the Nazi ban on *Mathis* furthered Hindemith's international career. His symphony *Mathis der Maler*, based on movements from the opera, was played everywhere, and the first complete performance of the opera (Zürich, 1938) was regarded as the artist's challenge to Hitler. However, this notoriety would have availed him nothing if the opera had not had those qualities of greatness which undoubtedly it possesses. There is a profound humanity in this work such as Hindemith had never before achieved. The idiom is more compromising and euphonious than previously, conforming readily with a more generally accepted standard of beauty. In short, this was " art " and not " craft ".

Under Nazi rule Hindemith's activity in Berlin soon ceased, and in 1934 he was forced to find employment abroad. For years he lived in Turkey, reorganising musical life on Western lines, but after touring the U.S.A. he settled there in 1939. American life seems to have influenced his music very little, apart from his settings of Walt Whitman's poems.

THE THEORIST

After the success of *Mathis*, Hindemith's work might well have been marked by an increasing humanism and a diminishing insistence on " craft ". But this was not so, and among the large number of works he has produced there are few which equal the emotional, spiritual greatness of *Mathis*, and many which fall far short. Some critics, noting the publication in 1937 of the first of the two volumes of *Unterweisung im Tonsatz* (published in English as *The Craft of Musical Composition*), would attribute the diminution of his expressive powers to an over-preoccupation with technical considerations. There may be some truth in this, but Hindemith's idiom itself explains the aloof nature of much of his music. Hindemith's music is essentially as contrapuntal as it was in the 'twenties. Tonal effects are clearer and less harsh than formerly, but basically the idiom is the same. And the truth is that his brilliant counterpoint, which may be intellectually satisfying, is seldom emotionally appealing. The difference between Hindemith's works of the 'twenties and 'fifties can easily be exaggerated. The style is essentially the same, the difference only one of an increased degree in emotional expression (within the limits of his style) in some, but not all, of his works after 1933.

Hindemith is still as much a neo-classic as he was in the 'twenties. Lacking Stravinsky's flexibility of outlook and purpose, it seems unlikely that Hindemith will ever spring surprises on his listeners. During the post-war years his works have remained emotionally frigid. The orchestration is often lacking in colour, the solid craftsmanship has been more evident than has imaginative warmth. After *Mathis* the great landmarks of his career are those which seem most spontaneous or to have a more profound emotional basis—the *Symphonische Tänze*, the ballet *Nobilissima Visione* (1938), *When lilacs last in the dooryard bloomed* (1946), and the symphonic extracts entitled *Harmonie der Welt* (1951) from another opera.

Hindemith has had great influence as a teacher, and his *Craft of Musical Composition* is an extremely well-reasoned exposition of the scientific laws underlying harmony. He has established convincing principles for the analysis of modern harmony and its application in composition, and though his methods are complex, there is no doubt that this publication is a theoretical treatise of the first order.

XXIV

CURRENTS AND CROSS-CURRENTS

THE work of Stravinsky, Bartók, Hindemith, and of Schoenberg and his followers, though of paramount importance in this century's musical development, should not be assumed to represent all the numerous and varied styles of composers throughout the Western world at this time. It is, indeed, the complexity of this activity that makes it difficult to draw in proper perspective. The essence of an artist is that he has some personal vision to communicate ; and composers, who are individuals, cannot be successfully regimented into tidy ranks, to be numbered off and neatly docketed. Some have continued, though inevitably with varying techniques, the nationalist trends of the nineteenth century, or have reacted against them ; others have been influenced, one way or another, by the work of pioneers and revolutionaries like Debussy or the great figures of the last chapter.

FRANCE

In France, for example, there had been a reaction against Debussy's exquisite Impressionism even before the 1914–18 war, in the works of the eccentric Erik Satie (1866–1925). Even as early as the late 'eighties Satie had been writing piano pieces with strange names (*Gnossiennes*, *Gymnopédies*) in which a grave, semi-liturgical character was combined with startling use of unresolved chords of the ninth. A declared enemy of preciousness on the one hand and bombast on the other, Satie continued to produce short piano pieces and songs in which echoes of café music were carefully woven into a self-consciously austere texture and labelled with eccentric titles, such as *Automatic Descriptions*, *Dried Embryos*, or *Bureaucratic Sonata*. In all of this there was a large element of Parisian *blague*, but also a genuine desire to purify the language of music and to achieve a fresh simplicity of language. Satie during the last ten years of his life found himself suddenly the centre of a new school of " bright young things " anxious to break with the immediate past of music. The most gifted of these were the Frenchmen Darius Milhaud (*b*. 1892) and Francis Poulenc (*b*. 1899), and the Swiss

425

Arthur Honegger (1892–1955). With no very good reason these three very dissimilar composers and three lesser talents—Germaine Tailleferre (b. 1892), Louis Durey (b. 1888), and Georges Auric (b. 1899)—were nicknamed by a Parisian journalist "Les Six" and their music became the height of fashion for the decade following the end of the First World War. Concision, sparkle, and humour marked their first essays, such as Poulenc's *Mouvements Perpetuels*, Milhaud's *Le Bœuf sur le toit* ("The Ox on the Roof"), and Auric's *Les Fâcheux* ("The Bores"). Impatient with all expressions of emotion, they aimed at athletic muscularity of phrase and rhythm, and combined dissonant harmony—sometimes two keys employed simultaneously—with a return to the continuity and symmetry of eighteenth-century music. War was declared on Wagner and all his works, and it became once again fashionable to admire Gounod.

It was not long before both Milhaud and Honegger graduated from this school of youthful impertinence. Milhaud proved enormously fertile, and although his output is very uneven in quality and reveals a bewildering variety of superficially assimilated influences, his songs and chamber-music often combine great technical dexterity with a charming freshness of inspiration. His operas include the ambitious *Christophe Colomb* (1928), *Maximilien*, *Bolivar*, and a *David* first heard at Jerusalem in 1954.

Honegger's increasing seriousness and fundamental Teutonic affinities showed themselves clearly in his later works. After the brilliant and at the time controversial tone-poems *Pacific 231* (an early impression of a train) and *Rugby* and the dramatic psalm *King David* (1921), his most important works were the second symphony (for strings and trumpet) written in 1941, three symphonies written between 1945 and 1951 ("Liturgique", "Deliciae Basilienses", and "Di Tre Re") and the stage oratorio *Joan of Arc at the Stake* (first performed in 1938), in which he made skilful use of his experience of writing for the cinema. His chamber music includes three string quartets, and his songs show the tender and lyrical side of a musical character in which strength is generally more noticeable than delicacy.

A SENTIMENTAL HUMORIST

Poulenc has remained, of all "Les Six", the most faithful to his original style of composition. Parisian verve and humour and a sophisticated literary sense mark all his songs, the ballet *Les Biches* ("The House Party") (1923), and the *opéra-bouffe Les Mamelles de Tirésias* ("The Breasts of Tiresias") (1944). His religious music includes an unaccompanied Mass, *Litanies à la Vierge Noire*, *Quatre Motets pour un temps de pénitence*, and a *Stabat Mater*. These show a depth of feeling and a workmanship superior to anything else that he has written except the Éluard songs of *Tel Jour telle nuit* (1937). His opera *Dialogues des Carmélites* (1957) is a clever setting of Bernanos's play of the same name.

A more traditional composer, Albert Roussel (1869–1937), came to musical maturity only in the years after the First World War, when he was already middle-aged. Educated in the school of César Franck, his ballet *Le Festin de l'Araignée* (1913) and his opera *Padmâvati* (1923) show the influence of Debussy mingled with a strong and individual sense of orchestral colour. A genuine symphonic sense and a harmony owing something to Stravinsky are to be found in his later orchestral works, which show him at his best—the *Suite en Fa* (1926) and the third and fourth symphonies (1930 and 1934). A distinguished string quartet and a number of fastidious songs are among his finest works.

After the deaths of Ravel and Roussel the most interesting of the French composers is Olivier Messiaen (*b.* 1908). A professional organist, he has occupied himself with works of semi-religious or mystical character— *L'Ascension* (1933), *Vingt Regards sur l'Enfant Jésus* (1944), and a *Messe de la Pentecôte* (1950). His style is eclectic and owes much to his studies of Indian music, bird-song, and Gregorian chant. An explorer in the field of sonorities, he produced in 1948 an enormous orchestral work entitled *Turangalila-Symphonie* which recalls Scriabin's *Poème de l'Extase* by the scented profusion and mystical sensuality of its style.

SPAIN

Spain contributed almost no major figure to European literature between the seventeenth and the twentieth centuries—from Cervantes, Lope de Vega, and Calderón to Lorca. Her situation in music is somewhat similar, and is doubtless similarly related to her political eclipse as a major power in the seventeenth century. In the development of the classical sonata and symphony, Spain furnishes the lone example of Juan Arriaga (1806–26) who died before he was twenty ; not until the mid-twentieth century was there a general appreciation of his well-proportioned single symphony and his three string quartets. The nineteenth century saw, it is true, a flowering of the characteristically Spanish form of Spanish light opera or *zarzuela*— for instance in *The Little Barber of Lavapies* by Francisco Barbieri (1823–94) ; but the *zarzuela* never had more than a local audience.

The composer regarded as the father of modern Spanish music is Felipe Pedrell (1841–1922), not so much for his compositions (which were chiefly for theatre and concert-hall), but for his work as a teacher, writer, and musical editor. He propounded the idea of musical nationalism, and emphasised that it should be based not only on folk-music but on the nation's whole artistic treasure. He himself edited the complete works of Victoria and the keyboard works of Cabezón, two great Renaissance figures of Spanish music. Manuel de Falla (1876-1946) was a pupil of Pedrell's ; and so was Enrique Granados (1867-1916). These two, with an older composer, Isaac Albéniz (1860-1909), established modern Spanish music of a distinctive kind in the international concert-hall.

All three men were skilled pianists, and Albéniz was indeed a pupil of the reigning king of pianist-composers, Liszt. The piano has obviously been an evocative instrument to Spanish composers ; and though a little important music has been written for the guitar (such as Falla's *Homage* in memory of Debussy), much more has been written in which the piano was used in such a way as to suggest guitar-like sounds. It has been suggested that this practice goes back to Domenico Scarlatti, who wrote most of his harpsichord sonatas in Spain (where he spent the latter part of his life) ; and certain characteristically Spanish traits may be detected in these works, as we have mentioned.

Albéniz spent much of his career in Paris and London, and among his works are three operas in English ; but his principal achievement lies in his piano pieces (more than 250 of them), especially the cycle of twelve called *Iberia*. They can be classified as impressionistic in their depiction of Spanish subjects, and Spanish dance-rhythms are used. Granados is also chiefly famous for a set of piano pieces called *Goyescas*, inspired by the paintings and drawings of Goya ; and it is partly on these that he based an opera of the same name.

The most remarkable as well as the best known of the three composers is Falla. In the concert-hall he developed an individual and consciously Spanish style with *Nights in the Gardens of Spain* for piano and orchestra, and the rarely heard *Fantasia Bética* (" Andalusian Fantasy ") for piano solo. In the theatre he made his name with the ballets *El Amor Brujo* (" Love the Sorcerer ") (produced in Madrid, 1915) and *The Three-Cornered Hat* (produced in London, 1919) and the operas *La Vida Breve* (" Life is Short ") (produced in Nice, 1913) and *Master Peter's Puppet Show* (first heard in 1923 in Seville), which uses puppets as well as human characters in an episode taken from *Don Quixote*. This last work is more than Spanish, as if the composer were seeking a subtlety of expression beyond that of nationalist idiom ; and Falla entered a decisively new field with the concerto for harpsichord and five instruments (1923-26), which aligns him with the contemporary neo-classicism of such composers as Stravinsky.[1]

[1] The posthumous *Atlántida*, finished by Ernest Halffter and first heard in its entirety at La Scala in 1962, shows this same ability to transcend purely Spanish idioms and achieve a wider. more objective humanity.

It has been relatively easy for outsiders to counterfeit the dance-rhythms and even the melodic clichés (often coloured by Arab influence) of Spanish music—easy, that is, if the aim is to convince other outsiders. Russian composers from Glinka onwards took a hand at this, and Rimsky-Korsakov's *Spanish Caprice* is an outstandingly successful example. Such nineteenth-century French composers as Lalo, Saint-Saëns, and Bizet (in *Carmen*) also evoked the Spanish idiom as "local colour", much as Viennese composers had raided Hungarian gypsy music. With Debussy and Ravel, the outsiders seem to approach authenticity, and Debussy's evocations of Spain in his piano works and his orchestral *Ibéria* won him the unstinting admiration of Falla himself.

One further Spanish cultivator of the nationalist style is notable: Joaquín Turina (1882–1949), known for his *Symphonic Rhapsody* for piano and orchestra, his symphonic poem *La Procesión del Rocío* (" The Procession of the Virgin of the Dew "), and other works. It is noteworthy that perhaps the most distinguished living pupil of Pedrell writes music which, while retaining certain Spanish characteristics, is much more aligned with international twentieth-century tendencies than with Spanish nationalism. He is Roberto Gerhard (*b.* 1896), a pupil not only of Pedrell and Granados, but also of Schoenberg. After the Spanish Civil War Gerhard, a Catalan, took refuge in England, where he now lives. Such works as his violin concerto, his harpsichord concerto, and his opera *The Duenna* show great imaginative gifts which have hardly won due recognition.

HUNGARY

The disparity of individual styles between composers of the same nation and the same generation could scarcely be better exemplified than in Hungary. Ernst von Dohnányi (1877–1960), a pianist of brilliant gifts, showed an allegiance to German musical ways and an indebtedness to Brahms. He often expressed himself most forcefully through the piano—as in his well-known early *Rhapsody* in C major, and the popular *Variations on a Nursery Tune* for piano and orchestra. His chamber works and an orchestral suite in F sharp minor are also sometimes heard. Dohnányi spent most of his active life in official musical positions, but lived in the U.S.A. in his last years.

In his *Ruralia Hungarica* for piano (some of which pieces he later orchestrated) Dohnányi borrowed the flavour of his country's popular music, but in what seems now rather an old-fashioned way. The radical probing of Hungarian folk-music, and the mating of its idiom with bold twentieth-century harmony so as to form a powerful new musical language, was the work of Béla Bartók and of Zoltán Kodály (*b.* 1882). Bartók was in his music the more startling, and undoubtedly the more important of the two. An outspoken political radical and nationalist, he managed to escape from Hungary, as we have seen. Kodály, who remained in Hungary, has been officially honoured as the patriarch among his country's musicians, and has found it possible to continue his work as composer and as musical educator (a rôle in which he is very prominent) under Communist rule.

Kodály, like Bartók, wrote a *Concerto for Orchestra* ; but the principal works by which he has become famous are of earlier date. In 1926 Budapest saw Kodály's opera, *Háry János*, about a boastful Hungarian folk-hero, and the suite drawn from this has remained a concert favourite. Its readily understandable harmonic idiom and its immediately attractive tunes are presented in a piquant orchestration which includes a part for the *cimbalom*, the traditional Hungarian dulcimer (the strings, lying flat, are struck with hammers held in the player's hand). In 1923 Kodály produced, for a national celebration, his *Psalmus Hungaricus* for tenor solo, chorus (properly including children), and orchestra, which is among the masterpieces of modern choral music. The text, a sixteenth-century Hungarian version of Psalm 55, has Hungarian patriotic associations, and a burning quality of passion runs through the music.

Among Kodály's other notable works are a sonata for unaccompanied cello, a masterly piece of music as well as a technical *tour de force* ; a set of orchestral variations on a Hungarian folk-song, *The Peacock* ; a Mass (*Missa Brevis*) and the *Budavari Te Deum* for chorus and orchestra ; and many short choral pieces (for men's voices, women's voices, and mixed voices). He has also been a prolific writer on music, especially on its national aspects, and on educational questions.

Three other modern Hungarian composers may be mentioned. They are a younger associate of Bartók's, Sándor Veress (*b.* 1907), who after the 1939–45 war went to live in Switzerland, and whose music shows the influence of both Bartók and Stravinsky ; Leo Weiner (*b.* 1885), not a prolific composer, whose piano and orchestral works have shown a general romanticism not emphasising Hungarian characteristics ; and Mátyás Seiber (1905–1960), a pupil of Kodály, who after working in Germany settled in England, and is referred to on page 445. Hungary since 1945, conformably with Communist æsthetic doctrine, has encouraged the cultivation of nationalism in its composers, but has produced no music to capture the rest of the world.

CZECHOSLOVAKIA

In Czechoslovakia the traditions of musical nationalism were infused with a radical modernity and a fierce power of expression by Leoš Janáček

(1854–1928). His reputation was late in growing, and there is something pathetic about the fact that he visited London late in life and made no musical impression, only to receive performances and critical eulogy long after his death. His opera *Katya Kabanová* was introduced to Britain at Sadler's Wells in 1951 (thirty years after its first performance in Brno), and *Jenůfa* at Covent Garden in 1956 (fifty-two years after its première).

The Czech language in its Moravian dialect deeply influenced the characteristic melodic line of Janáček. His method was usually, indeed, to present a sung line as an intensification of ordinary speech, caring little for formal symmetry in the "sentence" of the music. In this he resembled Mussorgsky. Matched to plots of sometimes savage passion, this produces a gripping idiom in the theatre—as indeed, in *Jenůfa* (original title, *Her Foster-Daughter*) and *Katya Kabanová*, both concerned with tragedies of womanhood. But Janáček's music is equally effective in the pure fairy-tale atmosphere of *The Cunning Little Vixen*, in which men and animals both sing—a masterly score, tender and evocative, with the sounds of nature merged in those of the orchestra. Janáček's ten operas form a living part of the repertory in his own country and have been remarkably widely performed in Germany since the 1939–45 war.

Sometimes harshly discordant and often breaking older conventions of euphonious progression, Janáček's style is perhaps less convincing in the concert hall. But it is nearly always arrestingly individual—as in the *Sinfonietta* for orchestra, the orchestral rhapsody called *Taras Bulba* (after Gogol), and the *Glagolitic Mass* ("Glagolitic" is a form of old Church Slavonic which to-day carries patriotic associations), which has a fierce unconventionality liable (like Verdi's Requiem) to shock any hearer for whom the association of music with religious texts first suggests the hymns and chants of the Anglican church.

High among Janáček's work is ranked a curious song-cycle, mainly for tenor and piano but making subordinate use of a contralto and three other female voices. This is *The Diary of One Who Disappeared*. His other compositions include songs for male voice choir, a medium cultivated by many Czech composers, including Smetana and Dvořák. Janáček is a curiously isolated figure, who could almost be described as musically self-made.

After Janáček, the chief opera to be produced in Czechoslovakia has been *The Whirlpool* (1949) by Eugen Suchoň (*b.* 1908). But the only Czech composer to become internationally well known is Bohuslav Martinů (1890–1959), a pupil of Suk, who after 1923 lived mainly in France and the United States but is, nevertheless, regarded by Czechs as a Czech musician. He was a prolific composer whose descriptive orchestral works *Half Time* (alluding to Association Football) and *La Bagarre* (" Tumult ") first made him known about 1930. Later, his Double Concerto for two string orchestras with piano and timpani showed an urgent, rather thickly harmonised style (related perhaps to that of Honegger) ; and he also wrote five symphonies, as well as much chamber music. His opera *Comedy on a Bridge* (originally for radio, 1937) mocks frontier restrictions with aptly pointed music.

FINLAND

Finland in the nineteenth century was a " protesting ", not a satisfied, country. It passed into Russian hands after the war of 1808–9 between Sweden and Russia, and Finnish independence was not officially proclaimed until the end of 1917. As in Norway, Finnish nationalism showed itself in the nineteenth century in a literary revival which centred on the publication of the *Kalevala*, the Finnish national epic. This was the work of the philologist Elias Lönnrot (1802–84), who assembled the work into coherent form after gleaning it from the country's popular songs and oral traditions. Lönnrot's second edition (1849) contains some 22,900 verses. It is a tale of magic, related to, but not dependent on, Teutonic and Norse mythology, and is written in unrhymed alliterative verse.

Just as the literary work of Ibsen and Bjørnson stimulated Grieg in Norway, so the *Kalevala* stirred the man who came to represent Finland in music—Sibelius (1865–1957). Johan (or, to use the French form he adopted, Jean) Sibelius studied in Berlin and Vienna but came back to work in Finland, and soon earned such recognition at home that in 1897 a government pension set him free to concentrate his whole activity on composition. The *Kalevala* is the direct literary source of Sibelius's four *Legends* for orchestra (one of which is *The Swan of Tuonela*), of the symphonic fantasy *Pohjola's Daughter*, and several other works ; and it seems sensible to link the *Kalevala* also with Sibelius's early orchestral work, *En Saga*, and with his last known orchestral work, *Tapiola* (1925), which takes its name from Tapio, the forest god of Finnish mythology.

Direct Finnish patriotic associations are carried, needless to say, by the popular *Finlandia* and by another early work, the *Karelia* Suite (Karelia is a southern province of Finland). But neither here nor elsewhere does Sibelius use folk-music. His idiom is, nevertheless, recognised by the Finns as their own. His early works have some relationship with Tchaikovsky ; and Sibelius may more generally be placed as demonstrating (like Nielsen in Denmark, and Vaughan Williams as well as the Russian composers) that the originally German-Austrian form of the symphony is capable of new expansion under the impulse of nationalism. But Sibelius's musical language is almost self-made. He wrote some attractive songs (to Finnish and Swedish texts), and a string quartet with the sub-title *Voces intimae* ("Intimate Voices"), as well as an opera which was produced in 1896 but has never been published. He composed numerous pieces of varying originality for the pianoforte, but his reputation chiefly stands on his symphonies and other orchestral works.

Though Sibelius lived to pass his ninetieth birthday, he published nothing in his last thirty years, and his seven symphonies span less than three decades (1898–1924). They keep to the classical three or four movements until the seventh and last, which is in only one movement, whose absolute, bare logic seems to distil the essence of Sibelius's symphonic thought. After this it is hardly strange that the much-talked-of eighth symphony failed to appear. Logic (by which, in music, is meant the capacity for developing and unifying musical ideas without introducing any merely ornamental loose ends) is always a strong point in Sibelius's symphonies. The final statement of the big tune in the last movement of the second symphony is an obvious example of the exactly contrived placing of the overwhelming, clinching argument. Symphonies Nos. 1, 2, and 5 have memorable "big tunes" of this sort and are the most popular symphonies. The fourth has a rather exaggerated reputation for being difficult, although it certainly possesses an eerie or mysterious quality.

Sibelius in his symphonies makes great play with short motives of a few notes, and he is a composer with distinctive fingerprints—among them, rushing string passages in contrary motion (some parts moving up while others move down), and falling two-note figures with the first note accented. Moreover, although anything but an ostentatious orchestral colourist, he is a great master of orchestration. For example, *The Swan of Tuonela* is characterised by the special "dark" quality of the whole orchestral sound —with one oboe, a bass clarinet, bassoons, horns, and trombones, but no flutes, ordinary clarinets or trumpets ; with strings subdivided for a special, rich effect ; and with prominent parts for kettledrums and bass drum and harp.

Sibelius's brother-in-law, Armas Järnefelt (1869–1958), was also a composer, whose *Praeludium* and *Berceuse* for orchestra are sometimes heard. The only other Finnish composers of some international standing are Selim Palmgren (1878–1951), who wrote several effective picturesque piano solos and for a time taught in the United States ; and Yrjö Kilpinen (1892–1959), a distinguished and highly prolific song-writer to poems in Finnish, Swedish, and German. In characterisation, Kilpinen's songs have been compared to both Mussorgsky and Hugo Wolf; and, like Wolf's, they give high importance to the piano.

DENMARK

Denmark recognises as her greatest composer, and as a specifically national one, Carl Nielsen (1865–1931). Nineteen years after his death the Danish State Radio Symphony Orchestra visited the Edinburgh Festival and played Nielsen's fifth symphony, provoking among certain British critics and music-lovers a wave of enthusiasm for Nielsen, who is otherwise almost unknown outside Scandinavia. Nielsen wrote, among other works, six symphonies, an opera called *Maskarade* (much cherished by Danes), various pieces of chamber music, and a remarkable organ piece called *Commotio*.

Nielsen's first symphony, composed in 1891–92, begins in one key and ends in another. (In 1894, quite independently, Mahler's Symphony No. 2 did likewise.) This use of what theorists have called " progressive tonality " makes it possible to regard the total composition as a battle in which the key that is to end the piece vanquishes the key that began it. Whether or not the ordinary listener can aurally follow such a battle, he cannot miss the element of conflict in Nielsen's symphonic thinking—conflicts of themes and keys which eventually end in triumphant decisiveness.

What the ancients thought of as the " temperaments " of men (choleric, phlegmatic, melancholy, and sanguine) give their name to Nielsen's second symphony, *The Four Temperaments*. In the third symphony or *Sinfonia Espansiva*, Nielsen uses wordless solo soprano and baritone, thus anticipating by a dozen years the wordless voice in Vaughan Williams's *Pastoral Symphony* of 1922. The fourth symphony is named *The Unquenchable* or *Inextinguishable*—(" Music is life, and as such is unquenchable ", Nielsen said). The fifth, in only two movements, is perhaps the finest of the symphonies. Nielsen's suggestion of conflict was never stronger than here, where the side-drummer is instructed to improvise a cadenza, louder and louder, as if trying to drown the rest of the orchestra, whose playing continues without heeding him. The sixth or *Sinfonia Semplice* (the name *Simple Symphony* is surely ironic) is bitter and sardonic and ends inconclusively. Superficially, but only superficially, it seems miles apart from the previous five.

Though Nielsen has been an inspiration to the Danish composers who followed, and though a direct influence can be seen in (for instance) the earlier works of Finn Høffding (*b.* 1899), a striking feature of modern Danish music has been its contact with the wider European movements of our century. Thus Knudaage Riisager (*b.* 1897) studied in Paris under Albert Roussel, and has apparently been influenced also by Bartók. In a light vein his entertaining orchestral modernisations of Czerny's piano studies formed the music for the ballet *Études*. Bartók also influenced Vagn Holmboe (*b.* 1909), who has won distinction with some of his seven symphonies and his " chamber concertos ". Prominent among younger composers is Niels Viggo Bentzon (*b.* 1919), a fine pianist who has composed many works for the piano as well as three string quartets, a set of symphonic variations for orchestra, and other works. He uses twelve-note technique.

NORWAY AND SWEDEN

In Norway the music of Harald Saeverud (*b.* 1897) is closely in touch with nationalistic traditions. Other Norwegians have considered that Grieg was not nationalistic enough and that he too much diluted his music with German elements. A stickler for the " purity " of folk style is Geirr Tveitt (*b.* 1908), whose orchestral arrangements of Norwegian mountain airs are very effective. Tveitt has also gone so far as to write a concerto for the Hardanger fiddle, the Norwegian folk-instrument which has " sympathetic " strings in addition to ordinary ones. An isolated Norwegian figure was Fartein Valen (1887–1952), a thorough modernist who evolved an atonal musical language with some relationship to Schoenberg's. His works include five symphonies, a violin concerto, and *Le Cimetière Marin* (" The Cemetery by the Sea "), an orchestral work after a poem by Valéry.

The first important figure of modern Swedish music is Hilding Rosenberg (*b.* 1892). The achievement of his five symphonies and six string quartets (which deserve to be more widely known) has given him among his countrymen something of the status of a Swedish Vaughan Williams. The *Little Suite* by Dag Wirén (*b.* 1905) and the *Pastoral Suite* by Lars-Erik Larsson (*b.* 1908) are two rather light works which have drawn attention to their composers. Probably the most important Swedish composer now is Karl-Birger Blomdahl (*b.* 1916), the composer of three symphonies (No. 3 has the title *Facets*), a cantata called *In the Hall of Mirrors*, and the first " space-opera ", *Aniara*. He makes use of twelve-note technique, as does a younger gifted composer, Ingvar Lidholm (*b.* 1921).

SOVIET RUSSIA

Musical nationalism, so far from being dead, has been elevated into a dogma in Soviet Russia. Nor has the paradox of a supposedly " leftist " political régime encouraging " conservative " art gone unnoticed. Thus when Prokofiev, Shostakovich, and other composers were condemned by Soviet officialdom in 1948 for " formalism " and other supposed faults, a letter of recantation on behalf of a congress of Russian musicians included the sentence : "It is obvious to us that, having entered the path of formalistic pseudo-modernism, the representatives of the movement condemned in the Resolution of the Central Committee of the All-Union Communist Party (Bolsheviks) have dissociated themselves from folk-music and song, have forgotten the musical language of their native land, have debased themselves to the point of subjecting their talents to models and dogmas of western European and American modernism."

This statement may have been inspired by necessity, but it would be wrong to think that the Soviet subscribers to such apologias are necessarily obsequious time-servers. There are no doubt many who quite genuinely feel that musical nationalism still unites the composer with his immediate audience in a special and valid way. Sergei Prokofiev (1891–1953) deliberately chose in 1934, after previously living abroad, to return to Soviet Russia and to simplify and broaden his style, previously rather acid. The result was to give us not only the popular *Peter and the Wolf* (for children, using a narrator and orchestra), but also such works as the second violin concerto, the fifth and seventh symphonies, the final four of his nine piano sonatas, and the ballets *Romeo and Juliet* and *Cinderella*. These are counted as amongst his best works. On the other hand, to the pre-Soviet period belong, among other things, the popular third piano concerto, the *Classical Symphony* (Prokofiev's first symphony, a loving *jeu d'esprit* with a bow in the direction of Haydn and Mozart), and two remarkable operas—the comic satire *Love for Three Oranges* (produced in Chicago in 1921), and *The Fiery Angel*, a dramatic chronicle which was composed in 1922–25 but achieved production and acclaim only in the 1950s.

Prokofiev had started his career before the Soviet revolution, but came to terms with it. In his early piano pieces, the *Sarcasmes* and the *Visions Fugitives*, he introduced a welcome strain of irony into Russian music ; and his exhilaratingly dry music, though it later shed its spiky melody and youthful irreverence, never lost a refreshing boyishness. Though he had individual points of style that depend on a twentieth-century approach to harmony (especially his fondness for unexpected slips from one key into another), he continued to find inspiration in the key-system and in forms developed from the romantic era.

Older composers who also came to terms with the Soviet æsthetic outlook were Reinhold Glière (1875–1956), of Belgian descent, who won some fame with his ballet *The Red Poppy* (1927), and Nikolai Miaskovsky (1881–1950), who wrote no less than twenty-seven symphonies (all but unknown outside Russia) and an attractive, tenderly nostalgic cello concerto.

Of the composers who have grown up within Soviet Russia, easily the most distinguished is Dmitri Shostakovich (*b.* 1906), who shot into

STATE OPERA HOUSE, VIENNA

Destroyed by bombs in 1945, the original (1869) building was rebuilt as above with
modern improvements and opened with a performance of *Fidelio* on 5th November, 1955.

CARNEGIE HALL, NEW YORK

Opened in May, 1891, with a music festival at which Tchaikovsky was the guest of
honour. The main auditorium seats 2760, and there is a smaller hall for recitals and
chamber music.

prominence with his first symphony, composed at the age of nineteen, and who has never, despite some ups and downs, lost his position of importance. In all he has written twelve symphonies, the eleventh in honour of the abortive 1905 Revolution. Shostakovich's music has not always been free of bombast—probably no one knows this better than the composer himself—but he has written at least two masterpieces ; the fifth and tenth symphonies. Comparable with these is his cello concerto (1959). A gifted pianist, Shostakovich has also distinguished himself with piano solos (from the early *Three Fantastic Dances* to three sets of preludes and fugues) and with a piano quintet which is one of the best-known pieces of chamber music of this century. A " sensational " opera, *The Lady Macbeth of Mtsensk District*, was first acclaimed and then condemned by Soviet officialdom.

Other Soviet composers have mostly remained little known to the non-Communist world, but two exceptions are Dmitri Kabalevsky (*b.* 1904) and Aram Khachaturian (*b.* 1903). Kabalevsky's opera *The Master of Clamecy*, after a novel by Romain Rolland, opens with an overture which has become popular in the concert-hall but is a superficial piece of music-making ; some of his songs and piano works carry considerably greater weight. Khachaturian, an Armenian, is prodigiously gifted. The *Sabre Dance* from his ballet *Gayaneh* (1942) is almost the only piece by a serious composer to penetrate that field of musical activity which is dominated by Tin Pan Alley ; and the music to this ballet, as also to Lermontov's play *Masquerade*, also merits serious appreciation. Khachaturian's other work includes a romantically-inclined piano concerto which shows (like some of his other music) the influence of Armenian folk-melody. The orchestral accompaniment includes a flexatone (a rarely encountered member of the percussion department, rather like a " musical saw " but shaken, not bowed), to simulate an Armenian folk-instrument.

POLAND

A Polish composer who has won a firm place in the European music of the twentieth century is Karol Szymanowski (1882–1937). He studied in Berlin, underwent the influence of Richard Strauss and Debussy, but later adopted a rather simpler style with some debt to Polish folk-music. His works for violin are notable : they include two fine but neglected concertos and three *Myths* for violin and piano (the first is the well-known *Fountain of Arethusa*). His opera *King Roger* (produced 1926) and his ballet *Harnasie* are highly regarded by his countrymen and others, and the former is the source of *Roxana's Song*, a piece sometimes heard also in an instrumental arrangement.

O.O.M.—P

Since the 1939–45 war Poland, politically linked to the Soviet Union, has officially encouraged music that is popular, nationalistic, and not over-experimental. But the full rigour of Communist æsthetic doctrine does not seem to have been felt in Poland, which in the mid-1950s opened its doors (as Russia did not) to the music of Stravinsky and Schoenberg. Working within Poland, the composer Witold Lutoslawski (*b.* 1913) has made a name for himself among musicians elsewhere with some imaginative orchestral works. Andrzej Panufnik (*b.* 1914) chose to leave Poland in protest against political conditions and has lived in England (working partly as a conductor) since 1954. Panufnik's compositions include two symphonies, and some of his work is indebted to Polish folk-music.

RUMANIA

Certain other national movements remain to be mentioned. A Rumanian composer, and more than a composer, was Georges Enesco (1881–1955). His own instrument was the violin, and he was a principal teacher of Yehudi Menuhin ; but he also conducted, and on occasion he appeared in public as a pianist. Such a musical all-rounder, fairly common in the eighteenth century, and not unknown in the nineteenth (Mendelssohn had equal versatility), has few contemporary parallels. In his two *Rumanian Rhapsodies* for orchestra Enesco evokes the traditional musical spirit of his country, and he is treated in Rumania as its chief national musical figure. His opera *Œdipus* was successfully revived in Bucharest in 1958. Elsewhere, however, his music is little heard, nor have any later Rumanian composers made an international mark.

BELGIUM

Little impact has been made by anything that we may call a Belgian school of composers. Guillaume Lekeu (1870–94), who was born in Belgium but studied in France under César Franck and Vincent d'Indy, would probably, like Franck, also have developed into a decisively French composer had early death not struck him. Perhaps the three chief Belgian composers since then are Joseph Jongen (1873–1953), his brother Léon Jongen (*b.* 1884), and Jean Absil (*b.* 1893), whose work includes five symphonies and two saxophone quartets. It is also worth recalling that the great Belgian violinist Eugene Ysaÿe (1858–1931), who gave the first performance of many new works, including Franck's violin sonata, was also himself a composer of some standing, and his fellow-violinists still cherish his romantically effective music for their instrument.

HOLLAND

Dutch composers inclined towards German musical models in the nineteenth century, and sometimes afterwards. Such a composer was Johan Wagenaar (1862–1941). (His son Bernard, born in 1894 and also a composer, settled in America.) Later, Debussy and other French composers began to have an influence, for instance on Sem Dresden (1881–1957) and Willem Pijper (1894–1947). But Pijper, who is regarded as Holland's chief modern composer, later inclined to a more fiercely modern style, and sometimes towards polytonal writing. His work includes three symphonies and five string quartets, the last unfinished. Among his pupils is the most distinguished living Dutch composer, Henk Badings (*b.* 1907), whose work shows some affinity with Hindemith's contrapuntal style and includes five symphonies and (very rare for any composer) four violin concertos. Of recent years he has been much involved with electronic music.

SWITZERLAND

Switzerland in modern times has naturally felt the pull of the larger nations round her. Arthur Honegger, though Swiss by parentage, was actually born and educated in France. Similarly it is fair to group with German composers another Swiss composer, Willy Burkhard (1900–55), who was somewhat influenced by Hindemith and who wrote *The Vision of Isaiah* and other Protestant oratorios. Frank Martin (*b.* 1890), though Swiss-born, seems to have little national allegiance. He has lived much in Holland, has set French and German words to music, and his opera *The Tempest* (on Shakespeare's play, but in German) had its first performance at the Vienna State Opera. His *Petite Symphonie Concertante* for piano, harpsichord, harp, and two string orchestras, has enjoyed success. He has been influenced both by modern French music and by the twelve-note technique of Schoenberg. It seems, indeed, doubtful whether we can speak of a Swiss " national " composer, even though Ernest Bloch (1880–1959) composed an orchestral rhapsody entitled *Helvetia*.

A " JEWISH " COMPOSER

Bloch is often thought of as constituting almost a unique case among national musical movements. Swiss by birth, German by training, American by naturalisation and residence, he has written many works with Jewish associations and is commonly considered a specifically Jewish composer. Though a number of other composers of the last 150 years have been of Jewish descent (Mendelssohn, Mahler, Offenbach, Anton Rubinstein, Arthur Benjamin, Aaron Copland, Darius Milhaud, Mario Castelnuovo-Tedesco—to name a few from different countries), and one or two have written works connected with Jewish worship or Jewish subjects, Bloch is perhaps the sole example of a composer so closely identified with Jewish tradition.

Bloch's works include a *Sacred Service* (for an American " Reformed " Jewish rite) ; *Schelomo* (" Solomon "), a rhapsody for cello and orchestra ; *Israel*, a symphony with voices (though with the character of a symphonic poem rather than of a symphony); and a suite for violin and piano called *Baal Shem*, alluding to the nineteenth-century pietistic sect of Chassidim. His music is highly individual and emotional ; it makes strong use of fourths and fifths in harmony, and of the Oriental-sounding melodic interval of the augmented second. Yet Bloch does not, in general, utilise traditional Jewish melodies, and declared that he was " not an archæologist ". Some would add that his best works are his least " Jewish " ones—such as the four string quartets and the piano quintet of 1923, which certainly stand very high in twentieth-century chamber music.

Bloch, at any rate, stands alone. Neither Europe nor America knows a " Jewish school " of music, nor is it surprising that the State of Israel, so recently founded, has as yet produced no composer of standing. When he comes, we need not be surprised if he turns out to be the dark-skinned son of a North African Jew instead of a once-removed Viennese or a twice-removed Muscovite. In any case, the music of the new Israel need not be expected to be anything like the music of a Jew like Bloch, consciously European but consciously different from his fellow-Europeans. If musical nationalism in most old-fashioned countries seems to be ready to wither away, it is possibly in this " new " nation that we may see it push forth a late bloom.

DEVELOPMENTS IN BRITAIN

Although Sir Henry Wood had conducted Schoenberg's *Five Orchestral Pieces* at the Proms in 1912, not Schoenberg but Stravinsky was the twentieth-century modernist whose influence first made itself felt on British composers. Stravinsky's anti-romantic outlook and his idiomatic use of chamber ensembles led to Bliss's *Rout* (1919) for wordless voice and ten instruments, and to Walton's *Façade* (1922), a twenty-year-old composer's precocious setting for reciter and instruments of Edith Sitwell's near-nonsense verses, which gained him a reputation as a musical wit and satirist he later found some difficulty in shaking off. Sir Arthur Bliss (*b.* 1891) later took a different turn and adopted a non-ironic, forthright, often martial air that seemed to indicate an unabashed romanticism beneath—as in the successful ballet *Checkmate* (1937). His chamber music includes an able clarinet quintet. The fine opening of the slow movement of the piano concerto (1938) is in strong contrast to the more grandiloquent style of his " Colour " symphony.

The modernist impetus of Sir William Walton (*b.* 1902) lasted longer —through the racy overture *Portsmouth Point* (which in 1925 set the example of all the breezy British overtures which followed), the viola concerto (1929), the magnificent choral work *Belshazzar's Feast* (1931), and the first symphony (first performed complete in 1935). *Belshazzar's Feast* is indeed easily the best, as well as the most popular, big British choral work since Elgar's *The Dream of Gerontius.* His violin and cello concertos contain music of great beauty, and masterly writing for the solo instruments with elaborate and effective orchestral accompaniment.

His opera *Troilus and Cressida* was a remarkable first work in this field, and showed a natural instinct for the stage, with fine arias, effective choral writing, and stirring climaxes. Following the Puccini type of operatic convention, it has not been sensational in its impact, but it is hoped that more will come from this great talent. His second symphony (1960) has disappointed the critics who find in it no technical or emotional advance on his tumultuous first (they forget that Beethoven's eighth followed his shattering fifth and seventh), but its lighter appeal and more comfortable impact have already given it a large public.

RAWSTHORNE AND TIPPETT

Alan Rawsthorne (*b.* 1905) uses a contrapuntal texture influenced by Hindemith. Two piano concertos (the second, 1951, unusually in four movements) and the first of two violin concertos are among the best of his none too abundant works ; also notable are two works for piano solo —a set of *Bagatelles* and a sonatina— and a clarinet quartet. Michael Tippett, also born in 1905, likewise underwent the influence of Hindemith, but also that of Holst and of the Elizabethan contrapuntists. Like Holst's, Tippett's music has apparently some difficulty in " getting across " to audiences. Contrapuntal skill and passionate lyricism are admirably combined in his concerto for double string orchestra (1939). A work conceived with striking originality was *A Child of Our Time* (1941), in effect an oratorio ; its subject is not biblical but drawn from the Nazi persecutions of the Jews, and Negro spirituals are used as a commentary in the way that Bach used traditional German hymns in his Passions. Tippett's other works include an opera, *The Midsummer Marriage* (1955), in which the composer's own libretto proved fatally obscure, though the music includes some of his best pages, such as the *Ritual Dances*, which can be performed as a concert work. Two song cycles—*Boyhood's End* and *The Heart's Assurance*—also deserve mention.

BERKELEY AND LAMBERT

Lennox Berkeley (*b.* 1903) is the composer of the expressive, yet tautly made, cycle for voice and orchestra, *Four Poems of St. Teresa of Avila*, and also of a fine but less-known vocal work, the *Stabat Mater* for six solo voices and orchestra. His training in Paris under Nadia Boulanger contributed to the clear texture of his orchestral writing in a Divertimento and other works. Of his operas, *A Dinner Engagement* (1954) is the best (thanks in part to Paul Dehn's witty libretto) and would be better still but for the composer's natural reticence of manner. Constant Lambert (1905–51) was composer, pianist, conductor, and critic, whose greatest influence was exerted as musical director of the Sadler's Wells Ballet (now The Royal Ballet); but in his *The Rio Grande* (for chorus, orchestra, and piano solo) he brought to the concert-hall a surprisingly durable and poetic adaptation of the jazz idiom of the late 1920s.

RUBBRA AND OTHERS

Edmund Rubbra (*b.* 1901), a pupil of Vaughan Williams and Holst, has been a prolific composer of orchestral and other music, including seven symphonies. It is recognisably English music of a quality which is solid enough to earn respect but not, apparently, striking enough for any single work to maintain itself in the general repertory. Even less mark on the general public has been made by Elisabeth Lutyens (*b.* 1906), who adopted Schoenberg's twelve-note technique and whose works include six string quartets and various concertos. William Alwyn (*b.* 1905) and Benjamin Frankel (*b.* 1906) have written film scores of real artistic importance, but their concert works have not found a place in the repertory. Humphrey Searle (*b.* 1915) made a lyrically pleasing use of Schoenberg's twelve-note technique in such works as his *Poem for 22 Solo Strings*, but has more recently taken to a free atonal method of composition—in such works as his neo-Lisztian second piano concerto.

REVOLT IN THE OPERA-HOUSE

It is in the opera-house that the glimmerings of the composers' revolt against complexity, without relaxation of standards of quality, are to be seen most clearly. Music in the theatre must be effective with an audience. It is there to serve the drama and its rôle is at least in some degree subsidiary. Despite this, from Monteverdi's day to our own, there has been much experimentation in style in the orchestra pit.

After the last war it was nothing less than an operatic explosion which first convinced Europe that English music might, after all, once more be exportable. If Benjamin Britten's *Peter Grimes* (1945) made its overwhelming effect in many theatres besides Sadler's Wells, this was due primarily to the intrinsic excellence of the opera and its music. But wide perception of this excellence was possible only because Britten commanded theatrical effect, the technique of communication, the power of direct address to an audience. This technique, and a willingness to use it, have stood him in excellent stead through a series of major works in which the operatic sequence has been dominant.

BRITTEN

Measured by the performances he has received abroad as well as in his own country, no British composer born in this century can rival Britten (*b.* 1913). Although it was the performance of his *Variations on a theme of Frank Bridge* for string orchestra at Salzburg in 1937 which first established his mastery, most of his work has been for voices. His opera *Peter Grimes* was followed by four operas of smaller dimensions using a chamber-orchestral accompaniment. These were *The Rape of Lucretia* (1946), *Albert Herring* (1947), a new edition of *The Beggar's Opera* (1948), and an entertainment for children, *Let's Make an Opera* (1949), which incorporated a one-act opera, *The Little Sweep*. For these works, which utilise an instrumental group consisting of a string quintet, wind quintet, harp, and percussion, Britten organised his own company, the English Opera Group, which also became the pivot of his other enterprise, the Aldeburgh Festival, held annually in the Suffolk town in which he has made his home.

Britten's later operas are *Billy Budd* (1951) and *Gloriana* (1953), both full-scale works, and the chamber works *The Turn of the Screw* (1954) and *Midsummer Night's Dream* (1960). *Noye's Fludde* (1958) is a musical adaptation of the medieval Chester Miracle Play. Several of these works call for child performers, and some for the musical participation of the audience.

No less notable have been Britten's song-cycles—including three with orchestra, *Les Illuminations* (1939), *Serenade* (for tenor, horn, and strings, 1943), and *Nocturne* (1958). Britten's entirely individual vocal line partly revives the ideas of word-setting found in Purcell, and stands out against a modern harmonic idiom indebted to both Stravinsky and Mahler, though the result is wholly personal and arresting.

Matters not purely musical may determine the public response to an opera ; and the second half of the twentieth century may not in general be readily sympathetic to the drawing of Christian lessons from pagan stories (*The Rape of Lucretia*) or to ghosts presented in three dimensions (*The Turn of the Screw*). Similarly, an opera using no women and ending in an anti-climax (*Billy Budd*) handicaps itself from the start. Nevertheless, some of Britten's most forceful and most imaginative music is here. The choral and orchestral *Spring Symphony*, also bursting with inspiration, is really a development of the song-cycle rather than of symphonic form. The admirable orchestral *Variations and Fugue on a Theme of Purcell* was originally written for a film ("The Young Person's Guide to the Orchestra") demonstrating orchestral instruments.

NEW INTEREST IN OPERA

Britten's success has been only one element in the growth of a new interest in opera in Britain. The establishment of a permanent opera and ballet company at Covent Garden since 1946, and the regular provision of public subsidies to opera at both Covent Garden and Sadler's Wells, have made conditions for British opera much more favourable. (Between 1919 and 1939, by contrast, only five new full-length British operas were produced at Covent Garden, and only two at the Old Vic and Sadler's Wells Theatres, which at first were run conjointly.) It was also a new feature of post-war Britain that state and local subsidies were extended to symphony orchestras and to many new festivals, easily the largest of which was the Edinburgh International Festival, which opened in 1947. This was originally associated in management with the Glyndebourne (Sussex) Opera Festival, which had opened in 1934 (for short international seasons on a high artistic level), and was continued after the war. The annual Cheltenham Festival of British Contempory Music (started 1946) has given composers a useful and prominent new platform.

Nevertheless, Arthur Benjamin (1893–1960) had to wait fifteen years after composing his one-act opera *Prima Donna* before it was staged in 1949 —since when performances in several countries have proved it to possess a rare lyrical and comic touch. With the same gifted librettist, Cedric

Cliffe, Benjamin composed *A Tale of Two Cities*, a full-length opera on Dickens's novel. This is a work full of musical force and dramatic stage-craft, just the combination lacking in many other modern British operas. A certain obviousness, permissible and even desirable on the stage, has perhaps hampered Benjamin's concert work ; but he has distinguished himself in writing light music—notably the celebrated *Jamaican Rumba*, originally for two pianos—which is at once really light and really artistic.

Two operas by Alan Bush (*b.* 1900), *Wat Tyler* (1953) and *Men of Blackmoor* (1956), were successfully produced in East Germany. The circumstances of their production there were doubtless connected with Bush's avowed Communist beliefs, but his music is always written with solid craft, sometimes with ingenious counterpoint (as in the string quartet sub-titled *Dialectic*) and, rather less frequently, with an appealing lyrical impetus.

NEW BLOOD

The Nazi persecutions and expulsions of the 1930s, which happily had given Glyndebourne the services of Fritz Busch as conductor and Carl Ebert as producer, also brought two composers to settle in Britain. Franz Reizen-stein (*b.* 1911), a pupil of Hindemith and later of Vaughan Williams, is noted as a pianist and has written some vigorous chamber music and concertos. Mátyás Seiber (1905–60) was a Hungarian by birth and a pupil of Kodály. Distinguished as a composer (his music includes four string quartets and a cantata with a text from James Joyce's *Ulysses*), he was also much sought after as a teacher.

Seiber was the teacher of Peter Racine Fricker (*b.* 1920), whose earlier music showed the influence both of Bartók and of Schoenberg, and inclines to seriousness of mood and thickness of texture. His output includes two symphonies, two violin concertos, and two string quartets ; but with the choral *Vision of Judgment* and the second symphony (1960) Hindemith's influence seems stronger. Completely removed from Fricker's approach is Malcolm Arnold (*b.* 1921), a former orchestral trumpeter whose music is deliberately "easy on the ear " ; and he is also the first important British composer since Elgar to write serious instrumental music in a genuinely " popular " (as distinct from an artificially " folk ") style. Five symphonies, a descriptive overture on Burns's *Tam o' Shanter*, and some simply con-structed but notably imaginative *English Dances* and *Scottish Dances* are among Arnold's orchestral works.

Antony Hopkins (*b.* 1921) has a light touch and a gift for musical mockery which have made delightful musical soufflés in operettas such as *Three's Company* (1953). A serious outlook and a discriminating ear marks

Iain Hamilton (*b.* 1922), whose work includes a curious but attractive cantata, *The Bermudas.* We may also note the names of Anthony Milner (*b.* 1925), whose melodiously wrought cantata *Salutatio Angelica* is one of several works with specific Catholic associations, and of John Joubert (*b.* 1927 in South Africa), a gifted song-writer. John Addison (*b.* 1920) and Donald Swann (*b.* 1922) have successfully harnessed serious musical resources to the composing of original light music.

It would be either invidious, or a mere indulgence in unqualified prophecy, if names of still younger composers were picked out here. Certainly no subsequent composer of twenty-five has shown the definite mastery which the twenty-four-year-old Britten showed with the *Variations on a Theme of Frank Bridge.* Such a youngster, should he or she arise, will find a musical England receptive to new ideas and ready in its musical and social institutions to give such ideas a hearing. Nothing can produce a musical Milton to order, but there seems no probability that such a Milton would be left mute and inglorious.

THE U.S.A.

In the U.S.A. German music reigned supreme in the concert-hall throughout the nineteenth century, and Germany attracted American composers for study. Of these, the most notable was Edward MacDowell (1861–1908), but the regard with which he is now held in his own country is largely sentimental, and only a few picturesquely romantic miniatures for the piano remain in the repertory. The first real consciousness of America in the musical life of Europe came not through any of these European-trained musicians but through something that most of them regarded as amusing at best and disgusting at worst : ragtime and jazz. Debussy borrowed from it in *Golliwogg's Cake-Walk* for piano, as early as 1908 ; and Ravel, Stravinsky, Milhaud, Hindemith, Constant Lambert and others soon followed. The first American work to capture the international concert-hall was an attempt to reconcile jazz with Liszt : the *Rhapsody in Blue* (1924) for piano and orchestra by George Gershwin (1898–1937). (The orchestration is by Ferde Grofé, though Gershwin's later works are orchestrated by himself.)

It was Paris, the centre of so much musical activity in the 1920s, that replaced the German cities as the Americans' Mecca for musical study. Virgil Thomson (*b.* 1896) and Aaron Copland (*b.* 1900), both of whom were pupils in Paris of the gifted Frenchwoman, Nadia Boulanger (*b.* 1887), are perhaps the two most important figures in the American music of their generation. They learnt in Paris to value simplicity of texture and clarity of sound, and to suspect the German urge to 'develop' themes. What is more, they found that this outlook favoured a specifically American music, which could borrow from traditional sources at will. Perhaps the chief American inspiration to Thomson has been the revivalist hymn-tune—in, for instance, his cello concerto ; and his chief non-American influence has been the French composer Erik Satie, as shown in the artful artlessness of Thomson's opera *Four Saints in Three Acts* (1928), written for a Negro cast to an apparently nonsensical text by Gertrude Stein.

Copland has been able to enrich his idiom with jazz (*Music for the Theatre*), cowboy songs and the like (the ballets *Rodeo* and *Appalachian Spring*), Latin-American tunes (*El Salón México* and the clarinet concerto)—or, on another occasion, to write music which seems completely non-derivative yet completely American, for instance the fine third symphony. This " American-ness " is hard to define. It is linked with something in the rhythmic formation of phrases, and something in an " open-sounding " harmony with prominent consecutive triads. In certain works even this disappears, and this protean composer can be completely atonal.

In the United States to-day, where music is well endowed at universities, there are probably hundreds (rather than just dozens) of composers actually at work. Probably the one who is most performed—perhaps even more than Copland—is an American only by residence. Gian-Carlo Menotti (*b.* 1911) was born in Italy but has lived in America since 1928. His extremely successful operas, with librettos by himself (all in English, except for *Amelia Goes to the Ball*, originally Italian), have a sure theatrical touch and a wide range—from *The Consul* (1950), a political drama, to the skittish *The Telephone* (1947) with only two characters, and the touching Christmas story *Amahl and the Night Visitors* (1951, originally for television). For all the skill of their presentation, the music of *The Medium* and *The Consul* is very thin ; but the lively and unpretentious music of *The Telephone* shows Menotti at his best.

SYMPHONISTS

Like Copland, Walter Piston (*b.* 1894) and Roy Harris (*b.* 1898) were pupils of Nadia Boulanger. Piston has combined considerable academic work with a steady output of direct and immediately impressive symphonies, totally unconcerned with any dogmas of language or message. His text-books on harmony, counterpoint, and orchestration equal anything in that field produced in Europe ; and of his sixth symphony he has said that it was composed " with no intent other than to make music to be played and listened to ". The symphonies of Paul Creston (*b.* 1906) are linked

447

more directly to the European tradition ; the third is based on Gregorian plainchant.

Other American composers whose work has lain mainly in the symphonic field and who show what are generally thought to be American national characteristics in their music are Howard Hanson (b. 1896), William Schuman (b. 1910), and Samuel Barber (b. 1910). Barber, who first sprang to attention with his *Adagio for Strings* (originally a movement for string quartet), has a style perhaps less overtly American and more inclined towards European romanticism than his fellows. Something of a lone figure who writes absolutely uncompromising, often atonal, music, is Roger Sessions (b. 1896).

It should be added that American composers to-day have discovered the founder of their line in Charles Ives (1874–1954), who composed music before 1920 in which, working quite independently of European musicians, he used such devices as polytonality, quarter-tones, and multiple simultaneous rhythms of great complexity. Here, apparently, was an American prophecy of Europe's revolutionary expansion of the resources of music. However, Ives also made full use of hymn-tunes and other traditional American musical elements. He was little recognised at first, and two major works, the *Concord* sonata for piano and the third symphony, achieved their first complete performances only in 1939 and 1946 respectively. Even now, Ives's music has made little headway outside America, except where there is a tendency to identify music that is unusual with music that is important.

THE AMERICAN MUSICAL SCENE

Symphonies are not the whole of American music, and it is indeed principally the scope and vitality in that wider field which calls for comment. In Europe, folk-music traditions are local : they are also for the most part dying or dead, their survival or revival depending on individual enthusiasm or specialist activity. In the United States the European traditions are not local, for each has been carried there at some time and dispersed thinly but generally, to mingle with other influences—Latin-American, American-Indian, or African. The resulting mixture has produced jazz, which is the only twentieth-century folk-music still alive in the sense that it is allowed its own development alongside the development of the folk concerned with it. For this reason it enjoys by far the strongest influence on popular music, now largely an international language, that any national folk-music has ever had.

Of their undisputed pre-eminence in this field the Americans are justifiably proud, but their achievement by no means ends there. Independence of outlook and an inherent vitality are turning a lack of tradition to good purpose and creating a musical culture that looks forward rather than backward. Standards of performance are high, and growing higher. The symphony orchestras are the most technically accomplished in the world, and standards of interpretation improve, an improvement reflected in the recent growth of first-class American chamber-music performances. The military band is now regarded seriously as a contributor to concert music in America, where it has been re-christened the " concert band " and sprung to great popularity. (In England, once a leader in this field, its style and repertory continue to linger in the past.) Light orchestras everywhere increasingly follow the American model. Educational standards are reflected in the appointment to the highest posts of such musicians as Piston, Milhaud, and Hindemith. Largely as the result of the influx into the United States of refugee musicians from Europe, the once-fashionable centres of Leipzig or London or Paris now appear less self-evidently superior to many much less traditional names in the New World.

LATIN AMERICA

In Latin America the only major figure of much more than national importance was the Brazilian, Heitor Villa-Lobos (1887-1959). His work does not quote folk-music but is specifically national in content, and frequently uses the special percussion instruments of Brazilian popular music. The works (more than a dozen) entitled *Chôros*, for various combinations ranging from a solo guitar (No. 1) to orchestra, band, and chorus (No. 14), are intended to synthesise the various Brazilian, South American Indian, and popular musical traditions, having for principal elements rhythm and melody of typical popular character. The instrumental works (at least nine) called *Bachianas Brasileiras* are intended to synthesise Bach-like elements with those of traditional Brazilian music.

Villa-Lobos's enormous output is the despair of cataloguers. Some of his works have been found deficient in enough interest to repay a second performance, but in others Villa-Lobos shows a lively melodic gift, great rhythmic invention, and charm, even in the apparently hackneyed field of illustrative music ; the musical picture of *The Little Train* (from the second *Bachiana Brasileira*) is deservedly a favourite. On the more intimate side. some of his studies for guitar have a finely balanced classical line, and his piano music is also often effective.

Other Brazilian composers of note are Camargo Guarnieri (*b.* 1907) and Eleazar de Carvalho (*b.* 1915), known in the United States as a conductor.

449

Carlos Chávez (*b.* 1899) of Mexico has also attempted, though in a slightly less exuberant style and a smaller output, a mating of his country's national traditions with the general heritage of a twentieth-century composer. His works include five symphonies (the *Sinfonia India* is the best known) and, for an ensemble of Mexican national instruments, a piece named *Xochipili-Macuilxochitl* after the Aztec god of war.

Much encouragement has been given in various Latin-American countries to the development of a specifically national kind of music. In Argentina composers of some standing include José Maria Castro (*b.* 1892), his brother Juan José Castro (*b.* 1895), and Alberto Ginastera (*b.* 1916).

XXV

MUSIC AND THE DANCE

WHETHER it accompanies a session of rock-'n'-roll or a ballerina's flawless rendering of a great *adagio* in classical ballet, all dance music is marked by its intensely rhythmical quality. The body of melody, clad in however rich harmonies, is suitable for dancing only if we are aware of an untiring rhythm which controls, inspires, and to some extent colours the dance movements.

The word "dance" is of great antiquity, deriving from a basic word found in most of the Germanic languages : its Greek variant comes from a Sanskrit root (*tan*) meaning tension. The fact of dancing is something as universal and spontaneous as the fact of vocal utterance ; peoples of an absolutely primitive standard of simplicity in architecture, clothing, and social methods use some kind of rhythmically patterned movements or gestures, to an accompaniment of drumming or chanting, as a means of giving pleasure, of invoking magic powers, and of worship. In its simplest form, as a spontaneous happening, dancing is a pattern of exercising certain groups of muscles (which produce exaggerated gestures of head, limbs, and torso) under a strong emotional influence. Dancing has both soothing and exciting qualities ; and whether the aim is to stimulate or relax the spirit, it forms simple and regular patterns. Sequences of steps and gesture are reiterated to an accompaniment of chanting, regular vocal expletives, and often percussive effects of drumming or hand-claps.

From this self-hypnotic activity there gradually grows the idea of making steps and gestures more elaborate, which leads the performer to develop a consciousness of skill. Usually much later in a people's cultural development comes the idea of making the dance-patterns more complex, not only to test the performer's skill but to draw admiration from spectators who are not participating. These stages in the choreographic development of a culture can occupy many hundreds of years of racial development.

EARLY HISTORY OF THE DANCE

Lacking the solidly documented evidence that we possess for the other arts, we must trace the history of dancing and of dance music indirectly—

through comparisons and suggestions derived from the history of drama, art music, and social custom.

We are so used to watching, or ourselves performing, dancing which uses music of some quality and interest of texture that we easily forget that the use of such music for dancing is a comparatively recent growth. Dancing, we know, is so old that it may be one of man's first purely pleasurable activities ; but we do not yet know whether he already used for urgent daily communication a form of rhythmic vocal utterance (such as would be found suitable to mark the " beat " of his dancing steps).

Our history of dance music coincides with the first reliable record we have of a European dance-form ; we know that dancing in Greece grew out of religious ceremonial into the more highly stylised ceremonial of the theatre. There were strong links between music, poetry, and dancing ; on most public occasions they were blended together to form the lyric, dramatic, or comic event.

As the drama became more elaborate and the number of chief actors was multiplied, the singing-and-dancing chorus took on a new importance. They pointed the play's situations and bridged the intervals between the great speeches with stylised " explanations " of what was supposed to be happening off-stage. Thus there grew up certain conventions of choreography, particular dance-forms suitable for accompanying lyric, tragic, or comic tales.

DANCING AS ENTERTAINMENT

After the decline of Greece, the Romans were quick to turn the hitherto sacred theatre-art into a wholly entertaining spectacle. The very nature and temperament of the peoples of the Mediterranean world are histrionic. The Greek forms of theatre had been transplanted to the Greek colonies in Sicily and Southern Italy. The wedding of Greek clarity of thought and austerity of communication with the exuberance and still predominantly unsophisticated taste of Italy produced a more spectacular, riotous, undisciplined, and vulgar form of theatrical entertainment. Dance and its accompanying music exploited all the shades of wit, farce, buffoonery, and near-obscenity that were permissible. Probably the first clear separation of music from stylised acting (and dancing) in the theatre came with the growth of skill in miming, which became one of the most popular theatrical *genres*. It was in the Roman theatre, too, that there appeared that significant division by which the audience ceases, either actually or in spirit, to participate directly in the narrative. The Romans were, in fact, the first wholehearted " spectators ".

452

We have no precise choreographic detail of Roman dancing. Apart from man's persistent destructive tendency, which accounts for us possessing so few of the art-objects of previous periods, there was for centuries no notion of putting dance steps on literary record. When musical and dance notations meant laborious and exacting work for skilled scribes and illustrators, it must have seemed scarcely worth while to place on written record what everyone knew, practised, and regularly watched others doing.

THE CHURCH AND DANCING

When the Christian Church assumed power over, and a large degree of responsibility for, the peoples of Europe, actors, mimes, dancers, musicians, and comedians were condemned for their moral licence, and their activities were regarded as unequivocally evil. Players were excommunicated, and what could not be brought somehow into the service of the Church was condemned—at least officially. Dancing, of course, went on. It was not possible to prevent people indulging in the most easily accessible form of social communion.

So far as the story of dance and dance music is concerned, however, the Dark Ages are veritably dark. We know that because mankind in Europe, as elsewhere on the globe, had since earliest times marked the turn of the seasons, the feasts of religion, and the hard facts of work and play through rituals (however simple) which involved music and dancing of a primitive kind, these rituals were kept alive. But we do not know what steps they danced, how the dance pursued certain patterns, what precise melodies they played to guide and regulate the dancers. From what we know of dancing and its music some centuries later, all we can guess is that the dancing of the first eleven or twelve Christian centuries would, to our eyes and ears, seem unbearably repetitive in pattern, since it used very few and very simple steps, and elementary melodies were played on simple instruments of the pipe and lute types.

The dance's connection with the theatre had not been lost, and the first forms from which grew European theatre, and thence our contemporary drama, are the plays and spectacles created to serve a primarily religious purpose—the medieval mysteries, miracles, and moralities. The story of Man's Fall, of Christ's Birth, Passion, and Crucifixion, the lures of Satan, and the pains or blisses of the future life—all these were the material of dramas (and of comedies, too) acted out in churchyards and church porches or in the market-place. Mime and dancing played a large part in these spectacles ; and musicians would be as indispensable as the other performers to drive home lessons that were taught most powerfully through acting, dancing, and declamation before the printed page (for both literature and musical script) became a commonplace of the European's daily existence.

In the repetitive and clumsy patterns of our early European folk-dancing there is for the performer the primary element of pleasure, even though it be only the physical satisfaction of rhythmic movement. All dancing is somehow entertaining, although in the more modern meaning of entertainment as " affording pleasure to the mind", dancing becomes transmuted into so sophisticated an activity as " ballet " only through slow, cautious processes of experiment which occupy centuries.

THE ORIGINS OF " BALLET "

To-day ballet is widely looked upon as the highest development that European dancing can reach. Certainly its present popularity grows out of the appeal of its complexities, added to the purely sensuous pleasure of watching beautiful bodies in graceful or significant movement. The dancing is geared to, is enmeshed with, or grows out of the music. Yet we have to realise that the forms in which ballet exists to-day were devised less than 150 years ago. Probably the most important new factor then introduced was the notion of the composer contributing by the form, tempi, rhythms, and dynamics of his music to the total effect desired.

Before we discuss the history of ballet, dancing, and dance music generally since 1800, we must look at the early history of ballet. During many centuries it was hard to distinguish where social dance ended and where " ballet " began. Very simply, ballet as a distinctive form of art-dancing can properly be said to emerge only when two conditions have been fulfilled. First, its techniques and their expressive use must have become so elaborate that they can be properly displayed only by full-time professional dancers : and, secondly, the idea must have arisen that it has to be performed before spectators. This, further, entails such matters as suitably fitted stages or dance areas, with a separation between performers and spectators. Even before these elementary conditions were achieved, however, so-called " ballets " were being given, and the name itself was used for those vast ceremonial spectacles which princes ordered on great occasions in the fourteenth and fifteenth centuries.

By the end of the sixteenth century some of these had become sensational news-items to be passed all round Europe, by letter or word of mouth. But even if their titles used the word " ballet " (as in *Le Ballet Polonais*, Paris, 1573, or *Le Ballet Comique de la Reine Louise*, Paris, 1581), this referred to the whole spectacle, in which complex formations of courtiers paraded, verses were declaimed, songs were sung, lutenists and viol-players played, and masses of dancers formed themselves into squares, crescents, or entwined circles. All this was staged in the largest indoor space available, with groves of transplanted orange-trees, colonnades of green branches, and working fountains as surroundings. This sort of ceremony meant that the performing of dances was beginning to be treated, in however primitive a way, as a science, as a method of organising human movement into patterns which should create pleasing results for both performer and spectator.

THE EARLY SET DANCES

For the common man and woman dancing had been the purely physical pleasure of self-directed movements performed as ceremonial, to express grief at death's presence or to announce joy at good fortune. After centuries in which Europeans had performed their simple trotting, bumping, and jogging around to the music of the *carole*, the novelty of a fresh kind of dance and a new dance music arose in one small corner of the continent. The carole-dancing took two forms (we must remember that there is little firm evidence of precisely when any change took place in dancing) ; these two forms were the *farandole* and the *bransle*, both to sung accompaniment by the dancers themselves, and both group-dances. In the *farandole* a single line of dancers, linked by the hands, followed whatever path or pattern the leader chose. The *bransle* was a closed circle, still hand-linked, whose patterns were more limited than those of the *farandole*. Both depended on team-work, and every dancer had to be as able as his fellows, otherwise there was little amusement for anyone.

The new dance form and its music were the *estampie*, whose influence was prodigious and far-reaching ; for it was the beginning of every form of social dance in which the unit was a soloist or a pair of dancers. The new freedom to make intricate patterns and figures led to the abandonment of vocal accompaniment, which was replaced by instrumental music. This freeing of secular instrumental music from its function of supporting or sustaining the voice opened the way to all those later exploitations of instrumental playing and composition from which European art music arose. On the other hand the liberation of the dance from the group-idea and the new notion of a man and woman dancing in unison, and then in opposition, led gradually to that vast catalogue of dances on which are based the contemporary techniques of ballroom, ballet, and " expressive " dancing.

"GOTHIC" AND "MEDITERRANEAN" TYPES

Some time after the *estampie* had spread over most of civilised Europe, a new line of choreographic progress became obvious. Dances for couples in partnership were mainly developed in Northern France—and in Northern Europe generally—while the idea of individual dancers tracing their own figures and designs found its proper milieu in Italy. From about the thirteenth century, when the scattered troubadours from Provence had carried the *estampie* round Europe, dance forms seem to grow along two distinct lines, which we may call the Gothic and the Mediterranean. A diagonal line across the face of Europe, reaching from north-west Spain to mid-Russia, neatly divides these two areas. In the southern region the ferment of what was to become the Renaissance was already in agitation, while northern Europe lay shrouded in a mist of Gothic twilight, of romance and of allegory. The north, although admitting the form of the *estampie*, still kept group dances in strong favour, whereas in Italy and Provence there grew up an intense interest in the mathematical and geometric aspects of music—and therefore of dancing. The link between dance forms and instrumental music is a primary one ; the process of growth was slow, but by about the fifteenth century composers were writing instrumental music for several dances successively. At first the convention was to link together only two dances—one each in the commonest forms, a slow (duple time) and a fast (triple time). By the next century in Italy composers were writing suites of three, four, and five dances. With the growth of the idea of the variation, these suites supplied the foundation on which, later, the overture and symphony and the different types of chamber music were created.

GALLIARD AND PAVANE

Gradually the Italian ideas spread northwards, though it was not the intricate and subtle *balli* (dances each to special music) which took the fancy of the French and English, but the *galliard* of French origin, the *pavane* (Italian or Spanish), and the *volta*, a brisker form of the galliard. For many centuries yet, social dancing in England was to be about equally divided between derivations from the *estampie* and complex group dances. These latter were in the form of *bransles* (pronounced commonly in England "brawls"), which were stylised French folk-dances still retaining the old linked line or closed circle form. They lasted well, too, for a suite of them persisted as the introductory item in any important court or society dancing occasion right into the eighteenth century.

The *pavane*—a stately dance in 4/4 time—is important because in England it seems to have been the first dance in a new form through which elegance and dignity could be displayed with a minimum of tiresome technique. But in contrast to the figuring of the group-dances (not very dissimilar to the sort of anonymous promenade common enough in a modern ball-room), the *pavane* allowed the individual, either male or female, to display a bright assertiveness. And at the *galliard*, a fast dance in 3/4 time, the English really excelled. Its very distinct rhythm is to a count of six accented on the fifth—this in order that the basic five steps could be performed. The characteristic jumps and springs were eminently suitable for young men who could best demonstrate the acrobatic element in its performance.

Soon these were superseded in popularity by the *allemande* and *courante*, which were to form the first two numbers in any dance-suite. The *allemande* (literally "German dance") was a *bransle* in duple time, with hand gestures and stiff hops which distinguished it from the commoner, simple form of the dance. The *courante* became a basic favourite all over Europe, and its popularity lasted for at least two centuries. As to differences of dance speed, Shakespeare has a telling comment in *Twelfth Night*, where Sir Toby remarks : "To church in a galliard and home in a coranto ".

The varieties of dance-types seem fantastic, but there were very few metres in which they were written and not many variations of speed at which they could be performed. Moreover—and this is probably the most valuable point that can be made about all our early forms of social dancing— throughout the centuries those forms were subtly influenced by the sort of places in which they were danced, the occasions for dancing, and the costumes in vogue.

In the twelfth and thirteenth centuries the costume of the aristocracy and nobility was fairly light in weight and not too cumbersome in shape. Women's and men's gowns could be tucked into a belt or held up in the hand, and the *estampie* grew partly from the fact that it was physically possible to move rapidly and neatly, in comparison with the solemn processional kind of dancing in fashion until then. In the next century all costume was more elaborate, weightier, and accentuated by enlarged head-dresses ; so the dance fashion moved back to the solemn processional movements of *basse-danses* or *bransles*. By Renaissance times, in Italy, men were wearing much lighter and closer-fitting garments, and silk was coming into wider use. Shoes were fitted like gloves and were almost as delicate and light. Whichever idea came first, certainly fast dancing with a lot of jumping and turning coincided with the wearing of clothes suitable for a lot of breath-consuming activity.

HALL AND COURT

Through these centuries we can also see how the northern nobleman's house, centred on a hall in which everybody gathered for meals and the relaxations following, permitted the continuance of the processional type of dancing. Italian houses were split up into more, and smaller, rooms ; the servants were kept at arms' length, and lords and ladies could disport themselves in the subtle and suave dances of the kind invented (and, happily for us, recorded) by Domenico of Ferrara. When we reach the eighteenth century we find such names as *sarabande, gigue, chaconne, passecaille, minuet, gavotte, rigaudon, passepied, bourrée* among the dances which were not only the commonest social recreation but were the basis on which theatrical dancing was being slowly developed into the ballet of the time. These titles, almost all interchangeable for the dance or the music to which it was performed, are not always of clear derivation. Again we must recall that when dancing was something that everyone *did*, all the time, very few people thought it necessary to record all the changes and fashions for posterity. Although there is probably as much dance literature throughout this time as there is documentation on the arts of painting and sculpture, too much of it is left unexplained—more particularly the occasions and reasons and persons associated with a new departure in dance style.

These later dances achieved popularity and international currency from their popularity at the court of Louis XIV, and it was from that centre that dance and music fashions spread over Europe. Every one of these dances had originated as some humble peasant or folk dance, some of them brought back from the Spanish colonies in the New World and prettified into stately indoor dances by professional dancing-masters. Examples of dances in 3/4 (the commonest) time were : *saltarello, sarabande, courante, passacaglia, chaconne, volta, minuet*—some slow and stately, some very quickly performed. *Allemande* was in 4/4 time, *bourrée* also 4/4. The *gavotte* and *rigaudon* were 2/2, while the *gigue* could be 3/8, 6/8, or 9/8. And style was all. An analysis of all the dance-forms surviving to the end of the eighteenth century shows that their total vocabulary consisted of not more than a dozen separate steps, jumps, and turns. What counted was how one danced, with what grace, self-possession, and air of calm dignity one led the patterned group or held the eye of all beholders in an ingenious solo.

FOLK-DANCE

"Folk-dancing" to-day too often suggests earnest people who come together on set occasions with great deliberation to perform the antique dances of our forefathers. Folk-dancing lasts longest in countries where the majority of people live close to the land. Simply, folk-dancing is an easy-come, easy-go way of relaxing among friends and neighbours, and in those communities still unmarked by an excess of sophistication it is a perfectly spontaneous way of behaving when people gather to celebrate such occasions as birth, betrothal, marriage, or death. Therefore folk-dancing is still a common, vigorous, and highly enjoyable activity in the rural parts of most European countries and Russia. In our own country the social changes of the Industrial Revolution quickly broke down the old patterns of country life and drove multitudes into the towns and cities, where they lost both the skill and the sense of occasion which have kept dancing alive as the primary social art in other countries.

The jig, the carol, and the morris seem to have lasted longest as the basic forms of our own country dancing ; they are the forms on which a majority of revived, or luckily preserved, English folk-dances are based. But the threads of all dance developments are too closely interwoven for anyone to say at what point in dance history some curious figure, or step-sequence, or trick of jumping in a new way, was taken over direct from a peasants' dance and inserted into what was being taught, either to a private circle or in a local " dance academy " somewhere, as the newest ballroom trick. While for hundreds of years polite society was amusing itself—and also performing an inescapable social duty—by performing more or less correctly all the dances already mentioned, peasants, herdsmen, labourers, and craftsmen were lustily dancing precisely the same rounds, brawls, jigs, and reels that their fathers had taught them, having had the skill and the technique handed down from their fathers for as long as men could remember. A formal analysis of the music used in ballroom and on village green could trace a common ancestry for most of the rhythms and styles in use.

Contemplating to-day the full-dress ballet, modern expressive stage dancing, musical comedy style, tap dancing, and the more elaborate developments practised in modern ballrooms, we often look too closely at the trees and fail to see the wood. All that the most highly trained ballet-dancer learns is based on what were, first, the steps, movements, and accompanying gestures of primitive people. It has all been elaborated, subjected to ratiocination and artful development by professional teachers. It has been merged with styles of acting and mime so that the " joins " between straight dance-steps and mimetic gesture, facial expression, body tension, use of balance, are marvellously hidden from the untrained eye. We should not forget, either, that ballet is a comparatively recent growth. The " ballets " of early Renaissance days were, as we noted earlier, spectacles in which the dancing was almost an incidental element. Ballet, in a form approximating to what we have now (though considerably changed between the middle of the eighteenth century and the beginning of the nineteenth), was an inevitable, almost unconsciously achieved transference of court or society dancing to a stage.

IMPORTANCE OF FRANCE

Almost from earliest Renaissance days, the theatre had become a feature of any important European city. The period of the late sixteenth and early seventeenth centuries was that in which the secular theatre became permanently established, and in this period all the diverse forms of theatrical art were being moulded into fresh (or, at least, fresh-seeming) shapes by dramatists, dancers, choreographers, composers, singers, and scenic designers. There is no clearly marked date on which the first recognisable ballet was danced, nor evidence as to what sort of theatre was used. Certainly if we are considering a spectacle consisting mainly of dancing—if that serves well enough as a definition of ballet—then such shows were a commonplace in the French theatre from the early seventeenth century to the end of the eighteenth. Early opera had much dancing interspersed among the arias, declamatory verses, and instrumental interludes ; and the separation of ballet from opera was first effected in some of the court entertainments written for Anne of Austria and the young Louis XIV. Indeed, the first important phase in the history of ballet is the reign of that monarch, for he was sufficiently enamoured of dancing to set up the world's first suitably organised Dance Academy in 1661. Out of this event grew certain inevitable developments.

The dancing-masters of Paris had a monopoly of teaching the fashionable dances requisite at court, and they first formulated the techniques of the dances, embodied in a terminology of their own (hence the fact that the basic language of ballet is French) and in their own notations. They gathered new dance ideas, steps and patterns from whatever sources they could—including, as we have noted, their own peasantry's dancing and whatever they could ascertain from travellers into strange lands—to maintain the supply of dance novelties for the court. All cultured Europe followed the lead of the French court, so that these strange variants of still-extant folk-dances from the fields of Burgundy, the marshes of the Landes, the mountains of Bavaria, and plains of Middle Europe were the raw material on which the dance-mania of polite society was nourished.

What in Louis XIV's day were called " ballets " were the great social dance events at court. In these the chief rôles were always danced by amateurs—members of the Royal Family and their suites and closest friends —while professionals were used for grotesque or undignified rôles. There was, most of the time, very little difference between a court entertainment (consisting of such a " ballet ") and a court ball. The ball was an occasion at which the main figures in the dances were performed by a couple at a time, with the other guests looking on, so they were both social and spectacular dances at one and the same time.

THE MUSIC OF THE DANCE

Ballet music had not yet achieved a special form of its own, such as we know to-day. The scores written for these early ballets still consisted of series of *rigaudons, bourrées, musettes, gavottes*, and *minuets*. This association —identification or opposition—that grew up between music and dance is noticeable all through the history of European dance music. The common element of rhythm, shared by dances and instrumental music, at first allows them to feed off one another's idioms. Then, as dancing assumes greater social importance, we find a limited number of basic forms maintained, almost all written in rigid styles and to few and, naturally, unvarying rhythms. The first kind of dance suite leads to the orchestral suite, which in its Baroque developments attains to one of the highest kinds of art music. Musical theory presses past the formal limitations imposed by practical dancing needs ; and art music expands into many rich styles and variants during a period of years in which dance music has become too rigidly stylised.

Not until society was shaken from end to end by the social upheaval of the Revolution of 1789 and the activities of Napoleon (which preceded the industrial revolution over most of Europe) was there a significant change in the ideas and idioms of Europe's dance music. Then, after the Napoleonic as after so many other wars, a species of " dance mania " swept the continent, manifesting itself in a wild enthusiasm for the new type of ballroom dancing typified in the *waltz*, and in the brilliantly imaginative concept of the Romantic ballet. This process, startling though it was in its effects, was not an entirely fresh chapter in the story of dance music developments. Trial-and-error methods had been applied before this to the problem of making ballet more dramatic, principally by Jean-Georges Noverre (1727–1810).

NOVERRE'S REFORMS

Noverre's chief distinction is that he attempted to create a ballet which should unite dancing with skilled naturalistic acting, using music written more or less to his directions. His reforms were partly frustrated by the arrogance of the leading dancers with whom he worked, who wished to dance only in the highly personal styles which had made their reputations. But he did work with Gluck, successfully, on the *ballet d'action* to *Iphigénie en Aulide* (1774), the composer having agreed to create music as specified by the choreographer. Gluck's score for the ballet *Don Juan* (1761), too, though entirely a dance suite, was written to fit the dance action as planned. Salvatore Viganò (1769–1821) was another reformer, a contemporary of Noverre, who tried to reform ballet by making the dancing more expressive of human passions, and also by what to-day would be called stylised production of the acting and mime. His work is shot through, moreover, with a novel tendency to create asymmetrical patterns and ensembles. He composed much of his own ballet music.

THE WALTZ

The value of the *waltz*, when it had won its place (against some opposition) in the ballrooms of Europe, was that it reinvigorated popular folk-dancing, though now in cities rather than among rustics. It had started as a dance (the *ländler*) of mountain folk in South Germany, gained a great vogue in Vienna, and had swept all Europe. Its importance lay in the fact that with it was reintroduced, for the first time since the Middle Ages, the notion of social dancing with single partners face to face—hence its original reputation of indecency. Also, and paradoxically, it swung ballroom dancing once and for all completely away from any close connection with ballet. Now ballroom dancing (with the further incentives supplied by *polka*, *schottische*, and later *quadrille*) became a purely personal dance activity, while ballet, once and for all, became stage dancing.

The advances in the structure of ballet in the nineteenth century were spectacular. As with so many developments in dance music, slight local tendencies seemed suddenly to amalgamate to achieve what at first looks like a violent innovation of style or technique. Fashion, partly following and partly leading public fancy, found the means to promulgate the novel idea, and men were convinced that a totally new manifestation of art had come upon them. A parallel growth in the ballet world, of the technique of training female dancers to dance on the point of the foot, and of the Romantic formula of the new type of ballet scenario, combined to launch the art of stage dancing upon a new lease of life—a rejuvenation it badly needed after the collapse of the old ballet ideals of the French court, which had been swept away at the Revolution.

For us, the chief interest in this period is in the composers who arose to fulfil the need that the new ballet had created—nothing less than the construction of scores of a duration of anything up to 150 minutes and of a pronouncedly dramatic nature. These scores were not only to supply actual dance-rhythms but to give those dances melodic characteristics, and provide appropriate atmosphere and background to the characters and places of action. A good deal of this music, throughout the century, consisted of theatrical adaptation and ingenious development of the *waltz*, *polka, polonaise, march, mazurka*, etc. But almost at the beginning of the Romantic era of ballet, a composer was at hand to create one of the outstanding ballet scores whose quality has undoubtedly had much to do with keeping the ballet in the repertoire.

THE ROMANTIC BALLET

In *Giselle*, Adolphe Adam (1803–56) built firmly on the requirements of the plot as stated by the choreographer and librettist for their story. This tells of a simple peasant girl who is wooed by a disguised prince; when his duplicity is made plain to Giselle, she goes mad and dies of grief. As an unmarried, betrothed maiden she passes into a sort of limbo; she becomes a " willi ", a species of spirit from German mythology. The " willis " haunt graveyards at night to ensnare any passing males, and Albrecht, the mourning prince, almost falls victim to them. He is saved by Giselle, who forces him to seek the protection of the cross marking her grave, but at dawn she vanishes with the other " willis " and he is left heartbroken. In accordance with the taste of the day, the novelty of the project and the orchestral and theatrical conventions, Adam created a neatly suitable score with a primitive form of leading-motive, a use of reminiscent melodies, and some engaging dances, both solo and ensemble. The music is built up mostly of short sections, with each dance treated differently in speed and expressive style. This results in a score of intensely dramatic quality, a mosaic of small pieces mostly too brief in themselves to attract much interest, but blended into a whole that enriches and enlarges the dance patterns, the characterisations and the dramatic content of each scene. No other ballets of that period survive in to-day's repertoire; for even in Russia, where the largest number of nineteenth-century ballets have been retained, they have been so arranged and re-choreographed that all that exists of the originals is the libretto and score—the latter often heavily cut in modern productions. Of all the hundreds of other ballets of the period 1840–1900 there is little reliable documentation which tells us enough about their plots, scenarios, scores, and styles of choreography. Perhaps we must accept the verdict that good ballets survive largely through good music.

From what we know of the operatic efforts of some composers of the Romantic era, obviously their ballet scores did not belong to the same genre as Adam's for *Giselle*. In Russia, where vast numbers of ballets were created during the century, literally dozens of compositions were supplied by Ludwig Minkus (1827–90), a Vienna-born Pole, and Cesare Pugni (1805–70), an Italian who had first worked in Paris and London. The choreography of these works—to judge from contemporary accounts—was of even less intrinsic worth than the hack-work supplied as music.

We look upon the nineteenth century as a great period of creative ballet activity, yet of a total output of nearly 500 full-length ballets in the main European capitals, to-day fewer than thirty are to be found still being performed, and those mostly in truncated or re-produced form. A small-scale ballet revival which dates from the Diaghilev renaissance (1909–29) finds its tradition of classicism in precisely five ballets which have endured over a period of a hundred years. The five are : *Giselle* (1841, Adam), *Coppélia* (1870, Delibes), *The Sleeping Beauty* (1890), *Casse-Noisette* (1892), and *Swan Lake* (1895) in its revised version (these three by Tchaikovsky). About a dozen others, in whole or in part, survive to-day in Russia, where they are continually re-produced, re-decorated, and in large part re-choreographed. Their scores are mostly by Pugni, Minkus, and Drigo. Of the remaining prolific composers of that era, only one stands in the same category as his master, Adam, and his successor, Tchaikovsky. This is Léo Delibes, a Frenchman, who after studying composition with Adam worked as accompanist and répétiteur at the Opéra while composing successful operettas. In 1866 he collaborated with Minkus (at that time working in Paris) on the score of *La Source*, for which each wrote two of the four acts. Delibes's two acts and some dances he had written for an earlier ballet were later the basis of a new version of *La Source*, now called *Naïla*.

His work at the Théâtre Lyrique allowed him to develop his acquaintance with the ballet music of the time and to study its conventions. He followed the practice of the day in using basic national dance-forms—*mazurka, waltz, czardas, reel, bolero*, etc.—which he expressed in melodies of real originality and great vivacity; his orchestration has vigour but never deserts the elegant.

In 1870 he wrote a full-length ballet score for the choreographer Saint-Léon, *Coppélia*, which was an immediate success, has become his most famous score, and has rarely been out of production since the day it was first danced. He wrote only one other ballet, *Sylvia* (1876), which is historically important because of its symphonic style of composition. Here, too, as in his other ballet scores, he remembered the lesson of Adam and made good dramatic use of leading-motives.

The Italian ballet dwindled in importance as opera more and more proved the popular theatre art of the nation. After Viganò's attempts at reform, the other outstanding Italian contribution to the art of ballet was the work of Carlo Blasis (1797–1878), a pupil of Viganò. His technical treatise on training for ballet dancing, *The Code of Terpsichore* (1830), created standards for academic training which are still valid. His influence persisted throughout the century and set an Italian signature on the growth of a classical dance style all over Europe. But this was the last major contribution made to ballet by Italy, which had started the first experiments in dance and music forms at the dawn of the Renaissance.

RUSSIA

French ballet, the European fountain-head, lost its ascendancy because of the complex social changes in French life during the nineteenth century. The *opéra-ballet* was arranged and regimented on a plan similar to that which had prevailed under the Bourbons, but this proved unworkable under the First and Second Empires and the Third Republic. The lead passed to Russia, and for the most cogent of reasons. Only in Russia was there, by 1850, a first-class dance academy, a regulated system of dance training, and a wealthy court supporting ballet both morally and financially.

Whatever the quality of scenarios, music, and choreography in Russia then, by all accounts the standard of dancing was far superior to that to be found elsewhere—though we should note that the lure of Russian ballet prestige and of handsome contracts drew most of the star dancers of France and Italy there (and so to influence Russian style) during the century. By now ballet had grown far beyond the forms in which it had existed at the French court up to 1789 ; but it was (as it remains to-day) phenomenally expensive to produce and to stage. Its best theatre-systems (such as had long existed in the Russian capitals, in Stockholm, Copenhagen, and Paris) need enormous staffs, theatres, stages, and orchestras, and battalions of dancers. During the latter half of the nineteenth century, it is safe to assert, ballet was staged anywhere in Europe only at enormous cost. Almost the only place in which it was a popular theatre spectacle drawing a big public *and making profits* was London, where there arose a special genre which was a spectacular revue larded with vast quantities of dancing rather than a pure ballet—the " Empire " and " Alhambra " spectacles of the 'eighties and 'nineties.

Whatever the help that music can give to dance, music alone does not sustain the art, as is shown by the nineteenth-century Russian example. The greatest heights to which that era's choreographic and musical imaginations could reach was that attained in the three masterpieces listed above for which Tchaikovsky wrote the scores. Like Adam, who was creating *Giselle* in the year of Tchaikovsky's birth, the Russian was a master of that essential quality which good, danceable, and memorable ballet music must have—lively and varied rhythms, each of which is vivid enough to suggest originality and musical coherence in each dance, interlude, or atmospheric scene. *Casse-Noisette* and *The Sleeping Beauty* were written in accordance with the scenario's needs, as outlined in considerable detail by the choreographer Petipa. *Swan Lake*, indifferently produced at first with hack choreography, seemed a dismal failure. Only after Tchaikovsky's death did Petipa realise what a splendid score this was, and the first version of the ballet as we know it was Act 2 by Ivanov (1834–1901), who was an assistant choreographer to Petipa. This was staged in 1894, and the remainder of the ballet was made by Petipa the next year. Tchaikovsky's gift of memorable and opulent melody is exactly suited to the symbolic, lyrical, and imaginative scenarios of these ballets. The melodies identify themselves with the dances, and the use of leading-motives is made the more dramatic thereby.

ISADORA DUNCAN

The art of ballet might well have died of artistic sterility at the beginning of this century, for three Tchaikovsky ballets were not sufficient to maintain the prestige of Russia's greatest choreographer, Petipa, who was at the end of his career. That revitalising force which had set the ballerina firmly in the public eye at the time of the Romantic resurgence had by 1900 dwindled to a series of cheap circus tricks which all but the very greatest ballerinas used regularly. Technique had once again won an ascendancy over expressiveness, even in Russia, and the art of theatre dance was badly in need of some reviving force all over the world.

But people outside the ballet world had been questioning the validity of a theatre-movement style whose chief defect was that it had in fact no style. Isadora Duncan (1878–1927), a Californian, had come to Europe to preach a new kind of dancing, a species of revived Hellenism devoutly created from an admiration of Greek sculpture, vases, and architecture. She was the forerunner of many kinds of so-called " expressive " dance systems, in which the performer seeks to communicate his highly personal experience to music. Although she publicised new ideas about what kinds of music could be used for dancing, these ideas were not her original property ; for by now innumerable ballets and dances had been made to music written simply as programme music without any suggestion of theatrical use.

SERGE DIAGHILEV

The reform of ballet came when the limits of usefulness of nineteenth-century classicism had been reached, after this classical style had been developed through the ballet of the Romantic era.

466

Later, Western choreographers began to create a species of neo-classicism, which was nothing other than an intelligent reappraisal of the uses that could be made of certain neglected or hitherto unnoticed elements from folk and popular dancing. The break away from Russia and its sterilities was instigated by Serge Diaghilev (1872–1929), whose strength it was to command respect, a modest capital, and the faithful services of such revolutionaries and innovators as the choreographer Fokine, the composer Stravinsky, and the designers Benois and Bakst.

Fokine had tried to interest the ballet directorate in St. Petersburg in a scheme for reforming the manner in which ballets were made. The scheme was rejected, but he made these new principles a foundation on which he built over sixty ballets between 1908 and 1942, when he died. Musically, the most significant of the "Five Principles" states that the ballet should allow for the perfect co-ordination of choreography, décor, and music, i.e. no more should one use the services of hack composers such as had served ballet in Russia for too long. Lacking a constant supply of Tchaikovskys, one could use existing programme music, provided that no violence were done to its structure or implicit character—a condition which Fokine believed that he observed in his first famous creation, Les Sylphides, to Chopin piano music orchestrated—and soon after, Carnaval, to Schumann piano music. Fokine was well served by Arensky, Tcherepnin, Hahn, Ravel, and Schmitt and, above all, by Stravinsky with The Firebird and Petrushka. Later, for Fokine ballets and also for Massine, Balanchine, and Nijinsky, Diaghilev obtained the collaboration of Satie, Falla, Prokofiev, Poulenc, Auric, Milhaud, Rieti, Sauguet, and the Englishmen Lambert and Berners.

Who can say what started the interest in the ballet revival conjured up by Diaghilev? Was it the fabulous quality of the dancing of Karsavina, Pavlova, Nijinsky, and Massine? Or the décors of such masters as Bakst and Benois whose like had not been seen in the European theatre since the days of Boquet and Berain? Or the music of Stravinsky and the rediscovered theatrical music of Tchaikovsky? To-day we still feel the repercussions flowing from that first Paris season fifty years ago, when every component of ballet had been re-assimilated, re-planned, and re-valued by these astonishing Russians.

Of the eleven ballets that Stravinsky has composed, each differs sharply from its nearest predecessor. The Firebird seems to derive its "magical" passages from Rimsky-Korsakov and its "human" situations from, perhaps, Tchaikovsky. Petrushka is loaded with quasi-themes from popular music of several kinds, including French, Viennese, Muscovite, and an echo from Tchaikovsky. The early works are marked by harsh and percussive harmonies, violently contrasted melodic lines, and the manipulation of rhythms through what seems every imaginable mutation. Yet each work presents differing and immediately acknowledged qualities ; no part of any one can be confused with another. *The Rite of Spring* is an unsatisfactory ballet score, inasmuch as its strength and unique quality grow entirely from its novel use of rhythm as such, and up to now it seems to have resisted successful assimilation with the dance forms accompanying it.

COMPOSER AND CHOREOGRAPHER

Stravinsky cannot be absolved from the charge of writing ballet music too self-contained—too intrinsically musical—always to form a sensible alliance with something so materially obvious as human bodies moving in space. Whether or not they have taken Stravinsky as their exemplar, either deliberately or unconsciously, most modern writers of ballet music seem to have assumed some of the fierce arrogance of that master, expressed in a determination that the music shall command interest and make a strong emotional impression in its own right. Many of to-day's young composers for ballet are writing music modelled on that of Stravinsky, in forcefulness of rhythm, in subtle and rarefied harmony, in dynamically unconventional orchestration. Yet, of those active enough in this field to be reckoned seriously, how many can be said to have achieved a happy balance of collaboration with the choreographer they presumably serve ? In too many instances we are aware of the music's insistence on a life of its own. Is this an inevitable condition of to-day's music-making ? The freedom in musical thought and in composition that accrued from the impact of Impressionism (with its emphasis on mood rather than on order) has led many composers of modern ballet music to a violent reaction which finds expression in what we may call the " abstract orgy ".

It is in no sense a failure on the part of a choreographer if he feels that effective ballets can be made as well to existing music as to specially commissioned scores. Financial, managerial, and even æsthetic considerations may incline a choreographer to use music he already knows, for frequently a known score can suggest choreographic possibilities. It is also obvious that some choreographers cannot achieve effective co-operation with composers. Further, many composers reveal an inability to accept the notion of collaboration ; too often they regard the music as being the incentive (*i.e.* the greater ingredient) in a ballet, whereas its function is to support, to suggest, and to provide a rhythmic framework. As always in the theatre, economics weigh heavily in any planning for ballet ; thousands of scores are available for free use, while the living musician must be paid for his trouble.

ROYAL FESTIVAL HALL, LONDON

Opened on 3rd May, 1951, with a performance of Beethoven's ninth symphony. Replaces
the earlier Queen's Hall, irreparably destroyed by bombs in 1941.

Fox Photos Ltd.

ROYAL ALBERT HALL, LONDON

Planned in 1851 for the purpose of " promotion of scientific and artistic knowledge ", this huge
building was not completed until 1871.   It has been the home of the famous Promenade Concerts
since 1941.

DIAGHILEV'S COMMISSIONS: FOKINE AND MASSINE

In Diaghilev's twenty years of activity he presented about sixty ballets (excluding the classics), and of these well over half were to scores specially written. Yet some of the most brilliant ballets were arranged on existing music—as for instance *Le Spectre de la Rose* (" Invitation to the Dance ", Weber), *Les Femmes de Bonne Humeur* (Scarlatti, arranged), *La Boutique Fantasque* (Rossini, arranged), and *Pulcinella* (Pergolesi, arranged). These latter three are not very dissimilar from various nineteenth-century ballets —tales of mixed fact and fantasy or complex amorous intrigues with deceptions and mistaken identities. Their music, arranged and orchestrated with tact and taste, is perfectly matched by their choreography.

Of the Diaghilev ballets, apart from Stravinsky's, perhaps the outstanding are : *Jeux* (Debussy, 1913), *Daphnis and Chloe* (Ravel, 1912), *The Three-Cornered Hat* (Falla, 1919), *Chout* (Prokofiev, 1920), *Les Biches* (Poulenc, 1924), and *The Prodigal Son* (Prokofiev, 1929). Apart from Fokine's early works to ready-made music, *Les Sylphides* (Chopin), *Carnaval* and *Papillons* (both Schumann), *Prince Igor* (Borodin), *Sadko* (Rimsky-Korsakov), many of the best works of Massine and Balanchine up to 1929, and since, have used existing music. Massine, using scores by Scarlatti, Rossini, Cimarosa, Bizet, Offenbach, Strauss, Lecocq, has devised some of his best successes, in a variety of genres—fantasy, comedy, fairy-tale, romance. In the 1930s, partly inspired by his revolutionary work *Ode* (1928), he essayed spectacular dance-dramas on big philosophical or romantic themes to symphonies by, respectively, Tchaikovsky, Brahms, Berlioz, Beethoven, and Shostakovich. These were : *Les Présages* (Tchaikovsky 5th), *Choreartium* (Brahms 4th), *Symphonie Fantastique* (Berlioz), *Seventh Symphony* (Beethoven), *Rouge et Noir* (Shostakovich 1st).

Not all these were equally successful as ballets. *Les Présages*, being the first, was the most sensational, and its " Man against Fate " theme drew a certain topicality from the political uncertainties in Europe at that period. *Rouge et Noir* (not seen in this country) is reported as providing the happiest blend of musical and choreographic dramatics. Of the first group, *Choreartium* was the most ambitious, and was almost wholly successful in creating a series of dance pictures or episodes corresponding with the ideas or moods suggested by the music. There were some superb dance and movement inventions here, whereby whole groups in motion were used in wholly new ways to create a spectacle half-tragic, half-lyric—and choreographically wholly exciting.

Massine's *Le Beau Danube*, to a potpourri of waltzes, polkas, quadrilles, and mazurkas by the three Strauss brothers, is one of the most successful and popular ballets of our time. After its first version, produced in 1924, it was revised in 1933, has come into the repertoire of five other companies, and has been danced thousands of times all over the world.

BALANCHINE AND TUDOR

Balanchine has made much use of Tchaikovsky's instrumental music with real choreographic success—*Ballet Imperial* (Piano concerto No. 2), *Serenade* (Serenade for Strings), *Theme and Variations* (Suite No. 3 in G). His most perfect romantic story-ballet is *Night Shadow* to an arrangement of Bellini pieces, and one of his greatest inventions in the abstract-pattern ballet genre is *Symphony in C* (to Bizet's only symphony). Antony Tudor has created, in a career of unparalleled brilliance, exactly one ballet to commissioned music (*Undertow*, William Schuman): his fame rests on such works as *Jardin aux Lilas* (Chausson's *Poème*), *Pillar of Fire* (Schoenberg's *Verklärte Nacht*), *The Planets* (Holst's suite), *Gala Performance* (Prokofiev piano concerto No. 3 and " Classical " symphony), *Dim Lustre* (Strauss's *Burleske*), and *Dark Elegies* (Mahler's *Kindertotenlieder*). In all cases of the use of existing music the test of suitability must be an empirical one : if the choreographer has evolved an original dance-structure which illuminates his theme and characters and also does no violence to the structure or quality of the music, then he cannot be accused of barbarism.

BALLET MUSIC NOW

Of composers now or recently active in ballet composition, a few have won approval of their work from judges highly competent to assess their scores but not always the most dispassionate or best-informed critics of ballet. This situation arises quite simply from a dearth of ballet critics, whose primary judgments are of the alliance between dance form, music form, and decorative framework. Music critics are commonly employed as critics of ballet over most of the Western world. They naturally rate a ballet's success by the close integration of musical and dance forms, often without exercising close visual appraisal of the dance and mime elements in the choreography. Of the composers, many are obviously skilled creators of musical structures which often merge happily with patterns of movement. Names that suggest themselves at once are : Denis ApIvor, Malcolm Arnold, Sir Arthur Bliss, Benjamin Britten, Aaron Copland, Roberto Gerhard, Francis Poulenc, and, in the recent past, Constant Lambert and Sergei Prokofiev.

Each of these has repeatedly shown a keen awareness of the special needs of ballet music and an appreciation of the fact that choreography is not merely a stringing together of existing dance steps to a rhythmically suitable score of a certain proportionate length. But other points require consideration at this stage of ballet's development. In no important ballet centre anywhere (and they are few enough to-day, comprising only London, New York, Copenhagen, Moscow, Leningrad, Paris) does there appear to be any working scheme whereby young musicians receive training in the requirements for writing, rehearsing, and conducting ballet music. In their writings and public utterances many composers express a sincere interest in ballet ; yet most of them seem to see ballet exclusively from the conductor's podium. No man can write well except out of what he has learned, and learned the long, hard way. We are at a point in ballet history where there is no world-known figure who can, even by indirect means and influence, guide those composers who sincerely wish to serve the dance theatre. The fact that ballet enjoys its present vast popularity entails much clever propaganda and a fashionable public with little intelligent interest in the future of the art. Not many of those attracted to the ballet have acquired any criterion whereby they can assess each component in a well-balanced work of theatre dancing. This would almost certainly not be the case if we had not achieved so complete a separation, years ago, between our own forms of popular social dancing and our theatre dance.

The curious fact is that art-music came to the service of ballet at a time when music itself was passing through a series of mutations, each of which—impressionism, expressionism, atonality, serialism—implied a negation of the basic relationship between music and dancing. The strong pulse of rhythm, out of which men were first able to correlate their unformed, spontaneous, and joy-giving physical movements, was the first element to be weakened in the newer music which followed that of Tchaikovsky and Stravinsky for the ballet.

THE BALLROOM

The vogue upon which ballroom dancing entered with the introduction of the *waltz* endured through the nineteenth century at nearly all social levels. As ballet had paused on the verge of a period of decline around 1900, so the ballroom styles which had enjoyed popularity seemed also to have become exhausted by that date. The reviving influence came from two sources, Latin-American folk-dances and American Negro jazz. Both types injected a new vital kind of rhythm into the desiccated formula of ballroom dancing ; and, as before in the history of dancing, each was strongly marked, in its patterns, variations of figures, and rhythmic flexibility, by national idioms deriving from the simple folk-dances of primitive peoples. The more or less balletic type of grouping and rhythm carried over by the popular ballroom dance of the past century from the Romantic period gave way to a species of "free patterning" comparable with the first, vivid dance experiments in Italy in the fifteenth century.

JAZZ

Negro jazz in the U.S.A. had grown out of ragtime, the music "invented" by brass-band players in New Orleans. The new dances were the *one-step* (2/4) and *fox-trot* (4/4), followed, in the 1920s and 1930s, by many bizarre forms including the *Charleston*, *Big Apple*, and *Black Bottom*. The Latin-American impact was through the introduction to Europe around 1912 of the *tango*, which is based on *habanera* rhythm (2/4), but danced very slowly. This opened the way for the later and more popular forms of *rumba*, *samba*, *paso-doble* ; and by now both kinds of American influence are blended in such types as *mambo*, *conga*, *rock-'n'-roll*. Ballroom dancing has achieved an amazing revival in Great Britain since the early 1920s. The first full impact of jazz, coming soon after the end of the war, coincided with that outbreak of dance-mania which seems always to be part of the reaction after a protracted war, as we saw the vogue for the *waltz* sweep over Europe after the Napoleonic Wars.

It would perhaps be too facile to trace some inevitability of connection between the cult of ballroom dancing (particularly on the lower social levels) and the cult of ballet, first by the intelligentsia and then by the bourgeois world, during the inter-war period. The most notable fact of our dance-culture to-day is that both parties appear to hold each other's interest in contempt. Few ballet-goers know how to comport themselves in a ballroom, and the working-class, artisan, and middle-class citizens who commonly fill public dance-halls rarely have any interest in watching ballet dancing. Such a complete separation between stage and ballroom can rarely have occurred before, and Albert Smith's book *Natural History of the Ballet Girl* (1847) shows the ballet dancer of a century ago avid for visiting public dance-halls when off duty ; then, apparently, professional dancers could not have too much of a good thing.

To-day, ballroom dancing is our form of folk-dancing, followed and enjoyed by the largest number of people. Despite the transfusions from the wilder stocks of American Negro and Latin music and dance, it has styles, idioms, and conventions of its own. All over Europe the English are regarded as the master ballroom dancers of to-day just as, four centuries ago, we had a reputation as " the dancing English ".

472

Conga, mambo, rumba, and the many variants which, season after season, become the fashionable dances of the day have shown once again that whatever may be the " folk-dance " of a period depends for popularity on its strong rhythmic basis rather than on its individual steps. We are at a moment in history when our folk-dance and our stage dance are almost totally out of touch with each other. Ballet composers write " atmospheric " scores using arbitrary and frequently changing rhythms, while popular dance-writers spin endless, but formally very limited, variations on four or five basic dance rhythms. Some faint sign of a *rapprochement* between the two fields of activity can be found in the work of a few " advanced " young choreographers who, exploiting the contemporary scene in naturalistic terms, choose to employ music with lengthy passages of unchanging rhythms. Such a trend might lead eventually to the writing of ballet-scores modelled on the earlier practice of Adam, Minkus, and Delibes, though with more cunning use of leading-motives, richer instrumental colour, and more symphonic structure.

473

XXVI

THE LATEST DEVELOPMENTS

WE must now consider the position of music in general to-day. As in most departments of life in this age of transition, there is a deep gulf between the musical *avant-garde* and the public, with the rank and file of musicians ranged uneasily somewhere between the two parties but inclining for the most part towards the conservative camp. The question at issue is no longer simply that of "difficult" or "ugly" sounds and the absence of "melody". The latest conception of music is one in which the idea of emotional communication is repudiated; "harmony" and "melody" have no meaning any longer. Science has been called in to amplify the tonal spectrum and mathematics to supply forms that can be objectively judged. In many cases the machine replaces the human performer, with his minute variations of mood reflected in tempo and dynamics, and his characteristically human fallibility. Music, in fact, has been approximated to a science and its status as an art has sunk. How has this come about?

SERIALISM

Ever since the Middle Ages, music has evolved with increasing momentum. The various stages of technical and stylistic developments, which were at first spaced hundreds of years apart, have followed each other increasingly rapidly. Whereas sixteenth-century polyphony took nearly 300 years to mature from the *ars nova* of 1300, in the twentieth century developments have become bewilderingly swift. Already not only Mahler and Strauss but even Schoenberg are regarded by young composers as belonging to a distant tradition.

The end of the Second World War began a period of feverish activity, and developments have followed each other with extreme rapidity. The invention of electronic music has indicated possibilities in instrumental music which only ten years ago were utterly unforeseeable. We are, in fact, living through a period of experimentation. Some even pursue experiment for its own sake. The American, John Cage, has acquired international notoriety with his " prepared piano " which produces thumps, twangs, clangs, buzzes, and thuds at what seem to him appropriate intervals, ending with a grand slam on the keyboard cover. We may safely say that this is not serious art but studio improvisation, sometimes no doubt " inspired " but more often tasteless.

Other experimentalists compose their creations " through the imperfection of the blank page ". This high-sounding jargon cloaks the cheap-jack trick of holding manuscript paper up to the light, marking the imperfections on or near the staves as " sounds ", and elaborating the random result as a " composition ". Such haphazard methods as these denote charlatans who have neither artistic sensibility nor seriousness of purpose. Experiment which is not rooted in reasoning and serious artistic morality is invalid. Unfortunately, the charlatan is often one of to-day's most successful men.

On the other hand there is, and has always been, a valid experimentalism which *creates* tradition. This, to-day, is the work of the best of the *avant-garde*, whose " post-Webernian " music is based on an intimate knowledge of the poetic possibilities of every technical and compositional factor, used with scrupulous artistic principles. True, the *avant-garde* composer is likely to be condemned by the ordinary music-lover on the grounds that his work is cerebral, calculated, and smacks of " constructivism ". *Avant-garde* compositions are in general based on the more or less complete serialisation of the musical material. To understand methods of construction it is necessary to grasp the principles of serial permutation.

Any series of notes or numbers can be varied by permutations. Thus 135246 is an elementary permutation of 123456. A series of only two numbers has only two permutations (*e.g.*, 1.2 : 2.1), three numbers have 6, four numbers have 24, and so on, until we find that 12 numbers have 479,001,600 permutations. The twelve-note series is therefore capable of over 479 million permutations, which from a practical viewpoint means that any note-row can be varied indefinitely without repetition occurring. By establishing a chain of series-permutations, the note-order of a composition can be predetermined from start to finish. The Schoenbergian series, with its definite vertical and horizontal values, can be abandoned in favour of an ever-changing, virtually infinite quantity of material. But this material must still be organised into rhythmic patterns ; it must be given form and, through expression marks and instrumental colour, emotive force. There are many ways of organising the rhythmic configuration of the material, and we can here only indicate some elementary procedures. In general, the methods fall into two classes—(1) a rhythmic structure may be imposed on the material from without, or (2) the material itself may dictate its own rhythmic configuration.

RHYTHMIC ORGANISATION

An example may be taken from the opening of Pierre Boulez's *Structures* for two pianos. In the first seven bars, the first piano plays the original series in such a way that the time-value of each note is some different multiple of the demi-semiquaver. Between the extremes of 1 and 12, each note has a different value, and the order of duration is 12.11.9.10.3.6.7.1.2.8. 4.5 (x♪). At the same time the second piano plays the inversion of the series with the note values in the proportions 5.8.6.4.3.9.2.1.7.11.10.12 (x♪).

This might seem to be a very mechanical, unpromising beginning to a composition which fills more than 90 pages. But in the course of this long work, which seems to sum up the entire resources of his technique, Boulez has written music of surprising power and variety, which gives no hint of its cerebral origin.

In case the reader entertains a legitimate doubt whether the cerebral composer really has control over his material, whether he can really guarantee an expressive result by predetermined formula, we will work a hypothetical example. Let us suppose that a composer wishes to create a short musical period in which sounds begin with minimum intensity and movement and quickly pile up to a maximum of intensity and excitement. A series of duration-proportions of the nature of 13.8.5.3.2.1 will guarantee slow movement at first and a precipitation of motion towards the end. It is sufficient to indicate a crescendo, and to allot orchestration to each note so that smooth-toned instruments gradually give way, chord by chord, to harsher sounds ; and he has an absolutely guaranteed result of a crescendo of extraordinary force and precipitation. Here we do not pretend to have created music, but to have illustrated in an elementary way that the composer's predetermined plan can be designed to give a definite result. Inspiration has given way to calculation, and this is characteristic of the age in which we live.

Let us now turn back for a moment to the second method of organising material into rhythmic patterns—that in which material itself may dictate its own rhythmic configuration. The most simple method is to make the duration of each note in a series proportionate to the interval which separates it from the next note. Notwithstanding the apparent rigidity of such a method, it is possible, with the organisation of silences, to mould note-groupings into significant phrases with just as much freedom as that enjoyed by the composer who works within the framework of diatonic harmony. Familiarity with such a system soon brings absolute control, and there is just as much room here for originality, vision, and inspiration as anywhere else. Many other methods are constantly being discovered by which material can determine its own rhythmic configuration. Some composers even use serial procedures to determine not only the duration and composition of each sound, but also to "organise" expression marks, instrumentation, metronome indications—in fact every element of a composition. It goes without saying that greater organisation does not necessarily mean greater æsthetic value.

Naturally, in this music there is a complete abandonment of most of the traditional musical practices. Harmony, melody, polyphony, and metre hardly exist in a traditional sense. Often all that can be grasped is *total* effect. The main concern of the composer is now the alternation of periods of relaxation and tension. Sounds have no longer any individual value except that determined by their height, depth, or intensity and by the part they play in building up tension or relaxation through harmonic and rhythmic stress and détente.

The rhythmic complexity of this music can be such that any sense of metre is destroyed. In this case a strange phenomenon occurs : the rhythmic articulation is so free that it gives the illusion of extemporisation beyond the bounds of metre. Any sense of the "mechanical" or "cerebral" origins is shed, and this music seems the very essence of freedom. Yet such complexity sets enormous problems for the performer, and it is plainly a short step from music of this nature to electronic music. Mechanical means are the only way to resolve such far-fetched rhythmic requirements, and this is why some *avant-garde* composers have, for a time at least, abandoned instrumental performance and taken refuge in the electronic sound studio.

CALCULATION OR IMPROVISATION ?

Where is all this enormous cerebral industry taking us ? It is difficult to see any physical end to it, for the number of possible methods of computing music are as infinite as the millions of permutations of a twelve-note series. But there is one important consideration which may well cancel out these constructivist procedures and make them, in the last analysis, of relatively small importance. This is the fact that however attentively we may listen to this music, no slightest hint of the structural foundation is ever apparent. Furthermore, music written according to the most diverse systems appears to have not only the same ethos, but also the same *extempore* character. The system itself has little value, and the quality of the music still depends on the artistic ingenuity and skill of the composer.

That constructivist procedures are after all of only relative importance is confessed by Stockhausen. In his recent *Zeitmässe* for five wind instruments, calculation is thrown to the winds. The instrumentalists are given a certain amount of material to play with, in their own time, and are brought together at certain points by a conductor. This is obviously the negation of calculated principles, and the establishment of the principle of "indeterminacy". That the "constructivists" are already reaching a crisis is suggested by certain excesses which are being resorted to. For instance, Stockhausen has written *Groups for three orchestras* in which the orchestras are conducted separately, at different tempi. We may suspect that such extreme means are used not only to achieve novelty at all costs, but simply because the composer has reached the *ne plus ultra* of more moderate instrumental combinations. The system is in fact already becoming exhausted. Especially is this evident when a highly intelligent, "cerebral" composer like the Belgian Henri Pousseur writes his music in small segments to be rearranged and "composed" by the performer in any form he cares to choose.

What are the inferences? It would seem that in only ten years integral serialism, or "computational composition", as we may call it, shows signs of a decline. There are only two alternatives—a super-cerebralism, or a return to more spontaneous, "inspired" forms of composition. As music in the past has constantly swung between the extremes of cerebralism and free, uninhibited "inspiration", there is no reason why the same should not happen now. In fact, it looks as though this must happen, if a real equilibrium between intellectual and humanist values is to be retained in our music. The *avant-garde* serialists have created a new, enormously rich language, which for the moment cannot be further technically advanced. Now is the time for composers of sensibility and vision to enrich this language with greater poetic and human values.

"MUSIQUE CONCRÈTE"

Musique concrète—"concrete music"—is a term applied to music built up on tape recordings from actual, "concrete" sources, to differentiate it from "electronic" music or music recorded directly on to tape from electronic frequency-generators. In the first case a microphone is used to record external sound phenomena. In the second the sound frequencies are generated electrically and pass straight on to tape.

It was soon after the last war that *musique concrète* came to public notice, largely as a result of the activities of Pierre Schaeffer and a Parisian group of musicians including Pierre Boulez, Pierre Henry, and Olivier Messiaen. Though much of the technique of making concrete music had already been discovered through experimentation on film sound-tracks, it was only through Schaeffer's efforts that the possibilities of recording techniques were exploited to produce complete works which pretend to artistic worth. A typical example of their efforts is the *Symphonie pour un homme seul* prepared by Schaeffer and Henry in 1951. The authors refer to this as a " symphony of human sounds, of noises appertaining to man's existence : panting, whistling, fragments of vocal sounds, shouts, footsteps, the banging of doors, orchestral instruments, and so on. The whole recorded by microphone, manipulated, and subdivided into such sequences as : Prosopopée, Partita, Waltz, Scherzo, Collectif, Erotica, Cadenze, Apostrofe, Stretto."

It was soon realised that sounds must be reproduced in changed forms, far removed from their banal, everyday aspects, for the " noises appertaining to man's existence " are too familiar to be taken seriously as art. The whole basis of concrete music rests on the principle of hiding the commonplace origin of sounds and turning them into completely new, unrecognisable phenomena. How is this done ? In tape-recording techniques there are many easy, practical ways of " mutating " sounds. First, many sounds which have a percussive origin, easily recognised, generate a quite different after-sound or reverberation. If the percussive portion of a sound is cut out of a tape, only the after-sound remains, and we may not be able to identify its source. This after-sound may then be manipulated and deformed in many ways. Suppose, for instance, that the clang of a bell has been recorded. The tape may be reversed so that the sound increases in volume to a percussive climax. It can be accelerated or braked to provide glissandos. The sound can be altered in pitch by running the tape faster or slower. If the moment of impact is cut off, the effect is of an organ-like sound, no longer that of a bell. If a portion of this is isolated and the tape-ends are joined into an " endless tape ", there is a sustained, infinite chord which can then be subjected to further treatment. By tone-controls and filters the upper partials can be isolated into a weird, discordant jangle ; or they can be eliminated to leave only the booming bourdon-tone of the low fundamental. The process does not end here. Through ring-modulators, echo chambers, etc., the chosen sound can further be modified into forms very far removed in character from the original source of sound.

When the technician has isolated and recorded the exact sound he wants, this may form only a fraction of the finished work. He has next to build up a " master " tape by *collages* or *montages*, fastening hundreds of snippets of tape together, and perhaps superimposing further sounds on sections which already contain manipulated recordings. Extremely varied pieces of concrete music have been made up from a single, extremely simple, original sound—a single piano chord, a drop of water falling into a bucket, the roar of a tube train. Especially " Piano-tape music ", which the Americans took up quite seriously, has produced results, some of which are amusing, some violently disturbing.

In general, however, concrete music is limited in artistic value. As independent music it is not worthy of serious attention, but it can be very useful in film sound-tracks, or as a background to radio plays.

ELECTRONIC MUSIC

Fifty years ago Busoni, referring to the future development of music, said, " Exhaustion awaits at the end of a road, the best part of which we have already traversed ". He considered the potentialities of diatonic and chromatic space to be well-nigh used up. He continued, " The development of our art is being stagnated by our musical instruments ". Though he could never have foreseen the prodigious skill of some modern instrumentalists, even these are severely taxed when confronted with problems such as we have noted in Stockhausen's music. *Avant-garde* music not only presses instrumentalists very hard, but its complexities often go beyond the possibility of instrumental performance.

It is hardly a coincidence that, at a moment when composers were losing contact with performers, electronic developments should have provided them with exactly the equipment needed to continue their researches into " cerebral " compositional developments. The modern recording studio has now become the composer's workshop, where he can write and record his own music, bringing it before the public without the mediation of performers, conductors, or publishers. This, for the composer, is an ideal situation, for he can ensure that the composition is prepared with scrupulous attention to every detail. He can make certain that every performance is perfect and identical, that nothing will ever be changed. Strangely enough, electronic composition, which at first seemed to by-pass the impasse of instrumental limitations, has in turn influenced instrumental music. Many contemporary instrumental compositions could never have been written without the experience of electronic music. One can only infer that the performer is keeping up with the composer much better than Busoni anticipated, and that perhaps, after all, instrumental music still has a big future.

After humble beginnings at Bonn University and Cologne Radio, where Herbert Eimert was its most distinguished pioneer in the early 'fifties, electronic music has now invaded most European radio studios. But though it has already advanced technically (in fact the progress in only a few years has been staggering) it is still in its infancy as a means of artistic expression. One can hardly expect a real *magnum opus* so soon.

Electronic music has had to make a fresh start. It can not be considered a descendant of pre-existing music, because every element of traditional music has had to be cut away at the roots. It was soon realised that electronic resources can in no way imitate instrumental music—the result is *ersatz*, a hopeless and flagrant falsity. Other territory has had to be explored, and the electronic music composer, instead of trying to re-create something with which he was already familiar (*i.e.* tradition), had to begin with the most elementary aspect of sound—a simple uncomplex vibration—and build up his sound structures from it in completely new dimensions. No wonder that at first he tended to rely on purely mathematical principles as a lifeline in this new world of astronomical dimensions. For it must be understood that electronic possibilities open up a territory which is frightening in its immensity. There is an enormous cosmos of sound-worlds which have never been explored, and there is no chart for the would-be space-traveller. This is why, so far, creative instinct (or " inspiration ") has hardly entered into the picture. The composer has had to be content either with calculated, predetermined compositions, or works in which he has experimented with only a small amount of known material.

BUILDING MATERIAL

It may interest the reader to learn something of the basic principles of electronic music. The raw material consists of pure " sine tones " made by frequency generators. These can produce tones from 16 to 20,000 Herz frequencies, but in practice a more limited range is used, mostly within the six octaves between 64 and 4096 Herz. (The Herz frequency is equal to the number of pitch vibrations per second.) These " sine tones " have no harmonics, and therefore no positive timbre, rather like a soft bourdon organ tone. In the electronic studio, there are banks of frequency generators (*e.g.*, the Milan studio has nine) so that various combinations of sine-tones can be produced simultaneously. By setting the pitch and volume of each tone on the various dials controlling the generators, any sound-form may be prepared and then recorded on tape. In this way very complex sounds may be prepared with the utmost accuracy.

A further sound source is that known as *white sound* or *white noise*. This is produced from a generator which emits simultaneously all audible frequencies, that is, a solid wall of sound in which no single tone predominates. By means of filters any zone or number of zones of *white sound* can be isolated from the rest. In fact, *white sound* can be filtered to such an extent that only one frequency is allowed to emerge.

There are therefore two basic methods of producing sound, and they are completely opposed. By the first method, simple sine tones can be combined into a complex sound. By the second, *white sound* (the most complex sound-form) can be simplified to produce a single sine tone. In practice both these methods are often used simultaneously.

Sound material from both sources may be further manipulated by means of ring modulators, dynamic suppressors, the *telefonbau normalzeit*, echo chambers, etc. For instance, two different signals may be recorded on separate tapes and fed into the ring modulator. This eliminates the original signals and replaces them by several distinct and varied complexes of sound. The result is often quite unpredictable. It is possible to re-pass this through the dynamic suppressor and ring modulator several times, and obtain constantly new material. The machines could continue for ever without repeating themselves, producing fantastic varieties of effects and constantly varied rhythmic patterns.

Of course to " compose " in this way is to leave everything to sheer chance. In practice some composers prepare a mass of material by these mechanical means. They select what seems most striking or most suited to their work, and then set about moulding this small selection of sounds into a more ample composition. The composer is thus able to work with the raw material of sound in his hands, and he has to control the audible effect over every centimetre of tape. Perhaps the composer's ear has never been such an essential factor in composition.

PREDETERMINATION AND CHANCE

Some works are mathematically predetermined in every detail. Graph-paper sketches are prepared which indicate the three dimensions (duration, intensity, and pitch) of every tone and combination of tones. The attack, decline and " expression " of every note has to be indicated, so that the work can be built up piece by piece. Many early works were constructed in this way, such as Stockhausen's *Two Studies*, Eimert's *Five Pieces*, Berio's *Mutations*, and Maderna's *Nocturne*.

Other works, such as Pousseur's *Scambi*, Maderna's *Syntaxis*, and Berio's *Perspectives* are so complex that they could never have begun with a mere graph-paper existence. Such works have been built up from combinations of effects obtained by chance (as described above) and treated with a certain improvisatory technique.

Electronic music has been used very successfully in compositions which include voice parts, either sung or spoken. Ernst Křenek's " pentecostal oratorio ", *Spiritus Intelligentiae Sanctus* (" The Holy Spirit of Understanding "), is a work of considerable proportions. Only two voices are used (tenor and soprano), but these are multiplied enormously by superimposition, so that astonishing choral effects are obtained. The accompaniment is composed of fairly simple electronic sine-tone structures which are rather lacking in subtlety. Stockhausen's *Gesang der Jünglinge* (" The Song of the Young Men ") is a much more complex and successful work. Only a boy's voice is used, again multiplied by superimposition to give an astonishing illusion of plurality to the vocal parts. The electronic music accompaniment is built up of very complex sound structures, and the interest is maintained in such a lengthy work by a variety of *bravura* effects.

We have previously mentioned various means by which electronic music of an *unpredictable* nature may be obtained by using such devices as ring modulators, dynamic suppressors, etc. But we cannot close this chapter without mentioning the electronic brain and electronic composing machines, which could go on " composing " music for ever without repetition. This would seem to be a serious threat to the composer !

But of course composing machines and methods have been invented by the dozen for the last three hundred years. By a certain " Tabular System ", ten thousand minuets could be composed without any knowledge of music. Another " set of cards " would provide 428,000,000 quadrilles ! In 1824 the " Componium " was exhibited at Paris, playing variations on a theme " not only during years and ages " but for eternity. Yet none of these machines has ever lost a composer a single day's work. There is a reason, of course, why no composer need fear even the electronic composing machines, for he expresses himself as a human being, through emotive and spiritual values which no machine can ever simulate.

Music has an immense future. Even electronic music and the most *avant-garde* computational compositions may well become primitivisms, too unimportant to recall or record. Music is as infinite as space ; it will never be exhausted ; but it must always be a humanist art. This is why mechanical methods must never be allowed to have supremacy over the composer's own free fantasy and inspiration. If ever they do, music as a humanist art is doomed.

THE PRESENT SITUATION

The new techniques of writing music are revolutionary, but they are techniques of language, of a tool of communication, and their very novelty has two attendant dangers. One is that a concentration on the mechanics of unfamiliar language often obscures the much greater importance of the quality of the message itself ; thus, the awe with which the simple-minded listen to any twelve-note string quartet makes them slow to condemn it as inferior. The other is that the use by a composer of unfamiliar language may in fact result in no communication being made at all, save to a handful of expert colleagues and supporters, a difficulty which is of course an occupational hazard of experimenters in all fields. But in music it has led to a progressive deterioration in the general esteem of contemporary music. In the eighteenth century this output was the whole of the repertory, in the nineteenth its staple ; but in our own it has tended to be segregated into a small and unloved corner, to be explored from a sense of duty rather than from inclination.

EXPANSION OF AUDIENCES

It is ironical that this should have happened at a time when music as a whole enjoys a wider popularity than ever before. The rise of broadcasting and the gramophone as distributors of music has led to an unparalleled expansion of audiences ; and a much greater difficulty lies nowadays in discovering silence than in finding music to listen to. Familiarity has in this instance led not to contempt but to an appetite for more, an appetite promoted by the very high standards of performance—instrumental, if not vocal—which the new mechanical distribution has established.

Measured quantitively, the expansion in listening, though great in every branch of music, has been greatest in the popular field : music for the entertainment of listeners, or for dancers. Indeed, this has expanded until all too clearly it has become separated from the main stream. It is no longer a branch of concert music, but a world inhabited by its own specialists. One thing the specialists have inherited from their classical ancestors is a fluency of technique. The speed and skill with which Mozart turned out a concert aria for a soprano is matched to-day by the speed and skill with which Robert Russell Bennet turns out a recording arrangement, not by the delays and psychological difficulties with which Walton ultimately turns out a symphony.

Another inheritance is a regard for their audiences, a realisation that if music is to be at all widely enjoyed it must first be intelligible. That is to say, that the language must be reasonably familiar and its communication skilful. Startling, original techniques lend themselves only reluctantly to such communication ; a successful atonal ballad or a *concrète* samba may not be contradictions in terms, but they are at present at least improbable.

POPULARITY

This is, of course, not to suggest that all music should entertain, still less that popular success is the only yardstick. If a composer is to be worth listening to, he must follow his natural bent, whether this leads him to *Pierrot Lunaire* or to *Oklahoma*. Most composers aim somewhere between these two extremes, and many have recently attempted to win back for serious contemporary music some of the popularity lost by the extremists. In this endeavour they have not been greatly helped by professional critical opinion. This is considerably more intellectual than in the past, and at least as conscientious ; but the standards which it endeavours to uphold often seem to be continuous novelty of idiom rather than musical quality as such.

INDEX

A

Abel, Karl Friedrich, 146, 167
Absil, Jean, 438
Acis and Galatea (Handel), 103
Accompaniment, 19, 29, 45
Adagio for Strings (Barber), 448
Adam, Adolphe, 463
Addison, John, 446
Addison, Joseph, 100
Aesthetic theory, 127 *et seq.*
   Rameau, 120
   Noverre, 129
   Winckelmann and Durazzo, 131
   Gluck, 133
   Grétry, 210
   See also under Theory of Composition
Agon (Stravinsky), 414
Agrippina (Handel), 99, 111
Aida (Verdi), 310 *et seq.*
Albeniz, Isaac, 428
Albinoni, Tommaso, 117
Alceste (Gluck), 132 *et seq.*, 135
Alcina (Handel), 106
Aldeburgh Festival, 443
Alfven, Hugo, 337
Algarotti, Francesco, 127
Allemande, 457
Alwyn, William, 442
Amahl and the Night Visitors (Menotti), 447
America, music of, 189, 446 *et seq.*
   Gershwin and Copland, 446
   Menotti, 447
   symphonists, 447
Amor Brujo, El (Falla), 428
Antiphons, 9, 27
Apostles, The (Elgar), 389
Appalachia (Delius), 390

"*Appassionata*" sonata (Beethoven), 199
Après-midi d'un faune, L' (Debussy), 377, 381
Argentina, music of, 450
Aria, 55 ; *da capo* form, 68 ; in *opera buffa*, 118 ; *cavatina*, 131
   Gluck, 135
   Mozart, 184
Ariadne auf Naxos (R. Strauss), 366
Arioso, 55, 309
Arlésienne, L' (Bizet), 317
Armide (Gluck), 137, 209
Arne, Michael, 115
Arne, Thomas Augustine, 105, 114
Arnold, Malcolm, 445
Arnold, Samuel, 115
Arriaga, Juan, 427
Ars Nova, 18, 20
Art of Fugue, The (Bach), 86
Atlántida (Falla), 428
Atonality, 396 *et seq.*, 410
Attwood, Thomas, 188
Auber, Daniel, 304
Auric, Georges, 426
Austria, music of, 20, 351 *et seq.*
   See also under Vienna

B

Bach, Carl Philipp Emanuel, 64, 86, 94, 145 *et seq.*, 150
Bach, Johann Christian, 95, 114, 146, 167
Bach, Johann Sebastian, 63 *et seq.*, 73 *et seq.*
   Brandenburg concertos, 80, 89 *et seq.*
   cantatas, 84, 91